Popular Names of U.S. Government Reports

A Catalog

Popular Names of U.S. Government Reports

A Catalog

FOURTH EDITION

Compiled by
Bernard A. Bernier, Jr.
Karen A. Wood

SERIAL AND GOVERNMENT PUBLICATIONS DIVISION
RESEARCH SERVICES

LIBRARY OF CONGRESS   WASHINGTON   1984

Library of Congress Cataloging in Publication Data

United States. Library of Congress. Serial and Government
    Publications Division.
    Popular names of U.S. Government reports.

    Includes indexes.
    SuDocs no.: LC 6.2:G74/984
    1. United States—Government publications—Bibliography. I.
Bernier, Bernard A., Jr. II. Wood, Karen A. III. Title.
Z1223.A199U54 1984   015'.73
ISBN 0-8444-0174-9

For sale by the Superintendent of Documents
U.S. Government Printing Office
Washington, D.C. 20402

Table of Contents

Foreword

Since many government publications become known by short titles that appear nowhere on the piece, and since libraries catalog them under institutional titles, a device for tying the two together is needed. The present catalog is the fourth edition of a work the Library of Congress first issued in 1966.

Entries in this edition, as in the previous edition, have been greatly expanded to include extensive annotations and other added information useful to both reference librarians and researchers. A subject index has been added to further facilitate its use.

The demand for the earlier editions has been heavy. We hope the present one will be even more useful.

Donald F. Wisdom
Chief, Serial and Government
Publications Division

Introduction

The fourth edition of this catalog presents a revised and updated key to popular names used in citing U.S. government reports. Published and/or computerized bibliographic records are usually structured under the corporate author, title, series, or subject. The name by which a report is cited in the news media or requested in libraries may not reflect this structure. Often such reports become known by the name of a person associated with the authoritative body, whether this be a congressional committee, federal advisory group, or private enterprise. Other reports may become known by a nonpersonal designation based upon such facets as subject matter or geographical descriptor.

As in the third edition, inclusion is not limited to reports issued by the Government Printing Office or specific government agencies. Private imprints issued for a sponsoring government agency and commercial reprints are included. If a report has been published in more than one edition, each is listed.

The section entitled "Impeachment Inquiry," which appeared in the third edition, has not been retained.

The appearance of this section in the 1976 edition, a departure from the listing solely of government reports, was in response to the contemporary demand for all reports and documents related to the Watergate affair.

The index provided in this edition includes entries for both corporate authors and subjects. Corporate authors are also listed in a subject format to facilitate identification (e.g., President's Committee on Foreign Aid is also listed as Foreign Aid, President's Committee on).

The section entitled "Unidentified Reports" updates the listing of reports about which we have insufficient information. Any assistance in identifying or locating these reports would be most welcome.

The editors continue to solicit new report titles for inclusion in future editions, as well as responses to the current edition. We are indebted to all those who have provided us with such bibliographic information in the past. In addition, we wish to thank Kathleen Y. Hinkle for her untiring assistance in the physical preparation of this publication.

Bernard A. Bernier, Jr.
Karen A. Wood

Popular Name —————— **ALBERT REPORT** [Albert, Carl]

Entry Number ————— **19**

Main Entry ————— U.S. *Congress. House. Committee on Agriculture.*

Title ———— United States agricultural exports to Western Europe. A report on the competitive position of United States agricultural products in the hard currency countries of Western Europe. Washington, U.S. Govt. Print. Off., 1960.

   iii, 10 p. 24 cm.
   At head of title: 86th Cong., 2d sess. Committee print.
   1. Produce trade — U.S.

Monthly Catalog Citation (date-entry number)* ———— HD9005.A527   1960   338.10973   60 — 60691 ———— L.C. Card Number

MC#: 1960-5012

SuDocs no.: Y 4.Ag8/1:Ex7/6

Superintendent of Documents Classification Number

*For older documents reference is made to citations in either the *Checklist of United States Public Documents, 1789-1909* or the *Document Catalog.*

Reports

A–ARMS REPORT

1

Lowenstein, James G.

U.S. security issues in Europe: burden sharing and offset, MBFR and nuclear weapons: September 1973; a staff report prepared for the use of the Subcommittee on U.S. Security Agreements and Commitments Abroad of the Committee on Foreign Relations, United States Senate [by James G. Lowenstein and Richard M. Moose] Washington, U.S. Govt. Print. Off., 1973.

v, 27 p. 24 cm.

At head of title: 93d Congress, 1st session. Committee print.

1. North Atlantic Treaty Organization—Finance. 2. Europe—Defenses. 3. United States—Armed Forces—Europe. 4. Atomic weapons. I. Moose, Richard M., joint author. II. United States. Congress. Senate. Committee on Foreign Relations. Subcommittee on United States Security Agreements and Commitments Abroad. III. Title.

UA646.3.L68   355.03′1   73-603434
                                                                                   MARC

Not located in Monthly Catalog

ABBE REPORT

2

Abbe, Leslie Morgan.

The nation's health facilities; ten years of the Hill-Burton hospital and medical facilities program, 1946-1956, prepared by Leslie Morgan Abbe and Anna Mae Baney. [Washington] U.S. Dept. of Health, Education, and Welfare, Public Health Service, Division of Hospital and Medical Facilities, Program Evaluation and Reports Branch [1958]

181 p. diagrs., tables. 26 cm. ([U.S.] Public Health Service. Publication no. 616)

1. Hospitals—U.S. I. Baney, Anna Mae, joint author. II. Title. (Series)

RA981.A2A52   362   58-61904
MC#: 1958-15319
SuDocs no.: FS2.2:F11/946-56

ABBOTT REPORT [Abbott, Edith]

see

WICKERSHAM COMMISSION [Wickersham, George Woodward]

Report on crime and the foreign born, no. 10

ABBOTT REPORT [Abbott, Frederick H.]

3

U.S. *Board of Indian commissioners.*

The administration of Indian affairs in Canada, by Frederick H. Abbott, secretary to the Board of Indian commissioners. Report of an investigation made in 1914, under the direction of the Board of Indian commissioners. Washington, D.C., 1915.

148 p. incl. forms. front., plates, ports. 25 cm.

1. Indians of North America—Canada. 2. Indians of North America—Government relations. I. Abbott, Frederick H., 1872- II. Title.

E92.U5   15-26386
Not located in Monthly Catalog
SuDocs no.: [I 20.5]

ABERCROMBIE REPORT [Abercrombie, Roland Knights]

4

U.S. *Civil Aeronautics Board.*

Survey of United States overseas mail. Prepared by Roland K. Abercrombie, principal analyst. Washington, 1943.

iii, 43 p. maps, diagrs. 28 x 44 cm.

Cover title.

At head of title: Civil Aeronautics Board. Economic Bureau. Research and Analysis Division.

1. Air mail service—U.S. I. Abercrombie, Roland Knights, 1900-

HE6496.A5 1943M   383.4973   43-50625* rev
MC#: 1943-page 1167
SuDocs no.: C31.202:M28/2

ACHESON REPORTS [Acheson, Dean Gooderham]

5

U.S. *Dept. of state. Committee on atomic energy.*

A report on the international control of atomic energy. Prepared for the secretary of state's Committee on atomic energy by a board of consultants . . . Washington, D.C. [U.S. Govt. print. off.] 1946.

xiii, 61 p. 23 cm. [U.S. Dept. of state. Publication 2498] Dean Acheson, chairman of the committee.

1. Atomic energy. 2. Atomic bomb. I. Acheson, Dean Gooderham, 1893- II. Title: International control of atomic energy.

UF767.U58 1946   341   46-26004
MC#: 1946-page 552
SuDocs no.: S 1.2:At7

6

U.S. *Attorney general's committee on administrative procedure.*

. . . Administrative procedure in government agencies. Report of the Committee on administrative procedure, appointed by the attorney general, at the request of the President, to investigate the need for procedural reform in various administrative tribunals and to suggest improvements therein. Washington, U.S. Govt. print. off., 1941.

viii, 474 p. incl. tables. 23 cm. ([U.S.] 77th Cong., 1st sess. Senate. Doc. 8)

Running title: Final report of the Attorney general's committee, administrative procedure.

Dean Acheson, chairman.

1. U.S.—Executive departments. 2. Administrative courts—U.S. 3. U.S.—Pol. & govt. I. Acheson, Dean Gooderham, 1893- II. Title.

JK416.A5 1941   353   41-50129
MC#: 1941-page 197
SuDocs no.: 77th Cong., 1st sess. S. Doc. 8

ACHINSTEIN REPORTS [Achinstein, Asher]

7

U.S. *Congress. Senate. Committee on Banking and Currency.*

Factors affecting the stock market. Staff report to the Committee on Banking and Currency, United States Senate. April 30, 1955. Washington, U.S. Govt. Print. Off., 1955.

vii, 201 p. illus. 24 cm.

At head of title: 84th Cong., 1st sess. Committee print.

1. Stock-exchange—U.S.

HG4556.U5A545 1955   332.61   55-61148
MC#: 1955-7981
SuDocs no.: Y4.B22/3:St6/9

8

U.S. *Library of Congress. Legislative Reference Service.*

Federal reserve policy and economic stability, 1951-57; report [to the] Committee on Banking and Currency. Study prepared by Asher Achinstein, Legislative Reference Service, together with Comments of staff of Federal Reserve Board. Washington, U.S. Govt. Print. Off., 1958.

xiii, 85 p. tables. 24 cm. (85th Cong., 2d sess. Senate. Report no. 2500)

1. Currency question—U.S. I. Achinstein, Asher, 1900- II. U.S. Congress. Senate. Committee on Banking and Currency. III. U.S. Federal Reserve Board. IV. Title. (Series: U.S. 85th Cong., 2d sess., 1958. Senate. Report no. 2500)

HG538.A314   332.4973   58-62192
MC#: 1958-15826

SuDocs no.: 85th Cong., 2d sess. S. Rept. 2500

ACKERMAN REPORT

9

Ackerman, Edward Augustus, 1911-

The impact of new techniques on integrated multiple-purpose water development; a report to the United States Senate Select Committee on National Water Resources. Washington, 1960.

2 v. (viii, 201 1) maps, diagrs., tables. 28 cm.
Bibliographical footnotes.

1. Water resources development—U.S. 2. Hydraulic engineering—U.S. I. U.S. Congress. Senate. Select Committee on National Water Resources. II. Title.

HD 1694.A5A62   333.910973   60-62980
Not located in Monthly Catalog

10

Ackerman, Edward Augustus, 1911-

The impact of new techniques on integrated multiple-purpose water development; water resources activities in the United States. [Report prepared at the request of the Select Committee on National Water Resources, United States Senate, pursuant to S. Res. 48, Eighty-sixth Congress]. Washington, U.S. Govt. Print. Off., 1960.

ix, 97 p. illus., maps (1 fold.) 27 cm.
At head of title: 86th Cong., 2d sess. Committee print no. 31.
Bibliographical footnotes.

1. Water resources development—U.S. 2. Hydraulic engineering—U.S. I. U.S. Congress. Senate. Select Committee on National Water Resources. II. Title.

HD 1694.A5A62 1960A   333.910973   60-61927
MC#: 1961-426 (LC card 60-4419 cancelled in favor of 60-61927)
SuDocs no.: Y 4.N21/8:86/31

ACKERMAN REPORT [Ackerman, William G.]

11

U.S. *Committee on Water Resources Research.*

Federal water resources research program; a progress report. 1964/65-

Washington, Office of Science and Technology, Executive Office of the President; for sale by the Superintendent of Documents, U.S. Govt. Print. Off.

v. 24 cm. ([U.S.] Federal Council for Science and Technology. Publication)

Report year ends June 30.

1. Water conservation—Research I. Title. (Series)

TC423.A26   64-60834 rev
MC#: 1964-9755 (Fiscal year 1965)
       1965-11673 (Fiscal year 1966) submitted by Robert L. Smith, Chairman
       1966-11215 (Fiscal year 1967) submitted by Leonard B. Dworsky, Chairman
       1967-11781 (Fiscal year 1968) submitted by Bernard B. Berger, Chairman

       1969-4919 (Fiscal year 1969) submitted by Leonard B. Dworsky, Chairman
       1970-10541 (Fiscal year 1970) submitted by H. Guyford Stever, Chairman
SuDocs no.: PrEx8.9:(year)

ACKLEY REPORT [Ackley, Gardner]

12

U.S. *Committee on the Economic Impact of Defense and Disarmament.*
Report. Washington, For sale by the Superintendent of Documents, U.S. Govt. Print. Off., 1965.

ix, 92 p. 24 cm.
Bibliographical footnotes.

1. Disarmament-Economic aspects—U.S.

HC110.D4A5   65-62742
MC#: 1966-1398 (LC card 66-60269 cancelled in favor of 65-62742)
SuDocs no.: Pr 36.8:Ec7/R29/965

ADAMS REPORT [Adams, John Quincy]

13

U.S. *Dept. of state.*

Report upon weights and measures, by John Quincy Adams, secretary of state of the United States. Prepared in obedience to a resolution of the Senate of the third March, 1817. Washington, Printed by Gales & Seaton, 1821.

245 p. 3 fold. tab. 23½ cm.

Printed also as Senate document 119 and House document 109, 16th Congress, 2d session, under titles beginning: Report of the secretary of state, upon weights and measures.

Papers in the Appendix (p. [137]-241) include tables of weights and measures as used in the United States, and laws of the several states, 1734-1819.

This copy is printed on fine paper, and has ms. note at head of title: U.S. Department of state, 4. May 1821.

1. Weights and measures. I. Adams, John Quincy, pres. U.S., 1767-1848. II. Title.

QC88.A22   3-23446
- - - - - Copy 2. Printed on ordinary paper, with ms. note on fly leaf: 1436. John Quincy Adams to the Columbian institute, May 1821.
Checklist of United States Public Documents, 1789-1909, page 903
Supt. of Docs. no.: S1.2:W42
Checklist of United States Public Documents, 1789-1909, page 6
16th Cong., 2d sess. S. Doc. 199. In Serial no. 45, vol. 4
16th Cong., 2d sess. H. Doc. 109. In Serial no. 55, vol. 8

ADLER REPORT [Adler, Julius Ochs]

14

U.S. National Security Training Commission.
20th century minutemen; a report to the President on a reserve forces training program. [Washington, U.S. Govt. Print. Off.] 1953 [i.e. 1954]

ix, 159 p. illus. 24 cm.

1. U.S.—Armed Forces—Reserves. I. Title.

UA42.A596   * 355.37   355.351   54-61082
MC#: 1954-2064
SuDocs no.: Y3.N21/19:2T91

ADLER REPORT [Adler, Julius Ochs]
National Security Training.
see also
WADSWORTH REPORT [Wadsworth, James W.]

AIKEN REPORTS [Aiken, George David]

15

United Nations. *General Assembly. 15th sess., 1960-61. Delegation from the United States.*

The United States in the United Nations, 1960—a turning point; report to the Committee on Foreign Relations, United States Senate by George D. Aiken [and] Wayne Morse, members of the Delegation of the United States to the 15th session of the General Assembly of the United Nations. Washington, U.S. Govt. Print. Off., 1961.

v, 32 p. 24 cm.
At head of title: 87th Cong., 1st sess., Committee print.
1. United Nations—U.S. I. Aiken, George David, 1892- II. Morse, Wayne Lyman, 1900- III. U.S. Congress. Senate. Committee on Foreign Relations. IV. Title.
JX1977.2.U5U55 1960-61   61-60726
MC#: 1961-5868
SuDocs no.: Y4.F76/2:Un35/5

See also MORSE REPORT [Morse, Wayne Lyman]
United States in the United Nations, 1960.

16

United Nations. *General Assembly. 15th sess., 1960-61. Delegation from the United States.*

The United States in the United Nations, 1960—a turning point; supplementary report to the Committee on Foreign Relations, United States Senate, by George D. Aiken, member of the Delegation of the United States to the 15th session of the General Assembly of the United Nations. Washington, U.S. Govt. Print. Off., 1961.

6 p. 24 cm.
At head of title: 87th Cong., 1st sess. Committee print.
1. United Nations—U.S. I. Aiken, George David, 1892- II. U.S. Congress. Senate. Committee on Foreign Relations. III. Title.
JX1977.2.U5U55 1960-61a   61-60727
MC#: 1961-5868
SuDocs no.: Y4.F76/2:Un35/5

17

U.S. *Congress. Senate. Committee on Foreign Relations.*

Latin America: Venezuela, Brazil, Peru, Bolivia, and Panama; report of George D. Aiken on a study mission. Washington, U.S. Govt. Print. Off., 1960.

v, 17 p. table, 24 cm.
At head of title: 86th Cong., 2d sess. Committee print.
1. U.S.—Relations (general) with South America. 2. South America—Relations (general) with the U.S. 3. U.S.—Relations (general) with Panama. 4. Panama—Relations (general) with the U.S. I. Aiken, George David, 1892-
F2237.U5   327.7308   60-60731
MC#: 1960-5188
SuDocs no.: Y4.F76/2:L34/2

18

U.S. *Congress. Senate. Committee on Foreign Relations.*

Study mission in the Caribbean area, December, 1957; report of George D. Aiken to the Committee on Foreign Relations, United States Senate. Washington, U.S. Govt. Print. Off., 1958.

vi, 22 p. map. 24 cm.
At head of title: 85th Cong., 2d sess. Committee print.
1. U.S.—Relations (general) with the Caribbean area. 2. Caribbean area—Relations (general) with the U.S. I. Aiken, George David, 1892- II. Title.

F1418.U4488   58-60286
MC#: 1958-3333
SuDocs no.: Y4.F76/2:C19

ALBERT REPORT [Albert, Carl]

19

U.S. *Congress. House. Committee on Agriculture.*

United States agricultural exports to Western Europe. A report on the competitive position of United States agricultural products in the hard currency countries of Western Europe. Washington, U.S. Govt. Print. Off., 1960.

iii, 10 p. 24 cm.
At head of title: 86th Cong., 2d sess. Committee print.
1. Produce trade—U.S.
HD9005.A527 1960   338.10973   60-60691
MC#: 1960-5012
SuDocs no.: Y4.Ag8/1:Ex7/6

ALCOHOL REPORT

20

U.S. *Dept. of Transportation.*

1968 alcohol and highway safety report; a study transmitted by the Secretary of the Department of Transportation to the Congress, in accordance with the requirements of section 204 of the Highway safety act of 1966, Public law 89-564. Washington, U.S. Govt. Print. Off., 1968.

v, 182 p. illus., maps. 24 cm.
At head of title: 90th Congress, 2d session. Committee print. "90-34."
"Printed for the use of the Committee on Public Works [Subcommittee on Roads, House of Representatives]"
Bibliography: p. 127-143.
1. Drinking and traffic accidents. I. U.S. Congress. House. Committee on Public Works. Subcommittee on Roads. II. Title.
HE5620.D7U5   614.8'62   68-67045
MC#: 1968-15293
SuDocs no.: Y4.P96/11:90-34

ALDERFER REPORT [Alderfer, Harold Freed]

21

U.S. *Mutual Security Agency. Mission to Greece.*

Report on Greek local government [prepared by Harold F. Alderfer] Athens, Greece, Civil Government Division, Mutual Security Agency, 1952.

491. 26 cm.
Cover title.
Commonly known as the Alderfer report.
1. Local government—Greece, Modern. I. Alderfer, Harold Freed, 1903- II. Title. III. Title: Alderfer report on Greek local government.
JS5608.U65   352.0495   53-61704
MC#: 1953-16354
SuDocs no.: Pr 33.918/2:G74

ALDRICH COMMISSION [Aldrich, Nelson Wilmarth]

Publications of the Aldrich Commission are listed according to the contents of the first entry (the 24-volume set, LC card 12-35259). Each report in the Publications series is followed by its respective separate edition or editions. Other reports of the commission are arranged alphabetically by title after the listing of the Publications.

22

U.S. *National monetary commission.*

Publications of National monetary commission . . . Washington, Govt. print. off., 1911 [i.e. 1909-12]

24 v. map, facsims., tables, forms, diagrs. 23 1/2-40 cm. (v. 21, 29½ cm.; v. 22, 29 cm.; v. 23, 40 cm).

Many folded tables, diagrs., etc.

The special title-pages are dated from 1909 to 1912, and, except in a few instances, bear Senate document numbers of the 61st Congress, 2d session.

This is one of the sets which were bound in dark red buckram, and distributed by the Office of superintendent of documents in accordance with the original plan, and in preference to the change announced in a circular of the National monetary commission, March 15, 1912, which eliminated v. 24, combined the material which was to have composed it with v. 1, and added to v. 23 a "Tabular summary of the laws, practices and statistics of the principal banks of the leading countries, prepared . . . by A. Piatt Andrew" (2 fold. sheets in pocket) The "Tabular summary" is not included in this set.

CONTENTS—I. Interviews on banking in England, France, Germany, Switzerland, and Italy: Doc. 405. Interviews on the banking and currency systems of England, Scotland, France, Germany, Switzerland, and Italy; under the direction of Hon. Nelson W. Aldrich, chairman. 1910.

II. Financial laws of the United States, 1778-1909: Doc. 580. Laws of the United States concerning money, banking and loans, 1778-1909, comp. by A. T. Huntington and Robert J. Mawhinney. 1910.

III. Digest of state banking laws: Doc. 353. Digest of state banking statutes, comp. by Samuel A. Welldon. 1910.

IV. Banking in United States before civil war: Doc. 571. The first and second banks of the United States, by John Thom Holdsworth and Davis R. Dewey. 1910.—Doc. 581. State banking before the civil war, by Davis R. Dewey, and The safety fund banking system in New York 1829-1866, by Robert E. Chaddock. 1910.

V. The national banking system: Doc. 582. The origin of the national banking system, by Andrew McFarland Davis [with Supplement] 1910-11.—Doc. 572. History of the national-bank currency, by Alexander Dana Noyes. 1910.—Doc. 538. History of crises under the national banking system, by O. M. W. Sprague. 1910.

VI. Clearing houses and credit instruments: Doc. 491. Clearing houses, by James Graham Cannon. 1910.—Doc. 399. The use of credit instruments in payments in the United States; report comp. by David Kinley. 1910.

VII. State banks, trust companies, and Independent treasury system: Doc. 659. State banks and trust companies since the passage of the national-bank act, by George E. Barnett. 1911.—Doc. 587. The Independent treasury of the United States and its relations to the banks of the country, by David Kinley. 1910.

VIII. The English banking system: Doc. 492. The English banking system, by Hartley Withers, Sir R. H. Inglis Palgrave, and other writers. 1910.—Doc. 591. History of the Bank of England and its financial services to the state. 2d ed., rev., by Eugen von Philippovich. Tr. by Christabel Meredith, with an introduction by H. S. Foxwell, 1911.

IX. Banking in Canada: Doc. 332. The history of banking in Canada, by Roeliff Morton Breckenridge. 1910.—Doc. 583. The Canadian banking system, by Joseph French Johnson. 1910.—Doc. 584. Interviews on the banking and currency systems of Canada, by a subcommittee of the National monetary commission [Edward B. Vreeland, chairman] 1910.

X. The Reichsbank and renewal of its charter: Doc. 408. The Reichsbank 1876-1900. 1910.—Doc. 507. Renewal of Reichsbank charter. 1910.

XI. Articles on German banking and German banking laws:

Docs. 508. Miscellaneous articles on German banking. 1910.—Doc. 574. German imperial banking laws, ed. by Dr. R. Koch, former president of the Reichsbank; together with the German stock exchange regulations. 1910.

XII-XIII. The German bank inquiry of 1908: Doc. 407. German bank inquiry of 1908. Stenographic reports. Proceedings of the entire commission [vol. I] on points I to V of the question sheet; vol. II on point VI of the question sheet (The deposit system) 1910-11.

XIV. The great German banks: Doc. 593. The German great banks and their concentration in connection with the economic development of Germany, by Dr. J. Riesser. 3. ed. completely revised and enlarged. 1911.

XV. Banking in France and the French Bourse: Doc. 522. Evolution of credit and banks in France, from the founding of the Bank of France to the present time, by André Liesse. 1909.—Doc. 494. The Bank of France in its relation to national and international credit, by Maurice Patron, and an article upon French savings, by Alfred Neymarck. 1910.—Doc. 573. The history and methods of the Paris Bourse, by E. Vidal. 1910.

XVI. Banking in Belgium and Mexico: Doc. 400. The National bank of Belgium, by Charles A. Conant. 1910.—Doc. 493. The banking system of Mexico, by Charles A. Conant. 1910.

XVII. Banking in Sweden and Switzerland: Doc. 576. The Swedish banking system, by A. W. Flux. 1910.—Doc. 401. The Swiss banking law, study and criticism of the Swiss legislation respecting banks of issue, and especially of the federal act of October 6, 1905, concerning the Swiss national bank, by Dr. Julius Landmann. 1910.

XVIII. Banking in Italy, Russia, Austro-Hungary, and Japan: Doc. 575. The banks of issue in Italy, by Tito Canovai, with an article by Carlo F. Ferraris, and the text of the Italian banking law. 1911.—Doc. 586. Banking in Russia, Austro-Hungary, the Netherlands, and Japan. 1911.

XIX. Administrative features of national banking and European fiscal and postal savings systems: Doc. 404. Suggested changes in the administrative features of the national banking laws. Replies to circular letter of inquiry of September 26, 1908, and Hearings, December 2 and 3, 1908. 1910.—Doc. 403. Report to the National monetary commission on the fiscal systems of the United States, England, France, and Germany. [By J. O. Manson, chief of division in office of treasurer of the United States] 1910.—Doc. 658. Notes on the postal savings-bank systems of leading countries. 1910.

XX. Miscellaneous articles: Doc. 406. An address by Senator Nelson W. Aldrich before the Economic club of New York, November 29, 1909, on the work of the National monetary commission. 1910.—Doc. 402. The discount system in Europe, by Paul M. Warburg. 1910.—Doc. 569. Bank acceptances, by Lawrence Merton Jacobs. 1910.—Doc. 579. The credit of nations, by Francis W. Hirst, and the trade balance of the United States, by George Paish. 1910.—Doc. 589. Bank loans and stock exchange speculation, by Jacob H. Hollander. 1911.

XXI. Statistics for United States, Great Britain, Germany, and France: Doc 570. Statistics for the United States, 1867-1909, comp. by A. Piatt Andrew. 1910.—Doc. 225. Special report from the banks of the United States, April 28, 1909 [with Supplement] 1909-10.—Doc. 578. Statistics for Great Britain, Germany, and France, 1867-1909. 1910.

XXII. Seasonal variations in demands for currency and capital: Doc. 588. Seasonal variations in the relative demand for money and capital in the United States, a statistical study, by Edwin Walter Kemmerer. 1910.

XXIII. Financial diagrams: Doc. 509. Financial diagrams, comp. by A. Piatt Andrew. 1910.

XXIV. Report of National monetary commission, including related papers, appendices, etc.: 62d Cong., 2d sess. Senate. Doc. 243. National monetary commission. Letter from secretary of the National monetary commission transmitting, pursuant to law, the report of the commission [Jan. 8, 1912] January 9, 1912, referred to the Committee on finance and ordered to be printed. 1912. – 61st Cong., 3d sess. Senate. Doc. 784. Suggested plan for monetary legislation submitted to the National monetary commission by Hon. Nelson W. Aldrich [January 16, 1911] 1911. 20 p. – 61st Cong., 3d sess. Senate. Doc. 784, pt. 2. Suggested plan for monetary legislation . . . Rev. ed., October, 1911. 1911. 24 p.

- - - - - Washington, Govt. print. off., 1911 [i.e. 1909-12]

24 v. map, facsims., tables, forms, diagrs. 23-39½ cm. (v. 21, 30 cm.; v. 22, 29 cm.; v. 23, 39½ cm.)

Many folded tables, diagrs., etc.

This set was collected and bound by the Library of Congress. Vol. xxiv has a general t.-p., "Publications of National monetary commission. Vol. xxiv. Report of National monetary commission including related papers appendices, etc., Washington 1911," and contains (1) "National monetary commission. Report of the National monetary commission. Washington, Govt. print. off., 1912" (an edition of the report of Jan. 8, 1912, differing in title from that issued as 62d Cong., 2d sess. Senate. Doc 243) – (2) "61st Cong., 3d sess. Senate. Doc. no. 784. Suggested plan for monetary legislation submitted to the National monetary commission by Hon. Nelson W. Aldrich [Jan. 16, 1911] Washington, Govt. print. off., 1911." 20 p. – (3) "The plan of the National monetary commission for the revision of our banking and currency laws. Speech of Hon. Edward B. Vreeland . . . February 6, 1912."

A copy of vol. xxiv, bound in dark red buckram, in the office of the superintendent of documents, has general t.-p. ". . . Recommendations of National monetary commission including Suggested plan for monetary legislation by Nelson W. Aldrich. Report of the National monetary commission. Washington 1912," and contains (1) "61st Cong., 3d sess. Senate. Doc. 784. Suggested plan for monetary legislation . . . By Hon. Nelson W. Aldrich [Jan. 16, 1911] Washington, Govt. print. off., 1911." 20 p. – (2) "61st Cong., 3d sess. Senate. Doc. 784, pt. 2. Suggested plan . . . Rev. ed. October, 1911. Washington, 1911. 24 p. – (3) "62d Cong.,2d sess. Senate. Doc. 243. National monetary commission. Letter from secretary of the National monetary commission transmitting, pursuant to law, the Report of the commission [dated Jan. 8, 1912] January 9, 1912 referred to the Committee on finance and ordered to be printed. Washington, Govt. print. off., 1912." 72 p.

HG471.A4 1911b

1. Banks and banking – U.S. 2. Currency question – U.S. 3. Finance – U.S. 4. Money. 5. Banks and banking. I. Aldrich, Nelson Wilmarth, 1841-1915. II. Title.

HG471.A4 1911a   12-35259

MC#: "Notes of General Interest" Mar. 1912-pages 538-539

MC#: Feb. 1912-page 478

23

U.S. *National monetary commission.*

Publications of National monetary commission . . . Washington, Govt. print. off., 1911-12 [i.e. 1909-12]

23 v. map, facsims., tables, forms, diagrs. 23-39½ cm. (v. 21, 30 cm; v. 22, 29 cm; v. 23, 39½ cm.)

Many folded tables, diagrs., etc.

The general title-pages of vols. 1 and 23 are dated 1912. The special title-pages are dated from 1909 to 1912 and, except in a few instances, bear Senate document numbers of the 61st Congress, 2d session.

Nelson W. Aldrich, chairman.

This is one of the sets which was bound in dark green buckram and issued in accordance with a circular of the National monetary commission dated March 15, 1912, which announced that the set would consist of 23 vols., instead of 24 vols., as projected. The material intended for v. 24 was combined with v. 1; and to

v. 23 was added "Tabular summary of the laws, practices and statistics of the principal banks of the leading countries, prepared . . . by A. Piatt Andrew" (2 fold. sheets in pocket)

Other sets, bound in dark red buckram, were distributed by the office of superintendent of documents, in accordance with the original plan. The general title-pages of those sets are dated 1911, and the "Tabular summary" [etc.] is not included.

Contents – I. Report of the National monetary commission. Interviews on banking in Europe: 62d Cong., 2d sess. Senate. Doc. 243. National monetary commission. Letter from secretary of the National monetary commission transmitting, pursuant to law, the report of the commission [Jan. 8, 1912] January 9, 1912, referred to the Committee on finance and ordered printed. – 61st Cong., 3d sess. Senate. Doc. 784. Suggested plan for monetary legislation submitted to the National monetary commission by Hon. Nelson W. Aldrich [Oct. 14, 1911] 24 p. – Suggested plan for monetary legislation . . . Rev. ed. October, 1911. 24 p. – 61st Cong., 2d sess. Senate. Doc. 405. Interviews on the banking and currency systems of England, Scotland, France, Germany, Switzerland, and Italy; under the direction of Hon. Nelson W. Aldrich, chairman. 1910.

II. Financial laws of the United States, 1778-1909: Doc. 580. Laws of the United States concerning money, banking, and loans, 1778-1909, comp. by A. T. Huntington and Robert J. Mawhinney. 1910.

III. Digest of state banking laws: Doc. 353. Digest of state banking statutes, comp. by Samual A. Welldon. 1910.

IV. Banking in United States before civil war: Doc. 571. The first and second banks of the United States, by John Thom Holdsworth and Davis R. Dewey. 1910. – Doc. 581. State banking before the civil war, by Davis R. Dewey, and The safety fund banking system in New York, 1829-1866, by Robert E. Chaddock. 1910.

V. The national banking system: Doc. 582. The origin of the national banking system, by Andrew McFarland Davis [with Supplement] 1910-11. – Doc. 572. History of the national-bank currency, by Alexander Dana Noyes. 1910. – Doc. 538. History of crises under the national banking system, by O. M. W. Sprague. 1910.

VII. State banks, trust companies, and Independent treasury system: Doc. 659. State banks and trust companies since the passage of the national-bank act, by George E. Barnett. 1911. – Doc 587. The Independent treasury of the United States and its relations to the banks of the country, by David Kinley. 1910.

VIII. The English banking system: Doc. 492. The English banking system, by Hartley Withers, Sir R. H. Inglis Palgrave, and other writers. 1910. – Doc. 591. History of the Bank of England and its financial services to the state. 2d ed., rev., by Eugen von Philippovich. Tr. by Christabel Meredith, with an introduction by H. S. Foxwell. 1911.

IX. Banking in Canada: Doc. 332. The history of banking in Canada, by Roeliff Morton Breckenridge. 1910. – Doc. 583. The Canadian banking system, by Joseph French Johnson. 1910. – Doc. 584. Interviews on the banking and currency systems of Canada, by a subcommittee of the National monetary commission [Edward B. Vreeland, chairman] 1910.

X. The Reichsbank and renewal of its charter: Doc. 408. The Reichsbank, 1876-1900. 1910. – Doc. 507. Renewal of Reichsbank charter. 1910.

XI. Articles on German banking and German banking laws: Doc. 508. Miscellaneous articles on German banking. 1910. – Doc. 574. German imperial banking laws, ed. by Dr. R. Koch, former president of the Reichsbank; together with the German stock exchange regulations. 1910.

XII-XIII. The German bank inquiry of 1908: Doc. 407. German bank inquiry of 1908. Stenographic reports. Proceedings of the entire commission [vol. 1] on points I-V of the question sheet; vol. II on point VI of the question sheet (The deposit system) 1910-11.

XIV. The great German banks: Doc. 593. The German great banks and their concentration in connection with the economic development of Germany, by Dr. J. Riesser. 3d ed. completely revised and enlarged. 1911.

XV. Banking in France and the French Bourse: Doc. 522. Evolution of credit and banks in France from the founding of the Bank of France to the present time, by Andre Liesse. 1909. — Doc. 494. The Bank of France in its relation to national and international credit, by Maurice Patron, and an article upon French savings, by Alfred Neymarck. 1910. — Doc. 573. The history and methods of the Paris Bourse, by E. Vidal. 1910.

XVI. Banking in Belgium and Mexico: Doc. 400. The National bank of Belgium, by Charles A. Conant. 1910. — Doc. 493. The banking system of Mexico, by Charles A. Conant. 1910.

XVII. Banking in Sweden and Switzerland: Doc. 576. The Swedish banking system, by A. W. Flux. 1910. — Doc. 401. The Swiss banking law, study and criticism of the Swiss legislation respecting banks of issue, and expecially of the federal act of October 6, 1905, concerning the Swiss national bank, by Dr. Julius Landmann. 1910.

XVIII. Banking in Italy, Russia, Austro-Hungary, and Japan: Doc. 575. The banks of issue in Italy, by Tito Canovai, with an article by Carlo F. Ferraris, and the text of the Italian banking law. 1911. — Doc. 586. Banking in Russia, Austro-Hungary, the Netherlands, and Japan. 1911.

XIX. Administrative features of national banking laws and European fiscal and postal savings systems: Doc. 404. Suggested changes in the administrative features of the national banking laws. Replies to circular letter of inquiry of September 26, 1908, and Hearings, December 2 and 3, 1908. 1910. — Doc. 403. Report to the National monetary commission of the fiscal systems of the United States, England, France, and Germany [by J. O. Manson, chief of division in office of treasurer of the United States] 1910. — Doc. 658. Notes on the postal savings-bank systems of the leading countries. 1910.

XX. Miscellaneous articles: Doc. 406. An address by Senator Nelson W. Aldrich before the Economic club of New York, November 29, 1909, on the work of the National monetary commission. 1910. — Doc. 402. The discount system in Europe, by Paul M. Warburg. 1910. — Doc. 569. Bank acceptances, by Lawrence Merton Jacobs. 1910. — Doc. 579. The credit of nations, by Francis W. Hirst, and The trade balance of the United States, by George Paish. 1910. — Doc. 589. Bank loans and stock exchange speculation, by Jacob H. Hollander. 1911.

XXI. Statistics for United States, Great Britain, Germany, and France: Doc. 570. Statistics for the United States, 1867-1909, comp. by A. Piatt Andrew. 1910. — Doc. 225. Special report from the banks of the United States, April 28, 1909 [with Supplement] 1909-10. — Doc. 578. Statistics for Great Britain, Germany, and France, 1867-1909. 1910.

XXII. Seasonal variations in demands for currency and capital: Doc. 588. Seasonal variations in the relative demand for money and capital in the United States, a statistical study, by Edwin Walter Kemmerer. 1910.

XXIII. Financial diagrams and European bank summaries, prepared by A. Piatt Andrew: Doc. 509. Financial diagrams, comp. by A. Piatt Andrew. 1910. — Tabular summary of the laws, practices and statistics of the principal banks of the leading countries, prepared for the National monetary commission by A. Piatt Andrew. (January 1912) 2 fold. sheets, in pocket.

1. Banks and banking — U.S. 2. Currency question — U.S. 3. Finance — U.S. 4. Money. 5. Banks and banking. I. Aldrich, Nelson Wilmarth, 1841-1915. II. Title.
HG471.A4 1911   16-15251
MC#: "Notes of General Interest" Mar. 1912-pages 538-539

24

U.S. *National monetary commission.*

. . . Interviews on the banking and currency systems of England, Scotland, France, Germany, Switzerland, and Italy, under the direction of Hon. Nelson W. Aldrich, chairman National monetary commission. Washington, Govt. print. off., 1910 [i.e. 1911]

541 p. fold. tables. 23 cm. (Publications of National monetary commission. vol. I)

61st Cong., 2d sess. Senate. Doc. 405.

Issued also separately, 1910.

1. Banks and banking. 2. Currency question. 3. Money. I. Aldrich, Nelson Wilmarth, 1841- II. Title.
HG471.A4 1911 vol. 1   12-35260
MC#: Feb. 1912-page 478
SuDocs no.: 61st Cong., 2d sess. S. Doc. 405

25

U.S. *National monetary commission.*

. . . Interviews on the banking and currency systems of England, Scotland, France, Germany, Switzerland, and Italy, under the direction of Hon. Nelson W. Aldrich, chairman National monetary commission. Washington, Govt. print. off., 1910.

541 p. fold. tables. 23½ cm. (61st Cong., 2d sess. Senate. Doc. 405)

Issued also, 1911, in Publications of National monetary commission. Vol. I.

1. Banks and banking. 2. Currency question. 3. Money — Europe. I. Aldrich, Nelson Wilmarth, 1841-1915. II. Title.
HG1576.U6   10-35470
- - - - - Copy 2.
MC#: Apr. 1910-page 612
SuDocs no.: 61st Cong., 2d sess. S. Doc. 405

26

U.S. *Laws, statutes, etc.*

. . . Laws of the United States concerning money, banking, and loans, 1778-1909; comp. by A. T. Huntington . . . and Robert J. Mawhinney . . . Washington, Govt. print. off., 1910 [i.e. 1911]

iii, iii-xxii p., 1 l., 267 p., 1 l., 269-812 p. 23 cm. (Publications of National monetary commission. vol. II) 61st Cong., 2d sess. Senate. Doc. 580.

Issued also separately, 1910.

1. Finance — U.S. 2. Banking law — U.S. 3. Coinage — U.S. 4. Paper money — U.S. 5. Debts, Public — U.S. I. Huntington, Andrew T. II. Mawhinney, Robert J., joint comp. III. Title.
HG471.A4 1911 vol. 2   12-35261
- - - - - Copy 2.
MC#: Feb. 1912-page 478
SuDocs no.: 61st Cong., 2d sess. S. Doc. 580

27

U.S. *Laws, statutes, etc.*

. . . Laws of the United States concerning money, banking, and loans, 1778-1909; comp. by A. T. Huntington . . . and Robert J. Mawhinney . . . [with Table of contents . . .] Washington, Govt. print. off., 1910.

v, 267 p., 1 l., 269-812, xxii p. 23 cm. (61st Cong., 2d sess. Senate. Doc. 580)

At head of title: . . . National monetary commission.

"Table of contents" has special t.-p.

1. Money — U.S. 2. Banking law — U.S. 3. Debts, Public — U.S. 4. Finance — U.S. I. Huntington, Andrew T., comp. II. Mawhinney, Robert J., comp. III. U.S. National monetary commission.
HG481.A2 1910   10-36032 Additions

- - - - Copy 2.
MC#: Oct. 1910-page 157
SuDocs no.: 61st Cong., 2d sess. S. Doc. 580
MC#: Nov. 1910-page 210
SuDocs no.: 61st Cong., 2d sess. S. Doc. 580, pt. 2

28

Welldon, Samuel Alfred, 1882- *comp.*
  . . . Digest of state banking statutes, comp. by Samual A. Welldon . . . Washington, Govt. print. off., 1910 [i.e. 1911]
  746 p. 3 fold. tab. 23 cm. (Publications of National monetary commission. vol. III)
  [U.S.] 61st Cong., 2d sess. Senate. Doc. 353.
  Presented by Mr. Aldrich; ordered printed February 8, 1910.
  Issued also separately, 1910.
  1. Banking law—U.S. 2. Banks and banking—U.S. 3. Trust companies—U.S. I. Title.
HG471.A4 1911 vol. 3   12-35262 rev.
- - - - Copy 2.
MC#: Feb. 1912-page 478
SuDocs no.: 61st Cong., 2d sess. S. Doc. 353

29

Welldon, Samual A. comp.
  . . . Digest of state banking statutes, comp. by Samuel A. Welldon . . . Washington, Govt. print. off., 1910.
  746 p. 3 fold. tab. 23 cm. ([U.S.] 61st Cong., 2d sess. Senate. Doc. 353)
  At head of title: . . . National monetary commission.
  Presented by Mr. Aldrich; ordered printed, February 8, 1910.
  1. Banking law—U.S. 2. Banks and banking—U.S. I. U.S. National monetary commission. II. U.S. 61st Cong., 2d sess., 1909-1910. Senate.
HG2424 1910   10-35377
- - - - Copy 2.
MC#: Apr. 1910-page 612
SuDocs no.: 61st Cong., 2d sess. S. Doc. 353

30

Holdsworth, John Thom.
  . . . The first and second banks of the United States, by John Thom Holdsworth . . . and Davis R. Dewey . . . Washington, Govt. print. off., 1910 [i.e. 1911]
  311 p. fold. tables. 23 cm. (Publications of National monetary commission. vol. IV [no. 1])
  [U.S.] 61st Cong., 2d sess. Senate. Doc. 571
  Issued also separately, 1910.
  1. Bank of the United States, 1791-1811. 2. Bank of the United States, 1816-1836. 3. Banks and banking—U.S. I. Dewey, Davis Rich, 1858- II. Title.
HG471.A4 1911 vol. 4, no. 1   12-35263
- - - - Copy 2.
MC#: Feb. 1912-page 478
SuDocs no.: 61st Cong., 2d sess. S. Doc. 571

31

Holdsworth, John Thom.
  . . . The first and second banks of the United States, by John Thom Holdsworth . . . and Davis R. Dewey . . . Washington, Govt. print. off., 1910.
  311 p. fold. tables. 23½ cm. ([U.S.] 61st Cong., 2d sess. Senate. Doc. 571)
  At head of title: . . . National monetary commission.
  1. Bank of the United States, 1791-1811. 2. Bank of the United States, 1816-1836. 3. Banks and banking—U.S. I. Dewey, Davis Rich, 1858- II. U.S. National monetary commission. III. U.S.

61st Cong., 2d sess., 1909-1910. Senate.
HG2525.H7   10-35942
- - - - Copy 2.
MC#: Aug. 1910-page 71
SuDocs no.: 61st Cong., 2d sess. S. Doc. 571

32

Dewey, Davis Rich, 1858-
  . . . State banking before the civil war, by Davis R. Dewey . . . and The safety fund banking system in New York, 1829-1866, by Robert E. Chaddock . . . Washington, Govt. print. off., 1910 [i.e. 1911]
  1 p. 1., 388 p. fold. map, fold. diagr. 23 cm. (Publications of National monetary commission. vol. IV [no. 2])
  [U.S.] 61st Cong., 2d sess. Senate. Doc. 581.
  Issued also separately, 1910.
  Bibliographical foot-notes.
  1. Banks and banking—U.S. 2. Banks and banking—New York (State) I. Chaddock, Robert Emmet, 1879- II. Title. III. Title: Safety fund banking system in New York.
HG471.A4 1911 vol. 4, no. 2   12-35264 Revised
- - - - Copy 2.
MC#: Feb. 1912-page 478
SuDocs no.: 61st Cong., 2d sess. S. Doc. 581

33

Dewey, Davis Rich, 1858-
  . . . State banking before the civil war, by Davis R. Dewey . . . and The safety fund banking system in New York, 1829-1866, by Robert E. Chaddock . . . Washington, Govt. print. off., 1910.
  1 p. 1., 388 p. fold. map, fold. diagr. 23 cm. ([U.S.] 61st sess. Senate. Doc. 581)
  At head of title: . . . National monetary commission.
  Bibliographical foot-notes.
  1. Banks and banking—U.S. 2. Banks and banking—New York (State) I. Chaddock, Robert Emmet, 1879- II. U.S. National monetary commission.
HG2581.D5   10-36029
- - - - Copy 2.
MC#: Oct. 1910-page 157
SuDocs no.: 61st Cong., 2d sess. S. Doc. 581

34

Davis, Andrew McFarland, 1833-1920
  . . . The origin of the national banking system, by Andrew McFarland Davis [and Supplement . . .] Washington, Govt. print,. off., 1910-11 [i.e. 1911]
  1 p. 1., 213 p., 1 1., 215-246 p. 23½ cm. (Publications of National monetary commission. vol. v [no. 1])
  [U.S.] 61st Cong., 2d sess. Senate. Doc. 582.
  Issued also separately, 1910-11.
  "The material upon which this research rests was collected . . . by Mr. Clyde O. Ruggles."
  Appendices: A. The Hooper bill. A bill to provide a national currency [1862]—B. The Sherman act. An act to provide a national currency [1863]—C. Section seven of "An act to provide ways and means for the support of the government," approved March 3, 1863.—D. The Moorhead bill.
  1. National banks—U.S. 2. Currency question—U.S. I. Title. II. Title: Hooper bill. III. Title: National banking system. IV. Title: Moorhead bill. V. Title: Sherman act.
HG471.A4 1911 vol. 5, no. 1   12-35265
- - - - Copy 2.
MC#: Feb. 1912-page 478
SuDocs no.: 61st Cong., 2d sess. S. Doc. 582

35

Davis, Andrew McFarland, 1833-1920.
   The origin of the national banking system. Washington, Govt. Print. Off., 1910-11.

   2 pts. (246 p.) 24 cm. ([U.S.] 61st Cong., 2d sess., 1909-1910. Senate. Document no. 582)
   At head of title: National Monetary Commission.
   Pt. 2 has title: Supplement . . .
   Issued also in Publications of National Monetary Commission, v. 5, no. 1.
   "The material upon which this research rests was collected . . . by Mr. Clyde O. Ruggles."
   1. National banks—U.S. 2. Currency question—U.S. I. U.S. National Monetary Commission. II. Title. (Series)
HG2555.D3   10-36030 rev *
MC#: Oct. 1910-page 157
        Mar. 1911-page 516
SuDocs no.: 61st Cong., 2d sess. S. Doc. 582

36

Noyes, Alexander Dana, 1862-
   . . . History of the national-bank currency, by Alexander Dana Noyes. Washington, Govt. print. off., 1910 [i.e. 1911]

   20 p. 23½ cm. (Publications of National monetary commission. vol. v [no. 2])
   [U.S.] 61st Cong., 2d sess. Senate. Doc. 572.
   Issued also separately, 1910.
   1. National bank notes. I. Title. II. Title: National-bank currency.
HG471.A4 1911 vol. 5, no. 2   12-35266
- - - - - Copy 2.
MC#: Feb. 1912-page 478
SuDocs no.: 61st Cong., 2d sess. S. Doc. 572

37

Noyes, Alexander Dana, 1862-
   . . . History of the national-bank currency, by Alexander Dana Noyes. Washington, Govt. print. off., 1910.

   20 p. 23 cm. ([U.S.] 61st Cong., 2d sess. Senate. Doc. 572)
   At head of title: . . . National monetary commission.
   1. National bank notes. I. U.S. National monetary commission. II. U.S. 61st Cong., 2d sess., 1909-1910. Senate.
HG607.N7   10-35949
- - - - - Copy 2.
MC#: Aug. 1910-page 71
SuDocs no.: 61st Cong., 2d sess. S. Doc. 572

38

Sprague, Oliver Mitchell Wentworth, 1873-
   . . . History of crises under the national banking system, by O. M. W. Sprague . . . Washington, Govt. print. off., 1910 [i.e. 1911]

   v, 484 p. fold. tables. 23½ cm. (Publications of National monetary commission. vol. v [no. 3])
   [U.S.] 61st Cong., 2d sess. Senate. Doc. 538.
   Issued also separately, 1910.
   1. Panics. 2. National banks—U.S. I. Title. II. Title: National banking system.
HG471.A4 1911 vol. 5, no. 3   12-35267
- - - - - Copy 2.
MC#: Feb. 1912-page 478
SuDocs no.: 61st Cong., 2d sess. S. Doc. 538

39

Sprague, Oliver Mitchell Wentworth. 1873-
   . . . History of crises under the national banking system, by

O. M. W. Sprague . . . Washington, Govt. print. off., 1910.
   v. 484 p. fold, tables. 23½ cm. (U.S. 61st Cong., 2d sess. Senate. Doc. 538)
   At head of title: National monetary commission.
   1. Panics. 2. National banks—U.S. I. U.S. National monetary commission. II. U.S. 61st Cong., 2d sess., 1909-1910. Senate.
HB3743.S7   10-35899
- - - - - Copy 2.
MC#: July 1910-page 24
SuDocs no.: 61st Cong., 2d sess. S. Doc. 538

40

Cannon, James Graham, 1858-
   . . . Clearing houses. By James Graham Cannon . . . Washington, Govt. print. off., 1910 [i.e. 1911]

   viii, 335 p. map, forms (2 fold.) facsims., tables (2 fold.) 23 cm. (Publications of National monetary commission. vol. vi [no. 1])
   [U.S.] 61st Cong., 2d sess. Senate. Doc. 491.
   Issued also separately, 1910.
   1. Clearing-house.
HG471.A4 1911 vol. 6, no. 1   12-35268
- - - - - Copy 2.
MC#: Feb. 1912-page 478
SuDocs no.: 61st Cong., 2d sess. S. Doc. 491

41

Cannon, James Graham, 1858-
   . . . Clearing houses. By James Graham Cannon . . . Washington, Govt. print. off., 1910.

   viii, 335 p. forms (2 fold.) facsims., tables (2 fold.) 23 cm. ([U.S.] 61st Cong., 2d sess. Senate. Doc. 491)
   At head of title: National monetary commission.
   1. Clearing-house. I. U.S. National monetary commission. II. U.S. 61st Cong., 2d sess., 1909-1910. Senate.
HG2306.C3   10-35726
- - - - - Copy 2.
MC#: May 1910-page 700.
SuDocs no.: 61st Cong., 2d sess. S. Doc. 491

42

Kinley, David, 1861-
   . . . The use of credit instruments in payments in the United States. Report comp. by David Kinley . . . Washington, Govt. print. off., 1910 [i.e. 1911]

   vi, 229 p. incl. 3 fold. diagr. 23 cm. (Publications of National monetary commission. vol. VI [no. 2])
   [U.S.] 61st Cong., 2d sess. Senate. Doc. 399.
   Issued also separately, 1910.
   "Select bibliography": p. 223-224.
   1. Credit—U.S. 2. Money—U.S. 3. Banks and banking—U.S. I. Title. II. Title: Credit instruments . . . United States.
HG471.A4 1911 vol. 6, no. 2   12-35269
- - - - - Copy 2.
MC#: Feb. 1912-page 478
SuDocs no.: 61st Cong., 2d sess. S. Doc. 399

43

Kinley, David, 1861-
   . . . The use of credit instruments in payments in the United States. Report comp. by David Kinley . . . Washington, Govt. print. off., 1910.

   vi, 229 p. incl. 3 fold. diagr. 23½ cm. ([U.S.] 61st Cong., 2d sess. Senate. Doc. 399)
   At head of title: . . . National monetary commission.

Issued also, 1911, in Publications of National monetary commission. vol. VI [no. 2]
"Select bibliography": p. 223-224.
1. Credit—U.S. 2. Money—U.S. 3. Banks and banking—U.S. I. U.S. National monetary commission. II. Title. III. Title: Credit instruments.
HG355.K5   10-35282
- - - - - Copy 2.
MC#: Mar. 1910-page 515
SuDocs no.: Y4.In/8:C91

44

Barnett, George Ernest.
. . . State banks and trust companies since the passage of the National-bank act, by George E. Barnett . . . Washington, Govt. print. off., 1911.
366 p. fold. tables, fold. diagr. 23 cm. (Publications of National monetary commission. vol. VII [no. 1])
[U.S.] 61st Cong., 3d sess. Senate. Doc. 659.
Issued also separately.
"Appendix B. The insurance of bank deposits in the West, by Thornton Cooke": p. 261-352.
1. Banking law—U.S. 2. Banks and banking—U.S. 3. Trust companies—U.S. I. Cooke, Thornton. II. Title. III. Title: National-bank act . . .
HG471.A4 1911 vol. 7, no. 1   12-35270
- - - - - Copy 2.
MC#: Feb. 1912-page 478
SuDocs no.: 61st Cong., 3d sess. S. Doc. 659

45

Barnett, George Ernest.
. . . State banks and trust companies since the passage of the National-bank act, by George E. Barnett . . . Washington, Govt. print. off., 1911.
366 p. fold. tables, fold. diagr. 23 cm. ([U.S.] 61st Cong., 3d sess. Senate. Doc. 659)
At head of title: National monetary commission.
1. Banking law—U.S. 2. Banks and banking—U.S. 3. Trust companies—U.S. I. U.S. National monetary commission. II. U.S. 61st Cong., 3d sess., 1910-1911. Senate.
HG2581.B33   11-35092
- - - - - Copy 2.
MC#: Jan. 1911-page 340
SuDocs no.: 61st Cong., 3d sess. S. Doc. 659

46

Kinley, David, 1861-
. . . The Independent treasury of the United States and its relations to the banks of the country, by David Kinley . . . Washington, Govt. print. off., 1910 [i.e. 1911]
370 p. diagrs. (part fold.) 23 cm. (Publications of National monetary commission. vol. VII [no. 2])
[U.S.] 61st Cong., 2d sess. Senate. Doc. 587.
Issued also separately, 1910.
"This monograph is a revision and continuation of the work of the present writer, published by Crowell & co., New York, in 1893, under the title: The Independent treasury of the United States."—Prefatory note.
"References": p. 331-333.
1. Independent treasury. 2. U.S. Treasury dept. I. Title.
HG471.A4 1911 vol. 7, no. 2   12-35271
- - - - - Copy 2.
MC#: Feb. 1912-page 478
SuDocs no.: 61st Cong., 2d sess. S. Doc. 587

47

Kinley, David, 1861-
. . . The Independent treasury of the United States and its relations to the banks of the country, by David Kinley . . . Washington, Govt. print. off., 1910.
370 p. diagrs. (partly fold.) 23 cm. (61st Cong., 2d sess. Senate. Doc. 587)
At head of title: . . . National monetary commission.
"This monograph is a revision and continuation of the work of the present writer, published by Crowell & co., New York, in 1893, under the title: The Independent treasury of the United States."—Prefatory note.
"References": p. 331-333.
1. Independent treasury. 2. U.S. Treasury dept. I. U.S. National monetary commission. II. U.S. 61st Cong., 2d sess., 1909-1910. Senate.
HG2535.K52   11-35046
- - - - - Copy 2.
MC#: Jan. 1911-page 339
SuDocs no.:61st Cong., 2d sess. S. Doc. 587

48

Withers, Hartley, 1867-
. . . The English banking system, by Hartley Withers, Sir R. H. Inglis Palgrave and other writers. Washington, Govt. print. off., 1910 [i.e. 1911]
1 p. l., 294 p. incl. 3 fold. tab. 23 cm. (Publications of National monetary commission. vol. VIII [no. 1])
[U.S.] 61st Cong., 2d sess. Senate. Doc. 492.
Issued also separately.
Contents.—The English banking system, by Hartley Withers.—The history of the separation of the departments of the Bank of England, by Sir R. H. Inglis Palgrave.—English banking organizations, by Ernest Sykes.—The London bankers clearing house, by R. M. Holland.
1. Banks and banking—Gt. Brit. 2. Bank of England. 3. London bankers' clearing house. I. Palgrave, Sir Robert Harry Inglis, 1827- II. Sykes, Ernest. III. Holland, Robert Martin. IV. Title.
HG471.A4 1911 vol. 8, no. 1   12-35272
- - - - - Copy 2.
MC#: Feb. 1912-page 478
SuDocs no.: 61st Cong., 2d sess. S. Doc. 492

49

Withers, Hartley, 1867-
. . . The English banking system, by Hartley Withers, Sir R. H. Inglis Palgrave and other writers. Washington, Govt. print. off., 1910.
1 p. l., 294 p. incl. 3 fold. tab. 23 cm. ([U.S.] 61st Cong., 2d sess. Senate. Doc. 492)
At head of title: . . . National monetary commission.
Contents.—The English banking system, by Hartley Withers—The history of the separation of the departments of the Bank of England, by Sir R. H. Inglis Palgrave.—English banking organizations, by Ernest Sykes.—The London bankers clearing house, by R. M. Holland.
1. Banks and banking—Gt. Brit. 2. Bank of England. 3. London bankers' clearing house. I. Palgrave, Sir Robert Harry Inglis, 1827- II. Sykes, Ernest. III. Holland, Robert Martin. IV. U.S. National monetary commission. V. U.S. 61st Cong., 2d sess., 1909-1910. Senate.
HG2988.W78   10-35995
- - - - - Copy 2.
MC#: Sept. 1910-page 113
SuDocs no.: 61st Cong., 2d sess. S. Doc. 492

50

Philippovich von Philippsberg, Eugen, 1858-
. . . History of the Bank of England and its financial services
to the state. 2d ed., rev., by Eugen von Philippovich . . . tr. by
Christabel Meredith, with an introduction by H. S. Foxwell.
Washington, Govt. print. off., 1911.

297 p. 23 cm. (Publications of National monetary commission.
vol. VIII [no. 2])
[U.S.] 61st Cong., 2d sess. Senate. Doc. 591.
Issued also separately.
1. Bank of England. 2. Finance—Gt. Brit.—Hist. I. Meredith,
Mrs. Christabel, tr. II. Foxwell, Herbert Somerton, 1849- III.
Title.
HG471.A4 1911 vol. 8, no. 2   12-35273
- - - - - Copy 2.
MC#: Feb. 1912-page 478
SuDocs no.: 61st Cong., 2d sess. S. Doc. 591

51

Philippovich von Philippsberg, Eugen, 1858-
. . . History of the Bank of England and its financial services
to the state. 2d ed., rev., by Eugen von Philippovich . . . tr. by
Christabel Meredith, with an introduction by H. S. Foxwell.
Washington, Govt. print. off., 1911.

297 p. 23 cm. ([U.S.] 61st Cong., 2d sess. Senate. Doc. 591)
At head of title: National monetary commission.
Issued also in Publications of National monetary commission.
vol. VIII [no. 2]
1. Bank of England. 2. Finance—Gt. Brit.—Hist. I. Meredith,
Mrs. Christabel, tr. II. Foxwell, Herbert Somerton, 1849- III.
U.S. National monetary commission. IV. Title.
HG2994.P6   11-35868
- - - - - Copy 2.
MC#: Oct. 1911-page 196
SuDocs no.: 61st Cong., 2d sess. S. Doc. 591

52

Breckenridge, Roeliff Morton.
. . . The history of banking in Canada, by Roeliff Morton
Breckenridge . . . Washington, Govt. print. off., 1910 [i.e. 1911]

vi, 3-308 p. 6 fold. tab. 23 cm. (Publications of National
monetary commission. vol. IX [no. 1])
[U.S.] 61st Cong., 2d sess. Senate. Doc. 332.
Presented by Mr. Burrows; ordered printed January 28, 1910.
Issued also separately, 1910.
1. Banks and banking—Canada. 2. Banking law—Canada. I.
Title.
HG471.A4 1911 vol. 9, no. 1   12-35274
- - - - - Copy 2.
MC#: Feb. 1912-page 478
SuDocs no.: 61st Cong., 2d sess. S. Doc. 332

53

Breckenridge, Roeliff Morton.
. . . The history of banking in Canada, by Roeliff Morton
Breckenridge . . . Washington, Govt. print. off., 1910.

vi, 3-308 p. 6 fold. tab. 23 cm. ([U.S.] 61st Cong., 2d sess.
Senate. Doc. 332)
At head of title: . . . National monetary commission.
Presented by Mr. Burrows; ordered printed, January 28, 1910.
1. Banks and banking—Canada. 2. Banking law—Canada. I.
U.S. National monetary commission. II. U.S. 61st Cong., 2d
sess., 1909-1910. Senate.
HG2701.B8   10-35223

- - - - - Copy 2.
MC#: Feb. 1910-page 417
SuDocs no.: 61st Cong., 2d sess. S. Doc. 332

54

Johnson, Joseph French, 1853-
. . . The Canadian banking system, by Joseph French Johnson . . . Washington, Govt. print. off., 1910 [i.e. 1911]

191 p. incl. fold. tables, fold. forms. fold diagrs. 23 cm. (Publica-
tions of National monetary commission. vol. IX [no. 2])
[U.S.] 61st Cong., 2d sess. Senate. Doc. 583.
Issued also separately, 1910.
Bibliography: p. 138.
1. Banks and banking—Canada. I. Title.
HG471.A4 1911 vol. 9, no. 2   12-35275
- - - - - Copy 2.
MC#: Feb. 1912-page 478
SuDocs no.: 61st Cong., 2d sess. S. Doc. 583

55

Johnson, Joseph French, 1853-
. . . The Canadian banking system, by Joseph French Johnson . . . Washington, Govt. print. off., 1910.

191 p. incl. fold. tables, fold. forms. fold. diagrs. 23 cm. ([U.S.]
61st Cong., 2d sess. Senate. Doc. 583)
At head of title: . . . National monetary commission.
Bibliography: p. 138.
1. Banks and banking—Canada. I. U.S. National monetary
commission.
HG2704.J7   10-36034
- - - - - Copy 2.
MC#: Oct. 1910-page 157
SuDocs no.: 61st Cong., 2d sess. S. Doc. 583

56

U.S. *National monetary commission.*
. . . Interviews on the banking and currency systems of
Canada, by a subcommittee of the National monetary commis-
sion. Washington, Govt. print. off., 1910 [i.e. 1911]

219 p. tables (1 fold.) 23 cm. (Publications of National monetary
commission. vol. IX [no. 3]
61st Cong., 2d sess. Senate Doc. 584.
E. B. Vreeland, chairman of subcommittee.
Issued also separately, 1910.
1. Banks and banking—Canada. 2. Money—Canada. I. Vree-
land, Edward Butterfield, 1857- II. Title.
HG471.A4 1911 vol. 9, no. 3   12-35276
- - - - - Copy 2.
MC#: Feb. 1912-page 478
SuDocs no.: 61st Cong., 2d sess. S. Doc. 584

57

U.S. *National monetary commission.*
. . . Interviews on the banking and currency systems of
Canada, by a subcommittee of the National monetary commis-
sion. Washington, Govt. print. off., 1910.

219 p. tables (1 fold.) 23 cm. (61st Cong., 2d sess. Senate. Doc.
584)
E. B. Vreeland, chairman of subcommittee.
Issued also 1911, in Publications of National monetary commission. Vol. IX [no. 3]
1. Banks and banking—Canada. 2. Money—Canada. I. Vreeland, Edward Butterfield, 1857- II. Title.
HG2704.U5   11-35047

- - - - - Copy 2.
MC#: Dec. 1910-page 267
SuDocs no.: 61st Cong., 2d sess. S. Doc. 584

58

Reichsbank, *Berlin.*
   . . . The Reichsbank, 1876-1900. Washington, Govt. print. off., 1910 [i.e. 1911]
   362 p. 23 cm. (Publications of National monetary commission. Vol. X [no. 1])
   [U.S.] 61st Cong., 2d sess. Senate. Doc. 408.
   Issued also separately, 1910.
   The German original of this work was published in 1900; English translation by F. W. C. Lieder. cf. p. 2.
   Appendix: Law of June 1, 1909, concerning changes in the bank act: p. 357-362.
   I. Lieder, Frederick William Charles, 1881- tr. II. Title.
HG471.A4 1911 vol. 10, no. 1   12-35277 Revised
MC#: Feb. 1912-page 478
SuDocs no.: 61st Cong., 2d sess. S. Doc. 408

59

Reichsbank, *Berlin.*
   . . . The Reichsbank, 1876-1900. Washington, Govt. print. off., 1910.
   362 p. 23 cm. ([U.S.] 61st Cong., 2d sess. Senate. Doc. 408)
   At head of title . . . National monetary commission.
   Issued also, 1911, in Publications of National monetary commission. Vol. X [no. 1]
   The German original of this work was published in 1900; English translation by F. W. C. Lieder. cf. p. 2.
   Appendix: Law of June 1, 1909, concerning changes in the bank act: p. 357-362.
   I. Lieder, Frederick William Charles, 1881- tr. II. U.S. National monetary commission. III. Title.
HG3054.A32   10-35476 Revised
MC#: Apr. 1910-page 612
SuDocs no.: 61st Cong., 2d sess. S. Doc. 408

60

U.S. *National monetary commission.*
   . . . Renewal of Reichsbank charter. Washington, Govt. print. off., 1910 [i.e. 1911]
   268 p. tables (part fold.) 23 cm. (Publications of National monetary commission. vol. X [no. 2])
   61st Cong., 2d sess. Senate. Doc. 507.
   Nelson W. Aldrich, chairman.
   Issued also separately, 1910.
   Contents. — Results of the German bank inquiry of 1908 (articles published in the "Frankfurter zeitung" during December, 1908) — Draft of a bill for the amendment of the German bank act with explanations. — Excerpts from the proceedings of the Third German bankers' convention, held in Hamburg in September, 1907. The discussion of deposit banking (speeches by Dr. Jaffé, Dr. Dammé, Dr. Solomonsohn, Max Schinckel, and Geh. Mueller) — Credit at the Reichsbank, by R. Koch. — Concerning the collateral loan business of the Reichsbank, especially the lending on imperial and state securities, by R. Koch. — Concerning the renewal of the Reichsbank privilege, by W. Lexis. — Concerning the renewal of the privilege of the Reichsbank and of the private note banks, by Moriz Stroell. — Law of June 1, 1909, amending the Bank act.
   I. Germany. Reichsbank. II. Germany. Bankenquetekommission. III. Koch, Richard, 1834- IV. Lexis, Wilhelm Hector Richard Albrecht, 1837- V. Stroll, Moritz. VI. Title.
HG471.A4 1911 vol. 10, no. 2   12-35278

61

U.S. *National monetary commission.*
   . . . Renewal of Reichsbank charter. Washington, Govt. Print. off., 1910.
   268 p. tables (part fold.) 23 cm. (61st Cong., 2d sess. Senate. Doc. 507)
   At head of title: National monetary commission.
   Nelson W. Aldrich, chairman.
   Issued also, 1911, in Publications of National monetary commission. Vol. X [no. 2]
   Contents. — Results of the German bank inquiry of 1908 (articles published in the "Frankfurter zeitung" during December, 1908) — Draft of a bill for the amendment of the German bank act with explanations. — Excerpts from the proceedings of the Third German bankers' convention, held in Hamburg in September, 1907. The discussion of deposit banking (speeches by Dr. Jaffé, Dr. Dammé, Dr. Solomonsohn, Max Schinckel, and Geh. Mueller) — Credit at the Reichsbank, by R. Koch. — Concerning the collateral loan business of the Reichsbank, especially the lending on imperial and state securities, by R. Koch. — Concerning the renewal of the Reichsbank privilege, by W. Lexis. — Concerning the renewal of the privilege of the Reichsbank and of the private note banks, by Moriz Stroell. — Law of June 1, 1909, amending the Bank act.
   I. Germany. Reichsbank. II. Germany. Bankenquetekommission. III. Koch, Richard, 1834- IV. Lexis, Wilhelm Hector Richard Albrecht, 1837-1914. V. Stroll, Moritz. VI. Title.
HG3055.U5   10-35783
- - - - - Copy 2.
MC#: June 1910-page 799
SuDocs no.: 61st Cong., 2d sess. S. Doc. 507

62

U.S. *National monetary commission.*
   . . . Miscellaneous articles on German banking. Washington, Govt. print. off., 1910 [i.e. 1911]
   478 p. 4 fold. tab. 23 cm. (Publications of National monetary commission. vol. XI [no. 1])
   61st Cong., 2d sess. Senate. Doc. 508.
   Issued also separately, 1910.
   1. Banks and banking — Germany. I. Title.
HG471.A4 1911 vol. 11, no. 1   12-35279
- - - - - Copy 2.
MC#: Feb. 1912-page 478
SuDocs no.: 61st Cong., 2d sess. S. Doc. 508

63

U.S. *National monetary commission.*
   . . . Miscellaneous articles on German banking. Washington, Govt. print. off., 1910.
   478 p. 4 fold. tab. 23½ cm. (61st Cong., 2d sess. Senate. Doc. 508)
   At head of title: National monetary commission.
   Issued also, 1911, in Publications of National monetary commission. Vol. XI [no. 1]
   1. Banks and banking — Germany. I. Title.
HG3048.U6   10-35886
- - - - - Copy 2.
MC#: July 1910-page 24
SuDocs no.: 61st Cong., 2d sess. S. Doc. 508

64

Koch, Richard, 1834-
. . . German imperial banking laws, ed. by Dr. R. Koch . . .
Together with the German stock exchange regulations.
Washington, Govt. print. off., 1910 [i.e. 1911]

v, 330 p. 2 fold. forms. 23 cm. (Publications of National
monetary commission. vol. XI [no. 2])

[U.S.] 61st Cong., 2d sess. Senate. Doc. 574.

Issued also separately, 1910.

Translated by F. F. Rosenblatt.

Introduction includes history of conditions prevailing in Germany, with regard to media of circulation — coins, paper money
and bank notes — etc.

1. Banking law — Germany. 2. Stock-exchange — Germany. I.
Rosenblatt, Frank F., tr. II. Title.

HG471.A4 1911 vol. 11, no. 2   12-35280

- - - - - Copy 2.

MC#: Feb. 1912-page 478

SuDocs no.: 61st Cong., 2d sess. S. Doc. 574

65

Koch, Richard, 1834-
. . . German imperial banking laws, ed. by Dr. R. Koch . . .
Together with the German stock exchange regulations. Washing-
ton, Govt. print. off., 1910.

v, 330 p. fold. forms. 23 cm. ([U.S.] 61st Cong., 2d sess.
Senate. Doc. 574)

At head of title: National monetary commission.

Translated by F. F. Rosenblatt.

Introduction includes history of conditions prevailing in Germany, with regard to media of circulation — coins, paper money
and bank notes — etc.

1. Banking law — Germany. 2. Stock-exchange — Germany. I.
U.S. National monetary commission. II. U.S. 61st Cong., 2d
sess., 1909-10. Senate. III. Rosenblatt, Frank F., tr.

HG3043.K8   10-35937

- - - - - Copy 2.

MC#: July 1910-page 24

SuDocs no.: 61st Cong., 2d sess. S. Doc. 574

66

Germany. *Bankenquete-kommission.*
. . . German bank inquiry of 1908: stenographic reports . . .
Washington, Govt. print. off., 1910-11 [i.e. 1911]

2 v. fold. tab. 23 cm. (Publications of National monetary commission. vol. XII-XIII)

[U.S.] 61st Cong., 2d sess. Senate. Doc. 407.

[Vol. I] pub. at Berlin, 1909, with title: Bankenquete 1908 . . .
vol. II, Berlin, 1910, with title: Bankenquete 1908/09 . . .

Vol. II has title: German bank inquiry of 1908-9 . . .

Rudolf Havenstein, chairman.

Issued also separately, 1910-11.

1. Banks and banking — Germany. 2. Germany. Reichsbank.
I. Havenstein, Rudolf, 1855- II. Title.

HG471.A4 1911 vol. 12-13   12-35281

- - - - - Copy 2.

MC#: Feb. 1912-page 478

SuDocs no.: 61st Cong., 2d sess. S. Doc. 407

67

Germany. *Bankenquete-kommission.*
. . . German bank inquiry of 1908: stenographic reports . . .
Washington, Govt. print. off., 1910-11.

2 v. fold. tab. 23 cm. ([U.S.] 61st Cong., 2d sess. Senate. Doc.
407)

At head of title: . . . National monetary commission.

[Vol. I] pub. at Berlin, 1909, with title: Bankenquete 1908 . . .
vol. II, Berlin, 1910, with title: Bankenquete 1908/09 . . .

Vol. II has title: German bank inquiry of 1908-9 . . .

Rudolf Havenstein, chairman.

1. Banks and banking — Germany. 2. Germany. Reichsbank.
I. Havenstein, Rudolf, 1855- II. U.S. National monetary commission.

HG3042.A5 1908d   10-35473 Additions

- - - - - Copy 2.

MC#: Apr. 1910-page 612 (Vol. 1)

SuDocs no.: 61st Cong., 2d sess. S. Doc. 407, pt. 1

Aug. 1911-page 95 (Vol. 2)

SuDocs no.: 61st Cong., 2d sess. S. Doc. 407, pt. 2

68

Riesser, Jacob, 1853-
. . . The German great banks and their concentration in connection with the economic development of Germany, by Dr. J.
Riesser . . . 3d ed. completely rev. and enl. Washington, Govt.
print. off., 1911.

xvi, 1042 p. 23 cm. (Publications of National monetary commission. vol. XIV)

[U.S.] 61st Cong., 2d sess. Senate. Doc. 593.

Issued also separately.

Translation of "Die deutschen grossbanken und ihre konzentration," by Morris Jacobson.

"Appendix I. Bibliography": p. 883-892.

1. Banks and banking — Germany. 2. Trusts, Industrial. I.
Jacobson, Morris. II. U.S. National monetary commission. III.
Title.

HG471.A4 1911 vol. 14   12-35282

- - - - - Copy 2.

MC#: Feb. 1912-page 478

SuDocs no.: 61st Cong., 2d sess. S. Doc. 593

69

Riesser, Jacob, 1853-
. . . The German great banks and their concentration in connection with the economic development of Germany, by Dr. J.
Riesser . . . 3d ed., completely rev. and enl. Washington, Govt.
print. off., 1911.

xvi, 1042 p. incl. tables. 23 cm. ([U.S.] 61st Cong., 2d sess.
Senate. Doc. 593)

At head of title: National monetary commission.

Issued also in Publications of National monetary commission.
vol. XIV.

Translation by Morris Jacobson of "Die deutschen grossbanken
und ihre konzentration."

"Appendix I. Bibliography": p. 883-892.

1. Banks and banking — Germany. 2. Trusts, Industrial. I.
Jacobson, Morris Lazarev, 1868- tr. II. U.S. National monetary
commission. III. Title.

HG3048.R65   11-35821

- - - - - Copy 2.

MC#: Oct. 1911-page 196

SuDocs no.: 61st Cong., 2d sess. S. Doc. 593

70

Liesse, André, 1854-
. . . Evolution of credit and banks in France from the found-
ing of the Bank of France to the present time, by André
Liesse . . . Washington, Govt. print. off., 1909 [i.e. 1911]

267 p. fold. tab. 23 cm. (Publications of National monetary
commission. vol. XV [no. 1])

[U.S.] 61st Cong., 2d sess. Senate. Doc. 522.

Issued also separately, 1909 [i.e. 1910]

1. Banks and banking—France. 2. Credit—France. 3. Finance—France. I. U.S. National monetary commission. II. Title.
HG471.A4 1911 vol. 15, no. 1   12-35283
- - - - - Copy 2.
MC#: Feb. 1912-page 478
SuDocs no.: 61st Cong., 2d sess. S. Doc. 522

71

Liesse, André, 1854-
. . . Evolution of credit and banks in France from the founding of the Bank of France to the present time, by André Liesse . . . Washington, Govt. print. off., 1909 [1910]
267 p. fold. tab. 23 cm. (U.S. 61st Cong., 2d sess. Senate. Doc. 522)
At head of title: National monetary commission.
Issued also, 1911, in Publications of National monetary commission. Vol. XV. [no.1]
1. Banks and banking—France. 2. Credit—France. 3. Finance—France. I. U.S. National monetary commission. II. Title.
HG3028.L5   10-35929
- - - - - Copy 2.
MC#: July 1910-page 24
SuDocs no.: 61st Cong., 2d sess. S. Doc. 522

72

Patron, Maurice.
. . . The Bank of France in its relation to national and international credit, by Maurice Patron . . . and an article upon French savings, by Alfred Neymarck . . . Washington, Govt. print. off., 1910.
181 p. fold. diagr. 23 cm. (Publications of National monetary commission. vol. XV [no. 2])
[U.S.] 61st .Cong., 2d sess. Senate. Doc. 494.
Issued also separately.
Bibliography: p. 160-161.
1. Banque de France, Paris. 2. Credit—France. 3. Finance—France. 4. Banks and banking. I. Neymarck, Alfred, 1848- II. U.S. National monetary commission. III. Title.
HG471.A4 1911 vol. 15, no. 2   12-35284
- - - - - Copy 2.
MC#: Feb. 1912-page 478
SuDocs no.: 61st Cong., 2d sess. S. Doc. 494

73

Patron, Maurice.
. . . The Bank of France in its relation to national and international credit, by Maurice Patron . . . and an article upon French savings, by Alfred Neymarck . . . Washington, Govt. print. off., 1910.
181 p. fold. diagr. 23 cm. ([U.S.] 61st Cong., 2d sess. Senate. Doc. 494)
At head of title: . . . National monetary commission.
Bibliography: p. 160-161.
1. Banque de France, Paris. 2. Credit—France. 3. Finance—France. 4. Banks and banking. I. Neymarck, Alfred, 1848- II. U.S. National monetary commission. III. U.S. 61st Cong., 2d sess., 1909-1910. Senate.
HG3035.P45   10-35784
- - - - - Copy 2.
MC#: June 1910-page 799
SuDocs no.: 61st Cong., 2d sess. S. Doc. 494

74

Vidal, Emmanuel.
. . . The history and methods of the Paris bourse, by E. Vidal. Washington, Govt. print. off., 1910.
1 p. 1., 276 p. facsims. 23½ cm. (Publications of National

monetary commission. vol. XV [no. 3])
[U.S.] 61st Cong., 2d sess. Senate. Doc. 573.
Issued also separately.
1. Paris. Bourse. I. U.S. National monetary commission. II. Title.
HG471.A4 1911 vol. 15, no. 3   12-35285
- - - - - Copy 2.
MC#: Feb.1912-page 478
SuDocs no.: 61st Cong., 2d sess. S. Doc. 573

75

Vidal, Emmanuel.
. . . The history and methods of the Paris bourse, by E. Vidal. Washington, Govt. print. off., 1910.
1. p. 1., 276 p. facsims. 23½ cm. ([U.S.] 61st Cong., 2d sess. Senate. Doc. 573)
At head of title: . . . National monetary commission.
Issued also, 1911, in Publications of National monetary commission. Vol. XV [no. 3]
1. Paris, Bourse. I. U.S. National monetary commission.
HG4582.V3   10-36031
MC#: Oct. 1910-page 157
SuDocs no.: 61st Cong., 2d sess. S. Doc. 573

76

Conant, Charles Arthur, 1861-1915.
. . . The National bank of Belgium. By Charles A. Conant . . . Washington, Govt. print. off., 1910 [i.e. 1911]
238 p. 23 cm. (Publications of National monetary commission. vol. XVI [no. 1])
[U.S.] 61st Cong., 2d sess. Senate. Doc. 400
Issued also separately, 1910.
1. Banque nationale de Belgique, Brussels. I. Title.
HG471.A4 1911 vol. 16, no. 1   12-35286
- - - - - Copy 2.
MC#: Feb. 1912-page 478
SuDocs no.: 61st Cong., 2d sess. S. Doc. 400

77

Conant, Charles Arthur, 1861-1915.
. . . The National bank of Belgium. By Charles A. Conant . . . Washington, Govt. print. off., 1910.
238 p. 23 cm. ([U.S.] 61st Cong., 2d sess. Senate. Doc. 400)
At head of title: . . . National monetary commission.
Issued also, 1911, in Publications of National monetary commission. vol. XVI [no. 1]
1. Banque nationale de Belgique, Brussels. I. U.S. National monetary commission. II. Title.
HG3106.C6   10-35308
- - - - - Copy 2.
MC#: Mar. 1910-page 515
SuDocs no.: Y4.W36:C64

78

Conant, Charles Arthur, 1861-1915.
. . . The banking system of Mexico, by Charles A. Conant . . . Washington, Govt. print. off., 1910 [i.e. 1911]
284 p. 4 fold. tab. 23 cm. (Publications of National monetary commission. vol. XVI [no. 2])
[U.S.] 61st Cong., 2d sess. Senate. Doc. 493.
Issued also separately, 1910.
"The banking laws of Mexico": p. 169-213.
1. Banks and banking—Mexico. 2. Banking law—Mexico. I. U.S. National monetary commission. II. Mexico. Laws, statutes, etc. III. Title.
HG471.A4 1911 vol. 16, no. 2   12-35287

- - - - - Copy 2.
MC#: Feb. 1912-page 478
SuDocs no.: 61st Cong., 2d sess. S. Doc. 493

79

Conant, Charles Arthur, 1861-1915.
  . . . The banking system of Mexico, by Charles A. Conant . . .
Washington, Govt. print. off., 1910.

  284 p. 4 fold. tab. 23 cm. ([U.S.] 61st Cong., 2d sess. Senate. Doc. 493)
  At head of title: National monetary commission.
  "The banking laws of Mexico": p. 169-213.
  Issued also, 1911, in Publications of National monetary commission. vol. XVI [no. 2]
  1. Banks and banking—Mexico. 2. Banking law—Mexico. I. U.S. National monetary commission. II. Mexico. Laws, statutes, etc. III. Title.
HG2714.C7   10-35744
- - - - - Copy 2.
MC#: May 1910-page 700
SuDocs no.: 61st Cong., 2d sess. S. Doc. 493

80

Flux, Alfred William, 1867-
  . . . The Swedish banking system, by A. W. Flux. Washington, Govt. print. off., 1910 [i.e. 1911]

  248 p. fold. diagr. 23 cm. (Publications of National monetary commission. vol. XVII [no. 1])
  [U.S.] 61st Cong., 2d sess. Seante. Doc. 576.
  Issued also separately, 1910.
  "Works consulted": p. 9-10.
  1. Banks and banking—Sweden. I. U.S. National monetary commission. II. Title.
HG471.A4 1911 vol. 17, no. 1   12-35288
- - - - - Copy 2.
MC#: Feb. 1912-page 478
SuDocs no.: 61st Cong., 2d sess. S. Doc. 576

81

Flux, Alfred William, 1867-
  . . . The Swedish banking system, by A. W. Flux. Washington, Govt. print. off., 1910.

  248 p. fold. diagr. 23½ cm. (U.S. 61st Cong., 2d sess. Senate. Doc. 576)
  At head of title: National monetary commission.
  "Works consulted": p. 9-10.
  Issued also, 1911, in Publications of National monetary commission. vol. XVII [no. 1]
  1. Banks and banking—Sweden. I. U.S. National monetary commission. II. Title.
HG3174.F6   10-35898
- - - - - Copy 2.
MC#: July 1910-page 24 (LC card 10-35899 referred to in error)
SuDocs no.: 61st Cong., 2d sess. S. Doc. 576

82

Landmann, Julius, 1877-
  . . . The Swiss banking law; study and criticism of the Swiss legislation respecting banks of issue, and especially of the federal act of October 6, 1905, concerning the Swiss national bank. By Dr. Julius Landmann. Washington, Govt. print. off., 1910 [i.e. 1911]

  269 p. 2 fold. tab. 23 cm. (Publications of National monetary commission. vol. XVII [no. 2])
  [U.S.] 61st Cong., 2d sess. Senate. Doc. 401.

Issued also separately, 1910.
  "The new Swiss central note bank," by A. Erdely: p. 238-249; Address of M. R. Comtesse: p. 264-268; "References": p. 269.
  1. Schweizerische national bank. 2. Banks and banking—Switzerland. 3. Banking law—Switzerland. I. Title.
HG471.A4 1911 vol. 17, no. 2   12-35289
- - - - - Copy 2.
MC#: Feb.1912-page 478
SuDocs no.: 61st Cong., 2d sess. S. Doc. 401

83

Landmann, Julius, 1877-
  . . . The Swiss banking law; study and criticism of the Swiss legislation respecting banks of issue, and especially of the federal act of October 6, 1905, concerning the Swiss national bank. By Dr. Julius Landmann. Washington, Govt. print. off., 1910.

  269 p. 2 fold. tab. 23 cm. ([U.S.] 61st Cong., 2d sess. Senate. Doc. 401)
  At head of title: . . . National monetary commission.
  "The new Swiss central note bank," by A. Erdely: p. 238-249; Address of M. R. Comtesse: p. 264-268; "References": p. 269.
  1. Schweizerische national bank. 2. Banks and banking—Switzerland. 3. Banking law—Switzerland. I. U.S. National monetary commission. II. U.S. 61st Cong., 2d sess., 1909-1910. Senate.
HG1870.S9L32   10-35354
- - - - - Copy 2.
MC#: Mar. 1910-page 515
SuDocs no.: Y4.In8/8:G46/2

84

Canovai, Tito.
  . . . The banks of issue in Italy, by Tito Canovai . . . with an article by Carlo F. Ferraris . . . and the text of the Italian banking law. Washington, Govt. print. off., 1911.

  1 p. 1., 345 p. fold. tab 23 cm. (Publications of National monetary commission. vol. XVIII [no. 1])
  [U.S.] 61st Cong., 2d sess. Senate. Doc. 575.
  Issued also separately.
  "The Italian banks of issue by Carlo F. Ferraris" is taken from Conrad' Handwörterbuch der staatswissenschaften, 3d ed.
  1. Banks and banking—Italy. 2. Banking law—Italy. I. Ferraris, Carlo Francesco, 1850- II. Italy. Laws, statutes, etc. III. Title.
HG471.A4 1911 vol. 18, no. 1   12-35290
- - -,- - Copy 2.
MC#: Feb. 1912-page 478
SuDocs no.: 61st Cong., 2d sess. S. Doc. 575

85

Canovai, Tito.
  . . . The banks of issue in Italy by Tito Canovai . . . with an article by Carlo F. Ferraris . . . and the text of the Italian banking law. Washington, Govt. print. off., 1911.

  1 p. 1., 345 p. fold. tab. 23 cm. ([U.S.] 61st Cong., 2d sess. Senate. Doc. 575)
  At head of title: . . . National monetary commission.
  "The Italian banks of issue by Carlo F. Ferraris" is taken from Conrad' Handwörterbuch der staatswissenschaften, 3d ed.
  1. Banks and banking—Italy. 2. Banking law—Italy. I. Ferraris, Carlo Francesco, 1850- II. U.S. Monetary commission. III. Italy. Laws, statutes, etc. IV. U.S. 61st Cong., 2d sess., 1909-1910. Senate.
HG1870.I8C3   11-35367
- - - - - Copy 2.
MC#: Apr. 1911-page 569
SuDocs no.: 61st Cong., 2d sess. S. Doc. 575

86

U.S. *National monetary commission.*
. . . Banking in Russia, Austro-Hungary, the Netherlands and
Japan. Washington, Govt. print. off., 1911.

v, 214 p. 23 cm. (Publications of National monetary commis-
sion. vol. XVIII [no. 2])
61st Cong., 2d sess. Senate. Doc. 586.
Issued also separately.
Articles I-III (p. 1-118) are from Conrad's Handwörterbuch
der staatswissenschaften, 3d ed.
Contents. — I. Organization of banking in Russia. By Professors
Idelson and Lexis. — II. The Bank of the Netherlands. By R.
vander Borght. — III. The Austro-Hungarian bank. By Professor
Zuckerkandl. — IV. The banking system of Japan. By Marquis
Katsura, Baron Sakatani, S. Naruse, O. M. W. Sprague.
1. Banks and banking — Russia. 2. Banks and banking —
Austria. 3. Oesterreichisch-ungarische bank, Vienna. 4. Banks
and banking — Netherlands. 5. Netherlandsche bank, Amsterdam.
6. Banks and banking — Japan. I. Title.
HG471.A4 1911 vol. 18, no. 2   12-35291
- - - - - Copy 2.
MC#: Feb. 1912-page 478
SuDocs no.: 61st Cong., 2d sess. S. Doc. 586

87

U.S. *National monetary commission.*
. . . Banking in Russia, Austro-Hungary, the Netherlands and
Japan. Washington, Govt. print. off., 1911.

v, 214 p. 23 cm. (61st Cong., 2d sess. Senate. Doc. 586)
At head of title: . . . National monetary commission.
Issued also 1911, in Publications of National monetary com-
mission. Vol. XVIII [no. 2]
Articles I-III (p. 1-118) are from Conrad's Handwörterbuch
der staatswissenschaften, 3d ed.
Contents. — I. Organization of banking in Russia. By Professors
Idelson and Lexis. — II. The Bank of the Netherlands. By R. van
der Borght. — III. The Austro-Hungarian bank. By Professor
Zuckerkandl. — IV. The banking system of Japan. By Marquis
Katsura, Baron Sakatani, S. Naruse, O. M. W. Sprague.
1. Banks and banking — Russia. 2. Banks and banking —
Austria. 3. Oesterreichisch-ungarische bank, Vienna. 4. Banks
and banking — Netherlands. 5. Nederlandsche bank, Amsterdam.
6. Banks and banking — Japan. I. Title.
HG1576.U62   11-35211
- - - - - Copy 2.
MC#: Feb. 1911-page 432
SuDocs no.: 61st Cong., 2d sess. S. Doc. 586

88

U.S. *National monetary commission.*
. . . Suggested changes in the administrative features of the na-
tional banking laws. Replies to circular letter of inquiry of
September 26, 1908, and hearings, December 2 and 3, 1908.
Washington, Govt. print. off., 1910 [i.e. 1911]

3,743 p. 23 cm. (Publications of National monetary commis-
sion. Vol. XIX [no. 1])
61st Cong., 2d sess. Senate. Doc. 404.
Issued also separately, 1910.
Hearings were also issued separately in 1908.
Nelson W. Aldrich, chairman. 1. Banking law — U.S. 2. Na-
tional banks — U.S. I. Title.
HG471.A4 1911 vol. 19, no. 1   12-35292
- - - - - Copy 2.
MC#: Feb. 1912-page 478
SuDocs no.: 61st Cong., 2d sess. S. Doc. 404

89

U.S. *National monetary commission.*
. . . Suggested changes in the administrative features of the na-
tional banking laws. Replies to circular letter of inquiry of
September 26, 1908, and hearings. December 2 and 3, 1908.
Washington, Govt. print. off., 1910.

374 p. 23 cm. (61st Cong., 2d sess. Senate. Doc. 404)
At head of title: . . . National monetary commission.
Nelson W. Aldrich, chairman.
Issued also, 1911, in Publications of National monetary com-
mision. Vol. XIX [no. 1]
Hearings were also issued separately in 1908.
1. Banking law — U.S. 2. National banks — U.S. I. Title.
HG471.A4 1908 b   10-35478
- - - - - Copy 2.
MC#: Apr. 1910-page 612
SuDocs no.: 61st Cong., 2d sess. S. Doc. 404

90

U.S. *National Monetary commission.*
National monetary commission: replies to circular letter of inquiry of September 26, 1908, on suggested changes in administrative features of the national banking laws. Washington,
Govt. print. off., 1908.

175 p. 23 cm.
1. National banks — U.S. 2. Banking law — U.S.
HG471.A4 1908 a   9-35768
Document Catalogue, vol. 10-page 1093

91

U.S. *National monetary commission.*
Hearings before the National monetary commission on changes
in the administrative features of the national banking laws. Dec.
2-3, 1908. Washington, Govt. print. off., 1908.

184 p. 23 cm.
1. National banks — U.S. 2. Banking law — U.S.
HG471.A4 1908   9-35165
- - - - - Copy 2.
MC#: Jan. 1909-page 322
SuDocs no.: Y3.N21/2:B22/1

92

U.S. *National monetary commission.*
Report to the National monetary commission on the fiscal
systems of the United States, England, France, and Germany.
Washington, Govt. print. off., 1910 [i.e. 1911]

86 p. 23 cm. (Publications of National monetary commission.
vol. XIX. [no. 2])
61st Cong., 2d sess. Senate. Doc. 403.
By J. O. Manson, of the Treasury department.
Issued also separately, 1909 and 1910.
1. Finance. 2. Finance — U.S. 3. Finance — Gt. Brit. 4.
Finance — France. 5. Finance — Germany. I. Manson, Joseph O.
II. Title. III. Title: Fiscal systems.
HG471.A4 1911   12-35293
- - - - - Copy 2.
MC#: Feb. 1912-page 478
SuDocs no.: 61st Cong., 2d sess. S. Doc. 403

93

U.S. *National monetary commission.*
. . . Report to the National monetary commission on the fiscal
systems of the United States, England, France, and Germany.
Washington, Govt. print. off., 1910.

86 p. 23 cm. (61st Cong., 2d sess. Senate. Doc. 403)
By J. O. Manson, of the Treasury department.

Issued also in 1911 in Publications of National monetary commission, vol. XIX [no. 2] and in 1909, without document series note.

1. Finance. 2. Finance—U.S. 3. Finance—Gt. Brit. 4. Finance—France. 5. Finance—Germany. I. Manson, Joseph O. II. Title. III. Title: Fiscal systems.
HJ197.U6 1910   10-35378
- - - - - Copy 2.
MC#: Mar. 1910-page 515
SuDocs no.: 61st Cong., 2d sess. S. Doc. 403

94

U.S. *National monetary commission.*
Report to the National monetary commission on the fiscal systems of the United States, England, France, and Germany. Washington, Govt. print. off., 1909.

86 p. 23½ cm.
By J. O. Manson, of the Treasury department.
1. Finance. I. Manson, Joseph O.
HJ197.U6 1909   9-35349
- - - - - Copy 2.
MC#: Mar. 1909-page 498
SuDocs no.: Y4.N21/2:F52

95

U.S. *National monetary commission.*
. . . Notes on the postal savings-bank systems of the leading countries. Washington, Govt. print. off., 1910.

128 p. tables (part fold.) 23 cm. (Publications of National monetary commission. vol. XIX [no. 3])
61st Cong., 3d sess. Senate. Doc. 658.
Issued also separately.
1. Postal savings-banks. I. Title.
HG471.A4 1911 vol. 19, no. 3   12-35294
- - - - - Copy 2.
MC#: Feb. 1912-page 478
SuDocs no.: 61st Cong., 3d sess. S. Doc. 658

96

U.S. *National monetary commission.*
. . . Notes on the postal savings-bank systems of the leading countries. Washington, Govt. print. off., 1910.

128 p. tables (part fold.) 23 cm. (61st Cong., 3d sess. Senate. Doc. 658)
At head of title: . . . National monetary commission.
Issued also, 1911, in Publications of National monetary commission. vol. XIX [no. 3]
1. Postal savings-banks. I. Title.
HG1951.U6 1910   10-35028
- - - - - Copy 2.
MC#: Dec. 1910-page 267
SuDocs no.: 61st Cong., 3d sess. S. Doc. 658

97

Aldrich, Nelson Wilmarth, 1841-1915.
. . . An address by Senator Nelson W. Aldrich before the Economic club of New York, November 29, 1909, on the work of the National monetary commission. Washington, Govt. print. off., 1910 [i.e. 1911]

29 p. 23 cm. (Publications of National monetary commission. vol. XX [no. 1])
[U.S.] 61st Cong., 2d sess. Senate. Doc. 406.
Issued also separately, 1910.
1. Banks and banking—U.S. 2. Currency question—U.S. 3. Panics. I. Title.
HG471.A4 1911 vol. 20, no. 1   12-35295

- - - - - Copy 2.
MC#: Feb. 1912-page 478
SuDocs no.: 61st Cong., 2d sess. S. Doc. 406

98

Aldrich, Nelson Wilmarth, 1841-1915.
. . . An address by Senator Nelson W. Aldrich before the Economic club of New York, November 29, 1909, on the work of the National monetary commission. Washington, Govt. print. off., 1910.

29 p. 23 cm. ([U.S.] 61st Cong., 2d sess. Senate. Doc. 406)
At head of title: National monetary commission.
Issued, 1911, in Publications of National monetary commission, vol. XX [no. 1] and in 1909, without document series note.
1. Banks and banking—U.S. 2. Currency question—U.S. 3. Panics. I. U.S. National monetary commission. II. Title.
HG472.A52   10-35477
- - - - - Copy 2.
MC#: Apr. 1910-page 612
SuDocs no.: 61st Cong., 2d sess. S. Doc. 406

99

Aldrich, Nelson Wilmarth, 1841-1915.
. . . An address by Senator Nelson W. Aldrich before the Economic club of New York, November 29, 1909, on the work of the National monetary commission. Washington, Govt. print. off., 1909.

29 p. 23 cm.
At head of title: National monetary commission.
Issued also, 1910, as Senate Doc. 406, 61st Cong., 2d sess; and in 1911 as Publications of National monetary commission. Vol. XX [no. 1]
1. Banks and banking—U.S. 2. Currency question—U.S. 3. Panics. I. U.S. National monetary commission.
HG472.A5   10-3025 Revised
Not located in Monthly Catalog

100

Warburg, Paul Moritz, 1868-
. . . The discount system in Europe, by Paul M. Warburg. Washington, Govt. print. off., 1910 [i.e. 1911]

43 p. 23 cm. (Publications of National monetary commission. vol. XX [no. 2])
[U.S.] 61st Cong., 2d sess. Senate. Doc. 402.
Issued also separately, 1910.
1. Discount. 2. Banks and banking. 3. Acceptances. I. Title.
HG471.A4 1911   12-35296 Revised
- - - - - Copy 2.
MC#: Feb. 1912-page 478
SuDocs no.: 61st Cong., 2d sess. S. Doc. 402

101

Warburg, Paul Moritz, 1868-
. . . The discount system in Europe, by Paul M. Warburg. Washington, Govt. print. off., 1910.

43 p. 23 cm. ([U.S.] 61st Cong., 2d sess. Senate. Doc. 402)
At head of title: . . . National monetary commission.
Issued also, 1911, in Publications of National monetary commission. vol. XX [no. 2]
1. Discount. 2. Banks and banking. 3. Acceptances. I. U.S. National monetary commission. II. Title.
HG1651.W3   10-35393 Revised
- - - - - Copy 2.
MC#: Mar. 1910-page 515
SuDocs no.: Y4.W36:R24/1-2

102

Jacobs, Lawrence Merton.
   . . . Bank acceptances, by Lawrence Merton Jacobs. Washington, Govt. print. off., 1910 [i.e. 1911]
   20 p. 23 cm. (Publications of National monetary commission. vol. XX [no. 3])
   [U.S.] 61st Cong., 2d sess. Senate. Doc. 569.
   Issued also separately, 1910.
   1. Banks and banking. 2. Banks and banking—U.S. I. Title.
HG471.A4 1911 vol. 20, no. 3   12-35297
- - - - - Copy 2.
MC#: Feb. 1912-page 478
SuDocs no.: 61st Cong., 2d sess. S. Doc. 569

103

Jacobs, Lawrence Merton.
   . . . Banks acceptances, by Lawrence Merton Jacobs. Washington, Govt. print. off., 1910.
   20 p. 23 cm. ([U.S.] 61st Cong., 2d sess. Senate. Doc. 569)
   At head of title: . . . National monetary commission.
   1. Banks and banking—Europe. 2. Banks and banking—U.S. I. U.S. National monetary commission. II. U.S. 61st Cong., 2d sess., 1909-1910. Senate.
HG1641.J2   10-35943
- - - - - Copy 2.
MC#: Aug. 1910-page 71
SuDocs no.: 61st Cong., 2d sess. S. Doc. 569

104

Hirst, Francis Wrigley, 1873-
   . . . The credit of nations, by Francis W. Hirst . . . and The trade balance of the United States, by George Paish . . . Washington, Govt. print. off., 1910 [i.e. 1911]
   iv, 213 p. tables (1 fold.) 23 cm (Publications of National monetary commission. vol. XX [no. 4])
   [U.S.] 61st Cong., 2d sess. Senate. Doc. 579.
   Issued also separately, 1910.
   Contents.—The credit of nations. Introduction [a comparative study of recent developments in Europe and the United States] The debt and credit of Great Britain. The debt and credit of Germany.The debt and credit of France. The debt and credit of the United States. The trade balance of the United States.
   1. Credit. 2. Debts, Public. 3. Balance of trade. 4. Finance—U.S. I. Paish, George, 1867- II. Title. III. Title: The trade balance of the United States.
HG471.A4 1911 vol. 20, no. 4   12-35298
- - - - - Copy 2.
MC#: Feb. 1912-page 478
SuDocs no.: 61st Cong., 2d sess. S. Doc. 579

105

Hirst, Francis Wrigley, 1873-
   . . . The credit of nations, by Francis W. Hirst . . . and The trade balance of the United States, by George Paish . . . Washington, Govt. print. off., 1910.
   iv, 213 p. tables (1 fold.) 23½ cm. ([U.S.] 61st Cong., 2d sess. Senate. Doc. 579)
   At head of title: . . . National monetary commission.
   Issued also, 1911, in Publications of National monetary commission. Vol. XX [no. 4]
   Contents.—The credit of nations. Introduction [a comparative study of recent developments in Europe and the United States] The debt and credit of Great Britain. The debt and credit of Germany. The debt and credit of France. The debt and credit of the United States.—The trade balance of the United States.
   1. Credit. 2. Debts, Public. 3. Balance of trade. 4. Finance—

U.S. I. Paish, George, 1867- II. U.S. National monetary commission. III. Title. IV. Title: The trade balance of the United States.
HJ8015.H6   10-36110
- - - - - Copy 2.
HF3029.H6
MC#: Nov. 1910-page 210
SuDocs no.: 61st Cong., 2d sess. S. Doc. 579

106

Hollander, Jacob Harry, 1871-
   . . . Bank loans and stock exchange speculation, by Jacob H. Hollander . . . Washington [Govt. print. off.] 1911.
   27 p. 23 cm. (Publications of National monetary commission. vol. XX [no. 5])
   [U.S.] 61st Cong., 2d sess. Senate. Doc. 589.
   Issued also separately.
   1. Banks and banking—U.S. 2. Speculation—U.S. I. Title.
HG471.A4 1911 vol. 20, no. 5   12-35299
- - - - - Copy 2.
MC#: Feb. 1912-page 478
SuDocs no.: 61st Cong., 2d sess. S. Doc. 589

107

Hollander, Jacob Harry, 1871-
   . . . Bank loans and stock exchange speculation, by Jacob H. Hollander . . . Washington [Govt. print. off.] 1911.
   27 p. 23½ cm. ([U.S.] 61st Cong., 2d sess. Senate. Doc. 589)
   At head of title: National monetary commission.
   Issued also in Publications of National monetary commission. vol. XX [no. 5]
   1. Banks and banking—U.S. 2. Speculation. I. U.S. National monetary commission. II. Title.
HG1813.U5H6   11-35928
- - - - - Copy 2.
MC#: Nov. 1911-page 248
SuDoc no.: 61st Cong., 2d sess. S. Doc. 589

108

U.S. *National monetary commission.*
   . . . Statistics for the United States, 1867-1909. Comp. by A. Piatt Andrew. Washington, Govt. print. off., 1910 [i.e. 1911]
   282 p. (part fold.) 30 cm. (Publications of National monetary commission. vol. XXI [no. 1]
   61st Cong., 2d sess. Senate. Doc. 570.
   Issued also separately, 1910.
   Contents.—pt. I. General statistics illustrating the growth of population, wealth, business, and commerce, 1867-1909.—pt. II. Statistics of banks and banking in the United States.—pt. III. Statistics of money, gold supply, foreignand domestic cash movements, and rates of foreign and domestic exchange.—pt. IV. Statistics of United States Treasury, including government receipts and expenditures . . . etc.
   1. U.S.—Stat. 2. Banks and banking—U.S. 3. Money—U.S.—Stat. I. Andrew, Abram Piatt, 1873- comp. II. Title.
HG471.A4 1911 vol. 21, no. 1   12-35300
- - - - - Copy 2.
- - - - - Copy 3.
MC#: Feb. 1910-page 478
SuDocs no.: 61st Cong., 2d sess. S. Doc. 570

109

U.S. *National monetary commission.*
   . . . Statistics for the United States, 1867-1909. Compiled by A. Piatt Andrew. Washington, Govt. print. off., 1910.

282 p. (part fold.) 29 cm. (61st Cong., 2d sess. Senate. Doc. 570)

Issued also, 1911, in Publications of National monetary commission. Vol. XXI [no. 1]

Contents. — pt. I. General statistics illustrating the growth of population, wealth, business, and commerce, 1867-1909. — pt. II. Statistics of banks and banking in the United States. — pt. III. Statistics of money, gold supply, foreign and domestic cash movements, and rates of foreign and domestic exchange. — pt. IV. Statistics of United States Treasury, including government receipts and expenditures . . . etc.

1. U.S. — Stat. 2. Banks and banking — U.S. 3. Money — U.S. — Stat. I. Andrew, Abram Piatt, 1873- comp. II. Title.
HG546.A4 1909   10-36024
- - - - - Copy 2.
MC#: Oct. 1910-page 157
SuDocs no.: 61st Cong., 2d sess. S. Doc. 570

110

U.S. *National monetary commission.*
. . . Special report from the banks of the United States, April 28, 1909 [and Supplement . . . Additional tables] Washington, Govt. print. off., 1909-1910 [i.e. 1911]

65 p., 1 l., 67-90 p. incl. tables (part fold.) 30 cm. (Publications of National monetary commission. vol. XXI [no. 2-3])
61st Cong., 2d sess. Senate. Doc. 225.
Presented by Mr. Aldrich; ordered printed December 21, 1909.
Issued also separately, 1909-10.
1. Banks and banking — U.S. I. Aldrich, Nelson Wilmarth, 1841- II. Title.
HG471.A4 1911 vol. 21, no. 2-3   12-35301
- - - - - Copy 2.
- - - - - Copy 3.
MC#: Feb. 1912-page 478
SuDocs no.: 61st Cong., 2d sess. S. Doc. 225

111

U.S. *National monetary commission.*
. . . Special report from the banks of the United States, April 28, 1909 [and Supplement . . . Additional tables] Washington, Govt. print. off., 1909-10.

65 p., 1 l., 67-90 p. incl. tables (part fold.) 29½ cm. (61st Cong., 2d sess. Senate. Doc. 225)
At head of title: National monetary commission.
Presented by Mr. Aldrich; ordered printed, December 21, 1909.
Issued also, 1911, in Publications of National monetary commission. Vol. XXI [no. 2-3]
1. Banks and banking — U.S. I. Aldrich, Nelson Wilmarth, 1841-1915. II. Title.
HG2406.A5 1909   9-35022 Revised
- - - - - Copy 2.
MC#: Jan. 1910-page 321
SuDocs no.: 61st Cong., 2d sess. S. Doc. 225
MC#: Nov. 1910-page 210
SuDocs no.: 61st Cong., 2d sess. S. Doc. 225, pt. 2

112

U.S. *National monetary commission.*
. . . Statistics for Great Britain, Germany, and France, 1867-1909. Washington, Govt. print. off., 1910 [i.e. 1911]

354 p. (part fold.) 30 cm. (Publications of National monetary commission. vol. XXI [no. 4])
61st Cong., 2d sess. Senate. Doc. 578.
Issued also separately, 1910.
Contents. — Statistics for Great Britain, 1867-1909. Furnished by "The Economist," F. W. Hirst, editor, and Sir Robert Harry

Inglis Palgrave. pt. I. General statistics. pt. II. Statistics of joint-stock and other banks. pt. III. Statistics of money, gold movements, rates of exchange, etc. pt. IV. Statistics of the Bank of England. — Statistics for Germany, 1870-1908. Furnished by the Centralverband des deutschen bank- und bankiergewerbes and the Deutsche oekonomist. pt. I. General statistics. pt. II. Statistics of banks and banking in Germany. pt. III. Statistics of money, gold supply, gold movements, and foreign exchange. — Statistics for France, 1870-1909. Furnished mainly by the Bank of France and the Credit lyonnais. pt. I. General statistics. pt. II. Statistics of banks and banking in France. pt. III. Statistics of money, gold supply, gold movements, and foreign exchange.

Other editions under author.
1. Gt. Brit. — Stat. 2. Germany — Stat. 3. France — Stat. 4. Banks and banking. I. Title.
HG471.A4 1911 vol. 21, no. 4   12-35302
- - - - - Copy 2.
- - - - - Copy 3.
MC#: Feb. 1912-page 478
SuDocs no.: 61st Cong., 2d sess. S. Doc. 578

113

U.S. *National monetary commission.*
. . . Statistics for Great Britain, Germany, and France, 1867-1909. Washington, Govt. print. off., 1910.

354 p. (part fold.) 29 cm. (61st Cong., 2d sess. Senate. Doc. 578)

Issued also, 1911, in Publications of National monetary commission. Vol. XXI [no. 4]

Contents. — Statistics for Great Britain, 1867-1909. Furnished by "The Economist," F. W. Hirst, editor, and Sir Robert Harry Inglis Palgrave. pt. I. General statistics. pt. II. Statistics of joint-stock and other banks. pt. III. Statistics of money, gold movements, rates of exchange, etc. pt. IV. Statistics of the Bank of England. — Statistics for Germany, 1870-1908. Furnished by the Centralverband des deutschen bank- und bankiergewerbes and the Deutscheoekonomist. pt. I. General statistics. pt. II. Statistics of banks and banking in Germany. pt. III. Statistics of money, gold supply, gold movements, and foerign exchange. — Statistics for France, 1870-1909. Furnished mainly by the Bank of France and the Crédit lyonnais. pt. I. General statistics. pt. II. Statistics of banks and banking in France. pt. III. Statistics of money, gold supply, gold movements, and foreign exchange.

1. Gt. Brit. — Stat. 2. Germany — Stat. 3. France — Stat. 4. Banks and banking. I. Title.
HG259.U5   10-36023
- - - - - Copy 2.
MC#: Oct. 1910-page 157
SuDocs no.: 61st Cong., 2d sess. S. Doc. 578

114

Kemmerer, Edwin Walter, 1875-
. . . Seasonal variations in the relative demand for money and capital in the United States; a statistical study, by Edwin Walter Kemmerer . . . Washington, Govt. print. off., 1910 [i.e. 1911]

517 p. incl. tables, diagrs. 29 cm. (Publications of National monetary commission. vol. XXII)
[U.S.] 61st Cong., 2d sess. Senate. Doc. 588.
Issued also separately, 1910.
"List of books and articles cited in report": p. 232.
Other editions under author.
1. Money — U.S. 2. Finance — U.S. I. Title.
HG471.A4 1911 vol. 22   12-35303
- - - - - Copy 2.
MC#: Feb. 1912-page 478
SuDocs no.: 61st Cong., 2d sess. S. Doc. 588

115

Kemmerer, Edwin Walter, 1875-

. . . Seasonal variations in the relative demand for money and capital in the United States; a statistical study, by Edwin Walter Kemmerer . . . Washington, Govt. print. off., 1910.

517 p. incl. tables, diagrs. 29 x 23 cm. ([U.S.] 61st Cong., 2d sess. Senate. Doc. 588)

At head of title: . . . National monetary commission.

Issued also, 1911, in Publications of National monetary commission. vol. XXII.

"List of books and articles cited in report": p. 232.

1. Money—U.S. 2. Finance—U.S. I. U.S. National monetary commission. II. Title.

HG538.K3   11-35145

- - - - - Copy 2.

MC#: Feb. 1911-page 432

SuDocs no.: 61st Cong., 2d sess. S. Doc. 588

116

Andrew, Abram Piatt, 1873-1936, comp.

. . . Financial diagrams, comp. by A. Piatt Andrew . . . Washington, Govt. print. off., 1910 [i.e. 1911]

2 p. l., 24 col. fold. diagr. 39½ cm. (Publications of National monetary commission. vol. XXIII)

[U.S.] 61st Cong., 2d sess. Senate. Doc. 509.

Presented by Mr. Aldrich April 26, 1910. Ordered to be printed, with illustrations.

Issued also separately, 1910.

Other editions under author.

1. Finance—U.S. 2. Finance. I. Title.

HG471.A4 1911 vol. 23   12-35304

- - - - - Copy 2.

MC#: Feb. 1912-page 478

SuDocs no.: 61st Cong., 2d sess. S. Doc. 509

117

Andrew, Abram Piatt, 1873-1936, comp.

. . . Financial diagrams, comp. by A. Piatt Andrew . . . Washington, Govt. print. off., 1910.

2 p. l., 24 col. fold. diagr. 39½ cm. ([U.S.] 61st Cong., 2d sess. Senate. Doc. 509)

At head of title: . . . National monetary commission.

Presented by Mr. Aldrich April 26, 1910. Ordered to be printed, with illustrations.

1. Finance—U.S. 2. Finance—Europe. I. U.S. National monetary commission. II. U.S. 61st Cong., 2d sess. 1909-1910. Senate.

HG175.A6   10-35941

- - - - - Copy 2.

MC#: Aug. 1910-page 71

SuDocs no.: 61st Cong., 2d sess. S. Doc. 509

118

U.S. *National monetary commission.*

. . . Report of the National monetary commission. Washington, Govt. print. off., 1912.

72 p. 23½ cm. (Publications of National monetary commission. vol. XXIV [no. 1])

Includes also "A bill to incorporate the National reserve association of the United States, and for other purposes," p. 43-72.

1. Banks and banking—U.S. 2. Finance—U.S. 3. National reserve association of the United States. I. Title.

HG471.A4 1911 vol. 24   13-8445

MC#: Apr. 1912-page 657

119

U.S. *National monetary commission.*

. . . Letter from secretary of the National monetary commission, transmitting, pursuant to law, the report of the commission . . . [Jan. 8, 1912] Washington, Govt. print. off., 1912.

72 p. 23½ cm. (62d Cong., 2d sess. Senate. Doc. 243)

At head of title: National monetary commission.

Referred to the Committee on finance and ordered printed, January 9, 1912.

Nelson W. Aldrich, chairman.

Published also, 1912, without document series note, with title, "Report of the National monetary commission". That edition was included also in "Publications of National monetary commission" (the set in 24 vols., 1911. vol. XXIV [no. 1])

"A bill to incorporate the National reserve association of the United States, and for other purposes": p. 43-72.

1. Banks and banking—U.S. 2. Currency question—U.S. 3. Finance—U.S. 4. National reserve association of the United States. I. Aldrich, Nelson Wilmarth, 1841-1915. II. Title.

HG471.A4 1912   12-35122 Revised

- - - - - Copy 2.

MC#: Jan. 1912-page 389

SuDocs no.: 62d Cong., 2d sess. S. Doc. 243

120

U.S. *National Monetary Commission.*

Suggested plan for monetary legislation, by Nelson W. Aldrich [chairman. Jan. 16, 1911] Washington, Govt. Print. Off., 1911.

2 pts. 24 cm. (61st Cong., 3d sess. Senate. Document no. 784)

Pt. 2, rev. ed., Oct. 1911.

1. Currency question—U.S. 1910- 2. National Reserve Association of the United States. 3. Banks and banking—U.S. I. Title. (Series: U.S. 61st Cong., 3d sess. 1910-11. Senate. Document no. 784)

HG538.A315 1911   11-35135 rev*

MC#: Feb. 1911-page 432

SuDocs no.: 61st Cong., 3d sess. S. Doc. 784

121

Aldrich, Nelson Wilmarth, 1841-1915.

Suggested plan for monetary legislation, submitted to the National monetary commission by Hon. Nelson W. Aldrich. Washington, Govt. print. off., 1911.

15 p. 23 cm.

Outline for a tentative plan for revision of national-banking legislation. Proposition to charter the Reserve association of America, to be the principal fiscal agent of the government of the United States.

1. Banks and banking—U.S. 2. National banks—U.S.

HG538.A53   11-35086

MC#: Jan. 1911-page 340

SuDocs no.: Y3.N21/2:L53

122

U.S. National Monetary Commission.

Suggested plan for monetary legislation, by Nelson W. Aldrich [chairman. Revision, Oct. 14, 1911] Washington, Govt. Print. Off., 1911.

2 pts. 24 cm. (61st Cong., 3d sess. Senate. Document no. 784)

1. Currency question—U.S.—1910. 2. National Reserve Association of the United States. 3. Banks and Banking—U.S. I. Title. (Series: U.S. 61st Cong., 3d sess., 1910-1911. Senate. Document no. 784)

HG538.A315 1911a   12-15902 rev*

MC#: Nov. 1911-page 248 (LC card 11-35825 referred to in error)

SuDocs no.: 61st Cong., 3d sess. S. Doc. 784, pt. 2

123

Aldrich, Nelson Wilmarth, 1841-1915.

Suggested plan for monetary legislation, submitted to the National monetary commission by Hon. Nelson W. Aldrich. Rev. ed., October, 1911. Washington, 1911.

24 p. 23½ cm.

Caption title: The National reserve association of the United States.

1. Banks and banking—U.S. 2. Banking law—U.S. I. U.S. National monetary commission.

HG538.A5143   11-35825

- - - - - Copy 2.

MC#: Oct. 1911-page 196

End of Publications series

124

Aldrich, Nelson Wilmarth, 1841-1915.

. . . Address of Hon. Nelson W. Aldrich, chairman of the National monetary commission, before the annual convention of the American bankers' association, at New Orleans, Tuesday, November 21, 1911. Washington [Govt. print. off.] 1911.

30 p. 23½ cm.

At head of title: National monetary commission.

1. Banks and banking—U.S. 2. Currency question—U.S. I. U.S. National monetary commission.

HG2481.A48   12-2146

- - - - - Copy 2.

Document Catalogue, vol. 11-page 1259

125

Aldrich, Nelson Wilmarth, 1841-1915.

. . . Address of Hon. Nelson W. Aldrich, chairman of the National monetary commission, before the City club at Kansas City, Mo., Wednesday, November 15, 1911. Washington [Govt. print. off.] 1911.

13 p. 23 cm.

1. Banks and banking—U.S. 2. Currency question—U.S. I. U.S. National monetary commission.

HG2481.A48 1911 d   12-35171

- - - - - Copy 2.

Document Catalogue, vol. 11-page 1259

126

Aldrich, Nelson Wilmarth, 1841-1915.

. . . Address of Hon. Nelson W. Aldrich, chairman of the National monetary commission, before the Trans-Mississippi commercial congress at Kansas City, Mo., Tuesday, November 14, 1911. Washington [Govt. print. off.] 1911.

15 p. 23 cm.

1. Banks and banking—U.S. I. U.S. National monetary commission.

HG2481.A48 1911 c   12-35172

- - - - - Copy 2.

Not located in Monthly Catalog.

127

Aldrich, Nelson Wilmarth, 1841-1915.

. . . Address of Hon. Nelson W. Aldrich, chairman of the National monetary commission, before the Western economic society, at Chicago, Saturday, November 11, 1911. Washington [Govt. print. off.] 1911.

21 p. 23 cm.

Relates especially to the organization of the National reserve association.

1. Banks and banking—U.S. I. U.S. National monetary commission.

HG2481.A48 1911 b   12-35173

- - - - - Copy 2.

Document Catalogue, vol. 11-page 1259

128

Aldrich, Nelson Wilmarth, 1841-1915.

Addresses by Senator Nelson W. Aldrich on the work of the National monetary commission before the Academy of political science, New York city, November 11, 1910, and the American academy of political and social science, Philadelphia, Pa., December 8, 1910. Washington, Govt. print. off., 1911.

14 p. 23 cm.

1. Currency question—U.S. 2. Banking law—U.S. 3. Banks and banking-U.S. I. U.S. National monetary commission.

HG2481.A48 1911 a   12-35174

- - - - - Copy 2.

Not located in Monthly Catalog

129

U.S. *Treasury dept.*

. . . Expenses of the National monetary commission. Letter from the secretary of the treasury, transmitting, in response to House resolution of May 8, 1911, statement of expenditures on account of the National monetary commission from June 5, 1908, to March 31, 1911. [Washington, Govt. print. off., 1911]

7 p. 23½ cm. (62d Cong., 1st sess. House. Doc. 56)

May 16, 1911.-Referred to the Committee on expenditures in the Treasury department and ordered to be printed.

Contains list of monographs published by the commission.

1. U.S. National monetary commission.

HG472.A4 1911   11-35425

MC#: May 1911-page 656

SuDocs no.: 62d Cong., 1st sess. H. Doc. 56

130

U.S. *National monetary commission.*

List of conferences in London, Paris, and Berlin, held by representatives of the National monetary commission, and of papers and statistics to be prepared for the Commission. Corrected up to January 30, 1909. Washington, Govt. print. off., 1909.

22 p. 23 cm.

1. Currency question—U.S.

HG471.A4 1909   9-35196

- - - - - Copy 2.

MC#: Feb. 1909-page 414

SuDocs no.: Y4.1N21/2:C76/1

131

U.S. *National monetary commission.*

List of conferences in London, Paris, and Berlin, held by representatives of the National monetary commission . . . corrected up to Mar. 18, 1909. 1909.

1 v. 8

MC#: Mar. 1909-page 498

SuDocs no.: Y4.N21/2:C76/2

132

[U.S. *National monetary commission*]

Notes on proposed codification and revision of the National bank act. Washington [Govt. print. off.] 1912.

51 p. 23½ cm.

Running title: National monetary commission. Proposed revision of the National bank act.

1. National banks (U.S.) 2. Banking law — U.S. I. U.S. Laws, statutes, etc. II. Title.
HG2547.A54 1912   12-35401
Document Catalogue, vol. 11-page 1259

133

Vreeland, Edward Butterfield, 1857-
   The plan of the National monetary commission for the revision of our banking and currency laws. Speech of Hon. Edward B. Vreeland, of New York, in the House of representatives, February 6, 1912. Washington [Govt. print. off.] 1912.

   47 p. 23½ cm.
   1. U.S. National monetary commission. 2. Banks and banking — U.S. 3. Currency question — U.S. — Speeches in Congress. I. Title.
HG2481.V84   12-35353
Not located in Monthly Catalog

134

U.S. *National monetary commission.*
   . . . Proposed codification of the national banking laws. Washington, Govt. print. off., 1912.

   cover-title, 107 p. 29½ cm.
   At head of title: National monetary commission.
   1. National banks — U.S. 2. Banking law — U.S. I. U.S. laws, statutes, etc. II. Title.
HG2547.A54 1912 a   12-35384
- - - - - Copy 2.
MC#: Mar. 1912-page 567

135

U.S. *National monetary commission.*
   Publications in course of preparation for the National monetary commission, November 1, 1909. Washington, Govt. print. off., 1909.

   19 p. 23½ cm.
   "European conferences held by representatives of the National monetary commission": p. 15-17.
   1. Banks and banking — Bibl. 2. Finance — Bibl.
Z7164.F5U69   9-35946
MC#: Nov. 1909-page 198
SuDocs no.: Y3.N21/2:P96/1

136

U.S. *National monetary commission.*
   Publications in course of preparation for the National Monetary Commission, December 1, 1909. Washington, Govt. print. off., 1909.

   19 p.
MC#: Dec. 1909-page 243
SuDocs no.: Y3.N21/2:P96/2

137

U.S. *National monetary commission.*
   Publications in course of preparation for the National Monetary Commission, March 17, 1910. Washington, Govt. print. off., 1910.

   14 p.
MC#: Mar. 1910-page 515
SuDocs no.: Y3.N21/2:P96/3

138

U.S. *National monetary commission.*
   Publications issued by and in preparation for the National monetary commission. September 1, 1910. Washington, Govt. print. off., 1910.

15 p. 23 cm.
   1. Banks and banking — Bibl. 2. Finance — Bibl.
Z7164.F5U69 1910   10-35988
- - - - - Copy 2.
MC#: Sept. 1910-page 113
SuDocs no.: Y3.N21/2:P96/4

139

U.S. *National monetary commission.*
   Publications issued by and in preparation for the National monetary commission, October 1, 1910. Washington, Govt. print. off., 1910.

   31 p. 23½ cm.
   1. Banks and banking — Bibl. 2. Finance — Bibl.
Z7164.F5U69 1910 a   11-28774
- - - - - Copy 2.
MC#: Sept. 1910-page 113
SuDocs no.: Y3.N21/2:P96/5

140

U.S. *National monetary commission.*
   Publications of the National monetary commission, September 1, 1911. Washington, Govt. print. off., 1911.

   31 p. 23½ cm.
- - - - - Washington, Govt. print. off., 1912.

   31 p. 23½ cm.
   1. Banks and banking — Bibl. 2. Finance — Bibl.
Z7164.F5U69 1911   11-35725
MC#: Sept. 1911-page 149
Mar. 1912-page 567

141

Andrew, Abram Piatt, 1873-1936.
   Tabular summary of laws, practices, and statistics of principal banks of leading countries. Washington, Govt. print. off., 1912.

   2 fold. tab.
HG1576.A6
Not located in Monthly Catalog

142

U.S. *National monetary commission.*
   . . . Savings departments of national banks and real estate loans. Summary of replies from bank officers relating thereto. Washington [Govt. print off.] 1912.

   50 p. 23½ cm.
   At head of title: National monetary commission.
   1. National banks (U.S.) 2. Savings banks — U.S. 3. Agricultural credit — U.S. 4. Mortgages. I. Title.
HG1922.A4   12-35402
MC#: Mar. 1912-page 567

ALDRICH REPORTS [Aldrich, Nelson Wilmarth]

143

U.S. *Congress. Senate. Committee on finance.*
   . . . Retail prices and wages. Report by Mr. Aldrich, from the Committee on finance, July 19, 1892 . . . Washington, Govt. print. off., 1892.

   3 v. 23½ cm. (52d Cong., 1st sess. Senate. Rept. 986)
   Paged continuously.
   Contents. — v. 1. Partial report submitted by Mr. Aldrich from the committee. Appendices: A. Report of the statistician, R. P. Falkner. B. Report of the commissioner of labor, C. D. Wright. C. Report of the statistician of the Department of agriculture, J. R. Dodge. Supplemental matter. Exhibits. — v. 2-3. Exhibits.

1. Prices—U.S. 2. Wages—U.S. 3. Cost and standard of living—U.S. 4. Food. I. Aldrich, Nelson Wilmarth, 1841-1915. II. Falkner, Roland Post, 1866- III. Wright, Carroll Davidson, 1840-1909.
HD6983.A35   8-1180
Checklist of United States Public Documents, 1789-1909, page 89
52d Cong., 1st sess. S. Rept. 986. In Serial no. 2916-2918, vol. 6-8

144

U.S. *Congress. Senate. Committee on finance.*
   . . . Wholesale prices, wages, and transportation. Report by Mr. Aldrich, from the Committee on finance, March 3, 1893 . . . Washington, Govt. print. off., 1893.
   4 v. 23 cm. (52d Cong., 2d sess. Senate. Rept. 1394)
   Added t.-p.: Reports of committees of the Senate of the United States . . .
   Vol. 1 has note on t.-p.: This volume embodies in a condensed form everything contained in volumes 2, 3, and 4. v. 2-4 paged continuously.
   "Statements of wholesale prices . . . and of rates of wages in U.S. for 52 years, and of prices in European countries for 40 years; also of changes in railway freight rates for 40 years."—Ames, Comprehensive index of the publication of the U.S. govt., 1889-93.
   Contents—I. Introductory report of committee: views of majority, views of minority.—Appendices. A. Report of the statistician, R. P. Falkner.—B. Report of the commissioner of labor. C. D. Wright.—C. Report of the statistician, Dept. of agriculture, T. R. Dodge.—D. Report of the commissioner of education, W. T. Harris.—E. Report of S. N. D. North on wool manufacture.—F. Report of Messrs. Mauger and Avery on prices of wool.—G. Report of T. Reece, jr. on prices of various textile articles.—H. Report of E. Stanwood on cotton goods.—I. Report of H. Bower on prices of drugs and chemicals.—J. Prices of miscellaneous articles.—K. Report upon changes in railway transportation rates on freight traffic throughout the United States, 1852 to 1893, by C. C. McCain.
   II-IV. Exhibits.
   1. Prices—U.S. 2. Wages—U.S. 3. Transportation—U.S.—Rates. 4. Railroads—U.S.—Rates. I. Aldrich, Nelson Wilmarth, 1841-1915. II. Falkner, Roland Post, 1866- III. McCain, Charles Curtice, 1856-
HD6983.A42   5-40397
- - - - - Another issue. 4v. HD6983.A43
   Without document series note ("Bureau ed.")
Checklist of United States Public Documents, 1789-1909, page 93
52d Cong., 2d sess. S. Rept. 1394. In Serial no. 3074, vol. 3

ALEXANDER REPORT [Alexander, John H.]

145

United States. *President's Task Force on Business Taxation.*
   Business taxation; the report. [Washington, For sale by the Supt. of Docs., U.S. Govt. Print. Off.] 1970.
   v, 82 p. illus. 24 cm.
   Includes bibliographical references.
   1. Corporations—United States—Taxation. I. Title.
HD2753.U6A4 1970   336.2'43'0973   79-609903
                                                MARC
MC#: 1971-2922
SuDocs no.: Pr37.8:B96/R29

ALLAN REPORT [Allan, Virginia R.]

146

United States. *President's Task Force on Women's Rights and Responsibilities.*

A matter of simple justice; the report of the President's Task Force on Women's Rights and Responsibilities. [Washington; For sale by the Supt. of Docs., U.S. Govt. Print. off.] 1970.
   ix, 33 p. 24 cm.
   Virginia R. Allan, Chairman.
   Includes bibliographical references.
   1. Women—Legal status, laws, etc.—United States. I. Allan, Virginia R. II. Title.
KF478.A68   340   77-607729
                                               MARC
MC#: 1970-10510
SuDocs no.: Pr 37.8:W84/R29

ALLEN REPORT [Allen, Francis A.]

147

U.S. *Attorney General's Committee on Poverty and the Administration of Federal Criminal Justice.*
   Report. Submitted to Robert F. Kennedy, Attorney General of the United States, Feb. 25, 1963. [Washington, 1963]
   x, 154 p. 23 cm.
   Cover title: Poverty and the administration of Federal criminal justice.
   Includes text of the bill and commentary on the proposed Criminal justice act of 1963.
   Commonly known as the Allen report.
   1. Criminal justice, Administration of—U.S. 2. Public defenders—U.S. I. Title: Poverty and the administration of Federal criminal justice. II. Allen report on poverty and the administration of Federal criminal justice.
                                                          64-60971
MC#: 1964-7351
SuDocs no.: J 1.2:P86

U.S. *Attorney General's Committee on Poverty and the Administration of Federal Criminal Justice.*
   Report. Submitted to Robert F. Kennedy, Attorney General of the United States, Feb. 25, 1963. Washington, U.S. Govt. Print. Off. [1964]
   xvi, 154 p. 24 cm.
   Cover title : Poverty and the administration of Federal criminal justice.
   Includes text of the bill and commentary on the proposed Criminal justice act of 1963.
   1. Criminal justice, Administration of—U.S. 2. Public defenders—U.S. I. Title : Poverty and the administration of Federal criminal justice.
                                                          65-60326

ALTMAN REPORT

148

[Altman, Oscar Louis] 1909-
   . . . Savings, investment, and national income . . . Washington, U.S. Govt. print. off., 1941.
   x, 135 p. incl. tables. 23 cm. ([U.S.] Temporary national economic committee. Investigation of concentration of economic power . . . Monograph no. 37)
   At head of title: 76th Cong., 3d sess. Senate committee print.
   Running title: Concentration of economic power.
   "A study made for the Temporary national economic committee, Seventy-sixth Congress, third session, pursuant to Public resolution no. 113 (Seventy-fifth Congress), authorizing and directing a select committee to make a full and complete study and investigation with respect to the concentration of economic power in, and financial control over, production and distribution of goods and services."
   By Oscar L. Altman. cf. Acknowledgment.

Printed for the use of the Temporary national economic committee.
1. Savings and investment. 2. Investments—U.S. 3. Income—U.S. 4. U.S.-Econ. condit.—1918- I. Title.
HC106.3.A5127 no. 37   339.4973   41-50315
MC#: 1941-page 415
SuDocs no.: Y 4.T24:M75, no. 37

See also under O'MAHONEY REPORTS [O'Mahoney, Joseph Christopher]

AMMEN REPORT [Ammen, Daniel]
see
MENOCAL REPORT [Menocal, Aniceto Garcia]

ANDERSON REPORT [Anderson, Henry Watkins]
see
WICKERSHAM COMMISSION [Wickersham, George Woodward]
Report on the causes of crime, no. 13

ANDERSON REPORT [Anderson, Hobson Dewey]
see under
O'MAHONEY REPORTS [O'Mahoney, Joseph Christopher]

ANDREW REPORTS [Andrew, Abram Piatt]
see under
ALDRICH COMMISSION [Aldrich, Nelson Wilmarth]
Statistics for the United States.

Andrew. Financial diagrams.

Andrew. Tabular summary of laws.

ANDREWS REPORT
149

Andrews, Frank Emerson, 1902-
Scientific research expenditures by the larger private foundations; prepared for the National Science Foundation. Washington, U.S. Govt. Print. Off., 1956.
21 p. illus. 26 cm. (National science studies)
1. Research—U.S. 2. Endowments—U.S. I. Title.
Q180.U5A75   507.2   56-60370 rev
MC#: 1956-4167
SuDocs no.: NS1.2:R31/4

ANFUSO REPORT [Anfuso, Victor L.]
150

U.S. *Congress. House. Committee on Agriculture.*
Food for civilian survival in event of war. Interim report of the Consumers Study Subcommittee. Washington, U.S. Govt. Print. Off., 1957.
ii, 4 p. 24 cm.
At head of title: Committee print.
1. Food supply—U.S. 2. U.S.—Military policy. I. Title.
HD9006.A515 1957   57-62005
MC#: 1957-16529
SuDocs no.: Y 4.Ag8/1:F73/16

ANGELL REPORT [Angell, Montgomery B.]
151

U.S. *Congress. Joint Committee on Internal Revenue Taxation.*
The Internal Revenue Service; its reorganization and administration. Washington, U.S. Govt. Print. Off., 1955.
iii, 111 p. illus. 24 cm.
1. U.S. Internal Revenue Service.

HJ5018.A535   55-61864
MC#: 1955-15007
SuDocs no.: Y 4.In8/11:In8/7

APPLEY REPORT [Appley, Lawrence A.]
152

U.S. *Office of Defense Mobilization. Committee on Manpower Resources for National Security.*
Manpower resources for national security; a report to the Director of the Office of Defense Mobilization. [Washington] 1953.
1 v. (various pagings) illus. 28 cm.
1. Manpower—U.S. I. Title.
UA17.5.U5A535   56-19666
Not located in Monthly Catalog

See also FLEMMING REPORT [Flemming, Arthur S.]

ARMY PEARL HARBOR BOARD
see
ROBERTS COMMISSION [Roberts, Owen Josephus]

ARNESON REPORT [Arneson, Gordon]
see under
O'MAHONEY REPORTS [O'Mahoney, Joseph Christopher]
James. Industrial concentration and tariffs.

ASH REPORTS [Ash, Roy L.]
153

United States. *President's Advisory Council on Executive Organization.*
Establishment of a Department of Natural Resources. Organization for social and economic programs. Memoranda for the President of the United States. [Washington, 1971]
vii, 160 p. map. 26 cm.
Includes bibliographical references.
SuDocs no.: Pr 37.8:Ex3/N21
1. United States. Dept. of Natural Resources. 2. United States—Politics and government—1969- 3. United States—Economic policy—1971- 4. United States—Social policy. I. Title. II. Title: Organization for social and economic programs.
HC103.7.A528 1971   353.04   72-602333
                                                  MARC
MC#: 1972-4663
SuDocs no.: Pr 37.8:Ex3/N21

154

United States. *President's Advisory Council on Executive Organization.*
A new regulatory framework; report on selected independent regulatory agencies. [Washington; For sale by the Supt. of Docs., U.S. Govt. Print. Off.] 1971.
ix, 198 p. illus. 23 cm.
Bibliography: p. 191-198.
1. Independent regulatory commissions—United States. I. Title
JK901.A58   353'.09'1   70-510810
                                                  MARC
MC#: 1971-5681
SuDocs no.: Pr 37.8:Ex3/R26

ASHEIM REPORT [Asheim, Lester]
155

Stanford University. *Institute for Communication Research.*
Educational television, the next ten years; a report and summary of major studies on the problems and potential of educational television, conducted under the auspices of the U.S. Office of Education. [Studies by Asheim and others] Stanford, 1962.

xi, 375 p. illus., fold. map. 24 cm.
Includes bibliographies.
1. Television in education. I. Asheim, Lester. II. Title.
LB1044.7.S8   371.3358   62-13346
Not located in Monthly Catalog

ASPINALL REPORTS [Aspinall, Wayne N.]

156

U.S. *Congress. House. Committee on Public Lands.*
Slum clearance, urban redevelopment and low rent housing in Alaska, Hawaii, Puerto Rico, and the Virgin Islands; reports to accompany S.3635. [Washington, U.S. Govt. Print. Off., 1950]
6 p. (U.S. 81st Cong., 2d sess., 1950-1951. House. Report no. 2276)
MC#: 1950-13257
SuDocs no.: 81st Cong., 2d sess. H. Rept. 2276

157

U.S. *Public Land Law Review Commission.*
One third of the Nation's land; a report to the President and to the Congress. Washington; [For sale by the Supt. of Docs., U.S. Govt. Print. Off.] 1970.
xiii, 342 p. illus. (part col.), col maps (1 fold. inserted) 27 cm.
Includes bibliographical references.
1. U.S. — Public lands. I. Title.
KF5601.A55P8   333.1'0973   70-607944
                                         MARC
MC#: 1970-11837
SuDocs no.: Y 3.P96/7:2 On2

AULL REPORT [Aull, Ruth]
see under
O'MAHONEY REPORTS [O'Mahoney, Joseph Christopher]
Lorwin. Technology in our economy.

AYRES REPORT [Ayres, Leonard P.]

158

U.S. *War dept. General staff.*
The war with Germany; a statistical summary, by Leonard P. Ayres . . . chief of the Statistics branch of the General staff. Washington, Govt. print. off., 1919.
154 p. incl. illus. (maps) tables, diagrs. 23½ cm.
Issued also as House doc. 174, 66th Cong., 1st sess.
1. European war, 1914-1918 — Stat. I. Ayres, Leonard Porter, 1879-1946. II. Title.
D570.1.A5 1919   19-26778
MC#: July 1919-page 52
SuDocs no.: W2.2:G31

159

U.S. *War dept. General staff.*
. . . The war with Germany; a statistical summary, by Leonard P. Ayres . . . chief of the Statistics branch of the General staff. Washington, Govt. print. off., 1919.
154 p. incl. illus. (maps) tables, diagrs. 23 cm. ([U.S.] 66th Cong., 1st sess. House. Doc. 174)
Issued also without congressional series numbering.
1. European war, 1914-1918 — Stat. I. Ayres, Leonard Porter, 1879-1946. II. Title.
D570.1.A5 1919b   20-5931
MC#: July 1919-page 52
SuDocs no.: 66th Cong., 1st sess. H. Doc. 174

160

U.S. *War dept. General staff.*
The war with Germany; a statistical summary, by Leonard P. Ayres, . . . chief of the Statistics branch of the General staff. 2d ed., with data rev. to August 1, 1919. Washington, Govt. print. off., 1919.
154 p. incl. illus. (maps) tables, diagrs. 23½ cm.
1. European war, 1914-1918 — Stat. I. Ayres, Leonard Porter, 1879-1946./II. Title.
D570.1.A5 1919a   19-25995
MC#: Nov. 1919-page 281
SuDocs no.: W2.2:G31

BAIN REPORT

161

Bain, Henry M. 1926-
The governing of Metropolitan Washington. Staff study for the Joint Committee on Washington Metropolitan Problems, Congress of the United States. Washington, U.S. Govt. Print. Off., 1958.
v, 98 p. 24 cm.
At head of title: 85th Cong., 2d sess. Joint committee print.
1. District of Columbia — Pol. & govt. — 1878- I. U.S. Congress. Joint Committee on Washington Metropolitan Problems. II. Title.
JK2725 1958.B3   352.0753   58-62496
MC#: 1959-342
SuDocs no.: Y4.W27/2:G74/3

BAKER REPORT [Baker, George P.]

162

U.S. *Congress. Senate. Committee on military affairs.*
War plants disposal — aircraft plants. Hearings before the Surplus property subcommittee of the Committee on military affairs and Industrial reorganization subcommittee of the Special committee on economic policy and planning, United States Senate, Seventy-ninth Congress, first session, pursuant to S. Res. 46 and S. Res. 33 . . . Washington, U.S. Govt. print. off., 1945-
v. maps (part fold.) fold. diagrs. 23 cm.
Joseph C. O'Mahoney, chairman of subcommittee.
Contents. — pt. I. Hearings, Oct. 29, 1945.
1. Aeroplane industry and trade — U.S. 2. Mill and factory buildings. I. U.S. Congress. Senate. Special committee on post-war economic policy and planning. II. Title.
TL724.1.F3A5 1945   338.4762913   45-37842
MC#: 1946-page 57
SuDocs no.: Y 4.M59/2:W19/14/pt.1

The "Report to the Air Coordinating Committee of the Subcommittee on Demobilization of the Aircraft Industry," known as the Baker report, appears on pages 28-65 of the hearings.

BAKER REPORT [Baker, Jacob]

163

U.S. *Inquiry on cooperative enterprise.*
. . . Report of the Inquiry on cooperative enterprise in Europe, 1937. Washington, D.C. [U.S. Govt. print. off.] 1937.
5 p. l., 321 p. incl. illus., tables, diagrs. 26 cm.
At head of title: United States Government printing office. Jacob Baker, chairman.
"The meaning of cooperative enterprise in America. Individual comments by Jacob Baker, Charles E. Stuart, Clifford Gregory, Leland Olds, Robin Hood [and] Emily Cuathorn [!] Bates": p. [79]-137.
1. Cooperation — Europe. I. U.S. Government printing office. II. *Baker, Jacob, 1895- III. Stuart, Charles Edward, 1881- IV. Gregory, Clifford Verne, 1883- V. Olds, Leland, 1890- VI. Hood,

Robin. VII. Bates, Emily Cauthorn. VIII. Title. IX. Title: Cooperative enterprise in Europe.
HD3484.A4U6 1937   334.094   37-26564
MC#: 1937-page 600
SuDocs no.: Y 3.C78/2:2R29

BAKER REPORT [Baker, Newton Diehl]

164

U.S. *Special commitee on Army air corps.*
    Final report of War department Special committee on Army air corps. July 18, 1934. Washington, U.S. Govt. print. off., 1934.
    iv, 86 p. incl. tables. 23½ cm.
    Newton D. Baker, chairman.
    1. U.S.—Army air corps. 2. Aeronautics—U.S. I. Baker, Newton Diehl, 1871-1937. II. Title.
UG633.A4 1934c   358.3   34-26909
MC#: July 1934-page 82
SuDocs no.: W 1.2:Ai7

BAKER REPORT [Baker, William O.]

165

U.S. *President's Science Advisory Committee.*
    Improving the availability of scientific and technical information in the United States, report. [Washington] 1958.
    9 1. (U.S. President. Press release, December 7, 1958)
SuDocs no.: Pr 34.7:(date)

BALL REPORT

166

Ball, Robert M.
    Pensions in the United States; a study prepared for the Joint Committee on the Economic Report by the National Planning Association. Washington, U.S. Govt. Print. Off., 1952.
    viii, 106 p. 24 cm.
    At head of title: 82d Cong., 2d sess. Joint Committee Print.
    1. Pensions—U.S. I. National Planning Association. II. U.S. Congress. Joint Committee on the Economic Report.
HD7106.U5B28   331.25   53-60108
MC#: 1953-2177
SuDocs no.: Y4.Ec7:P38

BALL REPORTS [Ball, Joseph Hurst]

167

[Swafford, Rosa Lee]
    . . . Wartime record of strikes and lock-outs, 1940-1945. Study of the number, causes and effects of strikes during the period of 1940-1945 . . . Washington, U.S. Govt. print. off., 1946.
    ix, 38 p. incl. tables, diagrs. 23 cm. ([U.S.] 79th Cong., 2d sess. Senate. Doc. 136)
    "By Rosa Lee Swafford."
    1. Strikes and lockouts—U.S. I. Title.
HD5324.S9   331.892973   46-26007
MC#: 1946-page 485
SuDocs no.: 79th Cong., 2d sess. S. Doc. 136

168

U.S. *Congress. Joint Committee on Labor-Management Relations.*
    Labor-management relations; report. Washington, U.S. Govt. Print. Off., 1948.
    5 pts. in 2 v. 23 cm. (80th Cong., 2d sess. 1948. Senate. Report no. 986)
    Pt. 2, corrected print. has subtitle: Minority views.
    1. Industrial relations—U.S. (Series: U.S. 80th Cong., 2d sess., 1948. Senate. Report no. 986)

HD8051.B17 1948   331.15   48-45851 rev 2*
MC#: 1948-7753—Committee Print Edition
SuDocs no.: Y4.L11/3:L11
MC#: 1948-7865
     1948-10591—part 2
     1949-3011—parts 3-5
SuDocs no.: 80th Cong., 2d sess. S. Rept. 986, pts. 1-5

169

U.S. *Congress. Senate. Committee on Appropriations.*
    Sick and annual leave. Report of the Committee on Appropriations, United States Senate on sick and annual leave in the Executive Branch. Washington, U.S. Govt. Print. Off., 1948.
    v, 41 p. tables. 24 cm.
    At head of title: 80th Cong., 2d sess. Senate committee print.
    1. U.S.—Officials and employees—Leave regulations. I. Title. II. Title: Ball report on sick and annual leave in the Executive Branch.
JK649 1948ca   *351.5 351.1   53-60115
MC#: 1948-7765
SuDocs no.: 80th Cong., 2d sess. S. Doc. 126

170

U.S. *Congress. Senate. Committee on education and labor.*
    . . . Formation of an international health organization . . . Report. "To accompany S. J. Res. 89" [Washington, U.S. Govt. print. off., 1945]
    18 p. illus. (maps) 23 cm. ([U.S.] 79th Cong., 1st sess. Senate. Rept. 782)
    Caption title.
    Submitted by Mr. Ball (for Mr. Smith) from the Committee on education and labor.
    1. Hygiene, Public—Societies, etc. I. Ball, Joseph Hurst, 1905- II. Title: International health organization.
RA421.I47 1945   614.0621   45-37799
MC#: 1946-page 55
SuDocs no.: 79th Cong., 1st sess. S. Rept. 782

BALLOU REPORT [Ballou, Sidney M.]
     see
CULLOM REPORT [Cullom, Shelby Moore]

BALOGH REPORT

171

[Balogh, Thomas,] Baron Balogh, 1905-
    . . . Investment trusts and investment companies. Letter from the chairman of the Securities and exchange commission transmitting, pursuant to law, a report on investment trusts in Great Britain . . . Washington, U.S. Govt. print. off., 1939.
    ix, 75 p. incl. tables. 23½ cm. ([U.S.] 76th Cong., 1st sess. House. Doc. 380)
    Running title: Investment trusts in Great Britain.
    Commonly known as the Balogh report.
    Issued also, in mineographed form, without document series note.
    Referred to the Committee on interstate and foreign commerce and ordered printed June 28, 1939.
    "This report was prepared in London, England, for the commission by two economists, Dr. Thomas Balogh and Dr. Ernest Doblin; and the material and opinions contained therein are solely those of the authors."—p. iii.
    1. Investment trusts. 2. Investments—Gt. Brit. I. Doblin, Ernest Martin, 1904 joint author. II. U.S. Securities and Exchange Commission. III. Title. IV. Title: Balogh report on investment trusts and investment companies.
HG4530.B28   332.140942   39-29228

MC#: 1939-page 1501
SuDocs no.: 76th Cong., 1st sess. H. Doc. 380

BANE REPORT [Bane, Frank]

172

U.S. *Surgeon General's Consultant Group on Medical Education.*
  Physicians for a growing America; report. [Washington] Public Health Service, U.S. Dept. of Health, Education, and Welfare, 1959.
  xiv, 95 p. maps, diagrs., tables. 26 cm. (U.S. Public Health Service. Publication no. 709)
  Bibliography: p. 90-95.
  1. Medical colleges—U.S. 2. Physicians—U.S. 3. Medicine—Study and teaching—U.S. I. Title (Series)
R745.U5   610.71173   59-62451
MC#: 1959-17046
SuDocs no.: FS2.2:P56/3

BANEY REPORT [Baney, Anna Mae]
  see
ABBE REPORT [Abbe, Leslie Morgan]

BANTA REPORT [Banta, John]
  see
BOSSELMAN REPORT [Bosselman, Fred P.]
  Taking issue.

BARBASH REPORT [Barbash, Jack]

173

U.S. *Congress. Senate. Committee on Labor and Public Welfare.*
  The problem of delay in administering the Labor-management relations act. Staff report to the Subcommittee on Labor and Labor-Management Relations of the Committee on Labor and Public Welfare, United States Senate, Eighty-second Congress, second session . . . Washington, U.S. Govt. Print. Off., 1952.
  iii, 34 p. 24 cm.
  At head of title: Committee print. 82d Cong., 2d sess. Senate.
  1. U.S. National Labor Relations Board. I. Title: Labor-management relations act.
                    331.15   52-61543 rev
MC#: 1953-15852
SuDocs no.: Y4.L11/2:L11/9

BARBOUR REPORT [Barbour, Dana Mills]
  see under
O'MAHONEY REPORTS [O'Mahoney, Joseph Christopher]
  Linninberg. Government purchasing.

BARDEN REPORT [Barden, Graham Arthur]

174

U.S. *Advisory committee on the study of higher education.*
  . . . Effect of certain war activities upon colleges and universities. Report from the Committee on education, House of representatives, pursuant to H. Res. 63, a resolution authorizing a study by the Committee on education of the effect of certain war activities upon colleges and universities . . . Washington, U.S. Govt. print. off., 1945.
  1 p., 1., 57 p. incl. tables, diagrs. 23 cm. ([U.S.] 79th Cong., 1st sess. House. Rept. 214)
  Report of the Advisory committee on the study of higher education. cf. Letter of transmittal.
  Submitted by Mr. Barden from the Committee on education. Cloyd H. Marvin, chairman.

  1. Universities and colleges—U.S. 2. World war, 1939—Education and the war. I. Barden, Graham Arthur, 1896-
LA226.A53 1945a   378.73   45-35651
MC#: 1945-page 366
SuDocs no.: 79th Cong., 1st sess. H. Rept. 214

BARKER REPORTS

175

Barker, Preston Wallace, 1896-
  . . . Rubber industry of the United States, 1839-1939, by P. W. Barker, business specialist for rubber and rubber manufactures, Leather and rubber division. Prepared under the direction of E. G. Holt, chief, Leather and rubber division. Washington, U.S. Govt. print. off., 1939.
  vi, 42 p. incl. illus., tables, diagrs. 23 cm. (U.S. Bureau of foreign and domestic commerce (Dept. of commerce) Trade promotion series, no. 197)
  At head of title: U.S. Department of commerce. Harry L. Hopkins, secretary. Bureau of foreign and domestic commerce. N. H. Engle, acting director . . .
  "Alphabetic list of rubber products": p. 35-42.
  1. Rubber industry and trade—U.S. I. Title.
HD9161.U52B28   338.4   39-26868
- - - - - Copy 2.
MC#: 1939-page 961
SuDocs no.: C 18.27:197

176

Barker, Preston Wallace, 1896-
  . . . Rubber statistics, 1900-1937; production, absorption, stocks and prices, by P. W. Barker, business specialist for rubber and rubber manufactures, Leather and rubber division. Prepared under the direction of E. G. Holt, Acting chief, Leather and rubber division. Washington, U.S. Govt. print. off., 1938.
  iv, 55 p. incl. tables, diagrs. 23 cm. (U.S. Bureau of foreign and domestic commerce (Dept. of commerce) Trade promotion series, no. 181)
  At head of title: U.S. Department of commerce. Daniel C. Roper, secretary. Bureau of foreign and domestic commerce. Alexander V. Dye, director . . .
  "Sources of statistics": p. 55.
  1. Rubber—Stat. I. Title.
HD9161.U52B3   338.4   38-26665
- - - - - Copy 2.
MC#: 1938-page 953
SuDocs no.: C 18.27:181

BARKLEY REPORTS [Barkley, Alben William]

177

U.S. *Congress. Joint committee on conditions in concentration camps in Germany.*
  . . . Atrocities and other conditions in concentration camps in Germany. Report of the committee requested by Gen. Dwight D. Eisenhower through the Chief of staff, Gen. George C. Marshall to the Congress of the United States relative to atrocities and other condition in concentration camps in Germany . . . Washington, U.S. Govt. print. off., 1945.
  1 p. l., 16 p. 23 cm ([U.S.] 79th Cong., 1st sess. Senate. Doc. 47)
  Running title: Conditions in concentration camps in Germany.
  Signed: Alben W. Barkley . . . [and others]
  1. Concentration camps—Germany. 2. World War, 1939-1945—Atrocities. I. Barkley, Alben William, 1877- II. Title.
DD253.U4867   940.54743   45-36129
MC#: 1945-page 591
SuDocs no.: 79th Cong., 1st sess. S. Doc. 47

178

U.S. *Congress. Joint committee on the investigation of the Pearl harbor attack.*

. . . Investigation of the Pearl harbor attack. Report of the Joint committee on the investigation of the Pearl harbor attack, Congress of the United States, pursuant to S. Con. Res. 27, 79th Congress, a concurrent resolution to investigate the attack on Pearl harbor on December 7, 1941, and events and circumstances relating thereto, and additional views of Mr. Keefe, together with Minority views of Mr. Ferguson and Mr. Brewster . . . Washington, U.S. Govt. print. off., 1946.

xvi p., 1 1., 580 (i.e. 604) p. 3 fold. maps. 23 cm. ([U.S.] 79th Cong., 2d sess. Senate Doc. 244)

Includes extra numbered pages.

Alben W. Barkley, chairman.

1. Pearl harbor, Attack on, 1941. 2. World War, 1939-1945—Japan. I. Barkley, Alben William, 1877- II. Ferguson, Homer, 1889- III. Brewster, Ralph Owen, 1888- IV. Title.

D767.92.A5 1945d   940.542   46-26972
MC#: 1946-page 1061
SuDocs no.: 79th Cong., 2d sess. S. Doc. 244

United States. *Congress. Joint Committee on the Investigation of the Pearl Harbor Attack.*

Report of the Joint Committee on the Investigation of the Pearl Harbor Attack. Including the Minority report. New York, Da Capo Press, 1972.

xvi, 492, 79 p. fold. chart, maps. 23 cm. (Franklin D. Roosevelt and the era of the New Deal)

At head of title: United States. 79th Congress, 2nd Session. Reprint of the 1946 ed.

Commonly known as the Barkley report.

1. Pearl Harbor, Attack on, 1941. 2. World War, 1939-1945—Japan. I. Title. II. Title: Barkley report on the Pearl Harbor attack. III. Series.

D767.92.A531972   940.542′6   74-166954
ISBN 0-306-70331-9   MARC
Not listed in Monthly Catalog

179

U.S. *Congress. Senate. Library.*

Domestic stability, national defense and World War II; legislative and executive background, 1933-1946. [Reprinted from Senate Document 224, Seventy-seventh Congress, with additions and revisions] Washington, U.S. Govt. Print. Off., 1947.

III, 163 p. 24 cm. 79th Cong., 2d sess. Senate. Document no. 261

Previous editions compiled by Alben W. Barkley.

1. U.S.—Defenses. 2. World War, 1939-1945—U.S. 3. Industrial mobilization—U.S. I. Barkley, Alben William, 1877- comp. Domestic stability, national defense and prosecution of World War II. II. Title. (Series: U.S. 79th Cong., 2d sess., 1946 Senate Document no. 261)

UA23.3.A585   973.917   47-46264*
MC#: 1947-4658
SuDocs no.: 79th Cong., 2d sess. S. Doc. 261

BARNETT REPORT [Barnett, George Ernest]
 see under
ALDRICH COMMISSION [Aldrich, Nelson Wilmarth]

BARNEY REPORT [Barney, Gerald O.]
 see
GLOBAL 2000 STUDY (U.S.)

BARR REPORT [Barr, John A.]

180

U.S. *Secretary's Advisory Committee on Hospital Effectiveness.*

Report. [Washington] U.S. Dept. of Health, Education, and Welfare; [for sale by Supt. of Docs., U.S. Govt. Print. Off., 1968]

x, 37 p. 24 cm.

1. Hospital care—U.S.

RA410.7.A56   362.1′1′0973   68-61278
MC#: 1968-9165 (LC card HEW68-66 cancelled in favor of 68-61278)
SuDocs no.: FS1.2:H79

BARROW REPORT [Barrow, Roscoe L.]

181

U.S. *Congress. House. Committee on Interstate and Foreign Commerce.*

Network broadcasting; report pursuant to section 136 of the Legislativge reorganization act of 1946, Public Law 601, 79th Congress, and House resolution 99, 85th Congress. Washington, U.S. Govt. Print. Off., 1958.

xxii, 737 p. forms, tables. 24 cm. (85th Cong., 2d sess. House report no. 1297)

1. Radio broadcasting—U.S. 2. Television broadcasting—U.S. I. Title. (Series: U.S. 85th Cong., 2d sess., 1958. House. Report no. 1297)

HE8698.A42 1958   58-60269
MC#: 1958-3097 (LC card 58-60239 listed in error)
SuDocs no.: 85th Cong., 2d sess. H. Rept. 1297

BARTLETT REPORT

182

Bartlett, Frederic P.

Report to the Governor of the Virgin Islands on population and economic factors for planning in the Virgin Islands. Original rev. draft [n.p., 1947]

80 p. 27 cm.

Cover title.

1. Virgin Islands of the United States—Econ. condit. 2. Virgin Islands of the United States—Population.

HC157.V6B3   330.97297   47-46278*
Not located in Monthly Catalog

BARTON REPORT [Barton, George W.]

183

U.S. *President's Task Force on Highway Safety.*

Mobility without mayhem; the report of the President's Task Force on Highway Safety. Washington, For sale by the Supt. of Docs., U.S. Govt. Print. Off., 1970.

vi, 58 p. 24 cm.

Bibliography: p. 56-58.

1. Traffic safety—U.S. I. Title.

HE5614.2.A58   614.8′62   73-610878
                MARC
MC#: 1971-7213
SuDocs no.: Pr37.8:H53/M71

BARTON REPORT [Barton, Walter E.]

184

United States. *First Mission on Mental Health to the U.S.S.R.*

Special report. Chevy Chase, Md., U.S. Dept. of Health, Education, and Welfare, National Institute of Mental Health; [for sale by the Supt. of Docs., U.S. Govt. Print. Off.] 1969.

viii, 181 p. illus., ports. 26 cm. (Public Health Service publication no. 1893)

1. Mental hygiene — Russia. 2. Psychiatry — Russia. I. Series: United States. Public Health Service. Publication no. 1893.
RA790.7.R9U5   614.58′0947   71-601378
                                      MARC
MC#: 1969-7427
SuDocs no.: FS2.22:Un3/3

BARUCH REPORTS

185

Baruch, Bernard Mannes, 1870-
    The international control of atomic energy, speech by Bernard M. Baruch . . . New York city, Freedom house, 1946.
    1. p. 1., 8 p. 20 cm. [U.S. Dept. of state. Publication 2681]
    1. Atomic energy. I. Title.
HD9698.A3B3   341   46-27940
MC#: 1946-page 1423
SuDocs no.: S1.2:At7/3

186

United Nations. *Atomic Energy Commission. Representative from the United States.*
    The international control of atomic energy, scientific information transmitted to the United Nations Atomic Energy Commission. Prepared in the office of Bernard M. Baruch. [Washington] Dept. of State [1946-47]
    7 v. in 2. 23 cm. ([U.S.] Dept. of State. [Publication 2661, 2775] United States and United Nations report series, 5, 9)
    Vol. 3: Bibliography and check list.
    1. Atomic power. 2. Atomic energy. I. Title. (Series: U.S. Dept. of State. Publication 2661, 2775. Series: U.S. Dept. of State. United States and United Nations report series, 5, 9)
TK9145.U4 1946   541.2   46-26835*
Not located in Monthly Catalog

187

United nations. *Atomic Energy Commission.*
    The international control of atomic energy; report. 1st-Dec. 31, 1946 Washington, U.S. Govt. Print. Off.
    v. 23 cm. ([U.S.]Dept. of State. Publication 2737 [etc.])
    Reports dated Dec. 31, 1946-Sept. 11, 1947 issued as U.S. Dept. of State. United States and United Nations report series, 8 [etc.]; reports, May 17, 1948 as U.S. Dept. of State. International organization and conference series, III, 7 [etc.].
    1. Atomic energy. I. Title. (Series. Series: U.S. Dept. of State. United States and United Nations report series 8 [etc.] Series: U.S. Dept. of State. International organization and conference series, III, 7 [etc.])
HD9698.A24 I 5   341   47-32641*
MC#: 1947-page 456
SuDocs no.: S 1.49:8

    The first report of the United Nations Atomic Energy Commission to the Security Council.
    The United States and the United Nations Report Series 8.

188

U.S. *Office of war mobilization.*
    Report on war and post-war adjustment policies. February 15, 1944. Bernard M. Baruch, John M. Hancock. [Washington, U.S. Govt. print. off., 1944]
    iv, 108 p. 23½ cm.
    Letter of transmittal signed: Bernard M. Baruch . . . John M. Hancock, Advisory unit for war and post-war adjustment policies, Office of war mobilization.
    Issued also as Senate doc. 154, 78th Cong., 2d sess., under title: War and post-war adjustment policy. Report . . .

1. U.S. — Economic policy. 2. World war, 1939-1945- — Economic aspects — U.S. 3. Reconstruction (1939-1951) — U.S. I. Baruch, Bernard Mannes, 1870- II. Hancock, John Milton, 1883-
HC106.4.A2867 1944c   338.91   44-40736
MC#: 1944-page 430
SuDocs no.: Pr32.5902:W19/5

189

U.S. *Office of war mobilization.*
    . . . War and post-war adjustment policy. Report on war and post-war adjustment policy, submitted by Bernard M. Baruch and John M. Hancock to James F. Byrnes, director, Office of war mobilization on February 15, 1944. Washington, U.S. Govt. print. off., 1944 .
    iv, 108 p. 23½ cm. ([U.S.] 78th Cong., 2d sess. Senate. Doc. 154)
    Issued also without congressional series numbering under title: Report on war and post-war adjustment policies . . .
    1. U.S. — Economic policy. 2. World war, 1939-1945- — Economic aspects — U.S. 3. Reconstruction (1939-) — U.S. I. Baruch, Bernard Mannes, 1870- II. Hancock, John Milton, 1883-
HC106.4.A2867 1944b   338.91   44-40680
MC#: 1944-page 430
SuDocs no.: 78th Cong., 2d sess. S. Doc. 154

190

U.S. *Special committee to study the rubber situation.*
    . . . The rubber situation. Message from the President of the United States transmitting a digest and report of the Special committee to study the rubber situation and to recommend action . . . Washington, U.S. Govt. print. off., 1942.
    1 p. 1., 46 p. incl. tables. 23 cm. ([U.S.] 77th Cong., 2d sess. House Doc. 836)
    Bernard M. Baruch, chairman.
    Issued also without document series note under title: Report of the Rubber survey committee.
    1. Rubber industry and trade-U.S. 2. Rubber, Artificial. I. Baruch, Bernard Mannes, 1870- II. Title.
HD9161.U52A5 1942p   338.4   42-38618
MC#: 1942-page 1181
SuDocs no.: 77th Cong., 2d sess. H. Doc. 836

191

U.S. *War industries board.*
    American industry in the war; a report of the War industries board (March 1921) by Bernard M. Baruch, chairman, including, besides a reprint of the report of the War industries board of world war I, Mr. Baruch's own program for total mobilization of the nation as presented to the War policies Commission in 1931, and current material on priorities and price fixing. With a foreward by Bernard M. Baruch, and an introduction by Hugh S. Johnson. Edited by Richard H. Hippelheuser. New York, Prentice-Hall, inc., 1941.
    xii, 498 p. fold. diagr. 23½ cm.
    1. European war, 1914-1918 — Economic aspects — U.S. 2. War — Economic aspects. 3. U.S. — Economic policy. I. Baruch, Bernard Mannes, 1870- Taking the profit out of war. II. Hippelheuser, Richard H., ed. III. Title.
HC106.2.A3 1941   330.973   41-10350
Not located in Monthly Catalog

BATES REPORT [Bates, Emily Cauthorn]
see
BAKER REPORT [Baker, Jacob]

BATTLE ACT REPORT [Battle, Laurie C.]

192

U.S. *Dept. of State.*

Mutual defense assistance control act of 1951; report to Congress. 1st- Jan. 24/July 24, 1952- [Washington, U.S. Govt. Print. Off.]

v. 24 cm. semiannual.

Vol. 1 issued by the Mutual Security Agency; v. 2-6 by the Foreign Operations Administration; v. 7-10 by the International Cooperation Administration.

Title varies slightly.

Each report has also a distinctive title.

1. East-West trade (1945-) 2. U.S.—Commercial policy. 3. Russia—Commercial policy.
HF1416.U5   *382.6   52-61994 rev 3
MC#: 1952-17978-1st report
SuDocs no.: Pr33.901/2:1
MC#: 1953-2693-2d report
SuDocs no.: Pr33.901/2:2
MC#: 1953-19172-3d report
SuDocs no.: FO1.1/2:3
MC#: 1954-8790-4th report
SuDocs no.: FO1.1/2:4
MC#: 1955-665-5th report (LC card 52-60646 referred to in error)
SuDocs no.: FO1.1/2:5
MC#: 1955-12485-6th report
SuDocs no.: FO1.1/2:6
MC#: 1956-4037-7th report
SuDocs no.: S17.1/2:7
MC#: 1956-19131-8th report
SuDocs no.: S17.1/2:8
MC#: 1957-11651-9th report
SuDocs no.: S17.1/2:9
MC#: 1958-6105-10th report
SuDocs no.: S17.1/2:10
MC#: 1958-13156-11th report (LC card SD50-66 referred to in error)
SuDocs no.: S1.71:132
MC#: 1959-6948-12th report
SuDocs no.: S1.71:136
MC#: 1960-6066-13th report
SuDocs no.: S1.71:147
MC#: 1961-5105-14th report (LC card 52-1194 referred to in error)
SuDocs no.: S1.71:156
MC#: 1962-10671-15th report
SuDocs no.: S1.71:175
MC#: 1964-3144-16th report
SuDocs no.: S1.71:182
MC#: 1965-5391-17th report
SuDocs no.: S1.71:196
MC#: 1966-6631-18th report
SuDocs no.: S1.71:210
MC#: 1967-7147-19th report
SuDocs no.: S1.71:218
MC#: 1968-8338-20th report
SuDocs no.: S1.71:223
MC#: 1969-4963-21st report
SuDocs no.: S1.71:228
MC#: 1970-17332-22d report
SuDocs no.: S1.71:242
MC#: 1971-10165-23d report
SuDocs no.: S1.71:253
MC#: 1972-10324-24th report
SuDocs no.: S1.71:261
MC#: 1973-26858-25th report
SuDocs no.: S1.71:275

BATTLE REPORT

193

Battle, Laurie C

Progress in the control of strategic exports to the Soviet bloc; report [submitted to] the [House of Representatives] Committee on Foreign Affairs. Washington, U.S. Govt. Print. Off., 1953.

v, 50 p. 23 cm.

At head of title: 83d Cong., 1st sess. Committee print.

1. U.S.—Commercial policy. 2. Embargo. 3. Munitions. I. U.S. Congress. House. Committee on Foreign Affairs. II. Title.
HF3031.B3   382   53-61003
MC#: 1953-8990
SuDocs no.: Y4.F76/1:Ex7

BATZELL REPORT [Batzell, Elmer E.]
see under
O'MAHONEY REPORTS [O'Mahoney, Joseph Christopher]
Hamilton. Patents and free enterprise.

BAYNE-JONES REPORT [Bayne-Jones, Stanhope]

194

U.S. *Dept. of Health, Education, and Welfare.*

The advancement of medical research and education through the Department of Health, Education, and Welfare; final report of the Secretary's consultants on medical research and education. [Washington] Office of the Secretary, Dept. of Health, Education, and Welfare, 1958.

xiv, 82 p. diagrs., tables. 26 cm.

1. Medical research—U.S. 2. Medicine—Study and teaching—U.S. I. Title.
R854.U5A54   610.72   58-61594
MC#: 1958-12877
SuDocs no.: FS1.2:M46

BAZELON REPORT [Bazelon,David L.]

195

U.S. *President's Panel on Mental Retardation.*

Report of the Task Force on Law [by] David L. Bazelon, chairman [and others. Washington, 1963?]

71 p. 27 cm.

1. Mental health laws—U.S. 2. Criminal liability—U.S. I. Bazelon, David L.
                                                  63-60030
MC#: 1963-21075
SuDocs no.: Pr 35.8:M52/L41

BEACH REPORT [Beach, William Dorrance]
see
UPTON REPORTS [Upton, Emory]

BEAN REPORT [Bean, Louis Hyman]
see
EZEKIEL REPORT [Ezekiel, Mordecai]

BECK REPORT [Beck, William Hopkins]

196

U.S. *Dept. of State.*

Occupation of Germany, policy and progress 1945-46. Washington, U.S. Govt. Print. Off. [1947]

viii, 241 p. maps. 24 cm. (Its Publication 2783. European series, 23)

1. Germany—Hist.—Allied occupation, 1945-2. Reconstruction (1939-1951)-Germany. I. Title. (Series: U.S. Dept. of State.

Publication 2783. Series: U.S. Dept. of State. European series, 23)
D802.G3U51947a   940.5343   S D 47-47*
U.S. Dept. of State. Library
MC#: 1947-5459
SuDocs no.: S1.45:23

BELL REPORT [Bell, David E.]
197

U.S. *Bureau of the Budget.*
Report to the President on Government contracting for research and development. Prepared by the Bureau of the Budget and referred to the Committee on Government Operations, United States Senate. Washington, U.S. Govt. Print. Off., 1962.

xiii, 92 p. diagrs., tables. 24 cm. (87th Cong., 2d sess. Senate. Document no. 94)
"Annotated bibliography on Federal contracting-out of research and development": p. 69-92.
1. Research and development contracts—U.S. 2. Research and development contracts—U.S.—Bibl. I. U.S. Congress. Senate. Committee on Government Operations. II. Title: Government contracting for research and development. (Series: U.S. 87th Cong., 2d sess. 1962. Senate. Document no. 94)
Q180.U5A44 1962   62-61537
MC#: 1962-13554
SuDocs no.: 87th Cong., 2d sess. S. Doc. 94

BELL REPORTS [Bell, Daniel Wafena]
198

United States. *Dept. of Health, Education, and Welfare.*
Toward a social report. Washington, For sale by the Supt. of Docs. U.S. Govt. Print. Off. [1969]

xxii, 101 p. illus. 24 cm.
Bibliographical footnotes.
1. United States—Social conditions-1960- I. Title.
HN56.A47   309.1'73   70-601158
                                     MARC
MC#:1969-5736
SuDocs no.: FS1.2:Sol/2

199

U.S. *Economic Survey Mission to the Philippines.*
Report to the President of the United States. Washington [Govt. Print. Off.] 1950.

ii, 107 p. 32 cm. (U.S. Dept. of State. Publication 4010. Far Eastern series, 38)
Daniel W. Bell, chief of mission.
1. Philippine Islands—Economic policy. I. Bell, Daniel W. (Series: U.S. Dept. of State. Publication 4010. Series: U.S. Dept. of State. Far Eastern series, 38)
HC455.A43 1950   330.9914   50-61628
MC#: 1951-1572
SuDocs no.: S1.38:38

200

U.S. *Economic Survey Mission to the Philippines.*
Report to the President of the United States. Washington, 1950.
ii, 107 p. 32 cm.
Daniel W. Bell, chief of mission.
Issued also as Publication 4010, Far Eastern series 38 of the Dept. of State.
1. Philippine Islands—Economic policy. I. Bell, Daniel Wafena.
HC455.A43 1950f   330.9914   51-60649
Not located in Monthly Catalog

201

U.S. *Public Advisory Board for Mutual Security.*
A trade and tariff policy in the national interest. [A report to the President] Washington, 1953.

v, 78 p. diagrs., tables. 26 cm.
1. U.S.-Commercial Policy. I. Title.
HF1455.A56   337   53-60935 rev
MC#: 1953-9581
SuDocs no.: Pr33.902:T67

BELLAMY REPORT [Bellamy, Paul]
202

U.S. *President's committee on deferment of federal employees.*
. . . Report of the President's committee on deferment of federal employees. Message from the President of the United States transmitting copy of the report of the President's committee on deferment of federal employees and his executive order giving effect to the committee's recommendations . . . Washington, U.S. Govt. print. off., 1943.

iii, 44 p. 23 cm. ([U.S.] 78th Cong., 1st sess. House. Doc. 127)
Running title: Deferment of federal employees.
1. Military service, Compulsory. 2. U.S.—Army—Recruiting, enlistment, etc. 3. U.S.—Officials and employees. I. Title: Deferment of federal employees.
UB343.A53 1943e   355.22   43-51912
MC#: 1943-page 491
SuDocs no.: 78th Cong., 1st sess. H. Doc. 127

BENDER REPORTS [Bender, George H.]
see under
HOFFMAN REPORTS [Hoffman, Clare E.]
Eighteenth intermediate report.

Twenty-second intermediate report.

BENDETSON REPORTS [Bendetson, Karl R.]
203

Army War College
Reorganization of the Army establishment; address by Mr. K. R. Bendetson before the Army War College, Carlisle Barracks, Penna., 1 December 1952. Carlisle Barracks, Pa. 1952.

2v. in 1, various pagings, charts.
Bound with a Review and Analysis of the Proposal presented.
1. United States. Army — Organization. I. Bendetson, Karl R. II. United States. Army War College.

204

United States. *War Relocation Authority.*
An obligation discharged: the Army transfers to the Relocation Authority, a civilian organization, Japanese evacuated from the Pacific coast. An address delivered to the personnel of Wartime Civil Control, by Col. Karl R. Bendetson, Nov. 3, 1942. San Francisco, 1942.

9 p. 23 cm.
1. World War, 1939-1945—Evacuation of Civilians. 2. Japanese in the United States. I. Bendetson, Karl R.

BENNET REPORT [Bennet, William S.]
see under
DILLINGHAM COMMISSION [Dillingham, William Paul]
Abstracts of reports of the Immigration commission, vols. 1-2.

Brief statement of the conclusions and recommendations.

BENNETT REPORTS [Bennett, Ivan L.]
205

U.S. *Panel on the World Food Supply.*
The world food problem; a report. Washington, For sale by the Supt. of Docs., U.S. Govt. Print. Off., 1967.

3 v. illus. 23 cm.
1. Food supply. I. Title.
HD9000.5.U54   338.1'9   67-61653
MC#: 1967-11706-707
SuDocs no.: Pr35.8:Sci2F73/v. (nos.)
MC#: 1968-1067
SuDocs no.: Pr35.8:Sci2F73/v.3

206

United States. *President's Science Advisory Committee. Panel on Biological and Medical Science.*
Scientific and educational basis for improving health; report. [Washington] Office of Science and Technology; [for sale by the Supt. of Docs., U.S. Govt. Print. Off.] 1972.

viii, 66 p. illus. 27 cm.
1. Medical care — United States. 2. Medical research — United States. 3. Medical policy — United States. I. Title.
RA395.A3U54 1972   362.1   72-602368
                                                          MARC
MC#: 1972-14187
SuDocs no.: PrEx8.2:H34

BENSON REPORTS [Benson, George C. S.]
207

U.S. *Dept. of Defense. Special Committee on ROTC.*
Report. Washington, 1969.

61 p.
1. U.S. Army. Reserve Officers' Training Corps.
[U428.5.A58]
Dept. of the Army Library
Not located in Monthly Catalog

208

United States. *Special Board to Study Negro Participation in the Army National Guard and the United States Army Reserve.*
Participation of Negroes in the reserve components of the Army. (Washington) 1967.

3v. tables (ASDIRS 1675)
Report of the Board appointed of Chief of Staff Memorandum 67-347 and 67-413.
1. U.S. Army Reserve. 2. Negro soldiers. I. Title. II. Series.
[UA42.A574]
Dept. of the Army Library
Not located in Monthly Catalog

BENTLEY REPORT [Bentley, Alvin M.]
see
GALLAGHER REPORT [Gallagher, Cornelius E.]

BENTON REPORT [Benton, Mildred Catherine]
209

George Washington University, Washington, D.C. Biological Sciences Communication Project.
A study of resources and major subject holdings available in U.S. Federal libraries maintaining extensive or unique collections of research materials; final report. By Mildred Benton, project supervisor, assisted by Signe Ottersen [and others] Washington, U.S. Office of Education, Bureau of Research, 1970.

ix, 670 p. 28 cm.

Title on spine: Federal libraries resources study.
"OE Bureau of Research project no. 8-0310, contract no. OEC-0-8080310-3742(095)"
Includes bibliographical references.
1. Libraries, Governmental, administrative, etc. — United States. 2. Catalogs, Union — United States. I. Benton, Mildred Catherine, 1902- II. Title. III. Title: Federal libraries resources study.
Z881.A1G4 1970b   011   79-609579
                                                          MARC
MC#: 1971-903
SuDocs no.: HE5.2:L61/10

BERG REPORT [Berg, Sherwood O.]
210

U.S. *National Advisory Commission on Food and Fiber.*
Food & fiber for the future; [final] report. Washington, For sale by the Supt. of Docs, U.S. Govt. Print. Off., 1967.

xiii, 361 p. illus. 23 cm.
Submitted to the President through his Committee on Food and Fiber.
1. Agriculture — Economic aspects — U.S. 2. Agriculture and state — U.S.I. U.S. President's Committee on Food and Fiber. II. Title.
HD1753 1967d   338.1'0973   67-61919
MC#: 1967-13063
SuDocs no.: Pr8:F73/F73

BERGER REPORT [Berger, Bernard B.]
see
ACKERMAN REPORT [Ackerman, William G.]
Federal water resources research program, fiscal year 1968.

BERGMANN REPORT
211

Bergmann, Barbara R.
Structural unemployment in the United States. Prepared by Barbara R. Bergmann and David E. Kaun, the Brookings Institution, for the U.S. Dept. of Commerce, Economic Development Administration. [Washington, U.S. Dept. of Commerce, Economic Development Administration; for sale by the Supt. of Docs, U.S. Govt. Print Off., 1967]

ix, 122 p. illus. 26 cm.
Bibliographical footnotes.
1. Labor supply — U.S. I. Kaun, David E., joint author. II. Brookings Institution, Washington, D.C. III. U.S. Economic Development Administration. IV. Title.
HD5724.B39   331.1'12'0973   67-61218
MC#: 1967-7872
SuDocs no.: C46.2:Un2

BERNSTEIN REPORT [Bernstein, Blanche]
Income-tested social benefits in New York.
see under
GRIFFITHS REPORTS [Griffiths, Martha W.]
Studies in public welfare, paper no. 8.

BERNSTEIN REPORT [Bernstein, Edward M.]
212

U.S. *Review Committee for Balance of Payments Statistics.*
The balance of payments statistics of the United States, a review and appraisal; report to the Bureau of the Budget. [Washington, U.S. Govt. Print. Off.] 1965.

xiii, 194 p. illus. 29 cm.

1. Balance of payments — U.S. 2. Commercial statistics. I. Title.
HG3883.U7A63   65-61454
MC#: 1965-8569
SuDocs no.: PrEx2.2:B18

BERTRAND REPORT [Bertrand, Daniel]
see under
O'MAHONEY REPORTS [O'Mahoney, Joseph Christopher]

BESSON BOARD [Besson, Frank S., Jr.]
213

United States. *Joint Logistics Review Board.*
Logistic support in the Vietnam era; a report. [Washington? 1970]
3 v. illus., maps. 26 cm.
Bibliography: v. 2, p. C3-C16.
CONTENTS: v. 1. A summary assessment with major findings and recommendations. — v. 2. A review of logistic support in the Vietnam era. — v. 3. Monograph summaries and recommendations.
1. United States — Armed Forces — Supplies and stores. 2. Logistics. I. Title.
UC263.A5175   355.4'1'0873   76-609704
                                                      MARC
Not Located in Monthly Catalog

BETTMAN REPORT [Bettman, Alfred]
see
WICKERSHAM COMMISSION [Wickersham, George Woodward]
Report on prosecution, no. 4.

BEVIS REPORTS [Bevis, Howard L.]
214

U.S. *President's Committee on Scientists and Engineers.*
Interim report. 1st-1956-Washington.
v. 27 cm.
Report for 1956- issued by the committee under its earlier name: National Committee for the Development of Scientists and Engineers.
1. Scientists, American. 2. Engineers, American.
Q125.U48   57-60554
Not located in Monthly Catalog

215

U.S. *President's Committee on Scientists and Engineers.*
United local action; schools, scientists, engineers, civic groups, universities, employers. Washington [1957]
21 1.28 cm.
1. Scientists, American. 2. Engineers, American. 3. Technical education — U.S. I. Title.
Q125.U49   507   58-60303
Not located in Monthly Catalog

BIGGERS REPORT [Biggers, John D.]
216

U.S. *Office of administrator of the census of partial employment, unemployment and occupations.*
. . . Final report on total and partial unemployment, 1937 . . . Washington, U.S. Govt. print. off., 1938.
4 v. illus. (maps) tables, diagrs., forms. 29 cm.
At head of title: Census of partial employment, unemployment and occupations: 1937. John D. Biggers, administrator.

Title appears on covers of vol. I-IV and on special t.-p. of vol. IV only.
Contents. — I. United States summary, geographic divisions, and states from Alabama to Indiana. — II. States from Iowa to New York. — III. States from North Carolina to Wyoming, Alaska, and Hawaii. — IV. The enumerative check census, by C. L. Dedrick and M. H. Hansen.
1. Unemployed — U.S. — Stat. I. Dedrick, Calvert Lampert. II. Hansen, Morris Howard, 1910-
HD5723.A5 1937d   331.137973   38-26231
MC#: 1938-page 1183
SuDocs no.: Y3.C33/5:2R29/3

BLACK REPORT
217

Black, Eugene Robert, 1898-
[Report on the supersonic transport program, made as a result of President Kennedy's appointment to look into this problem and to advise him thereon, by Eugene R. Black and Stanley de J. Osborne. Washington, 1963]
2, 11, 105 p. illus. 27 cm.
Title from letter of transmittal. — p. 1 (2d group)
1. Supersonic transport planes. 2. Aeronautics and state — U.S. I. Osborne, Stanley de J. II. Title.
HE9770.J4B5   65-60356
Not located in Monthly Catalog

BLACK REPORT [Black, Hugo L.]
218

U.S. *Congress. Senate. Special committee to investigate air and ocean mail contracts.*
. . . Investigation of air mail and ocean mail contracts. Preliminary report with recommendations pertaining to ocean mail contracts . . . Washington, U.S. Govt. print. off., 1935.
ii, 47 p. 23½ cm.
At head of title: 74th Cong., 1st sess. Senate committee print. "Printed for the use of the Special committee to investigate air mail and ocean mail contracts."
1. Mail steamers — U.S. 2. Air mail service — U.S. 3. Shipping bounties and subsidies — U.S. I. Title.
HE6477.A4 1935   383.4973   35-26479
MC#: 1935-page 661
SuDocs no.: 74th Cong., 1st Sess. S. Rept. 898

BLAIR REPORT [Blair, John Malcolm]
see under
O'MAHONEY REPORTS [O'Mahoney, Joseph Christopher]
Blair. Price discrimination in steel.
Lorwin. Technology in our economy.
Nelson. Price behavior and business policy.

BLAISDELL REPORT [Blaisdell, Donald Christy]
see under
O'MAHONEY REPORTS [O'Mahoney, Joseph Christopher]

BLANCHARD REPORT [Blanchard, Edna L.]
see under
O'MAHONEY REPORTS [O'Mahoney, Joseph Christopher]
Bertrand. Motion picture industry.

BLAUCH REPORT

219

Blauch, Lloyd E., 1889-

Public education in the territories and outlying possesions, by Lloyd E. Blauch, assisted by Charles F. Reid . . . Prepared for the Advisory committee on education. Washington, U.S. Govt. print. off., 1939.

xv. 243 p. illus. (maps) 23 cm. ([U.S.] Advisory committee on education. Staff study no. 16)

"Bibliographical note" at the end of each chapter except I and IX: "General bibliographical note." :p. 240.

"Publications of the committee": p. 243.

1. Education—U.S.—Territories. I. Reid, Charles Frederick. 1901- II. Title.

L111.A93 no. 16	370.973	39-26775
LA396.B6	(370.973)	

- - - - - Copy 2.

MC#: 1939-page 757

SuDocs no.: Y3.Ad9/2:7/16

BLUE RIBBON DEFENSE PANEL REPORT
see
FITZHUGH REPORT [Fitzhugh, Gilbert W.]

BLUESTONE REPORT [Bluestone, David W.]
see
WILLIAMS REPORT [Williams, Ernest William]

BOAS REPORT [Boas, Franz]
see under
DILLINGHAM COMMISSION [Dillingham, William Paul]
Changes in bodily form of descendants of immigrants.

BOLLING REPORT [Bolling, Richard]

220

U.S. *Congress. House. Select Committee on Committees.*

Committee reform amendments of 1974. Report of the Select Committee on Committees, U.S. House of Representatives to accompany H. Res. 988 together with supplemental views. Washington, U.S. Govt. Print. Off., 1974.

1 v, 460 p. 22 cm. (93d Cong., 2d sess. H. Rept. no. 916, part II)

Richard Bolling, Chairman.

MC#: 1974-07392, 07393

SuDocs no.: Y4.C73/6:R25/974/pt.1 & pt.2

BOLTE REPORTS [Bolte, Charles L.]

221

U.S. *Dept. of Defense.*

A concept of career management for officer personnel of the armed services; a report and recommendation for the Secretary of Defense by the Department of Defense Ad Hoc Committee to Study and Revise the Officer Personnel Act of 1947. [Washington] 1960.

226 p. illus. 26 cm.

1. U.S.—Armed Forces—Officers. 2. U.S.—Armed Forces—Personnel management. I. Title.

[UB413.A23]

Dept. of the Army Library

Not located in Monthly Catalog

222

U.S. *Dept. of Defense. Ad Hoc Committee to Study and Revise the Officer Personnel Act of 1947.*

[Concept of career management for officer personnel of the Armed Services.] Supplementary report. 19 April 1961. Detailed comments and Legislative draft. [Washington, D.C.] 1961.

31 lvs.

1. U.S.—Armed Forces—Officers. 2. U.S.—Armed Forces—Pay, allowances, etc.

[UB412.A46 1961]

Industrial College of the Armed Forces

Not Located in Monthly Catalog

BOLTON REPORT [Bolton, Frances P.]

223

U.S. *Congress. House. Committee on Foreign Affairs.*

The strategy and tactics of world communism. Report [of] Subcommittee No. 5, National and International Movements, with Supplement I, One hundred years of communism, 1848-1948, and Supplement II, Official protests of the United States Government against Communist policies or actions, and related correspondence. [July 1945-Dec. 1947] Washington, U.S. Govt. Print. Off., 1948.

1 v. (various pagings) 24 cm. (80th Cong., 2d sess. House. Document no. 619)

Each supplement has special t.p.

Issued also without Congressional series numbering under title: Report [on] the strategy and tactics of world communism.

- - - - - Supplement 3. Country studies. Washington, U.S. Govt. Print. Off., 1949.

3 v. 24 cm. (81st Cong., 1st sess. House. Document no. 154)

Contents.—A. The coup d'etat in Prague.—B. Communism in the Near East.—C. Communism in China.

HX40.U6 1948a Suppl. 3

- - - - - Supplement 4. Five hundred leading Communists in the Eastern Hemisphere, excluding the U.S.S.R. Washington, U.S. Govt. Print. Off., 1948.

xv, 129 p. 24 cm. (80th Cong., 2d sess. House. Document no. 707)

HX40.U6 1948a Suppl. 4

1. Communist strategy. I. Title. (Series: U.S. 80th Cong., 2d sess., 1948. House. Document no. 619. Series: U.S. 80th Cong., 2d sess., 1948. House. Document no. 707. Series: U.S. 81st Cong., 1st sess., 1949. House. Document no. 154)

HX40.U6 1948a	335.4	48-46279*

MC#: 1948-12990

SuDocs no.: 80th Cong., 2d sess. H. Doc. 619

MC#: 1948-18680

SuDocs no.: 80th Cong., 2d sess. H. Doc. 707

MC#: 1949-8982 (LC card 49-46300 cancelled in favor of 48-46279)

SuDocs no.: 81st Cong., 1st sess. H. Doc. 154

MC#: 1949-2988

SuDocs no.: Y4.F76/1:C73/2/supp. 3A-3C

BONBRIGHT REPORT [Bonbright, James Cummings]
see
PARKER REPORT [Parker, James Southworth]

BOONE REPORT [Boone, Joel T.]

224

U.S. *Coal mines administration.*

A medical survey of the bituminous-coal industry. Report of the Coal mines administration. Washington [U.S. Govt. print. off.] 1947.

xxiv, 244 p. 1 l., 67 p., incl. illus. (incl. group port., maps) tables, diagrs. pl. 29 cm.

"The coal miner and his family. Supplement to the report":
1 l., 67 p.

Bibliography: p. 229-231.

1. Coal-miners—Diseases and hygiene. 2. Coal-miners—U.S.
3. Hospitals—U.S. I. Title.
HD7269.M63U6 1947   331.822331.822   Med 47-993
MC#: 1947-page 527
SuDocs no.: I1.2:B54

BOOZ, ALLEN, HAMILTON REPORT

225

Booz, Allen and Hamilton, inc.

Management survey of activities of the Veterans Administration by the firm of Booz-Allen-Hamilton. Recommendations of the Administrator of Veterans' Affairs. Washington, U.S. Govt. Print. Off., 1952.

vi, 990 p. illus., maps (part fold) 24 cm.

At head of title: 82d Cong., 2d sess. House committee print no. 322.

Commonly known as the Booz, Allen, Hamilton report.

"Printed for the use of the Committee on Veterans' Affairs."

1. U.S. Veterans Administration. I. U.S. Congress. House. Committee on Veterans' Affairs. II. Title. III. Title: Booz, Allen, Hamilton report on activities of the Veterans Administration.
UB373.B657   353.8   52-63226
MC#: 1953-838
SuDocs no.: Y4.V64/3:M31

BORCHARDT REPORT [Borchardt, Kurt]

226

U.S. Congress. House. Committee on Interstate and Foreign Commerce.

Medical school inquiry; staff report to the Committee on Interstate and Foreign Commerce, House of Representatives, Eighty-fifth Congress, first session, containing background information relating to schools of medicine, dentistry, osteopathy, and public health. Washington, U.S. Govt. Print. Off., 1957.

xiv, 479 p. illus., maps. 24 cm.

At head of title: Committee print.

1. Medical colleges—U.S. I. Title.
R745.A5151957   610.71173   57-60608
MC#: 1957-13598
SuDocs no.: Y4.In8/4:M46/5

BORMAN REPORT [Borman, Frank]

227

United States. *Special Commission on the United States Military Academy.*

Report to the Secretary of the Army/by the Special Commission on the United States Military Academy.—[Washington]: U.S. Dept. of the Army, 1976.

91 p.; 27 cm.

1. United States. Military Academy, West Point. 2. Self-government (in education)
U410.F7U561976   355'.007'1174731   77-600977
                                      MARC
MC#: 1977-14745
SuDocs no.: D101.2:M59/4

BOSSELMAN REPORT [Bosselman, Fred P.]
    see
DOUGLAS REPORT [Douglas, Paul H.]
National Commission on Urban Problems.

Research report, no. 15

BOSSELMAN REPORTS

228

Bosselman, Fred P. 1934-

The quiet revolution in land use control. Prepared for the Council on Environmental Quality by Fred Bosselman and David Callies. [Washington; For sale by the Supt. of Docs, U.S. Govt. Print. Off., 1972]

vii, 327, [44] p. illus. 28 cm.

Includes bibliographical references.

Supt. of Docs., no.: PrEx 14.2:L22

1. Land—United States—States. 2. Land tenure—United States—States—Law. I. Callies, David, joint author. II. United States. Council on Environmental Quality. III. Title.
HD2051972.B66   333.7'0973   70-616368
                                      MARC
MC#: 1972-1594
SuDocs no.: PrEx 14.2:L22

229

Bosselman, Fred P. 1934-

The quiet revolution in land use control; summary report. Prepared for the Council on Environmental Quality by Fred Bosselman and David Callies. [Washington, U.S. Govt. Print. Off., 1971]

34 p. 28 cm.

1. Land—U.S. 2. Cities and towns—Planning—U.S. I. Callies, David. II. United States. Council on Environmental Quality. III. Title.

                                    NUC73-32417
MC#: 1972-1595
SuDocs no.: PrEx 14.2:L22/sum.

230

Bosselman, Fred P. 1934-

The taking issue; a study of the Constitutional limits of governmental authority to regulate the use of privately-owned land without paying compensation to the owners. Written for the Council on Environmental Quality, by Fred Bosselman, David Callies [and] John Banta. [Washington, For sale by the Supt. of Docs., U.S. Govt. Print. Off., 1973]

xxiii, 329 p. 24 cm.

Includes bibliographical references.

1. Land use—Law and legislation—United States. 2. Police power—United States. I. Callies, David, joint author. II. Banta, John, joint author. III. United States. Council on Environmental Quality. IV. Title.
KF5692.B68   346'.73'046   73-602495
                                      MARC
MC#: 1973-31174
SuDocs no.: PrEx 14.2:T13

BOWEN REPORT [Bowen, Howard]

231

U.S. *National Commission on Technology, Automation, and Economic Progress.*

Technology and the American economy; report. [Washington, U.S. Govt. Print. Off.] 1966.

xiv, 115 p. illus. 26 cm.

- - - - - Appendix. Studies prepared for the National Commission on Technology, Automation, and Economic Progress [and edited for publication by Judith Huxley, editorial consultant] Washington, For sale by the Superintendent of Documents, U.S. Govt. Print. Off., 1966.

6 v. illus. 26 cm.

Includes bibliographies. Bibliographical footnotes.

Contents.—v. 1. The outlook for technological change and employment.—v. 2. The employment impact of technological change.—v. 3. Adjusting to change.—v. 4. Statements relating to the impact of technological change.—v. 5. Applying technology to unmet needs.—v. 6. Educational implications of technological change.

HC106.6.A4785 Appendix

1. U.S.—Economic conditions—1945- 2. Unemployment, Technological. 3. Machinery in industry. I. Title.

HC106.6.A4785   330.973   66-61519

MC#: 1966-7923

SuDocs no.: Y3.T22:2T22/v.1

MC#: 1966-13872

SuDocs no.: Y3.T22:2T22/app./v.1-6

BOWER REPORT [Bower, Ward Taft]

1896
Known as TINGLE REPORT [Tingle, George R.]

1897-1906
Known as KUTCHIN REPORT [Kutchin, Howard M.]

1907-1910
Known as MARSH REPORT [Marsh, Millard C.]

1911-1913 (1911 report under EVERMANN)
Known as EVERMANN REPORT [Evermann, Barton Warren]

1914-1944
Known as BOWER REPORT [Bower, Ward Taft]

232

U.S. *Fish and Wildlife Service*

Alaska fishery and fur-seal industries.

Washington, U.S. Govt. Print. Off. [etc.]

v. in illus., maps (part fold.) 23-25 cm. annual.

Began publication with 1893 issue.

Reports for 1899-1902 issued in the congressional series as House or Senate Documents; 1896-98 issues as Treasury Dept. Document no. 1925, 2010; 1903-05 issued as Dept. of Commerce and Labor Document no. 12, 35; 1905-29 issued as Bureau of Fisheries Document no. 618, 632, 645, 730, 746, 766, 780, 797, 819, 834, 838, 847, 872, 891, 909, 933, 951, 973, 992, 1008, 1023, 1040, 1064, 1086; 1930-39 issued as the Bureau's Administrative report no. 2, 7, 11, 16, 19, 23, 28, 31, 36, 40; 1940- issued as the Service's Statistical digest no. 2, 5, 8, 10, 13

Reports for 1913-39 issued also as appendix to the Report of the Commissioner of Fisheries.

Title varies: 18 -98, 1900- Report on the salmon fisheries of Alaska (varies slightly)—1899, Report of the special agent for the protection of the Alaska salmon fisheries.—1906-10, The fisheries of Alaska.—1912, Fishery and fur industries of Alaska.

Other slight variations in title.

Reports for 18 -1902 issued by the Treasury Dept., Special Agents Division; 1903- by the Division of Alaskan Fisheries; 1906-39, by the Bureau of Fisheries.

1. Fisheries—Alaska. 2. Fish-culture—Alaska. 3. Sealing. I. U.S. Bureau of Fisheries. Report. Appendix. II. Title. (Series: U.S. Bureau of Fisheries. Document no. 603 [etc.] Series: U.S. Bureau of Fisheries. Administrative report no. 2 [etc.] Series: U.S. Fish and Wildlife Service. Statistical digest no. 2 [etc.])

SH11.A7A3   59-46872

1896
Document Catalogue, 54th Congress-page 15
Treasury Document 1925

1897
Document Catalogue, 55th Congress-page 29
Treasury Document 2010

1899
Checklist of United States Public Documents, 1789-1909-page 120
56th Cong., 1st sess. S. Doc. 153. In Serial no. 4039, vol. 11

1900
Checklist of United Public Documents, 1789-1909-page 120
56th Cong., 2d sess. S. Doc. 168. In Serial no. 4042, vol. 14

1901
Checklist of United States Public Documents, 1789-1909-page 125
57th Cong., 1st sess. S. Doc. 138. In Serial no. 4231, vol. 13

1902
Checklist of United States Public Documents, 1789-1909-page 130
57th Cong., 2d sess. S. Doc. 113. In Serial no. 4424, vol. 9

1903
MC#: 1904-page 433
Dept. of Commerce and Labor Doc. no. 12

1904
MC#: Mar. 1905-page 250
Dept. of Commerce and Labor Doc. no. 35

1906
MC#: May 1907-page 650 (LC card 7-35263 cancelled in favor of 59-46872)
Bureau of Fisheries Doc. no. 618

1907
MC#: Apr. 1908-page 431 (LC card 7-35263 cancelled in favor of 59-46872)
Bureau of Fisheries Doc. no. 632

1908
MC#: Apr. 1909-page 547 (LC card 7-35263 cancelled in favor of 59-46872)
Bureau of Fisheries Doc. no. 645

1909
MC#: Apr. 1910-page 581 (LC card 7-35263 cancelled in favor of 59-46872)
Bureau of Fisheries Doc. no. 730

1910
MC#: Apr. 1911-page 565 (LC card 7-35263 cancelled in favor of 59-46872)
Bureau of Fisheries Doc. no. 746

1912
MC#: Nov. 1913-page 216 (LC card F13-212 cancelled in favor of 59-46872)
Bureau of Fisheries Doc. no. 780

1913
MC#: Aug. 1914-page 88 (LC card F13-212 cancelled in favor of 59-46872)
Bureau of Fisheries Doc. no. 797

1914
MC#: Sept. 1915-page 106 (LC card F13-212 cancelled in favor of 59-46872)
Bureau of Fisheries Doc. no. 819

1915
MC#: Jan. 1917-page 404 (LC card F13-212 cancelled in favor of 59-46872)
Bureau of Fisheries Doc. no. 834

1916
MC#: Aug. 1917-page 73 (LC card F17-246 cancelled in favor of 59-46872)
Bureau of Fisheries Doc. no. 838

1917
MC#: Dec. 1918-page 260 (LC card F13-212 cancelled in favor of 59-46872)
Bureau of Fisheries Doc. no. 847

1918
MC#: Dec. 1919-page 295 (LC card F13-212 cancelled in favor
    of 59-46872)
Bureau of Fisheries Doc. no. 872

1919
MC#: Dec. 1920-page 228 (LC card F13-212 cancelled in favor
    of 59-46872)
Bureau of Fisheries Doc. no. 891

1920
MC#: Dec. 1921-page 312 (LC card F13-212 cancelled in favor
    of 59-46872)
Bureau of Fisheries Doc. no. 909

1921
MC#: Dec. 1922-page 324 (LC card F13-212 cancelled in favor
    of 59-46872)
Bureau of Fisheries Doc. no. 933)

1922
MC#: Dec. 1923-page 283 (LC card F13-212 cancelled in favor
    of 59-46872)
Bureau of Fisheries Doc. no. 951

1923
MC#: Apr. 1925-page 739 (LC card F13-212 cancelled in favor
    of 59-46872)
SuDocs no.: C6.1:924/app.3

1924
MC#: Dec. 1925-page 328 (LC card F13-212 cancelled in favor
    of 59-46872)
SuDocs no.: C6.1:925/app.4

1925
MC#: Nov. 1926-page 279 (LC card F13-212 cancelled in favor
    of 59-46872)
SuDocs no.: C6.1:926/app.3

1926
MC#: July 1927-page 16 (LC card F13-212 cancelled in favor
    of 59-46872)
SuDocs no.: C6.1:927/app.4

1927
MC#: Jan. 1929-page 434 (LC card F13-212 cancelled in favor
    of 59-46872)
SuDocs no.: C6.1:928/app.4

1928
MC#: Nov. 1929-page 290 (LC card F13-212 cancelled in favor
    of 59-46872)
SuDocs no.: C6.1:929/app.6

1929
MC#: Oct. 1930-page 223 (LC card F13-212 cancelled in favor
    of 59-46872)
SuDocs no.: C6.1:930/app.10

1930
MC#: Oct. 1931-page 222 (LC card F13-212 cancelled in favor
    of 59-46872)
SuDocs no.: C6.1:931/app.1

1931
MC#: Aug. 1932-page 103 (LC card F13-212 cancelled in favor
    of 59-46872)
SuDocs no.: C6.1:932/app.1

1932
MC#: Oct. 1933-page 263 (LC card F13-212 cancelled in favor
    of 59-46872)
SuDocs no.: C6.1:933/app.1

1933
MC#: Nov. 1934-page 361 (LC card F13-212 cancelled in favor
    of 59-46872)
SuDocs no.: C6.1:934/app.2

1934
MC#: 1935-page 1021 (LC card F13-212 cancelled in favor of
    59-46872)
SuDocs no.: C6.1:935/app.1

1935
MC#: 1936-page 1109 (LC card F13-212 cancelled in favor of
    59-46872)
SuDocs no.: C6.1:936/app.1

1936
MC#: 1938-page 26 (LC card F13-212 cancelled in favor of
    59-46872)
SuDocs no.: C6.1:937/app.2

1937
MC#: 1938-page 1310 (LC card F13-212 cancelled in favor of
    59-46872)
SuDocs no.: C6.1:938/app.2

1938
MC#: 1940-page 829 (LC card F13-212 cancelled in favor of
    59-46872)
SuDocs no.: C6.1:939/app.2

1939
MC#: 1941-page 499 (LC card F13-212 cancelled in favor of
    59-46872)
SuDocs no.: I45.1:940/app.2

1940
MC#: 1942-page 927 (LC card 42-38361 cancelled in favor of
    59-46872)
SuDocs no.: I49.32:2

1941
MC#: 1943-page 853 (LC card F13-212 cancelled in favor of
    59-46872)
SuDocs no.: I49.32:5

1942
MC#: 1944-page 657 (LC card F13-212 cancelled in favor of
    59-46872)
SuDocs no.: I49.32:8

1943
MC#: 1945-page 178 (LC card F13-212 cancelled in favor of
    59-46872)
SuDocs no.: I49.32:10

1944
MC#: 1946-page 932 (LC card F13-212 cancelled in favor of
    59-46872)
SuDocs no.: I49.32:13

BOWLER REPORT [Bowler, Alida Cynthia]
    see
    WICKERSHAM COMMISSION [Wickersham,
George Woodward]
    Report on crime and the foreign born, no. 10.

BOWMAN REPORT [Bowman, Wallace]
233

United States. *Congress. Senate. Committee on Interior and Insular
Affairs.*
    The Council on Environmental Quality—oversight report.—
Washington: U.S. Govt. Print. Off., 1977.
    vii, 167 p.; 24 cm.
    At head of title: 94th Congress, 2d session. Committee print.

"Printed at the request of Henry M. Jackson, chairman, Committee on Interior and Insular Affairs, United States Senate."
Bibliography: p. 43-45.
1. United States. Council on Environmental Quality. 2. Environmental policy—United States. I. Title.
HC110.E5U535 1977   353.007′7   77-601317
MARC
MC#: 1977-9074
SuDocs no.: Y4.In8/13:C83/2

BRADLEY COMMISSION [Bradley, Omar N.]
234

U.S. *Congress. House. Committee on Veterans' Affairs.*
Findings and recommendations of the President's Commission on Veterans' Pensions (Bradley Commision). Hearings before the Committee on Veterans' Affairs, House of Representatives, Eighty-fourth Congress, second session, on the report of President's Commission on Veterans' Pensions. Washington, U.S. Govt. Print. Off., 1956.
iii, 3557-3862 p. illus. 24 cm.
1. Veterans—U.S. 2. U.S. President's Commission on Veterans' Pensions. Veterans' benefits in the United States, findings and recommendations; a report to the President.
UB357.A593 1956a   351.5   56-61453
MC#: 1956-10395
SuDocs no.: Y4.V64/3:P38/16

235

U.S. *President's Commission on Veterans' Pensions.*
Veterans' benefits in the United States, findings and recommendations; a report to the President. [Washington, U.S. Govt. Print. Off.] 1956.
415 p. 23 cm.
1. Veterans—U.S. I. Title.
UB357.A63   355.115   56-61009
MC#: 1956-9360
SuDocs no.: Pr34.8:V64

BRANSCOMB REPORT [Branscomb, Lewis M.]
236

U.S. *President's Science Advisory Committee. Space Science and Technology Panel.*
The next decade in space; a report of the Space Science and Technology Panel of the President's Science Advisory Commitee. [Washington, Executive Office of the President, Office of Science and Technology; for sale by the Supt. of Docs., U.S. Govt. Print. Off.] 1970.
ii, 63 p. 26 cm.
1. Astronautics—U.S. I. Title.
TL789.8.U5A6 1970   629.4′0973   77-606539
MARC
MC#: 1970-7729
SuDocs no.: PrEx8.2:Spl

BREATHITT REPORTS [Breathitt, Edward T.]
237

United States. National Advisory Commission on Rural Poverty.
The people left behind, a report. Washington, For sale by the Supt. of Docs., U.S. Govt. Print. Off., 1967.
xiv, 160 p. illus. 27 cm.
Commonly known as the Breathitt report.
Includes bibliographies.
1. U.S.—Rural conditions. 2. Poor—United States. I. Title. II. Title: Breathitt report on rural poverty.
HN58.A29   339.4′6′091734   67-62676

MC#: 1968-1065
SuDocs no.: Pr 36.8:R88/P39

238

U.S. *National Advisory Commission on Rural Poverty.*
Rural poverty in the United States; a report. Washington, For sale by the Supt. of Docs., U.S. Govt. Print. Off., 1968.
xii, 601 p. illus. 27 cm.
Includes bibliographies.
1. Poor—U.S. 2. U.S.—Rural Conditions. I. Title.
HC110.P6A485   309.1′73   68-62367
MC#: 1968-14563
SuDocs no.: Pr36.8:R88/R88/2

BRECKINRIDGE REPORT [Breckinridge, M. S.]
see
PARKER REPORT [Parker, James Southworth]

BRECKINRIDGE REPORT [Breckinridge, Roeliff Morton]
see under
ALDRICH COMMISION [Aldrich, Nelson Wilmarth]

BREWSTER REPORT [Brewster, Daniel B.]
239

United States. Commission on Political Activity of Government Personnel.
A Commission report. [Washington, U.S. Govt. Print. Off., 1968]
3 v. 24 cm.
Cover title.
Commonly known as the Brewster report.
Includes bibliographies.
Contents: v. 1. Findings and recommendations.—v. 2. Research.—v. 3. Hearings.
1. Civil service—Political activity. I. Title: Brewster report on political activity of Government personnel.
KF5344.A85   353′.004   68-60477
MARC
MC#: 1968-4351
SuDocs no.: Y3.P75:1/968/v. 1-3

BREWSTER REPORT [Brewster, Ralph Owen]
Investigation of the Pearl Harbor Attack.
see
BARKLEY REPORT [Barkley, Alben William]

BREWSTER REPORT [Brewster, Ralph Owen]
240

U.S. *Congress. Aviation Policy Board.*
National aviation policy. Report pursuant to Public law 287, 80th Cong . . . .Washington, U.S. Govt. Print. Off., 1948.
vi, 57 p. diagr. 24 cm. ([U.S.] 80th Cong., 2d sess., 1948. Senate. Report no. 949)
Owen Brewster, chairman.
1. Aeronautics—U.S. 2. Aeroplane industry and trade—U.S. I. Brewster, Ralph Owen, 1888- (Series)
TL521.A5 1948d   629.1306173   48-45808*
MC#: 1948-7829
SuDocs no.: 80th Cong., 2d sess. S. Rept. 949

BRILEY REPORT [Briley, John Marshall]

241

U.S. *President's Task Force on Prisoner Rehabilitation.*
The criminal offender-what should be done? The report of the President's Task Force on Prisoner Rehabilitation. [Washington; For sale by the Supt. of Docs., U.S. Govt. Print. Off.,] 1970.

vii, 24 p. 24 cm.
1. Rehabilitation of criminals—U.S. I. Title.
HV9304.A5 1970   364.7'6   73-607578
                                        MARC
MC#: 1970-1050
SuDocs no.: Pr37.8:P93/R29

BRIM REPORT [Brim, Orville G., Jr.]

242

United States. National Science Foundation. National Science Board. Special Commission on the Social Sciences.
Knowledge into action: improving the Nation's use of the social sciences; report of the Special Commission on the Social Sciences of the National Science Board. [Washington] National Science Foundation; [for sale by the Supt. of Docs., U.S. Govt. Print. Off.] 1969.

xxiv, 95 p. 24 cm.
"NSB 69-3."
Bibliographical footnotes.
1. Social sciences—History—United States. 2. Social sciences and state—United States. 3. United States—Social policy. I. Title.
H53.U5A5   300'.973   70-603195
                                   MARC
MC#: 1969-13202
SuDocs no.: NS1.28:69-3

BROACH REPORT [Broach, Howell Hamilton]
see
RUSSELL REPORT [Russell, John Dale]

BRONK REPORT [Bronk, Detlev W.]

243

U.S. *President's Science Advisory Committee. Panel on Food Additives.*
Report. [Washington, 1960]
16 p. 16 x 24 cm.
1. Food additives.
TX553.A3U54   614.3   60-62210 rev
Not located in Monthly Catalog

BROOKINGS REPORT

244

Brookings Institution, *Washington, D.C. International Studies Group.*
The administration of foreign affairs and overseas operation; a report prepared for the Bureau of the Budget, Executive Office of the President. Washington, 1951.

xxv, 880 p. 24 cm.
1. U.S.—For. rel.—1945- 2. Economic assistance, American. 3. Technical assistance, American. I. U.S. Bureau of the Budget. II. Title.
JX1705.B7   353.1   51-61182
Not located in Monthly Catalog

BROOKINGS REPORT
Investigation of executive agencies of the government.
see
BYRD REPORT [Byrd, Harry Flood]

BROOKS REPORT [Brooks, Alfred H.]

1904-1916; 1919-1923
Known as BROOKS REPORT [Brooks, Alfred H.]
1917-1918
Known as MARTIN REPORT [Martin, G. C.]
1924; 1926-1930
Known as SMITH REPORT [Smith, Philip S.]
1925
Known as MOFFITT REPORT [Moffitt, Fred H.]

245

U.S. *Geological Survey.*
Mineral resources of Alaska; report on progress of investigations. 1904- Washington, U.S. Govt. Print. Off.
v. illus., maps (part fold., part col.) 24 cm. (Its Bulletin) vols. for 1941-42 and 1943-44 are combined issues.
Title varies: 1904-06 Report on progress of investigations of mineral resources of Alaska.
Reports for 1902-03 included in U.S. Geological Survey Bulletins 213 and 225, which have special title: Contributions to economic geology (TN23.U62)
Vols. for 1931- issued in parts, each part with special t.p.
1. Mines and mineral resources—Alaska. I. Title. (Series)
QE75.B9   (557.3) 553.4   GS5-752 rev 2*
- - - - - 2d set
TN24.A4A2
1904
MC#: 1905-page 292
Geological Survey Bulletin 259
Also issued as:
58th Cong., 3d sess. H. Doc. 400
1905
MC#: Oct.1906-page 365
Geological Survey Bulletin 284
Also issued as:
59th Cong., 1st sess. H. Doc. 832
1906
MC#: Aug. 1907-page 50
Geological Survey Bulletin 314
Also issued as:
59th Cong., 2d sess. H. Doc. 797
1907
MC#: July 1908-page 22
Geological Survey Bulletin 345
Also issued as:
60th Cong., 1st sess. H. Doc. 977
1908
MC#: July 1909-page 30
Geological Survey Bulletin 379
Also issued as:
60th Cong., 2d sess. H. doc. 1522
1909
MC#: Jan. 1911-page 352
Geological Survey Bulletin 442
Also issued as:
61st Cong., 3d sess. H. Doc. 1019
1910
MC#: July 1911-page 32; Aug. 1911-page 101
Geological Survey Bulletin 480
Also issued as:
61st Cong., 3d sess. H. Doc. 1474
1911
MC#: Nov. 1912-page 231

Geological Survey Bulletin 520
Also issued as:
62d Cong., 2d sess. H. Doc. 845

1912
MC#: Nov. 1913-page 223
Geological Survey Bulletin 542
Also issued as:
63d Cong., 2d sess. H. Doc. 308

1913
MC#: Oct. 1914-page 206
Geological Survey Bulletin 592
Also issued as:
63d Cong., 2d sess. H. Doc. 1068

1914
MC#: Oct.1915-page 153
Geological Survey Bulletin 622
Also issued as:
64th Cong., 1st sess. H. Doc. 44

1915
MC#: Sept. 1916-page 182
Geological Survey Bulletin 642
Also issued as:
64th Cong., 1st sess. H. Doc. 1251

1916
MC#: Aug. 1918-page 74
Geological Survey Bulletin 662
Also issued as:
65th Cong., 2d sess. H. Doc. 607

1917
MC#: Jan. 1920-page 384
Geological Survey Bulletin 692
Also issued as:
65th Cong., 3d sess. H. Doc. 1872

1918
MC#: Oct. 1920-page 142
Geological Survey Bulletin 712
Also issued as:
66th Cong., 3d sess. H. Doc. 833

1919
MC#: Aug. 1921-page 94
Geological Survey Bulletin 714
Also issued as:
66th Cong., 3d sess. H. Doc. 1001

1920
MC#: Sept. 1922-page 150
Geological Survey Bulletin 722
Also issued as:
67th Cong., 2d sess. H. Doc. 309

1921
MC#: Aug. 1923-page 70
Geological Survey Bulletin 739
Also issued as:
67th Cong., 3d sess. H. Doc. 461

1922
MC#: Feb. 1925-page 587
SuDocs no.: I 19.3:755
Also issued as:
68th Cong., 1st sess. H. Doc. 326

1923
MC#: Nov. 1925-page 273
SuDocs no.: I 19.3:773
Also issued as:
68th Cong., 2d sess. H. Doc. 503

1924
MC#: Feb. 1927-page 609
SuDocs no.: I 19.3:783
Also issued as:
69th Cong., 1st sess. H. Doc. 88

1925
MC#: Dec. 1927-page 360
SuDocs no.: I 19.3:792
Also issued as:
69th Cong., 2d sess. H. Doc. 543

1926
MC#: Aug. 1929-page 80
SuDocs no.: I 19.3:797
Also issued as:
69th Cong., 2d sess. H. Doc. 796

1927
MC#: June 1930-page 1129
SuDocs no.: I 19.3:810
Also issued as:
70th Cong., 2d sess. H. Doc. 557

1928
MC#: Jan. 1931-page 537
SuDocs no.: I 19.3:813
Also issued as:
71st Cong., 1st sess. H. Doc. 86

1929
MC#: Mar. 1932-page 751
SuDocs no.: I 19.3:824
Also issued as:
71st Cong., 1st sess. H. Doc. 120

1930
MC#: June 1933-page 994
SuDocs no.: I 19.3:836
Also issued as:
72d Cong., 1st sess. H. Doc. 110

BROTMAN REPORT [Brotman, Richard Emanuel]
see
WILLIAMSBURG PAPERS

BROWN BOARD [Brown, Frederic J.]
246

United States. Dept. of the Army. Board of Inquiry on the Army Logistics System.
   Report by the Department of the Army Board of Inquiry on the Army Logistics System.
   [Washington, 1966-67]
   7 v. charts. (ASDIRS 0834)
   Contents. v. 1. Introduction, summary and guide to implementation. v. 2. Assets management. v. 3. Annex A. v. 4. Acquisition management. v. 5. General management. v. 6. Personnel, training, and organization. v. 7. Logistics systems.
   1. United States. Army.—Organization. 2. Logistics. I. Title. II. Title: Brown Board.
[UA24.A778]
Dept. of the Army Library
Not Located in Monthly Catalog

BROWN REPORT [Brown, Douglass Vincent]
   see under
   O'MAHONEY REPORTS [O'Mahoney, Joseph Christopher]

BROWN REPORT [Brown, Edmund G.]

247

U.S. National Commission on Reform of Federal Criminal Laws.
Final report: a proposed new Federal criminal code (title 18,
United States Code) Washington, U.S. Govt. Print. Off., 1971.

xxv, 364 p. 24 cm.
1. Criminal law—U.S. I. Title: A proposed new Federal
criminal code (title 18, United States Code)
KF9219.A345   345′.73′02632   78-610591
                                                        MARC
MC#: 1971-5569
SuDocs no.: Y3.N21/26:1/971

BROWN REPORT [Brown, J. Lee]

248

U.S. *Office of community war services.*
Planning for recreation areas and facilities in small towns and
cities, prepared by J. Lee Brown . . . [Washington] Federal
security agency, Office of community war services, Recreation
division, 1945 [i.e. 1946]

vii, 51 p. plans (1 fold.) 23 cm.
"Bibliography of recreation planning": p. 50-51.
1. Recreation. I. Brown, J. Lee, 1908-
GV171.U63 1945f   790   46-25505
MC#: 1946-page 175
SuDocs no.: FS9.2:R24/14

BROWN REPORT [Brown, Laura Mae]

see under
O'MAHONEY REPORTS [O'Mahoney, Joseph Christopher]

Nelson. Price behavior and business policy.

BROWN REPORT [Brown, Malcolm Johnston]

see
WEBB REPORT [Webb, John Nye]

BROWN REPORT [Brown, Walter F.]

249

U.S. *Congress. Joint committee on reorganization of the administrative branch of the government.*
Reorganization of executive departments. Hearings before the
joint committee on the reorganization of the administrative branch
of the government. Congress of the United States, Sixty-eighth
Congress, first session, on S. J. Res. 282, Sixty-seventh Congress,
a resolution to amend the resolution of December 29, 1920, entitled "Joint resolution to create a joint committee on the
reorganization of the administrative branch of the government
[and supplement]" January 7 to 31, April 8, 1924. Printed for
the use of the Joint committee on reorganization of the administrative branch of the government. Washington, Govt. print.
off., 1924.

iii, 786, iii, 787-834 p. 23½ cm.
Issued also in parts.
Walter F. Brown, chairman.
1. U.S.—Executive departments. I. Title.
JK649 1924   24-7725 Revised
- - - - - Copy 2.
MC#: May 1924-page 721
SuDocs no.: Y4.R29:H35

BROWNELL REPORT [Brownell, John A.]

see under
O'MAHONEY REPORTS [O'Manoney, Joseph Christopher]

Brown. Industrial wage rates.

BROWNLOW REPORTS [Brownlow, Louis]

250

U.S. *President's committee on administrative management.*
Administrative management in the government of the United
States. January 1937. The President's committee on administrative
management. [Washington, U.S. Govt. print. off., 1937]

v, 47 p. 29 cm.
On cover: Administrative management. Report of the Presi-
dent's committee.
Issued also as Senate doc. 8, 75th Cong., 1st sess., with title:
Reorganization of the executive departments. Message from the
President of the United States transmitting a report on reorganiza-
tion of the executive departments of the government.
Louis Brownlow, chairman.
1. U.S.—Executive departments. 2. U.S.—Pol. &
govt.—1933-1945, I. Brownlow, Louis, 1879- II. Title.
JK643.C36b   37-26063
MC#: 1937-page 94
SuDocs no.: Y3.P92/2:2Ad6 and Y3.P92/3:2/Ad6/2

251

U.S. *President's committee on administrative management.*
. . . Reorganization of the executive departments. Message
from the President of the United States transmitting a report on
reorganization of the executive departments of the government . . . Washington, U.S. Govt. print. off., 1937.

1 p. l., 84 p. 23½ cm. (75th Cong., 1st sess. Senate. Doc. 8)
Read; ordered to lie on the table and be printed January 12,
1937.
Issued also without document series note with title: Ad-
ministrative management in the government of the United States.
Louis Brownlow, chairman.
1. U.S.—Executive departments. 2. U.S.—Pol. &
govt.—1933-1945. I. Brownlow, Louis, 1879- II. Title. (III. Doc.
title.)
JK643.C36c   37-26079
- - - - - Copy 2.
MC#: 1937-page 94
SuDocs no.: 75th Cong., 1st sess. S. Doc. 8

252

U.S. *President's committee on administrative management.*
. . . Report of the committee, with studies of administrative
management in the federal government. Submitted to the President and to the Congress in accordance with Public law no. 739,
74th Congress, 2d session. Washington, U.S. Govt. print. off.,
1937.

xiii, 382 p. incl. tables, diagrs. 29 cm.
At head of title: The President's committee on administrative
management.
On cover: . . . Report with special studies.
Part II, Studies of administrative management in the federal
government, is issued also separately with title: Studies on ad-
ministrative management in the government of the United States.
Louis Brownlow, chairman.
Contents.—pt. I. Report of the President's committee.—pt. II.
Studies of administrative management in the federal government.
Personnel administration in the federal service, by F. W. Reeves
and P. T. David. Financial control and accountability, by A. E.
Buck. The General accounting office, by H. C. Mansfield. The
problem of the independent regulatory commissions, by R. E.
Cushman. Departmental management, by A. W. Macmahon.
Executive management and the federal field service, by J. W.
Fesler. Government corporations and independent supervisory
agencies, by Herbert Emmerich. The exercise of rulemaking

power, by James Hart. The preparation of proposed legislative measures by administrative departments, by E. E. Witte.

1. U.S.—Pol. & govt.—1933- 2. U.S.—Executive departments. I. Brownlow, Louis, 1879- II. Reeves, Floyd Wesley, 1890- III. David, Paul T. IV. Buck, Arthur Eugene, 1888- V. Mansfield, Harvey Claflin, 1905- VI. Cushman, Robert Eugene, 1889- VII. Macmahon, Arthur Whittier, 1890- VIII. Fesler, James William, 1911- IX. Emmerich, Herbert. X. Hart, James, 1896- XI. Witte, Edwin Emil, 1887-

JK421.A45 1937   353   37-26978
MC#: 1937-page 1106
SuDocs no.: Y3.P92/3:2Ad6/3

253

U.S. *President's committee on administrative management.*

. . . Studies on administrative management in the government of the United States . . . Washington, U.S. Govt. print. off., 1937.

5 v. tables, diagrs. 29 cm.

On cover: Administrative management . . .

Issued also as part II of the Report of the committee, with studies of administrative management in the federal government. (U.S. President's committee on administrative management)

Contents.—no. I. Personnel administration in the federsal service, by F. W. Reeves and P. T. David.—no. II. Fiscal management in the national government. 1. Financial control and accountability, by A. E. Buck. 2. The General accounting office, by H. C. Mansfield.—no. III. The problem of the independent regulatory commissions, by R. E. Cushman.—no. IV. Problems of administrative management. 1. Departmental management, by A. W. Macmahon. 2. Executive management and the federal field service, by J. W. Fesler. 3. Government corporations and independent supervisory agencies, by Herbert Emmerich.—no. V. The exercise of rule-making power and the preparation of proposed legislative measures by administrative departments. 1. The exercise of rule-making power and the preparation of proposed legislative measures by administrative departments, by James Hart. 2. The preparation of proposed legislative departments, by E. E. Witte.

1. U.S.—Pol. & govt. 2. U.S.—Executive departments. I. Reeves, Floyd Wesley, 1890- II. David, Paul Theodore, 1906- III. Buck, Arthur Eugene, 1888- IV. Mansfield, Harvey Claflin, 1905- V. Cushman, Robert Eugene, 1889- VI. Macmahon, Arthur Whittier, 1890- VII. Fesler, James William, 1911- VIII. Emmerich, Herbert. IX. Hart, James, 1896- X. Witte, Edwin Emil, 1887- XI. Title. XII. Title: Administrative management.

JK421.A45 1937b   353   37-26684
- - - - - Copy 2.
MC#: 1937-pages 799-800
SuDocs no.: Y3.P92/3:7(nos.)

BUCK REPORT [Buck, Aurthur Eugene]
    see
BROWNLOW REPORT [Brownlow, Louis]

BULLITT REPORT

254

Bullitt, William Christian, 1891-

Report to the Joint Committee on Foreign Economic Cooperation concerning China, pursuant to section 124 of Public law 472, 80th Congress. Washington, U.S. Govt. Print. Off., 1948.

ii, 13 p. 24 cm.

At head of title: 80th Cong., 2d sess. Committee print.

1. China—Econ. condit.—1918- 2. Reconstruction (1939-)—China.

HC427.B8   338.951   49-45818*
Not located in Monthly Catalog

BUNTING REPORT [Bunting, Mary I.]

255

U.S. *President's Commission on the Status of Women. Committee on Education.*

Report of the Committee on Education to the President's Commission on the Status of Women. Washington, For sale by the Superintendent of Documents, U.S. Govt. Print. Off. [1964]

vi, 71 p. diagr., table. 26 cm.

Bibliographical references included in "Notes" (p. 43-50) "Background papers prepared for the Committee on Education": p. 60. "Selected bibliography on women's education and careers prepared by the Radcliffe Institute for Independent Study, September 1963": p. 61-66.

1. Education of women.

LC1752.U5   64-60845
MC#: 1964-7679
SuDocs no.: Pr35.8:W84/Ed8

BURNS REPORT [Burns, Eveline Mabel Richardson]
    see under
GRIFFITHS REPORTS [Griffiths, Martha W.]
    Studies in public welfare, paper no. 8.

BURNS REPORT [Burns, J. Gail]

256

United States. International Trade Commission.

Footwear : report to the President on Investigation no. TA-201-18, under section 201 of the Trade act of 1974 / United States International Trade Commission, [prepared by J. Gail Burns, Barbara Guth, assisted by Bernard A. Peterson, Thomas L. Donnelly, William Gearhart; Charles W. Ervin, senior investigator]. —Washington : The Commission, 1977.

ix, 54, [177] p. :graphs; 27 cm. —(USITC publication; 799) Cover title.

Includes bibliographical references.

1. Tariff on boots and shoes—United States. I. Burns, J. Gail. II. Guth, Barbara. III. Title. IV. Series: United States. International Trade Commission. USITC publication; 799.

HF2651.B63U55   382'.45'68530973   77-601212
                                          MARC
MC#: 1979-18753
SuDocs no.: TC1.2:F73/66

BURTON REPORT [Burton, Benjamin T.]

257

U.S. *Public Health Service.*

Kidney disease program analysis; a report to the Surgeon General. Washington, U.S. Govt. Print. Off., 1967.

xiv, 211 p. (Its Publication no. 1745)

Benjamin T. Burton, Chairman.

     68-60656
MC#: 1968-4361
SuDocs no.: FS2.2:K54/3

BUSH REPORTS

258

Bush, Vannevar, 1890-

Proposals for improving the patent system; [study] of the Committee on the Judiciary, United States Senate, pursuant to S. Res. 167 of the Eighty-fourth Congress, second session. Washington, U.S. Govt. Print. Off., 1957.

v, 30 p. 24 cm. (Study of the Subcommittee on Patents, Trademarks, and Copyrights, study no. 1)

85th Cong., 1st sess. Senate. Document no. 21.
Commonly known as the Bush report.

1. Patent laws and legislation—U.S. I. Title. II. Title. Bush report on improving the patent system. (Series: U.S. Congress. Senate. Committee on the Judiciary. Study of the Subcommittee on Patents, Trademarks and Copyrights, study no. 1. Series: U.S. 85th Cong., 1st sess. 1957. Senate. Document no. 21)

57-60187

MC#: 1957-1852
SuDocs no.: Y4.J89/2:P27/3/no. 1
MC#: 1957-3724
SuDocs no.: 85th Cong., 1st sess. S. Doc. 21

259

U.S. *Office of scientific research and development.*

Science, the endless frontier. A report to the President by Vannevar Bush, director of the Office of scientific research and development. July 1945. Washington, U.S. Govt. print. off., 1945.

ix, 184 p. incl. tables, diagrs. 23 cm.

On cover: Report to the President on a program for postwar scientific research.

Appendices: Committees consulted.—Report of the Medical advisory committee.—Report of the Committee on science and the public welfare.—Report of the Committee on discovery and development of scientific talent.—Report of the Committee on publication of scientific information.

1. Science and state—U.S. 2. Research. 3. World war, 1939-1945—Science. I. Bush, Vannevar, 1890- II. Title.
Q127.U6A53 1945   507.2   45-36413
MC#: 1945-page 902
SuDocs no.: Pr32.413:Sci2

United States. Office of Scientific Research and Development.

Science, the endless frontier / Vannevar Bush.—New York: Arno Press, 1980.

xxvi, 220 p.:ill.;24 cm.—(Three centuries of science in America)
Reprint of the 1945 ed. published by U.S. Govt. Print. Off., Washington.

Commonly known as the Bush report.
ISBN 0-405-12534-8

1. Science and state—United States. 2. Research—United States. I. Bush, Vannevar, 1890- II. Title. III. Title: Bush report. IV. Series.
Q127.U6U49 1980   509'.73   79-7953
                                                    MARC

Not listed in Monthly Catalog

BUTTERWORTH REPORT [Butterworth, Benjamin]

260

U.S. *Patent Office.*

The growth of industrial art. Arranged and compiled under the supervision of the Hon. Benj. Butterworth, Commissioner of patents and representative of Interior department, Board U.S. executive departments, World's industrial and cotton centennial exposition. New Orleans: 1884-5. Washington, Govt. print. off., 1884.

2 v. 200 pl. 71½ cm.

Each volume made up of 3 p. l. and 100 plated representing primitive methods and modern patents.

1. Design, Industrial—United States. 2. Patents—United States. I. Butterworth, Benjamin, 1837-1898, comp. II. New Orleans. World's industrial and cotton centennial exposition, 1884-1885.

5-20244

Not located in Checklist of United States Public Documents, 1789-1909

261

U.S. *Patent Office.*

The growth of industrial art. Arranged and compiled under the supervision of the Hon. Benj. Butterworth, commissioner of patents . . . Reproduced and printed in pursuance of act of Congress March 3, 1886, and acts supplementary thereto. Washington, Govt. print. off., 1888.

2 p. l., 200 p. 51 x 40 cm.

Issued also as House miscellaneous documents, 2d sess., 52d Cong.—1892-93, v. 30.

200 pages of illustration, with descriptive letterpress, representing primitive methods and modern patents.

1. Design, Industrial—United States. 2. Patents—United States. I. Butterworth, Benjamin, 1837-1898, comp. II. U.S. 52d Cong., 2d sess., 1892-1893. House. III. Title.
T15.U6 1888   609   33-7433
Checklist of United States Public Documents, 1789-1909-page 95
52d Cong., 2d sess. H. Misc. Doc. [121]. In Serial no. 3139, Vol. 30

262

U.S. *Patent Office.*

The growth of industrial art. Arranged and compiled under the supervision of the Hon. Benj. Butterworth, commissioner of patents . . . Reproduced and printed in pursuance of act of Congress March 3, 1886, and acts supplementary thereto. Washington, Govt. print. off., 1892.

2 p. l., 200 p. 51 cm.

200 pages of illustrations, with descriptive letterpress, representing primitive methods and modern patents.

1. Industrial arts. 2. Patents. I. Butterworth, Benjamin, 1837-1898, comp. II. Title.
T15.U6 1892   609   5-20245 rev
- - - - - Copy 2. Imperfect: prelim. leaves (incl. t.-p.) wanting; p. 1-2 mutilated.
- - - - - Copy 3. Rosenwald Coll.
Checklist of United States Public Documents, 1789-1909—page 515
SuDocs no.: I23.2:In2

BYRD REPORT [Byrd, Harry Flood]
263

U.S. *Congress. Senate. Select committee to investigate the executive agencies of the government.*

. . . Investigation of executive agencies of the government. Preliminary report of the Select committee to investigate the executive agencies of the government pursuant to Senate resolution no. 217 (74th Congress) a resolution creating a Select committee to investigte executive agencies of the government with a view to coordination . . . Washington, U.S. Govt. print. off., 1937.

xxxi, 1229 p. incl. tables. diagrs. (part fold.) 23½ cm. (75th Cong., 1st sess. Senate. Rept. 1275)

Presented by Mr. Byrd. Ordered printed with illustrations August 16 (calendar day, August 19), 1937.

Includes the report prepared by the Brookings institution on the functional and fact-finding survey of the executive agencies of the government.

1. U.S.—Executive departments. I. Brookings institution, Washington, D.C. II. Title.
JK649 1937 i   353   38-26120
- - - - - Copy 2.
MC#: 1938-page 182
SuDocs no.: 75th Cong., 1st sess. S. Rept. 1275

BYRNES REPORT [Byrnes, James Francis]

264

U.S. *Office of war mobilization.*

. . . Reconversion. A report to the President from Director of war mobilization James F. Byrnes. Washington, U.S. Govt. print. off., 1944.

1 p. l., 14 p. 23 cm. ([U.S.] 78th Cong., 2d sess. Senate. Doc. 237)

Issued also without congressional series numbering.

1. U.S.Economic policy. 2. Reconstitution (1939-)—U.S. I. Byrnes, James Francis, 1879-
HC106.4.A292 1944c   338.91   44-41509
MC#: 1944-page 1190
SuDocs no.: 78th Cong., 2d sess. S. Doc. 237

265

U.S. *Office of war mobilization.*

Reconversion. A report to the President from Director of war mobilization James F. Byrnes. [Washington, U.S. Govt. print. off., 1944]

1 p. l., 14 p. 23 cm.

Issued also as Senate doc. 237, 78th Cong., 2d sess. 1. U.S.— Economic policy. 2. Reconstruction (1939-)—U.S. I. Byrnes, James Francis, 1879-
HC106.4.A292 1944d   338.91   44-41422
MC#: 1944-page 1190
SuDocs no.: Pr32.5902:R24

CALLIES REPORT [Callies, David]
see
BOSSELMAN REPORTS [Bosselman, Fred P.]
Quiet revolution in land use control.

Quiet revolution in land use control, summary.

Taking issue.

CALLMANN REPORT [Callmann, Rudolf]
see under
O'MAHONEY REPORTS [[O'Mahoney, Joseph Christopher]
Domeratzky. Regulation of economic activities in foreign countries.

CAMPBELL REPORT [Campbell, Angus]
Racial attitudes in 15 American cities.
see
KERNER COMMISSION [Kerner, Otto]
Supplemental studies.

CANADIAN-AMERICAN COMMITTEE REPORT
see
DAVIS REPORT [Davis, John]

CANCE REPORT [Cance, Alexander E.]
see under
DILLINGHAM COMMISSION [Dillingham, William Paul]
Abstract of the report on recent immigrants in agriculture.
Immigrants in industries.

CANNAN REPORT [Cannan, R. Keith]

266

U.S. *Veterans Administration. Dept. of Medicine and Surgery.*
Medical research in the Veterans' Administration. 1957-Washington, U.S. Govt. Print. Off.

v. 24 cm. annual.

Issued as House committee print.

Report year irregular for 1957-61; for 1961/62- , ends June 30.

Report submitted to the House Committee on Veterans' Affairs.

1. Medical research—U.S. I. U.S. Congress. House. Committee on Veterans' Affairs. II. Title.
RA11.F3   57-60875 rev 2

1957
Not located in Monthly Catalog
85th Cong., 1st sess. H. Comm. Print 50

1958
MC#: 1959-323
SuDocs no.: Y4.V64/3:M46/10
85th Cong., 2d sess. H. Comm. Print 188

1960
Not located in Monthly Catalog
86th Cong., 2d sess. H. Comm. Print 283

1961
MC#: 1962-6495
SuDocs no.: VA1.43:961
87th Cong., 1st sess. H. Comm. Print 161

1962-63
MC#: 1964-12159
SuDocs no.: Y4.V64/3:M46/10/962-63
88th Cong., 1st sess. H. Comm. Print 148

1963-64
MC#: 1965-6976
SuDocs no.: VA1.43:964
88th Cong., 2d sess. H. Comm. Print 252

1964-65
MC#: 1966-5209
SuDocs no.: VA1.43:965

1965-66
MC#: 1967-7218
SuDocs no.: VA1.43:966

1966 (Fiscal)
MC#: 1967-4563
SuDocs no.: Y4.V64/3:M46/10/965-66
89th Cong., 2d sess. H. Comm. Print 247

CANNON REPORT [Cannon, James Graham]
see under
ALDRICH COMMISSION [Aldrich, Nelson Wilmarth]

CANOVAI REPORT [Canovai, Tito]
see under
ALDRICH COMMISSION [Aldrich, Nelson Wilmarth]

CAPEHART REPORT [Capehart, Homer E.]

267

U.S. *Congress. Senate. Committee on Banking and Currency.*

Study of Latin American countries; interim report. A study of the operations in Latin American countries of the Export-Import Bank and the International Bank and their relationship to the expansion of international trade, pursuant to S. Res. 25, 83d Congress, 1st session. Washington, U.S. Govt. Print. Off., 1954.

vi, 648 p. illus., maps 23 cm. (83d Cong., 2d sess. Senate. Report no. 1082)

At head of title: Confidential committee print.

1. Spanish America—Comm.—U.S. 2. U.S.—Comm.— Spanish America. 3. Investments, American—Spanish America. 4. Spanish America—Econ. condit.—1918- 5. Export-Import

Bank of Washington. 6. International Bank for Reconstruction and Development. I. Title. (Series: U.S. 83d Cong., 2d sess., 1954. Senate. Report no. 1082)

HF3376.U485   330.98   54-61512
MC#: 1954-6911
SuDocs no.: 83d Cong., 2d sess. S. Rept. 1082

CARHART REPORT [Carhart, Arthur Hawthorne]
see
ORRRC REPORTS
ORRRC study report, 27

CARROLL REPORT [Carroll, John A.]
268

U.S. *Congress. Senate. Committee on the Judiciary.*
Administrative practice and procedure. Report of the Committee on the Judiciary, United States Senate made by its Subcommittee on Administrative Practice and Procedure pursuant to S. Res. 234, 86th Cong., 2d sess., as extended, together with individual views. Washington, U.S. Govt. Print. Off., 1961.

iii, 26 p. 24 cm. (87th Cong., 1st sess. Senate. Report no. 168)
1. Administrative procedure—U.S. (Series: U.S. 87th Cong., 1st sess., 1961. Senate. Report no. 168)

                                          61-61192
MC#: 1961-7261
SuDocs no.: 87th Cong., 1st sess. S. Rept. 168

CARTER REPORT [Carter, H. E.]
269

U.S. *National Science Foundation. National Science Board.*
Science and the challenge ahead. Report of the National Science Board. GPO 1974.

vii, 56 p. National Science Board (Series)
MC#: 75-08307
SuDocs no.: NS1.28:74-1

CARTER REPORT [Carter, Thomas H.]
270

Alaska *(Ter.) Laws, statutes, etc.*
The laws of Alaska, embracing the Penal code, the Code of criminal procedure, the Political code, the Code of civil procedure, and the Civil code, with the treaty of cession, and all acts and parts of acts relating to the district, annotated with references to decisions by the courts of the United States and the Supreme court of Oregon, by Thomas H. Carter . . . Chicago, Callaghan and Company, 1907.

xxxix, 533 p. 26½ cm.
I. Carter, Thomas Henry, 1854-1911, ed. II. U.S. Laws, statutes, etc. III. U.S. Courts. IV. Oregon. Supreme Court.
                                   11-7654 Revised

Not located in Monthly Catalog

CASE REPORT [Case, Henry Lawrence]
see
LELAND REPORT [Leland, Simeon Elbridge]

CASEY REPORT
271

Casey, Jesse F.
Observations on the treatment of the mentally ill in Europe, by J. F. Casey [and] Leon L. Rackow, in collaboration with August W. Sperry. [Washington, Veterans Administration, 1960]
63 p.

1. Psychiatry—Europe. 2. Mental illness—Europe. I. Rackow, Leon L., joint author. II. U.S. Veterans Administration. III. Title.

                                       NUC66-31876
Not located in Monthly Catalog

CHADDOCK REPORT [Chaddock, Robert Emmet]
see under
ALDRICH COMMISSION [Aldrich, Nelson Wilmarth]
Dewey. State banking before the Civil War.

CHAFEE REPORT [Chafee, Zechariah]
see
MOONEY-BILLINGS REPORT [Mooney, Thomas J. and Billings, Warren K.]
WICKERSHAM COMMISSION [Wickersham, George Woodward]
Report on lawlessness, no. 11

CHAMBERLAIN REPORT [Chamberlain, Frederic M.]
see
EVERMANN REPORT [Evermann, Barton Warren]

CHARPIE REPORT [Charpie, Robert A.]
272

United States. Panel on Invention and Innovation.
Technological innovation: its environment and management. Washington, U.S. Dept. of Commerce; for sale by the Supt. of Docs., U.S. Govt. Print. Off., 1967.

vii, 83 p. illus. (part col.) 26 cm.
Bibliographical footnotes.
1. Technological innovations—United States. 2. Research, Industrial—United States—Management. I. Title.

HC110.T4A55   658.5'7'0973   67-60538
                                                 MARC
MC#: 1967-5962
SuDocs no.: C1.2:T22

CHASE REPORT [Chase, Francis S.]
273

U.S. *President's Committee on Public Higher Education in the District of Columbia.*
A report to the President, June 1964; public higher education in the District of Columbia. [Washington, U.S. Govt. Print. Off., 1964]

v, 44 p. 24 cm.
1. Education—Washington, D.C. I. Title: Public higher education in the District of Columbia.

L134.C5 1964   64-61895
MC#: 1964-16821
SuDocs no.: Pr35.8:Ed8/R29

CHATELAIN REPORT [Chatelain, Leon, Jr.]
274

U.S. *National Commission on Architectural Barriers to Rehabilitation of the Handicapped.*
Design for all Americans: a report. Washington, For sale by the Supt. of Docs., U.S. Govt. Print. Off. [1968]

54 p. illus. 20 x 26 cm.

                                                   68-62540
                                                   MARC
MC#: 1968-14601
SuDocs no.: FS17.102:D45

275

United States. *National Commission on Architectural Barriers to Rehabilitation of the Handicapped.*

Message from the President of the United States; transmitting a report entitled "Design for all Americans." Washington, U.S. Govt. Print. Off., 1968.

v, 28 p. 23 cm. (90th Congress, 2d session. House Document no. 324)

1. Architecture and the physically handicapped. I. Title. II. Title: Design for all Americans. III. Series: United States. 90th Congress, 2d session, 1968. House. Document no. 324.

NA2545.P5U56   725   68-62333
                                       MARC

MC#: 1968-15097
SuDocs no.: 90th Cong., 2d sess. H. Doc. 324

CHENOWETH REPORTS [Chenoweth, J. Edgar]
see under
HOFFMAN REPORTS [Hoffman, Clare E.]
Fifth intermediate report.

Tenth intermediate report.

Fourteenth intermediate report.

CHERINGTON REPORTS

276

Cherington, Paul W.

Airline equipment investment program. Communication from the President of the United States, transmitting a report concerning the status and economic significance of the airline equipment investment program, dated June 30, 1958. [Prepared for the President's Special Assistant for Aviation] Washington, U.S. Govt. Print. Off., 1958.

iii, 52 p. 24 cm. (85th Cong., 2d sess. House document no. 430)
1. Air lines—U.S.—Finance. 2. Jet transports. 3. Aeronautics and state—U.S. I. U.S. Executive Office of the President. II. Title. (Series: U.S. 85th Cong., 2d sess., 1958. House. Document no. 430)

TL521.C43   58-61732
MC#: 1958-11839
SuDocs no.: 85th Cong., 2d sess. H. Doc. 430

277

Cherington, Paul W.

The status and economic significance of the airline equipment investment program, a report, by Paul W. Cherington, prepared for [E. R. Quesada] the President's special assistant for aviation. [Washington] 1958.

44 p. 26 cm.
1. Aeronautics, Commercial—U.S. 2. Aeronautics and state—U.S. 3. Aeronautics, Commercial—Finance. I. Title.

TL521.C44   387.7   58-61692
Not located in Monthly Catalog

CHERNIACK REPORT [Cherniack, Stacie]
see
STEINHART REPORT [Steinhart, John S.]

CHINA WHITE PAPER

278

U.S. *Dept. of State.*

United States relations with China, with special reference to the period 1944-1949, based on the files of the Department of State. [Washington, U.S. Govt. Print. Off., 1949]

xli, 1054 p. fold. col. map. 24 cm. (*Its* Publication 3573. Far Eastern series, 30)

"Errata": 2 p. inserted.

1. U.S.—For. rel.—China. 2. China—For. rel.—U.S. (Series: U.S. Dept. of State. Publication 3573. Series: U.S. Dept. of State. Far Eastern series, 30)

E183.8.C5U53 1949   327.730951   49-46773*
MC#: 1949-20549
SuDocs no.: S1.38:30

CHURCH COMMITTEE [Church, Frank]
279

United States. *Congress. Senate. Select Committee to Study Governmental Operations with Respect to Intelligence Activities.*

Final report of the Select Committee to Study Governmental Operations with Respect to Intelligence Activities, United States Senate: together with additional, supplemental, and separate views.-Washington: U.S. Govt. Print. Off., 1976.

6 v.; 24 cm. —(Report — 94th Congress, 2d session, Senate; no. 94-755)

Vol. 3-6 lack subtitle.

Includes bibliographical references.

Contents: book 1. Foreign and military intelligence. —book 2. Intelligence activities and the rights of Americans. —book 3. Supplementary detailed staff reports on intelligence activities and the rights of Americans. —book 4. Supplementary detailed staff reports on foreign and military intelligence. —book 5. The investigation of the assassination of President John F. Kennedy. —book 6. United States. Library of Congress. Congressional Research Service. Supplementary reports on intelligence activities.

1. Intelligence service—United States. 2. Civil rights—United States. I. United States. Library of Congress. Congressional Research Service. II. Title. III. Series: United States. 94th Congress, 2d session, 1976. Senate Report; no. 94-755.

KF31.5.G7 1976   327′.12′0973   76-601758
                                         MARC

MC#: 1977-1267
SuDocs no.: 94-2:S.rp.755/bk.3

CLARK PANEL [Clark, Mark]
280

United States. *Civilian Advisory Panel on Military Manpower Procurement.*

Report to the Committee on Armed Services, House of Representatives. Washington, U.S. Govt. Print. Off., 1967.

vi, 30 p. 24 cm.

At head of title: Committee print.

1. Military service, Compulsory—United States. I. United States. Congress. House. Committee on Armed Services.

UB343.A5 1967b   355.2′2′0973   67-60895
                                         MARC

MC#: 1967-6028
SuDocs no.: Y4.Ar5/2:M31

CLARK REPORT [Clark, Dean A.]
281

U.S. *Congress. Senate. Committee on Labor and Public Welfare.*

Health insurance plans in the United States. Report pursuant to S. Res. 273, 81st Cong., 2d sess. and S. Res. 39, 82d Cong., 1st sess., a resolution directing further study on health problems. Washington, U.S. Govt. Print. Off., 1951.

3 pts. 24 cm. (82d Cong., 1st sess. Senate. Report no. 359)

Pt. 2, Appendixes; pt. 3 has special subtitle: Activities of government in the field of health services.

1. Insurance, Health—U.S. 2. Medical care, Prepaid—U.S.
I. Title. (Series: U.S. 82d Cong., 1st sess., 1951. Senate. Report
no. 359)
HG9396.A5 1951d   368.42   51-60947
MC#: 1951-11125-part 1
1951-13411-parts 2-3
SuDocs no.: 82d Cong., 1st sess. S. Rept. 359

CLARK REPORT [Clark, John Maurice]
  see
  ROPER REPORT [Roper, Daniel Calhoun]

CLARKE INVESTIGATION [Clarke, Carter W.]
  see
  ROBERTS COMMISSION [Roberts, Owen
Josephus]

CLAUSEN INVESTIGATION [Clausen, Henry C.]
  see
  ROBERTS COMMISSION [Roberts, Owen
Josephus]

CLAUSEN REPORT [Clausen, Hugh T.]
  see
  WEST-CLAUSEN REPORT [West, Bland and
Clausen, Hugh T.]

CLAY REPORTS [Clay, Lucius D.]

282

Germany *(Territory under Allied occupation, 1945- U.S. Zone) Military
Governor.*
  Dresdner and Deutsche banks. Special report, June 1947. [n.p.,
Lithographed by the Adjutant General OMGUS] 1947.
  34 p. maps. 33 x 21 cm.
  At head of title: Military Government of Germany (U.S.)
  "Prepared by Finance Division."
  1. Dresdner Bank, Berlin. 2. Deutsche Bank, Berlin. I. Ger-
many (Territory under Allied occupation, 1945- U.S. Zone) Of-
fice of Military Government. Finance Division.
HG3060.B54D7 1947   332.1   48-12862*
Not located in Monthly Catalog
SuDocs no.: [W1.722:CT]

283

U.S. *Committee to Strengthen the Security of the Free World.*
  The scope and distribution of United States military and
economic assistance programs; report to the President of the
United States. Washington, Dept. of State; for sale by the
Superintendent of Documents, U.S. Govt. Print. Off., 1963.
  25 p. 24 cm.
  1. Economic assistance, American. 2. Military assistance,
American. 3. Technical assistance, American. I. Title.
HC60.U6A53 1963   63-61054
MC#: 1963-9401
SuDocs no.: S1.2:As7

284

U.S. President's Advisory Committee on a National Highway
Program.
  National highway program. Message from the President of the
United States relative to a national highway program.
Washington, U.S. Govt. Print. Off., 1955.
  xiv, 54 p. illus., maps (part fold.) 23 cm. (84th Congress, 1st
session. House document no. 93)
  Commonly known as the Clay report.

"A 10-year national highway program; a report to the Presi-
dent [by] the President's Advisory Committee on a National
Highway Program, January 1955": p. vii-xiv and 54 p.
  1. Roads—U.S. I. U.S. President, 1953-1961 (Eisenhower) II.
Title. III. Title: Clay report on a ten-year national highway pro-
gram. (Series: U.S. 84th Congress, 1st session, 1955. House.
Document no. 93)
HE355.A3A518 1955   55-60556
MC#: 1955-4220
SuDocs no.: 84th Cong., 1st sess. H. Doc. 93

285

U.S. *President's Advisory Committee on a National Highway Program.*
  A ten-year national highway program; a report to the Presi-
dent. [Washington, U.S. Govt. Print. Off.] 1955.
  vi, 57 p. illus., map. 24 cm.
  1. Roads—U.S. I. Title.
HE355.A3A55   55-60265
MC#: 1955-1770
SuDocs no.: Pr34.8:H53

CLEVELAND COMMISSION [Cleveland, Frederick
Albert]

  The reports of the Cleveland Commission are listed
alphabetically by title.

286

U.S. *President's commission on economy and efficiency.*
  . . . The administrative purpose of the accounting methods and
procedures which have been installed in the depart-
ments . . . Washington [Govt. print. off.] 1913.
  13 p. illus. 23 cm. (Circular no. 32)
  At head of title: The President's commission on economy and
efficiency.
  1. U.S.—Executive departments. 2. Finance—U.S.—
Accounting. I. Title.
JK643.C10c   13-35023
- - - - - Copy 2.
MC#: Jan. 1913-page 356
SuDocs no.: Y3.Ec7/4:32

287

U.S. *President's commission on economy and efficiency.*
  . . . Apportionment of appointments. Message from the President of the United States transmitting report of the President's
commission on economy and efficiency on the apportionment of
appointments made from the registers of the Civil service commission to the apportioned service at Washing-
ton . . . Washington [Govt. print. off.] 1913.
  70 p. 23½ cm. (63d Cong., 1st sess. Senate. Doc. 50)
  Referred to the Committee to audit and control the contingent
expenses of the Senate and ordered printed May 29, 1913.
  1. Civil service—U.S. I. Title.
JK766.A5 1913   13-35460
- - - - - Copy 2.
MC#: June 1913-page 669
SuDocs no.: 63d Cong., 1st sess. S. Doc. 50

288

U.S. *President's Commission on economy and efficiency.*
  Catalog and price list of supplies for use in the Bureau of the
Census, Department of Commerce and Labor [Compiled by C.
R. Bartlett]. Washington, U.S. Govt. Print. Off., 1911.
  2 p., 3-13 1. (Circular no. 12)
MC#: May 1911-page 637
SuDocs no.: Y3.Ec7/4:12

289

U.S. *President's Commission on Economy and Efficiency.*
    Circular. no. 1-35. Washington [Govt. Print. Off.] 1910-13.
    34 no. in v. 23-30 cm.
    No. 1 has no numbering or series title.
    No. 7 not published. Cf. U.S. Superintendent of Documents.
Catalogue of the public documents, 1909/11.
    No. 1-3 and 5-10 issued by the commission under a variant
name: President's Inquiry in Re Economy and Efficiency.
    L.C. set incomplete: no. 7-8, 16, 22, and 24 wanting.
    1. U.S. — Pol. & govt. — 1909-1913.
JK643.C10c   11-35740 rev*
Not located in Monthly Catalog

290

U.S. *President's commission on economy and efficiency.*
    Circular in reports to be prepared by committees on economy
and efficiency of Executive Departments and independent
establishments. Washington, U.S. Govt. Print. Off., 1911.
    20 p. (Circular no. 16)
MC#: June 1911-page 692
SuDocs no.: Y3.Ec7/4:16

291

U.S. *President's commission on economy and efficiency.*
    . . . Commission on economy and efficiency. Message from
the President of the United States, transmitting information in
response to Senate resolution of January 25, 1912, giving the
names of the members of the Commission on economy and efficiency in the government service . . . [Washington, Govt. print.
off., 1912]
    2 p. 24 cm. (62d Cong., 2d sess. Senate. Doc. 294)
    F. A. Cleveland, chairman.
    I. Title.
JK643.C10h 1912a
- - - - - Copy 2.
MC#: Feb. 1912-page 495
SuDocs no.: 62d Cong., 2d sess. S. Doc. 294

292

U.S. *President's commission on economy and efficiency.*
    Conclusions reached with respect to expenditure accounting and
reporting, discussion of information needed and of methods recom-
mended as means of producing it. Washington, U.S. Govt. Print.
Off. 1913.
    53 p. (Circular no. 33)
MC#: May 1913-page 614 (LC card 13-35437 cancelled)
SuDocs no.: Y3.Ec7/4:33

293

U.S. *President's commission on economy and efficiency.*
    Definition and classification of expenditures for services other
than personal, subsistence and support of persons. Washington,
U.S. Govt. Print. Off., 1911.
    21 p. (Circular no. 9)
MC#: May 1911-page 637
SuDocs no.: Y3.Ec7/4:9

294

U.S. *President's commission on economy and efficiency.*
    Definition and classification of expenditures for services other
than personal, transportation of persons. Washington, U.S. Govt.
Print. Off., 1911.
    5 p., 6-33 1. (Circular no. 8)
MC#: June 1911-page 692
SuDocs no.: Y3.Ec7/4:8

295

U.S. *President's commission on economy and efficiency.*
    Description of accounting forms suggested as means of obtaining
information needed about appropriations and funds, stores, expenses, capital outlays, etc. Washington, U.S. Govt. Print. Off.,
1911.
    14, [12] 1. (Circular no. 13)
MC#: June 1911-page 692
SuDocs no.: Y3.Ec7/4:13

296

U.S. *President's commission on economy and efficiency.*
    Description of expenditure documents and procedures for pur-
chase of supplies, materials, equipment, and services other than
personal and for distribution of supplies and materials from stores.
Washington, U.S. Govt. Print. Off., 1911.
    50 1. (Circular no. 6)
MC#: May 1911-page 637
SuDocs no.: Y3.Ec7/4:6

297

U.S. *President's commission on economy and efficiency.*
    . . . Economy and efficiency in the government service.
Message of the President of the United States, transmitting reports
of the Commission on economy and efficiency . . . Washington
[Govt. print. off.] 1912.
    1 p. 1., 565 p. 23 cm. (62d Cong., 2d sess. House. Doc. 670)
    F. A. Cleveland, chairman.
    Includes reports on the following subjects: Methods of appoint-
ment. Consolidation of Lighthouse and Life-savings services.
Revenue-cutter service. The consolidation of auditing offices. The
Returns office. Government expenses for travel. Handling and
filing of correspondence. Distribution of government documents.
Outlines of organization.
    1. U.S. — Executive departments. 2. U.S. — Officials and
employees. I. Cleveland, Frederick Albert, 1865- II. Title.
JK643.C10j 1912   12-35563
- - - - - Copy 2.
MC#: Apr. 1912-page 677
SuDocs no.: 62d Cong., 2d sess. H. Doc. 670

298

U.S. *President's commission on economy and efficiency.*
    . . . Establishment of an independent public health ser-
vice . . . Letter from the chairman of the President's commission
on economy and efficiency, submitting the report to the President on the establishment of an independent public health service . . . [Washington, Govt. print. off., 1913]
    4 p. 24½ cm. (62d Cong., 3d sess. Senate. Doc. 1002)
    Presented by Mr. Owen. Referred to the Committee on public
health and national quarantine and ordered printed Jan. 11, 1913.
    Appears also in "Message of the President . . . transmitting
reports of the Commission on economy and efficiency" [Jan. 8,
1913] p. 911-915.
    I. Title.
RA11.A3 1913   13-35029
- - - - - Copy 2.
MC#: Jan. 1913-page 356
SuDocs no.: 62d Cong., 3d sess. S. Doc. 1002

299

U.S. *President's commission on economy and efficiency.*
    Instructions to be followed in analysis of salaries and wages by
classes of employees and other compensation for personal services
paid by government. Washington, U.S. Govt. Print. Off., 1912.

24 p. (Circular no. 27)
MC#: Dec. 1912-page 282 (LC card 12-29939 cancelled)
SuDocs no.: Y3.Ec7/4:27

300

U.S. *President's commission on economy and efficiency.*
Instructions to be followed in preparation of analyses of estimates and expenditures called for by the President, July 10, 1912. Washington, U.S. Govt. Print. Off., 1912.
9 p. (Circular no. 25)
MC#: July 1912-page 42
SuDocs no.: [Y3.Ec7/4:25]

301

U.S. *President's commission on economy and efficiency.*
Interim report on plan of inquiry and progress of work, Sept. 27-Dec. 31, 1910. Washington, U.S. Govt. Print. Off., 1911.
13 p. (Circular no. 4)
Document Catalogue, v. 10-page 486

302

U.S. *President's commission on economy and efficiency.*
. . . Memorandum concerning the work completed and in progress by the President's commission on economy and efficiency, submitted for the information of the Committee on appropriations of the House of representatives . . . Washington [Govt. print. off.] 1912.
18 p. 23 cm. (Circular no. 23)
1. U.S. — Executive departments. 2. Finance — U.S. — Accounting. I. Title.
JK643.C10c   12-35819
- - - - - Copy 2.
MC#: May 1912-page 776
SuDocs no.: [Y3.Ec7/4:23]

303

U.S. *President's commission on economy and efficiency.*
. . . Memorandum of conclusions reached by the commission concerning the principles that should govern in the matter of handling and filing correspondence and preparing and mailing communications in connection with the work of the several departments of the government, together with suggestions for the use of labor-saving devices in preparing and mailing letters, etc . . . .Washington [Govt. print. off.] 1912.
36 p. 23 cm. (Circular no. 21)
1. U.S. — Executive departments — Record and correspondence files. I. Title.
JK643.C10c no. 21   12-35209
- - - - - Copy 2.
MC#: Feb. 1912-page 495
SuDocs no.: [Y3.Ec7/4:21]

304

U.S. *President's commission on economy and efficiency.*
. . . Memorandum of conclusions reached by the commission concerning the principles that should govern in the matter of handling and filing correspondence and preparing and mailing communications in connection with the work of the several departments of the government, together with suggestions for the use of labor-saving devices in preparing and mailing letters, etc. [Rev. ed.] Washington [Govt. print. off.] 1912.
42 p. 23½ cm. (Circular no. 21. [Rev. ed.])
1. U.S. — Executive departments — Record and correspondence files. I. Title.
JK643.C10c no. 21   12-35605

- - - - - Copy 2.
MC#: Apr. 1912-page 677
SuDocs no.: [Y3.Ec7/4:21]

305

U.S. *President, 1909-1913 (Taft)*
. . . Message of the President of the United States on economy and efficiency in the government service. In two volumes . . . Washington [Govt. print. off.] 1912.
2 v. 23 cm. (62d Cong., 2d sess. House Doc. 458)
Appendix: Report to the President on the reorganization of the government of the United States as it existed July 1, 1911, shown by an outline of organization with recommendations . . . Submitted by the Commission on economy and efficiency, November, 1911.
1. U.S. — Executive departments. 2. U.S. — Officials and employees. 3. Civil service — U.S. 4. Finance — U.S. — Accounting. I. U.S. President's commission on economy and efficiency. II. Title.
JK643.C10g 1912   12-35245
- - - - - Copy 2.
MC#: Feb. 1912-page 495
SuDocs no.: 62d Cong., 2d sess. H. Doc. 458

306

U.S. *President's commission on economy and efficiency.*
. . . Message of the President of the United States, transmitting the reports of the Commission on economy and efficiency . . . Washington [Govt. print. off.] 1913.
x, 923 p. 23 cm. (62d Cong., 3d sess. House. Doc. 1252)
Communicated to the two houses of Congress, referred to the Committee on appropriations, and ordered printed, January 8, 1913.
F. A. Cleveland, chairman.
Includes reports on the following subjects: Business methods of the office of the adjutant general. Office of the chief of engineers (Mail and record division) Bureau of insular affairs. Office of the surgeon-general. Office of the Signal corps. Office of the chief of ordnance. Departments of justice. Methods of keeping efficiency records of employees in the National bank redemption agency of the Department of the Treasury. Report on the electric lighting of federal buildings of Department of the Treasury. On the establishment of an independent public-health service. The recovery of fiber stock of canceled paper money.
"Establishment of an independent Public-health service" is also issued separately, as Senate doc. 1002.
1. U.S. — Executive departments. 2. U.S. — Officials and employees. I. Cleveland, Frederick Albert, 1865-1946. II. Title.
JK643.C10k   13-35024
- - - - - Copy 2.
MC#: Jan. 1913-page 356
SuDocs no.: 62d Cong., 3d sess. H. Doc. 1252

307

U.S. *President's commission on economy and efficiency.*
Message of the President transmitting reports of the Commission on economy and efficiency, January 8, 1913, together with a brief memorandum descriptive of the work of the commission since its organization . . . Washington [Govt. print. off.] 1913.
19 p. 23 cm. (Circular no. 31)
1. U.S. — Executive departments. 2. Finance — U.S. — Accounting. 3. U.S. War dept. I. Taft, William Howard, pres. U.S., 1857- II. Title.
JK643.C10c   13-35025
- - - - - Copy 2.
MC#: Jan. 1913-page 356
SuDocs no.: Y3.Ec7/4:31

308

U.S. *President's commission on economy and efficiency.*

. . . The need for a national budget. Message from the President of the United States, transmitting report of the Commission on economy and efficiency on the subject of the need for a national budget . . . Washington [Govt. print. off.] 1912.

vii, 568 p. 23 cm. (62d Cong., 2d sess. House. Doc. 854)

Frederick A. Cleveland, chairman.

"Bibliography of Congressional inquiries into the conduct of the business of executive departments other than by standing committees of Congress, 1789-1911": p. 477-485.

1. Budget—U.S. 2. U.S.—Executive departments. 3. U.S.—Government publications—Bibl. I. Cleveland, Frederick Albert, 1865-1946. II. Title.

HJ2051.A6 1912   12-35898

MC#: July 1912-page 42

SuDocs no.: 62d Cong., 2d sess. H. Doc. 854

309

U.S. *President's commission on economy and efficiency.*

Organization charts of the Department of the Navy. Washington, U.S. Govt. Print. Off., 1911.

3 p., [53] 1. (Circulation no. 17)

MC#: June 1911-page 692

SuDocs no.: Y3.Ec7/4:17

310

U.S. *President's commission on economy and efficiency.*

Outline for reclassification of estimates of Government expenditures on a uniform basis. Washington, U.S. Govt. Print. Off., 1910.

13 p. (Circular no. [1])

MC#: May 1911-page 637

SuDocs no.: Y3.Ec7/4:1

311

U.S. *President's commission on economy and efficiency.*

Outline illustrating the use of uniform classification of stationery, drafting, scientific, and educational supplies for purposes of correlating specification numbers with code for common analysis of accounts. Washington, U.S. Govt. Print. Off., 1911.

30 p. (Circular no. 11)

MC#: May 1911-page 637

SuDocs no.: Y3.Ec7/4:11

312

U.S. *President's commission on economy and efficiency.*

Outline of classification of objects of government on a uniform basis with symbols for convenient reference to price lists and catalogues suggested for use in making descriptive entries on documents and records, as a means of facilitating current work and of reducing cost of analyzing accounts and of making special reports. Washington, U.S. Govt. Print. Off., 1911.

2 p. 3-131 1. (Circular no. 19)

Document Catalogue, vol. 11, page 568

313

U.S. *President's commission on economy and efficiency.*

Proposed business and accounting procedure of the United States Indian Service, Department of the Interior. Washington, U.S. Govt. Print. Off., 1911.

2 p. 3-17 ¢[41] 1. (Circular no. 14)

MC#: June 1911-page 692

SuDocs no.: Y3.Ec7/4:14

314

U.S. *President's commission on economy and efficiency.*

Questions to be answered and instructions to be followed in preparation of report asked for on the subject of collection of cost data, keeping of cost accounts, and making of cost reports. Washington, U.S. Govt. Print. Off., 1911.

22 p. (Circular no. 15)

MC#: June 1911-page 692

SuDocs no.: Y3.Ec7/4:15

315

U.S. *President's commission on economy and efficiency.*

. . . Questions to be answered and instructions to be followed in the preparation of report asked for on the subject of telegraph and cable business and cipher coding systems . . . Washington [Govt. print. off.] 1913.

8 p. 23 cm. (Circular no. 28)

At head of title: President's commission on economy and efficiency.

Running title: Inquiry relative to telegraph and cable business.

1. Telegraph—U.S.—Stat. 2. Cables, Submarine. 3. Cipher and telegraph codes. I. Title.

JK643.C10c   13-35048

- - - - - Copy 2.

MC#: Jan. 1913-page 356

SuDocs no.: Y3.Ec7/4:28

316

U.S. *President's commission on economy and efficiency.*

Questions to be answered and memorandum of instructions to be followed in preparation of report, form 6, asked for on subject of handling and filing of correspondence. Washington, U.S. Govt. Print. Off., 1911.

13 p. (Circular no. 5)

MC#: May 1911-page 637

SuDocs no.: Y3.Ec7/4:5

317

U.S. *President's commission on economy and efficiency.*

Questions to be answered and memorandum of instructions to be followed in preparation of report, form 6, asked for on subject of keeping of service records and preparations and payment of pay rolls, etc. Washington, U.S. Govt. Print. Off., 1912.

11 1. (Circular no. 24)

Processed.

Document Catalogue, vol. 11, page 568

318

U.S. *President's commission on economy and efficiency.*

. . . Recovery of government waste paper. Message from the President of the United States, submitting, in response to Senate resolution of February 21, 1913, additional information relative to the saving in recovery of government waste paper. [Washington, Govt. print. off., 1913]

18 p. 23½ cm. (62d Cong., 3d sess. Senate. Doc. 1105)

Read, referred to the Committee on appropriations, and ordered printed Feb. 24, 1913.

Frederick A. Cleveland, chairman.

"Report on the collection, handling, and disposition of waste paper in the government service," and, "The recovery of fiber stock of canceled paper money," reports submitted Feb. 11, 1913, and Sept. 21, 1912, including a report on the Winestock process by F. C. Clark of the Bureau of standards.

1. Waste paper. I. Cleveland, Frederick Albert, 1865-1946. II. Title.

TS1109.U5 1913   13-35119
- - - - - Copy 2.
MC#: Feb. 1913-page 431
SuDocs no.: 62d Cong., 3d sess. S. Doc. 1105

319

U.S. *President's commission on economy and efficiency.*
    Report by the Commission on economy and efficiency submitted to the President December 18, 1912, and sent to Congress with the message of the President, January 8, 1913 . . . Washington [Govt. print. off.] 1913.
    28 p. 23 cm. (Circular no. 34)
    1. U.S.—Executive departments. 2. Civil service—U.S. 3. Finance—U.S.—Accounting. I. Title.
JK643.C10c   13-35083
- - - - - Copy 2.
MC#: Feb. 1913-page 431
SuDocs no.: Y3.Ec7/4:34

320

U.S. *President's commission on economy and efficiency.*
    . . . Report of the commission on economy and efficiency . . . Washington [Govt. print. off.] 1912.
    37 p. 3 fold. pl. 23 cm. (62d Cong., 2d sess. Senate. Doc. 293)
    F. A. Cleveland, chairman.
    Message from the President (Mr. Taft) transmitting three reports relative to the following subjects: 1. The centralization of the distribution of government publications.—2. The use of window envelopes in the government service.—3. The use of a photographic process for copying printed and written documents, maps, drawings, etc.
    1. U.S.—Government publications. 2. Envelopes (Stationery) 3. Photography—Reproduction of plans, drawings, etc. I. Cleveland, Frederick Albert, 1865-1946. II. Title.
JK643.C10h 1912c   12-35163
- - - - - Copy 2.
MC#: Feb. 1912-page 495 (LC card 12-35317 cancelled in favor of 12-35163)
SuDocs no.: 62d Cong., 2d sess. S. Doc. 293

321

U.S. *President's commission on economy and efficiency.*
    . . . Report of the investigation of the United States Patent Office made by the President's commission on economy and efficiency, December, 1912 . . . Washington [Govt. print. off.] 1912.
    624 p. fold. tab., diagrs. (1 fold.) 23 cm. (62d Cong., 3d sess. House. Doc. 1110)
    F. A. Cleveland, chairman.
    "Publications of the Patent office": p. 477-495.
    "Bibliography of the United States Patent office, 1789 to 1912": p. 521-535.
    1. U.S. Patent Office. I. Cleveland, Frederick Albert, 1865-1946. II. Title.
T223.S 1912b   13-35026
- - - - - Copy 2.
MC#: Jan. 1913-page 356
SuDocs no.: 62d Cong., 3d sess. H. Doc. 1110

322

U.S. *President's commission on economy and efficiency.*
    . . . Report on methods of keeping efficiency records of employees in the National bank redemption agency of the Department of the Treasury . . . Washington [Govt. print. off.] 1913.
    44 p. 23 cm. (Circular no. 35)
    At head of title: The President's commission on economy and efficiency.

    1. U.S. National bank redemption agency. I. Title.
JK643.C10c   13-35084
- - - - - Copy 2.
MC#: Feb. 1913-page 431
SuDocs no.: Y3.Ec7/4:35

323

U.S. *President's commission on economy and efficiency.*
    Report on the preliminary inquiry made under authority of the Sundry civil appropriation act of June 25, 1910, prior to the organization of the President's commission on economy and efficiency . . . Washington [Govt. print. off.] 1913.
    18 p. 23 cm. (Circular no. 29)
    Frederick A. Cleveland, chairman.
    Caption title: Report on the preliminary inquiry on economy and efficiency. September 27, 1910, to March 8, 1911.
    1. U.S.—Executive departments. 2. U.S.—Officials and employees. I. Cleveland, Frederick Albert, 1865-1946. II. Title.
JK643.C10c   13-35027
- - - - - Copy 2.
MC#: Jan. 1913-page 356
SuDocs no.: Y3.Ec7/4:29

324

U.S. *President's commission on economy and efficiency.*
    Report to the President by the Commission on economy and efficiency . . . Washington [Govt. print. off.] 1913.
    32 p. 23½ cm. (Circular no. 30)
    A report relative to the organization of the commission and its activities up to October 30, 1911.
    1. U.S.—Executive departments. 2. Finance—U.S.—Accounting. I. Cleveland, Frederick Albert, 1865-1946. II. Title.
JK643.C10c   13-35028
- - - - - Copy 2.
MC#: Jan. 1913-page 356
SuDocs no.: Y3.Ec7/4:30

325

U.S. *President's commission on economy and efficiency.*
    Report to the President on the use of outline of organization of Government prepared by the Commission as a means for showing currently the organization conditions of Government. Washington, Govt. Print. Off., 1912.
    8 p. (Circular no. 22)
MC#: June 1912-page 864 (LC card 12-35853 cancelled)
SuDocs no.: [Y3.Ec7/4:22]

326

U.S. *President's commission on economy and efficiency.*
    . . . Report to the President recommending the preparation of alphabetical lists or catalogues to be used in the several branches of the service in the preparation of requisitions, orders, and other expenditure documents . . . Washington [Govt. print. off.] 1912.
    22 p. 23 cm. (Circular no. 26)
    Frederick A. Cleveland, Walter W. Warwick, Merritt O. Chance, commissioners.
    "Suggested form of catalogue and price list of supplies prepared for use in the Bureau of the census . . . (Printed by the Commission . . . as Circular no. 12)": p. 11-22.
    1. U.S.—Executive departments-Equipment and supplies. I. Cleveland, Frederick Albert, 1865-1946. II. Title.
JK643.C10c no. 26   12-29025
- - - - - Copy 2.
MC#: Oct. 1912-page 189
SuDocs no.: Y3.Ec7/4:26

327

U.S. *President's commission on economy and efficiency.*

Reprint of message from the President of the United States and report of the commission on economy and efficiency relative to retirement from the classified civil service of superannuated employees. Washington, Govt. print. off., 1912.

1 p. 1., 62 p. 23 cm.

Frederick A. Cleveland, chairman.

The full report, including appendixes in detail, was pub. as House doc. 732, 62d Cong., 2d sess. with title: Retirement from the classified civil service, of superannuated employees . . .

1. Civil service—U.S. I. Cleveland, Frederick Albert, 1865-1946.

JK791.A5 1912a   12-35813

- - - - - Copy 2.

MC#: May 1912-page 777

328

U.S. *President's commission on economy and efficiency.*

Reprint of reports of the Commission on economy and efficiency regarding outlines of organization of the government. Washington [Govt. print. off.] 1912.

23, [1] p. 23 cm.

Frederick A. Cleveland, chairman.

The full report, including the outline of the organization of the government in detail, was pub. in 2 v. as House doc. 458, 62d Cong., 2d sess.

1. U.S.—Executive departments. 2. Civil service—U.S. I. Cleveland, Frederick Albert, 1865-1946. II. Title.

JK643.C10n 1912   12-35654

- - - - - Copy 2.

MC#: Apr. 1912-page 678

329

U.S. *President's commission on economy and efficiency.*

. . . Retirement from the classified civil service of superannuated employees. Message from the President of the United States transmitting report of the commission . . . Washington [Govt. print. off.] 1912.

1 p. 1., 59, 225, 264, 49, 8, 5 p. incl. diagrs. 23½ cm. (62d Cong., 2d sess. House. Doc. 732)

Frederick A. Cleveland, chairman.

Appendices: A. (Senate doc. 745, 61st Cong., 3d sess.) Savings; an annuity plan proposed for retirement of superannuated civil-service employees, by Herbert D. Brown.—B. (Senate doc. 290, 61st Cong., 2d sess.) Civil-service retirement—Great Britain and New Zeland, by Herbert D. Brown. Prepared under the direction of Chas. P. Neill, commissioner of labor.—C. (Senate doc. 420, 61st Cong., 2d sess.) Civil-service retirement—New South Wales, Austrailia, by Herbert D. Brown. Prepared under the direction of Chas. P. Neill, commissioner of labor.—D. The Hamil, Maher, and Cummins bills.—E. Schedule calling for information with regard to employees.

1. Civil service pensions—U.S. 2. Civil service pensions—Gt. Brit. 3. Civil service pensions—New Zealand. 4. Civil service pensions—New South Wales. I. Cleveland, Frederick Albert, 1865-1946. II. Brown, Herbert D. III. Title.

JK791.A5 1912   12-35640

- - - - - Copy 2.

MC#: May 1912-page 777

SuDocs no.: 62d Cong., 2d sess. H. Doc. 732

330

U.S. *President's commission on economy and efficiency.*

Revised outline for reclassification of objects of Government expenditure on a uniform basis. Washington, U.S. Govt. Print. Off., 1911.

3 p., 4-20 1. (Circular no. 10)

Revision of Circular no. 2.

MC#: May 1911-page 637

SuDocs no.: Y3.Ec7/4:10

331

U.S. *President's commission on economy and efficiency.*

Suggested forms for reporting assets and liabilities, revenues and expenses, funds and appropriations with definitions of Governmental accounting and reporting terms. Washington, U.S. Govt. Print. Off., 1912.

4 p. + 5-16 1. + 17-21 p. (Circular no. 20)

MC#: June 1912-page 864

SuDocs no.: [Y3.Ec7/4:20]

332

U.S. *President's commission on economy and efficiency.*

Suggested outline for reclassification of estimates of Government expenditure on a uniform basis. Washington, U.S. Govt. Print. Off., 1910.

14 p.

MC#: May 1911-page 637

SuDocs no.: Y3.Ec7/4:1

333

U.S. *President's commission on economy and efficiency.*

Suggestions as to schedules of documents and registers of documents and schedules for use in developing a uniform system of controlling accounts and summary reports. Washington, U.S. Govt. Print. Off., 1911.

3 p., 5-16 numb. 1. (Circular no. 18)

MC#: June 1911-page 692

SuDocs no.: Y3.Ec7/4:18

334

U.S. *President's commission on economy and efficiency.*

. . . Suggestions as to schedules of documents and registers of documents and schedules, for use in developing a uniform system of controlling accounts and summary reports . . . Washington [Govt. print. off.] 1912.

3 p., 5-16 numb. 1. incl. forms. fold. form. 29½ cm. (Circular no. 18)

Printed on one side of leaf only.

An earlier ed. was pub. in 1911.

Frederick A. Cleveland, chairman.

1. U.S.—Executive departments. 2. Finance, Public—U.S.—Accounting. I. Cleveland, Frederick Albert, 1865-1946. II. Title.

JK643.C10c no. 18a   12-35917

Not located in Monthly Catalog

335

U.S. *President's commission on economy and efficiency.*

Tentative outline and numbering of bureaus and divisions of the Navy. Washington, U.S. Govt. Print. Off., 1910.

16 p. (Circular no. 3)

MC#: May 1911-page 637

SuDocs no.: Y3.Ec7/4:3

336

U.S. *President's commission on economy and efficiency.*

Tentative outline for reclassification of objects of Government expenditure on a uniform basis with detail classification and codification of war equipment. Washington, U.S. Govt. Print. Off., 1910.

22 p. (Circular no. 2)
MC#: May 1911-page 637
SuDocs no.: Y3.Ec7/4:2

337

U.S. *Congress. Senate. Committee on public buildings and grounds.*

Underground pneumatic tube system. Hearing before the Committee on public buildings and grounds, United States Senate . . . June 7, 1912 [and Jan. 9, 1913] Washington, Govt. print. off., 1912-13.

73 6 p. incl. plans. 23 cm.

George Sutherland, chairman.

Part 2, Jan. 9, 1913 consists of the Report of the President's commission on economy and efficiency of Jan. 9, 1913.

1. Pneumatic tube transportation. I. U.S. President's commission on economy and efficiency.
HE7521.A4   12-35888
- - - - - Copy 2.
MC#: Feb. 1913-page 428
SuDocs no.: Y4.P96/7:P74

CLEWLOW REPORT [Clewlow, Carl W.]

338

U.S. *Bureau of the Budget.*

Report to the President on the management of automatic data processing in the Federal Government. Submitted by the Committee on Government Operations, United States Senate. Washington, U.S. Govt. Print. Off., 1965.

vii, 111 p. illus. 24 cm. (89th Cong., 1st sess. Senate. Document no. 15)

1. Electronic data processing—Public administration. I. U.S. Congress. Senate. Committee on Government Operations. II. Title. III. Title: Management of automatic data processing in the Federal Government. (Series: U.S. 89th Cong., 1st sess., 1965. Senate. Document no. 15)
JK468.A8A512   65-60915
MC#: 1965-5987
SuDocs no.: 89th Cong., 1st sess. S. Doc. 15

COATES REPORT [Coates, John Boyd, Jr.]
see
McMINN REPORT [McMinn, John H.]

COBB REPORT [Cobb, John Nathan]
see
EVERMANN REPORT [Evermann, Barton Warren]

COCHRAN REPORT [Cochran, John Joseph]

339

U.S. *Congress. House. Select committee on government organization.*

. . . Government organization. Report. "To accompany S. 3331" . . . [Washington, U.S. Govt. print. off., 1938]

40 p. 23½ cm. (75th Cong., 3d sess. House. Rept. 2033)

Submitted by Mr. Cochran. Committee to the Committee of the whole House on the state of the Union and ordered printed March 30, 1938.

"Minority views" (p. 39-40) signed: John Taber, Charles L. Gifford.

1. U.S.—Executive departments. I. Cochran, John Joseph, 1880- II. Taber, John, 1880- III. Gifford, Charles L., 1871- IV. Title.
JK649 1938b   353   38-26282
- - - - - Copy 2.
MC#: 1938-page 302
SuDocs no.: 75th Cong., 3d sess. H. Rept. 2033

COCKRELL REPORTS [Cockrell, Francis Marion]

340

U.S. *Congress. Senate. Select committee on methods of business and work in the executive departments.*

. . . Additional report of the Select committee of the United States Senate, appointed under Senate resolution of March 3, 1887, to inquire into and examine the methods of business and work in the executive departments, etc., and the causes of delays in transacting the public business, etc . . . .Washington, Govt. print. off., 1889.

1 p. l., 78 p., 1 l., iii, 3-220 p. 23½ cm. ([51st Cong.] special sess., 1889. Senate. Report. 3)

On verso of t.-p.: Treasury document no. 1218. Secretary. Presented by Mr. Cockrell. Ordered printed March 28, 1889.

1. U.S.—Executive departments. 2. Civil service—U.S. I. Cockrell, Francis Marion, 1834-1915. II. U.S. 51st Cong., special sess., 1889. Senate. III. Title: Methods of business and work in executive departments, Additional report on.
JK649 1889   10-29467
Checklist of United States Public Documents, 1789-1909, page 82
51st Cong., Special Sess. S. Rept. 3. In Serial no. 2619, vol. 2

341

U.S. *Congress. Senate. Select committee on methods of business and work in the executive departments.*

. . . Report [of] the Select committee of the United States Senate, appointed under Senate resolution of March 3, 1887, to inquire into and examine the methods of business and work in the executive departments, etc., and the causes of delays in transacting the public business, etc . . . .Washington, Govt. print. off., 1888.

3 v. 23½ cm. (50th Cong., 1st sess. Senate. Rept. 507)

Presented by Mr. Cockrell. Ordered printed March 8, 1888. An additional report was published in 1889.

Contents.—[pt. 1] Report.—pt. 2. The Department of the Treasury; the Department of the interior.—pt. 3. The Department of state; the Department of justice; the Department of war; the Department of the navy; the Post-office department; the Department of agriculture; the Government printing office.

1. U.S.—Executive departments. 2. Civil service—U.S. I. Cockrell, Francis Marion, 1834-1915. II. Title. III. Title: Dockery-Cockrell reports. IV. Title: Methods of business and work in executive departments, Report on.
JK649 1888   9-27209
Checklist of United States Public Documents, 1789-1909, page 79
50th Cong., 1st sess. S. Rept. 507. In Serial nos. 2521-2522, vols. 3-4, pts. 1-3

COFFIN REPORTS [Coffin, Frank M.]

342

U.S. *Congress. House. Committee on Foreign Affairs.*

Report of the special study mission to Canada of the Committee on Foreign Affairs pursuant to H. Res. 29 . . . Washington, U.S. Govt. Print. Off., 1958.

vii, 15 p. tables. 24 cm. (85th Cong., 2d sess., House report no. 1766)

1. U.S.—Relations (general) with Canada. 2. Canada—Relations (general) with the U.S. (Series: U.S. 85th Cong., 2d sess. 1958. House. Report no. 1766)
E183.8.C2U6   327.73071   58-61100
MC#: 1958-11970
SuDocs no.: 85th Cong., 2d sess. H. Rept. 1766

343

U.S. *Congress. Committee on Foreign Affairs.*

Special study mission to Europe. Report, part I, by Edna F. Kelly [and others] Report, part II, A study of European economic regionalism, a new era in free world economic politics, by Frank M. Coffin, Cornelius E. Gallagher [and] Alvin M. Bentley. Washington, U.S. Govt. Print. Off., 1960.

xi, 176 p. map, diagrs., tables. 24 cm. (86th Cong., 2d sess. House report no. 1226)

Each part published also separately.

Bibliography: p. 136-146.

1. U.S. — Foreign economic relations. 2. Economic assistance, American. 3. Europe — Economic policy. 4. European economic community. I. Kelly, Edna F. II. U.S. Congress. House Committee on Foreign Affairs. A study of European economic regionalism, a new era in free world economic politics. III. Title. IV. Title: A study of European regionalism, a new era in free world politics. (Series: U.S. 86th Cong., 2d sess., 1960. House. Report no. 1226)

HF1455.A53 1960a   337.914   60-60532

MC#: 1960-3575

SuDocs no.: 86th Cong., 2d sess. H. Rept. 1226

344

U.S. *Congress. House. Committee on Foreign Affairs.*

A study of European economic regionalism: a new era in free world economic politics; report of a special study mission of the Subcommittee on Europe. Washington, U.S. Govt. Print. Off., 1960.

vii, 136 p. map, diagrs., tables. 24 cm.

At head of title: 86th Cong., 2d sess. Committee print.

"Selective bibliography on the common market": p. 96-106.

1. Europe — Economic policy. 2. European common market (1955-) I. Title: European economic regionalism.

HC240.U565   338.94   60-60381

MC#: 1960-1637

SuDocs no.: Y4.F76/1:Eu7/7

See also

MC#: 1960-1636

SuDocs no.: Y4.F76/1:Eu7/6

COHEN REPORT

345

Cohen, Elias S

Mental illness among older Americans. Prepared for consideration by the Special Committee on Aging, United States Senate. Washington, U.S. Govt. Print. Off., 1961.

iii, 20 p. 24 cm.

At head of title: 87th Cong., 1st sess. Committee print.

Bibliographical references included in "Footnotes" (p. 20)

1. Mental illness. 2. Aged. I. U.S. Congress. Senate. Special Committee on Aging.

RC952.5.C6   61-64932

MC#: 1961-20623

SuDocs no.: Y4.Ag4:M52

COHEN REPORT

346

Cohen, Felix S 1907-1953.

Handbook of Federal Indian law, with reference tables and index. Foreword by Harold I. Ickes, Introd. by Nathan R. Margold. 4th print. 1945. Washington, U.S. Govt. Print. Off., 1945.

xxiv, 662 p. illus., fold. map (on cover) 30 cm.

At head of title: United States Department of the Interior. Office of the Solicitor.

"Tribal index of materials on Indian law": p. 457-484.

Bibliography: p. 638-650.

1. Indians of North America — Legal status, laws, etc. 2. Indians of North America — Treaties. I. U.S. Solicitor for the Dept. of the Interior. II. Title.

KF8205.A33 1945   45-6928

MC#: 1945-page 751 (LC card 45-36321 cancelled in favor of 45-6928)

SuDocs no.: I48.6:In2/4th print.

COHEN REPORT

347

Cohen, Irvin J

Observation on care of the aging in Europe. Printed for the use of the Committee on Veterans' Affairs. Washington, U.S. Govt. Print. Off., 1961.

v, 144 p. illus. 24 cm.

At head of title: 87th Cong., 1st sess. House committee print no. 152.

1. Old age assistance — Europe. I. U.S. Congress. House. Committee on Veterans' Affairs. II. Title.

HV1481.A2C6   362.6094   62-60339

MC#: 1962-7104

SuDocs no.: Y4.V64/3:Ag3

COHEN REPORT [Cohen, Milton]

348

U.S. *Securities and Exchange Commission. Special Study of Securities Markets.*

Report. Washington, U.S. Govt. Print. Off., 1963-

v. diagrs., forms. 24 cm. (88th Cong., 1st sess. House document no. 95, pt. 1)

"Referred to the Committee on Interstate and Foreign Commerce." Bibliographical footnotes.

1. Securities — U.S. I. U.S. Congress. House. Committee on Interstate and Foreign Commerce. (Series: U.S. 88th Cong., 1st sess. 1963. House. Document no. 95, pt. 1)

HG4556.U5A57 1963   63-61766

MC#: 1963-11753, pt. 1

1963-11754, pt. 3

1963-18798, pt. 2

1963-18799, pt. 4

SuDocs no.: 88th Cong., 1st sess. H. Doc. 95, pt. 1, 2, 3, 4

COHEN REPORT [Cohen, Wilbur Joseph]

Toward a long-range plan for federal financial support for higher education.

see

RIVLIN REPORT [Rivlin, Alice M.]

COHEN REPORTS [Cohen, Wilbur Joseph]

349

United States. Dept. of Health, Education, and Welfare. Office of the Secretary.

Health in America: the role of the Federal government in bringing high quality health care to all the American people; a report to the President by the Secretary of Health, Education, and Welfare. [Washington, 1968]

2, 35 p. 27 cm.

Caption title.

1. Medical care — United States. 2. Hygiene, Public — United States. [1. Medical care — United States. 2. Public health — United States] I. Cohen, Wilbur Joseph, 1913- II. Title. III. Title: The role of the Federal government in bringing high quality health care to all the American people.

RA445   hew 68-124

MARC

Not located in Monthly Catalog
SuDocs no.: [FS1.2:H3/4]

350

U.S. *President's Committee on Population and family Planning.*
   Population and family planning; the transition from concern to action; report. [Washington, U.S. Dept. of Health, Education, and Welfare] 1968.

   43 p. 23 cm.
   1. Birth control—U.S. 2. U.S.—Population. I. Title.
HQ766.5.U5A57   301.3′2   70-602155
                                                         MARC

MC#: 1969-6165
SuDocs no.: Pr36.8:P81/P81

COKE REPORT [Coke, James Guthrie]
   see
DOUGLAS REPORTS [Douglas, Paul H.]

   National Commission on Urban Problems.
   Research report no. 18

COLE REPORT

351

Cole, David L
   Report to the Director-General on the proposed programs for improving labor-management co-operation. Washington, D.C., U.S. Dept. of Labor. 1955.

   38 p. (typescript)
   Report of the Director-General to the Thirty-eighth session of the International Labor Conference at Geneva in June 1955.
Not located in Monthly Catalog

COLE REPORTS [Cole, Albert M.]

352

U.S. *President's Advisory Committee on Government Housing Policies and Programs.*
   Recommendations on Government housing policies and programs, a report. [Washington] 1953.

   ix, 377 p. tables. 23 cm.
   1. Housing—U.S. I. Title: Government housing policies and programs.
HD7293.A587   331.833   53-63272
MC#: 1954-1024
SuDocs no.: Pr34.8:H81

353

U.S. *President's Advisory Committee on Government Housing Policies and Programs.*
   A report to the President of the United States, December 14, 1953. [n.p., 1954?]

   1 v. (various pagings) 27 cm.
   Cover title.
   1. Housing—U.S.
HD7293.A5 1954e   60-24203
Not located in Monthly Catalog

COLEMAN REPORTS

354

Coleman, James Samuel, 1926-
   Equality of educational opportunity, by James S. Coleman [and others. Washington] U.S. Dept. of Health, Education, and Welfare, Office of Education; [for sale by the Superintendent of Documents, U.S. Govt. Print. Off., 1966]

   vi, 737, vii, 548 p. illus. 26 cm.

"OE-38001" and "OE-38001 (Supplement)"
"A publication of the National Center for Educational Statistics."
Bound in 2 parts; the second part has special t.p.: Supplemental appendix to the survey; section 9.10/correlation tables.
   1. Negroes—Education. [1. Segregation in education] 2. Education—U.S.—1945- I. U.S. Office of Education. II. U.S. National Center for Educational Statistics. III. Title. IV. Title: Supplemental appendix to the survey on Equality of educational opportunity.
L112.C6   370′.973   HEW66-127
MC#: 1966-14551
SuDocs no.: FS5.238:38001
MC#: 1966-14552
SuDocs no.: FS5.238:38001/supp.

355

[Coleman, James Samuel] 1926-
   Equality of educational opportunity [summary report. Washington] U.S. Dept. of Health, Education, and Welfare, Office of Education; [for sale by the Superintendent of Documents, U.S. Govt. Print. Off., 1966]

   v, 33 p. illus. 26 cm.
   "OE-38000."
   A slightly different version of the summary included, as section 1, in the main report of the survey.
   "The survey was carried out by the National Center for Educational Statistics of the U.S. Office of Education."
   1. Education—U.S.—1945- -Stat. 2. Negroes—Education—Stat. I. U.S. Office of Education. II. U.S. National Center for Educational Statistics. III. Title.
LA209.2.C58   370.19′344   66-62837
MC#: 1966-13271 (LC card HEW66-126 cancelled in favor of 66-62837)
SuDocs no.: FS5.238:38000

COLLAMER REPORT [Collamer, Jacob]
   see
MASON REPORTS [Mason, James Murray]

COLMAN REPORT [Colman, William G.]

356

U.S. *Advisory Commission on Intergovernmental Relations.*
   Report. Washington.
   v. 27 cm. annual.
   1. Federal government—U.S.
JK325.A2   62-62329
1961
MC#: 1962-16238
SuDocs no.: Y3.Ad9/8:1/961

1962
MC#: 1963-4324
SuDocs no.: Y3.Ad9/8:1/962

1963
MC#: 1963-4325
SuDocs no.: Y3.Ad9/8:1/963

1964
MC#: 1964-5782
SuDocs no.: Y3.Ad9/8:1/964

COLORADO REPORT
   see
CONDON REPORT [Condon, Edward Uhler]

COMPTON REPORT [Compton, Karl]

357

U.S. *President's Advisory Commission on Universal Training.*
   A program for national security, May 29, 1947. Report. Washington, U.S. Govt. Print. Off., 1947.

   vii, 453 p. 24 cm.
   1. Military service, Compulsory—U.S. 2. Military education—U.S. I. Title. II. Title: National security.
UB353.A5 1947a   355.22   47-31670*
MC#: 1947-page 935
SuDocs no.: Y3.Ad9/5:2N21

COMSTOCK REPORT [Comstock, George A.]
      see
   RUBINSTEIN-COMSTOCK REPORT [Rubinstein, Eli Abraham and Comstock, George A.]

CONANT REPORT [Conant, Charles Arthur]
      see under
   ALDRICH COMMISSION [Aldrich, Nelson Wilmarth]

CONDON REPORT [Condon, Edward Uhler]

358

Colorado. University.
   Final report of the scientific study of unidentified flying objects conducted by the University of Colorado. Edward U. Condon, scientific director. Daniel S. Gillmor, editor. [Boulder, Colo.] 1968.

   3 v. (xi, 1465 p.) illus. 28 cm.
   "This research was supported by the Air Force Office of Scientific Research, Office of Aerospace Research, USAF, under contract F44620-67-C-0035."
   Includes bibliographies.
   1. Flying saucers. I. Condon, Edward Uhler, 1902- II. Title. III. Title: Scientific study of unidentified flying objects.
TL789.C658   001'.9   72-625998
                                     MARC

Not located in Monthly Catalog

Colorado. University.
   Final report of the scientific study of unidentified flying objects. Edward U. Condon, scientific director. Daniel S. Gillmor, editor. With an introd. by Walter Sulliven. New York, Dutton, 1969.

   xxiv, 967 p. illus. 22 cm.
   Commonly known as the Condon report.
   Conducted by the University of Colorado under contract F44620-67-C-0035 with the Air Force Office of Scientific Research, Office of Aerospace Research, USAF.
   Includes bibliographical references.
   1. Flying saucers. I. Condon, Edward Uhler, 1902- II. Title. III. Title: Scientific study of unidentified flying objects. IV. Title: Condon report on unidentified flying objects.
TL789.C658 1969   001'.94   73-77914
                                     MARC

Not listed in Monthly Catalog

CONDON REPORT [Condon, Edward Uhler]
   Aliens in the skies.
      see
   FULLER REPORT [Fuller, John Grant]

CONLON REPORT

359

Conlon Associates, ltd.
   United States foreign policy: Asia. Studies prepared at the request of the Committee on Foreign Relations, United States Senate. No. 5. Washington, U.S. Govt. Print. Off., 1959.

   ix, 157 p. 24 cm.
   At head of title: Committee print. 86th Cong., 1st sess.
   1. U.S.—For. rel.—Asia. 2. Asia—Politics. I. U.S. Congress. Senate. Committee on Foreign Relations. II. Title.
DS33.4.U6C6   327.7305   60-60164 rev
MC#: 1960-464
SuDocs no.: Y4.F76/2:F76/12/no. 5

CONNALLY REPORTS

360

Connally, Thomas Terry, 1877-
   Report on western Europe. Printed for the use of the Senate Foreign Relations Committee. Washington, U.S. Govt. Print. Off., 1952.

   iii, 31 p. 24 cm.
   At head of title: 82d Cong., 2d sess. Committee print.
   1. Europe-Politics-1945- 2. Europe-Defenses. I. U.S. Congress. Senate. Committee on Foreign Relations.
D1053.C6   940.55   52-60071
Not located in Monthly Catalog

361

U.S. *Congress. Senate. Committee on Foreign Relations.*
   A decade of American foreign policy; basic documents, 1941-49, prepared at the request of the Senate Committee on Foreign Relations by the staff of the committee and the Dept. of State. Washington, U.S. Govt. Print. Off., 1950.

   xiv, 1381 p. maps (1 fold.) 23 cm. ([U.S.] 81st Cong., 1st sess. [1950] Senate. Document no. 123)
   1. U.S.—For. rel.—1933-1945. 2. U.S.—For. rel.—1945- I. U.S. Dept. of State. (Series)
JX1416.A47   327.73   50-60544
MC#: 1950-9183
SuDocs no.: 81st Cong., 1st sess. S. Doc. 123

CONROY REPORT [Conroy, Katherine H.]
      see under
   GRIFFITHS REPORTS [Griffiths, Martha W.]
      Studies in public welfare, paper no. 16.

COOK REPORT [Cook, Roy Clyde]
      see under
   O'MAHONEY REPORTS [O'Mahoney, Joseph Christopher]
      Cook. Control of the petroleum industry.
      Review and criticism on behalf of Standard oil co.

COOKE REPORT [Cooke, Thornton]
      see under
   ALDRICH COMMISSION [Aldrich, Nelson Wilmarth]
      Barnett. State Banks and trust companies.

COOLIDGE REPORT [Coolidge, Charles A.]

362

U.S. *Dept. of Defense.*
   Department of Defense implementation of recommendations of Coolidge Committee on Classified Information. [Washington] 1957.

2 v. 26 cm.

Cover title.

1. U.S. Dept. of Defense. Committee on Classified Information. 2. Defense information, Classified—U.S.

UB247.A53   *355.42 355.34   58-60658

Not located in Monthly Catalog

COOPER COMMITTEE REPORTS [Cooper, Theodore]

363

U.S. Dept. of Health, Education, and Welfare. Study Group on Medical Devices.

Medical devices: a legislative plan. September 1970. [Washington: Department of Health, Education, and Welfare. Study Group of Medical Devices] 1970.

i, 18 leaves (typescript)

Appendix: 1-5.

1. Medical devices.

Not located in Monthly Catalog

364

U.S. *NIH Program Mechanisms Committee.*

Report of NIH Program Mechanisms Committee. February 14, 1973. [Washington: Department of Health, Education, and Welfare. Public Health Service. National Institutes of Health]. 1973.

ii, 28 leaves (typescript)

Appendix: 1-6.

Minority Report.

1. National Institutes of Health-Program administration.

Not located in Monthly Catalog.

COOPER REPORT [Cooper, Charles P.]

365

U.S. *Dept. of Defense. Advisory Committee on Fiscal Organization and Procedures.*

Commercial Activities Working Group report[s] Washington, 1954-

v. illus. 27 cm.

Cover title.

1. U.S.—Armed Forces—Finance. 2. U.S.—Armed Forces—Facilities.

UC20.A513   55-60689

MC#: 1955-4582

SuDocs no.: D1.2:Ex2

MC#: 1955-4583

SuDocs no.: D1.2:C65

MC#: 1955-4584

SuDocs no.: D1.2:C73

MC#: 1955-4585

SuDocs no.: D1.2:L37

MC#: 1955-4586

SuDocs no.: D1.2:M59

MC#: 1955-4587

SuDocs no.: D1.2:P83

MC#: 1955-6335

SuDocs no.: D1.2:P93

COOPER REPORT [Cooper, Joseph David]

366

U.S. *Federal personnel council. Committee on employee relations.*

Accident and health insurance for federal employees. An informative statement by the Committee on employee relations, U.S. Council of personnel administration, Washington, D.C.

Prepared by Joseph D. Cooper, secretary, Committee on employee relations. [Washington] 1944.

1 p. 1., 54 numb. 1. 27 cm.

Reproduced from type-written copy.

1. Insurance, Health—U.S. 2. Insurance, Accident—U.S. 3. Civil service—U.S. I. Cooper, Joseph David, 1917- II. Title.

HG9697.U5A5 1944   368.41   45-2672 rev

Not located in Monthly Catalog

COPELAND REPORT [Copeland, Royal S.]

367

U.S. *Forest service.*

. . . A national plan for American forestry. Letter from the secretary of agriculture transmitting in response to S. Res. 175 (Seventy-second Congress) the report of the Forest service of the Agricultural department on the forest problem of the United States . . . Washington, U.S. Govt. print. off., 1933.

2 v. maps, tables, diagrs. 23½ cm. (73d Cong., 1st sess. Senate. Doc. 12)

Paged continuously.

Referred to the Committee on printing March 13 (calendar day, March 30), 1933.

Another issue of this report is published without document series note as "Separate, no. 1-

References interspersed.

1. Forests and forestry—U.S. I. Title.

SD11.A47 1933   634.90973   33-26292

MC#: May 1933-page 863

SuDocs no.: 73d Cong., 1st sess. S. Doc. 12

CORBETT REPORT [Corbett, Robert J.]

368

U.S. *Congress. House. Committee on Post Office and Civil Service.*

Study of civilian manpower utilization in the Federal Government. Preliminary report by the Subcommittee on Manpower Utilization. Washington, U.S. Govt. Print. Off., 1953.

iii, 11 p. 23 cm.

At head of title: Subcommittee print.

1. Civil service—U.S.

JK649 1953 1   *351.3 351.1   53-61983

MC#: 1953-15587

SuDocs no.: Y4.P84/10:C49/3

CORDASCO REPORT [Cordasco, Francesco]
see
MONDALE REPORT [Mondale, Walter F.]

CORDINER REPORT [Cordiner, Ralph]

369

U.S. *Defense Advisory Committee on Professional and Technical Compensation.*

Report [and recommendation for the Secretary of Defense] Washington, U.S. Govt. Print. Off., 1957.

2 v. diagrs., tables. 26 cm.

Contents.—v. 1. Military personnel; a modern concept of manpower management and compensation for personnel of the uniformed services.—v. 2. Civilian personnel; a plan of action to attract and retain professional, technical, and managerial employees for defense.

1. U.S.—Armed Forces-Recruiting, enlistment, etc. 2. U.S.—Armed Forces—Pay, allowances, etc. 3. U.S. Dept. of Defense—Officials and employees—Salaries, allowances, etc. 4. Manpower—U.S.

UB323.A5 1957   355.1   57-60268

MC#: 1957-8461, 8462

SuDocs no.: D1.2:P94/3/v.1-2

CORDON REPORT [Cordon, Guy]
370

U.S. *Congress. Senate. Committee on Interior and Insular Affairs.*
Contributions to local governments on account of nontaxable Federal lands. Report. [Washington, U.S. Govt. Print. Off., 1947]

12 p. 24 cm. ([U.S.] 80th Cong., 1st sess., 1947. Senate. Report no. 270)

Caption title.
Submitted by Mr. Cordon from the Committee on Public Lands.
1. U.S. — Public lands. 2. Land — Taxation — U.S. 3. Taxation, Exemption from — U.S. I. Cordon, Guy, 1890- II. Title. (Series)
HJ4182.A27A5 1947   336.294   47-31628 rev*
MC#: 1947-page 828
SuDocs no.: 80th Cong., 1st sess. S. Rept. 270

371

U.S. *Congress. Senate. Committee on Interior and Insular Affairs.*
Contributions to local governments on account of nontaxable Federal lands. Report to accompany S.582. [Washington, U.S. Govt. Print. Off., 1948]

27 p. 23 cm. [U.S.] 80th Cong., 2d sess., 1948. Senate. Report no. 1267)

Caption title.
Submitted by Mr. Cordon.
1. Land — Taxation — U.S. 2. Taxation, Exemption from — U.S. 3. U.S. — Public lands. I. Cordon, Guy, 1890- (Series)
HJ4182.A27A5 1948   336.1   48-46238*
MC#: 1948-13437
SuDocs no.: 80th Cong., 2d sess. S. Rept. 1267

CORSI REPORT [Corsi, Jerome R.]
   see
MASOTTI REPORT [Masotti, Louis H.]

COSTELLO REPORT [Costello, John Martin]
   see
EBERHARTER REPORT [Eberharter, Herman P.]

COVER REPORT [Cover, John Higson]
   see under
O'MAHONEY REPORTS [O'Mahoney, Joseph Christopher]

COX REPORT [Cox, Archibald]
372

U.S. *Advisory Panel on Labor-Management Relations Law.*
Organization and procedure of the National Labor Relations Board; report to the Senate Committee on Labor and Public Welfare pursuant to S. Res. 66 and S. Res. 141, Eighty-sixth Congress. Washington, U.S. Govt. Print. Off., 1960.

ii, 26 p. 24 cm. (86th Cong. 2d sess. Senate. Document no. 81)
1. U.S. National Labor Relations Board. I. U.S. Congress. Senate. Committee on Labor and Public Welfare. (Series: U.S. 86th Cong., 2d sess., 1960. Senate. Document no. 81)
         331.1506173   60-60589
MC#: 1960-3648
SuDocs no.: 86th Cong., 2d sess. S. Doc. 81

COX REPORT [Cox, Edward Eugene]
373

U.S. *Congress. House. Special committee on government competition with private enterprise.*

. . . Government competition with private enterprise. Report of the Special committee appointed to investigate government competition with private enterprise, House of representatives, pursuant to H. Res. 235, a resolution creating a Special committee to investigate government competition with private enterprise . . . Washington, U.S. Govt. print. off., 1933.

253 p. incl. tables. 23½ cm. ([U.S.] 72d Cong., 2d sess. House. Rept. 1985)
On cover: House reports on public bills, etc., II. House report 1985, 72d Cong., 2d sess.
Mr. Shannon, chairman.
"Minority views" (p. 26-29) signed: E. E. Cox.
Issued also in type-written (carbon copy) from under title: Report (pursuant to H. Res. 235) of the Special committee to investigate government competition with private interprise.
1. Industry and state — U.S. 2. Competition, Unfair — U.S. 3. Competition. I. Cox, Edward Eugene, 1880-1951. II. Title.
HD3616.U45A5 1933   380.167522   33-26114
MC#: Feb. 1933-page 597
SuDocs no.: 72d Cong., 2d sess. H. Rept. 1985

COX REPORT [Cox, Irene]
Handbook of public income transfer programs.
  see under
GRIFFITHS REPORTS [Griffiths, Martha W.]
Studies in public welfare, paper no. 2.

Studies in public welfare, paper no. 6.

Studies in public welfare, paper no. 10.

COX REPORT [Cox, Kenneth A.]
374

U.S. *Congress. Senate. Committee on Interstate and Foreign Commerce.*
The television inquiry; television network practices. Staff report prepared [by Kenneth A. Cox, special counsel] for the Committee on Interstate and Foreign Commerce, United States Senate. Washington, U.S. Govt. Print. Off., 1957.

iii, 102 p. 23 cm.
At head of title: 85th Cong., 1st sess. Committee print no. 2.
1. Television stations — U.S. 2. Television broadcasting — U.S.
HE8698.A43 1957b   58-60547
MC#: 1958-4582
SuDocs no.: Y4.In8/3:T237/9

CRAVENS REPORT [Cravens, Kenton R.]
375

U.S. *Congress. Senate. Committee on Banking and Currency.*
Study of banking laws; legislative recommendations of the Federal supervisory agencies to the Committee on Banking and Currency, United States Senate. Washington, U.S. Govt. Print. Off., 1956.

vii, 212 p. 24 cm.
1. Banking law — U.S. 2. Banks and banking — U.S.
         56-63869 rev
MC#: 1956-20125
SuDocs no.: Y4.B22/3:L44

CRAWFORD REPORT [Crawford, James H., Jr.]
376

United States.
Scientific and technological communication in the Government; a government research report. [Task force members: chairman, James H. Crawford, Jr., and others] Washington [Distributed by] U.S. Dept. of Commerce, Office of Technical Services [1962]

iii, 81 p. diagrs. 27 cm.

Cover title.
Commonly known as the Crawford report.
"AD 299545."
Bibliography: p. 74-81.
1. Communication in science. 2. Science—U.S. I. Title. II. Title: Crawford report on scientific and technical communication in the Government.
Q223.U54   63-65025
Not located in Monthly Catalog

CREEL REPORT [Creel, George]

377

U.S. *Committee on public information.*
Complete report of the chairman of the Committee on public information. 1917: 1918: 1919. Washington, Govt. print. off., 1920.

iv, 290 p. incl. tables, form. 23 cm.
George Creel, chairman.
Running title: Report Committee on public information.
1. U.S. Committee on public information. 2. European war, 1914-1918—Public opinion. 3. Propaganda, American. I. Creel, George, 1876- II. Title. III. Title: Report . . .
D632.A5 1919   20-26826
MC#: Sept. 1920-page 113
SuDocs no.: P96/3:1/917-19

CRIME COMMISSION REPORTS

378

U.S. *President's Commission on Law Enforcement and Administration of Justice.*
The challenge of crime in a free society; a report. Washington, U.S. Govt. Print. Off., 1967.

xi, 340 p. illus. 28 cm.
1. Crime and criminals—U.S. I. Title.
HV6789.A33   364'.9'73   67-60748
MC#: 1967-7044
SuDocs no.: Pr36.8:L41/C86

379

U.S. *Task Force on the Police.*
Task Force report: the police. [Washington, For sale by the Supt. of Docs., U.S. Govt. Print. Off., 1967]

xi, 239 p. illus. 28 cm.
Bibliographical footnotes.
1. Police—U.S. I. Title. II. Title: The police.
HV7568.A5 1967   363.2'0973   67-61326
MC#: 1967-10034
SuDocs no.: Pr36.8:L41/P75

380

U.S. *Task Force on the Administration of Justice.*
Task Force report : the courts. [Washington, For sale by the Supt. of Docs., U.S. Govt. Print. Off., 1967]

x, 178 p. illus. 28 cm.
Bibliographical footnotes.
1. Criminal justice, Administration of. 2. Criminal courts—U.S. 3. Criminal procedure—U.S. I. Title. II. Title: The courts.
KF9223.A86   343'.0973'03   67-61471
MC#: 1967-10032
SuDocs no.: Pr36.8:L41/C83

U.S. *Task Force on the Administration of Justice.*
Task Force report : the courts. Westport, Conn. : Greenwood Press, 1978.

x, 178 p., 29 cm.

Reprint of the 1967 ed. published by the U.S. Govt. Print. Off. Includes bibliographical references and index.
1. Criminal justice, Administration of. 2. Criminal courts—U.S. 3. Criminal procedure—U.S. I. Title. II. Title: The courts.
[KF9223.A86]   345'.73'05   77-28367

381

U.S. *Task Force on Corrections.*
Task Force report : corrections. [Washington, For sale by the Supt. of Docs., U.S. Govt. Print. Off., 1967]

xiii, 222 p. illus. 28 cm.
Bibliographical footnotes.
1. Punishment—U.S. I. Title. II. Title: Corrections.
HV9304.A5 1967   364'.9'73   67-61469
MC#: 1967-10031
SuDocs no.: Pr36.8:L41/C81

382

United States. Task Force on Juvenile Delinquency.
Task Force report : juvenile delinquency and youth crime ; report on juvenile justice, and consultants' papers. [Washington, For sale by the Supt. of Docs., U.S. Govt. Print. Off., 1967]

xii, 428 p. illus. 28 cm.
Includes bibliographies.
1. Juvenile delinquency—United States. 2. Juvenile courts—United States. I. Title. II. Title: Juvenile delinquency and youth crime.
HV9304.A5 1967b   364.36'0973   67-61654
                                              MARC
MC#: 1967-11703
SuDocs no.: Pr36.8:L41/J98

383

United States. Task Force on Organized Crime.
Task Force report ; organized crime, annotations and consultants' papers. [Washington, For sale by the Supt. of Docs., U.S. Govt. Print. Off., 1967]

vii, 126 p. illus. 28 cm.
Bibliographical footnotes.
1. Organized crime—United States. I. Title. II. Title: Organized crime.
HV6789.A343   364.1'0973   67-61470
                                              MARC
MC#: 1967-10033
SuDocs no.: Pr36.8:L41/Or3

384

Institute for Defense Analyses.
Task force report : science and technology ; a report to the President's Commission on Law Enforcement and Administration of Justice. [Washington, For sale by the Supt. of Docs., U.S. Govt. Print. Off., 1967]

xiv, 228 p. illus., maps. 28 cm.
1. Criminal justice, Administration of—United States. 2. Police—United States. I. United States. President's Commission on Law Enforcement and Administration of Justice. II. Title. III. Title: Science and technology.
HV8031.I5   364.12'0973   67-61570
MC#: 1967-11704
SuDocs no.: Pr36.8:L41/Sci2

385

United States. Task Force on Assessment of Crime.
Task Force report : crime and its impact—an assessment. [Washington, Task Force on Assessment, the President's Com-

mission on Law Enforcement and Administration of Justice ; for sale by the Supt. of Docs., U.S. Govt. Print. Off., 1967]

xi, 220 p. illus., maps. 28 cm.
On spine: Task Force report : assessment of crime.
Includes bibliographical references.
1. Crime and criminals—United States. I. Title. II. Title : Crime and its impact—an assessment. III. Title: Assessment of crime.

HV6789.A34   364′.9′73   67-61792
                                                              MARC
MC#: 1967-13065
SuDocs no.: Pr36.8:L41/C86/3

386

U.S. *Task Force on Narcotics and Drug Abuse.*
Task Force report : narcotics and drugs abuse ; annotations and consultants' papers. [Washington, For sale by the Supt. of Docs., U.S. Govt. Print. Off., 1967]

vii, 158 p. 28 cm.
Includes bibliographies.
1. Narcotic habit—U.S. 2. Narcotics, Control of—U.S. I. Title. II. Title : Narcotics and drug abuse.
HV5825.A63   67-61713
MC#: 1967-13067
SuDocs no.: Pr36.8:L41/N16

387

United States. Task Force on Drunkenness.
Task Force report : drunkenness ; annotations, consultants' papers, and related materials. [Washington, For sale by the Supt. of Docs., U.S. Govt. Print. Off., 1967]

vii, 131 p. illus. 28 cm.
Bibliography : p. 46-49.
1. Alcoholism—United States. 2. Drunkenness (Criminal law)—United States. I. Title. II. Title: Drunkenness.
HV5292.A36   364.17′3′0973   67-61712
                                                              MARC

MC#: 1967-13066
SuDocs no.: Pr36.8:L41/D84/2

CRIME REPORTS
see
PETERSON REPORTS [Peterson, Russell W.]

CRITICAL MATERIALS REPORT

388

Special Report : critical imported materials. — [Washington] : Council on International Economic Policy : [for sale by the Supt. of Docs., U.S. Govt. Print. Off.], 1974.

iii, 49, 61 p. : graphs ; 27 cm.
1. Raw materials—United States. 2. Raw materials. I. United States. Council on International Economic Policy. II. Title: Critical imported materials.
HF1052.S57   382′.5′0973   75-600863
                                                              MARC

MC#: 1975-01651
SuDocs no.: Pr38.8:In8/Im7

CRONKITE REPORT [Cronkite, E. P.]
389

U.S. *Naval Medical Research Institute.*
Some effects of ionizing radiation on human beings; a report on the Marshallese and Americans accidentally exposed to radiation from fallout and a discussion of radiation injury in the human being, from the Naval Medical Research Institute, U.S. Naval

Radiological Defense Laboratory, and Medical Dept., Brookhaven National Laboratory. Edited by E.P. Cronkite, V.P. Bond, and C.L. Dunham. [Washington] U.S. Atomic Energy Commission, 1956.

viii, 106 p. illus (part col.) diagrs., tables. 27 cm. ([U.S. Atomic Energy Commission] TID 5358)
Includes bibliographies.
1. Radiation—Physiological effect. I. Title. II. Title: Ionizing radiation. (Series)
QC770.U63 no. 5358   612.014482   56-63920
MC#: 1957-461
SuDocs no.: Y3.At7:22/TID5358

CROWDER REPORT [Crowder, Walter Frederick]
see under
O'MAHONEY REPORTS [O'Mahoney, Joseph Christopher]
Thorp. Structure of Industry.

CROWELL REPORT [Crowell, Benedict]
390

U.S. *War dept.*
America's munitions 1917-1918. Report of Benedict Crowell, the assistant secretary of war, director of munitions. Washington, Govt. print. off., 1919.

592 p. incl. tables, diagrs. front., plates (1 fold) 23½ cm.
Most plates printed on both sides.
Contents.—Introduction.—book I. Ordnance.—book II. The air service.—book III. The Engineer corps.—book IV. Chemical warfare.—book V. Quartermaster activities.—book VI. The Construction division.—book VII. The Signal corps.—Conclusion.
1. Munitions. 2. U.S. Army—Supplies and stores. I. Title.
UC263.A53   19-26646
MC#: June 1919-page 707
SuDocs no.: W1.2:M92

CROXTON REPORT [Croxton, Frederick Cleveland]
see under
DILLINGHAM COMMISSION [Dillingham, William Paul]
Children of immigrants in schools.

Statistical review of immigration, 1820-1910.

CRUMPACKER REPORT [Crumpacker, Shepard J.]
391

U.S. *Congress. House. Committee on the Judiciary.*
Providing for the admissibility in certain criminal proceedings of evidence obtained by interception of communications; report to accompany H. R. 8649. [Washington, U.S. Govt. Print. Off., 1954]

6 p. 24 cm. (83d Cong., 2d sess. House of Representatives. Report no. 1461)
Caption title.
1. Wire-tapping. I. Title. (Series: U.S. 83d Cong., 2d sess., 1954. House. Report no. 1461)
                            *364.12351.74   54-61566
MC#: 1954-6767
SuDocs no.: 83d Cong., 2d sess. H. Rept. 1461

CULLOM REPORT [Cullom, Shelby Moore]
392

U.S. *Hawaiian commission.*
. . . Message from the President of the United States, transmitting the report of the Hawaiian commission, appointed in pursuance of the "Joint resolution to provide for annexing the

Hawaiian islands to the United States," approved July 7, 1898; together with a copy of the civil and penal laws of Hawaii . . . Washington, Govt. print. off., 1898.

iii, 164, 560 p. 23 cm. (55th Cong., 3d sess. Senate. Doc. 16) S. M. Cullom, chairman.

Includes: The Laws of Hawaii, compiled by Sidney M. Ballou, and published by authority in 1897, and the session laws of 1898, modified in conformity to the recommendations of the commission.

1. Hawaii—Annexation. 2. Law—Hawaii. I. Cullom, Shelby Moore, 1829-1914. II. Hawaiian islands. Laws, statutes, etc. III. Ballou, Sidney M.

DU627.3.U52   8-25327
MC#: 1898-page 691
SuDocs no.: 55th Cong., 3d sess. S. Doc. 16

CULLUM REPORT [Cullum, Robert M.]
393

U.S. *Dept. of the Interior. Division of Budget and Administrative Management.*

People in motion, the postwar adjustment of the evacuated Japanese Americans. United States Dept. of the Interior, War Agency Liquidation Unit, formerly War Relocation Authority. Washington, U.S. Govt. Print. Off. [1947]

270 p. 26 cm.
"References cited": p. 263-269.
1. Japanese in the U.S. I. Title.
E184.J3U52 1947   325.2520973   47-46105*
MC#: 1947-5629
SuDocs no.: I52.2:J27/7

CURRAN REPORT [Curran, Charles D.]
394

U.S. *Study Commission on the Neches, Trinity, Brazos, Colorado, Guadalupe, San Antonio, Nueces, and San Jacinto River Basins and Intervening Areas.*

The report of the U.S. Study Commission—Texas. [Washington] 1962.

4 pts. illus., maps (part fold., part col.) 28 cm. (87th Cong., 2d sess. House document no. 494)

Contents.—pt. 1. The Commission plan.—pt. 2. Resources and problems.—pt 3. The eight basins.—pt. 4. Summary and recommendations.

1. Water resources development—Texas. (Series: U.S. 87th Cong., 2d sess., 1962. House. Document no. 494)

HD1694.T4A6   333.9109764   62-62496
MC#: 1962-19027
SuDocs no.: 87th Cong., 2d sess. H. Doc. 494

CURRIER STUDY
395

United States. *Office of the Comptroller of the Army.*

Analysis of the operation and maintenance; Army appropriation: final report. Washington: The Comptroller, 1971.

ca. 150 leaves. (ASDIRS; 3904)
Known as the "Currier study."
1. United States. Army—Appropriations and expenditures.I. Title. II. Title: Operation and maintenance, Army appropriations. III. Title: The Currier study. IV. Series.
[UA17.U582]
Dept. of the Army Library
Not Located in Monthly Catalog

CURTIS REPORT [Curtis, Carl Thomas]
see
TOLAN COMMITTEE [Tolan, John Harvey]
National defense migration. Final report . . .

CURTIS REPORTS [Curtis, Edward P.]
396

Mineola, N.Y. Airborne Instruments Laboratory.

National requirements for aviation facilities: 1956-75; final report prepared by Airborne Instruments Laboratory, Aeronautical Research Foundation, and Cornell Aeronautical Laboratory for Edward P. Curtis, special assistant to the President for aviation facilities planning. [Washington, U.S. Govt. Print. Off., 1957]

v. maps, diagrs., tables. 26 cm.
Cover title.
Contents.—v. 1. Summary.—v. 2. Air traffic, by Airborne Instruments Laboratory.—v. 3. Aircraft characteristics. pt. 1 Civil aircraft, by Cornell Aeronautical Laboratory.—
v. 4. Forecast of aviation activity, by Aeronautical Research Foundation.

1. Aeronautics—U.S. 2. Aids to air navigation—U.S. I. Cambridge, Mass. Aeronautical Research Foundation. II. Cornell Aeronautical Laboratory, inc., Buffalo. III. U.S. Special Assistant to the President for Aviation Facilities Planning. IV. Title.

TL521.M48   387.7   57-60756
MC#: 1957-11806
SuDocs no.: Pr34.8:Av5/2/v.1
MC#: 1957-11807
SuDocs no.: Pr34.8:Av5/2/v.3/pt.1
MC#: 1957-11808
SuDocs no.: Pr34.8:Av5/2/v.4
MC#: 1957-14524
SuDocs no.: Pr34.8:Av5/2/v.2

397

U.S. *Executive Office of the President.*

Modernizing the national system of aviation facilities; a plan by the systems engineering team of the Office of Aviation Facilities Planning, the White House. [Washington, U.S. Govt. Print. Off.] 1957.

vii, 64 p. illus. 27 cm.
Cover title.
1. Aids to air navigation—U.S. 2. Air traffic control—U.S. 3. Airways—U.S. I. Title.
TL726.2.A5415   *629.125 629.1325   57-60769 rev
MC#: 1957-11805
SuDocs no.: Pr34.8:Av5/3

CUSHMAN REPORT [Cushman, Robert Eugene]
see
BROWNLOW REPORT [Brownlow, Louis]

DADDARIO REPORT [Daddario, Emilio Q.]
398

United States. Congress. House. Committee on Science and Astronautics. Subcommittee on Science, Research, and Development.

Utilization of Federal laboratories; report. Ninetieth Congress, second session. Washington, U.S. Govt. Print. Off., 1968.

v, 68 p. 24 cm.
At head of title: Committee print.
"Serial U."
Bibliographical footnotes.
1. Laboratories—United States. I. Title.
Q183.3.U55   502'.8   68-67095
                                                    MARC
MC#: 1969-422
SuDocs no.: Y4.Sci2:90-2/U

DANIELIAN REPORT [Danielian, Noobar R.]
399

U.S. *Dept. of commerce.*
  . . . The St. Lawrence survey . . . N.R. Danielian, director, St. Lawrence survey. Washington, U.S. Govt. print. off., 1941.
  7 v. illus., plates (1 fold) maps (part fold.; 1 in pocket) charts, tables. 23 cm.
  At head of title: United States Dept. of commerce. Jesse H. Jones, secretary.
  "Addendum to part VII":1 leaf laid in.
  Contents. — I. History of the St. Lawrence project. — II. Shipping services on the St. Lawrence river. — III. Potential traffic on the St. Lawrence seaway. — IV. The effect of the St. Lawrence seaway upon existing harbors. — V. The St. Lawrence seaway and future transportation requirements. — VI. The economic effects of the St. Lawrence power project. — VII. Summary report of the St. Lawrence survey, including the National defense aspects of the St. Lawrence project.
  1. St. Lawrence river — Navigation. 2. St. Lawrence river — Power utilization. 3. St.Lawrence river — Comm. I. Title.
TC427.S3U48   386.2097   41-50012
MC#: 1941-page 127
SuDocs no.: C1.22:1
MC#: 1941-page 268
SuDocs no.: C1.22:2 and C1.22:6
MC#: 1941-page 620
SuDocs no.: C1.22:5
MC#: 1941-page 790
SuDocs no.: C1.22:4
MC#: 1941-page 1393
SuDocs no.: C1.22:3
MC#: 1942-page166
SuDocs no.: C1.22:7

DAUGHERTY REPORT [Daugherty, Mary]
see
WICKERSHAM COMMISSION [Wickersham, George Woodward]
Report on the cost of crime, no. 12.

DAVENPORT REPORT [Davenport, Donald Hills]
see under
O'MAHONEY REPORTS [O'Mahoney, Joseph Christopher]

DAVENS REPORT [Davens, Edward]
400

U.S. *President's Panel on Mental Retardation.*
  Report of the Task Force on Prevention, Clinical Services, and Residential Care. Edward Davens, chairman, Robert E. Cooke [and others] August, 1962. Washington, Published for the President's Panel on Mental Retardation by the U.S. Dept. of Health, Education, and Welfare, Public Health Service [1963]
  57 p. 27 cm.
  1. Mental deficiency. 2. Mentally handicapped. I. Davens. Edward. II. Title: Task Force on Prevention, Clinical Services, and Residential Care.
RC570.U5   63-62402
MC#: 1963-18273
SuDocs no.: Pr35.8:M52/P92

DAVID REPORT [David, Paul T.]
see
BROWNLOW REPORT [Brownlow, Louis]

DAVIDSON REPORT
401

Davidson, George, 1825-1911.
  Irrigation and reclamation of land for agricultural purposes as now practiced in India, Egypt, Italy, etc., 1875. [Washington, U.S. Govt. Print. Off., 1876?]
  73 p. (U.S. 44th Cong., 1st sess., 1875-1876. Senate Executive document no. 94)
Checklist of United States Public Documents, 1789-1909-page 55
44th Cong., 1st sess. S. Ex. Doc. 94. In Serial no. 1664

DAVIES REPORT [Davies, Paul L.]
402

U.S. *Dept. of the Army. Advisory Committee on Army Organization.*
  Organization of the Army; report. [Washington] 1953.
  1 v. (various pagings) 26 cm.
  Cover title.
  1. U.S. Army — Organization. I. Title.
UA24.A7752   355.3   54-61077
MC#: 1954-3163
SuDocs no.: D101.2:Or3

DAVIS REPORT [Davis, Andrew McFarland]
see under
ALDRICH COMMISSION [Aldrich, Nelson Wilmarth]

DAVIS REPORT [Davis, Arthur Powell]
see
WALKER COMMISSION [Walker, John Grimes]

DAVIS REPORT [Davis, Halford G.]
403

Davis, Halford G.
  . . . Public policy in postwar aviation.Report on public policy in postwar aviation, by Halford G. Davis . . . Washington, U.S. Govt. print. off., 1945.
  vi, 56 p. fold. map. 23 cm. ([U.S.] 79th Cong., 1st sess. Senate. Doc. 56)
  1. Aeronautics, Commercial — U.S. I. Title. II. Title: Postwar aviation.
TL521.D3   387.7   45-36411
MC#: 1945-page 854
SuDocs no.: 79th Cong., 1st sess. S. Doc. 56

DAVIS REPORT [Davis, James C.]
404

U.S. *Congress. House. Committee on Post Office and Civil Service.*
  Legislative control of Federal positions and salaries; report. Washington, U.S. Govt. Print. Off., 1958.
  ix, 24 p. tables. 24 cm. (85th Cong., 2d sess. House report no. 2706)
  1. Civil service — U.S. 2. U.S. — Officials and employees — Salaries, allowances, etc. (Series: U.S. 85th Cong., 2d sess., 1957. House. Report no. 2706)
JK649 1958c   351.1   59-60109 rev
MC#: 1959-306
SuDocs no.: 85th Cong., 2d sess. H. Rept. 2706

DAVIS REPORT [Davis, James John]
see
DONAHEY REPORT [Donahey, Vic]

DAVIS REPORT
405

Davis, John, July 31, 1916-
   Oil and Canada — United States relations; [report prepared for] Canadian-American Committee. [Washington? 1959]
    xii, 36 p. maps, diagrs., tables. 23 cm. (Reports on Canada-United States relations)
    Bibliographical footnotes.
    1. Petroleum industry and trade — Canada. 2. Petroleum industry and trade — U.S. I. Canadian-American Committee. II. Title. (Series)
HD9574.C22D3   338.27282   59-13700
Not located in Monthly Catalog

DAVIS REPORT [Davis, William Hammatt]
    National recovery administration.
    see
ROPER REPORT [Roper, Daniel Calhoun]

DAVIS REPORTS [Davis, William Hammatt]
406

U.S. *President's Commission on Labor Relations in the Atomic Energy Installations.*
   Report. [Washington] U.S. Atomic Energy Commission, 1949.
    13 p. 24 cm.
    William H. Davis, chairman.
    1. Atomic workers.
HD8039.A62U5 1949b   331.1   49-46429*
MC#: 1949-11048
SuDocs no.: Y3.At7:2L11

407

U.S. *President's committee on the cost of living.*
   . . . Report of the President's committee on the cost of living. [Washington] U.S. Govt. print. off., 1945 [i.e. 1946]
    1 p. 1., v, 423 p. incl. tables, diagrs. 23 cm.
    At head of title: Office of economic stabilization.
    William H. Davis, chairman.
    1. Cost and standard of living — U.S. I. Davis, William Hammatt, 1879- II. U.S. Office of economic stabilization.
HD6983.A53 1946   331.831   46-26695
MC#: 1946-page 977
SuDocs no.: Pr32.6002:C82

DeBAKEY REPORT [DeBakey, Michael E.]
408

U.S. *President's Commission on Heart Disease, Cancer and Stroke.*
   A national program to conquer heart disease, cancer and stroke; report to the President. [Washington] 1964-65.
    2 v. illus. 26 cm.
    Vol. 1 is a summary report, while v. 2 consists of subcommittee reports and staff papers.
    Bibliography: v. 1, p. 102-113.
    1. Heart — Diseases. 2. Cancer. 3. Cerebrovascular disease. I. Title.
RC682.U49   65-60405 rev
MC#: 1965-2978, 9861
SuDocs no.: Pr36.8:H35/P94/v. 1-2

DEDRICK REPORT [Dedrick, Calvert Lampert]
    see
BIGGERS REPORT [Biggers, John D.]

DeFOREST REPORT [DeForest, Ralph E.]
409

United States. President's Task Force on the Physically Handicapped.
   A national effort for the physically handicapped; the report of the President's Task Force on the Physically Handicapped. Washington; For sale by the Supt. of Docs., U.S. Govt. Print.Off., 1970.
    vi, 34 p. 24 cm.
    1. Physically handicapped — United States. I. Title.
HV3023.A1P7   362.4'0973   74-609295
                                            MARC
MC#: 1970-17219
SuDocs no.: Pr37.8:P56/R29

DeKNIGHT REPORT [DeKnight, William F.]
410

U.S. *Register of the Treasury.*
   . . . History of the currency of the country and of the loans of the United States from the earliest period to June 30, 1900. Prepared by William F. DeKnight . . . under the direction of J.F. Tillman, register of the Treasury. [2d ed., with Appendix, prepared under the direction of Judson W. Lyons, register of the Treasury] Washington, Govt. print. off., 1900.
    277 p. 31 cm. (Treasury department. Document no. 1943. Second edition . . .)
    1. Money — U.S. — Hist. 2. Debts, Public — U.S. I. DeKnight, William F. II. Title.
HG501.A3 1900   2-1615
MC#: Oct. 1900-page 525
SuDocs no.: T32.2:C93/2

DELANEY REPORT [Delaney, James J.]
411

U.S. *Congress. House. Select Committee to Investigate the Use of Chemicals in Food Products.*
   Investigation of the use of chemicals in food products; report pursuant to H. Res. 323, 81st Cong., 1st sess. [Washington, U.S. Govt. Print. Off., 1951]
    11 p. 24 cm. (81st Cong., 2d sess. House of Representatives. Report no. 3254)
    Caption title.
    1. Food adulteration and inspection. (Series: U.S. 81st Cong., 2d sess., 1950-51. House. Report no. 3254)
TX531.U5 1951b   614.31   51-60254
MC#: 1951-3172
SuDocs no.: 81st Cong., 2d sess. H. Rept. 3254

DELANO REPORT [Delano, Frederic Adrian]
412

U.S. *National planning board.*
   . . . Final report-1933-34 . . . Washington, U.S. Govt. print. off., 1934.
    vii, 119 p. incl. maps, tab., diagr. 29 cm.
    At head of title: National planning board. Federal emergency administration of public works. Harold L. Ickes, administrator.
    Frederick A. Delano, chairman.
    1. U.S. — Economic policy. 2. Industry and state — U.S. I. Delano, Frederic Adrian, 1863-
HC106.3.A5 1934h   330.973   34-28262
- - - - - Copy 2.
MC#: Dec. 1934-page 455
SuDocs no.: F3.F31/4:2N21

DENBY REPORT [Denby, Charles]

see

SCHURMAN REPORT [Schurman, Jacob Gould]

DENTON REPORT [Denton, Robert Harold]

see under

O'MAHONEY REPORTS [O'Mahoney, Joseph Christopher]

Stone. Toward more housing.

DERTHICK REPORTS [Derthick, Lawrence Gridley]

413

U.S. *Education Mission to the U.S.S.R.*

Soviet commitment to education; report of the first official U.S. Education Mission to the U.S.S.R., with an analysis of recent educational reforms. [Washington] U.S. Dept. of Health, Education, and Welfare, Office of Education [1959]

xi, 135 p. illus., ports., map. 24 cm. ([U.S. Office of Education] Bulletin 1959, no. 16)

1. Education—Russia—1945- I. Title. (Series)

L111.A6 1959, no. 16   HEW59-82

- - - - - Copy 2.

LA832.U65

MC#: 1959-14590

SuDocs no.: FS5.3:959/16

414

U.S. *Office of Education.*

Status report on the National defense education act at midpoint: June 1960. Submitted to Subcommittee on Special Education by Lawrence G. Derthick, Commissioner of Education, U.S. Dept. of Health, Education, and Welfare. Committee on Education and Labor, House of Representatives, Eighty-sixth Congress, second session. Washington, U.S. Govt. Print. Off., 1960.

ii, 21 p. tables. 24 cm.

At head of title: Committee print.

1. National defense education act. I. Derthick, Lawrence Gridley, 1905- II. U.S. Congress. House. Committee on Education and Labor.

LB2825.A49 1960   379.12   60-64658

MC#: 1961-7136

SuDocs no.: Y4.Ed8/1:N21d/2

DEWEY REPORT [Dewey, George]

see

SCHURMAN REPORT [Schurman, Jacob Gould]

DEWEY REPORTS [Dewey, Davis Rich]

see under

ALDRICH COMMISSION [Aldrich, Nelson Wilmarth]

Holdsworth. First and second banks of the United States.

Dewey. State banking before the civil war.

DeWITT REPORT [De Witt, John Lesesne]

415

U.S. *Army. Western defense command and fourth army.*

Final report, Japanese evacuation from the West coast.1942. Washington, U.S. Govt.print. off., 1943.

xxiii, 618 p. incl. plates, tables, diagrs. maps (part fold) 23½ cm.

Letterhead (p. vii): Headquarters Western defense command and fourth army. Office of the commanding general.

Signed (p. x): J. L. DeWitt, lieutenant general, U.S. army, commanding.

1. World war, 1939- —Evacuation of civilians. 2. Japanese in the U.S. 3. World war, 1939- —U.S. I. De Witt, John Lesesne, 1880-

D769.8.A6A37 1942   940.547273   44-40486

MC#: 1944-page 215

SuDocs no.: W2.2:J27

DICKENS REPORT [Dickens, Paul DeWitt]

see under

O'MAHONEY REPORTS [O'Mahoney, Joseph Christopher]

Gilbert. Export prices and export cartels.

DIES COMMITTEE [Dies, Martin]

416

U.S. *Congress. House. Special committee on un-American activities. 1938-*

. . . Investigation of un-American propaganda activities in the United States . . . Report. "Pursuant to H. Res. 282, 75th Cong." and H. Res. 26, 76th Cong. . . . [Washington, U.S. Govt. print. off., 1941]

25 p. incl. tab. 23 cm. (77th Cong., 1st sess. House. Rept.1)

Union calendar no. 1

Submitted by Mr. Dies. Committed to the Committee of the whole House on the state of the Union and ordered printed January 3, 1941.

Running title: Un-American propaganda activities.

1. National socialism. 2. Propaganda, German. 3. Germans in the U.S. 4. Communism. 5. Propaganda, Russian. 6. Fascism. 7. Propaganda, Italian. I. Dies, Martin, 1901- II. Title. III. Title: Un-American propaganda activities.

E743.5.A5 1941   335.0973   41-50015

MC#: 1941-page 34

SuDocs no.: 77th Cong., 1st sess. H. Rept. 1

417

U.S. *Congress. House. Special committee on un-American activities (1938-1944)*

. . . Investigation of un-American propaganda activities in the United States. Report of the Special committee on un-American activities, House of representatives, Seventy-eighth Congress, second session, on H. Res. 282, to investigate (1) the extent, character, and objects of un-American propaganda activities in the United States, (2) the diffusion within the United States of subversive and un-American propaganda that is instigated from foreign countries or of a domestic origin and attacks the principle of the form of government as guaranteed by our Constitution, and (3) all other questions in relation thereto that would aid Congress in any necessary remedial legislation. Report on the C.I.O. Political action committee . . . Washington, U.S. Govt. print. off., 1944.

iii p., 1 l., 215 p. 23½ cm. ([U.S.] 78th Cong., 2d sess. House. Rept. 1311)

Running title: Un-American propaganda activities.

Submitted by Mr. Dies from the Special committee on un-American activities.

1. Congress of industrial organizations. Political action committee. 2. U.S.—Pol. & govt.—1933-1945. 3. Communism—U.S.-1917- I. Dies, Martin, 1901- II. Title: Un-American propaganda activities.

HD8055.C75U6 1944c   335   44-40794

MC#: 1944-page 509

SuDocs no.: 78th Cong., 2d sess. H. Rept. 1311

418

U.S. *Congress. House. Special committee on un-American activities (1938-1944)*

. . . Investigation of un-American propaganda activities in the United States. Report of the Special committee on un-American activities, House of representatives, Seventy-eighth Congress, second session, on H. Res. 282, to investigate (1) the extent, character, and objects of un-American propaganda activities in the United States, (2) the diffusion within the United States of subversive and un-American propaganda that is instigated from foreign countries or of a domestic origin and attacks the principle of the form of government as guaranteed by our Constitution, and (3) all other questions in relation thereto that would aid Congress in any necessary remedial legislation. Report on the Peace now movement . . . Washington, U.S. Govt. print. off., 1944.

ii, 13 p. 23 ½ cm. ([U.S.] 78th Cong., 2d sess. House. Rept. 1161)

Submitted by Mr. Dies from the Special committee on un-American activities.

1. Collett, John Albert, 1911- 2. Peace now movement. I. Dies, Martin, 1901-
JX1908.U6P4 1944a   351.75   44-40650
MC#: 1944-page 252
SuDocs no.: 78th Cong., 2d sess. H. Rept. 1161

DIES COMMITTEE [Dies, Martin]
see also
STARNES REPORT [Starnes, Joe]
VOORHIS REPORT [Voorhis, Horace Jeremiah]
WOOD REPORT [Wood, John Stephens]

DILLINGHAM COMMISSION [Dillingham, William Paul]

Reports of the Dillingham Commission are filed according to the contents note of the first entry. Other related reports are interfiled.

419

U.S. *Immigration commission, 1907-1910.*
. . . Reports of the Immigration commission . . . Washington, Govt. print. off., 1911.

41 v. maps, tables, diagrs. 23 cm.
William P. Dillingham, chairman.
Published as Senate documents of the 61st Congress, 2d and 3d sessions. A general index was announced, as v. 42, to be Senate doc. 785, 61st Cong., 3d sess. It has not been printed.
Contents.—[v. 1-2] Abstracts of reports of the Immigration commission (in two volumes) (61st Cong., 3d sess. Senate. Doc. 747)—[v. 3] Statistical review of immigration, 1820-1910. Distribution of immigrants, 1850-1900. [Prepared by Fred C. Croxton] (61st Cong., 3d sess. Senate. Doc. 756)—[v. 4] Emigration conditions in Europe. (61st Cong., 3d sess. Senate. Doc. 748)—[v. 5] Dictionary of races or peoples. [Prepared by Daniel and Elnora C. Folkmar] (61st Cong., 3d sess. Senate. Doc. 662)—[v. 6-25] Immigrants in industries (in twenty-five parts) [Pt. 1-23, by W. J. Lauck; pt. 24, by A. E. Cance; pt. 25, by H. A. Millis] (61st Cong., 2d sess. Senate. Doc. 633)—[v. 26-27] Immigrants in cities: a study of the population of selected districts in New York, Chicago, Philadelphia, Boston, Cleveland, Buffalo, and Milwaukee. [Prepared by Emanuel A. Goldenweiser and Mary L. Mark, assisted by Nellie F. Sheets] (61st Cong., 2d sess. Senate. Doc. 338)—[v. 28] Occupation of the first and second generations of immigrants in the United States. Fecundity of immigrant women. Prepared by Joseph A. Hill, assisted by Julius H. Parmelee] (61st Cong., 2d sess. Senate. Doc. 282)—[v. 29-33] The children of immigrants in schools (in five volumes) [Prepared from data collected by Roland P. Falkner: I. Summary, by Fred C. Croxton; II-V. General tables] (61st Cong., 3d sess. Senate. Doc. 749)—[v. 34-35] Immigrants as charity seekers. [Prepared by Jessie C. Lloyd, assisted by Francis H. McLean]

(61st Cong., 3d sess. Senate. Doc. 665)—[v. 36] Immigration and crime. [Prepared by Leslie Hayford] (61st Cong., 3d sess. Senate. Doc. 750)—[v. 37] Steerage conditions, importation and harboring of women for immoral purposes, immigrant homes and aid societies, immigrant banks. [Report on steerage conditions, by Anna Herkner; on immigrant homes and aid societies, by Martha E. Dodson: on immigrant banks, by W. K. Ramsey, jr.] (61st Cong., 3d sess. Senate. Doc. 753)—[v. 38] Changes in bodily form of descendants of immigrants. (Final report) [Prepared by Franz Boas] (61st Cong., 2d sess. Senate. Doc. 208)—[v. 39] Immigration legislation. 1. Federal immigration legislation. 2. Digest of immigration decisions. 3. Steerage legislation, 1819-1908. 4. State immigration and alien laws. [Prepared by Frank L. Shaw] (61st Cong., 3d sess. Senate. Doc. 758)—[v. 40] The immigration situation in other countries: Canada, Australia, New Zealand, Argentina, Brazil. [Prepared by W. W. Husband, Mary Helen Eagan, and Mary Mills West] (61st Cong., 3d sess. Senate. Doc. 761)—[v. 41] Statements and recommendations submitted by societies and organizations interested in the subject of immigration. (61st Cong., 3d sess. Senate. Doc. 764)

1. U.S.—Emig. & immig. 2. Emigration and immigration. 3. Emigration and immigration law—U.S. I. Dillingham, William Paul, 1843-1923. II. Title.
JV6415.A3   14-19769

420

U.S. *Immigration commission, 1907-1910.*
. . . Abstracts of reports of the Immigration commission, with conclusions and recommendations and views of the minority. (In two volumes) Washington, Govt. print. off., 1911.

2 v. 23 ½ cm. (Reports of the Immigration commission, v. 1-2)
61st Cong., 3d sess. Senate. Doc. 747.
William P. Dillingham, Chairman.
"Views of the minority" by William S. Bennet.
Referred to the Committee on immigration and ordered printed, Dec. 5, 1910.
List of reports of the immigration commission, p. iv.
Included are complete reports on: Immigration conditions in Hawaii; Immigration and insanity; Immigrants in charity hospitals; Alien seamen and stowaways; Contract labor and induced and assisted immigration; The Greek padrone system in the United States; Peonage.
1. U.S.—Emig. & immig. 2. Emigration and immigration law—U.S. 3. Hawaiian Islands—Emig. & immig. 4. Aliens—U.S. 5. Sailors. 6. Stowaways. 7. Contract labor-U.S. 8. Padrone system. 9. Peonage—U.S. I. Dillingham, William Paul, 1843-1923. II. Bennet, William S. III. Title.
JV6415.A4 1911a   11-35034
- - - - - Copy 2.
JV6417.C07a
MC#: Feb. 1911-pages 431-432
      Mar. 1911-page 516
      Dec. 1911-page 311

421

U.S. *Immigration commission, 1907-1910.*
. . . Abstract of the report on immigration and crime . . . Washington, Govt. print. off., 1911.

65 p. incl. tables. 23 ½ cm.
At head of title: The Immigration commission.
W.P. Dillingham, chairman.
"List of reports of the Immigration commission": p. 3.
1. U.S.—Emig. & immig. 2. Crime and criminals—U.S. I. Dillingham, William Paul, 1843-1923.
HV6181.U5   11-35230
- - - - - Copy 2.
MC#: Feb. 1911-page 431
SuDocs no.: Y3.Im6:C86

422

U.S. *Immigration commission,* 1907-1910.
. . . Abstract of the report on recent immigrants in agriculture . . . Washington, Govt. print. off., 1911.

75 p. incl. tables. 23 cm.
At head of title: The immigration commission.
On cover: Prepared by Alexander E. Cance, PH.D. Department of agricultural economics, Massachusetts agricultural college.
Senator William P. Dillingham, chairman.
"List of reports of the Immigration commission": p. 3.
1. U.S.—Emig. & immig. 2. Agriculture—U.S. 3. Agricultural laborer—U.S. I. Cance, Alexander E. II. Dillingham, William Paul, 1843-1923.
JV6606.A4A5 1911   11-15357
MC#: Mar. 1911-page 516
SuDocs no.: Y3.Im6:Ag8

423

U.S. *Immigration commission,* 1907-1910.
. . . Abstract of the report on the children of immigrants in schools . . . Washington, U.S. Govt. Print. Off., 1911.

99 p. 23 cm.
At head of title: The Immigration Commission
"List of reports of the Immigration Commission": p. 3.
1. Immigrant children—Education.
LC3731.U5   E11-1595
MC#: Feb. 1911-page 431
SuDocs no.: Y3.Im6:C43

424

U.S. *Immigration commission,* 1907-1910.
. . . Statistical·review of immigration, 1820-1910. Distribution of immigrants, 1850-1900 . . . Washington, Govt. print. off., 1911.

viii, 587 p. 23 cm. (Reports of the Immigration commission, v. 3)
61st Cong., 3d sess. Senate. Doc. 756.
Referred to the Committee on immigration and ordered printed, with illustrations, December 5, 1910.
William P. Dillingham, chairman.
Prepared for the commission by Fred C. Croxton.
"List of reports of the Immigration commission": p. iii.
1. U.S.—Emig. & immig. 2. U.S.—Foreign population. I. Dillingham, William Paul, 1843-1923. II. Croxton, Frederick Cleveland, 1871- III. Title. IV. Title: Distribution of immigrants, 1850-1900.
JV6415.A3 v.3   13-35052
- - - - - Copy 2.
JV6461.A8 1911
MC#: Feb. 1913-page 418
SuDocs no.: 61st Cong., 3d sess. S. Doc. 756

425

U.S. *Immigration commission,* 1907-1910.
. . . Emigration conditions in Europe . . . Washington, Govt. print. off., 1911.

x, 424 p. diagr. 23½ cm. (Reports of the Immigration commission, v. 4)
61st Cong., 3d sess. Senate. Doc. 748.
Referred to the Committee on immigration and ordered printed, with illustrations, December 5, 1910.
William P. Dillingham, chairman.
"List of Reports of the Immigration commission": p. iii.
1. Emigration and immigration. 2. U.S.—Emig. & immig. I. Dillingham, William Paul, 1843-1923. II. Title.
JV6415.A3 v. 4   12-40009

- - - - - Copy 2.
JV6080.U6
MC#: Aug. 1912-page 106
SuDocs no.: 61st Cong., 3d sess. S. Doc. 748

426

U.S. Immigration commission, 1907-1910.
. . . European immigration, 1899-1909 . . . Table showing European immigration, by race or people, into the United States from 1899 to 1909. [Washington, Govt. print. off., 1912]

1 p. 24 cm. (62d Cong., 2d sess. Senate. Doc. 401)
Presented by Mr. Lodge. Ordered printed March 11, 1912.
1. Emigration and immigration. 2. U.S.—Emig. & immig. I. Lodge, Henry Cabot, 1850- II. Title.
JV6461.A8 1909d   12-35344
- - - - - Copy 2.
Not located in Monthly Catalog
SuDocs no.: 62d Cong., 2d sess. S. Doc. 401

427

U.S. *Immigration commission,* 1907-1910.
. . . Dictionary of races or peoples . . . Washington, Govt. print. off., 1911.

vii, 150 p. incl. maps. 2 fold. maps. 23½ cm. (Reports of the Immigration commission, v. 5)
61st Cong., 3d sess. Senate. Doc. 662.
William P. Dillingham, chairman.
Prepared for the commission by Dr. Daniel Folkmar, assisted by Dr. Elnora C. Folkmar.
"Selected bibliography of general works": p. 8-12.
1. Ethnology—Dictionaries. 2. Ethnology—Bibl. 3. U.S.—Emig. & immig. I. Dillingham, William Paul, 1843-1923. II. Folkmar, Daniel, 1861- III. Folkmar, Elnora Cuddeback, 1863- IV. Title.
JV6415.A3 v. 5   12-35140
- - - - - Copy 2.
MC#: Feb. 1912-page 477
SuDocs no.: 61st Cong., 3d sess. S. Doc. 662

428

U.S. *Immigration commission,* 1907-1910.
. . . Immigrants in industries. (In twenty-five parts) . . . Washington, Govt. print. off., 1911.

20 v. 23 cm. (Reports of the Immigration commission, v. 6-25)
61st Cong., 2d sess. Senate. Doc. 633.
William P. Dillingham, chairman.
Pt. 1-23 by W.J. Lauck; pt. 24 by A.E. Cance; pt. 25 by H.A. Millis.
Contents.—pt. 1 (v. 6-7) Bituminous coal mining.—pt. 2 (v. 8-9) Iron and steel manufacturing.—pt. 3-4 (v. 10) Cotton goods manufacturing in the north Atlantic states. Woolen and worsted goods manufacturing.—pt. 5-7 (v. 11) Silk goods manufacturing and dyeing. Clothing manufacturing. Collar, cuff, and shirt manufacturing.—pt. 8-10 (v. 12) Leather manufacturing. Boot and shoe manufacturing. Glove manufacturing.—pt. 11 (v. 13) Slaughtering and meat packing.—pt. 12-13 (v. 14) Glass manufacturing. Agricultural implement and vehicle manufacturing.—pt. 14-16 (v. 15) Cigar and tobacco manufacturing. Furniture manufacturing. Sugar refining.—pt. 17-20 (v. 16) Copper mining and smelting. Iron ore mining. Anthracite coal mining. Oil refining.—pt. 21-22 (v. 17-18) Diversified industries: pt. 21, General tables; pt. 22, The floating immigrant labor supply.—pt. 23 (v. 19-20) Summary report on immigrants in manufacturing and mining.—pt. 24 (v. 21-22) Recent immigrants in agriculture.—pt. 25 (v. 23-24) Japanese and other immigrant races in the Pacific Coast and Rocky Mountain states: v. 1, Japanese and East Indians; v. 2, Agriculture; v. 3, Diversified industries.

1. U.S.—Emig. & immig. 2. U.S.—Indus. I. Dillingham, William Paul, 1843-1923. II. Lauck, William Jett, 1879- III. Cance, Alexander E. IV. Millis, H.A. V. Title.
JV6415.A3   11-35989
- - - - - 2d set.
HD8081.A3
Parts 1, 5-13, 17-20, 22
MC#: Jan. 1912-page 389
Parts 2 (vol. 9), 3-4, 14-16
MC#: Feb. 1912-page 477
Part 2 (vol. 8)
MC#: Mar. 1912-page 567
Part 21 (vol. 17)
MC#: Dec. 1911-page 312
Part 21 (vol. 18)
MC#: Jan. 1912-page 389
Part 23
MC#: June 1912-page 849
Part 24
MC#: Dec. 1912-page 277
Part 25 (vol. 23)
MC#: Apr. 1912-page 657
Part 25 (vols. 24-25)
MC#: May 1912-page 759
SuDocs no.: 61st Cong., 2d sess. S. Doc. 633

429

U.S. *Immigration commission,* 1907-1910.
. . . Immigrants in cities: a study of the population of selected districts in New York, Chicago, Philadelphia, Boston, Cleveland, Buffalo, and Milwaukee . . . Washington, Govt. print.off., 1911.

2 v. tables, diagrs. 23½ cm. (Reports of the Immigration commission. v. 26-27)
61st Cong., 2d sess. Senate. Doc. 338.
William P. Dillingham, chairman.
Prepared by E. A. Goldenweiser and Mary Louise Mark, assisted by Nellie F. Sheets.
"List of Reports of the Immigration commission": p. iii.
Vol. II: Tables.
1. U.S.—Foreign population. I. Dillingham, William Paul, 1843-1923. II. Goldenweiser, Emanual Alexandrovich, 1883- III. Mark, Mary Louise. IV. Title.
JV6415.A3 v. 26-27   12-35107
- - - - Copy 2.
JV6475.A5 1911
MC#: Jan. 1912-page 389
SuDocs no.: 61st Cong., 2d sess. S. Doc. 338

430

U.S. *Immigration commission,* 1907-1910.
. . . Occupations of the first and second generations of immigrants in the United States. Fecundity of immigrant women . . . Washington, Govt. print. off., 1911.

v, 826 p. 23 cm. (Reports of the Immigration commission, v. 28)
61st Cong., 2d sess. Senate. Doc. 282.
William P. Dillingham, chairman.
Prepared under the direction of the commission by Joseph A. Hill, chief statistician, Division of revision and results, Bureau of the census. The report entitled Fecundity of immigrant women is based on unpublished census schedules of the Twelfth census, and prepared by Joseph A. Hill, assisted by Julius H. Parmelee.
1. U.S.—Emig. & immig. 2. U.S.—Occupations. 3. Fecundity. 4. U.S.—Statistics, Vital. I. Dillingham, William Paul, 1843-1923. II. Hill, Joseph Adna, 1860- III. Parmelee, Julius H. IV. Title.
JV6415.A3 v. 28   12-35827

- - - - - Copy 2.
JV6471.A5 1911
MC#: June 1912-page 849
SuDocs no.:61st Cong., 2d sess. S. Doc. 282

431

U.S. *Immigration commission,* 1907-1910.
. . . The children of immigrants in schools. (In five volumes . . .) Washington, Govt. print. off., 1911.

5 v. tables. 23 cm. (Reports of the Immigration commission, v. 29-33)
61st Cong., 3d sess. Senate Doc. 749.
William P. Dillingham, chairman.
Vol. I, prepared by Fred C. Croxton and Frances W. Simonds, is a summary of data collected in 37 cities by Roland P. Falkner. Vol. II-V contain general tables in which the various data are shown by cities, with explanatory text and comment by Dr. Falkner.
1. U.S.—Emig. & immig. 2. U.S.—Foreign population. 3. School attendance—U.S. 4. Schools—U.S. 5. Universities and colleges—U.S. I. Dillingham, William Paul, 1843-1923. II. Falkner, Roland Post, 1866- III. Croxton, Frederick Cleveland, 1871-IV. Simonds, Frances W. V. Title.
JV6415.A3 v. 29-33   12-35965
- - - - - Copy 2.
LC3731.A5 1911
MC#: Feb. 1913-page 418 (vol. 1)
      July 1912-page 34 (vols. 2, 3, 5)
      Aug. 1912-page 106 (vol. 4)
SuDocs no.: 61st Cong., 3d sess. S. Doc. 749

432

U.S. *Immigration commission,* 1907-1910.
. . . Immigrants as charity seekers (in two volumes) Washington, Govt. print. off., 1911.

2 v. tables. 23½ cm. (Reports of the Immigration commission. v. 34-35).
61st Cong., 3d sess. Senate. Doc. 665.
William P. Dillingham, chairman.
Ordered printed December 5, 1910.
Report prepared by Jessie C. Lloyd, special agent of the Immigration commission; inquiry conducted with the assistance of Francis H. McLean, field secretary of the Field dept. for the extension of organized charity in the United States. Vol. 2. General tables.
1. U.S.—Emig. & immig. 2. U.S.—Foreign population. 3. Charities—U.S. I. Dillingham, William Paul, 1843-1923. II. Lloyd, Jessie C. III. Title.
JV6415.A3 v. 34-35   11-35020
- - - - - Copy 2.
HV4010.A5 1911
MC#: Jan. 1912-page 389
SuDocs no.: 61st Cong., 3d sess. S. Doc. 665

433

U.S. *Immigration commission,* 1907-1910.
. . . Immigration and crime . . . Washington, Govt. print. off., 1911.

vii, 449 p. 23 cm. (Reports of the Immigration commission, v. 36)
61st Cong., 3d sess. Senate. Doc. 750.
William P. Dillingham, chairman.
Prepared under the direction of the commission by Leslie Hayford, special agent.
1. U.S.—Emig. & immig. 2. Criminal statistics—U.S. I. Dillingham, William Paul, 1843-1923. II. Hayford, Leslie. III. Title.
JV6415.A3 v. 36   12-35824

- - - - Copy 2.
HV6181.U5 1911 a
MC#: June 1912-page 849
SuDocs no.: 61st Cong., 3d sess. S. Doc. 750

434

U.S. *Immigration commission,* 1907-1910.
. . . Steerage conditions, importation and harboring of women for immoral purposes, immigrant homes and aid societies, immigrant banks . . . Washington, Govt. print. off., 1911.
v, 350 p. fold tab. 23 cm. (Reports of the Immigration commission, v. 37)
61st Cong., 3d sess. Senate. Doc. 753.
William P. Dillingham, chairman.
Ordered printed December 5, 1910.
Report on steerage conditions by Miss Anna Herkner; on immigrant homes and aid societies, by Martha E. Dodson; on immigrant banks, by W. K. Ramsey, jr., special agents of the commission.
1. Steamboats—Passenger accommodations. 2. Prostitution. 3. U.S.—Emig. & immig. 4. Banks and banking—U.S. I. Dillingham, William Paul, 1843-1923. II. Herkner, Anna. III. Dodson, Martha E. IV. Ramsey, W. K., jr. V. Title.
JV6415.A3 v. 37   11-35990
- - - - Copy 2.
JV6481 1911
MC#: Dec. 1911-page 312
SuDocs no.: 61st Cong., 3d sess. S. Doc. 753

435

U.S. *Immigration commission,* 1907-1910.
. . . Steerage conditions. Partial report, on behalf of the Immigration commission, on steerage conditions . . . Washington, Govt. print. off., 1909.
46 p. 23 cm. (61st Cong., 2d sess. Senate. Doc. 206)
Presented by Mr. Dillingham, chairman; referred to Committee on immigration and ordered printed, December 13, 1909.
Laws of the United States relating to steerage accommodations: p. 40-46.
1. Steamboats—Passenger accommodation. I. Dillingham, William Paul, 1843-1923.
HE601.U4A5 1909   9-35970
- - - - Copy 2.
MC#: Dec. 1909-page 243
SuDocs no.: 61st Cong., 2d sess. S. Doc. 206

436

U.S. *Immigration commission,* 1907-1910.
. . . Importing women for immoral purposes. Report from the Immigration commission transmitting, in response to Senate resolution no. 86, by Senator Lodge, a partial report to Congress on the importation and harboring of women for immoral purposes . . . Washington, Govt. print. off., 1909.
iii, 3-61, p. 23 cm. (61st Cong., 2d sess. Senate. Doc. 196)
Presented by Mr. Dillingham, chairman. Ordered printed, December 10, 1909.
1. Prostitution.
HQ281.U6   9-35971
- - - - Copy 2.
MC#: Dec. 1909-page 243
SuDocs no.: 61st Cong., 2d sess. S. Doc. 196

437

U.S. *Immigration commission,* 1907-1910.
. . . Immigrant banks . . . Washington, Govt. print. off., 1910.

167 p. 23 cm. (61st Cong., 2d sess. Senate. Doc. 381)
At head of title: . . . The Immigration commission.
Referred to Committee on immigration and ordered printed, Feb. 24, 1910.
W. P. Dillingham, chairman.
Prepared by W. K. Ramsey, jr., special agent of the Commission, under direction of W. Jett Lauck, superintendent of agents.
1. U.S.—Emig. & immig. 2. Banks and banking—U.S. I. Ramsey, W. K., jr. II. Dillingham, William Paul, 1843-1923. III. U.S. 61st Cong., 2d sess., 1909-1910. Senate.
HG2002.A5 1910   10-35994
- - - - Copy 2.
MC#: Sept. 1910-page 113
SuDocs no.: 61st Cong., 2d sess. S. Doc. 381

438

U.S. *Immigration commission,* 1907-1910.
. . . Changes in bodily form of descendants of immigrants. (Final report) . . . Washington, Govt. print. off., 1911.
xii, 573 p. incl. tables, diagrs. 23½ cm. (Reports of the Immigration commission. v. 38)
61st Cong., 2d sess. Senate. Doc. 208.
William P. Dillingham, chairman.
Prepared for the Commission by Franz Boas.
A partial report on this subject, by the same author, was transmitted to Congress December 16, 1909. (S. doc. no. 208, 61st Cong., 2d sess.)
Ordered reprinted, with corrections and illustrations, June 8, 1911.
1. U.S.—Foreign population. 2. Anthropometry—U.S. I. Dillingham, William Paul, 1843-1923. II. Boas, Franz, 1858- III. Title.
JV6415.A3 v. 38   12-35066
- - - - Copy 2.
GN58.U5A4 1911
MC#: Jan. 1912-page 388
SuDocs no.: 61st Cong., 2d sess. S. Doc. 208

439

U.S. *Immigration commission,* 1907-1910.
. . . Changes in bodily form of descendants of immigrants . . . Washington, Govt. print. off., 1910.
ii, 113 p. diagrs. 23 cm. (61st Cong., 2d sess. Senate. Doc. 208)
At head of title: . . . The Immigration commission.
Presented by Mr. Dillingham, referred to Committee on immigration, and ordered printed, December 16,1909.
Based on investigations by Franz Boas, chiefly among Sicilians and east European Hebrews in New York public schools.
1. U.S.—Foreign population. 2. Anthropometry—U.S. I. Boas, Franz, 1858-
GN58.U5A4 1910   10-35609
- - - - Copy 2.
MC#: Apr. 1910-page 611
SuDocs no.: 61st Cong., 2d sess. S. Doc. 208

440

U.S. *Immigration commission,* 1907-1910.
. . . Immigration legislation. 1. Federal immigration legislation. 2. Digest of immigration decisions. 3. Steerage legislation, 1819-1908. 4. State immigration and alien laws . . . Washington, Govt.print. off., 1911.
vi, 956 p. 23 cm. (Reports of the Immigration commission, v. 39)
61st Cong., 3d sess. Senate. Doc. 758.
William P. Dillingham, chairman.
Prepared under the direction of the commission by Frank L. Shaw.

1. Emigration and immigration law—U.S. 2. U.S.—Emig. &
immig. I. Dillingham, William Paul, 1843-1923. II. Shaw, Frank
L.
JV6415.A3 v. 39   12-35845
- - - - - Copy 2.
JV6421.A5 1911
MC#: June 1912-page 849
SuDocs no.: 61st Cong., 3d sess. S. Doc. 758

441

U.S. *Immigration commission,* 1907-1910.
. . The immigration situation in other countries: Canada,
Australia, New Zealand, Argentina, Brazil . . . Washington,
Govt. print. off., 1911.
    ix, 229 p. 23½ cm. (Reports of the Immigration commission.
v. 40)
    61st Cong., 3d sess. Senate. Doc. 761.
    William P. Dillingham, chairman.
    Ordered printed Dec. 5, 1910.
    That part of the report which deals with Canada, prepared by
W. W. Husband, is a revision of "The immigration situation in
Canada," pub. 1910 as Senate doc. 469, 61st Cong., 3d sess. The
part relating to Australia and New Zealand was prepared by Mary
Helen Eagan, and that relating to Argentina and Brazil by Mary
Mills West.
    1. Canada—Emig. & immig. 2. Australia—Emig. & immig.
3. New Zealand—Emig. & immig. 4. Argentine Republic—Emig.
& immig. 5. Brazil—Emig. & immig. I. Dillingham, William
Paul, 1843-1923. II. Husband, Walter W. III. Eagan, Mary
Helen. IV. West, Mary Mills.
JV6415.A3 v. 40   11-35019
- - - - - Copy 2.
JV6033.U6 1911
MC#: Dec. 1911-page 312
SuDocs no.: 61st Cong., 3d sess. S. Doc. 761

442

U.S. *Immigration commission,* 1907-1910.
. . . The immigration situation in Canada. Presented by Mr.
Dillingham . . . Washington, Govt. print. off., 1910.
    218 p. 23½ cm. (61st Cong., 2d sess. Senate. Doc. 469)
    Ordered printed April 1, 1910.
    Prepared by W. W. Husband.
    1. Canada—Emig. & immig. I. Dillingham, William Paul,
1843-1923. II. Husband, Walter W. III. Title.
JV7225.U6   10-35862
- - - - - Copy 2.
MC#: June 1910-page 799
SuDocs no.: 61st Cong., 2d sess. S. Doc. 469

443

U.S. *Immigration commission,* 1907-1910.
. . . Statements and recommendations submitted by societies
and organizations interested in the subject of immigration . . . Washington, Govt. print. off., 1911.
    vii, 431 p. 23 cm. (Reports of the Immigration commission,
v. 41)
    61st Cong., 3d sess. Senate. Doc. 764.
    William P. Dillingham, chairman. Referred to the Commit-
tee on immigration and ordered printed Dec. 5, 1910.
    Statements of Committee on information for aliens, Sons of
the American revolution; Council of Jewish women; Immigrants'
protective league; International committee of the Young men's
Christian associations; American federation of labor, etc., etc.
    "List of reports of the Immigration commission": p. iii.
    1. U.S.—Emig. & immig. 2. Aliens—U.S. 3. Emigration and

immigration law—U.S. 4. Naturalization--U.S. I. Dillingham,
William Paul, 1843-1923. II. Title.
JV6415.A3 v. 41   13-35114
- - - - - Copy 2.
JV6415.A4 1911b
MC#: Feb. 1913-page 418
SuDocs no.: 61st Cong., 3d sess. S. Doc. 764

444

U.S. *Immigration commission,* 1907-1910.
. . . Estimate of appropriation for continuing work of Immigration commission. Letter from the chairman . . . showing the progress of the work . . . with an estimate of the appropriation
necessary to complete its report . . . [Washington, Govt. print.
off., 1910]
    10 p. 23 cm. (61st Cong., 2d sess. Senate. Doc. 280)
    Referred to Committee on appropriations, and ordered printed,
January 11, 1910.
    William P. Dillingham, chairman.
    1. U.S.—Emig. & immig. I. Dillingham, William Paul,
1843-1923.
JV6415.A4 1910   10-35111
MC#: Jan. 1910-page 321
SuDocs no.: 61st Cong., 2d sess. S. Doc. 280

445

U.S. *Immigration commission,* 1907-1910.
. . . Statement relative to the work and expenditures of the Im-
migration commission created under section thirty-nine of the im-
migration act of February 20, 1907 . . . Washington, Govt. print.
off., 1909.
    44 p. 23 cm. (60th Cong., 2d sess. House. Doc. 1489)
    Ordered to be printed, February 27, 1909.
    William P. Dillingham, chairman.
    1. U.S.—Emig. & immig. I. Dillingham, William Paul,
1843-1923. II. Title.
JV6415.A4 1909   9-35357
- - - - - Copy 2.
MC#: Mar. 1909-page 498
SuDocs no.: 60th Cong., 2d sess. H. Doc. 1489

446

U.S. *Immigration commission,* 1907-1910.
. . . Brief statement of the conclusions and recommendations
of the Immigration commission, with views of the minor-
ity . . . Washington, Govt. print. off., 1911.
    40 p. 23½ cm. (61st Cong., 3d sess. Senate. Doc. 783)
    Presented by Mr. Dillingham, chairman. Ordered printed Jan.
24, 1911.
    "List of reports of the Immigration commission": p. 12-13.
    Views of the minority, signed by William S. Bennet: p. 40.
    1. U.S.—Emig. & immig. I. Dillingham, William Paul,
1843-1923. II. Bennett, William S., 1870-
JV6416.A8 1911   11-35120
- - - - - Copy 2.
MC#: Jan. 1911-page 339
SuDocs no.: 61st Cong., 3d sess. S. Doc. 783

DILLON REPORT [Dillon, Clarence Douglas]
447

U.S. *Committee on Federal Credit Programs.*
    Report to the President of the United States. Washington, U.S.
Govt. Print. Off., 1963.
    vii, 67 p. tables. 24 cm.
    1. Government lending—U.S. 2. Insurance,
Government—U.S.

HG3729.U5A442 1963   63-60933
MC#: 1963-7389
SuDocs no.: Pr35.8:C86/R29

DIMOCK REPORT [Dimock, Marshall Edward]
see under
O'MAHONEY REPORTS [O'Mahoney, Joseph Christopher]

DISNEY REPORT [Disney, Wesley Ernest]
448

U.S. *Congress. House. Committee on ways and means.*
. . . Increasing the debt limit of the United States and further amending the Second liberty bond act and establishing a salary limitation . . . Report. "To accompany H.R. 1780" [Washington, U.S. Govt. print. off., 1943]

13 p. 23½ cm. ([U.S.] 78th Cong., 1st sess. House. Rept. 181)
Caption title.
Submitted by Mr. Disney for the Committee on ways and means.
1. Debts, Public—U.S. 2. Bonds—U.S. 3. Wages—U.S. I. Disney, Wesley Ernest, 1883-
HJ8119.A48 1943c   336.3   43-51768
MC#: 1943-page 294
SuDocs no.: 78th Cong., 1st sess. H. Rept. 181

DOBLIN REPORT [Doblin, Ernest Martin]
see
BALOGH REPORT [Balogh, Thomas]

DOCKERY REPORT [Dockery, Alexander Monroe]
see
COCKRELL REPORT [Cockrell, Francis Marion]

DODD INVESTIGATION [Dodd, Thomas J.]
449

United States. Congress. Select Committee on Standards and Conduct.
Investigation of Senator Thomas J. Dodd of Connecticut; report to accompany S. Res. 112. Washington, U.S. Govt. Print. Off., 1967.

iii, 32 p. 24 cm. (90th Congress, 1st session. senate. Report no. 193)
"Under the authority of S. Res. 338, (88th Congres, second session)"
1. Dodd, Thomas J., 1907- I. Title. II. Series: United States. 90th Congress, 1st session, 1967. Senate. Report no. 193.
KF31.5.S7 1956   328.73'0924   67-61440
                                              MARC
MC#: 1967-9296
SuDocs no.: 90th Cong., 1st sess. S. Rept. 193

DODD REPORT [Dodd, Norman]
450

U.S. *Congress. House. Special Committee to Investigate Tax Exempt Foundations.*
The report of Norman Dodd, director of research, covering his direction of the staff of the Special Committee of the House of Representatives to Investigate Tax Exempt Foundations for the six months' period, November 1, 1953-April 30, 1954. New York, Long House, inc., © 1954.

15 p. 23 cm.
On cover: The Dodd report to the Reece Committee on Foundations.

1. Charitable uses, trusts, and foundations—U.S. I. Dodd, Norman.
AS911.A2U522   061   54-11186
Not listed in Monthly Catalog

451

U.S. *Congress. House. Special Committee to Investigate Tax Exempt Foundations.*
A report from Norman Dodd, director of research, covering his direction of the staff of the Special Committee of the House of Representatives to Investigate Tax Exempt Foundations, for the six months' period, November 1, 1953-April 30, 1954. [Washington, 1954]

i, 25 l. 27 cm.
"Prepared in accordance with the suggestion which the director of research made to the committee at its meeting in Washington, D.C. on Thursday, the 29th of April, 1954."
1. Charitable uses, trusts, and foundations—U.S. I. Dodd, Norman.
AS911.A2U523   54-60059
MC#: 1954-9985
SuDocs no.: Y4.T19/3:R29

DODDS REPORT [Dodds, Harold Willis]
452

James Madison Memorial Commission.
James Madison Memorial Commission; a summary account of the Commission's part in the planning of the Library of Congress James Madison Memorial Building. Harold W. Dodds, chairman, October 15, 1972. [Washington, 1973]

9 p. 23 cm.
1. United States. Library of Congress. James Madison Memorial Building. I. Dobbs, Harold Willis, 1889-
Z733.U6J35 1973   353.008'52   73-601736
                                              MARC
MC#: 1973-23510
SuDocs no.: Y3.M26:2L61

DODGE REPORT [Dodge, Grenville M.]
453

U.S. *Commission appointed by the President to investigate the conduct of the War dept. in the war with Spain.*
Report of the Commission appointed by the President to investigate the conduct of the War department in the war with Spain . . . Washington, Govt. print. off., 1900.

8 v. 23 cm. (U.S. 56th Cong., 1st sess. Senate. Doc. no. 221)
Members of the commission: Gen. Grenville M. Dodge, Iowa, president; Col. James A. Sexton, Illinois; Col. Charles Denby, Indiana; Capt. Evan P. Howell, Georgia; Ex-Gov. Urban A. Woodbury, Vermont; Brig. Gen. John M. Wilson, U.S.A.; Gen. James A. Beaver, Pennsylvania; Maj. Gen. Alexander McD. McCook, U.S.A.; Dr. Phineas S. Conner, Ohio; Richard Weightman, secretary; Lieut. Col. F. B. Jones, disbursing officer; Maj. Stephen C. Mills, recorder.
Contents.—v. 1. Minutes of meetings. Report to President. Appendices.—v. 2. Appendices.—v. 3-7. Testimony.—v. 8. Correspondence.
1. U.S.—Hist.—War of 1898—Sources. 2. U.S. War dept. I. U.S. 56th Cong., 1st sess. 1899-1900. Senate.
E725.U62   1-19676
MC#: 1900-page 189
SuDocs no.: 56th Cong., 1st sess. Doc. 221

DODSON REPORT [Dodson, Martha E.]
    see under
  DILLINGHAM COMMISSION [Dillingham, William Paul]
    Steerage conditions, importation and harboring of women for immoral purposes.

DOMERATZKY REPORT [Domeratzky, Louis]
    see under
  O'MAHONEY REPORTS [O'Mahoney, Joseph Christopher]

DONAHEY REPORT [Donahey, Vic]

454

U.S. *Congress. Joint committee to investigate Tennessee valley authority.*
  . . . Investigation of the Tennessee valley authority. Report of the Joint committee on the investigation of the Tennessee valley authority, Congress of the United States, pursuant to Public resolution no. 83 (75th Congress) creating a special joint congressional committee to make an investigation of the Tennessee valley authority together with the Minority views of Mr. Davis, Mr. Jenkins, and Mr. Wolverton, and the Individual views of Mr. Jenkins . . . Washington, U.S. Govt. print. off., 1939.
  3 v. illus., maps (part fold., 1 in pocket) tables, diagrs. (part fold.) 23 1/2 cm. (76th Cong., 1st sess. Senate. Doc. 56)
  Ordered printed with illustrations April 3, 1939.
  Vic Donahey, chairman.
  Contents. — Report. — Appendix A. Reports and exhibits. — Appendix B. Report of chief engineer.
  1. Tennessee valley authority. I. Davis, James John, 1873-1947. II. Jenkins, Thomas Albert, 1880- III. Wolverton, Charles Anderson, 1880- IV. Donahey, Vic, 1873-1946. V. Title.
TK1425.M8A5 1939d   [627.10975]   39-26689
                    621.309761
MC#: 1939-page 665
SuDocs no.: 76th Cong., 1st sess. S. Doc. 56

DONALDSON REPORT

455

Donaldson, Thomas Corwin, 1843-1898.
  . . . The public domain. Its history, with statistics . . . Public land commission. Committee on codification. Prepared in pursuance of the acts of Congress of March 3, 1879, and June 16, 1880, by Thomas Donaldson, of the commission and committee, and giving the result of the several land laws for the sale and disposition of the public domain to June 30, 1880. Revised July 16, 1881. Washington, Govt. print. off., 1881.
  v, 544 p. 2 fold maps (incl. front.) diagrs. (part fold.) 23½ cm. (46th Cong., 3d sess. House. Ex. doc. 47, pt.4)
  1. U.S. — Public lands. I. U.S. Public lands commission, 1879-1880. II. Title.
                                      15-17357
Checklist of United States Public Documents, 1789-1909, page 64
46th Cong., 3d sess. H. Ex. doc. 47, pt. 4. In serial no. 1975, vol. 25

DONNELLY REPORT [Donnelly, Charles H.]
    see
  PRICE REPORT [Price, Charles Melvin]

DOOLITTLE REPORTS [Doolittle, James H.]

456

U.S. *Air Coordinating Committee.*
  Airport safety, an Air Coordinating Committee review of policies and action in the fields covered by the Doolittle Airport Commission, May 16, 1952. [Washington] 1954.

36 p. 27 cm.
  1. U.S. President's Airport Commission. 2. Aeronautics-Safety measures. 3. Airports — U.S. I. Title.
TL726.2.A515   55-61500
MC#: 1955-13588
SuDocs no.: Y3.Ai7/3:2Sal

457

U.S. *President's Airport Commission.*
  The airport and its neighbors; the report. Washington, U.S. Govt. Print. Off., 1952.
  x, 116 p. illus. 26 cm.
  Bibliography: p. 113-116.
  1. Airports — U.S. I. Title.
TL521.A544 1952   *387.73 629.136   52-61225
MC#: 1952-11418
SuDocs no.: Pr33.16:952

458

U.S. *War dept. Board on officer-enlisted man relationships.*
  . . . Officer-enlisted man relationships. Report of the secretary of war's Board on officer-enlisted man relationships to Hon. Robert P. Patterson, the secretary of war, May 27, 1946 . . . Washington, U.S. Govt. print. off., 1946.
  iii, 23 p. 23 cm. ([U.S.] 79th Cong., 2d sess. Senate. Doc. 196)
  James H. Doolittle, chairman.
  Issued also under title: The complete Doolittle report; the report of the secretary of war's Board on officer-enlisted man relationships.
  1. U.S. Army. 2. U.S. Army — Officers. 3. Military discipline — U.S. I. Doolittle, James Harold, 1896- II. Title.
UA24.A7 1946k   355.33   46-26497
MC#: 1946-page 842
SuDocs no.: 79th Cong., 2d sess. S. Doc. 196

DORR REPORT [Dorr, Goldthwaite Higginson]
    see
  WICKERSHAM COMMISSION [Wickersham, George Woodward]
    Report on the cost of crime, no. 12.

DOUGLAS COMMISSION [Douglas, William O.]

459

U.S. *Securities and exchange commission.*
  . . . Report on the study and investigation of the work, activities, personnel and functions of protective and reorganization committees. Prusuant to section 211 of the Securities exchange act of 1934 . . . Washington, D.C . . . . Washington, U.S. Govt. print. off., 1936-40.
  8 v. tables. 23 cm.
  At head of title: Securities and exchange commission.
  Contents. — I. Strategy and techniques of protective and reorganization committees. 1937. — II. Committees and conflicts of interest. 1937. — III. Committees for the holders of real estate bonds. 1936. — IV. Committees for the holders of municipal and quasi-municipal obligations. 1936. — V. Protective committees and agencies for holders of defaulted foreign governmental bonds. 1937. — VI. Trustees under indentures. 1936. — VII. Management plans without aid of committees. 1938. — VIII. A summary of the law pertaining to equity and bankruptcy reorganizations and of the commission's conclusions and recommendations. 1940.
  1. Securities — U.S. 2. Stock-exchange — U.S. I. Hasse, Adelaide Rosalia, 1868-
HG4929.A2A4   332.630973   36-26649 revised
- - - - - Copy 2.
MC#: 1937-page 651
SuDocs no.: SE1.2:C73/pt.1

MC#: 1937-page 801
SuDocs no.: SE1.2:C73/pt.2
MC#: 1936-page 894
SuDocs no.: SE1.2:C73/pt.3
MC#: 1936-page 894
SuDocs no.: SE1.2:C73/pt.4
MC#: 1937-page 651
SuDocs no.: SE1.2:C73/pt.5
MC#: 1936-page 894
SuDocs no.: SE1.2:C73/pt.6
MC#: 1938-page 720
SuDocs no.: SE1.2:C73/pt.7
MC#: 1940-page 1407
SuDocs no.: SE1.2:C73/8

DOUGLAS REPORT [Douglas, Lewis W.]

460

U.S. *President's Committee for Hungarian Refugee Relief.*
   Report to the President. [Washington, U.S. Govt. Print. Off.] 1957.
   7 p. 24 cm.
   1. Refugees, Hungarian.
HV640.5.H8U55   361.53   57-60269
MC#: 1957-8915
SuDocs no.: Pr34.8:H89

DOUGLAS REPORTS [Douglas, Paul H.]

461

U.S. *Congress. Joint Economic Committee.*
   A compendium of materials on monetary, credit, and fiscal policies; a collection of statements submitted to the Subcommittee on Monetary, Credit, and Fiscal Policies by Government officials, bankers, economists and others [for the use of the] Joint Committee on the Economic Report. Washington, U.S. Govt. Print. Off., 1950.
   v, 443 p. 23 cm. (81st Cong., 2d sess. Senate. Document no. 132)
   1. Finance—U.S. (Series: U.S. 81st Cong., 2d sess. 1950-1951. Senate. Document no. 132)
HG181.A4 1950a   332   50-60344 rev
MC#: 1950-7354
SuDocs no.: 81st Cong., 2d sess. S. Doc. 132

462

United States. National Commission on Urban Problems.
   Building the American city; report. New York, Praeger [1969]
   xi, 500 p. illus. 26 cm. (Praeger special studies in U.S. economic and social development)
   Bibliographical footnotes.
   1. Housing—United States. 2. Municipal government—United States. I. Title.
HD7293.A56 1969b   333.7'7   73-85922
                                              MARC

Not listed in Monthly Catalog

463

United States. National Commission on Urban Problems.
   Building the American city; report to the Congress and to the President of the United States. Washington, For sale by the Supt. of Docs., U.S. Govt. Print. Off. [1969]
   xi, 504 p. illus. 27 cm. (91st Congress, 1st session. House Document no. 91-34)
   1. Housing—United States. 2. Local government—United States. I. Title. II. Series: United States. 91st Congress, 1st session, 1969. House. Document no. 91-34.

HD7293.A56 1969   333.7'7   76-601162
                                              MARC
MC#: 1969-5326
SuDocs no.: 91st Cong., 1st sess. H. Doc. 34

The reports of the National Commission on Urban Problems are listed numerically.

464

Netzer, Dick, 1928-
   Impact of the property tax: its economic implications for urban problems [by Dick Netzer] [Research report] supplied by the National Commission on Urban Problems to the Joint Economic Committee, Congress of the United States. Washington, U.S. Govt. Print. Off., 1968.
   xiii, 48 p. illus. 24 cm.
   At head of title: 90th Congress, 2d session. Joint committee print.
   Bibliographical footnotes.
   1. Property tax—United States. 2. Cities and towns—United States. 3. Housing—United States. I. United States. National Commission on Urban Problems. II. United States. Congress. Joint Economic Committee. III. Title.
HJ4120.N38   336.2'022'0973   68-62613
                                              MARC
MC#: 1968-13829
SuDocs no.: Y4.Ec7:P94/14

465

American Society of Planning Officials.
   Problems of zoning and land-use regulation. Washington, 1968.
   iv, 80 p. 26 cm. (National Commission on Urban Problems. Research report no. 2)
   "Prepared for the consideration of the National Commission on Urban Problems."
   1. Land—United States. 2. Zoning law—United States. 3. Land subdivision—Law and legislation—United States. I. Title. II. Series: United States. National Commission on Urban Problems. Research report no. 2.
HT123.A25 no. 2   352'.96'0973   68-62130
                                              MARC
MC#: 1968-11542
SuDocs no.: Pr36.8:Ur1/2/R31/no. 2

466

Hodge, Particia Leavey.
   The challenge of America's metropolitan population outlook, 1960 to 1985, by Patricia Leavey Hodge and Philip M. Hauser. Prepared for the consideration of the National Commission on Urban Problems. Washington, For sale by the Supt. of Docs., U.S. Govt. Print. Off., 1968.
   vi, 90 p. 26 cm. (National Commission on Urban Problems. Research report no. 3)
   1. United States—Population. 2. Metropolitan areas—United States. I. Hauser, Philip Morris, 1909- joint author. II. Title. III. Series: United States. National Commission on Urban Problems. Research report no. 3.
HT123.A25 no. 3   301.3'29'73   68-67299
                                              MARC
MC#: 1968-18020
SuDocs no.: Pr36.8:Url/2/R31/no.3

Hodge, Patricia Leavey.
   The challenge of America's metropolitan population outlook, 1960 to 1985 [by] Patricia Leavey Hodge [and] Philip M. Hauser. Foreword by Paul H. Douglas. New York, Praeger [1968]

xiii, 90 p. illus. 27 cm. (Praeger special studies in U.S. economic and social development)

"Prepared for the National Commission on Urban Problems." Bibliographical footnotes.

1. United States—Population. 2. Metropolitan area—United States. I. Hauser, Philip Morris, 1909- joint author. II. United States. Ntional Commission on Urban Problems. III. Title.

HB2175.H63   301.3′29′73   68-56907
                                                          MARC

Not listed in Monthly Catalog

467

Smart, Walter.

The large poor family: a housing gap, by Walter Smart, Walter Rybeck [and] Howard E. Shuman. Prepared for the consideration of the National Commision on Urban Problems. Washington, 1968.

iv, 28 p. 27 cm. (National Commission on Urban Problems. Resarch report no. 4)

1. Housing—United States. 2. Poor—United States. I. Rybeck, Walter, joint author. II. Shuman, Howard E., joint author. III. Title. IV. Series: United States. National Commission on Urban Problems. Research report no. 4.

HT123.A25 no. 4   301.5′4′0973   68-62716
                                                          MARC

MC#: 1968-14560
SuDocs no.: Pr36.8:Ur1/2/R31/no. 4

468

Hodge, Patricia Leavey.

The Federal income tax in relation to housing [by] Patricia Leavey Hodge and Philip M. Hauser. Prepared for the consideration of the National Commission on Urban Problems. Washington, For sale by Supt. of Docs, U.S. Govt. Print. Off., 1968.

vi, 162 p. 26 cm. (National Commission on Urban Problems. Research report, no. 5)

Bibliographical footnotes.

1. Housing—United States. 2. Urban renewal—United States. 3. Income tax—United States. I. Hauser, Philip Morris, 1909- joint author. II. Title. III. Series: United States. National Commission on Urban Problems. Research report, no. 5.

HT123.A25 no. 5   353.007′242   68-67084
                                                          MARC

MC#: 1968-16456
SuDocs no.: Pr36.8:Ur1/2/R31/no. 5

469

Manvel, Allen D. 1912-

Local land and building regulation: How many agencies? What practices? How much personnel? By Allen D. Manvel. Prepared for the consideration of the National Commission on Urban Problems. Washington, For sale by the Supt. of Docs., U.S. Govt. Print. Off., 1968.

v, 48 p. 27 cm. (National Commission on Urban Problems. Research report, no. 6)

1. Building laws—United States. 2. Zoning law—United States. I. Title. II. Series: United States. National Commission on Urban Problems. Research report no. 6.

HT123.A25 no. 6   340   68-67303
                                                          MARC
MC#:   1968-18021
SuDocs no.: Pr36.8:Ur1/2/R31/no.6

470

Keith, Nathaniel Schnieder, 1906-

Housing America's low- and moderate-income families; progress and problems under past programs, prospects under Federal act of 1968, by Nathaniel Keith. Prepared for the consideration of the National Commission on Urban Problems. Washington, for sale by the Supt. of Docs., U.S. Govt. Print. Off., 1968.

v, 30 p. 27 cm. (National Commission on Urban Problems. Research report no. 7)

1. Housing—U.S. I. Title. (Series: U.S. National Commission on Urban Problems. Research report no. 7)

HT123.A25 no. 7   301.5′4   68-67284
MC#: 1968-18022
SuDocs no.: Pr36.8:Ur1/2/R31/no.7

471

George Schermer Associates.

More than shelter; social needs in low- and moderate-income housing. Prepared for the consideration of the National Commission on Urban Problems. Washington, For sale by the Supt. of Docs., U.S. Govt. Print. Off., 1968.

xi, 213 p. 26 cm. (National Commission on Urban Problems. Research report no. 8)

1. Public housing—United States. 2. Public housing—Social aspects. I. Title. II. Series: United States. National Commission on Urban Problems. Research report no. 8.

HT123.A25 no. 8   301.5′4   71-600074
                                                          MARC
MC#: 1969-1314
SuDocs no.: Pr36.8:Ur1/2/R31/no.8

472

Manvel, Allen D. 1912-

Housing conditions in urban poverty areas, by Allen D. Manvel. Washington, For sale by the Supt. of Docs., U.S. Govt. Print. Off., 1968.

iv, 21 p. 26 cm. (National Commission on Urban Problems. Research report no. 9)

"Prepared for the consideration of the National Commission on Urban Problems."

1. Slums—United States. I. Title. II. Series: United States. National Commission on Urban Problems. Research report no. 9.

HT123.A25 no. 9   301.5′4   71-600137
                                                          MARC
MC#: 1969-1315
SuDocs no.: Pr36.8:Ur1/2/R31/no. 9

473

Kristof, Frank S.

Urban housing needs through the 1980's: an analysis and projection, by Frank S. Kristof. Washington, For sale by the Supt. of Docs., U.S. Govt. Print. Off., 1968.

xvi, 92 p. illus. 26 cm. (National Commission on Urban Problems. Research report no. 10)

"Prepared for the consideration of the National Commission on Urban Problems."

Bibliographical footnotes.

1. Housing—United States. I. Title. II. Series: United States. National Commission on Urban Problems. Research report no. 10.

HT123.A25 no. 10   301.5′4   78-600101
                                                          MARC
MC#: 1969-2402
SuDocs no.: Pr36.8:Ur1/2/R31/no. 10

474

Raymond & May Associates.

Zoning controversies in the suburbs: three case studies. Prepared for the consideration of the National Commission on Urban Problems. [Washington] For sale by the Supt. of Docs., U.S. Govt. Print. Off., 1968.

v, 82 p. illus., plans. 26 cm. (National Commission on Urban Problems. Research report no. 11)

1. Zoning—United States—Case studies. I. Title. II. Series: United States. National Commission on Urban Problems. Research report no. 11.

HT123.A25 no. 11   352'.961'0973   79-600068
                                                                                    MARC

MC#: 1969-1316
SuDocs no.: Pr36.8:Ur1/2/R31/no.11

475

Manvel, Allen D. 1912-

Three land research studies: Trends in value of real estate and land, 1956-66, Land use in 106 large cities, by Allen D. Manvel; Estimating California land values from independent statistical indicators, by Robert H. Gustafson and Ronald B. Welch. Prepared for the consideration of the National Commission on Urban Problems. Washington, For sale by the Supt. of Docs., U.S. Govt. Print. Off., 1968.

vi, 72 p. 26 cm. (U.S. National Commission on Urban Problems, Research report no. 12.)

1. Land research—United States. I. Title. II. Series: United States. National Commission on Urban Problems. Research report no. 12.

HT123.A25 no. 12
MC#: 1969-1317
SuDocs no.: Pr36.8:Ur1/2/R31/no. 12

476

Milgram, Grace (Smelo)

U.S. land prices; directions and dynamics, by Grace Milgram. Assisted by Michael Bach, Thomas A. Barrington [and] Liam Shortall. Prepared for the consideration of National Commission on Urban Problems. Washington, For sale by the Supt. of Docs., U.S. Govt. Print. Off., 1968 [i.e. 1969]

v, 77 p. 26 cm. ([United States. National Commission on Urban Problems] Research report no. 13)

Bibliography: p. 71-77.

1. Real property—Prices—United States. I. Title. II. Series.

HT123.A25 no. 13   333.3'32   70-601438
                                                                                    MARC

MC#: 1969-7405
SuDocs no.: Pr36.8:Ur1/2/R31/no. 13

477

Grad, Frank P.

Legal remedies for housing code violations, by Frank P. Grad. Prepared for the consideration of the National Commission on Urban Problems. Washington, For sale by the Supt. of Docs., U.S. Govt. Print. Off., 1968.

vii, 264 p. 26 cm. (National Commission on Urban Problems. Research report no. 14)

Bibliographical references included in "Footnotes" (p. 155-264)

1. Landlord and tenant—United States. 2. Building laws—United States. I. Title. II. Series: United States. National Commission on Urban Problems. Research report no. 14.

HT123.A25 no. 14   340   77-600192
                                                                 MARC

MC#: 1969-1318
SuDocs no.: Pr36.8:Ur1/2/R31/no.14

478

Bosselman, Fred P.

Alternatives to urban sprawl: legal guidelines for Governmental action. Prepared for the consideration of the National Commission on Urban Problems. Washington, For sale by the Supt. of Docs., U.S. Govt. Print. Off., 1968.

iv, 69 p. (National Commission on Urban Problems. Research report no. 15)

Includes bibliographic references.

1. Housing—United States. I. Title. II. Series: United States. National Commission on Urban Problems. Research report no. 15.

HT123.A25 no. 15
MC#: 1969-4860
SuDocs no.: Pr36.8:Ur1/2/R31/no.15

479

Eaves, Elsie.

How the many costs of housing fit together. Prepared for the consideration of the National Commission on Urban Problems. Washington, For sale by the Supt. of Docs., U.S. Govt. Print. Off., 1969.

viii, 103 p. 26 cm. (National Commission on Urban Problems. Research report no. 16)

Bibliographic references included in "Sources" (p. 102-103)

1. Housing—United States. I. Title. II. Series:United States. National Commission on Urban Problems. Research report no. 16.

HT123.A25 no. 16   301.5'4'0973   76-601434
                                                                                      MARC

MC#: 1969-7406
SuDocs no.: Pr36.8:Ur1/2/R31/no. 16

480

Slavet, Joseph S.

New approaches to housing code administration, by Joseph S. Slavet and Melvin R. Levin. Prepared for the consideration of the National Commission on Urban Problems. Washington, For sale by the Supt. of Docs., U.S. Govt. Print. Off., 1969.

vi, 217 p. 26 cm. (National Commission on Urban Problems. Research report no. 17)

Includes bibliographic references.

1. Housing—United States—Law and legislation. I. Levin, Melvin R., 1924- joint author. II. United States. National Commission on Urban Problems. III. Title. IV. Series: United States. National Commission on Urban Problems. Research report no. 17.

HT123.A25 no. 17   340   75-602309
                                                                 MARC

MC#: 1969-8778
SuDocs no.: Pr36.8:Ur1/2/R31/no. 17

481

Coke, James Guthrie.

Fragmentation in land-use planning and control, by James G. Coke and John J. Gargan. Prepared for the consideration of the National Commission on Urban Problems. Washington [For sale by the Supt. of Docs., U.S. Govt. Print. Off.] 1969.

v, 91 p. 26 cm. (National Commission on Urban Problems. Research report no. 18)

Bibliographical references included in "Notes" (p. 81-91)

1. Land use—Planning—United States. I. Gargan, John J., 1934- joint author. II. United States. National Commission on Urban Problems. III. Title. IV. Series: United States. National Commission on Urban Problems. Research report no. 18.

HT123.A25 no. 18   333.3'37   75-602333

MC#: 1969-10284
SuDocs no.: Pr36.8:Ur1/2/R31/no. 18

482

Mood, Eric W.

Housing code standards; three critical studies: The development, objective, and adequacy of current housing code standards, by Eric W. Mood. Administrative provisions of housing codes, by Barnet Lieberman. Inadequacies and inconsistencies in the definition of substandard housing, by Oscar Sutermeister. Washington; For sale by the Supt. of Docs., U.S. Govt. Print. Off., 1969.

vi, 108 p. 26 cm. (National Commission on Urban Problems. Research report no. 19)

"Prepared for the consideration of the National Commission on Urban Problems."

Includes bibliographical references.

1. Building laws—United States. I. Lieberman, Barnet, 1903- II. Sutermeister, Oscar, 1912- III. Title. IV. Series: United States. National Commission on Urban Problems. Research report no. 19.

HT123.A25 no. 19   340   75-602857
                                          MARC

MC#: 1969-11599
SuDocs no.: Pr36.8:Ur1/2/R31/no. 19

DOWNEY REPORT [Downey, Sheridan]

483

U.S. *Congress. Senate. Special committee to investigate the old-age pension system.*

. . . Old-age pension system. Preliminary report of the Special committee to investigate the old-age pension system pursuant to Senate resolution no. 129 (77th Congress) a resolution to investigate the operation of the old-age pension system and means for securing minimum pensions there under together with the Minority views of Mr. Green. August 28, 1941. Washington, U.S. Govt. print. off., 1941.

iv, 46 p. incl. tables. 23 cm. ([U.S.] 77th Cong., 1st sess. Senate. Rept. 666)

Sheridan Downey, chairman.

1. Old age pensions—U.S. I. Downey, Sheridan, 1884- II. Green, Theodore Francis, 1867-

HD7106.U5A5 1941d   331-254430973   41-51144
MC#: 1941-page 1268
SuDocs no.: 77th Cong., 1st sess. S. Rept. 666

DOWNING REPORT [Downing, Thomas N.]

484

Downing, Thomas N.

Report of the Hon. Thomas N. Downing, chairman, Subcommittee on Merchant Marine on the oversight hearings of the Subcommittee on Merchant Marine, Committee on Merchant Marine and Fisheries, with respect to the U.S.-flag merchant marine.— Washington: U.S. Govt. Print. Off., 1977.

vi, 142 p.: maps; 24 cm.

"Serial no. 94-M."

At head of title: 94th Congress, 2d session. Committee print.

"Printed for the use of the Committee on Merchant Marine and Fisheries."

1. Merchant marine—United States. 2. United States—National security. I. United States. Congress. House. Committee on Merchant Marine and Fisheries.

HE745.A212 1977a   387.5'0973   77-601036

MC#: 1978-12152
SuDocs no.: Y4.M53:94-M

DOWNING REPORT [Downing, Walter]
see
KIRKPATRICK REPORT [Kirkpatrick, Patti]

DOYLE REPORT

485

Doyle, George Aloysius, 1917-

Foundations for a national policy to preserve private enterprise in the 1980's: a study/prepared for the use of the Subcommittee on Economic Growth and Stabilization of the Joint Economic Committee, Congress of the United States [by George A. Doyle].—Washington: U.S. Govt. Print. Off., 1977.

v, 40 p.; 24 cm.

At head of title: 95th Congress, 1st session. Joint committee print.

1. Small business. 2. Industry and state—United States. I. United States. Congress. Joint Economic Committee. Subcommittee on Economic Growth and Stabilization. II. Title.

HD2346.U5D69   338.973   77-601941
                                          MARC

MC#: 1977-12533
SuDocs no.: Y4.Ec7:En8/2/980

DOYLE REPORT [Doyle, John P.]

486

U.S. *Congress. Senate. Committee on Commerce.*

National transportation policy. Report of the Committee on Commerce, United States Senate, by its special study group on transportation policies in the United States, pursuant to S. Res. 29, 11, and 244 of the 86th Congress. Washington, U.S. Govt.Print.Off., 1961.

xxi, 732 p. maps, diagrs., tables. 24 cm. (87th Cong., 1st sess. Senate. Report no. 445)

1. Transportation—U.S. I. Title. (Series: U.S. 87th Cong., 1st sess. 1961. Senate. Report no. 445)

HE18 1961.A528   385.0973   61-61872
MC#: 1961-12457
SuDocs no.: 87th Cong., 1st sess. S. Rept. 445

DRAPER REPORTS

487

Draper, William Henry, 1894-

Coordination of procurement between the War and Navy Departments, prepared at the direction of the Secretary of the Navy and the Under Secretary of War by William H. Draper and Lewis L. Strauss. [Washington] 1945.

3 v. diagrs. 33 cm.

Contents.—v. 1. Final and interim reports—v. 2. Functional studies—v. 3. Materiel studies.

1. U.S. Army—Supplies and stores. 2. U.S. Navy—Supplies and stores. I. Strauss, Lewis L., joint author.

UC263.D7   355.8   52-27547
Not located in Monthly Catalog

488

U.S. *President's Committee to Study the United States Military Assistance Program.*

Composite report. Washington, 1959.

2 v. illus., maps, group port. 24 cm.

Vol. 2, Supplement: annexes.

1. Military assistance, American. 2. Economic assistance, American.
UA12.U535 1959c   355.0973   59-62197
MC#: 1959-15153
SuDocs no.: Pr34.8:M59/2/v.1-2

489

U.S. *President's Committee to Study the United States Military Assistance Program.*
    Conclusions concerning the Mutual security program. Communication from the President of the United States transmitting the final report . . . with the several studies which are annexes thereto. Washington, U.S. Govt. Print. Off., 1959.
    2 v. map, diagrs., tables. 24 cm. (86th Cong., 1st sess. House. Document no. 215)
    1. Mutual security program, 1951- I. Title. (Series: U.S. 86th Cong., 1st sess., 1959. House. Document no. 215)
UA12.U484 1959   59-64228
MC#: 1959-14115
SuDocs no.: 86th Cong., 1st sess. H. Doc. 215, pt. 1
MC#: 1959-14116
SuDocs no.: 86th Cong., 1st sess. H. Doc. 215, pt. 2

490

U.S. *President's Committee to Study the United States Military Assistance Program.*
    Interim report. Washington, 1959.
    16 p. 24 cm.
    1. Military assistance, American.
UA12.U535 #195a   355   59-61109
MC#: 1959-10557
SuDocs no.: Pr34.8:M59/rp.2

491

U.S. *President's Committee to Study the United States Military Assistance Program.*
    Letter to the President of the United States and the Committee's final report. Conclusions concerning the mutual security program. Washington, 1959.
    56 p. map, diagrs., tables. 24 cm.
    Cover title.
    1. Military assistance, American. 2. Economic assistance, American.
UA12.U535 1959d   59-64239
MC#: 1959-15156 (refers erroneously to LC card 59-61109)
SuDocs no.: Pr34.8:M59/3

492

U.S. *President's Committee to Study the United States Military Assistance Program.*
    Letter to the President of the United States and the Committee's third interim report. Economic assistance programs and administration. Washington, 1959.
    71 p. maps, diagrs. 24 cm.
    Cover title.
    1. Economic assistance, American.
HC60.U6P72   59-64227
MC#: 1959-13550 (refers erroneously to LC card 59-61109)
SuDocs no.: Pr34.8:M59/rp.3

493

U.S. *President's Committee to Study the United States Military Assistance Program.*
    Preliminary conclusions submitted to the President with the Committee's letter of March 17, 1959. [Washington, 1959]

4, 10 p. 27 cm.
    1. Military assistance, American.
UA12.U535 1959b   355   59-61005
MC#: 1959-6899
SuDocs no.: Pr34.8:M59

494

U.S. *President's Committee to Study the United States Military Assistance Program.*
    Preliminary report and letter of transmittal. Washington, U.S. Govt. Print. Off., 1959.
    v, 8 p. 24 cm. (86th Cong., 1st sess. Senate. Document no. 18)
    1. Military assistance, American. (Series: U.S. 86th Cong., 1st sess., 1959. Senate. Document no. 18)
UA12.U535   355   59-60891 rev
MC#: 1959-5943
SuDocs no.: 86th Cong., 1st sess. S. Doc. 18

495

U.S. *President's Committee to Study the United States Military Assistance Program.*
    Report on the organization and administration of the military assistance program submitted to the President on June 3, 1959. Communication from the President of the United States, transmitting a report . . . Washington, U.S. Govt. Print. Off., 1959.
    v, 36 p. 24 cm. (86th Congress, 1st session, House document no. 186)
    "Second interim report."
    Commonly known as the Draper report.
    1. Military Assistance, American. I. U.S. President, 1953-1961 (Eisenhower) II. Draper report on the United States military assistance program. III. Title. IV. Series: U.S. 86th Cong., 1st sess., 1959. House Document no. 186.
UA12.U535 1959e   70-30563
                                     MARC
MC#: 1959-9809
SuDocs no.: 86th Cong., 1st sess. H. Doc. 186

DUNHAM REPORT [Dunham, Charles L.]
496

National Academy of Sciences. *Washington, D.C.*
    Evaluation of biomedical research and education in the Veterans Administration. Washington, The Academy, 1968.
    75 p.
Not located in Monthly Catalog

DUNLAP REPORT [Dunlap and Associates, Inc.]
497

U.S. *National Highway Safety Bureau.*
    Economics of highway emergency ambulance services. March 1969. Washington, D.C. U.S. Govt. Print. Off., 1969.
    [4], 63 p. illus.
    Cover title.
    Prepared under contract FH- 11-6541, by Dunlap Associates, Inc., Darien, Conn.
                                       72-602394
MC#: 1969-10187 (LC card 72-602394 assigned, not printed, under Dunlap and Associates, inc.)
SuDocs no.: TD2.202:Am1

DUNLOP REPORT [Dunlop, John Thomas]
    see under
  O'MAHONEY REPORTS [O'Mahoney, Joseph Christopher]
    Brown. Industrial wage rates.

DUNN REPORT

498

Dunn, Edgar S., Jr.

Review of proposal for a national data center: a report by Edgar S. Dunn. Washington, D.C.: Office of Statistical Standards, Bureau of the Budget, Executive Office of the President. 1965.

68 p. in various pagings; 27 cm. (Statistical evaluation report; v. no. 6).

Cover title.

"December 1965."

1. Statistics. 2. United States—Statistics. I. United States. Bureau of the Budget. Office of Statistical Standards. II. Title: Statistical evaluation report.

DUNNING REPORT [Dunning, Gordon M.]

499

U.S. *Atomic Energy Commission.*

Radioactive contamination of certain areas in the Pacific Ocean from nuclear tests; a summary of the data from the radiological surveys and medical examinations. Edited by Gordon M. Dunning. [Washington] 1957.

ix, 53 p. diagrs., tables. 27 cm.

Bibliography: p. 53.

1. Atomic weapons—Testing. 2. Pacific Ocean. 3. Radioactive fallout.

UF767.U48 1957a   *574.191   57-60908

MC#: 1957-12916

SuDocs no.: Y3.At7:2R11/20

DWORSKY REPORT [Dworsky, Leonard B.]

see

ACKERMAN REPORT [Ackerman, William G.]

Federal water resources research program, Fiscal years 1967 and 1969.

DYBWAD REPORT

500

Dubwad, Rosemary F.

International directory of mental retardation resources. Edited by Rosemary F. Dybwad. [Washington, President's Committee on Mental Retardation] 1971.

ix, 316 p. 27 cm.

Supt. of Docs. no.: Pr36.8:M52/R31/4

1. Mental retardation facilities—Directories. 2. Mentally handicapped—Directories. I. United States. President's Committee on Mental Retardation. II. Title.

HV3004.D97   362.3′025   72-614168

                                     MARC

MC#: 1971-15963

SuDocs no.: Pr36.8:M52/R31/4

DYKSTRA REPORTS [Dykstra, Clarence Addison]

501

U.S. *National resources committee. Research committee on urbanism.*

Interim report to the National resources committee by the Research committee on urbanism. National resources committee. July, 1936. [Washington? 1936]

4 p. 1., ii-iv numb. 1., 18, 18a, 19-36, 36a-36c, 37-189 p. incl. tables (part fold.) forms. diagrs. 26½ cm.

Mimeographed.

C. A. Dykstra, chairman.

1. Cities and towns—U.S. I. Dykstra, Clarence Addison. II. Title.

HT123.A5 1936   323.3520973   36-26645

- - - - - Copy 2.

MC#: 1936-page 884

SuDocs no.: Y3.N21/12:2Ur1/2

United States. National Resources Committee. Research Committee on Urbanism.

Interim report to the National Resources Committee / Research Committee on Urbanism.-New York: Arno Press, 1978.

iv, 189 p.: forms; 24 cm.-(American federalism)

Reprint of the 1936 ed. published by National Resources Committee, Washington.

Commonly known as the Dykstra report.

C. A. Dykstra, Chairman.

ISBN 0-405-10508-8

1. Cities and towns—United States. I. Dykstra, Clarence Addison, 1883-1950. II. Title. III. Title: Dykstra report. IV. Series.

HT123.U45 1978   301.36′0973   77-74966

                                     MARC

Not listed in Monthly Catalog

DYNES REPORT [Dynes, Russell Rowe]

see

KEMENY COMMISSION REPORT [Kemeny, John G.]

Staff report to the President's Commission on the Accident at Three Mile Island.

EAGAN REPORT [Eagan, Mary Helen]

see under

DILLINGHAM COMMISSION [Dillingham, William Paul]

Immigration situation in other countries.

EAVES REPORT [Eaves, Elsie]

see

DOUGLAS REPORTS [Douglas, Paul H.]

National Commission on Urban Problems. Research report no. 16.

EBERHARTER REPORT [Eberharter, Herman Peter]

502

U.S. *Congress. House. Special committee on un-American activities, 1938-*

. . . Report and Minority views of the Special committee on un-American activities on Japanese war relocation centers . . . Report. [Washington, U.S. Govt. print. off., 1943]

28 p. 23½ cm. ([U.S.] 78th Cong. 1st sess. House. Rept. 717)

Caption title.

Running title: Investigation, un-American propaganda activities.

Submitted by Mr. Costello from the Special committee on un-American activities.

"Minority views of the Honorable Herman P. Eberharter": p. 17-28.

1. U.S. War relocation authority. I. Costello, John Martin, 1903- II. Eberharter, Herman Peter, 1892- III. Title: Japanese war location centers. IV. Title: Investigation, un-American propaganda activities.

D769.8.A6A57 1943k   940.547273   43-50829

MC#: 1943-page 1291

SuDocs no.: 78th Cong., 1st sess. H. Rept. 717

EBERSTADT REPORT

503

[Eberstadt, Ferdinand] 1890-

. . . Unification of the War and Navy departments and postwar organization for national security. Report to Hon. James Forrestal, secretary of the Navy, on unification of the War and Navy departments and postwar organization for national security. October 22, 1945 . . . Washington, U.S. Govt. print. off., 1945.

x, 251 p. diagrs. (part fold.) 23 cm.

At head of title: 79th Congress, 1st session. Senate committee print.

"Report made by Mr. Ferdinand Eberstadt."-Letter of submittal.

"Printed for the use of the Committee on naval affairs, United States Senate."

1. U.S. War dept. 2. U.S. Navy dept. I. U.S. Congress. Senate. Committee on naval affairs. II. Title.

UA23.E2   355   46-27761
Not located in Monthly Catalog

EDDY REPORTS [Eddy, Manton S.]

504

U.S. *Adjutant General's Office.*
Survey of the educational program of the Command and Staff College. Report and recommendations on program no. PR-4097 by a special survey commission. Feb. 1947. [Washington, D.C., 1947]

121 p. il.
[U415.U7]
Industrial College of the Armed Forces
Not located in Monthly Catalog

505

U.S. *Dept. of the Army. Board on Educational System for Officers.*
Report of the Department of the Army Board on educational system for officers. [Washington] 1949.

59 p. illus. 27 cm.
Cover title.
1. Military education—U.S. 2. U.S. Army—Officers. I. Title.
[U408.3.A53]
Dept. of the Army Library
Not located in Monthly Catalog

506

U.S. *War Dept. Military Education Board on Educational System for Officers of the Army.*
Report [Washington, D.C. 1946]

90 p.
[U415.U5 1946 res.]
Industrial College of the Armed Forces
Not located in Monthly Catalog

EDWARDS REPORT [Edwards, Alice Leora]
see under
O'MAHONEY REPORTS [O'Mahoney, Joseph Christopher]
Kaidanovsky. Consumer standards.

EHLE REPORT [Ehle, Boyd]
see
WALKER COMMISSION [Walker, John Grimes]

EISENBUD REPORT [Eisenbud, Merrill]

507

U.S. *National Center for Radiological Health. Enviromnental Radiation Exposure Advisory Committee.*
Report to the Director, National Center for Radiological Health, Public Health Service, on environmental contamination by radioactive substances. [Washington] U.S. Dept. of Health, Education, and Welfare, Public Health Service [1968]

iii, 24 p. 26 cm.

1. Radiation—Safety measures. 2. Radioactive substances—Safety measures. I. Title: Environmental contamination by radioactive substances.

TK9152.U52   614.83'9   68-62842
MC#: 1968-16487
SuDocs no.: FS2.2:R11/23

EISENHOWER REPORT [Eisenhower, Dwight David]
see
STEARNS-EISENHOWER REPORT [Stearns, Robert L. and Eisenhower, Dwight David]

EISENHOWER REPORTS

508

Eisenhower, Milton Stover, 1899-
United States-Latin America relations [1953-1958]: report to the President, December 27, 1958. [Washington] Dept. of State [1959]

16 p. 26 cm. (Department of State publication 6764. Inter-American series, 55)

Cover title.

"Reprinted from the Department of State bulletin of January 19, 1959."

1. U.S.—Relations (general) with Spanish America. 2. Spanish America—Relations (general) with the U.S. I. Title. (Series: U.S. Dept. of State. Publication 6764. Series: U.S. Dept. of State. Inter-American series, 55)

F1418.E45   327.7308   59-60465
- - - - - Copy 2.
F1401.U65 no. 55
MC#: 1959-4071
SuDocs no.: S1.26:55

509

United States. National Commission on the Causes and Prevention of Violence.
Progress report to President Lyndon B. Johnson, January 9, 1969. [Washington, For sale by the Supt. of Docs., U.S. Govt. Print. Off., 1969]

7, A52 p. 27 cm.

Commonly known as the Eisenhower report.

1. Violence. 2. United States—Social conditions. 3. Crime and criminals—United States. I. Title: Eisenhower report on the causes and prevention of violence.

HV6493.U5   364'.9'73   79-600530
                                                        MARC
MC#: 1969-4862
SuDocs no.: Pr36.8:V81/R29/969

510

United States. National Commission on the Causes and Prevention of Violence.
To establish justice, to insure domestic tranquility; final report. Washington; For sale by the Supt. of Docs., U.S. Govt. Print. Off. [1969]

xxxii, 338 p. illus., ports. 24 cm.

Includes bibliographical references.

1. Violence—United States. I. Title.

HN59.A514   301   75-604476
                                                        MARC
MC#: 1970-2203
SuDocs no.: Pr36.8:V81/J98/2

511

U.S. *Task Force on Law and Law Enforcement.*

Rights in concord: the response to the counter-inaugural protest activities in Washington, D.C., January 18-20, 1969; a special staff study submitted to the National Commission on the Causes and Prevention of Violence. [Washington, For sale by the Supt. of Docs., U.S. Govt. Print. Off., 1969]

xvi, 120, A5 p. illus., maps, ports. 24 cm. ([U.S. National Commission on the Causes and Prevention of Violence] Investigative reports)
Number 4 on spine.
1. Washington, D.C. — Demonstration, January 18-20, 1969. 2. Nixon, Richard Milhous, 1913- — Inauguration. I. Title. (Series)
E855.A5   975.3′04   77-602828
                                                        MARC

MC#: 1969-13325
SuDocs no.: Pr36.8:V81/R44

ELIOT REPORT

512

Eliot, Charles William, 1899-
Land planning considerations in the Washington metropolitan area. Staff study for the Joint Committee on Washington Metropolitan Problems, Congress of the United States. Washington, U.S. Govt. Print. Off., 1958.

v, 12 p. 24 cm.
At head of title: 85th Cong., 2d sess. Joint Committee print.
1. Regional planning — Washington metropolitan area. I. U.S. Congress. Joint Committee on Washington Metropolitan Problems. II. Title.
NA9127.W2E58   711.409753   59-60303
MC#: 1959-3400
SuDocs no.: Y4.W27/2:L22

ELKIND REPORT [Elkind, Arnold B.]

513

United States. National Commission on Product Safety.
Final report presented to the President and Congress. [Washington; For sale by the Supt. of Docs., U.S. Govt. Print Off.] 1970.

xiv, 167, 32 p. illus., ports. 27 cm.
Includes bibliographical references.
1. Consumer protection — United States. 2. Accidents — Prevention. 3. Safety appliances. 4. Safety regulations — United States. I. Title.
HC110.C63A54   658.83   76-606753
                                                     MARC

MC#: 1970-11768
SuDocs no.: Y3.N21/25:1/970

ELLENDER REPORTS

514

Ellender, Allen Joseph, 1891-
Review of United States Government operations in South Asia, by Allen J. Ellender [report to the Committee on Appropriations, United States Senate] Washington, U.S. Govt. Print. Off., 1968.

vii, 380 p. 24 cm. (90th Congress, 2d session. Senate. Document no. 77)
1. Technical assistance, American — South Asia. 2. Economic assistance, American — South Asia. I. United States. Congress. Senate. Committee on Appropriations. II. Title. III. Series:

United States. 90th Congress, 2d session, 1968. Senate. Document no. 77.
HC60.E43   338.91′73′054   68-62075
                                                     MARC
MC#: 1968-10471
SuDocs no.: 90th Cong., 2d sess. S. Doc. 77

515

U.S. *Congress. Senate. Committee on Appropriations.*
Report on overseas operations of the United States Government, by Allen J. Ellender, U.S. Senator, from the State of Louisiana. Washington, U.S. Govt. Print. Off., 1957.

vii, 525 p. tables. 24 cm. (85th Cong., 1st sess. Senate. Document no. 31)
1. U.S. — Foreign economic relations. 2. Economic assistance, American. 3. Technical assistance, American. 4. Military assistance, American. I. Ellender, Allen Joseph, 1891- (Series: U.S. 85th Cong., 1st sess., 1957. Senate. Document no. 31)
HC60.U51334   57-61261
MC#: 1957-5193
SuDocs no.: 85th Cong., 1st sess. S. Doc. 31

516

U.S. *Congress. Senate. Committee on Appropriations.*
A report on United States foreign operations in Africa, by Allen J. Ellender, U.S. Senator, from the State of Louisiana. Washington, U.S. Govt. Print. Off., 1963.

ix, 803 p. map, tables. 24 cm. (88th Cong., 1st sess. Senate. Dcoument no. 8)
1. Africa — Hist. 2. Africa — Descr. & trav. — 1951- 3. U.S. — Relations (general) with Africa. 4. Africa — Relations (general) with the U.S. I. Title: United States foreign operations in Africa. (Series: U.S. 88th Cong., 1st sess., 1963. Senate. Document no. 8)
DT38.U488   63-61053
MC#: 1963-8021
SuDocs no.: 88th Cong., 1st sess. S. Doc. 8

517

U.S. *Congress. Senate. Committee on Appropriations.*
A review of United States Government operations in Latin America, by Allen J. Ellender, U.S. Senator from the State of Louisiana. Washington, U.S. Govt. Print. Off., 1959.

xix, 535 p. tables. 24 cm. (86th Cong., 1st sess. Senate. Document no. 13)
1. U.S. — Relations (general) with Spanish America. 2. Spanish America — Relations (general) with the U.S. I. Ellender, Allen Joseph, 1891- II. Title (Series: U.S. 86th Cong., 1st sess., 1959. Senate. Document no. 13)
F1418.U434 1959   327.73098   59-60632
MC#: 1960-8162
SuDocs no.: 86th Cong., 1st sess. S. Doc. 13

518

U.S. *Congress. Senate. Special committee to investigate administration and operation of civil service laws.*
. . . Investigation of administration and operation of civil service laws. Report of the Special committee to investigate administration and operation of civil service laws, pursuant to S. Res. 68 (78th Congress, extending S. Res. 198, 75th Congress) . . . Washington, U.S. Govt. print. off., 1945.

iii, 16 p. 23½ cm. ([U.S.] 79th Cong., 1st sess. Senate. Rept. 24)
Running title: Administration and operation of civil service laws.
Submitted by Mr. Ellender.

1. Civil service—U.S. I. Ellender, Allen Joseph, 1891- II. Title: Administration and operation of civil service laws.
JK649 1945   351.1   45-35461
MC#: 1945-page 167
SuDocs no.: 79th Cong., 1st sess. S. Rept. 24

ELLIOTT REPORT [Elliott, Foster F.]
519

U.S. *Dept. of agriculture. Interbureau committee on state legislation for better land use.*
State legislation for better land use, a special report by an interbureau committee of the United States Department of Agriculture. [Washington] U.S. Govt. print. off., 1941.

xix, 122 p. 26½ cm.
"The Interbureau committee on state legislation for better land use."—p. v.
"Selected bibliography": p. 118-122.
1. Land [utilization—Law] 2. (Regional planning—U.S.) 3. Agriculture—Economic aspects—U.S. 4. (U.S.—Public lands) 5. [Land utilization—U.S.] I. Title.
HD186.A15 1941   333.70973   Agr41-392
MC#: 1941-page 607
SuDocs no.: A36.2:L22/13

ELLIOTT REPORT [Elliott, Robin]
see
LUTES REPORT [Lutes, Le R.]

ELY REPORT
520

Ely, Northcutt, 1903-
. . . Light on the Mexican water treaty from the ratification proceedings in Mexico. A report to the Colorado river water users' association. February 11, 1946, Salt Lake City, Utah. By Northcutt Ely . . . Washington, U.S. Govt. Print. off., 1946.

iii, 23 p. 23 cm. ([U.S.] 79th Cong., 2d sess. Senate. Doc. 249)
Running title: Mexican water treaty.
1. Colorado river. 2. Water-supply—Colorado valley. I. Colorado river water users' association. II. Title. III. Title: Mexican water treaty.
HD1694.C6E4   333.91   46-26902
MC#: 1946-page 1061
SuDocs no.: 79th Cong., 2d sess. S. Doc. 249

EMERSON REPORT [Emerson, Lynn Arthur]
see
WILLIS REPORT [Willis, Benjamin C.]

EMMERICH REPORT [Emmerich, Herbert]
see
BROWNLOW REPORT [Brownlow, Louis]

ENGLE REPORT [Engle, Nathanael Howard]
see under
O'MAHONEY REPORTS [O'Mahoney, Joseph Christopher]
Cover. Problems of small business.

ERSKINE REPORT [Erskine, Graves B.]
521

U.S. *Federal interagency committee on migrant labor.*
Migrant labor . . . a human problem. Report and recommendations, Federal interagency committee on migrant labor. [Washington] U.S. Dept. of labor, Retraining and reemployment administration [1947]

vi, 58 p. incl. illus., tables. 19 x 25 cm.
1. Migrant labor—U.S. I. U.S. Retraining and reemployment administration.
HD5856.U5A53 1947   331.796   L47-68
MC#: 1947-page 701
SuDocs no.: L24.2:M58

EVANS REPORT [Evans, S. S.]
see
WALKER COMMISSION [Walker, John Grimes]

EVANS REPORT [Evans, Wilmoth Duane]
see under
O'MAHONEY REPORTS [O'Mahoney, Joseph Christopher]
Bertrand. Motion picture industry.

EVERMANN REPORT
522

Evermann, Barton Warren, 1853-1932.
. . . Alaska fisheries and fur industries in 1911. [By] Barton Warren Evermann . . . Washington, Govt. print. off., 1912.

1 p. l., 99 p. 23 cm. ([U.S.] Bureau of fisheries. Doc. 766)
At head of title: Department of commerce and labor . . .
Contents.—General administrative report, by B. W. Evermann and F. M. Chamberlain.—Statistics of the fisheries of Alaska for 1911, by J. N. Cobb and F. M. Chamberlain.—Fish culture in Alaska, by W. T. Bower.—The fur-seal service in 1911, by W. I. Lembkey.
1. Fisheries—Alaska. 2. Fish-culture—Alaska. 3. Seals (Animals) 4. Fox. I. Chamberlain, Frederic M., 1867- II. Cobb, John Nathan, 1868- III. Bower, Ward Taft, 1881- IV. Lembkey, Walter I., 1870- V. Title.
                                                      F12-388
MC#: Dec. 1912-page 270
Bureau of Fisheries Doc. No. 766

See also BOWER REPORT [Bower, Ward T.]

EWING REPORT
523

Ewing, Oscar Ross, 1889-
The Nation's health [a ten year program]; a report to the President. [Washington, U.S. Govt. Print. Off., 1948]

xiv, 186 p. illus., map. 25 cm.
1. Hygiene, Public—U.S. 2. Medicine, State—U.S.
RA445.E85   614.0973   48-47008*
MC#: 1948-22270
SuDocs no.: FS1.2:H34/3

EZEKIEL REPORT [Ezekiel, Mordecai]
524

U.S. *Dept. of agriculture.*
. . . Economic bases for the Agricultural adjustment act, by Mordecai Ezekiel, economic advisor to the secretary of agriculture and Louis H. Bean, economic adviser Agricultural adjustment administration. Washington, U.S. Govt. print. off., 1933.

iv, 67 p. incl. map, diagrs. 23 cm.
At head of title: United States Department of agriculture, Washington, D.C. December, 1933.
Contribution from the Office of the secretary and the agricultural adjustment administration.
1. Agriculture—Economic aspects. 2. (Agriculture—U.S.) I. *Ezekiel, Mordecai, 1899- II. Bean, Louis Hyman, 1896- joint author. III. Title. IV. Title: Agricultural adjustment act.

HD9005.A5 1933   338.10973   Agr33-927
MC#: Dec. 1933-page 423
SuDocs no.: A1.2:Ag8/7

FAHY REPORT [Fahy, Charles]

525

U.S. *President's Committee on Equality of Treatment and Opportunity in the Armed Services.*

Freedom to serve, equality of treatment and opportunity in the armed services; a report. Washington, U.S. Govt. Print. Off., 1950.

xii, 82 p. 25 cm.

1. U.S. Army—Appointments and retirements. 2. U.S. Navy—Appointments and retirements. 3. U.S. Air Force—Appointments and retirements. 4. Negroes—Segregation. I. Title.
UB412.A4 1950   355.3   50-60728
MC#: 1950-13511
SuDocs no.: D1.2:F87

FAIRBANKS REPORT [Fairbanks, H. S.]

526

U.S. *National interregional highway committee.*

. . . Interregional highways. Message from the President of the United States, transmitting a report of the National interregional highway committee, outlining and recommending a national system of interregional highways . . . Washington, U.S. Govt. print. off., 1944.

xi, 184 p. incl. tables, diagrs. XIV pl. on 7 l., maps (1 fold.) 24 cm. ([U.S.] 78th Cong., 2d sess. House. Doc. 379)

"Final report."—Letter of transmittal.

Issued also, in mimeographed form, without congressional series numbering under title: Interregional highways. Report of . . . .

1. Roads—U.S. I. Title.
TE23.A5 1944   625.71   44-40705
MC#: 1944-page 556
SuDocs no.: 78th Cong., 2d sess. H. Doc. 379

FAIRLESS REPORT [Fairless, Benjamin F.]

527

U.S. *President's Citizen Advisers on the Mutual Security Program.*

Report to the President, March 1, 1957. Washington, U.S. Govt. Print Off., 1957.

vii, 36 p. illus. 24 cm.

1. Military assistance, American. 2. Economic assistance, American.
UA12.U534   355   57-61248
MC#: 1957-5812
SuDocs no.: Pr34.8:M98

FALK REPORT

528

Falk, Leslie K.

Procurement of library materials in the Federal Government; an orientation aid prepared for the Federal Library Committee by Leslie K. Falk. Washington, Federal Library Committee, 1968.

42 p. 27 cm. (FLC publication no. 1)

Commonly known as the Falk report.

A project of the Task Force on Procedures in Federal Libraries of the Federal Library Committee.

Bibliographical references included in "Notes" (p. 37-39.)

1. Libraries, Governmental, administrative, etc.—United States. 2. Acquisitions (Libraries) I. United States. Task Force on Procurement Procedures in Federal Libraries. II. Title. III. Title: Falk report on procurement of library materials in the

Federal Government. I. Series: United States. Federal Library Committee. FLC publication no. 1.
Z675.G7F3   025.2   68-62486
                                  MARC
MC#: 1969-4614
SuDocs no.: LC1.32/2:L61

FALKNER REPORT [Falkner, Roland Post]
see
ALDRICH REPORT [Aldrich, Nelson Wilmarth]
Retail prices and wages.

Wholesale prices, wages, and transportation.

DILLINGHAM COMMISSION [Dillingham, William Paul]
Children of immigrants in schools.

FARBSTEIN REPORTS

529

Farbstein, Leonard.

Special study mission to the Far East; report pursuant to H. Res. 113, a resolution authorizing the Committee on Foreign Affairs to conduct thorough studies and investigations of all matters coming within the jurisdication of such committee. Washington, U.S. Govt. Print. Off., 1961.

v, 7 p. 24 cm.

At head of title: 86th Cong., 2d sess. Committee print.

1. East (Far East)—Politics. I. U.S. Congress. House. Committee on Foreign Affairs.
DS518.1.F3   61-60878
MC#: 1961-5745
SuDocs no.: Y4.F76/1:Ea7/2

530

U.S. *Congress. House. Committee on Foreign Affairs.*

Arab refugees from Palestine. Report of a special study mission to the Near East of the Committee on Foreign Affairs, by Leonard Farbstein, pursuant to H. Res. 55, 88th Congress . . . Washington, U.S. Govt. Print. Off., 1963.

vii, 9 p. 24 cm. (88th Cong., 1st sess. House report no. 196)

1. Refugees, Arab. 2. Near East—Politics. I. Farbstein, Leonard. II. Title. (Series: U.S. 88th Cong., 1st sess., 1963. House. Report no. 196)
DS38.U53   63-61412
MC#:1963-7957
SuDocs no.: 88th Cong., 1st sess. H. Rept. 196

531

U.S. *Congress. House. Committee on Foreign Affairs.*

Report of the special study mission to the Mediterranean and Near East, comprising Leonard Farbstein, New York, of the Committee on Foreign Affairs, pursuant to H. Res. 29, a resolution authorizing the Committee on Foreign Affairs to conduct thorough studies and investigations of all matters coming within the jurisdiction of such committee. Washington, U.S. Govt. Print. Off., 1958.

vii, 4 p. 24 cm. (85th Cong., 2d sess. House report no. 1407)

1. Mediterranean region—Politics. I. Title: Special study mission to the Mediterranean and Near East. (Series: U.S. 85th Cong., 2d sess., 1958. House. Report no. 1407)
DE98.U5   956   58-60406
MC#: 1958-4351
SuDocs no.: 85th Cong., 2d sess. H. Rept. 1407

FELDMAN REPORT

532

Feldman, Herman, 1894-

. . . A personnel program for the federal civil service, by Herman Feldman . . . economic adviser to the Field survey division, Personnel classification board. A report transmitted by the director of the Personnel classification board . . . Washington, U.S. Govt. print. off., 1931.

ix, 289 p. tables (1 fold.) fold. form. 23½ cm. ([U.S.] 71st Cong., 3d sess. House. Doc. 773)

Referred to the Committee on the civil service and ordered printed, with illustrations, February 16, 1931.

1. U.S.—Officials and employees—Salaries, allowances, etc. 2. Civil service—U.S. I. U.S. Personnel classification board. II. Title.

JK765.F4   351.10973   31-27039
- - - - - Copy 2.
MC#: May 1931-page 997
SuDocs no.: 71st Cong., 3d sess. H. Doc. 773

FERGUSON REPORT [Ferguson, Garland S.]

533

U.S. *Committee to Review the Decartelization Program in Germany.*
Report to the Honorable Secretary of the Army. [Washington, 1949]

129, 6 l. 32 cm.
Caption title.
Garland S. Ferguson, chairman.
1. Trusts, Industrial—Germany.
HD2857.U6 1949   388.85   49-46674*
Not located in Monthly Catalog

FERGUSON REPORT [Ferguson, Homer]

534

U.S. *Congress. Senate. Committee on Government Operations.*
Interim report of the Investigations Subcommittee of the Committee on Expenditures in the Executive Departments pursuant to S. Res. 189, 80th Congress, a resolution authorizing the Committee on Expenditure in the Executive Departments to carry out certain duties. Washington, U.S. Govt. Print. Off., 1948.

3 pts. 23 cm. (80th Cong., 2d sess. Senate. Report no. 1775)
Contents.—pt. 1. Investigation of Federal employees loyalty program.—pt. 2. The administration of export controls.—pt. 3. Conduct of Ilse Koch war crimes trial.
1. Allegiance—U.S. 2. U.S.—Officials and employees. 3. Koch, Ilse, 1906- 4. Export controls—U.S. (Series: U.S. 80th Cong., 2d sess., 1948. Senate. Report no. 1775)
JK730.A5 1948a   351.1   48-4674 rev*
MC#: 1948-22134, pt. 1
MC#: 1949-754, pt. 2
MC#: 1949-3012, pt. 3
SuDocs no.: 80th Cong., 2d sess. S. Rept. 1775

FERGUSON REPORT [Ferguson, Homer]
     Investigation of the Pearl Harbor attack.
     see
BARKLEY REPORTS [Barkley, Alben William]

FERRARIS REPORT [Ferraris, Carlo Francesco]
     see under
ALDRICH COMMISSION [Aldrich, Nelson Wilmarth]
     Canovai. Banks of issue in Italy.

FERRISS REPORT [Ferriss, Abott Lamoyne]
     see
ORRRC REPORTS
     ORRRC study report, 19.

FESLER REPORT [Fesler, James William]
     see
BROWNLOW REPORT [Brownlow, Louis]

FINDLEY REPORT [Findley, David E.]

535

U.S. *Commission of Fine Arts.*
Art and government; report to the President on activities of the Federal Government in the field of art. Washington [U.S. Govt. Print. Off.] 1953.

v, 141 p. 26 cm.
1. Art and state—U.S. 2. State encouragement of science, literature and art. I. Title.
N8710.A1U62   706.9   53-61728
MC#: 1953-13231
SuDocs no.: FA1.2:G74

FINE REPORT [Fine, Selma Evelyn]
     see
KNEELAND REPORT [Kneeland, Hildegarde]

FINLETTER REPORTS [Finletter, Thomas Knight]

536

U.S. *Economic Cooperation Administration. Special Mission to the United Kingdom.*
Report. London, 1948.

3 v. illus., maps. 22 x 28-28 cm.
Contents.—v. 1. The highlights.—v. 2. Supporting facts.—v. 3. Statistical supplement.
1. Gt. Brit.—Econ. condit.—1945-
HC256.5.U5 1948   330.942   51-20300 rev
Not located in Monthly Catalog

537

U.S. *Economic Cooperation Administration. Special Mission to the United Kingdom.*
The Sterling area; an American analysis. Prepared under direction of John M. Cassels, director, Research and Statistics Division. London, 1951.

672 p. illus., maps (part col.) 28 cm.
1. Sterling area. 2. Economic conditions—1945- 3. Currency question.
HC59.U53 1951   330.904   52-61779
Not located in Monthly Catalog

538

U.S. *President's Air Policy Commission.*
Survival in the air age, a report. Washington, U.S. Govt. Print. Off., 1948.

ix, 166 p. 25 cm.
Thomas K. Finletter, chairman.
1. Aeronautics—U.S. 2. Aeronautics, Military—U.S. I. Finletter, Thomas Knight, 1893- II. Title.
TL521.A5 1948   629.1306173   48-45516*
MC#: 1948-4415
SuDocs no.: Pr33.2:Ai71

FISHER REPORT [Fisher, William Alfred]
     see
HILL REPORT [Hill, David Spence]

FITZGERALD REPORT

539

FitzGerald, Benedict F.

A report to the Senate Interstate Commerce Committee on the need for investigation of cancer research organizations.

(*In* Congressional record. v. 99 (1953) pt. 12, p. A5350-5353)
1. U.S. Congress. Senate. Committee on Interstate and Foreign Commerce.
SuDocs no.: X/a.83/1:12

FITZGERALD REPORT [Fitzgerald, Joseph H.]

540

U.S. *Federal Field Committee for Development Planning in Alaska.*

Alaska natives & the land. Anchorage, Alaska; For sale by the Supt. of Docs., U.S. Govt. Print. Off., Washington, 1968.

iii, 565 p. illus., maps (part col., 1 fold. inserted) 28 x 38 cm.
1. Indians of North America—Alaska. 2. Natural resources—Alaska. I. Title.

E78.A3U65　　　　　333.1'09798　　　　　79-600959
　　　　　　　　　　　　　　　　　　　　　　　　　MARC
MC#: 1969-5604
SuDocs no.: Y3.A1 1s/4:2N21

FITZHUGH REPORT [Fitzhugh, Gilbert W.]

541

U.S. Blue Ribbon Defense Panel.

Report to the President and the Secretary of Defense on the Department of Defense. [Washington] Dept. of Defense; [for sale by the Supt. of Docs., U.S. Govt. Print. Off.] 1970.

ix, 237 p. 27 cm.
- - - - - Supplemental statement on the shifting balance of military power, September 30, 1970. [Washington, 1971]
xi, 35 p. 26 cm.
Signed by seven members of the panel.
UA23.3.A419 Suppl.
- - - - - Appendix
[Washington] 1970-
v. illus. (part fold.) 26 cm.
Cover title.
Bibliography: Appendix F, p. H1-H14.
UA23.3.A419 Suppl. 2
1. U.S. Dept. of Defense. 2. U.S.—Defenses. 3. Russia—Defenses. I. Title. II. Title: The shifting balance of military power.

UA23.3.A419　　　　　353.6　　　　　70-608286
　　　　　　　　　　　　　　　　　　　　　　　　　MARC
MC#: 1970-13816
SuDocs no.: D1.2:B62/970
MC#: 1971-12549 (LC card 79-613667 preassigned, not yet printed)
SuDocs no.: D1.2:B62/970/supp.

FLANDERS REPORTS [Flanders, Ralph Edward]

542

U.S. *Congress. Joint Committee on Housing.*

High cost of housing. Report of a subcommittee of the Joint Committee on Housing, Congress of the United States, pursuant to H. Con. Res. 104, 80th Congress. Washington, U.S. Govt. Print. Off., 1948.

vii, 185 p. fold. diagrs. 23 cm. ([U.S.] 80th Cong., 2d sess. 1948. House. Document no. 647)
Letter of transmittal signed: Ralph E. Flanders.
Issued also without Congressional series numbering as Joint Committee print.

1. Building—U.S. 2. Housing—U.S. I. Flanders, Ralph Edward, 1880- II. Title. (Series)

HD9715.U52A5 1948a　　　690.973　　　48-46261*
MC#: 1948-13000
SuDocs no.: 80th Cong., 2d sess. H. Doc. 647

543

U.S. *Congress. Joint Economic Committee.*

Profits. Report of a subcommittee of the Joint Committee on the Economic Report on profits hearings. Washington, U.S. Govt. Print. Off., 1949.

ix, 227 p. charts. 24 cm.
At head of title: 80th Cong., 2d sess. Joint committee print.
1. Profit—U.S.

HC110.P7A48　　　　338.7　　　　49-45713 rev*
MC#: 1949-19143
SuDocs no.: Y4.Ec7:P94

FLANIGAN REPORTS [Flanigan, Peter M.]

544

United States. Foreign Agricultural Service (1953-)

Agricultural trade and the proposed round of multilateral negotiations. Report prepared at the request of Peter Flanigan, Assistant to the President for International Economic Affairs, for the Council on International Economic Policy. Washington, U.S. Govt. Print. Off., 1973.

ix, 241 p. illus. 24 cm.
At head of title: 93d Congress, 1st session. Committee print.
Commonly known as Flanigan report.
"Prepared by a team assembled from the Foreign Agricultural Service, the Economic Research Service, and the Agricultural Stabilization and Conservation Service."
"Printed for the use of the [Senate] Committee on Agriculture and Forestry."
1. Produce trade—United States. 2. Produce trade. 3. United States—Commercial policy. I. United States. Dept. of Agriculture. Economic Research Service. II. United States. Agricultural Stabilization and Conservation service. III. United States. Council on International Economic Policy. IV. United States. Congress. Senate. Committee on Agriculture and Forestry. V. Title. VI. Title: Flanigan report.

HD9006.U56 1973　　　382'.41'0973　　　73-602534
　　　　　　　　　　　　　　　　　　　　　　　　　MARC
MC#: 1973-32126
SuDocs no.: Y4.Ag8/8:T67

545

United States. President.

International economic report of the President, transmitted to the Congress. 1973- Washington, For sale by the Supt. of Docs., U.S. Govt. Print. Off.

v. 27 cm.
Vols. for 1973- include the Annual report of the Council on International Economic Policy.
1. United States—Foreign economic relations—Yearbooks. 2. International economic relations—Yearbooks. 3. Economic history—1945- —Yearbooks. I. United States. Council on International Economic Policy. Annual report. II. Title.

HF1455.U47a　　　　382'.0973　　　73-643312
ISSN 0091-2492　　　　　　　　　　　　　　　　MARC-S
MC#: 1973-25671
SuDocs no.: Pr37.8:In8/3/R29/2/973

FLEISHMAN REPORT

546

Fleishman, Lawrence.

Report on survey of the Bureau of Customs for the United States Economic Survey Mission to the Philippines. Seattle, Dept. of Treasury, 1950.

23 1. 32 cm.

1. Philippines (Republic) Bureau of Customs. 2. Customs administration—Philippine Islands.
HJ7266.F55   336.262   52-60945
Not located in Monthly Catalog

FLEMING REPORT [Fleming, Robert V.]
547

U.S. *President's Advisory Commission on Presidential Office Space.*
Presidential office space; report. [Washington] 1957.

40 p. illus. 26 cm.
1. U.S. Executive Office of the President. I. Title.
JK518.A57   353.03   57-60486 rev
MC#: 1957-10314
SuDocs no.: Pr34.8:P92

FLEMMING REPORT [Flemming, Arthur S.]
548

U.S. *Office of Defense Mobilization.*
A report to the President by the Director. Washington, U.S. Govt. Print. Off., 1954.

xviii, 70 p. diagrs. 23 cm.
Cover title: Manpower resources for national security.
Report of the Committee on Manpower Resources for National Security, with recommendations of the Director of the Office of Defense Mobilization.
1. Manpower—U.S. I. U.S. Office of Defense Mobilization. Committee on Manpower Resources for National Security. II. Title: Manpower resources for national security.
UA17.5.U5A53   355.22   54-61122
Not located in Monthly Catalog

See also APPLEY REPORT [Appley, Lawrence A.]

FLETCHER REPORT [Fletcher, Alice Cunningham]
549

U.S. *Office of education.*
. . . Indian education and civilization; a report prepared in answer to Senate resolution of February 23, 1885, by Alice C. Fletcher, under direction of the commissioner of education. Washington, Govt. print. off., 1888.

2 p. 1., [3]-693 p. 23½ cm. ([U.S.] 48th Cong., 2d sess. Senate. Ex doc. 95)
At head of title: . . . Bureau of education. Special report, 1888.
Added t.—p.: The executive documents of the Senate of the United States for the second session of the Forty-eighth Congress and the special session of the Senate convened March 3, 1885 . . . volume 2, part 2 . . .
N.H.R. Dawson, commissioner.
1. Indians of North America—Education. 2. Indians of North America—Civilization. I. Fletcher, Alice Cunningham, 1845-1923. II. U.S. Office of education. Special report, 1888. III. Title.
E97.U55   7-2004
Checklist of United States Public Documents, 1789-1909, p. 72
48th Cong., 2d sess. S. Ex. Doc. 95. In Serial no. 2264, vol. 2, pt. 2

FLETCHER REPORT [Fletcher, Duncan Upshaw]
550

U.S. *Congress. Senate. Committee on banking and currency.*

. . . Stock exchange practices. Report to the Committee on banking and currency pursuant to S. Res. 84 (72d Congress) a resolution to investigate practices of stock exchanges with respect to the buying and selling and the borrowing and lending of listed securities and S. Res. 56 and S. Res. 97 (73d Congress) resolutions to investigate the matter of banking operations and practices, transactions relating to any sale, exchange, purchase, acquisition, borrowing, lending, financing, issuing, distributing, or other disposition of, or dealing in, securities or credit by any person or firm, partnership, company, association, corporation, or other entity, with a view to recommending necessary legislation, under the taxing power or other federal powers . . . Washington, U.S. Govt. print. off., 1934.

viii, 394 p. incl. tables. 23 cm. (73d Cong., 2d sess. Senate. Rept. 1455)
Submitted by Mr. Fletcher. Ordered printed June 6 (calendar day, June 16), 1934.
1. Stock-exchange—U.S. I. Fletcher, Duncan Upshaw, 1859- II. Title.
HG4556.U5A5 1934h   332.610973   34-28258
- - - - - Copy 2.
MC#: Nov. 1934-page 366
SuDocs no.: 73d Cong., 2d sess. S. Rept. 1455

FLUX REPORT [Flux, Alfred William]
    see under
    ALDRICH COMMISSION [Aldrich, Nelson Wilmarth]

FLYNN REPORT [Flynn, Leo J.]
551

U.S. *Interstate commerce commission.*
. . . Coordination of motor transportation. A report by Leo J. Flynn, attorney-examiner, to the Interstate commerce commission . . . Washington, U.S. Govt. print. off., 1932.

1 p. 1., 136 p. incl. tables. 23½ cm. (72d Cong., 1st sess. Senate. Doc. 43)
Presented by Mr. Metcalf. Ordered printed January 6, 1932.
1. Transportation, Automotive. I. Flynn, Leo J., 1879- II. Title.
HE5623.A4 1932   388.30973   32-26181
- - - - - Copy 2.
MC#: Feb. 1932-page 599
SuDocs no.: 72d Cong., 1st sess. S. Doc. 43

FOGELSON REPORT [Fogelson, Robert M.]
    Who riots? A study of participation in the 1967 riots.
    see
    KERNER COMMISSION [Kerner, Otto]
    Supplemental studies.

FOLKMAR REPORT [Folkmar, Daniel]
    see under
    DILLINGHAM COMMISSION [Dillingham, William Paul]
    Dictionary of races or peoples.

FOLKMAR REPORT [Folkmar, Elnora Cuddeback]
    see under
    DILLINGHAM COMMISSION [Dillingham, William Paul]
    Dictionary of races or people.

FOLSOM REPORTS [Folsom, Marion B.]

552

U.S. *Advisory Committee on Public Health Service Personnel Systems.*
  Report. [Washington] U.S. Dept. of Health, Education, and
Welfare, Public Health Service [1962]
    vii, 120 p. diagrs., tables. 24 cm.
    1. U.S. Public Health Service—Officials and employees.
RA11.B15 1962   62-61896
MC#: 1963-7411
SuDocs no.: FS2.2:P43/2

553

U.S. *President's Special Panel on Federal Salaries.*
  [Report]
    (*In* Pay increases for certain civilian employees and members
of the uniformed services. [Washington] 23 cm. p. 12-24. (U.S.
89th Cong., 1st sess., 1965. House. Document no. 170)
MC#: 1965-10397
SuDocs no.: 89th Cong., 1st sess. H. Doc. 170, p. 12-24

FORD REPORT [Ford, Worthington Chauncy]
see
KEEP COMMISSION [Keep, Charles Hallam]
    Documentary historical publications of the United States
    government.

FOREMAN REPORT [Foreman, Paul W.]

554

U.S. *General Services Administration.*
  Federal employee parking and transportation survey,
Washington metropolitan area. Washington, 1962-1963.
    3 v. col. maps (part fold.) tables. 27 cm.
    Contents.—1. Improvements in public transportation.—2. The
parking problem.—3. Staggered working hours.
    1. Automobile parking—Washington metropolitan area. 2.
Transportation—Washington metropolitan area. 3. Washington
metropolitan area—Transit systems. 4. Traffic surveys—
Washington metropolitan area. I. Title.
HE372.W3 1962   388.4   62-61059
Not located in Monthly Catalog

FORRESTAL REPORT [Forrestal, James A.]

555

U.S. *Navy Dept. Office of Management Engineer.*
  Personnel administration at the executive level. Annapolis,
United States Naval Institute, 1948.
    v, 45 p. diagrs. 26 x 30 cm.
    1. Executives. I. United States Naval Institute, Annapolis.
HF5500.U6 1948   658.3124   48-22128*
Not located in Monthly Catalog

FORSYTH REPORT [Forsyth, George]

556

The army's master program for the modern volunteer army; a
program for professionals. [Washington. Dept. of the Army] 1971.
    58 p. diagrs.
    Cover title: The modern volunteer army.
    1. U.S. Army—Recruiting, enlistment, etc. I. Title: The
modern volunteer army.
[UA25.A3]
Dept. of the Army Library
Not located in Monthly Catalog

FOWLER REPORT [Fowler, Henry]

557

U.S. *Task Force on Promoting Increased Foreign Investment in United
States Corporate Securities and Increased Foreign Financing for United States
Corporations Operating Abroad.*
  Report to the President of the United States. [Washington, For
sale by the Superintendent of Documents, U.S. Govt. Print. Off.,
1964]
    v, 36 p. 24 cm.
    Cover title.
    1. Investments, Foreign—U.S. 2. Investments, American.
HG4538.U79   64-61361
Not located in Monthly Catalog
SuDocs no.: [Pr35.8:F763/R29]

FOXWELL REPORT [Foxwell, Herbert Somerton]
see under
ALDRICH COMMISSION [Aldrich, Nelson Wilmarth]
    Philippovich von Philippsberg. History of the Bank of
    England.

FRAENKEL REPORT

558

Fraenkel, William A
  Guide to job placement of the mentally retarded. The President's Committee on Employment of the Handicapped in coopera-
tion with National Association for Retarded Children and the U.S.
Employment Service, Bureau of Employment Security, U.S.
Dept. of Labor. [Washington, U.S. Govt. Print. Off., 1963]
    iv, 16 p. 23 cm.
    Cover title.
    1. Mentally handicapped—Employment—U.S. I. U.S. Presi-
dent's Committee on Employment of the Handicapped. II. Ti-
tle: Job placement of the mentally retarded.
HV3006.A4F68   L63-72
MC#: 1963-14448
SuDocs no.: L16.44/2:M52/2

FRAMINGHAM HEART STUDY

559

The Framingham study; an epidemiological investigation of car-
diovascular disease. [Bethesda, Md., U.S. Dept. of Health,
Education, and Welfare, National Institutes of Health; for sale
by the Supt. of Docs., U.S. Govt. Print. Off., Washington, 1968-
    v. in 27 cm. (v. 12-22)
    Study under the direction of the National Heart Institute.
    Bibliography: v. 1, p. 1i1-1i7.
    1. Cardiovascular system—Diseases—Collected works. 2.
Epidemiology—Collected works. 3. Medical geography—
Massachusetts—Framingham. I. U.S. National Heart Institute.
RC667.F7   616.1   71-603009
                                                          MARC
Sections 1-8 not located in Monthly Catalog.
MC#: 1970-974-976 (Sections 9-11)
       1969-8686-8696, 16255 (Sections 12-23)
SuDocs no.: FS2.22:F84/sec. (nos.)
MC#: 1970-7620 (Section 24)
       1971-1319, 7099, 14172 (Sections 25-27)
       1974-1466 (Section 28)
       1974-08136 (Section 29)
       1975-04485 (Section 30)
       1977-3393 (Section 31)
       1977-11053 (Section 32)
       1979-15242 (Section 33)
SuDocs no.: HE20.3002:F84/sec. (nos.)

560

United States. National Heart Institute.
   The Framingham heart study: habits and coronary heart disease. [Bethesda, Md., 1966]
   [16] p. (incl. covers) illus. 20 x 26 cm. (Public Health Service publication no. 1515)
   Cover title.
   1. Coronary heart disease. I. Title. II. Series: United States. Public Health Service. Publication no. 1515.
RC669.U527   616.1'23   66-62686
                                                           MARC
MC#: 1966-18005
SuDocs no.: FS2.22:H35/12

FRANCK REPORT

561

Franck, Peter G.
   Obtaining financial aid for a development plan; the Export-Import Bank of Washington loan to Afghanistan. Washington, U.S. Govt. Print. Off., 1954.
   vii, 55 p. maps, tables. 24 cm.
   At head of title: 83d Cong., 2d sess. Committee print.
   1. Afghanistan—Economic policy. 2. Export-Import Bank of Washington. I. Title.
HC417.F7   338.958   54-61483
MC#: 1954-5437
SuDocs no.: Y4.B22/3:Ex7/9

FRANK REPORT

562

Frank, Bernard, 1902-
   Metropolitan water problems. Staff report prepared for the Joint Committee on Washington Metropolitan Problems on conservation and recreation in a comprehensive program for the Potomac River Basin with special reference to the National Capital region. Washington, U.S. Govt. Print. Off., 1958.
   v, 21 p. illus., fold. map. 24 cm.
   At head of title: 85th Cong., 2d sess. Committee print.
   Bibliography: p. 18-19.
   1. Water supply—Washington, D.C. I. U.S. Congress. Joint Committee on Washington Metropolitan Problems. II. Title.
TD225.W3F7   628.1   58-61233
MC#: 1958-16891
SuDocs no.: Y4.W27/2:W29/3

FRANK REPORT [Frank, Lawrence Kelso]
      see
ORRRC REPORTS
      ORRRC study report, 22.

FRANKE REPORT [Franke, William B.]
      see
GATES REPORT [Gates, Thomas S.]
      Report on the organization of the Dept. of the Navy.

FRANKLIN REPORTS

563

Franklin, William McHenry, 1913-
   Protection of foreign interests, a study in diplomatic and consular practice, by William McHenry Franklin . . . Washington, D.C., U.S. Govt. print. off. [1947]
   vii, 328 p. 23½ cm. ([U.S.] Dept. of state. [Publication 2693])
   1. Diplomatic protection. I. Title.
JX1683.F6F7   341.7   47-32298
MC#: 1947-page 740
SuDocs no.: S1.2:P94/2

564

U.S. *Dept. of State. Historical Office.*
   Documents on international aspects of the exploration and use of outer space, 1954-1962. Staff report, prepared for the Committee on Aeronautical and Space Sciences, United States Senate. Washington, U.S. Govt. Print. Off., 1963.
   xiii, 407 p. 24 cm. (88th Cong., 1st sess. Senate. Document no. 18)
   An expansion of pt. 3: International negotiations regarding the use of outer space, 1957-60, by the Historical Office, Dept. of State, published as document (S. Doc. 26, 87th Cong., 1st sess.) with title: Legal problems of space exploration: a symposium, prepared by the Legislative Reference Service of the Library of Congress.
   1. Astronautics—International cooperation—Addresses, essays, lectures. 2. Astronautics and civilization—Addresses, essays, lectures. I. U.S. Congress. Senate. Committee on Aeronautical and Space Sciences. II. U.S. Library of Congress. Legislative Reference Service. Legal problems of space exploration: a symposium. (Series: U.S. Cong., 1st sess., 1963. Senate. Document no. 18)
JX5768.U5   63-61570
MC#: 1963-9960
SuDocs no.: 88th Cong., 1st sess. S. Doc. 18

FRENCH REPORT [French, Robert W.]

565

U.S. *Committee on the Southwest Economy.*
   The Southwest; a report to the President's Council of Economic Advisers. [Washington, 1954]
   1 v. (various pagings) maps, tables. 29 cm.
   Cover title.
   Bibliographical footnotes.
   1. Southwest, New—Econ. condit. I. Title.
HC107.A165A48   55-60655
MC#: 1955-5151
SuDocs no.: Pr34.9:So8

FRENCH REPORT [French, William C.]
      see under
O'MAHONEY REPORTS [O'Mahoney, Joseph Christopher]
      Nelson. Price behavior and business policy.

FRENDZEL REPORT

566

Frendzel, Donald J.
   The Soviet seven-year plan (1959-65) for oil. [Washington] U.S. Dept. of the Interior, Bureau of Mines [1961]
   17 p. fold. map (in pocket) tables. 27 cm. (U.S. Bureau of Mines. Information circular, 8023)
   Bibliography: p. 16-17.
   1. Petroleum industry and trade—Russia. I. Title. (Series)
TN295.U4 no. 8023   61-61416
MC#: 1961-9445
SuDocs no.: I28.27:8023

FRIED REPORT [Fried, Larry C.]

567

U.S. *National Institute of Neurological Diseases and Blindness.*
   Progress in spinal cord injury research, FY 1967, by Larry C. Fried. Bethesda, Md., U.S. National Institutes of Health, 1968.
   109 1. (NINDB Program analysis reports no. 19)
Not located in Monthly Catalog

FRIEDMAN REPORT [Friedman, Jesse J.]
568

U.S. *Congress. Senate. Committee on the Judiciary.*

Corporate mergers and acquisitions. The Committee on the Judiciary of the United States Senate reports: a staff study of the Subcommittee on Antitrust & Monopoly [prepared by Jesse J. Friedman, economic consultant] pursuant to S. Res. 170, 84th Cong., 2d sess., as extended by S. Res. 84, 85th Cong . . . .Washington, U.S. Govt. Print. Off., 1957.

    v, 74 p. 24 cm. (85th Cong., 1st sess. Senate. Report no. 132)

    1. Consolidation and merger of corporations—U.S. I. Title. (Series: U.S. 85th Cong., 1st sess., 1957. Senate. Report no. 132)

                                                  57-61347

MC#: 1957-5283

SuDocs no.: 85th Cong., 1st sess. S. Rept. 132

FRIEND REPORT
569

Friend, Irwin.

    Study of the savings and loan industry, directed by Irwin Friend. Submitted to the Federal Home Loan Bank Board. Washington; [For sale by the Supt. of Docs., U.S. Govt. Print. Off.] 1969.

    4 v. (ix, 1822 p.) illus. 24 cm.

    Study conducted at the Wharton School of Finance and Commerce, University of Pennsylvania.

    Includes bibliographical references.

    1. Building and loan associations—United States—Addresses, essays, lectures. I. United States. Federal Home Loan Bank Board. II. Pennsylvania. University. Wharton School of Finance and Commerce. III. Title.

HG2151.F84   338.4′7′332320973   72-606665

                                                  MARC

MC#: 1970-14368

SuDocs no.: FHL1.2:Sa9/5/v.1-4

FRIEND REPORT [Friend, Irwin]
    Distribution of ownership in the 200 largest non-financial corporations.
    see under

O'MAHONEY REPORTS [O'Mahoney, Joseph Christopher]
    Goldsmith. Distribution of ownership in the 200 largest non-financial corporations.

FROST REPORT
570

Frost, George E. 1918-

    The patent system and the modern economy; [study] of the Committee on the Judiciary, United States Senate, pursuant to S. Res. 167 of the Eighty-fourth Congress, second session. Washington, U.S. Govt. Print. Off., 1957.

    v, 77 p. 24 cm. (Study of the Subcommittee on Patents, Trademarks, and Copyrights, study no. 2)

    85th Cong., 1st sess. Senate. Document no. 22.

    1. Patents—U.S. 2. Research, Industrial—U.S. I. Title. (Series: U.S. Congress. Senate. Committee on the Judiciary. Study of the Subcommittee on Patents, Trademarks, and Copyrights, study no. 2. Series: U.S. 85th Cong., 1st sess., 1957. Senate. Document no. 22)

57-60188

MC#: 1957-1851

SuDocs no.: Y4.J89/2:P27/3/no. 2

MC#: 1957-3725

SuDocs no.: 85th Cong., 1st sess. S. Doc. 22

FRY REPORT
571

Fry, Bernard Mitchell, 1915-

    Economics and interaction of the publisher-library relationship in the production and use of scholarly and research journals: final report/by Bernard M. Fry and Herbert S. White, with special additional material by Marjorie Shepley.—[Washington]: U.S. National Science Foundation, Office of Science Information Services: [Springfield, Va.]: distributed by National Technical Information Service, U.S. Dept. of Commerce, 1975.

    xiii, 401 p.: forms; 28 cm.

    "PB-249-108."

    Bibliography: p. 385-401.

    1. Libraries and publishing. 2. Scholarly periodicals—Publishing. 3. Acquisition of serial publications. I. White, Herbert S., joint author. II. Shepley, Marjorie, joint author. III. United States. National Science Foundation. Office of Science Information Service. IV. Title: Economics and interaction of the publisher-library relationship . . .

Z716.6.F77   338.4′7′070572   77-376451

                                                  MARC

Not located in Monthly Catalog

FRY REPORT
572

Fry (George) & Associated, inc.

    Salary study and proposed pay adjustment plan, Post Office Department field services; an independent report on current compensation problems prepared at the request of the U.S. Post Office Department. With a letter of transmittal from the Postmaster General to the Chairman of the Committee on Post Office and Civil Service of the U.S. Senate and House of Representatives. [Washington, U.S. Govt. Print. Off.] 1954.

    v, 65 p. 23 cm.

    1. U.S. Post Office Dept.—Appointments, promotions, salaries, etc. I. U.S. Post Office Dept.

HE6499.F78   383.4973   54-61253 rev

MC#: 1954-4430

SuDocs no.: P1.2:Sa3/2

FULLER REPORT [Fuller, John Grant]
573

U.S. *Congress. House. Committee on Science and Astronautics.*

    Aliens in the skies; the scientific rebuttal to the Condon Committee report. Testimony by six leading scientists before the House Committee on Science and Astronautics, July 29, 1968. Edited and with an introd. and commentary by John G. Fuller. New York, Putnam [1969]

    217 p. 22 cm.

    1. Colorado. University. Final report of the scientific study of unidentified flying objects. 2. Flying saucers. I. Fuller, John Grant, 1913- ed. II. Condon, Edward Uhler, 1902- III. Title.

TL789.U56   001′.9   70-86302

                                                  MARC

Not located in Monthly Catalog

FULLER REPORT [Fuller, Walter D.]
574

U.S. *Congress. Senate. Committee on Post Office and Civil Service.*

    Postal rates and postal policy of the Post Office Department; report pursuant to S. Res. 49, a resolution to investigate certain matters respecting postal rates and charges in handling certain mail matter. Washington, U.S. Govt. Print. Off., 1954.

ix, 364 p. illus. 24 cm. (83d Cong., 2d sess. Senate. Report no. 1086)

1. Postal service — U.S. — Rates. 2. Postal service — U.S. — (Service: U.S. 83d Cong., 2d sess., 1954. Senate. Report no. 1086.

HE6331 1954.A512   383.4973   54-61588
MC#: 1954-6912
SuDocs no.: 83d Cong., 2d sess. S. Rept. 1086

FULTON REPORTS [Fulton, James Grove]

575

U.S. *Congress. House. Committee on Foreign Affairs.*
Displaced persons and the International Refugee Organization. Report of a special subcommittee of the Committee on Foreign Affairs . . . Eightieth Congress, first session. Washington, U.S. Govt Print. Off., 1947.

iii, 88 p. 23 cm.
James G. Fulton, chairman.
1. International Refugee Organization. 2. World War, 1939-1945 — Displaced persons. I. Fulton, James Grove, 1903-
HV640.3.U6 1947b   940.53159   48-50032*
MC#: 1948-594
SuDocs no.: Y4.F76/1:D63/3

576

U.S. *Congress. House. Committee on Foreign Affairs.*
Voluntary foreign aid; the nature and scope of postwar private American assistance abroad with special reference to Europe. A study by a special subcommittee of the Committee on Foreign Affairs . . . Eightieth Congress, second session. Washington, U.S. Govt. Print. Off., 1948.

iii, 91 p. 24 cm.
At head of title: Subcommittee print.
James G. Fulton, chairman.
1. Charities — Europe. 2. Reconstruction (1939-) — Europe. I. Fulton, James Grove, 1903- II. Title.
HV238.U62 1948   940.531444   48-45635*
MC#: 1948-5702
SuDocs no.: Y4.F76/1:F76/11

GAITHER REPORT [Gaither, H. Rowan, Jr.]

577

United States. President's Science Advisory Committee. Security Resources Panel.
Deterrence and survival in the nuclear age (the "Gaither report" of 1957)/printed for the use of the Joint Committee on Defense Production, Congress of the United States.- — Washington : U.S. Govt. Print. Off., 1976.

iii, 45 p. : graphs; 23 cm.
At head of title: 94th Congress, 2d session.
Joint Committee print.
1. United States — Defenses. 2. United States — Military policy. 3. Deterrence (Strategy) 4. Atomic warfare. I. United States. Congress. Joint Committee on Defense Production. II. Title: Deterrence and survival in the nuclear age . . . III. Title: Gaither report.
UA23.U493 1976   355.03'307'3   76-601955
                                 MARC

Not located in Monthly Catalog

GALLAGHER REPORT [Gallagher, Cornelius E.]

578

U.S. *Congress. House. Committee on Foreign Affairs.*

Special study mission to Berlin; report, by Cornelius E. Gallagher (D., N.J.) and Alvin M. Bentley (R., Mich.) pursuant to H. Res. 113 . . . Washington, U.S. Govt. Print. Off., 1959.

vii, 27 p. 24 cm.
At head of title: 86th Cong., 1st sess. Committee print.
1. Berlin question (1945-) I. Gallagher, Cornelius E. II. Bentley, Alvin M.
DD881.U46   943.155   59-62194
MC#: 1959-14338
SuDocs no.: Y4.F76/1:B45

GALLATIN REPORT [Gallatin, Albert]

579

U.S. *Treasury Dept.*
Roads and canals. [Report] communicated to the Senate, April 6, 1808. (10th Cong., 1st sess. [Senate document] no. 250)

(*In* U.S. Congress. American state papers. Washington. 33 cm. Class X. Miscellaneous, [1834], p. 724-741)
Checklist of United States Public Documents, 1789-1909, page 4 10th Cong., 1st sess. S. Doc. 250. In Serial no. 014, vol. 1

GALVIN REPORT [Galvin, John E.]

580

U.S. *Commission on Judicial and Congressional Salaries.*
Judicial and congressional salaries; reports of the task forces of the Commission on Judicial and Congressional Salaries pursuant to Public law 220, 83d Congress. Washington, U.S. Govt. Print. Off., 1954.

iv, 80 p. illus. 24 cm. (83d Cong., 2d sess. Senate. Document no. 97)
1. Judges — U.S. — Salaries, pensions, etc. 2. U.S. Congress — Salaries, pensions, etc. I. Title. (Series: U.S. 83d Cong., 2d sess., 1954. Senate. Document no. 97)
                      328.333   54-61455
MC#: 1954-5319
SuDocs no.: 83d Cong., 2d sess. S. Doc. 97

GANNETT REPORT [Gannett, Henry]

581

National conservation commission, *Washington, D.C.*
. . . Report of the National conservation commission. February, 1909. Special message from the President of the United States transmitting a report of the National conservation commission, with accompanying papers . . . Ed. under the direction of the executive committee by Henry Gannett. Washington, Govt. print. Off., 1909.

3 v. plates, maps, diagrs. 23 cm. (60th Cong., 2d sess. Senate. Doc. no. 676)
Contents. — v. 1. Report, etc. — v. 2. Accompanying papers: Waters and forests. — v. 3. Accompanying papers: Lands, minerals, and national vitality.
1. U.S. — Econ. condit. 2. Natural resources. 3. U.S. — Statistics, Vital. 4. Hygiene, Public — U.S. I. U.S. President, 1901-1909 (Roosevelt) II. Gannett, Henry, 1846-1914, ed.
HC101.A4 1909a   9-35662
MC#: July 1909-page 39
SuDocs no.: 60th Cong., 2d sess. S. Doc. no. 676

GARDEN PLOT

582

United States. Dept. of the Army.
DA civil disturbance plan: garden plot / prepared by the Director of Military Support, Headquarters, Dept. of the Army for the DoD Executive Agent.- — Washington: Dept. of the Army, 1978.

xi, 289 p. in various pagings: ill.; 27 cm.
Cover title.
"The nickname applicable to this plan is GARDEN PLOT."—Pref.
1. United States. Army—Civic action. I. United States. Dept. of the Army. Directorate of Military Support. II. Title. III. Title: Garden Plot.
[UH723.U53 1978]
Dept. of the Army Library
Not located in Monthly Catalog

GARDNER REPORT

583

Gardner, John William, 1912-
A.I.D. and the universities; report to the Administrator of the Agency for International Development, by John W. Gardner. Washington, Agency for International Development [1964]

xii, 51 p. 23 cm.
1. Educational exchanges—U.S. 2. U.S. Agency for International Development. I. Title.
LB2283.G3 1964   64-61681
MC#: 1964-12561
SuDocs no.: S18.2:Un3

GARFINKEL REPORT [Garfinkel, Irwin]

see under

GRIFFITHS REPORTS [Griffiths, Martha W.]
Studies in public welfare, paper no. 13.

GARGAN REPORT [Gargan, John J.]

see

DOUGLAS REPORTS [Douglas, Paul H.]
National Commission on Urban Problems.

Research report no. 18

GARMENT REPORT [Garment, Leonard]

584

U.S. *National Goals Research Staff.*
Toward balanced growth: quantity with quality; report. Washington; [For sale by the Supt. of Docs., U.S. Govt. Print. Off.] 1970.

v, 228 p. illus., maps. 24 cm.
1. U.S.—Social conditions—1960- 2. U.S.—Economic conditions—1961- I. Title.
HN59.A515   309.1'73   78-608272
                                                                  MARC
MC#: 1970-12905
SuDocs no.: Pr37.8:N21g/R29/970

GARRETT REPORT [Garrett, Earle W.]

see

VOLLMER REPORT [Vollmer, August]

WICKERSHAM COMMISSION [Wickersham, George Woodward]
Report on police, no. 14.

GARRISON REPORT [Garrison, Lloyd K.]

585

U.S. *Fact-finding board in the General motors dispute,* 1945/46.
. . . Report to the President by the Fact-finding board in the General motors dispute [and Appendix A-G] [Washington, 1946]

2 pts. tables. 32-35½ cm.
Caption title.
Reproduced from type-written copy.

Release dated Jan. 10, 1946.
Appendices include Chronology of the GM-UAW case and Corporation statement of December 28, 1945 on withdrawal from proceedings.
1. General motors strike, 1945- 2. Wages—U.S. [3. Automobile workers-U.S.] I. International union, united automobile, aircraft and agricultural implement workers of America. II. General motors corporation.
                                                                  L46-77
MC#: 1946-page 524 (LC card L46-20 cancelled in favor of L46-77)
SuDocs no.: L1.16:G28

GATCHELL REPORT [Gatchell, Willard Waddington]

see

PARKER REPORT [Parker, James Southworth]

GATES REPORTS [Gates, Thomas S.]

586

U.S. *Committee on Organization of the Dept. of the Navy (1958-1959)*
Report. [Washington] 1959.

175 p. diagrs. 24 cm.
"NAVEXOS P-1996."
1. U.S. Navy Dept.
VA52.A184   353.7   59-60840
MC#: 1959-6868
SuDocs no.: D201.2:Or3/959

587

U.S. *President's Commission on an All-Volunteer Armed Force.*
The report of the President's Commission on an All-Volunteer Armed Force. [Washington, For sale by the Supt. of Docs., U.S. Govt. Print. Off., 1970]

xiii, 211 p. 24 cm.
Cover title.
Commonly known as the Gates report.
Includes bibliographical references.
1. U.S.—Armed Forces—Recruiting, enlistment, etc. I. Title: Gates report on an all-volunteer Armed Force.
UB323.A5 1970a   355.2'2   78-605447
                                                                  MARC
MC#: 1970-6127
SuDocs no.: Pr37.8:Ar5/R29/970

United States. President's Commission on an All-Volunteer Armed Force.
The report of the President's Commission on an All-Volunteer Armed Force. [New York] Collier Books [1970]

218 p. 22 cm.
Commonly known as the Gates report.
1. United States—Armed Forces—Recruiting, enlistment, etc. I. Title. II. Title: Gates report on an all-volunteer armed force.
UB323.A5 1970   355.2'23'0973   79-12775
                                                                  MARC

Not listed in Monthly Catalog

GEROW REPORT [Gerow, Leonard T.]

588

U.S. War Dept. Military education board.
Report of War Department Military Education Board on educational system for officers of the army. [Command and General Staff School, 1946]

90 p. illus. 35 cm.
[U408.3.A53 1946]
Dept. of the Army Library
Not located in Monthly Catalog

GESELL REPORT [Gesell, Gerhard Alden]

589

U.S. *President's Committee on Equal Opportunity in the Armed Forces.*
    Equality of treatment and opportunity for Negro military personnel stationed within the United States; initial report. [Washington] 1963.

    93 p. 27 cm.
    1. U.S.—Armed Forces—Negroes. 2. Negroes—Segregation. I. Title.
E185.63.U63   63-62364
Not located in Monthly Catalog

GESELL REPORT [Gesell, Gerhard Alden]
    Statement on life insurance.

    Study of legal reserve life insurance companies.
    see under
O'MAHONEY REPORTS [O'Mahoney, Joseph Christopher]

GIBSON REPORT [Gibson, John W.]

590

U.S. *Displaced Persons Commission.*
    Memo to America: the DP story; the final report of the U.S. Displaced Persons Commission. Washington, U.S. Govt. Print. Off., 1952.

    xi, 376 p. tables. 24 cm.
    1. U.S.—Emig. & immig. 2. World War, 1939-1945—Displaced persons. 3. Refugees, Political. I. Title. II. Title: The DP story.
JV6416.A83 1952   325.73   52-61541
MC#: 1952-15329
SuDocs no.: Y3.D63/2:1/952

GIFFORD REPORT [Gifford, Charles L.]
    see
COCHRAN REPORT [Cochran, John Joseph]

GILBERT REPORT [Gilbert, Milton]
    see under
O'MAHONEY REPORTS [O'Mahoney, Joseph Christopher]

GILLEM BOARD REPORT [Gillem, Alvan C.]

591

U.S. *Bureau of Public Relations (War Dept.)*
    Report of the Board of Officers on Utilization of Negro Manpower in the Post-War Army. Wash., D.C., 26 Feb 1946.

    11 lvs.
    1. Negroes—soldiers. 2. U.S.—Economic Policy. I. Gillem, Alvan C.
[E185.63U58]
Dept. of the Army Library
Not located in Monthly Catalog

GILLETTE REPORT [Gillette, Hyde]

592

U.S. *Congress. House. Committee on Government Operations.*
    Organization and management of missile programs; eleventh report. Washington, U.S. Govt. Print. Off., 1959.

vi, 156 p. 24 cm. (86th Cong., 1st sess. House report no. 1121)
    1. Guided missiles. 2. Ballistics. I. Title. (Series: U.S. 86th Cong., 1st sess., 1959. House. Report no. 1121)
UG633.A412 1959e   623.4519   59-62236
MC#: 1959-14311
SuDocs no.: 86th Cong., 1st sess. H. Rept. 1121

GIZA REPORT [Giza, Richard]

593

U.S. *National Institutes of Health. Resources Analysis Branch.*
    DHEW obligations to institutions of higher education. 1964/65- [Washington] Office of the Assistant Secretary for Health and Scientific Affairs, U.S. Dept. of Health, Education, and Welfare.

    v. illus. 27 cm. annual.
    Report year ends June 30.
    Vols. for 1964/65- issued in 2 pts.: p. 1. Summary data.—pt. 2. Detailed data.
    1. Federal aid to higher education—U.S. I. U.S. Office of the Assistant Secretary for Health and Scientific Affairs. II. Title.
                                                HEW67-16
MC#: 1966-12477, 12478 (Parts 1, 2)
SuDocs no.: FS2.22:Ed8/2/965/pt. (no.)

GLASS REPORT [Glass, Fred M.]

594

U.S. *Task Force on National Aviation Goals.*
    Project Horizon; report. [Washington] Federal Aviation Agency, 1961.

    xiii, 239 p. 25 cm.
    1. Aeronautics—U.S.
TL521.A546 1961   387.70943   61-62380
MC#: 1961-19292
SuDocs no.: FAA1.2:H78

GLOBAL 2000 STUDY (U.S.)

595

Global 2000 Study (U.S.)
    The global 2000 report to the President—entering the twenty-first century : a report / prepared by the Council on Environmental Quality and the Department of State; Gerald O. Barney, study director.—Washington, D.C.: For sale by the Supt. of Docs., U.S. Govt. Print. Off., 1980-1981.

    3 v.: ill.; 27 cm.
    Vol. 2 has also special title: The technical report.
    Vol. 3 has title: The global 2000 report to the President: documentation on the government's global sectoral models, the government's "global model."
    Includes bibliographies and index.
    1. Environmental policy. 2. Natural resources. 3. Food supply. 4. Twenty-first century—Forecasts. 5. Twentieth century—Forecasts. 6. Economic forecasting. I. Barney, Gerald O. II. United States. Council on Environmental Quality. III. United States. Dept. of State. IV. Title.
HC79.E5G59 1980b   333.7-dc19   80-602859
                                                MARC
MC#: 1980-22217
SuDocs no.: PrEx14.2:G51/2000/v.1-2
MC#: 1981-11144
SuDocs no.: PrEx14.2:G51/2000/v.3

Global 2000 Study (U.S.)
    The global 2000 report to the President of the U.S., entering the 21st century: a report / prepared by the Council on Environmental Quality and the Department of State; Gerald O. Barney, study director.—New York: Pergamon Press, [1980-

v. "1": ill. ; 25 cm. — (Pergamon policy studies on policy, planning, and modeling)

Includes bibliographical references and index.

Contents: v. 1. The summary report — special edition with the environment projections and the government's global model. ISBN 0-08-024617-6 (v.1.). ISBN 0-08-024616-8 (pbk.: v.1.)

1. Environmental policy. 2. Natural resources. 3. Food supply. 4. Twenty-first century — Forecasts. 5. Twentieth century — Forecasts. 6. Economic Forecasting. I. Barney, Gerald O. II. United States. Council on Environmental Quality. III. United States. Dept. of State. IV. Title. V. Title: Entering the 21st century. VI. Series.

HC79.E5G59 1980   333.7′0973-dc19   80-20264
                                                                                      MARC

Not listed in Monthly Catalog

596

Council on Environmental Quality (U.S.)

Global future: time to act: report to the President on global resources, environment and population / Council on Environmental Quality; United States Department of State. — [Washington, D.C.: The Council?]: For sale by the Supt. of Docs., U.S. G.P.O., 1981.

liii, 209 p.; 26 cm.
S/N 041-011-00056-4
Item 856-E Supt. of Docs. no.: PrEx 14.2:G51/3

1. Environmental policy — International cooperation. 2. Conservation of natural resources — International cooperation. 3. Economic assistance, American. 4. Technical assistance, American. I. United States. Dept. of State. II. Title.

HC79.E5C68 1981   333.7′0973-dc19   81-601263
                                                                              AACR 2 MARC

MC#: 1981-3841
SuDocs no.: PrEx14.2:G51/3

GLYNN REPORT [Glynn, Thomas]
597

United States. Vice President's Task Force on Youth Employment.

A review of youth employment problems, programs & policies / The Vice President's Task Force on Youth Employment. — [Washington, D.C. : U.S. Dept. of Labor, Employment and Training Administration], 1980.

3 v.; 28 cm.
Cover title.
Includes bibliographies.
Contents: v. 1. The youth employment problem. — v. 2. Special needs and concentrated problems. 3. Program experience.

1. Youth — Employment — United States — Addresses, essays, lectures. 2. Minority youth — Employment — United States — Addresses, essays, lectures. 3. Manpower policy United States — Addresses, essays, lectures. I. Title.

HD6273.U55 1980   331.3′411′0973-dc19   80-601825
                                                                                      MARC

MC#: 1980-10677
SuDocs no.: Pr39.8:Y8/Em7/v.1-3

GOLDBERG REPORTS [Goldberg, Authur J.]
598

U.S. *Missile Sites Labor Commission.*
  Report. 1st-
1961/62-
[Washington, U.S. Govt. Print. Off.]
v. illus. 27 cm. annual.
Report year for 1962 ends May 26; for 1963- June 1.
Title varies slightly.

Each report has also a distinctive title: 1961/62, United for America. — 1962/63. Success before countdown.

1. Strikes and lockouts — Guided missile industries — U.S.
HD5325.G8A3   62-61561 rev
1961/62, United for America
MC#: 1962-14563
SuDocs no.: Pr35.8:M69/Un3
1962/63, Success before countdown
MC#: 1963-20083
SuDocs no.: Pr35.8:M69/Su1

599

U.S. *President's Advisory Committee on Labor-Management Policy.*

The benefits and problems incident to automation and other technological advances; report. Washington [U.S. Govt. Print. Off.] 1962.

11 p. illus. 28 cm.
1. Automation — Economic aspects — U.S. I. Title.
HC110.A9A6   62-60925
MC#: 1962-8596
SuDocs no.: Pr35.8:/L11/Au8

600

U.S. *President's Advisory Committee on Labor-Management Policy.*

Collective bargaining; a report. [Washington, U.S. Govt. Print. Off., 1962]

iii, 12 p. illus. 28 cm.
1. Collective bargaining — U.S.
HD6483.U74   62-61476
MC#: 1962-14559
SuDocs no.: Pr35.8:L11/C68

GOLDENTHAL REPORT [Goldenthal, Aldolph James]
see under
O'MAHONEY REPORTS [O'Mahoney, Joseph Christopher]

GOLDENWEISER REPORT [Goldenweiser, Emanual Alexandrovich]
see under
DILLINGHAM COMMISSION [Dillingham, William Paul]
Immigrants in cities.

GOLDMUNTZ REPORT [Goldmuntz, Alexander]
601

United States. Dept. of Transportation. Air Traffic Control Advisory Committee.

Report of Department of Transportation Air Traffic Control Advisory Committee. [Washington; For sale by the Supt. of Docs., U.S. Govt. Print. Off.] 1969 [i.e. 1970]

2 v. illus., maps. 26 cm.
Includes bibliographical references.
1. Air traffic control — United States. I. Title.
TL725.3.T7U673   629.136′6′0973   71-606236
                                                                                      MARC

MC#: 1970-7866, 7867
SuDocs no.: TD1.2:A17/v.1-2

GOLDSMITH REPORT [Goldsmith, Raymond William]
see under
O'MAHONEY REPORTS [O'Mahoney, Joseph Christopher]

GOLDSTEIN REPORT [Goldstein, Jon H.]

Effectiveness of manpower training programs.
see under
GRIFFITHS REPORTS [Griffiths, Martha W.]

Studies in public welfare, paper no. 3.

GOLDSTEIN REPORT [Goldstein, Joseph]

see
PEERS COMMISSION [Peers, William R.]

GOLDWATER REPORT

602

Goldwater, Barry, 1938-
Congressman Barry Goldwater, Jr., reports on the United States Government and the American radio-television-motion picture industry / compiled by Gus Kaye. — [Washington?]: Goldwater, [1972?]

66 leaves; 28 cm.
1. Government publicity—United States. 2. Government competition—United States. I. Kaye, Gus.
JK849.A3G64   353.008′74   74-601125
                                                    MARC

Not located in Monthly Catalog

GOOCH REPORT [Gooch, Daniel Wheelwright]

see
WADE REPORT [Wade, Benjamin Franklin]

Report of the Joint Committee on the Conduct of the War.

GOODE REPORT

603

Goode, George Brown, 1851-1896.
. . . The fisheries and fishery industries of the United States. Prepared through the co-operation of the commissioner of fisheries and the superintendent of the tenth census by George Brown Goode . . . and a staff of associates . . . Washington, Govt. print. off., 1884-87.

8 v. in 7. plates, charts. 28 cm.
At head of title: U.S. Commission of fish and fisheries.
Contents.—sec. I. Natural history of useful aquatic animals, by G. B. Goode, J. A. Allen, H. W. Elliott, F. W. True, E. Ingersoll, J. A. Ryder, R. Rathbun. 2 v.—sec. II. A geographical review of the fisheries industries and fishing communities for the year 1880, by R. E. Earll, W. A. Wilcox, A. H. Clark, F. Mather, J. W. Collins, M. McDonald, S. Stearns, D. S. Jordan, F. W. True.—sec. III. The fishing grounds of North America, by R. Rathbun, J. W. Collins, D. S. Jordan, T. H. Bean, L. Kunlien, F. W. True.—sec. IV. The fishermen of the United States, by G. B. Goode, J. W. Collins.—sec. V. History and methods of the fisheries, by G. B. Goode, J. W. Collins, N. P. Scudder, T. H. Bean, A. H. Clark, R. E. Earll, S. Stearns, F. W. True, M. McDonald, W. A. Wilcox, C. G. Atkins, D. S. Jordan, C. H. Gilbert, L. Kumlien, A. H. Clark, J. T. Brown, H. W. Elliott, J. H. Swan, E. Ingersoll, R. Rathbun. 3 v.
1. Fisheries—U.S. I. U.S. Bureau of fisheries.
SH221.G59   F20-35
Checklist of United States Public Documents, 1789-1909, page 409
SuDocs no.: FC1.6:(sec. nos.)

GORDON REPORT [Gordon, Robert A.]

604

U.S. *President's Committee to Appraise Employment and Unemployment Statistics.*

Measuring employment and unemployment. [Washington, U.S. Govt. Print. Off., 1962]

412 p. map, diagrs., tables. 24 cm.
Bibliographical footnotes.
1. Labor supply—U.S.—Stat. 2. Unemployed—U.S.—Stat. I. Title.
HD5711.U57   331.112   62-64695
MC#: 1962-22715
SuDocs no.: Pr35.8:Em7/3/M46

GORDON REPORT [Gordon, Thomas S.]

605

U.S. *Congress. House. Committee on Foreign Affairs.*
Report of the special study mission to the Mediterranean area of the Committee on Foreign Affairs, submitted pursuant to H. Res. 29 . . . Washington, U.S. Govt. Print. Off., 1957.

vii, 12 p. maps. 24 cm. (85th Cong., 1st sess. House report no. 208)
1. Mutual security program, 1951- 2. Mediterranean region—Politics. 3. U.S.—For. rel. (Series: U.S. 85th Cong., 1st sess., 1957. House. Report no. 208)
UA12.U5 1957   57-61340
MC#: 1957-6866
SuDocs no.: 85th Cong., 1st sess. H. Rept. 208

GORE REPORT [Gore, Albert]

606

U.S. *Congress. Senate. Select Committee for Contribution Investigation.*
Report pursuant to S. Res. 205, as extended by S. Res. 218 and S. Res. 227, 84th Cong., 2d sess. Washington, U.S. Govt. Print. Off., 1956.

iii, 12 p. 24 cm. (84th Cong., 2d sess. Senate. Report no. 1724)
1. Case, Francis Higbee, 1896- 2. Elections—U.S.—Campaign funds. 3. Gas, Natural—U.S. (Series: U.S. 84th Cong., 2d sess. 1956. Senate. Report no. 1724)
JK1991.A4 1956   56-60957
MC#: 1956-7202
SuDocs no.: 84th Cong., 2d sess. S. Rept. 1724.

GORHAM REPORT [Gorham, William]

607

U.S. *Dept. of Health, Education, and Welfare.*
A report to the President on medical care prices. [Washington, For sale by the Supt. of Docs., U.S. Govt. Print. Off.] 1967.

vii, 38 p. illus. 24 cm.
1. Medical care, Cost of—U.S. [1. Medical care—Cost—U.S.] I. Title: Medical care prices.
RA410.U45   338.4′3   HEW67-61
                                                 MARC
MC#: 1967-8194A
SuDocs no.: FS1.2:M46/3

GORHAM STUDY

608

U.S. *Assistant Secretary of Defense (Manpower).*
Defense study on military compensation. [Gorham Study]. [Washington] 1962.

8 v. charts, graphs, tables (ASDIRS 1001)
AD - 474891 - AD - 474898
1. U.S.—Armed Forces—Pay, allowances, etc. I. Title. II. Title: Military compensation. III. Title: Gorham study. IV. Series. [UC74.A4 1962]
Dept. of the Army Library
Not located in Monthly Catalog

GORINSON REPORT [Gorinson, Stanley M.]
see
KEMENY COMMISSION REPORTS [Kemeny, John G.]
> Report of the Office of Chief Counsel on the Nuclear Regulatory Commission. Role of the managing utility and its suppliers.

GOROKHOFF REPORT

609

Gorokhoff, Boris Ivanovich, 1917-
> Providing U.S. scientists with Soviet scientific information. Rev. ed. [Washington? 1962]

> 46 p. map, diagrs., tables. 26 cm.
> Cover title.
> 1. Science — Russia — Information services. I. Title.
> Z7407.R9G6 1962   62-6784
> Not located in Monthly Catalog

GOTTFELD REPORT

610

Gottfeld, Gunther M
> Rapid transit systems in six metropolitan areas; staff report prepared for the Joint Committee on Washington Metropolitan Problems, Congress of the United States. Washington, U.S. Govt. Print. Off., 1959.

> v, 39 p. 24 cm.
> 1. Local transit — U.S. 2. Toronto — Transit systems. I. U.S. Congress. Joint Committee on Washington Metropolitan Problems. II. Title.
> HE4451.G6   388.40973   60-60447
> MC#: 1960-1696
> SuDocs no.: Y4.W27/2:T68/6

GOTTSCHALK COMMITTEE REPORT [Gottschalk, Carl W.]

611

Committee on Chronic Kidney Disease.
> Report of the Committee on Chronic Kidney Disease, submitted to the Bureau of the Budget by Carl W. Gottschalk, Chairman — [Washington s.n.] 1967.

> 197 leaves, 29 cm.
> Cover title.
> Bibliography: leaves 159-166.
> 1. Kidney — transplantation. 2. Dialysis. 3. Renal insufficiency. I. Gottschalk, Carl W. II. Gottschalk Committee Report.
> [RC901.5.C65 1967]
> Joseph and Rose Kennedy Institute of Ethics
> Not located in Monthly Catalog

GRACE REPORTS [Grace, J. Peter]

612

Commerce Committee for the Alliance for Progress.
> Proposals to improve the flow of U.S. private investment to Latin America; report. Washington, U.S. Dept. of Commerce, 1963.

> viii, 78, A29, B11 p. tables. 27 cm.
> "Report . . . presented to the Department [of Commerce] on January 4, 1963."
> 1. Investments, American — Spanish America. I. U.S. Dept. of Commerce. II. Title.
> HG5302.C58   63-61548
> MC#: 1963-9783
> SuDocs no.: C1.2:L34

613

U.S. *International Development Advisory Board.*
> An economic program for the Americas; report [prepared by one of its members, J. Peter Grace, Jr.] Washington, 1954.

> 30 p. illus. 28 cm.
> 1. Spanish America — Economic policy. I. Title.
> HC165.U47   55-60357
> Not located in Monthly Catalog

GRAD REPORT [Grad, Frank P.]
see
DOUGLAS REPORTS [Douglas, Paul H.]
> National Commission on Urban Problems.

> Research report no. 14

GRAHAM REPORT

614

Graham, Hugh Davis.
> Violence in America: historical and comparative perspectives; a report to the National Commission on the Causes and Prevention of Violence, by Hugh Davis Graham and Ted Robert Gurr. [Washington, For sale by the Supt. of Docs., U.S. Govt. Print. Off.] 1969.

> 2 v. (xxii, 644 p.) illus. 24 cm. ([NCCPV staff study series, 1-2])
> Commonly known as the Graham report.
> Report of the Task Force on Historical and Comparative Perspectives.
> Includes bibliographies.
> 1. Violence — United States. I. Gurr, Ted Robert, 1936- joint author. II. United States. National Commission on the Causes and Prevention of Violence. III. United States. National Commission on the Causes and Prevention of Violence. Task Force on Historical and Comparative Perspectives. IV. Title. V. Title: Graham report on violence in America. VI. Series: United States. National Commission on the Causes and Prevention of Violence. NCCPV staff study series, 1-2.
> HN90.V5G7 1969   301.2   76-601931
>   MARC
> MC#: 1969-13328
> SuDocs no.: Pr36.8:V81/H62/v.1-2

GRAHAM REPORT [Graham, Robert E.]

615

U.S. *Office of Business Economics.*
> Income in Alaska; a supplement to the Survey of current business, by Robert E. Graham, Jr., National Income Division. [Washington, U.S. Govt. Print. Off., 1960]

> 35 p. maps, diagrs., tables. 26 cm. "The information . . . will be updated each year and published . . . in the August issues of the Survey of current business."
> 1. Income — Alaska. I. Graham, Robert E. II. Survey of current business. Supplement. III. Title.
> HC107.A45A4 1960   339.4109798   60-64732
> MC#: 1961-256
> SuDocs no.: C43.8/3:Al 1s

GRAHAM REPORT [Graham, William Alexander]
see
RENO REPORT [Reno, Marcus Albert]

GRANBY REPORT [Granby, Helene]
see under
O'MAHONEY REPORTS [O'Mahoney, Joseph Christopher]

GRAVES REPORT [Graves, William Brooke]

see

KESTNBAUM COMMISSION [Kestnbaum, Meyer]

Summaries of survey reports.

GRAY REPORT [Gray, Carl R., Jr.]

616

U.S. *Veterans Administration.*

Reorganization of Veterans Administration; background and solution. [Washington? 1953]

ix, 49 p. illus., fold. col. maps. 33 cm.

Cover title.

1. U.S. Veterans Administration.

UB373.A45 1953   355.115   53-60192

MC#: 1953-2907

SuDocs no.: VA1.2:R29

GRAY REPORT [Gray, Lewis Cecil]

617

U.S. *Special committee on farm tenancy.*

. . . Farm tenancy. Message from the President of the United States transmitting the report of the Special committee on farm tenancy . . . Washington, U.S. Govt. print. off., 1937.

vii, 28 p. 23½ cm. (75th Cong., 1st sess. House. Doc. 149)

Referred to the Committee on agriculture and ordered printed February 16, 1937.

Prepared by a joint technical committee of the Special committee on farm tenancy and the National resources committee consisting of L. C. Gray, chairman, John D. Black, E. G. Nourse and others. *cf.* Letter of transmittal, p. v-vi.

Issued also without document series note, with supplementary material and title: Farm tenancy. Report of the President's committee.

H. A. Wallace, chairman.

1. Farm tenancy—U.S. 2. Agriculture—Economic aspects—U.S. 3. Land tenure—U.S. I. U.S. National resources committee. II. Gray, Lewis Cecil, 1881- III. Wallace, Henry Agard, 1888-

HD1511.U5A5 1937b   333.50973   37-26227

MC#: 1937-page 173

SuDocs no.: 75th Cong., 1st sess. H. Doc. 149

GRAY REPORTS

618

Gray, Gordon.

Report to the President on foreign economic policies. Washington, U.S. Govt. Print. Off., 1950.

vii, 131 p. 23 cm.

1. U.S.—Economic policy. 2. U.S.—Commercial policy. 3. Industrialization. 4. Economic policy.

HC106.5.G68   338.973   50-61567

MC#: 1950-25572

SuDocs no.: Pr33.2:F76

619

U.S. *Dept. of Defense. Committee on Civilian Components.*

Reserve forces for national security, report to the Secretary of Defense. [Washington, U.S. Govt. Print. Off., 1948]

v, 211 p. diagrs. 24 cm.

Cover title.

Seal of National Military Establishment, United States of America, on cover.

Bibliography: p. 195-199.

1. Armed Forces—U.S.—Reserves.

UA42.A52 1948   355   48-46999*

MC#: 1948-22655

SuDocs no.: M1.2:R31

GREEN REPORT [Green, Theodore Francis]

620

United Nations. *General Assembly. 7th sess., 1952- Delegation from the United States.*

Seventh General Assembly of the United Nations. Report of Senator Theodore Francis Green as a delegate to the Seventh General Assembly of the United Nations, October 14 to December 21, 1952, together with certain speeches made on the United Nations. Washington, U.S. Govt. Print. Off., 1953.

v, 42 p. illus. 24 cm. (83d Cong., 1st sess. Senate. Document no. 27)

1. United Nations. General Assembly. 7th sess., 1952- I. Green, Theodore Francis, 1867- (Series: U.S. 83d Cong., 1st sess., 1953. Senate. Document no. 27)

JX1977.A48U6 1952c   341.133   53-60825

MC#: 1953-7477

SuDocs no.: 83d Cong., 1st sess. S. Doc. 27

GREEN REPORT [Green, Theodore Francis]

Old-age pension system.

see

DOWNEY REPORT [Downey, Sheridan]

GREGORY REPORT [Gregory, Clifford Verne]

see

BAKER REPORT [Baker, Jacob]

GREVERUS REPORT [Greverus, Jane]

see under

O'MAHONEY REPORTS [O'Mahoney, Joseph Christopher]

Blaisdell. Economic power and political pressures.

GRIFFIN REPORT [Griffin, William]

621

U.S. *Dept. of State.*

Legal aspects of the use of systems of international waters, with reference to Columbia-Kootenay River system under customary international law and the Treaty of 1909. Memorandum [prepared by William Griffin] of the State Dept. Washington, U.S. Govt. Print. Off., 1958.

v, 92 p. 24 cm. (85th Cong., 2d sess. Senate. Document no. 118)

1. International rivers. 2. Water-rights (International law) 3. Columbia River. 4. Kootenai River. I. Title. (Series: U.S. 85th Cong., 2d sess., 1958. Senate. Document no. 118)

JX4150.U6   333.91   58-62096

MC#: 1958-15807

SuDocs no.: 85th Cong., 2d sess. S. Doc. 118

GRIFFITHS REPORTS [Griffiths, Martha W.]

622

Storey, James R

Public income transfer programs: the incidence of multiple benefits and the issues raised by their receipt; a study, by James R. Storey. Washington, U.S. Govt. Print. Off., 1972.

v, 51 p. 24 cm. (Studies in public welfare, paper no. 1)

At head of title: 92d Congress, 2d session. Joint committee print.

"Prepared for the use of the Subcommittee on Fiscal Policy of the Joint Economic Committee, Congress of the United States."

Includes bibliographical references.

1. Public welfare—United States. I. United States. Congress. Joint Economic Committee. Subcommittee on Fiscal Policy. II. Title. III. Series.

HV95.S83   361.6′2′0973   72-601836

                                                        MARC

MC#: 1972-10688

SuDocs no.: Y4.Ec7:W45/paper 1

623

Cox, Irene.

Handbook of public income transfer programs; a staff study prepared for the use of the Subcommittee on Fiscal Policy of the Joint Economic Committee, Congress of the United States. Washington, U.S. Govt. Print. Off., 1972.

vi, 336 p. 24 cm. (Studies in public welfare, paper no. 2)

At head of title: 92d Congress, 2d session. Joint committee print.

Bibliography: p. 334-336.

1. Public welfare—United States. 2. Insurance, Social—United States. 3. Income—United States. I. United States. Congress. Joint Economic Committee. Subcommittee on Fiscal Policy. II. Title. III. Series.

HV91.C68   361.6′2′0973   72-603346

                                                        MARC

MC#: 1973-16933

SuDocs no.: Y4.Ec7:W45/paper 2

624

Goldstein, Jon H

The effectiveness of manpower training programs: a review of research on the impact on the poor [by Jon H. Goldstein], A staff study prepared for the use of the Subcommittee on Fiscal Policy of the Joint Economic Committee, Congress of the United States. Washington, U.S. Govt. Print. Off., 1972.

vii, 70 p. 24 cm. (Studies in public welfare, paper no. 3)

At head of title: 92d Congress, 2d session. Joint committee print.

Bibliography: p. 68-70.

1. Occupational training—United States. 2. Hard-core unemployed—United States. 3. Manpower policy—United States. I. United States. Congress. Joint Economic Committee. Subcommittee on Fiscal Policy. II. Title. III. Series.

HD5715.2.G64   362.8′5   72-603706

                                                        MARC

MC#: 1973-16934

SuDocs no.: Y4.Ec7:W45/paper 3

625

Income transfer programs: how they tax the poor; a volume of studies prepared for the use of the Subcommittee on fiscal Policy of the Joint Economic Committee, Congress of the United States. Washington, U.S. Govt. Print. Off., 1972.

ix, 139 p. 24 cm. (Studies in public welfare, paper no. 4)

At head of title: 92d Congress, 2d session. Joint committee print.

"The compendium was compiled and edited by Robert I. Lerman."

Includes bibliographical references.

Contents: Lerman, R. I. Incentive effects in public income transfer programs.—Mirer, T. W. Alternative approaches to integrating income transfer programs.—Hausman, L. J. Cumulative tax rates in alternative income maintenance systems.

Supt. of Docs. no.: Y4.Ec7:W45/paper 4

1. Guaranteed annual income—United States. 2. Public welfare—United States. 3. Income—United States. I. Lerman, Robert I. Incentive effects in public income transfer programs.

1972. II. Mirer, Thad W. Alternative approaches to integrating income transfer programs. 1972. III. Hausman, Leonard J. Cumulative tax rates in alternative income maintenance systems. 1972. IV. United States. Congress. Joint Economic Committee. Subcommittee on Fiscal Policy. V. Series.

HC1101.I5I52   362.5   73-600950

                                                        MARC

MC#: 1973-21140

SuDocs no.: Y4.Ec7:W45/paper 4

626

Issues in welfare administration. A staff study prepared for the use of the Subcommittee on Fiscal Policy of the Joint Economic Committee, Congress of the United States. Washington, U.S. Govt. Print. Off., 1972-[73]

3 v. 24 cm. (Studies in public welfare, paper no. 5)

At head of title: 92d Congress, 2d session. Joint committee print; v. 2: 93d Congress, 1st session. Joint committee print. v. 3: 93d Congress, 1st session. Joint committee print.

Includes bibliographical references.

Contents: pt. 1. Galm, S. Welfare—an administrative nightmare.—pt. 2. Handler, J. F. and others. Intergovernmental relationships.—pt. 3. Kershaw, D. N., Allen, J. T. and Bawden, D. L. Implications of the income maintenance experiments.

1. Public welfare administration—United States—Collected works. I. United States. Congress. Joint Economic Committee. Subcommittee on Fiscal Policy. II. Series.

HV95.I88   361′.008   73-600933

                                                        MARC

MC#: 1973-21140 (LC card 73-161527 cancelled in favor of 73-600933)

SuDocs no.: Y4.Ec7:W45/paper 5, pt. 1

MC#: 1973-24309

SuDocs no.: Y4.Ec7:W45/paper 5, pts. 2,3

627

Storey, James R.

How public welfare benefits are distributed in low-income areas, based on data collected by the General Accounting Office; a staff study prepared for the use of the Subcommittee on Fiscal Policy of the Joint Economic Committee, Congress of the United States [by James R. Storey, Alair A. Townsend, and Irene Cox] Washington, U.S. Govt. Print. Off., 1973.

x, 144 p. 24 cm. (Studies in public welfare, paper no. 6)

At head of title: 93d Congress, 1st session. Joint committee print.

- - - - - Additional material for paper no. 6; a study prepared for the use of the Subcommittee on Fiscal Policy of the Joint Economic Committee, Congress of the United States. [Compiled by Alair A. Townsend] Washington, U.S. Govt. Print. Off., 1973.

vii, 114 p. illus. 26 cm. (Studies in public welfare)

At head of title: 93d Congress, 1st session. Joint committee print.

HV91.S73 Suppl.

1. Public welfare—United States. I. Townsend, Alair A., joint author. II. Cox, Irene, joint author. III. United States. Congress. Joint Economic Committee. Subcommittee on Fiscal Policy. IV. Title. V. Series.

HV91.S73   361.6′2′0973   73-601360

                                                        MARC

MC#: 1973-27096

SuDocs no.: Y4.Ec7:W45/paper 6

MC#: 1973-30939 (Additional material: LC card 73-602435 cancelled in favor of 73-601360)

SuDocs no.: Y4.Ec7:W45/paper 6

628

United States. Congress. Joint Economic Committee. Subcommittee on Fiscal Policy.

Issues in the coordination of public welfare programs. Washington, U.S. Govt. Print. Off., 1973.

vi, 255 p. 24 cm. (Studies in public welfare, paper no. 7)

At head of title: 93d Congress, 1st session. Joint committee print.

Includes bibliographical references.

1. Public welfare — United States. 2. Insurance, Social — United States. I. Title. II. Series.

HV95.U52 1973   362'.973   73-602728

                                          MARC

MC#: 1973-32023

SuDocs no.: Y4.Ec7:W45/paper 7

629

Bernstein, Blanche, 1912-

Income-tested social benefits in New York,: adequacy, incentives, and equity: [submitted to] Subcommittee on Fiscal Policy of the Joint Economic Committee, Congress of the United States: a study/by Blanche Bernstein, with Anne N. Shkuda and Eveline M. Burns. — Washington: U.S. Govt. Print. Off.; for sale by the Supt. of Docs., 1973.

viii, 167 p.; 24 cm. — (Studies in public welfare; paper no. 8)

At head of title: 93d Congress, 1st session. Joint Committee print.

Includes bibliographical references.

Supt. of Docs. no.: Y4.Ec7:W45/paper 8

1. Public welfare — New York (City) I. Shkuda, Anne N. II. Burns, Eveline Mabel Richardson, 1900- III. United States. Congress. Joint Economic Committee. Subcommittee on Fiscal Policy. IV. Title. V. Series.

HV99.N59B43   361.6'2'09747   73-602564

                                          MARC

MC#: 1973-29835

SuDocs no.: Y4.Ec7:W45/Paper 8

630

Concepts in welfare program design; a volume of studies.

Prepared for the use of the Subcommittee on Fiscal Policy of the Joint Economic Committee, Congress of the United States. August 20, 1973. Washington, U.S. Govt. Print. Off., 1973-

v. 24 cm. (Studies in public welfare, paper no. 9, pt. 1)

At head of title: 93d Congress, 1st session. Joint committee print.

Includes bibliographical references.

Contents: pt. 1. Okner, B. A. The role of demogrants as an income maintenance alternative. — Haveman, F. H. Work-conditioned subsidies as an income maintenance strategy. — Packer, A. H. Categorical public employment guarantees.

Supt. of Docs. no.: Y4.Ec7:W45/paper 9

1. Public welfare — United States — Addresses, essays, lectures. 2. Guaranteed annual income — United States — Addresses, essays, lectures. 3. Economic assistance, Domestic — United States — Addresses, essays, lectures. I. United States. Congress. Joint Economic Committee. Subcommittee on Fiscal Policy. II. Series.

HV95.C638   361.6'2'0973   73-178394

                                          MARC

MC#: 1973-30940 (LC card 73-602707 cancelled in favor of 73-178394)

SuDocs no.: Y4.Ec7:W45/paper 9, pt. 1

631

Storey, James R

The new supplemental security income program-impact on cur-

rent benefits and unresolved issues. A staff study prepared for the use of the Subcommittee on Fiscal Policy of the Joint Economic Committee, Congress of the United States [by James R. Storey and Irene Cox] Washington, U.S. Govt. Print. Off., 1973.

vi, 449 p. 24 cm. (Studies in public welfare, paper no. 10)

At head of title: 93d Congress, 1st session. Joint committee print.

1. Public welfare — United States. 2. Old age assistance — United States. 3. Guaranteed annual income — United States. I. Cox, Irene, joint author. II. United States. Congress. Joint Economic Committee. Subcommittee on Fiscal Policy. III. Title. IV. Series.

HV95.S829   362.5   73-603001

                                          MARC

MC#: 1974-05011

SuDocs no.: Y4.Ec7:W45/paper 10

632

Taggart, Robert.

The labor market impacts of the private retirement system; a study prepared for the use of the Subcommittee on Fiscal Policy of the Joint Economic Committee, Congress of the United States. Washington, U.S. Govt. Print. Off., 1973.

x, 125 p. 24 cm. (Studies in public welfare, paper no. 11)

At head of title: 93d Congress, 1st session. Joint committee print.

1. Old age pensions — United States. 2. Labor supply — United States. 3. Age and employment — United States. I. United States. Congress. Joint Economic Committee. Subcommittee on Fiscal Policy. II. Title. III. Series.

HD7106.U5T33   331.1'2'0973   73-603165

                                          MARC

MC#: 1974-04033

SuDocs no.: Y4.Ec7:W45/paper 11

633

The Family, poverty, and welfare programs; factors influencing family instability; a volume of studies prepared for the use of the Subcommittee on Fiscal Policy of the Joint Economic Committee, Congress of the United States. Washington, U.S. Govt. Print. Off., 1973-

v. 24 cm. (Studies on public welfare, paper no. 12)

1. Public welfare — United States — Addresses, essays, lectures. 2. Illegitimacy — United States — Addresses, essays, lectures. 3. Father — separated children — Addresses, essays, lectures. I. United States. Congress. Joint Economic Committee. Subcommittee on Fiscal Policy. II. Series.

HV91.F32   362.8'2'0973   73-603174

                                          MARC

MC#: 1974-04034

SuDocs no.: Y4.Ec7:W45/paper 12, pt. 1

MC#: 1974-06207

SuDocs no.: Y4.Ec7:W45/paper 12, pt. 2

MC#: 1975-05078

SuDocs no.: Y4.Ec7:W45/paper 12/pt. 1/rev.

MC#: 1975-05078

SuDocs no.: Y4.Ec7:W45/paper 12/pt. 2/rev.

634

How income supplements can affect work behavior; a volume of studies prepared for the use of the Subcommittee on Fiscal Policy of the Joint Economic Committee, Congress of the United States [by Irwin Garfinkel and others] Washington, U.S. Govt. Print. Off., 1974.

ix, 100 p. illus. 24 cm. (Studies in public welfare, paper no. 13)

At head of title: 93d Congress, 2d session. Joint Committee print.

Includes bibliographical references.

Contents: Garfinkel, I. Income transfer programs and work effort: a review. — Rea, S. A., Jr. Trade-offs between alternative income maintenance programs. — Cain, G. G., and Watts, H. W. An examination of recent cross-sectional evidence on labor force response to income maintenance legislation.

1. Income maintenance programs — United States — Addresses, essays, lectures. 2. Public welfare — United States — Addresses, essays, lectures. 3. Hard-core unemployed — United States — Addresses, essays, lectures. I. Garfinkel, Irwin. II. United States. Congress. Joint Economic Committee. Subcommittee on Fiscal Policy. III. Series.

HC110.I5H68   362.5   74-601249
                                                    MARC
MC#: 1974-06208
SuDocs no.: Y4.Ec7:W45/paper 13

635

Burke, Vee.

Public welfare and work incentives: theory and practice; a staff study prepared for the use of the Subcommittee on Fiscal Policy of the Joint Economic Committee, Congress of the United States [by Vee Burke and Alair A. Townsend] Washington, U.S. Govt. Print. Off., 1974.

vi, 55 p. illus. 24 cm. (Studies in public welfare, paper no. 14)

At head of title: 93d Congress, 1st session. Joint Committee Print.

"Prepared in chart book form as a short, nontechnical summary of subcommittee papers nos. 4 and 13 in the series Studies in public welfare."

1. Public welfare — United States. 2. Income maintenance programs — United States. 3. Labor supply — United States. I. Townsend, Alair A., joint author. II. United States. Congress. Joint Economic Committee. Subcommittee on Fiscal Policy. III. Title. IV. Series.

HV91.B87   362'.973   74-601452
                                                    MARC
MC#: 1974-09010
SuDocs no.: Y4.Ec7:W45/paper 14

636

Storey, James R

Welfare in the 70's: a national study of benefits available in 100 local areas: a staff study prepared for the use of the Subcommittee on Fiscal Policy of the Joint Economic Committee, Congress of the United States / [by James R. Storey]. — Washington: U.S. Govt. Print. Off., 1974.

ix, 300 p.; 24 cm. — (Studies in public welfare; paper no. 15)

At head of title: 93d Congress, 2d session. Joint committee print.

1. Public welfare — United States. I. United States. Congress. Joint Economic Committee. Subcommittee on Fiscal Policy. II. Title. III. Series.

HV91.S734   362'.973   74-602364
                                                    MARC
MC#: 1975-15006
SuDocs no.: Y4.Ec7:W45/paper 15

637

United States. Congress. Joint Economic Committee. Subcommittee on Fiscal Policy.

A model income supplement bill: a staff study: prepared for the use of the Subcommittee on Fiscal Policy of the Joint Economic Committee, Congress of the United States. - Washington: U.S. Govt. Print. Off., 1974.

v, 62 p.; 24 cm. — (Studies in public welfare; paper no. 16)

At head of title: 93d Congress, 2d session. Joint Committee print.

1. Income maintenance programs — United States. I. Title. II. Series.

HC110.I5U53 1974   344'.73'0325   75-600668
                                                    MARC
MC#: 1976-06760
SuDocs no.: Y4.Ec7:W45/paper 16

638

United States. Food and Nutrition Service.

National survey of food stamp and food distribution program recipients : a summary of findings on income sources and amounts and incidence of multiple benefits: a study prepared for the use of the Joint Economic Committee, Congress of the United States / [prepared by the Department of Agriculture's Food and Nutrition Service] — Washington: U.S. Govt. Print. Off., 1974.

v, 47 p.; 24 cm. — (Studies in public welfare; no. 17)

At head of title: 93d Congress, 2d session. Joint committee print.

1. Food relief — United States. 2. Welfare recipients — United States. 3. Income — United States. I. United States. Congress. Joint Economic Committee. Subcommittee on Fiscal Policy. II. Title. III. Series.

HV696.F6U66 1974   362.5   75-600667
                                                    MARC
MC#: 1975-11453
SuDocs no.: Y4.Ec7:W45/paper 17

639

Issues in financing retirement income : a volume of studies prepared for the use of the Subcommittee on Fiscal Policy on the Joint Economic Committee, Congress of the United States. — Washington : U.S. Govt. Print. Off., 1974.

v, 200 p.; 24 cm. — (Studies in public welfare; paper no. 18)

At head of title: 93d Congress, 2d session. Joint Committee print.

"Origin and development of social security financing in the United States, 1932-73: selected references, by Nacy Davenport": p. 102-158.

Contents: Korns, A. The future of social security. — Crowley, F. J. Financing the social security program — then and now. — Munnell, A. H. The impact of social security on personal saving. — Schmitt, R. Integration of private pension plans with social security.

1. Insurance, Social — United States — Finance — Addresses, essays, lectures. 2. Insurance, Social — United States — Addresses, essays, lectures. 3. Old age pensions — United States — Addresses, essays, lectures. I. United States. Congress. Joint Economic Committee. Subcommittee on Fiscal Policy. II. Series.

HD7125.I87   368.4'00973   75-601286
                                                    MARC
MC#: 1976-06761
SuDocs no.: Y4.Ec7:W45/paper 18

640

Public employment and wage subsidies: a volume of studies prepared for the use of the Subcommittee on Fiscal Policy of the Joint Economic Committee, Congress of the United States. — Washington : U.S. Govt. Print. Off., 1974.

v, 164 p.: graphs ; 24 cm. — (Studies in public welfare; paper no. 19)

At head of title: 93d Congress, 2d session. Joint committee print.

Bibliography: p. 119-121.

1. Welfare recipients — Employment — United States — Addresses, essays, lectures. 2. Hard-core unemployed — United

States—Addresses, essays, lectures. 3. Public welfare—United States—Addresses, essays, lectures. I. United States. Congress. Joint Economic Committee. Subcommittee on Fiscal Policy. II. Series.

HV95.P77   362.5   75-601433
                                                         MARC
MC#: 1976-10696
SuDocs no.: Y4.Ec7:W45/paper 19

641

United States. Congress. Joint Economic Committee. Subcommittee on Fiscal Policy.

Handbook of public income transfer programs, 1975 : a staff study prepared for the use of the Subcommittee on Fiscal Policy of the Joint Economic Committee, Congress of the United States.—Washington : U.S. Govt. Print. Off., 1974.

vi, 361 p. ; 24 cm.—(Studies in public welfare; paper no. 20)
At head of title: 93d Congress, 2d session. Joint committee print.
Revision of the 1972 ed. written by I. Cox.
Bibliography: p. 357-360.
1. Public welfare—United States. 2. Social security—United States. 3. Income maintenance programs—United States. I. Cox, Irene. Handbook of public income transfer programs. II. Title. III. Series.

HV91.U54 1974   362.5   75-602015
                                                         MARC
MC#: 1976-04920
SuDocs no.: Y4.Ec7:W45/paper 20

GRIFFITHS REPORTS [Griffiths, Martha W.]
see also
TAFT REPORT [Taft, Robert, Jr.]

GROSS REPORTS [Gross, Paul M.]

642

U.S. *Congress. House. Committee on Appropriations.*

Report on environmental health problems. Hearings before the subcommittee of the Committee on appropriations, House of Representatives, Eighty-sixth Congress, second session. Washington, U.S. Govt. Print. Off., 1960.

ii, 208, iii p. diagrs., tables. 24 cm.
Bibliography: p. 107.
1. Hygiene, Public—U.S. I. Title: Environmental health.

RA11.A3 1960b   614.0973   60-60889
MC#: 1960-6633
SuDocs no.: Y4.Ap/1:H34/2

643

U.S. *Public Health Service. Committee on Environmental Health Problems.*

Report to the Surgeon General. [Washington] U.S. Dept. of Health, Education, and Welfare, Public Health Service, 1962.

vii, 288 p. tables. 24 cm. (U.S. Public Health Service. Publication no. 908)
1. Hygiene, Public—U.S. (Series)

RA11.B18 1962   614.0973   62-60859
MC#: 1962-8610
SuDocs no.: FS2.2:En8/2

GROSSE REPORT [Grosse, Robert N.]

644

U.S. *Bureau of the Budget. Office of Statistical Standards.*

Capital requirements for the expansion of industrial capacity, prepared for the interindustry economic research program, by Robert N. Grosse [staff member. Washington] 1953-

v. 27 cm.
1. Capital investments. I. Grosse, Robert N. II. Title.
HD52.U52   54-61331 rev
This report is complete in two parts.
Not located in Monthly Catalog

GRUENING REPORT [Gruening, Ernest Henry]

645

U.S. *Congress. Senate. Committee on Government Operations.*

Report of a study of United States foreign aid in ten Middle Eastern and African countries: Turkey, Iran, Syria, Lebanon, Jordan, Israel, Greece, Tunisia, Libya, Egypt. Submitted by Ernest Gruening, Subcommittee on Reorganization and International Organization of the Committee on Government Operations, United States Senate. Washington, U.S. Govt. Print. Off., 1963.

v, 472 p. diagrs., tables. 24 cm.
At head of title: 88th Cong., 1st sess. Committee print.
1. Economic assistance, American—Near East. I. Title: Foreign aid in ten Middle Eastern and African countries.

HC412.U736   63-65283
MC#: 1963-19055
SuDocs no.: Y4.G74/6:F76a

GRUENING REPORT [Gruening, Ernest Henry]
Study mission to Eastern (American) Samoa.
see
LONG REPORT [Long, Oren E.]

GULLANDER REPORT [Gullander, W. P.]

646

U.S. *President's Committee on Employment of the Handicapped.*

Unparalleled opportunity for employment of the handicapped; address by W. P. Gullander, President, National Association of Manufacturers, before the 8th annual National Meeting of Employers sponsored by the Employer Committee of the President's Committee on Employment of the Handicapped, Nov. 1, 1966. Phoenix, Ariz. [1967]

7 p.
MC#: 1967-8618A
SuDocs no.: PrEx1.10/2:G95

GURR REPORT [Gurr, Ted Roberts]
see
GRAHAM REPORT [Graham, Hugh Davis]

GUSTAFSON REPORT [Gustafson, Robert H.]
see
DOUGLAS REPORTS [Douglas, Paul H.]
National Commission on Urban Problems.
Research report, no. 12

GUTH REPORT [Guth, Barbara]
see
BURNS REPORT [Burns, J. Gail]

HAAGEN—SMIT REPORT [Haagen—Smit, A. J.]

647

U.S. *President's Task Force on Air Pollution.*

Cleaner air for the Nation; the report of the President's Task Force on Air Pollution. Washington; For sale by the Supt. of Docs., U.S. Govt. Print. Off.,1970.

vi, 35 p. 24 cm.

1. Air — Pollution — U.S. I. Title.
TD883.2.A57   628.5'3'0973   76-611830
MARC
MC#: 1971-10092
SuDocs no.: Pr37.8:Ai7/R29

HABER REPORT [Haber, William]
648

U.S. *National resources planning board. Committee on long-range work and relief policies.*
Security, work, and relief policies. 1942. Report of the Committee on long-range work and relief policies to the National resources planning board. Washington, U.S. Govt. print. off., 1942.
xii, 640 p. illus. (incl. maps) tables (part fold.) diagrs. 29 cm.
William Haber, chairman.
Includes bibliographies.
1. Public welfare — U.S. 2. Insurance, State and compulsory — U.S. I. Title.
HV85.A53 1942   361.6   43-51851
MC#: 1943-page 636
SuDocs no.: Pr32.302:R31/943/pt. 3
Also issued as: 78th Cong., 1st sess. H. Doc. 128, pt. 3

HACKETT REPORT [Hackett, William H.]
649

U.S. *Congress. House. Committee on Interior and Insular Affairs.*
Alaska's vanishing frontier; a progress report, prepared by William H. Hackett, staff consultant, at the request of Monroe M. Redden, chairman, Subcommittee on Territories and Insular Possessions, Committee on Interior and Insular Affairs, United States House of Representatives. Washington, U.S. Govt. Print. Off., 1951.
v, 88 p. maps. 23 cm.
At head of title: Committee print.
1. Alaska — Econ. condit. 2. Alaska — Soc. condit. I. Hackett, William H. II. Title.
HC107.A45A4 1951   30.9798   52-60436
Not located in Monthly Catalog

HADDAWAY REPORT [Haddaway, George E.]
650

U.S. *Civil Aeronautics Administration. Aviation Development Advisory Committee.*
America's civil air power; a plan to obtain maximum national benefit from the resources of non-airline civil aviation, submitted to D. W. Rentzel, Administrator of Civil Aeronautics. [Washington] 1950.
41 1. 27 cm.
George E. Haddaway, chairman.
1. U.S. — Air defenses. 2. Aeronautics, Commercial — U.S.
UG633.A42 1950   355.23   50-61618
Not located in Monthly Catalog

HAGEN REPORT [Hagen, Harold C.]
651

U.S. *Congress. House. Committee on Post Office and Civil Service.*
Appeals and grievance procedures in the Federal government; report [of the Subcommittee on the Federal Civil Service] to the Committee on Post Office and Civil Service, House of Representatives. Washington, U.S. Govt. Print. Off., 1954.
iv, 27 p. 23 cm. (83d Cong., 2d sess. House report no. 1759)
1. Grievance procedures. 2. Civil service — U.S. I. Title. (Series: U.S. 83d Cong., 2d sess., 1954. House. Report no. 1759)

JK769.A52   *351.5 351.1   54-61971
MC#: 1954-9813
SuDocs no.: 83d Cong., 2d sess. H. Rept. 1759

HAGOOD REPORT [Hagood, Margaret Jarman]
652

U.S. *Bureau of Agricultural Economics.*
Farm-operator family level-of-living indexes for counties of the United States, 1930, 1940, 1945, and 1950 [by Margaret Jarman Hagood] Washington, 1952.
82 p. maps. 27 cm.
Cover title.
1. Cost and standard of living — U.S. 2. Farmers — U.S. I. Title.
HD6983.A513   339.42   53-60951
MC#: 1952-8205
SuDocs no.: A36.2:F22/36/930-50

HAINES BOARD REPORTS [Haines, Ralph E.]
653

U.S. *Adjutant General's Office.*
Report of the Department of the Army Board to review Army officer schools (Haines Board); record of completed actions. Wash., D.C., Dept. of the Army, 1970.
xxviii, 185 lvs. tables.
1. Military education — U.S. 2. U.S. Army — Officers. I. Haines Board report. II. Title. III. Department of the Army Board to review Army officer school (Haines Board)
[U415.U514 1970]
Industrial College of the Armed Forces
Not located in Monthly Catalog

654

U.S. *Dept. of the Army. Board to Review Army Officer Schools.*
Report. [Ralph E. Haines, Jr., President of the Board.] Washington, 1966.
5 v. charts; diagrs., tables. 26 cm.
Also in microfiche.
1. Military education — U.S. 2. U.S. Army — Officers. I. Haines, Ralph E. II. Title: Haines Board Report. III. Series.
[U408.3.A532 1966]
Dept. of the Army Library
Not located in Monthly Catalog

HAINS REPORT [Hains, Peter Conover]
see
WALKER COMMISSION [Walker, John Grimes]

HALSEY REPORTS [Halsey, Edwin Alexander]
655

U.S. *Congress. Senate.*
. . . The electoral college. Constitutional provisions and laws on election of President and vice president together with the nomination and election of presidential electors. Compiled under the direction of Edwin A. Halsey, secretary of the United States Senate. Washington, U.S. Govt. print. off., 1944.
ii, 26 p. 23 cm. ([U.S.] 78th Cong., 2d sess. Senate Doc. 243)
Data on "Nominations and election of presidential electors [by Samuel H. Still, State law index]" (p. 7-25) was furnished by the Legislative reference service of the Library of Congress and issued also separately.
1. Presidents — U.S. — Election. I. Halsey, Edwin Alexander, 1881-comp. II. Still, Samuel Hutchins, 1908- III. U.S. Library of Congress. Legislative reference service. IV. Title.
JK529.A5 1944b   324.249   44-41487
MC#: 1944-page 1131
SuDocs no.: 78th Cong., 2d sess. S. Doc. 243

656

U.S. *Congress. Senate.*
. . . Electoral college votes. Constitutional provisions and laws on election of President and vice president, together with the indicated electoral college vote November 1940. Compiled under the direction of Edwin A. Halsey, secretary of the United States Senate. Washington, U.S. Govt. print. off., 1940.

iii, 7 p. incl. tab. 23½ cm. (76th Cong., 3d sess. Senate. Doc. 311)
1. Presidents—U.S.—Election—1940. 2. Elections—U.S. I. Halsey, Edwin Alexander, 1881- comp. II. Title.
JK529.A5 1940b   324.2490973   40-29315
MC#: 1940-page 1583
SuDocs no.: 76th Cong., 3d sess. S. Doc. 311

HALVORSON REPORT [Halvorson, Harlow W.]

657

U.S. *Dept. of Agriculture.*
Report from the U.S. Dept. of Agriculture and a statement from the Land Grant Colleges IRM-1 Advisory Committee on farm price and income projections 1960-65 under conditions approximating free production and marketing of agricultural commidities. Washington, U.S. Govt. Print. Off., 1960.

xi, 30 p. tables. 24 cm. (86th Cong., 2d sess. Senate. Document no. 77)
1. Agricultural prices—U.S. 2. Agriculture—Economic aspects—U.S. I. Title: Farm price and income projections, 1960-65. (Series: U.S. 86th Cong., 2d sess., 1960. Senate. Document no. 77)
HB233.A3U514 1960   338.130973   60-60651
MC#: 1960-18434
SuDocs no.: ·86th Cong., 2d sess. S. Doc. 77

HAMILTON REPORT [Hamilton, Alexander]

658

U.S. *Treasury dept.*
Official reports on Publick credit, a national bank, manufactures, and a mint. By Alexander Hamilton. Philadelphia, W. M'Kean, 1821.

vii p., 1 l., 325 p. front. (port.) 22½ cm.
A reprint, with new t.-p. and different frontispiece, of v. 1 of Hamilton's works, New York, 1810.
1. Finance—U.S. 2. Banks and banking—U.S. 3. Bank of the United States, 1791-1811. 4. Tariff—U.S. 5. Free trade and protection—Protection. 6. U.S.—Manuf. 7. Mints—U.S. 8. Coinage—U.S. I. Hamilton, Alexander, 1757-1804.
HJ247.H25   8-137
Not located in Checklist of United States Public Documents, 1789-1909

HAMILTON REPORT [Hamilton, Charles]
see
WICKERSHAM COMMISION [Wickersham, George Woodward]
Report on criminal statistics, no. 3

HAMILTON REPORT [Hamilton, Walton Hale]
see under
O'MAHONEY REPORTS [O'Mahoney, Joseph Christopher]

HAMMOND REPORT

659

Hammond, Henry Schweitzer.
The performance of physically impaired workers in manufac-

turing industries, a report prepared by the Bureau of Labor Statistics for the Veterans Administration. Washington, U.S. Govt. Print. Off., 1948.

vii, 132 p. forms. 26 cm. (U.S. Bureau of Labor Statistics. Bulletin no. 923)
1. Disabled—Rehabilitation, etc.—U.S. 2. [Disabled—Occupations] I. U.S. Veterans Administration. II. Title. III. Title: Physically impaired workers in manufacturing industries. (Series)
HD8051.A62 no. 923   331.86   L48--46*
- - - - - Copy 3.
HD7256.U5H35
MC#: 1948-22543
SuDocs no.: L2.3:923

HANCOCK REPORT [Hancock, John Milton]
see
BARUCH REPORT [Baruch, Bernard Mannes]
War and post-war adjustment policy.

HANDLER REPORT [Handler, Milton]
see under
O'MAHONEY REPORTS [O'Mahoney, Joseph Christopher]

HANDLER REPORT [Handler, Phillip]

660

United States. President's Science Advisory Committee.
Handling of toxicological information; a report of the President's Science Advisory Committee. Washington; For sale by the Supt. of Docs., U.S. Govt. Print. Off., 1966.

iii, 21 p. 24 cm.
Commonly known as the Handler report.
Donald F. Hornig, chairman.
Includes bibliographical references.
1. Toxicology. I. Hornig, Donald F., 1917- II. Title. III. Title: Handler report on handling of toxicological information.
RA1216.U53   615.9   77-15905
                   MARC
MC#: 1966-12455
SuDocs no.: Pr35.8:Sci2/T66

HANKINS REPORT [Hankins, L.]
see
WALKER COMMISSION [Walker, John Grimes]

HANLEY REPORT [Hanley, James M.]

661

United States. Congress. House. Subcommittee on Position Classification.
Report on job evaluation and ranking in the Federal Government. Washington, U.S. Govt. Print. Off., 1969.

xv, 467 p. illus. 24 cm. (91st Congress, 1st session. House report no. 91-28)
Commonly known as the Hanley report.
Bibliographical footnotes.
1. Civil service positions—United States—Classification. I. Title. II. Title: Hanley report on job evaluation and ranking in the Federal Government. III. Series: United States. 91st Congress, 1st session, 1969. House. Report no. 91-28.
JK775 1969.A48   353.006'01'2   78-601255
                   · MARC
MC#: 1969-5359
SuDocs no.: 91st Cong., 1st sess. H. Rept. 28

HANNAH REPORTS [Hannah, John A.]

662

U.S. *Commission on Civil Rights.*

Freedom to the free: century of emancipation, 1863-1963; a report to the President. [Washington, For sale by the Superintendent of Documents, U.S. Govt. Print. Off., 1963]

viii, 246 p. 24 cm.

Bibliography: p. 209-240.

1. Negroes—Civil rights. 2. Negroes—Legal status, laws, etc. I. Title.

E185.61.U582　　　　　323.4　　　　　63-60591

MC#: 1963-4609

SuDocs no.: CR1.1:963

663

U.S. *Commission on Civil Rights.*

Racial isolation in the public schools; a report. Washington, For sale by the Supt. of Docs., U.S. Govt. Print. Off. [1967]

2 v. 24 cm.

Bibliographical footnotes.

- - - - - Appendices [for] Vol. 2 of a Report by the U.S. Commission on Civil Rights. Washington, For sale by the Supt. of Docs., U.S. Govt. Print. Off. [1967]

iii, 293 p. 23 cm.

LA210.A45 Appx.

1. Segregation in education—U.S. I.Title.

LA210.A45　　　　　370.19'342　　　　　67-60694

MC#: 1967-5918

SuDocs no.: CR1.2:Sch6/12/v.1,2

HANSEN REPORT [Hansen, Morris Howard]
see
BIGGERS REPORT [Biggers, John D.]

HANSEN-SAMUELSON REPORT [Hansen, Alvin H. and Samuelson, Paul A.]

664

U.S. *Office of temporary controls.*

Guaranteed wages. Report to the President by the Advisory board, Office of war mobilization and reconversion, Office of temporary controls. Murray W. Latimer, research director. January 31, 1947. Washington, U.S. Govt. print. off., 1947.

xx, 473 p. incl. tables, diagrs. 26 cm.

1. Wages—Annual wage. I. Title.

HD4928.A5U5 1947　　　331.23　　　　　47-32226

MC#: 1947-page 737

SuDocs no.: Pr33.302:W12

The report, "Economic Analysis of Guaranteed Wages," appears as Appendix F in the above cited report.

See also LATIMER REPORT [Latimer, Murray W.]

HARNESS REPORTS [Harness, Forest A.]
see under
HOFFMAN REPORTS [Hoffman, Clare E.]

Third intermediate report.

Fourth intermediate report.

Supplemental report to the fourth intermediate report.

Eighth intermediate report.

Fifteenth intermediate report.

Nineteenth intermediate report.

Twenty-third intermediate report.

HARNEY REPORT [Harney, Malachi L.]

665

United States. Congress. House. Special Subcommittee on the Metropolitan Police Dept.

Investigation and study of Metropolitan Police Department recruitment and retention problems and related matters. Report of the Committee on the District of Columbia, House of Representatives, Eighty-ninth Congress, second session, pursuant to the Legislative reorganization act of 1946. Washington, U.S. Govt. Print. Off., 1967.

v, 32 p. 24 cm. (90th Congress, 1st session. House report no. 12)

Commonly known as the Harney report.

1. District of Columbia. Police Dept. I. Title. II. Title: Harney report on Metropolitan Police Department recruitment and retention problems. III. Series: United States. 90th Congress, 1st session, 1967. House. Report no. 12.

HV7619.D3 1967　　　353.9753'007'4　　　67-60969
　　　　　　　　　　　　　　　　　　　　　　　　MARC

MC#: 1967-6011

SuDocs no.: 90th Cong., 1st sess. H. Rept. 12

HARRIMAN REPORTS [Harriman, William Averell]

666

Human rights, unfolding of the American tradition. [Washington] President's Commission for the Observance of Human Rights Year 1968; [for sale by the Supt. of Docs., U.S. Govt. Print. Off., 1968]

xiv, 127 p. 19 cm. (Department of State publication 8403)

"A selection of documents and statements compiled by the Historical Office, Bureau of Public Affairs, U.S. Department of State."

Issued in 1949 by the Office of Public Affairs, Dept. of State.

1. Liberty. 2. Civil rights—U.S. I. U.S. President's Commission for the Observance of Human Rights Year 1968. II. U.S. Dept. of State. Historical Office. III. U.S. Dept. of State. Office of Public Affairs. Human rights, unfolding of the American tradition.

JC571.H78 1968　　　323.4'0973　　　　68-67312

MC#: 1968-18135

SuDocs no.: S1.2:H88/968

667

United States. President's Commission for the Observance of Human Rights Year 1968.

To continue action for human rights; Human Rights Year, 1968. [Washington, For sale by the Supt. of Docs., U.S. Govt. Print. Off., 1969]

v, 62 p. ports. 24 cm.

On cover: Final report.

1. Civil rights. I. Title.

JC571.U63　　　　　323.4　　　　　70-601766
　　　　　　　　　　　　　　　　　　　　　　　　MARC

MC#: 1969-8782

SuDocs no.: Pr36.8:H88/Ac8

668

United States. President's Commission for the Observance of Human Rights Year 1968.

To deepen our commitment; interim report. [Washington, For sale by the Supt. of Docs., U.S. Govt. Print. Off., 1968]

iii, 39 p. illus., ports. 23 cm.

Cover title.

1. Civil rights—United States. I. Title.
JC599.U5A319 1968   323.4′0973   70-600134
                                                      MARC

MC#: 1969-1321
SuDocs no.: Pr36.8:H88/C73

669

U.S. *President's Committee on Foreign Aid.*
    European recovery and American aid, a report. Washington
[U.S. Govt. Print. Off.] 1947.

    x, 286 p. 24 cm.
    W. A. Harriman, chairman.
    1. Europe—Econ. condit.—1945- 2. Reconstruction (1939-)—
Europe. I. Harriman, William Averell, 1891- II. Title.
HC240.U62 1947a   330.94   47-46709*
MC#: 1948-4408
SuDocs no.: Pr33.2:Eu74

670

U.S. *President's Committee on Foreign Aid.*
    European recovery and American aid, a report. Washington,
1947.

    3 pts. in 2 v. 28 cm.
    W. Averell Harriman, chairman.
    1. Europe—Econ. condit.—1945- 2. Reconstruction (1939-)—
Europe. I. Harriman, William Averell, 1891- II. Title.
HC240.U62 1947   330.94   47-46656*
Not located in Monthly Catalog

HARRIS REPORT

671

Harris, Daniel, 1941-
    Staff study of campus riots and disorders, October 1967-May
1969. [Prepared by Daniel Harris and Joseph Honcharik for] Permanent Subcommittee on Investigations of the Committee on
Government Operations, U.S. Senate. Washington, U.S. Govt.
Print. Off., 1969.

    iii, 52 p. 24 cm.
    At head of title: 91st Congress, 1st session. Committee print.
    1. Student movements—United States. 2. College students—
United States—Political activity. I. Honcharik, Joseph, joint
author. II. United States. Congress. Senate. Committee on
Government Operations. Permanent Subcommittee on Investiga-
tions. III. Title.
LA229.H28   378.1′98′10973   76-602490
                                                      MARC

MC#: 1969-14037
SuDocs no.: Y4.G74/6:R47/3

HARRIS REPORT [Harris, Louis & Associates]

672

United States. Congress. Senate. Committee on Government
Operations. Subcommittee on Intergovernmental Relations.
    Confidence and concern: citizens view of American Govern-
ment; a survey of public attitudes. Washington, U.S. Govt. Print.
Off., 1973.

    2 v. 26 cm. (v. 2: 20 x 26 cm.)
    At head of title: 93d Congress, 1st session, Committee print.
    1. Public opinion—United States. I. Title.
HN90.P8U54 1973   301.15′43′320973   74-600590
                                                      MARC

MC#: 1974-04204, 04205
SuDocs no.; Y4.G74/6:Am3/3/pt. 1,2

HARRIS REPORT [Harris, Owen]

673

U.S. *Congress. House. Committee on Interstate and Foreign Commerce.*
    Broadcast ratings; report, pursuant to section 136 of the
Legislative reorganization act of 1946, Public law 601, 79th Cong.,
and House resolution 35, 89th Congress. Washington, U.S. Govt.
Print. Off., 1966.

    v, 22 p. 24 cm. (89th Congress, 2d sess. House report no. 1212)
    Caption title.
    "Based on an investigation conducted by its Special Subcom-
mittee on Investigations."
    1. Television programs—Rating. 2. Radio programs—Rating.
I. U.S. Congress. House. Committee on Interstate and Foreign
Commerce. Special Subcommittee on Investigations. II. Title.
(Series: U.S. 89th Cong., 2d sess., 1966. House. Report no. 1212)
HE8697.A8U62   384.54   66-60628
MC#: 1966-4082
SuDocs no.: 89th Cong., 2d sess. H. Rept. 1212

HARRIS REPORT [Harris, Stephen]
see
WALKER COMMISSION [Walker, John Grimes]

HARRISON REPORT [Harrison, George McGregor]
see
ROPER REPORT [Roper, Daniel Calhoun]

HART INQUIRY [Hart, Thomas C.]
see
ROBERTS COMMISSION [Roberts, Owen Josephus]

HART REPORT [Hart, Hastings Hornell]
see
WICKERSHAM COMMISSION [Wickersham, George Woodward]
    Report on penal institutions, no. 9.

HART REPORT [Hart, James]
see
BROWNLOW REPORT [Brownlow, Louis]

HARTWELL REPORT [Hartwell, Jonathan L.]
see
SHUBIK REPORT [Shubik, Philippe]

HAUPT REPORT [Haupt, Lewis Muhlenberg]
see
WALKER COMMISSION [Walker, John Grimes]

HAUSER REPORT [Hauser, Philip Morris]
see
DOUGLAS REPORTS [Douglas, Paul H.]
    National Commission on Urban Problems.

    Research report, no. 3

    Research report, no. 5

HAUSMAN REPORT [Hausman, Leonard J.]
    Cumulative tax rates in alternative income maintenance
        systems.
see under
GRIFFITHS REPORTS [Griffiths, Martha W.]
    Studies in public welfare, paper no. 4.

HAVENSTEIN REPORT [Havenstein, Rudolf]
see under
ALDRICH COMMISSION [Aldrich, Nelson Wilmarth]
    German bank inquiry of 1908.

HAYES REPORT [Hayes, Charles Willard]
   see
WALKER COMMISSION [Walker, John Grimes]

HAYES REPORT [Hayes, Everis Anson]
   see
PUJO REPORT [Pujo, Arsène Paulin]

HAYFORD REPORT [Hayford, Leslie]
   see under
DILLINGHAM COMMISSION [Dillingham, William Paul]
     Immigration and crime.

HAYNES REPORT [Haynes, Charles G.]

674

U.S. *Congress. House. Committee on Appropriations. Surveys and Investigations Subcommittee.*

A report to the Committee on Appropriations, House of Representatives, on procurement policies and practices, Department of Defense. January 1956.

(*In* U.S. Congress. House. Committee on Appropriations. Department of Defense appropriations for 1957: Procurement policies and practices of the Department of Defense. Hearings . . . 89th Congress, 2d session. Washington, 1956. 24 cm. p. 3-98)

MC#: 1956-7061
SuDocs no.: Y4.Ap6/1:D36/5/957-2

HEARD REPORT [Heard, Alexander]

675

U.S. *President's Commission on Campaign Costs.*

Financing presidential campaigns; report. [Washington, U.S. Govt. Print. Off.] 1962.

36 p. illus. 24 cm.
1. Elections—U.S.—Campaign funds. 2. Presidents—U.S.—Elections. I. Title.

JK1991.A4 1962   62-61089
MC#: 1962-10590
SuDocs no.: Pr35.8:C15/F49

HEARST REPORT [Hearst, W. R., Jr.]

676

U.S. *President's Committee for Traffic Safety.*

The action program: status of selected activities, the traffic challenge, the committee's activities; report to the President. [Washington. U.S. Govt. Print. Off.] 1965.

ix, 36 p. illus. (part col.) 27 cm.
Cover title.
"Prepared by the Advisory Council to the President's Committee for Traffic Safety as a status report to the committee."
Covers Jan. 1964 through Aug. 1965.
1. Traffic safety—U.S. I. U.S. Advisory Council to the President's Committee for Traffic Safety. II. Title.

HE5614.2.A5683   614.8620973   66-60304
MC#: 1966-1449
SuDocs no.: C37.7:Ac8/965

HECKSCHER REPORT [Heckscher, August]

677

U.S. *Special Consultant on the Arts.*

The arts and the National Government; report to the Presi-

dent, submitted by August Hackscher, Special Consultant on the Arts, May 28, 1963. Washington, U.S. Govt. Print. Off., 1963.

viii, 36 p. 24 cm. (88th Cong., 1st sess. Senate. Document no. 28)

1. Art and state—U.S. 2. State encouragement of science, literature, and art. I. Heckscher, August, 1913- II. Title. (Series: U.S. 88th Cong., 1st sess., 1963. Senate. Document no. 28)

N6512.A54 1963   63-65035
MC#: 1963-17192
SuDocs no.: 88th Cong., 1st sess. S. Doc. 28

HECTOR REPORT

678

Hector, Louis J
Problems of the CAB and the independent regulatory commissions; memorandum to the President. [Washington] 1958.

75 p. 27 cm.
1. U.S. Civil Aeronautics Board. I. Title.

TL521.H4   387.7173   60-60527
Not located in Monthly Catalog

HECTOR REPORT [Hector, Louis J.]
    Report of the Miami Study Team on Civil Disturbances.
   see
MIAMI REPORT

HEINEMAN REPORTS [Heineman, Ben W.]

679

U.S. *President's Commission on Income Maintenance Programs.*

Background papers. [Washington; For sale by the Supt. of Docs., U.S. Govt. Print. Off., 1970]

ix, 455 p. illus. 25 cm.
Ben W. Heineman, chairman.
Includes bibliographical references.
1. Guaranteed annual income—U.S. I. Heineman, Ben W., 1914- II. Title.

HC110.I5A564   331.2′3′0973   73-607945
                                       MARC
MC#: 1970-11830
SuDocs no.: Pr36.8:In2/B12

680

United States. President's Commission on Income Maintenance Programs.

Poverty amid plenty, the American paradox; report. [Washington; For sale by the Supt. of Docs., U.S. Govt. Print. Off.] 1969.

ix, 155 p. illus. 25 cm.
Commonly known as the Heineman report.
Includes bibliographical references.
1. Economic assistance, Domestic—United States. 2. Income—United States. 3. Poor—United States. I. Title. II. Title: Heineman report on income maintenance.

HC110.P63A59   362.5′0973   71-605334
                                       MARC
MC#: 1970-6126
SuDocs no.: Pr36.8:In2/P86

681

United States. President's Task Force on Government Organization.

The organization and management of Great Society programs: a final report of the President's Task Force on Government Organization.—[Washington, D.C.]; The Task Force, [1967]

20, 13, 28, [9] leaves of plates; map; 28 cm.
"June 15, 1967."
1. United States — Executive departments — Reorganization. 2. Administrative agencies — United States — Reorganization. 3. Economic assistance, Domestic — United States. 4. United States — Politics and government — 1963-1969. I. Title.
JK421.U58 1967   353.07'8-dc19   80-602642
                                                 AACR2 MARC

Not located in Monthly Catalog

682

White House Conference "To Fulfill These Rights," *Washington, D.C., 1966.*
Council's report and recommendations to the conference, June 1-2, 1966, Washington, D.C. [Washington, U.S. Govt. Print. Off., 1966]
vii, 104 p. 26 cm.
E185.615.W45 1966cb   362.8'4'0973   66-61594
MC#: 1966-11322
SuDocs no.: Y3.W58/15:2C83

683

White House Conference "To Fulfill These Rights," *Washington, D.C., 1966.*
Report. [Washington, 1966]
vii, 177 p. 26 cm.
1. Negroes — Civil rights — Congresses. 2. Negroes — Social conditions — 1964-
E184.5.W47 1966c   66-62390
                                                   MARC
MC#: 1966-15429
SuDocs no.: Y3.W58/15:1/966

684

White House Conference "To Fulfill These Rights," *Washington, D.C., 1966.*
Speeches. Washington [1966]
66 p. 24 cm.
Cover title.
1. Negroes — Civil rights — Addresses, essays, lectures.
E185.615.W45 1966c   323.4'09174'96   66-62601
MC#: 1966-12567
SuDocs no.: Y3.W58/15:2Sp3

HELLER REPORTS [Heller, Walter W.]

685

U.S. *Committee on Financial Institutions.*
Report to the President of the United States. Washington, U.S. Govt. Print. Off., 1963.
66 p. 24 cm.
1. Banks and banking — U.S. 2. Monetary policy — U.S.
HG2481.A413   63-61354
MC#: 1963-10028
SuDocs no.: PrEx6.2:F49

686

U.S. *Consumer Advisory Council.*
Report. 1st- 1962/63- [Washington] Executive Office of the President; [for sale by the Superintendent of Documents, U.S. Govt. Print. Off.]
v. tables. 24 cm.
1. Consumer protection — U.S. I. U.S. Executive Office of the President.
HC110.C6A3   63-65353
MC#: 1963-20615

SuDocs no.: PrEx6.10:963
1966 report entitled "Consumer Issues '66" submitted by ESTHER PETERSON.
MC#: 1967-5405
SuDocs no.: Pr36.8:C76/C76/2/966

HELLIWELL REPORT [Helliwell, Paul L. E.]
see
MIAMI REPORT

HEPBURN REPORT [Hepburn, Arthur Japy]

687

U.S. *Navy dept. Board on submarine, destroyer, mine and naval air bases.*
. . . Report on need of additional naval bases to defend the coasts of the United States, its territories, and possessions. Letter from the secretary of the navy transmitting report of the Board appointed to report upon the need, for purposes of national defense, of additional submarine, destroyer, mine, and naval air bases on the coasts of the United States, its territories, and possessions . . . [Washington, U.S. Govt. print. off., 1939]
39 p. 23½ cm. (76th Cong., 1st sess. House. Doc. 65)
Referred to the Committee on naval affairs and ordered printed January 3, 1939.
1. Fortification — U.S. 2. U.S. — Coast defenses. 3. U.S. — Navy. 4. Mines, Submarine. 5. Aeronautics, Military — U.S. 6. Navy-yards and naval stations — U.S. I. Hepburn, Arthur Japy, 1877- II. Title.
VA67.A3 1939   359.0973   39-26086
- - - - - Copy 2.
MC#: 1939-page 97
SuDocs no.: 76th Cong., 1st sess. H. Doc. 65

HERKNER REPORT [Herkner, Anna]
see under
DILLINGHAM COMMISSION [Dillingham, William Paul]
Steerage conditions.
Steerage conditions, importation and harboring of women for immoral purposes.

HERMANN REPORT [Hermann, Binger]

688

U.S. *General land office.*
The Louisiana purchase, and our title west of the Rocky mountains, with a review of annexation by the United States. By Binger Hermann, commissioner of the General land office. Washington, Govt. print. off., 1898.
87 p. 7 port., 5 maps. 26 cm.
1. Louisiana purchase. 2. U.S. — Territorial expansion. I. Hermann, Binger, 1843-
E333.U57   2-23754
MC#: 1898-page 583
SuDocs no.: I21.2:L93/1

HERTER REPORT [Herter, Christian A.]

689

Committee on Foreign Affairs Personnel.
Personnel for the new diplomacy, report. [Washington, Carnegie Endowment for International Peace] 1962.
xi, 161 p. 24 cm.
1. U.S. — Foreign relations administration. 2. U.S. — Diplomatic and consular service. 3. U.S. Dept. of State — Officials and employees. I. Title.
JX1706.Z5C6   353.1   62-22365
Not located in Monthly Catalog

HESBURGH REPORTS [Hesburgh, Theodore M.]
690

United States. Commission on Civil Rights.
    Federal civil rights enforcement effort; a report. [Washington;
For sale by the Supt. of Docs., U.S. Govt. Print. Off.] 1970.
    xxi, 1115 p. 27 cm.
    Cover title.
    1. Civil rights—United States. 2. Discrimination—United
States. I. Title.
    KF4755.A8337   323.4'0973   74-609051
                                                               MARC
    MC#: 1970-15683
    SuDocs no.: CR1.2:En2

691

United States. Select Commission on Immigration and Refugee
Policy.
    U.S. immigration policy and the national interest : the final
report and recommendations of the Select Commission on Im-
migration and Refugee Policy with supplemental views by com-
missioners, March 1, 1981. —[Washington, D.C.?] : The Select
Commission, 1981.
    xxxii, 453 p. ; 28 cm.
    "Submitted to the Congress and the president of the United
States pursuant to Public Law 95-412."
    Item 1089
    Supt. of Doc. no.: Y3.Im6/2:2Im6/981
    1. Emigration and immigration law—United States. 2.
Refugees—Legal status, laws, etc.—United States. 3. United
States—Emigration and immigration. 4. Refugees—United
States. I. Title.
    KF4819.A3218   353.0081'7-dc19   81-601744
                                                       AACR 2 MARC
    MC#: 1981-11302
    SuDocs no.: Y3.Im6/2:2Im6/981

692

United States. Select Commission on Immigration and Refugee
Policy.
    U.S. immigration policy and the national interest : staff report
of the Select Commission on Immigration and Refugee Policy,
April 30, 1981. —[Washington, D.C.?] : The Select Commission,
1981.
    10 v. ; 28 cm.
    Includes nine appendix volumes.
    "Supplement to the final report and recommendations of the
Select Commission on Immigration and Refugee Policy."
    Item 1089
    Includes bibliographies.
    Contents: appendix A. Papers on U.S. immigration history—
appendix B. Papers on international migration—appendix C.
Papers on refugees—appendix D. Papers on legal immigration
to the United States—appendix E. Papers on illegal migration
to the United States—appendix F. Papers on temporary
workers—appendix G. Papers on the administration of immigration law—recommendations and votes.
    Supt. of Docs. no.: Y3.Im 6/2:2Im6/staff ; Y3.Im6/2:2Im
6/app. A-I
    1. Emigration and immigration law—United States. 2.
Refugees—Legal status, laws, etc.—United States. 3. United
States—Emigration and immigration. 4. Refugees—United
States. I. Title.
    KF4819.A3218 Suppl   325.73-dc19   81-602159
                                                       AACR 2 MARC

    MC#: 1981-11301
    SuDocs no.: Y3.Im6/2:2Im6/staff
                       Y3.Im6/2:2Im6/app. A-I

HESS REPORT [Hess, Stephen]
693

White House Conference on Children, Washington, D.C., 1970.
    Report to the President. [Washington; For sale by the Supt.
of Docs., U.S. Govt. Print. Off., 1971]
    451 p. 28 cm.
    Includes bibliographical references.
    Supt. of Docs. No.: Y3.W58/3-2:1/970
    1. Children of the United States—Congresses.
    HQ792.U5W46 1970a   301.43'1'0973   77-612404
                                                               MARC
    MC#: 1971-11852
    SuDocs no.: Y3.W58/3-2:1/970

HESTER REPORT [Hester, James M.]
694

United States. President's Task Force on Higher Education.
    Priorities in higher education; the report. [Washington; For
sale by the Supt. of Docs., U.S. Govt. Print. Off.] 1970.
    xi, 31 p. 24 cm.
    1. Education, Higher—United States—1965- I. Title.
    LA227.3.A27   378.73   75-609255
                                                       MARC
    MC#: 1970-17220
    SuDocs no.: Pr37.8:Ed8/R29

HEWITT INQUIRY [Hewitt, H. Kent]
        see
    ROBERTS COMMISSION [Roberts, Owen
Josephus]

HICKEY REPORT [Hickey, Margaret]
695

U.S. *President's Commission on the Status of Women. Committee on Federal
Employment Policies and Practices.*
    Report of the Committee on Federal Employment to the Presi-
dent's Commission on the Status of Women. Washington, For
sale by the Superintendent of Documents, U.S. Govt. Print. Off.,
1963.
    viii, 195 p. diagrs., forms, tables. 26 cm.
    Bibliography: p. 61-62.
    1. Women in the civil service—U.S.
    JK721.A53   64-60362
    MC#: 1964-3090
    SuDocs no.: Pr35.8:W84/Em7

HILL REPORT [Hill, David Spence]
696

U.S. *National advisory committee on education.*
    Federal relations to education . . . Report of the National ad-
visory committee on education . . . Washington, D.C. [National
capital press, inc.] 1931.
    2 v. illus. (maps) diagrs. 23½ cm.
    Contents.—I. Committee findings and recommendations.—
II. Basic facts, prepared by David Spence Hill and William Alfred
Fisher.
    1. Education and state—U.S. 2. Education—U.S. I. Hill,
David Spence, 1873- II. Fisher, William Alfred. III. Title.
    LC89.A5 1931   379.73   31-34552
    - - - - - Copy 2.
    Not located in Monthly Catalog

HILL REPORT [Hill, Joseph Adna]
   see under
DILLINGHAM COMMISSION [Dillingham, William Paul]
     Occupations of the first and second generations of immigrants.

HILL REPORT [Hill, Lister]

697

U.S. *Congress. Senate. Committee on Armed Services.*
   The Army-Navy medical services corps act of 1947. Report to accompany H. R. 3215. [Washington, U.S. Govt. Print. Off., 1947]
   14 p. 24 cm. ([U.S.] 80th Cong., 1st sess., 1947. Senate. Report no. 464)
   Caption title.
   Submitted by Mr. Hill.
   1. U.S. Army — Sanit. affairs. 2. U.S. Navy — Sanit. affairs. I. Hill, Lister, 1894- II. Title. III. Series.
UH223.A39 1947a   355.34   47-31735*
MC#: 1947-page 984
SuDocs no.: 80th Cong., 1st sess. S. Rept. 464

HILL REPORT [Hill, R. B.]
     Who riots? A study of participation in the 1967 riots.
   see
KERNER COMMISSION [Kerner, Otto]
     Supplemental studies.

HIPPELHEUSER REPORT [Hippelheuser, Richard H.]
   see
BARUCH REPORT [Baruch, Bernard Mannes]
     American industry in the war.

HIRST REPORT [Hirst, Francis Wrigley]
   see under
ALDRICH COMMISSION [Aldrich, Nelson Wilmarth]

HODGE REPORT [Hodge, Patricia Leavey]
   see
DOUGLAS REPORTS [Douglas, Paul H.]
     National Commission on Urban Problems.
     Research report, no. 3
     Research report, no. 5

HODGES REPORT [Hodges, Luther H.]

698

U.S. *President's Advisory Committee on Labor-Management Policy.*
   Policies designed to ensure that American products are competitive in world markets; [report] Washington [1963]
   iii, 9 p. illus. 28 cm.
   Cover title: American products/world markets.
   1. U.S. — Commercial policy. I. Title. II. Title: American products/world markets.
HF1456 1963.A52   63-65147
MC#: 1963-18272
SuDocs no.: Pr35.8:L11/P94

HOELSCHER REPORT [Hoelscher, Leonard W.]

699

U.S. *Dept. of the Army.*
   Study of the functions, organization and procedure of the Department of the Army; OSD Project 80 [Army] Washington, 1961.

7 pts. in 9 v. illus. 26 cm.
   Contents: 1. Overall report. 2. Headquarters, Dept. of the Army. 3. The U.S. Continental Army Command. 4. ODCSLOG, The technical services and logistical functions. 5. Research and development. 6. Personnel functions. 7. Reserve components. 8. Supplement: Army aviation.
[UA24.A79]
Dept. of the Army Library
Not located in Monthly Catalog

HOEY REPORT [Hoey, Clyde R.]

700

U.S. *Congress. Senate. Committee on Government Operations. Permanent Subcommittee on Investigations.*
   Employment of homosexuals and other sex perverts in government; interim report submitted pursuant to S. Res. 280 (81st Congress) Washington, U.S. Govt. Print. Off., 1950.
   26 p. (81st Cong., 2d sess. Senate. Document no. 241)
   Submitted by the committee under its earlier name: Committee on Expenditures in the Executive Departments.
MC#: 1951-640
SuDocs no.: 81st Cong., 2d sess. S. Doc. 241

HOFFMAN REPORT [Hoffman, Austin Clair]
   see under
O'MAHONEY REPORTS [O'Mahoney, Joseph Christopher]

HOFFMAN REPORT [Hoffman, Paul G.]

701

U.S. *Economic Coopertion Administration.*
   A report on recovery progress and United States aid. Washington, 1949.
   ii, 267 p. 24 cm.
   1. Europe — Econ. condit. — 1945- 2. Economic assistance, American. I. Title: European recovery program. II. Title: Hoffman report on European recovery progress and United States Aid.
HC240.U7 1949   338.91   49-46412*
MC#: 1949-14366
SuDocs no.: Y3.E74/3:2Eu7'2'949

HOFFMAN REPORTS [Hoffman, Clare E.]

   Reports of the House Committee on Government Operations, issued under its earlier name, Committee on Expenditures in the Executive Departments, Clare E. Hoffman, Chairman, are listed in numerical order with an indication of the subcommittees and their respective chairmen submitting the reports.

702

U.S. *Congress. House. Committee on Government Operations.*
   Investigation of the effectiveness of antiracketeering laws and the administration thereof. First intermediate report of the Committee on Expenditures in the Executive Departments. Investigation of the effectiveness and administration of the Hobbs amendment, Public law 486, Seventy-ninth Congress, to the Antiracketeering act, approved June 8, 1934, 48 Stat. 979, U.S.C., 1940 ed., title 18, secs. 420A-420E. Washington, U.S. Govt. Print. Off., 1947.
   iii, 37 p. 24 cm. (80th Cong., 1st sess. H. Rept. 238)
   Includes supplemental report signed by Mr. Hoffman.
   Report of the Antiracketeering Subcommittee, Clare E. Hoffman, Chairman.
MC#: 1947-page 656
SuDocs no.: 80th Cong., 1st sess. H. Rept. 238

703

U.S. *Congress. House. Committee on Government Operations.*

Investigation of the effectiveness of antiracketeering laws and the administration thereof. Supplemental report to the first intermediate report of the Committee on Expenditures in the Executive Departments. Investigation of the effectiveness and administration of the Hobbs amendment, Public law 486, Seventy-ninth Congress, to the Antiracketeering act, approved June 8, 1934, 48 Stat. 979, U.S.C., 1940 ed., title 18, secs. 420A-420E. Washington, U.S. Govt. Print. Off., 1947.

iii, 5 p. 24 cm. (80th Cong., 1st sess. House report no. 1220)
1. Racketeering—Philadelphia. 2. Racketeering—U.S. (Series: U.S. 80th Cong., 1st sess., 1947. House. Report no. 1220)
HV6688.U6 1947   331.8808   48-50065 rev*
Report of the Antiracketeering Subcommittee, Clare E. Hoffman, Chairman.
MC#: 1948-3020
SuDocs no.: 80th Cong., 1st sess. H. Rept. 1220

704

U.S. *Congress. House. Committee on Government Operations.*

Investigation of the disposition of surplus property. Second intermediate report of the Committee on Expenditures in the Executive Departments . . . Washington, U.S.Govt. Print. Off., 1947.

v, 55 p. 24 cm. (80th Cong., 1st sess. House report no. 785)
1. Surplus government property—U.S. (Series: U.S. 80th Cong., 1st sess., 1947. House. Report no. 785)
JK1661.A5 1947b   336.12   47-31966 rev*
Report of the Surplus Property Subcommittee, Ross Rizley, Chairman.
MC#: 1947-page 965
SuDocs no.: 80th Cong., 1st sess. H. Rept. 785

705

U.S. *Congress. House. Committee on Government Operations.*

Investigation of the participation of Federal officials in the formation and operation of health workshops; third intermediate report of the Committee on Expenditures in the Executive Departments . . . Washington, U.S. Govt. Print. Off., 1947.

iii, 7 p. 24 cm. (80th Cong., 1st sess. House report no. 786)
1. Insurance, Health—U.S. 2. U.S.—Officials and employees. 3. U.S.—Appropriations and expenditures. (Series: U.S. 80th Cong., 1st sess., 1947. House. Report no. 786)
HD7102.U4A5 1947b   331.25442   47-31736 rev 2*
Report of the Subcommittee on Publicity and Propaganda, Forest A. Harness, Chairman.
MC#: 1947-page 964
       1947-4578 (Corrected print)
SuDocs no.: 80th Cong., 1st sess. H. Rept. 786

706

U.S. *Congress. House. Committee on Government Operations.*

Investigation of participation of Federal officials of the War Department in publicity and propaganda, as it relates to universal military training. Fourth intermediate report of the Committee on Expenditures in the Executive Departments, Publicity and Propaganda Subcommittee. Washington, U.S. Govt. Print. Off., 1947.

iii, 8 p. 24 cm. (80th Cong., 1st sess. House report no. 1073)
1. Military service, Compulsory—U.S. 2. U.S. War Dept.—Officials and employees. 3. Government publicity—U.S. (Series: U.S. 80th Cong., 1st sess., 1947. House. Report no. 1083)
UB353.A5 1947b   355.22   47-31971 rev*

Report of the Subcommittee on Publicity and Propaganda, Forest A. Harness, Chairman.
MC#: 1947-2853
SuDocs no.: 80th Cong., 1st sess. H. Rept. 1073

707

U.S. *Congress. House. Committee on Government Operations.*

Investigation of participation of Federal officials of the Department of the Army in publicity and propaganda, as it relates to universal military training. Supplemental report to the fourth intermediate report of the Committee on Expenditures in the Executive Departments. Washington, U.S. Govt. Print. Off., 1948.

iii, 9 p. 24 cm. (80th Cong., 2d sess. House report no. 1510)
1. Military service, Compulsory—U.S. 2. U.S. War Dept. 3. U.S. Dept. of the Army. 4. Government publicity—U.S. (Series: U.S. 80th Cong., 2d sess., 1948. House. Report no. 1510)
UA24.A7 1948f   355.22   48-45811 rev*
Report of the Subcommittee on Publicity and Propaganda, Forest A. Harness, Chairman.
MC#: 1948-7598
SuDocs no.: 80th Cong., 2d sess. H. Rept. 1510

708

U.S. *Congress. House. Committee on Government Operations.*

Investigation of the State Department; fifth intermediate report of the Committee on Expenditures in the Executive Departments. Washington, U.S. Govt. Print. Off., 1947.

iii, 5 p. 24 cm. (80th Cong., 1st sess. House report no. 1072)
1. U.S. Dept. of State. (Series: U.S. 80th Cong., 1st sess., 1947. House. Report no. 1072)
JK851.A45 1947a   353.1   47-31980 rev*
Report of the State Department Subcommittee, J. Edgar Chenoweth, Chairman.
MC#: 1947-2852
SuDocs no.: 80th Cong., 1st sess. H. Rept. 1072

709

U.S. *Congress. House. Committee on Government Operations.*

Investigation of the proposed sale of Naylor Gardens; sixth intermediate report of the Committee on Expenditures in the Executive Departments. Washington, U.S. Govt. Print. Off., 1948.

iii, 3 p. 23 cm. (80th Cong., 2d sess. House report no. 1235)
1. Washington, D.C. Naylor Gardens. (Series: U.S. 80th Cong., 2d sess., 1948. House. Report no. 1235)
HD7304.W3A5 1948   331.833   48-45524 rev*
Report of the Special Subcommittee to Investigate the Proposed Sale of Naylor Gardens, Clare E. Hoffman, Chairman.
MC#: 1948-3035
SuDocs no.: 80th Cong., 2d sess. H. Rept. 1235

710

U.S. *Congress. House. Committee on Government Operations.*

Investigation of the disposition of a steam-power-generating plant at Oklahoma ordnance works near Chouteau, Okla. Seventh intermediate report of the Committee on Expenditures in the Executive Departments. Washington, U.S. Govt. Print. Off., 1948.

iii, 9 p. 24 cm. (80th Cong., 2d sess. House report no. 1250)
1. Steam power—plants—Chouteau, Okla. 2. Surplus government property—U.S. (Series: U.S. 80th Cong., 2d sess., 1948. House. Report no. 1250)
HD9685.U605 1948   336.12   48-50022 rev*
Report of the Surplus Property Subcommittee, Ross Rizley, Chairman.
MC#: 11948-5548
SuDocs no.: 80th Cong., 2d sess. H. Rept. 1250

711

U.S. *Congress. House. Committee on Government Operations.*
    Investigation of Agricultural Adjustment Agency and Production and Marketing Administration publicity and propaganda in Nebraska. Eighth intermediate report of the Committee on Expenditures in the Executive Departments. Washington, U.S. Govt. Print. Off., 1948.
    iii, 19 p. 24 cm. (80th Cong., 2d sess. House report no. 1365)
    1. U.S. Agricultural Adjustment Agency. (Series: U.S. 80th Cong., 2d sess., 1948. House. Report no. 1365)
HD1753 1948e   338.14   48-45703 rev*
Report of the Subcommittee on Publicity and Propaganda, Forest A. Harness, Chairman.
MC#: 1948-5663
SuDocs no.: 80th Cong., 2d sess. H. Rept. 1365

712

U.S. *Congress. House. Committee on Government Operations.*
    Investigation of the Civil Service Commission investigators' leads file; ninth intermediate report of the Committee on Expenditures in the Executive Departments. Washington, U.S. Govt. Print. Off., 1948.
    v, 7 p. 24 cm. (80th Cong., 2d sess. House report no. 1498)
    1. U.S. Congress. 2. U.S. Civil Service Commission. (Series: U.S. 80th Cong., 2d sess., 1948. House. Report no. 1498)
JK1059 80th.A5   351.1   48-45831 rev*
Report of the Subcommittee Investigating the Civil Service Com mission, Clare E. Hoffman, Chairman.
MC#: 1948-7586
SuDocs no.: 80th Cong., 2 sess. H. Rept. 1498

713

U.S. *Congress. House. Committee on Government Operations.*
    Investigation of the State Department transfer of relief funds to the Luckman Citizens' Food Committee; tenth intermediate report of the Committee on Expenditures in the Executive Departments. Washington, U.S. Govt. Print. Off., 1948.
    iii, 11 p. 23 cm. (80th Cong., 2d sess. House report no. 1772)
    1. U.S. Citizens Food Committee. 2. U.S. Dept. of State. 3. Food supply—U.S. (Series: U.S. 80th Cong., 2d sess., 1948. House. Report no. 1772)
HD9006.A5 1948b   338.1   48-46170 rev*
Report of the State Department Subcommittee, J. Edgar Chenoweth, Chairman.
MC#: 1948-10493
SuDocs no.: 80th Cong., 2d sess. H. Rept. 1772

714

U.S. *Congress. House. Committee on Government Operations.*
    Investigation of the sale of Parkview Heights, housing project at Knox, Inc., by Public Housing Administration to Knox Homes, inc., a private corporation. Eleventh intermediate report of the Committee on Expenditures in the Executive Departments. Washington, U.S. Govt. Print. Off., 1948.
    v, 13 p. 23 cm. (80th Cong., 2d sess. House report no. 1900)
    1. Knox, Ind. Parkview Heights. (Series: U.S. 80th Cong., 2d sess., 1948. House. Report no. 1900)
HD7304.K6A5 1948a   331.833   48-46268 rev*
Report of the Subcommittee Investigating the Sale of Parkview Heights, Housing Project at Knox, Ind., Clare E. Hoffman, Chairman.
MC#: 1948-13129
SuDocs no.: 80th Cong., 2d sess. H. Rept. 1900

715

U.S. Congress. House. Committee on Government Operations.
    Investigation to ascertain scope of interpretation by General Counsel of National Labor Relations Board of the term affecting commerce as used in the Labor management relations act, 1947. Twelfth intermediate report of the Committee on Expenditures in the Executive Departments. Washington, U.S. Govt. Print. Off., 1948.
    iii, 11 p. 23 cm. (80th Cong., 2d sess. House report no. 2050)
    1. Interstate commerce. 2. Labor laws and legislation—U.S. (Series: U.S. 80th Cong., 2d sess., 1948. House. Report no. 2050)
HD7833.A452 1948a   331.15   48-46409 rev*
Report of the Subcommittee of the Committee on Expenditures in the Executive Departments, Clare E. Hoffman, Chairman.
MC#: 1948-15699
SuDocs no.: 80th Cong., 2d sess. H. Rept. 2050

716

U.S. *Congress. House. Committee on Government Operations.*
    Investigation of surplus real property and consolidation of facilities of the armed services in the San Francisco Bay area. Thirteenth intermediate report of the Committee on Expenditures in the Executive Departments. Washington, U.S. Govt. Print. Off., 1948.
    iii, 13 p. 23 cm. (80th Cong., 2d sess. House report no. 2164)
    1. U.S.—Defenses. 2. Surplus government property—U.S. (Series: U.S. 80th Cong., 2d sess., 1948. House. Report no. 2164)
UA23.A4 1948a   355   48-46612 rev*
Report of the Surplus Property Subcommittee, Ross Rizley, Chairman.
MC#: 1948-15813
SuDocs no.: 80th Cong., 2d sess. H. Rept. 2164

717

U.S. *Congress. House. Committee on Government Operations.*
    Investigation of the State Department Voice of America broadcasts; fourteenth intermediate report of the Committee on Expenditures in the Executive Departments. Washington, U.S. Govt. Print. Off., 1948.
    iii, 16 p. 23 cm. (80th Cong., 2d sess. House report no. 2350)
    1. Voice of America (Radio program) (Series: U.S. 80th Cong., 2d sess. 1949. House. Report no. 2350)
HE8698.A4 1948b   791.4   48-46553 rev*
Report of the State Department Subcommittee, J. Edgar Chenoweth, Chairman.
MC#: 1948-18701
SuDocs no.: 80th Cong., 2d sess. H. Rept. 2350

718

U.S. *Congress. House. Committee on Government Operations.*
    Investigation of the Public Housing Authority at San Diego and Los Angeles; fifteenth intermediate report of the Committee on Expenditures in the Executive Departments. Washington, U.S. Govt. Print. Off., 1948.
    iii, 9 p. 23 cm. (80th Cong., 2d sess. House report no. 2351)
    1. United States Housing Authority. (Series: U.S. 80th Cong., 2d sess., 1948. House. Report no. 2351)
HD7304.S8A5   331.833   48-46554 rev*
Report of the Subcommittee on Publicity and Propaganda, Forest A. Harness, Chairman.
MC#: 1948-18702
SuDocs no.: 80th Cong., 2d sess. H. Rept. 2351

719

U.S. *Congress. House. Committee on Government Operations.*

Investigation of the Views Mill Village Veterans' Housing Project, Montgomery County, Md.; sixteenth intermediate report of the Committee on Expenditures in the Executive Departments. Washington, U.S. Govt. Print. Off., 1948.

iii, 8 p. 24 cm. (80th Cong., 2d sess. House report no. 2373)
1. Viers Mill Village Veterans' Housing Project, Montgomery Co., Md. (Series: U.S. 80th Cong., 2d sess., 1948. House. Report no. 2373)

HD7304.V5A5 1948   331.833   48-46547 rev*
Report of the Subcommittee Investigating Viers Mill Village
  Veterans' Housing Project, Melvin C. Snyder, Chairman.
MC#: 1948-18724
SuDocs no.: 80th Cong., 2d sess. H. Rept. 2373

720

U.S. *Congress. House. Committee on Government Operations.*

Investigation as to the manner in which the United States Board of Parole is operating and as to whether there is a necessity for a change in either the procedure or basic law. Seventeenth intermediate report of the Committee on Expenditures in the Executive Departments. Washington, U.S. Govt. Print. Off., 1948.

iii, 35 p. 23 cm. (80th Cong., 2d sess. House report no. 2441)
1. U.S. Board of Parole. (Series: U.S. 80th Cong., 2d sess., 1948. House. Report no. 2441)

HV9304.A5 1948b   364.62   48-46607 rev*
Report of the Subcommittee Investigating Granting of Paroles,
  Clare E. Hoffman, Chairman.
MC#: 1948-18792
SuDocs no.: 80th Cong., 2d sess. H. Rept. 2441

721

U.S. *Congress. House. Committee on Government Operations.*

Investigation of General Accounting Office audit of wartime freight vouchers; eighteenth intermediate report of the Committee on Expenditures in the Executive Departments. Washington, U.S. Govt. Print. Off., 1948.

vi, 6 p. 24 cm. (80th Cong., 2d sess. House report no. 2457)
1. U.S. General Accounting Office. 2. Freight and freightage—U.S.

HE18 1948.A55   385.1324   48-46931 rev*
Report of the Procurement and Buildings subcommittee, George
  H. Bender, Chairman.
MC#: 1948-20647
SuDocs no.: 80th Cong., 2d sess. H. Rept. 2457

722

U.S. *Congress. House. Committee on Government Operations.*

Investigation of Bureau of Reclamation, Department of the Interior: nineteenth intermediate report of the Committee of Expenditures in the Executive Departments. Washington, U.S. Govt. Print. Off., 1948.

iii, 36 p. 23 cm. (80th Cong., 2d sess. House report no. 2458)
1. U.S. Bureau of Reclamation.

HD1721 1948k   631.606173   48-46932 rev*
Report of the Subcommittee on Publicity and Propaganda, Forest
  A. Harness, Chairman.
MC#: 1948-20648
SuDocs no.: 80th Cong., 2d sess. H. Rept. 2458

723

U.S. *Congress. House. Committee on Government Operations.*

Investigation of publication sponsored by the Department of the Army entitled Army talks; twentieth intermediate report of the Committee on Expenditures in the Executive Departments. Washington, U.S. Govt. Print. Off., 1948.

iii, 4 p. 23 cm. (80th Cong., 2d sess. House report no. 2463)

1. Army talks. (Series: U.S. 80th Cong., 2d sess., 1948. House. Report no. 2463)

U716.A5 1948a   355.1   49-45569 rev*
Report of the Subcommittee of the Committee on Expenditures
  in the Executive Departments, Clare E. Hoffman, Chairman.
MC#: 1949-2967
SuDocs no.: 80th Cong., 2d sess. H. Rept. 2463

724

U.S. *Congress. House. Committee on Government Operations.*

Investigation as to the administration of the laws affecting labor disputes, interstate and foreign commerce and the antiracketeering statute, the interstate transportation of pickets, and the activities of the Department of Justice, in connection with strikes in the meat-packing industry in twenty States. Twenty-first intermediate report of the Committee on Expenditures in the Executive Departments. Washington, U.S. Govt. Print. Off., 1948.

iii, 17 p. 23 cm. (80th Cong., 2d sess. House report no. 2464)
1. Strikes and lockouts—Meat industry—U.S. (Series: U.S. 80th Cong., 2d sess., 1948. House. Report no. 2464)

HD5325.M4A5 1948a   331.8928649   49-45570 rev*
Report of the Subcommittee Investigating Strikes in the Meat-
  Packing Industry in Twenty States, Clare E. Hoffman,
  Chairman.
MC#: 1949-2968
SuDocs no.: 80th Cong., 2d sess. H. Rept. 2464

725

U.S. *Congress. House. Committee on Government Operations.*

Report of the Subcommittee on Procurement and Buildings of the Committee on Expenditures in the Executive Departments on its activities for [calendar] year 1948. Twenty-second intermediate report of the Committee on Expenditures in the Executive Departments. Washington, U.S. Govt. Print. Off., 1949.

iii, 9 p. 24 cm. (80th Cong., 2d sess. House report no. 2473)
Report of the Procurement and Buildings Subcommittee, George
  H. Bender, Chairman.
MC#: 1949-2977 (LC card 49-45619 preassigned, not printed)
SuDocs no.: 80th Cong., 2d sess. H. Rept. 2473)

726

U.S. *Congress. House. Committee on Government Operations.*

Final report of the Subcommittee on Publicity and Propaganda. Twenty-third intermediate report of the Committee on Expenditures in the Executive Departments. Washington, U.S. Govt. Print. Off., 1949.

iii, 12 p. 24 cm. (80th Cong., 2d sess. House report no. 2474)
1. Government publicity—U.S. (Series: U.S. 80th Cong., 2d sess., 1948. House. Report no. 2474)

JK468.P8A5 1949   353   49-45571 rev*
Report of the Subcommittee on Publicity and Propaganda, Forest
  A. Harness, Chairman.
MC#: 1949-2978
SuDocs no.: 80th Cong., 2d sess. H. Rept. 2474

727

U.S. *Congress. House. Committee on Government Operations.*

Investigation of the Atomic Energy Commission at Los Alamos, N. Mex.; twenty-fourth intermediate report of the Committee on Expenditures in the Executive Departments. Washington, U.S. Govt. Print. Off., 1949.

iii, 5 p. 24 cm. (80th Cong., 2d sess. House report no. 2478)
1. U.S. Atomic Energy Commission. (Series: U.S. 80th Cong., 2d sess., 1948. House. Report no. 2478)

HD9698.U52A5 1949   541.2   49-45572 rev*

Report of the Subcommittee on Investigation of the Atomic Energy Commission at Los Alamos, N. Mex., Melvin C. Snyder, Chairman.
MC#: 1949-2979
SuDocs no.: 80th Cong., 2d sess. H. Rept. 2478

728

U.S. *Economic Cooperation Administration.*
A report on recovery progress and United States aid. Washington, 1949.

ii, 269 p. 24 cm.
On cover: European recovery program.
1. Europe—Econ. condit.—1945- 2. Economic assistance, American. I. Title: European recovery program. II. Title: Hoffman report on European recovery progress and United States aid.
HC240.U7 1949d   338.94   50-61694
Not located in Monthly Catalog

HOHAUS REPORT [Hohaus, Reinhard A.]

729

U.S. *Dept. of Health, Education, and Welfare.*
A report to the Secretary of Health, Education, and Welfare on extension of old-age and survivors insurance to additional groups of current workers [by the] consultants on social security. Washington, 1953.

vi, 32 p. 23 cm.
1. Old age pensions—U.S.
HD7106.U5A514   *368.43   53-63333
               331.25443
MC#: 1953-16278
SuDocs no.: FS1.2:O1 1

HOLDSWORTH REPORT [Holdsworth, John Thom]
    see under
  ALDRICH COMMISSION [Aldrich, Nelson Wilmarth]

HOLLAND REPORT [Holland, Robert Martin]
    see under
  ALDRICH COMMISSION [Aldrich, Nelson Wilmarth]
      Withers. English banking system.

HOLLANDER REPORT

730

Hollander, Jacob Harry, 1871-
. . . Debt of Santo Domingo . . . Report on the debt of Santo Domingo, submitted to the President of the United States by Jacob H. Hollander, special commissioner . . . [Washington, Govt. print. off., 1905]

1 p. 1., 250 p. incl. tables. 23 cm. ([U.S.] 59th Cong., 1st sess. [Senate] Ex. doc. 1)
Presented by Mr. Lodge. Referred to the Committee on foreign relations and, together with the accompanying papers, ordered printed in confidence for the use of the Senate, December 15, 1905.
Confidential.
"List of books, with reference to periodicals in the Library of Congress, relating to Santo Domingo": p. 234-250.
1. Debts, Public—Dominican republic. I. Lodge, Henry Cabot, 1850-1924. II. Title.
HJ8547.H6   336.3097293   35-36330 rev.
Not located in Monthly Catalog
SuDocs no.: 59th Cong., 1st sess. S. Ex. Doc. 1

HOLLANDER REPORT [Hollander, Jacob Harry]
    Bank loans and stock exchange speculations.
  see under
  ALDRICH COMMISSION [Adlrich, Nelson Wilmarth]

HOLLINGSWORTH REPORT [Hollingsworth, James F.]

731

U.S. *Dept. of the Army. Office of Reserve Components.*
Hollingsworth report; review of ARNG Federal recognition standards and procedures for Reserve component officers. [Washington] 1967.

2 v. charts, diagrs., tables. (ASDIRS 2134)
1. U.S. Army Reserve—Officers. I. Hollingsworth Board. II. Title. III. Series.
[UA42.A581]
Dept. of the Army Library
Not located in Monthly Catalog

HOLLISTER REPORT [Hollister, S. C.]

732

U.S. *Congress. House. Committee on Merchant Marine and Fisheries.*
Report of a long-range program for Isthmian Canal transits . . . pursuant to H. Res. 105, 86th Cong., 1st sess. Washington, U.S. Govt. Print. Off., 1960.

x, 831 p. illus., maps (part fold.) 24 cm. (86th Cong., 2d sess. House report no. 1960)
Includes bibliographies.
1. Panama Canal. (Series: U.S. 86th Cong., 2d sess., 1960. House. Report no. 1960)
HE537.65 1960.U54   386.444   60-62146
MC#: 1960-16860
SuDocs no.: 86th Cong., 2d sess. H. Rept. 1960

HOLLOWAY REPORT [Holloway, James Lemuel, III]

733

United States. Joint Chiefs of Staff. Special Operations Review Group.
Rescue mission report. [Washington: Joint Chiefs of Staff, 1980.]

"August 1980".
Accompanied by "Statement of Admiral J. L. Holloway, III . . . Chairman.
Special Operations Review Group".
1. Hostages—Iran. 2. United States—Armed Forces—Search and rescue operations. I. Holloway, James L. II. Title.
[U260.U62]
Dept. of the Army Library
MC#: 1981-6607
SuDocs no.: D5.2:R31/2

HONCHARIK REPORT [Honcharik, Joseph]
    see
  HARRIS REPORT [Harris, Daniel]

HOOD REPORT [Hood, Robin]
    see
  BAKER REPORT [Baker, Jacob]

HOOK REPORT [Hook, Charles R.]

734

U.S. *Advisory Commission on Service Pay.*

Career compensation for the uniformed forces; Army, Navy, Air Force, Marine Corps, Coast Guard, Coast and Geodetic Survey, Public Health Service. A report and recommendation for the Secretary of Defense. Washington, U.S. Govt. Print. Off., 1948.

2 v. 26 cm.

"Earnings of college graduates, a selective bibliography": v. 2, p. 56-65.

Vol. 2: Appendix.

1. U.S. Army — Pay, allowances, etc. 2. U.S. Navy — Pay, allowances, etc. I. Title.

UC74.A43 1948   355.135   49-45652*
MC#: 1949-5611
SuDocs no.: M1.2:C73
MC#: 1949-7962
SuDocs no.: M1.2:C73/app.

HOOKER REPORT [Hooker, Evelyn]

735

United States. National Institute of Mental Health. Task Force on Homosexuality.

National Institute of Mental Health Task Force on Homosexuality : final report and background papers. Edited by John M. Livingood. Rockville, Md., National Institute of Mental Health; [for sale by the Supt. of Docs., U.S. Govt. Print. Off., Washington, 1972]

vii, 79 p. 27 cm. (DHEW publication, no. (HSM) 72-9116)
Includes bibliographies.
Supt. of Docs. no.: HE20.2402:H75/2

1. Homosexuality — Addresses, essays, lectures. I. Livingood, John M. II. Title. III. Series : United States. Dept. of Health, Education, and Welfare. DHEW publication, no. (HSM) 72-9116.

HQ76.U55 1972   301.41′57   73-600955
                                                         MARC
MC#: 1973-22077
SuDocs no.: HE20.2402:H75/2

United States. National Institute of Mental Health. Task Force on Homosexuality.

National Institute of Mental Health Task Force on Homosexuality : final report and background papers / edited by John M. Livingood. - Rockville, Md. : U.S. Dept. of Health, Education, and Welfare, Public Health Service, Alcohol, Drug Abuse, and Mental Health Administration, National Institute of Mental Health ;Washington : for sale by the Supt. of Docs., U.S. Govt. Print. Off., [1976]

v, 79 p. ; 27 cm. — (DHEW publication ; no. (ADM) 76-357)
Includes bibliographies.

1. Homosexuality — Addresses, essays, lectures. I. Livingood, John M. II. Title. III. Series: United States. Dept. of Health, Education, and Welfare. DHEW publication ; no. (ADM) 76-357.

HQ76.25.U54 1976   306.7′6-dc19   77-602042
                                                         MARC
Not located in Monthly Catalog

HOOVER COMMISSION 1947-49 [Hoover, Herbert Clark]

The varying editions of the Hoover Commission Reports are grouped together in the following order: department edition, document edition, task force reports. These are arranged alphabetically by the title of the department edition.

736

U.S. Commision on Organization of the Executive Branch of the Government (1947-1949)

Administration of overseas affairs; a report to the Congress, March 1949. [Washington, U.S. Govt. Print. Off., 1949]

50 p. 23 cm.
"Federal-State relations; a report to the Congress, March 1949": p. [19]-39.
"Federal research; a report to the Congress, March 1949": p. [41]-50.
Herbert Hoover, chairman.
Issued also as House document no. 140, 81st Cong., 1st sess., under title: Overseas administration, Federal-State relations, Federal research. Letter from the chairman.

1. U.S. — Territories and possessions. 2. World War, 1939-1945 — Occupied territories. 3. Federal government — U.S. 4. Research — U.S. I. Hoover, Herbert Clark, Pres. U.S., 1874-1964. II. U.S. Commission on Organization of the Executive Branch of the Government (1947-1949) Federal-State relations. III. U.S. Commission on Organization of the Executive Branch of the Government (1947-1949) Federal research, a report.

JV562.A52 1949   353.8   49-46294
- - - - - Copy 2.
JK643.C47A55 no. 18
MC#: 1949-8900
SuDocs no.: Y3.Or3:20v2

U.S. *Commission on Organization of the Executive Branch of the Government* (1947-1949)

Overseas administration, Federal-State relations, Federal research. Letter from the chairman [Herbert Hoover], Commission on Organization of the Executive Branch of the Government transmitting its report on Federal-State relations, and separately, in typescript, volumes 1, 2, 3, and 4 of the task force report in this field. Washington, U.S. Govt. Print. Off., 1949.

50 p. 23 cm. (81st Cong., 1st sess. House document no. 140)
"Federal-State relations; a report to the Congress March 1949": p. [19]-39.
"Federal research; a report to the Congress, March 1949": p. [41]-50.
Issued also without congressional series numbering under title: Administration of overseas affairs; a report to the Congress, March 1949.

1. U.S. — Territories and possessions. 2. World War, 1939-1945 — Occupied territories. 3. Federal government — U.S. 4. Research — U.S. I. Hoover, Herbert Clark, Pres. U.S., 1874-1964. II. U.S. Commission on Organization of the Executive Branch of the Government (1947-1949) Federal-State relations. III. U.S. Commission on Organization of the Executive Branch of the Government (1947-1949) research. (Series: U.S. 81st Cong., 1st sess., 1949. House. Document no. 140)

JV562.A52 1949a   353.8   49-46246*
MC#: 1949-8971
SuDocs no.: 81st Cong., 1st sess. H. Doc. 140

Council of State Governments.

Federal-State relations by the Council of State Governments. Report of the Commission on Organization of the Executive Branch of the Government pursuant to Public law 162, 80th Congress. Washington, U.S. Govt. Print. Off., 1949.

x, 297 p. 23 cm. ([U.S.] 81st Cong., 1st sess., 1949. Senate. Document no. 81)
"Prepared for the Commission's consideration as a supplement to the Commission's report[s: Administration of overseas affairs; a report issued without congressional series numbering, and Overseas administration, Federal-State relations, Federal research. Letter, issued as House Document no. 140, 81st Cong., 1st sess.]"
Bibliography: p. 296-297.

1. Federal government — U.S. I. U.S. Commission on Organization of the Executive Branch of the Government. Administration of overseas affairs. II. U.S. Commission on

Organization of the Executive Branch of the Government. Overseas administration. (Series)
JK325.C63   353.9   49-46374*
MC#: 1949-17039
SuDocs no.: 81st Cong., 1st sess. S. Doc. 81

737

U.S. *Commission on Organization of the Executive Branch of the Government (1947-1949)*

Budgeting and accounting; a report to the Congress, February 1949. [Washington, U.S. Govt. Print. Off., 1949]

100 p. 23 cm.

"Statistical activities; a report to the Congress, February 1949": p. [85]-97.

Herbert Hoover, chairman.

Issued also as House document no. 84, 81st Cong., 1st sess., under title: Budgeting and accounting. Letter from the chairman.

1. Budget—U.S. 2. Finance, Public—U.S.—Accounting. I. Hoover, Herbert Clark, Pres. U.S., 1874-1964. II. U.S. Commission on Organization of the Executive Branch of the governnment (1947-1949) Statistical activities, a report.
HJ2051.A62 1949   351.72   49-45800 rev*
- - - - - Copy 2.
JK643.C47A55 no. 7
MC#: 1949-6870
SuDocs no.: Y3.Or3:2B85

U.S. *Commission on Organization of the Executive Branch of the Government (1947-1949)*

Budgeting and accounting. Letter from the chairman [Herbert Hoover], Commission on Organization of the Executive Branch of the Government, transmitting its report. Washington, U.S. Govt. Print. Off., 1949.

100 p. 23 cm. (81st Cong., 1st sess. House document no. 84)

"Statistical activities; a report to the Congress, February 1949": p. [85]-97.

Issued also without congressional series numbering under title: Budgeting and accounting; a report to the Congress, February 1949.

1. Budget—U.S. 2. Finance, Public—U.S.—Accounting. I. Hoover, Herbert Clark, Pres. U.S., 1874-1964. II. U.S. Commission on Organization of the Executive Branch of the Government (1947-1949) Statistical activities, a report. (Series: U.S. 81st Cong., 1st sess., 1949. House. Document no. 84)
HJ2051.A62 1949a   351.72   49-46083 rev*
MC#: 1949-6953
SuDocs no.: 81st Cong., 1st sess. H. Doc. 84

Mills, Frederick Cecil, 1892-

The statistical agencies of the Federal Government; a report with recommendations prepared for the Commission on Organization of the Executive Branch of the Government by Frederick C. Mills and Clarence D. Long. [Washington, U.S. Govt. Print. Off., 1948, i.e. 1949]

iii, 21 p. 23 cm.

On cover: Task force report on Statistical agencies, Appendix D.

An appendix to a report by the Commission on Organization of the Executive Branch of the Government with title, Statistical agencies published as p. 85-97 in Budgeting and accounting; a report to the Congress, February 1949.

1. U.S.—Stat. I. Long, Clarence Dickinson, 1908- joint author. II. U.S. Commission on Organization of the Executive Branch of the Government. Budgeting and accounting. III. Title: Task force report on Statistical agencies, Appendix D.

HA37.U55M5   310.6173   49-46010*
MC#: 1949-6883
SuDocs no.: Y3.Or3:7/D

Hanes, John Wesley, 1892-

Fiscal, budgeting, and accounting systems of Federal Government; a report with recommendations prepared for the Commission on Organization of the Executive Branch of the Government by John W. Hanes, A. E. Buck, and T. Coleman Andrews. [Washington, U.S. Govt. Print. Off., 1949]

ix, 110 p. 24 cm.

Cover title: Task force report on Fiscal, budgeting, and accounting activities, Appendix F.

An appendix to two reports by the Commission on Organization of the Executive Branch of the Government with titles, Budgeting and accounting and Treasury Department, respectively.

1. Budget—U.S. 2. Finance—U.S.—Accounting. I. U.S. Comission on Organization of the Executive Branch of the Government. Budgeting and accounting. II. U.S. Commission on Organization of the Executive Branch of the Government. Treasury Department; a report. III. Title: Task force report on Fiscal, budgeting, and accounting activities, Appendix F.
HJ2051.A62 1949b   351.72   49-45801*
MC#: 1949-6884
SuDocs no.: Y3.Or3:7/F

738

U.S. *Commission on Organization of the Executive Branch of the Government (1947-1949)*

Concluding report; a report to the Congress, May 1949. [Washington, U.S. Govt. Print. Off., 1949]

132 p. illus. 23 cm.

"Index of Commission reports and published task force reports, prepared by Legislative Reference Service, Library of Congress": p. [83]-132.

Herbert Hoover, chairman.

Issued also as House document no. 197, 81st Cong., 1st sess., under title: The nineteenth and concluding report. Letter from the chairman [Herbert Hoover] transmitting the nineteenth and concluding report.

1. U.S.—Executive departments. I. Hoover, Herbert Clark, Pres. U.S., 1874-1964. II. U.S. Library of Congress. Legislative Reference Service.
JK643.C47A5527   353   49-46149*
- - - - - Copy 2.
JK643.C47A55 no. 19
MC#: 1949-13601
SuDocs no.: Y3.Or3:2Or3

U.S. *Commission on Organization of the Executive Branch of the Government (1947-1949)*

The nineteenth and concluding report. Letter from chairman [Herbert Hoover] transmitting the nineteenth and concluding report. Washington, U.S. Govt. Print. Off., 1949.

132 p. illus. 24 cm. (81st Cong., 1st sess. House document no. 197)

"Index of Commission reports and published task force reports, prepared by Legislative Reference Service, Library of Congress": p. [83]-132.

Issued also without congressional series numbering under title: Concluding report; a report to the Congress, May 1949.

1. U.S.—Executive departments. I. Hoover, Herbert Clark, Pres. U.S., 1874-1964. II. U.S. Library of Congress. Legislative Reference Service. (Series: U.S. 81st Cong., 1st sess., 1949. House. Document no. 197)

JK643.C47A55272   353   49-46621 rev*
MC#: 1949-16683
SuDocs no.: 81st Cong., 1st sess. H. doc. 197

739

U.S. *Commission on Organization of the Executive Branch of the Government* (1947-1949)
    Department of Agriculture; a report to the Congress, February 1949. [Washington, U.S. Govt. Print. Off., 1949]
    41 p. 24 cm.
    Herbert Hoover, chairman.
    Issued also as House document no. 80, 81st Cong., 1st sess. under title: Department of Agriculture. Letter from the chairman [Herbert Hoover] transmitting the Commission's report on "Reorganization of the Department of Agriculture."
    1. U.S. Dept. of Agriculture. I. Hoover, Herbert Clark, Pres. U.S., 1874-1964.
S21.Z7 1949   630.6173   49-45842*
- - - - - Copy 2.
JK643.C47A55 no. 6
MC#: 1949-6871
SuDocs no.: Y39.Or3:2Ag8

U.S. *Commission on Organization of the Executive Branch of the Government* (1947-1949)
    Department of Agriculture. Letter from the chairman [Herbert Hoover] transmitting to the Congress the Commission's report on "Reorganization of the Department of Agriculture." Washington, U.S. Govt. Print. Off., 1949.
    41 p. 24 cm. (81st Cong., 1st sess. House document no. 80)
    Issued also without congressional series numbering under title: Department of Agriculture; a report to the Congress, February 1949.
    1. U.S. Dept. of Agriculture. I. Hoover, Herbert Clark, Pres. U.S., 1874-1964. (Series: U.S. 81st Cong., 1st sess., 1949. House Document no. 80)
S21.Z7 1949a   630.6173   49-46017 rev*
MC#: 1949-6952
SuDocs no.: 81st Cong., 1st sess. H. Doc. 80

U.S. *Commission on Organization of the Executive Branch of the Government* (1947-1949) Committee on Agricultural Activities.
    Agricultural functions and organization in the United States; a report with recommendations, prepared for the Commission on Organization of the Executive Branch of the Government, by a committee under chairmanship of H. P. Rusk and G. Harris Collingwood, research director. [Washington, U.S. Govt. Print. Off., 1949]
    xviii, 112 p. map. 23 cm.
    On cover: Task force report on agriculture activities, Appendix M.
    An appendix to Department of Agriculture; a report to the Congress, February 1949, by the Commission on Organization of the Executive Branch of the Government.
    1. U.S. Dept. of Agriculture. I. U.S. Commission on Organization of the Executive Branch of the Government (1947-1949) Department of Agriculture; a report.
S21.Z7 1949b   630.6173   49-46009 rev*
MC#: 1949-6889
SuDocs no.: Y3.Or3:7/M

740

U.S. *Commission on Organization of the Executive Branch of the Government* (1947-1949)
    Department of Commerce; a report to the Congress, March 1949. [Washington, U.S. Govt. Print. Off., 1949]
    34 p. 24 cm.
    Herbert Hoover, chairman.
    Issued also as House document no. 100, 81st Cong., 1st sess., under title: Department of Commerce. Letter from the chairman.
    1. U.S. Dept. of Commerce. I. Hoover, Herbert Clark, Pres. U.S., 1874-1964.
HF73.U5 1949c   353.8   49-45843 rev*
- - - - - Copy 2.
JK643.C47A55 no. 10
MC#: 1949-6872
SuDocs no.: Y3.Or3:2C73

U.S. *Commission on Organization of the Executive Branch of the Government* (1947-1949)
    Department of Commerce. Letter from the chairman [Herbert Hoover] transmitting the Commission's report on Reorganization of the Department of Commerce. Washington, U.S. Govt. Print. Off., 1949.
    34 p. 23 cm. (81st Cong., 1st sess. House document no. 100)
    Issued also without congressional series numbering under title: Department of Commerce; a report to the Congress, March 1949.
    1. U.S. Dept. of Commerce. I. Hoover, Herbert Clark, Pres. U.S., 1874-1964. (Series: U.S. 81st Cong., 1st sess., 1949. House. Document no. 100)
HF73.U5 1949d   353.8   49-46084 rev*
MC#: 1949-6964
SuDocs no.: 81st Cong., 1st sess. H. Doc. 100

U.S. *Commission on Organization of the Executive Branch of the Government (1947-1949) Committee on Independent Regulatory Commissions.*
    A report with recommendations prepared for the Commission on Organization of the Executive Branch of the Government. [Washington, U.S. Govt. Print. Off., 1949]
    x, 150 p. 23 cm.
    On cover: Task force report on regulatory commissions, Appendix N.
    An appendix to two reports by the Commission on Organization of the Executive Branch of the Government with titles Department of Commerce and The independent regulatory commissions, respectively.
    1. Independent regulatory commissions — U.S. I. U.S. Commission on Organization of the Executive Branch of the Government (1947-1949) Department of Commerce; a report. II. U.S. Commission on Organization of the Executive Branch of the Government (1947-1949) The independent regulatory commissions; a report.
JK 643.C47A5526   353   49-46008 rev*
MC#: 1949-6890
SuDocs no.: Y3.Or3:7/N

741

U.S. *Commission on Organization of the Executive Branch of the Government* (1947-1949)
    Department of Labor; a report to the Congress, March 1949. [Washington, U.S. Govt. Print. Off., 1949]
    22 p. 23 cm.
    Herbert Hoover, chairman.
    Issued also as House document no. 119, 81st Cong., 1st sess., under title: Department of Labor. Letter from the chairman.
    1. U.S. Dept. of Labor. I. Hoover, Herbert Clark, Pres. U.S., 1874-1964.
HD4835.U4A542 1949   353.8   49-46078 rev*
- - - - - Copy 2.
JK643.C47A55 no. 13
MC#: 1949-6874
SuDocs no.: Y3.Or3:2L11

U.S. *Commission on Organization of the Executive Branch of the Government* (1947-1949)

Department of Labor. Letter from the chairman [Herbert Hoover], Commission on Organization of the Executive Branch of the Government, transmitting its report on the Department of Labor, and separately, in typescript, a memorandum on the Department by George W. Taylor. Washington, U.S. Govt. Print. Off., 1949.

22 p. 23 cm. (81st Cong., 1st sess., House document no. 119)
Issued also without congressional series numbering under title: Department of Labor; a report to the Congress, March 1949.
1. U.S. Dept. of Labor. I. Hoover, Herbert Clark, Pres. U.S., 1874-1964. (Series: U.S. 81st Cong., 1st sess., 1949. House. Document no. 119)
HD4835.U4A542 1949a   353.8   49-46179 rev*
MC#:1949-8963
SuDocs no.: 81st Cong., 1st sess. H. Doc. 119

742

U.S. *Commission on Organization of the Executive Branch of the Government* (1947-1949)

Foreign affairs; a report to the Congress, February 1949. [Washington, U.S. Govt. Print. Off., 1949]

77 p. 23 cm.
Herbert Hoover, chairman.
Issued also as House document no. 79, 81st Cong., 1st sess., under title: Foreign affairs. Letter from the chairman [Herbert Hoover] transmitting the report on foreign affairs.
1. U.S. — For. rel. 2. U.S. Dept. of State. I. Hoover, Herbert Clark, Pres. U.S., 1874-1964.
JX234.A8 1949b   327.73   49-45782 rev*
- - - - - Copy 2.
JK643.C47A55 no. 5
MC#: 1949-6875
SuDocs no.: Y3.Or3:2F76

U.S. *Commission on Organization of the Executive Branch of the Government* (1947-1949)

Foreign affairs. Letter from the chairman [Herbert Hoover] transmitting the report on foreign affairs. Washington, U.S. Govt. Print. Off., 1949.

77 p. 24cm. (81st Cong., 1st sess. House document no. 79)
JX234.A8 1949c   327.73   49-46016 rev*
MC#: 1949-6951
SuDocs no.: 81st Cong., 1st sess. H. Doc. 79

Bundy, Harvey Hollister, 1888-

The organization of the Government for the conduct of foreign affairs; a report with recommendations prepared for the Commission on Organization of the Executive Branch of the Government, by Harvey H. Bundy and James Grafton Rogers. [Washington, U.S. Govt. Print. Off., 1949]

xi, 134 p. 24 cm.
Cover title: Task force report on Foreign affairs, Appendix H.
An appendix to Foreign affairs; a report to the Congress, February 1949, by the Commission on Organization of the Executive Branch of the Government.
1. U.S. — For. rel. 2. U.S. Dept. of State. I. Rogers, James Grafton, 1883- joint author. II. U.S. Commission on Organization of the Executive Branch of the Government. Foreign Affairs. III. Title: Task force report on Foreign affairs, Appendix H.
JX234.A8 1949d   327.73   49-45780*
MC#: 1949-6886
SuDocs no.: Y3.Or3:7/H

743

U.S. *Commission on Organization of the Executive Branch of the Government* (1947-1949)

General management of the Executive Branch; a report to the Congress, February 1949. Washington, U.S. Govt. Print. Off. [1949]

xii, 51 p. 23 cm.
Herbert Hoover, chairman.
Issued also as House document no. 55, 81st Cong., 1st sess., under title: First report. Letter from chairman [Herbert Hoover] transmitting the first report relating to the general management of the Executive Branch.
1. U.S. — Executive departments. I. Hoover, Herbert Clark, Pres. U.S., 1874-1964.
JK643.C47A552   353   49-45668 rev*
- - - - - Copy 2.
JK643.C47A55 no. 1
MC#: 1949-4590
SuDocs no.: Y3.Or3:2Ex3

U.S. *Commission on Organization of the Executive Branch of the Government* (1947-1949)

First report. Letter from chairman [Herbert Hoover] transmitting the first report relating to the general management of the Executive Branch. Washington, U.S. Govt. Print. Off., 1949.

xii, 51 p. 24 cm. (81st Cong., 1st sess. House document no. 55)
Issued also without congressional series numbering under title: General management of the Executive Branch; a report to the Congress, February 1949.
1. U.S. — Executive departments. I. Hoover, Herbert Clark, Pres. U.S., 1874-1964. (Series: U.S. 81st Cong., 1st sess., 1949. House. Document no. 55)
JK643.C47A5522   353   49-45597 rev*
MC#: 1949-4651
SuDocs no.: 81st Cong., 1st sess. H. Doc. 55

Hensel, Herman Struve, 1901-

Departmental management in Federal administration; a report with recommendations prepared for the Commission on Organization of the Executive Branch of the Government, by H. Struve Hensel and John D. Millett; staff: Walter Dunham, Jr. [and others. Washington, U.S. Govt. Print. Off., 1949]

ix, 60 p. 24 cm.
Cover title: Task force report on departmental management, Appendix E.
An appendix to General management of the Executive Branch; a report to the Congress, February 1949, by the Commission on Organization of the Executive Branch of the Government.
1. U.S. — Executive departments. I. Millett, John David, 1912- joint author. II. U.S. Commission on Organization of the Executive Branch of the Government. General management of the Executive branch. III. Title: Task force report on departmental management, Appendix E.
JK643.C47A5523   353   49-45758*
MC#: 1949-4594
SuDocs no.: Y3.Or3:7/E

744

U.S. *Commission on Organization of the Executive Branch of the Government* (1947-1949)

The independent regulatory commissions; a report to the Congress, March 1949. [Washington, U.S. Govt. Print. Off., 1949]

24 p. 24 cm.
Herbert Hoover, chairman.
Issued also as House document no. 116, 81st Cong., 1st sess., under title: The independent regulatory commissions. Letter from the chairman.

1. Independent regulatory commissions—U.S. I. Hoover, Herbert Clark, Pres. U.S., 1874-1964.
JK643.C47A5524   353   49-46076*
- - - - - Copy 2.
JK643.C47A55 no. 12
MC#: 1949-6880
SuDocs no.: Y3.Or3:2R26

U.S. *Commission on Organization of the Executive Branch of the Government* (1947-1949)

The independent regulatory commissions. Letter from the chairman [Herbert Hoover], Commission on Organization of the Executive Branch of the Government transmitting its report on the independent regulatory commissions and, separately, as Appendix N, the task force report on this subject. Washington, U.S. Govt. Print. Off., 1949.

23 p. 24 cm. (81st Cong., 1st sess. House document no. 116)

Issued also without congressional series numbering under title: The independent regulatory commissions; a report to the Congress, March 1949.

1. U.S.—Executive departments. I. Hoover, Herbert Clark, Pres. U.S., 1874-1964. (Series: U.S. 81st Cong., 1st sess., 1949. House. Document no. 116)
JK643.C47A5525   353   49-46178 rev*
MC#: 1949-8962
SuDocs no.: 81st Cong., 1st sess. H. Doc. 116

U.S. *Commission on Organization of the Executive Branch of the Government (1947-1949) Committee on Independent Regulatory Commissions.*

A report with recommendations prepared for the Commission on Organization of the Executive Branch of the Government. [Washington, U.S. Govt. Print. Off., 1949]

x, 150 p. 23 cm.

On cover: Task force report on regulatory commissions, Appendix N.

An appendix to two reports by the Commission on Organization of the Executive Branch of the Government with titles Department of Commerce and The independent regulatory commissions, respectively.

1. Independent regulatory commissions—U.S. I. U.S. Commission on Organization of the Executive Branch of the Government (1947-1949) Department of Commerce; a report. II. U.S. Commission on Organization of the Executive Branch of the Government (1947-1949) The independent regulatory commissions; a report.
JK643.C47A5526   353   49-46008 rev*
MC#: 1949-6890
SuDocs no.: Y3.Or3:7/N

745

U.S. *Library of Congress. Legislative Reference Service.*

Index to the reports of the Commission on Organization of the Executive Branch of the Government and to supporting task force reports, prepared at request of the Senate Committee on Expenditures in the Executive Departments. Washington, U.S. Govt. Print. Off., 1949.

vii, 77 p. 23 cm.

At head of title: 81st Cong., 1st sess. Senate committee print.

1. U.S.—Executive departments. I. U.S. Commission on Organization of the Executive Branch of the Government.
JK643.C47A5528   353   49-46360*
MC#: 1949-14291
SuDocs no.: Y3.Ex7/14:Or3/3

746

U.S. *Commission on Organization of the Executive Branch of the Government* (1947-1949)

The national security organization; a report to the Congress, February 1949. [Washington, U.S. Govt. Print. Off., 1949]

30 p. 24 cm.

Herbert Hoover, chairman.

Issued also as House document no. 86, 81st Cong., 1st sess., under title: The national security organization. Letter from the chairman [Herbert Hoover] transmitting to the Congress a study prepared for the Commission's consideration on the national security organization in the Federal Government.

1. U.S.—Defenses. I. Hoover, Herbert Clark, Pres. U.S., 1874-1964.
UA23.A413 1949   355   49-45841 rev*
- - - - - Copy 2.
JK643.C47A55 no. 8
MC#: 1949-6877
SuDocs no.: Y3.Or3:2N21/s

U.S. *Commission on Organization of the Executive Branch of the Government* (1947-1949)

The national security organization. Letter from the chairman [Herbert Hoover] transmitting to the Congress a study prepared for the Commission's consideration of the national security organization in the Federal Government. Washington, U.S. Govt. Print. Off., 1949.

30 p. 24 cm. (81st Cong., 1st sess. House document no. 86)

Issued also without congressional series numbering under title: The national security organization; a report to the Congress, February 1949.

1. U.S.—Defenses. I. Hoover, Herbert Clark, Pres. U.S., 1874-1964. (Series: U.S. 81st Cong., 1st sess., 1949. House. Document no. 86)
UA23.A413 1949a   355   49-46020 rev*
MC#: 1949-6955
SuDocs no.: 81st Cong., 1st sess. H. Doc. 86

U.S. *Commission on Organization of the Executive Branch of the Government (1947-1949) Committee on the National Security Organization.*

National security organization; a report with recommendations prepared for the Commission on Organization of the Executive Branch of the Government. [Washington, U.S. Govt. Print. Off., 1949]

xiv, 121 p. 23 cm.

On cover: Task force report on national security organization, Appendix G.

An appendix to The national security organization; a report to the Congress, February 1949, by the Commission on Organization of the Executive Branch of the Government.

E. Eberstadt, chairman of committee.

1. U.S.—Defenses. I. U.S. Commission on Organization of the Executive Branch of the Government (1947-1949) The national security organization; a report.
UA23.A413 1949b   355   49-46011 rev*
MC#: 1949-6885
SuDocs no.: Y3.Or3:7/G

747

U.S. *Commission on Organization of the Executive Branch of the Government* (1947-1949)

Office of General Services; a report to the Congress, February 1949. [Washington, U.S. Govt. Print. Off., 1949]

v, 52 p. 24 cm.

"The organization and management of Federal supply activities; a report to the Congress, February 1949": p. [17]-52.

Herbert Hoover, chairman.

Issued also as House document no. 73, 81st Cong., 1st sess., under title: Office of General Services, supply service. Letter from the chairman.

1. U.S. General Services Administration. 2. Government purchasing—U.S. 3. Archives—U.S. 4. U.S.—Government property. I. Hoover, Herbert Clark, Pres. U.S., 1874-1964. II. U.S. Commission on Organization of the Executive Branch of the Government (1947-1949) The organization and management of Federal supply activities.
JK1671.A32 1949   353.8   49-45761*
- - - - - Copy 2.
JK643.C47A55 no. 3
MC#: 1949-4591
SuDocs no.: Y3.Or3:2G28

U.S. *Commission on Organization of the Executive Branch of the Government* (1947-1949)
Office of General Services, supply activities. Letter from the chairman [Herbert Hoover] transmitting a report on the Office of General Services. Washington, U.S. Govt. Print. Off., 1949.

v, 52 p. 24 cm. (81st Cong., 1st sess. House document no. 73)
"The organization and management of Federal supply activities; a report to the Congress, February 1949": p. [17]-52.
Issued also without congressional series numbering under title: Office of General Services; a report to the Congress, February 1949.
1. U.S. General Services Administration. 2. Government purchasing—U.S. 3. Archives—U.S. 4. U.S.—Government property. I. Hoover, Herbert Clark, Pres. U.S., 1874-1964. II. U.S. Commission on Organization of the Executive Branch of the Government (1947-1949) The organization and management of Federal activities. (Series: U.S. 81st Cong., 1st sess., 1949. House. Document no. 73)
JK1671.A32 1949a   353.8   49-46022 rev*
MC#: 1949-4659
SuDocs no.: 81st Cong., 1st sess. H. Doc. 73

Forbes, Russell, 1896-
The Federal supply system; a report with recommendations prepared for the Commission on Organization of the Executive Branch of the Government. [Washington, U.S. Govt. Print. Off., 1949]

x, 116 p. 23 cm.
Cover title: Task force report on the Federal supply system, Appendix B.
An appendix to a report by the Commission on Organization of the Executive Branch of the Government with title: The organization and management of Federal supply activities published as p. 17 to 52 in Office of General Services; a report to the Congress, February 1949.
1. Buying. 2. U.S.—Government property. I. U.S. Commission on Organization of the Executive Branch of the Government. Office of General Services. II. Title: Task force report on the Federal supply system. Appendix B.
JK1671.A32 1949b   351.71   49-45759*
MC#: 1949-4593
SuDocs no.: Y3.Or3:7/B

Leahy, Emmett J
Records management in the United States Government; a report with recommendations prepared for the Commission on Organization of the Executive Branch of the Government. [Washington, U.S. Govt. Print. Off., 1949]

v, 48 p. 23 cm.
On cover: Task force report on Records management, Appendix C.
An appendix to a report by the Commission on Organization of the Executive Branch of the Government with title: Office of General Services; a report to the Congress, February.
1. Archives—U.S. I. U.S. Commission on Organization of the Executive Branch of the Government. Office of General Services.

II. Title: Task force report on Records management, Appendix C.
CD3023.L43   025.171   49-46074*
MC#: 1949-6882
SuDocs no.: Y3.Or3:7/C

748

U.S. *Commission on Organization of the Executive Branch of the Government.* (1947-1949).
Personnel management; a report to the Congress, February 1949. [Washington, U.S. Govt. Print. Off., 1949]

59 p. 24 cm.
Herbert Hoover, chairman.
Issued also as House Document no. 63, 81st Cong., 1st sess., under title: Personnel management. Letter from chairman [Herbert Hoover] transmitting the Commission's report.
1. Personnel management. 2. Civil service—U.S. I. Hoover, Herbert Clark, Pres. U.S., 1874-1964.
JK765.A52 1949   351.1   49-45783*
- - - - - Copy 2.
JK643.C47A55 no. 2
MC#: 1949-6878
SuDocs no.: Y3.Or3:P43

U.S. *Commission on Organization of the Executive Branch of the Government* (1947-1949)
Personnel management. Letter from chairman [Herbert Hoover] transmitting the Commission's report . . . Washington, U.S. Govt. Print. Off., 1949.

59 p. 23 cm. (81st Cong., 1st sess. House document no. 63)
Issued also without congressional series numbering under title: Personnel management; a report to the Congress, February 1949.
1. Personnel management. 2. Civil service—U.S. I. Hoover, Herbert Clark, Pres. U.S., 1874-1964. (Series: U.S. 81st Cong., 1st sess., 1949. House. Document no. 63)
JK765.A52 1949a   351.1   49-45749 rev*
MC#: 1949-4657
SuDocs no.: 81st Cong., 1st sess. H. Doc. 63

U.S. *Commission on Organization of the Executive Branch of the Government (1947-1949) Personnel Policy Committee.*
Programs for strengthening Federal personnel management; a report with recommendations prepared for the Commission on Organization of the Executive Branch of the Government. [Washington, U.S. Govt. Print. Off., 1949]

xv, 101 p. 24 cm.
Cover title: Task force report on Federal personnel, Appendix A.
An Appendix to Personnel management; a report to the Congress, February 1949, by the Commission on Organization of the Executive Branch of the Government.
John A. Stevenson, chairman of committee.
1. Personnel management—U.S. 2. Civil service—U.S. I. U.S. Commission on Organization of the Executive Branch of the Government (1947-1949) Personnel management, a report.
JK765.A52 1949b   351.1   49-45760 rev*
MC#: 1949-4592
SuDocs no.: Y3.Or:7/A

749

U.S. *Commission on Organization of the Executive Branch of the Government* (1947-1949)
The Post Office; a report to the Congress, February 1949. [Washington, U.S. Govt. Print. Off., 1949]

21 p. 23 cm.
Herbert Hoover, chairman.

Issued also as House document no. 76, 81st Cong., 1st sess., under title: The Post Office. Letter from the chairman [Herbert Hoover] transmitting the Commission's report on the Post Office Department.

1. U.S. Post Office Dept. I. Hoover, Herbert Clark, Pres. U.S., 1874-1964.
HE6331 1949.A523   383.4973   49-45781 rev*
- - - - - Copy 2.
JK643.C47A55 no. 4
MC#: 1949-6879
SuDocs no.: Y3.Or3:2P84

U.S. *Commission on Organization of the Executive Branch of the Government* (1947-1949)
The Post Office. Letter from the chairman [Herbert Hoover] transmitting the Commission's report on the Post Office Department. Washington, U.S. Govt. Print. Off., 1949.

21 p. 24 cm. (81st Cong., 1st sess. House document no. 76)
Issued also without congressional series numbering under title: The Post Office; a report to the Congress, February 1949.
1. U.S. Post Office Dept. I. Hoover, Herbert Clark, Pres. U.S., 1874-1964. (Series: U.S. 81st Cong., 1st sess., 1949. House. Document no. 76)
HE6331 1949.A524   383.4973   49-46003 rev*
MC#: 1949-6948
SuDocs no.: 81st Cong., 1st sess. H. Doc. 76

Heller, (Robert) and Associates, *Cleveland.*
Management organization and administration of the Post Office Department; a report, with recommendations prepared for the Commission on Organization of the Executive Branch of the Government. [Washington, U.S. Govt. Print. Off., 1949]

x, 74 p. maps (1 fold.) 24 cm.
Cover title: Task force report on The Post Office, Appendix I.
An appendix to The Post Office; a report to the Congress, February, 1949, by the Commission on Organization of the Executive Branch of the Government.
1. U.S. Post Office Dept. I. U.S. Commission on Organization of the Executive Branch of the Government. The Post Office. II. Title: Task force report on The Post Office, Appendix I.
HE6331 1949.A525   383.4973   49-45779*
MC#: 1949-6887
SuDocs no.: Y3.Or3:7/I

750

U.S. *Commission on Organization of the Executive Branch of the Government* (1947-1949)
Reorganization of Federal business enterprises; a report to the Congress, March 1949. [Washington, U.S. Govt. Print. Off., 1949]

129 p. 23 cm.
Herbert Hoover, chairman.
Issued also as House document no. 152, 81st Cong., 1st sess., under title: Federal business enterprises. Letter from the chairman.
1. Corporations, Government—U.S. I. Hoover, Herbert Clark, Pres. U.S., 1874-1964.
HD3881.A54 1949   380.1622   49-46173 rev*
- - - - - Copy 2.
JK643.C47A55 no. 17
MC#: 1949-8899
SuDocs no.: Y3.Or3:2B96

U.S. *Commission on Organization of the Executive Branch of the Government* (1947-1949)
Federal business enterprises. Letter from the chairman [Herbert Hoover], Commission on Organization of the Executive Branch of the Government transmitting its report on Federal business

enterprises, and separately, the task force reports on revolving funds, as Appendix J; on water resources projects, as Appendix K; and on lending agencies, as Appendix R. Washington, U.S. Govt. Print. Off., 1949.

129 p. 23 cm. (81st Cong., 1st sess. House document no. 152)
Issued also without congressional series numbering under title: Reorganization of Federal business enterprises; a report to the Congress, March 1949.
1. Corporations, Government—U.S. I. Hoover, Herbert Clark, Pres. U.S., 1874-1964. (Series: U.S. 81st Cong., 1st sess., 1949. House. Document no. 152)
HD3881.A54 1949a   380.1622   49-46313 rev*
MC#: 1949-8981
SuDocs no.: 81st Cong., 1st sess. H. Doc. 152

Haskins & Sells.
Revolving funds and business enterprises of the Government, exclusive of lending agencies; a report with recommendations prepared for the Commission on Organization of the Executive Branch of the Government. [Washington, U.S. Govt. Print. Off., 1949]

vi, 176 p. 24 cm.
On cover: Task force report on revolving funds and business enterprises of the Government, Appendix J.
An appendix to a report by the Commission on Organization of the Executive Branch of the Government with title: Reorganization of Federal business enterprises; a report to the Congress, March 1949.
1. Government business enterprises—U.S. 2. Electric utilities—U.S. I. U.S. Commission on Organization of the Executive Branch of the Government (1947-1949) Reorganization of Federal business enterprises. II. Title. III. Title: Task force report on revolving funds and business enterprises of the Government, Appendix J.
HD3887.H3   380.1622   49-46171 rev*
MC#: 1949-8901
SuDocs no.: Y3.Or3:7/J

Roberts, Arthur Boardman, 1884-
Certain aspects of power irrigation and flood control projects; a report with recommendations prepared for the Commission on Organization of the Executive Branch of the Government. [Washington, U.S. Govt. Print. Off., 1949]

x, 65 p. 24 cm.
On cover: Task force report on water resources projects, Appendix K.
An appendix to a report by the Commission on Organization of the Executive Branch of the Government with title: Reorganization of Federal business enterprises; a report to the Congress, March 1949.
Bibliography: p. 62-65.
1. U.S.—Public works. 2. Electric utilities—U.S. 3. Irrigation—U.S. 4. Floods—U.S. I. U.S. Commission on Organization of the Executive Branch of the Government. Reorganization of Federal business enterprises. II. Title: Task force report on water resources projects, Appendix K.
HD3881.A54 1949b   351.8   49-46172*
MC#: 1949-8902
SuDocs no.: Y3.Or3:7/K

Price, Waterhouse and Company.
Activities and organization of lending agencies of the Government; a report with recommendations prepared for the Commission on Organization of the Executive Branch of the Government. [Washington, U.S. Govt. Print. Off., 1949]

xx, 108 p. 24 cm.
On cover: Task force report on lending agencies, Appendix R.

An appendix to a report by the Commission on Organization of the Executive Branch of the Government with title: Reorganization of Federal business enterprises; a report to the Congress, March 1949.

1. Credit—U.S. I. U.S. Commission on Organization of the Executive Branch of the Government. Reorganization of Federal business enterprises. II. Title: Task force report on lending agencies, Appendix R.

HG3729.U5P7   332.31   49-46170*
MC#: 1949-8903
SuDocs no.: Y3.Or3:7/R

U.S. *Commission on Organization of the Executive Branch of the Government* (1947-1949)

Reorganization of Federal business enterprises; a report to the Congress, March, 1949. New York, Greenwood Press [1969]

129 p. 23 cm.

Herbert Hoover, chairman.

Title on spine: Federal business enterprises.

Reprint of the 1949 ed.

1. Government business enterprises—U.S. I. Hoover, Herbert Clark, Pres. U.S., 1874-1964. II. Title. III. Title: Federal business enterprises. IV. Title: Hoover Commission report on Federal business enterprises.

HD3881.A54 1969   353.09'2   71-90716
                                            MARC
ISBN8371-2271-6
Not listed in Monthly Catalog

751

U.S. *Commission on Organization of the Executive Branch of the Government* (1947-1949)

Reorganization of Federal medical activities; a report to the Congress, March 1949. [Washington, U.S. Govt. Print. Off., 1949]

57 p. 24 cm.

Herbert Hoover, chairman.

Issued also as House document no. 128, 81st Cong., 1st sess., under title: Reorganization of Federal medical activities. Letter from the chairman.

1. Medicine, State—U.S. 2. Medical research—U.S. I. Hoover, Herbert Clark, Pres. U.S., 1874-1964.

RA11.B14 1949   614.06173   49-46077*
- - - - - Copy 2.
JK643.C47A55 no. 16
MC#: 1949-6876
SuDocs no.: Y3.Or3:2M46

U.S. *Commission on Organization of the Executive Branch of the Government* (1947-1949)

Reorganization of Federal medical activities. Letter from the chairman [Herbert Hoover] Commission on Organization of the Executive Branch of the Government, transmitting its report on medical activities, and separately, as Appendix O, the task force report on organization of Federal medical services, and a supplemental task force report on an independent medical agency. Washington, U.S. Govt. Print. Off., 1949.

57 p. 24 cm. (81st Cong., 1st sess. House document no. 128)

Issued also without congressional series numbering under title: Reorganization of Federal medical activities; a report to the Congress, March 1949.

1. Medicine, State—U.S. 2. Medical research—U.S. I. Hoover, Herbert Clark, Pres. U.S., 1874-1964. (Series: U.S. 81st Cong., 1st sess., 1949. House. Document no. 128)

RA11.B14 1949d   614.06173   49-46217 rev*
MC#: 1949-8967
SuDocs no.: 81st Cong., 1st sess. H. Doc. 128

U.S. *Commission on Organization of the Executive Branch of the Government (1947-1949) Committee on Federal Medical Services.*

Federal medical services; a report with recommendations prepared for the Commission on Organization of the Executive Branch of the Government. [Washington, U.S. Govt. Print. Off., 1949]

xxi, 95 p. 23 cm.

On cover: Task force report on Federal medical services, Appendix O.

An appendix to Reorganization of Federal medical activities; a report to the Congress, March 1949, by the Commission on Organization of the Executive Branch of the Government.

Tracy S. Voorhees, chairman of committee.

1. Medicine, State—U.S. 2. Medical research—U.S. I. U.S. Commission on Organization of the Executive Branch of the Government (1947-1949) Reorganization of Federal medical activities, a report.

RA11.B14 1949e   614.06173   49-46080 rev*
MC#: 1949-6891
SuDocs no.: Y3.Or3:7/0

U.S. *Commission on Organization of the Executive Branch of the Government (1947-1949) Committee on Federal Medical Services.*

Federal medical services; a report with recommendations; [supplemental report on an independent medical agency] prepared for the Commission on Organization of the Executive Branch of the Government by the chairman [Tracy S. Voorhees] of the Committee on Federal Medical Services acting for the committee. [Washington, U.S. Govt. Print. Off., 1949]

2 p. 24 cm.

On cover: Task force report on Federal medical services. Supplement to Appendix O.

A supplemental appendix to Reorganization of Federal medical activities; a report to the Congress, March 1949, by the Commission on Organization of the Executive Branch of the Government.

1. Medicine, State—U.S. 2. Medical research—U.S. I. U.S. Commission on Organization of the Executive Branch of the Government (1947-1949) Reorganization of Federal medical activities, a report.

RA11.B14 1949f   614.06173   49-46250 rev*
MC#: 1949-6891
SuDocs no.: Y3.Or3:7/0

752

U.S. *Commission on Organization of the Executive Branch of the Government* (1947-1949)

Reorganization of the Department of the Interior; a report to the Congress, March 1949. [Washington, U.S. Govt.Print Off., 1949]

94 p. 24 cm.

Herbert Hoover, chairman.

Issued also as House document no. 122, 81st Cong., 1st sess., under title: Department of the Interior. Letter from the chairman.

1. U.S. Dept. of the Interior. I. Hoover, Herbert Clark, Pres. U.S., 1874-1964.

JK865 1949c   353.3   49-46079*
- - - - - Copy 2.
JK643.C47A55 no. 14
MC#: 1949-6873
SuDocs no.: Y3.Or3:2In8

U.S. *Commission on Organization of the Executive Branch of the Government* (1947-1949)

Department of the Interior. Letter from the chairman [Herbert Hoover], Commission on Organization of the Executive Branch of the Government transmitting its report on the Department of the Interior and, separately, as appendixes, L, M, and Q, the related task force reports on natural resources, agriculture, and public works. Washington, U.S. Govt. Print. Off., 1949.

94 p. 24 cm. (81st Cong., 1st sess. House document no. 122)

Issued also without congressional series numbering under title: Reorganization of the Department of the Interior; a report to the Congress, March 1949.

1. U.S. Dept. of the Interior. I. Hoover, Herbert Clark, Pres. U.S., 1874-1964. (Series: U.S. 81st Cong., 1st sess., 1949. House. Document no. 122)

JK865 1949d   353.3   49-46276 rev*
MC#: 1949-8964
SuDocs no.: 81st Cong., 1st sess. H. Doc. 122

U.S. *Commission on Organization of the Executive Branch of the Government (1947-1949) Committee on Natural Resources.*

Organization and policy in the field of natural resources; a report with recommendations, prepared for the Commission on Organization of the Executive Branch of the Government by Leslie A. Miller, chairman, and task force committee members and a special unit of the Legislative Reference Service of the Library of Congress. [Washington, U.S. Govt. Print. Off., 1949]

ix, 244 p. fold. map. 23 cm.

On cover: Task force report on natural resources, Appendix L.

An appendix to a report by the Commission on Organization of the Executive Branch of the Government with title: Reorganization of the Department of the Interior; a report to the Congress, March 1949.

1. Natural resources—U.S. 2. U.S. Dept. of the Interior. I. U.S. Library of Congress. Legislative Reference Service. II. U.S. Commission on Organization of the Executive Branch of the Government (1947-1949) Reorganization of the Department of the Interior; a report.

HC106.5.A47 1949b   333.72   49-46073 rev*
MC#: 1949-6888
SuDocs no.: Y3.Or3:7/L

Moses, Robert, 1888-

Department of Works; a report with recommendations prepared for the Commission on Organization of the Executive Branch of the Government. [Washington, U.S. Govt. Print. Off., 1949]

viii, 81 p. 23 cm.

On cover: Task force report on public works, Appendix Q.

An appendix to a report by the Commission on Organization of the Executive Branch of the Government with title: Reorganization of the Department of the Interior; a report to the Congress, March 1949.

1. U.S.—Public works. I. U.S. Commission on Organization of the Executive Branch of the Government. Reorganization of the Department of the Interior. II. Title: Task force report on public works, Appendix Q.

HD3887.M6   353.8   49-46072*
MC#: 1949-6893
SuDocs no.: Y3.Or3:7/Q

753

U.S. *Commission on Organization of the Executive Branch of the Government (1947-1949)*

Reorganization of veterans' affairs; a report to the Congress, February 1949. [Washington, U.S. Govt. Print. Off., 1949]

26 p. 23 cm.

Commonly known as the Hoover Commission report.

Herbert Hoover, chairman.

Issued also as House document no. 92, 81st Cong., 1st sess., under title: Reorganization of veterans' affairs. Letter from the chairman.

1. U.S. Veterans Administration. I. Hoover, Herbert Clark, Pres. U.S., 1874-1964. II. Title. III. Title: Hoover Commission report on veterans' affairs.

UB373.A4 1949   353.8   49-45835 rev*
- - - - - Copy 2.
JK643.C47A55 no. 9
MC#: 1949-6895
SuDocs no.: Y3.Or3:2V64

U.S. *Commission on Organization of the Executive Branch of the Government (1947-1949)*

Reorganization of veterans' affairs. Letter from the chairman [Herbert Hoover], Commission on Organization of the Executive Branch of the Government, transmitting its report on veterans' affairs. Washington, U.S. Govt. Print. Off., 1949.

26 p. 24 cm. ([U.S.] 81st Cong., 1st sess., 1949. House. Document no. 92)

Issued also without congressional series numbering under title: Reorganization of veterans' affairs; a report to the Congress, February 1949.

1. U.S. Veterans Administration. I. Hoover, Herbert Clark, Pres. U.S., 1874-1964. (Series)

UB373.A4 1949a   353.8   49-46085 rev*
MC#:1949-6957
SuDocs no.: 81st Cong., 1st sess. H. Doc. 92

U.S. *Commission on Organization of the Executive Branch of the Government (1947-1949) Committee on Veterans' Affairs.*

Report of the Hoover Commission Committee on Veterans' Affairs (Commission task force) Printed for the use of the Committee on Veterans' Affairs. Washington, U.S. Govt. Print. Off., 1949.

v, 36 p. diagrs. 24 cm.

At head of title: 81st Cong. 1st sess. House committee print no. 13.

1. U.S. Veterans Administration. I. U.S. Congress. House. Committee on Veterans' Affairs.

UB373.A4 1949b   62-4858
Not located in Monthly Catalog

754

U.S. *Commission on Organization of the Executive Branch of the Government (1947-1949)*

Social security and education, Indian affairs; a report to the Congress, March 1949. [Washington, U.S. Govt. Print. Off., 1949]

81 p. 23 cm.

"Indian affairs; a report to the Congress, March 1949": p. [53]-80.

Herbert Hoover, chairman.

Issued also as House document no. 129, 81st Cong., 1st sess., under title: Social security and education, Indian affairs. Letter from the chairman.

1. Public welfare—U.S. 2. Insurance, Social—U.S. 3. Education—U.S. 4. Indians of North America—Government relations. I. Hoover, Herbert Clark, Pres. U.S., 1874-1964. II. U.S. Commission on Organization of the Executive Branch of the Government (1947-1949) Indian affairs, a report.

HV85.A52 1949   331.2544   49-46075 rev*
- - - - - Copy 2.
JK643.C47A55 no. 15
MC#: 1949-6881
SuDocs no.: Y3.Or3:2So1

U.S. *Commission on Organization of the Executive Branch of the Government (1947-1949)*

Social security and education, Indian affairs. Letter from the chairman [Herbert Hoover], Commission on Organization of the Executive Branch of the Government, transmitting its report on Social security and education, and separately, as Appendix P, the task force report on welfare activities . . . Washington, U.S. Govt. Print. Off., 1949.

81 p. 24 cm. ([U.S.] 81st Cong., 1st sess., 1949. House. Document no. 129)

"Indian affairs; a report to the Congress, March 1949": p. [53]-80.

Issued also without congressional series numbering under title: Social security and education, Indian affairs; a report to the Congress, March 1949.

1. Public welfare—U.S. 2. Insurance, Social—U.S. 3. Education—U.S. 4. Indians of North America—Government relations. I. Hoover, Herbert Clark, Pres. U.S., 1874-1964. II. U.S. Commission on Organization of the Executive Branch of the Government (1947-1949) Indian affairs, a report. (Series)
HV85.A52 1949a   331.2544   49-46259 rev*
MC#: 1949-8968
SuDocs no.: 81st Cong., 1st sess. H. Doc. 129

Brookings Institution, *Washington, D.C.*
Functions and activities of the National Government in the field of welfare; a report with recommendations prepared for the Commission on Organization of the Executive Branch of the Government. [Washington, U.S. Govt. Print. Off., 1949]

xv, 590 p. 23 cm.

On cover: Task force report on public welfare, Appendix P.

An appendix to a report by the Commission on Organization of the Executive Branch of the Government with title: Social security and education, Indian affairs; a report to the Congress, March 1949.   •

1. Public welfare—U.S. 2. Insurance, Social—U.S. I. U.S. Commission on Organization of the Executive Branch of the Government. Social security and education, Indian affairs. II. Title: Task force report on public welfare, Appendix P.
HV85.A52 1949b   360.973   49-46071*
MC#: 1949-6892
SuDocs no.: Y3.Or3:7/P

755

U.S. *Commission on Organization of the Executive Branch of the Government* (1947-1949)
[Task force reports. n.p., 1947?-49?]

84 v. maps (part fold., part col.) diagrs., tables. 27-30 cm.

Consists of appendices, staff studies prepared as working tools for task forces, or data supplementing chapters of the Commission's report.

Includes "Index to the task force typescript reports of the Commission . . . " prepared by Legislative Reference Service, Library of Congress.

- - - - - Microfilm. 9 reels. 35 mm.
    Contents.—1. AA-EB.—2. EC-FD.—3. GA-HK.—4. HL-NC.—5. ND-NK.—6. NL-OK.—7. OL-SD.—8. SE-WE.—9. Index.
Microfilm 01928JK.
1. U.S.—Executive departments. I. U.S. Library of Congress. Legislative Reference Service.
JK643.C47A5537   62-34909
Not located in Monthly Catalog

756

U.S. *Commission on Organization of the Executive Branch of the Government* (1947-1949)
Treasury Department; a report to the Congress, March 1949. [Washington, U.S. Govt. Print. Off., 1949]

37 p. 23 cm.
Herbert Hoover, chairman.

Issued also as House document no. 115, 81st Cong., 1st sess., under title: Treasury Department. Letter from the chairman. I. U.S. Treasury Dept. I. Hoover, Herbert Clark, Pres. U.S., 1874-1964.
HJ263.A42 1949   353.2   49-46081 rev*
- - - - - Copy 2.
JK643.C47A55 no. 11
MC#: 1949-6894
SuDocs no.: Y3.Or3:2T72

U.S. *Commission on Organization of the Executive Branch of the Government* (1947-1949)
Treasury Department. Letter from the chairman [Herbert Hoover] transmitting a report on the Treasury Department, and separately, as Appendix F, the task force report on Fiscal, budgeting and accounting activities of the Federal Government. Washington, U.S. Govt. Print. Off., 1949.

37 p. 24 cm. (81st Cong., 1st sess. House document no. 115)

Issued also without congressional series numbering under title: Treasury Department; a report to the Congress, March 1949.

1. U.S. Treasury Dept. I. Hoover, Herbert Clark, Pres. U.S., 1874-1964. (Series: U.S. 81st Cong., 1st sess., 1949. House. Document no. 115)
HJ263.A42 1949a   353.2   49-46082 rev*
MC#: 1949-6967
SuDocs no.: 81st Cong., 1st sess. H. Doc. 115

For progress report see McCLELLAN REPORT

HOOVER COMMISSION 1953-55 [Hoover, Herbert Clark]

757

U.S. *Commission of the Executive Branch of the Government* (1953-1955)
Budget and accounting; a report to the Congress. [Washington, U.S. Govt. Print. Off.] 1955.

xii, 72 p. 24 cm.
1. Budget—U.S. 2. Finance, Public—U.S.—Accounting. I. Title.
HJ2051.A62 1955   *336.395 351.72   55-61374
MC#: 1955-10628
SuDocs no.: Y3.Or3/2:2B85
MC#: 1955-11445
SuDocs no.: 84th Cong., 1st sess. H. Doc. 192

U.S. *Commission on Organization of the Executive Branch of the Government (1953-1955) Task Force on Budget and Accounting.*
Report on budget and accounting in the United States Government, prepared for the Commission on Organization of the Executive Branch of the Government. [Washington, U.S. Govt. Print. Off.] 1955.

x, 87 p. diagr. 24 cm.
1. Budget—U.S. 2. Finance, Public—U.S.—Accounting. I. Title: Budget and accounting in the United States Government.
HJ2051.A62 1955a   55-61588
MC#: 1955-15974
SuDocs no.: Y3.Or3/2:8B85

758

U.S. *Commission on Organization of the Executive Branch of the Government* (1953-1955)
Business enterprises; a report to the Congress. [Washington, U.S. Govt. Print. Off.] 1955.

xviii, 113 p. 24 cm.
1. Government business enterprises—U.S.
HD3616.U45A577 1955   *338.7 380.1652   55-61186

MC#: 1955-10629
SuDocs no.: Y3.Or3/2:2B96
MC#: 1955-9454
SuDocs no.: 84th Cong., 1st sess. H. Doc. 162

U.S. *Commission on Organization of the Executive Branch of the Government (1953-1955) Special Committee on Business Enterprises in the Government Outside of the Department of Defense.*

Staff study on business enterprises outside of the Department of Defense. Prepared by the research staff of the Commission. [Washington] 1955.

xiii, 118 p. 24 cm.

1. Government business enterprises—U.S. I. Title. II. Title: Business enterprises outside of the Department of Defense.

HD3616.U45A577 1955b   55-61716
MC#: 1955-15980
SuDocs no.: Y3.Or3/2:8B96

759

U.S. *Commission on Organization of the Executive Branch of the Government* (1953-1955)

Business organization of the Department of Defense; a report to the Congress. [Washington, U.S. Govt. Print. Off.] 1955.

xxii, 149 p. diagrs. 24 cm.

1. U.S. Dept. of Defense. I. Title.

UA23.3A472 1955   353.6   55-61491
MC#: 1955-12649
SuDocs no.: Y3.Or3/2:2B96/2
MC#: 1955-11446
SuDocs no.: 84th Cong., 1st sess. H. Doc. 196

U.S. *Commission on Organization of the Executive Branch of the Government (1953-1955) Committee on Business Organization of the Dept. of Defense.*

Subcommittee report on business enterprises of the Department of Defense, prepared for the Committee on Business Organization of the Dept. of Defense of the Commission on Organization of the Executive Branch of the Government, by the Subcommittee on Business Enterprises. [Washington, U.S. Govt. Print. Off.] 1955.

xii, 200 p. tables. 24 cm.

1. Government business enterprises—U.S. I. Title: Business enterprises of the Department of Defense.

UA23.A415   55-61998
MC#: 1955-15981 (LC card 55-61835 cancelled in favor of 55-61998)
SuDocs no.: Y3.Or3/2:8B96/2

760

U.S. *Commission on Organization of the Executive Branch of the Government (1953-1955) Committee on Business Organization of the Dept. of Defense.*

Subcommittee report on special personnel problems in the Department of Defense. Prepared for the Commission on Organization of the Executive Branch of the Government by the Subcommittee on Special Personnel Problems in the Department of Defense of the Committee on Business Organization of the Department of Defense. [Washington, U.S. Govt. Print. Off.] 1955.

xii, 99 p. diagrs., tables. 24 cm.

1. U.S.—Armed Forces—Personnel management.

UB153.A515   55-61797
MC#: 1955-15982
SuDocs no.: Y3.Or3/2:8P43/2

U.S. *Commission on Organization of the Executive Branch of the Government (1953-1955) Committee on Business Organization of the Dept. of Defense.*

Subcommittee report on research activities in the Department of Defense and defense related agencies, prepared for the Commission on Organization of the Executive Branch of the Government by the Subcommittee on Research Activities in the Dept. of Defense and Defense Related Agencies of the Committee on Business Organization of the Dept. of Defense. [Washington, U.S. Govt. Print. Off.] 1955.

x, 91 p. 24 cm.

1. Military research—U.S. 2. U.S. Dept. of Defense. I. Title: Research activities in the Department of Defense.

U393.A5   55-61371
MC#: 1955-10633
SuDocs no.: Y3.Or3/2:8R31

761

U.S. *Commission on Organization of the Executive Branch of the Government* (1953-1955)

Depot utilization, warehousing and storage; a report to the Congress. [Washington, U.S. Govt. Print. Off.] 1955.

x, 27 p. 24 cm.

1. U.S.—Government property. 2. Warehouses—U.S. I. Title.

JK1671.A35   55-61334
MC#: 1955-10630
SuDocs no.: Y3.Or3/2:2D44
MC#: 1955-9457
SuDocs no.: 84th Cong., 1st sess. H. Doc. 170

U.S. *Commission on Organization of the Executive Branch of the Government (1953-1955) Committee on Business Organization of the Dept. of Defense.*

Report on depot utilization, prepared for the Commission on Organization of the Executive Branch of the Government by the Subcommittee on Depot Utilization of the Committee on Organization of the Department of Defense. [Washington, U.S. Govt. Print. Off.] 1955.

ix, 94 p. maps (part fold.) diagrs., tables. 24 cm.

1. U.S.—Government property. 2. Warehouses—U.S. I. Title: Depot utilization.

JK1671.A35 1955   55-61630
MC#: 1955-15975
SuDocs no.: Y3.Or3/2:8D44

762

U.S. *Commission on Organization of the Executive Branch of the Government* (1953-1955)

Final report to the Congress. [Washington, U.S. Govt. Print. Off.] 1955.

xi, 32 p. 24 cm.

1. U.S.—Executive departments.

JK643.C53A55 1955e   353   55-61490
MC#: 1955-12651
SuDocs no.: Y3.Or3/2:1/955
MC#: 1955-11456
SuDocs no.: 84th Cong., 1st sess. H. Doc. 209

763

U.S. *Commission on Organization of the Executive Branch of the Government* (1953-1955)

Five staff papers, prepared for the Task Force on Procurement. [Washington] 1955.

3 v. in 1. illus. 27 cm.

Cover title.

Contents.—v. 1. Defense procurement: the vital roles of the National Security Council and the Joint Chiefs of Staff. Translation of logistics programs into procurement requirements.—

v. 2. Contracting policies and administration. Coordinated procurement. — v. 3. Inventory control and distribution.
1. Government purchasing — U.S.
JK1671.A35 1955a   *336.39 351.71   57-61124
Not located in Monthly Catalog

764

U.S. *Commission on Organization of the Executive Branch of the Government* (1953-1955)
Federal medical services; a report to the Congress. [Washington, U.S. Govt. Print. Off.] 1955.
xiii, 88 p. tables. 24 cm. (84th Cong., 1st sess., 1955. House. Document no. 99)
1. Medicine, State — U.S. I. Title. (Series: U.S. 84th Cong., 1st sess., 1955. House. Document no. 99)
RA395.A3A44 1955b   55-60609
MC#: 1955-5139
SuDocs no.: Y3.Or3/2:2m46
MC#: 1955-4225
SuDocs no.: 84th Cong., 1st sess. H. Doc. 99

U.S. *Commission on Organization of the Executive Branch of the Government (1953-1955) Task Force on Federal Medical Services.*
Report on Federal medical services, prepared for the Commission on Organization of the Executive Branch of the Government. [Washington, U.S. Govt. Print. Off.] 1955.
xii, 139 p. illus. 24 cm.
- - - - - Appendix. Prepared for the Commission on Organization of the Executive Branch of the Government. [Washington] 1954.
v, illus. 27 cm.
RA395.A3A44 1955a Appx.
1. Medicine, State — U.S. I. Title: Federal medical services.
RA395.A3A44 1955a   55-60571 rev
MC#: 1955-5143
SuDocs no.: Y3.Or3/2:8M46
Appendix not located in Monthly Catalog

765

U.S. *Commission on Organization of the Executive Branch of the Government* (1953-1955)
Food and clothing in the Government; a report to the Congress. [Washington, U.S. Govt. Print. Off.] 1955.
x, 73 p. tables. 24 cm.
1. U.S. — Armed Forces — Commissariat. 2. U.S. — Armed Forces — Uniforms. 3. Government purchasing — U.S. I. Title.
UC703.A542 1955a   355.81   55-61103
MC#: 1955-8416
SuDocs no.: Y3.Or3/2:2F73
MC#: 1955-7563
SuDocs no.: 84th Cong., 1st sess. H. Doc. 146

U.S. *Commission on Organization of the Executive Branch of the Government (1953-1955) Task Force on Subsistence Services.*
Report on food and clothing in the Government, prepared for the Commission on Organization of the Executive Branch of the Government. [Washington, U.S. Govt. Print. Off.] 1955.
xiv, 198 p. maps (part fold.) tables. 24 cm.
Bibliography: p. 197-198.
1. U.S. — Armed Forces — Commissariat. 2. U.S. — Armed Forces — Uniforms. 3. Government purchasing — U.S. I. Title: Food and clothing in the Government.
UC703.A542   355.81   55-60950
MC#: 1955-8417
SuDocs no.: Y3.Or3/2:8F73

766

U.S. *Commission on Organization of the Executive Branch of the Government* (1953-1955)
Intelligence activities; a report to the Congress. [Washington, U.S. Govt.Print. Off.] 1955.
ix, 76 p. 23 cm.
1. Intelligence service — U.S. I. Title.
JK468.I6A52   55-61682
MC#: 1955-15972
SuDocs no.: Y3.Or3/2:2In8
MC#: 1955-14492
SuDocs no.: 84th Cong., 1st sess. H. Doc. 201

767

U.S. *Commission on Organization of the Executive Branch of the Government* (1953-1955)
Legal services and procedure; a report to the Congress. [Washington, U.S. Govt. Print. Off.] 1955.
xi, 115 p. 24 cm.
1. Government attorneys — U.S. 2. Representation in administrative proceedings — U.S. 3. Administrative procedure — U.S. I. Title.
55-60874
MC#: 1955-6724
SuDocs no.: Y3.Or3/2:2L52
MC#: 1955-5982
SuDocs no.: 84th Cong., 1st sess. H. Doc. 128

U.S. *Commission on Organization of the Executive Branch of the Government (1953-1955) Task Force on Legal Services and Procedure.*
Report on legal services and procedure, prepared for the Commission on Organization of the Executive Branch of the Government. [Washington, U.S. Govt. Print. Off.] 1955.
xi, 442 p. 24 cm.
Consists of 5 pts.
- - - - - Appendices and charts. [Washington, 1954?]
1 v. (various pagings) diagrs., tables. 27 cm.
Constitutes pt. 6 of the main work.
1. Government attorneys — U.S. 2. Representation in administrative proceedings — U.S. 3. Administrative procedure — U.S. I. Title: Legal services and procedure.
55-60871   353
MC#: 1955-6725
SuDocs no.: Y3.Or3/2:8L52
Appendix not located in Monthly Catalog

768

U.S. *Commission on Organization of the Executive Branch of the Government* (1953-1955)
Lending, guaranteeing, and insurance activities; a report to the Congress. [Washington, U.S. Govt. Print. Off.] 1955.
xi, 126 p. tables. 24 cm.
Issued also as House document no. 107, 84th Cong., 1st sess., under title: Lending agencies.
1. Government lending — U.S. 2. Insurance, Government — U.S. I. Title.
HG3729.U5A44 1955a   55-60608
MC#: 1955-5140
SuDocs no.: Y3.Or3/2:2L54

U.S. *Commission on Organization of the Executive Branch of the Government* (1953-1955)
Lending agencies. Letter from chairman, Commission on Organization of the Executive Branch of the Government, transmitting a report on lending, guaranteeing, and insurance

activities of the Federal Government, pursuant to Public law 108, 83d Congress. Washington, U.S. Govt. Print. Off., 1955.

xi, 126 p. tables. 24 cm. (84th Cong., 1st sess. House document no. 107)

Issued also without congressional series numbering under title: Lending, guaranteeing, and insurance activities.

1. Government lending—U.S. II. Title. (Series: U.S. 84th Cong., 1st sess., 1955. House Document no. 107)

HG3729.U5A44 1955b   332.3   55-60690
MC#: 1955-4232
SuDocs no.: 84th Cong., 1st sess. H. Doc. 107

U.S. *Commission on Organization of the Executive Branch of the Government (1953-1955) Task Force on Lending Agencies.*

Report on lending agencies, prepared for the Commission on Organization of the Executive Branch of the Government. [Washington, U.S. Govt. Print. Off.] 1955.

ix, 257 p. diagrs., tables. 24 cm.

1. Government lending—U.S. 2. Insurance, Government—U.S. I. Title: Lending agencies.

HG3729.U5A44 1955   55-60493
MC#: 1955-6726
SuDocs no.: Y3.Or3/2:8L54

769

U.S. *Commission on Organization of the Executive Branch of the Government (1953-1955)*

Overseas economic operations; a report to the Congress. [Washington, U.S. Govt. Print. Off.] 1955.

xiv, 75 p. tables. 24 cm.

1. U.S.—Foreign economic relations. 2. Economic assistance, American. 3. Technical assistance, American. 4. Military assistance, American. I. Title.

HF1455.A57   338.973   55-61480
MC#: 1955-12652
SuDocs no.: Y3.Or3/2:2Ec7
MC#: 1955-11443
SuDocs no.: 84th Cong., 1st sess. H. Doc. 175

U.S. *Commission on Organization of the Executive Branch of the Government (1953-1955) Task Force on Overseas Economic Operations.*

Report on overseas economic operations, prepared for the Commission on Organization of the Executive Branch of the Government. [Washington, U.S. Govt. Print. Off.] 1955.

ix, 854 p. diagrs., tables. 24 cm.

1. U.S.—Foreign economic relations. 2. Economic assistance, American. 3. Technical assistance, American. 4. Military assistance, American. I. Title: Overseas economic operations.

HF1455.A573   55-61909
MC#: 1955-17576
SuDocs no.: Y3.Or3/2:8Ec7

U.S. *Commission on Organization of the Executive Branch of the Government (1953-1955) Task Force on Overseas Economic Operations.*

Overseas economic operations; a report to the Congress by the Commission on Organization of the Executive Branch of the Government. New York, Greenwood Press [1968]

ix, 854 p. illus. 24 cm.

First published in 1955 under title: Report on overseas economic operations.

1. U.S.—Foreign economic relations. 2. Economic assistance, American. 3. Technical assistance, American. 4. Military assistance, American. I. Title.

HF1455.A573 1968   309.2'23   68-55107
                                             MARC

Not in Monthly Catalog

770

U.S. *Commission on Organization of the Executive Branch of the Government (1953-1955)*

Paperwork management; a report to the Congress. [Washington, U.S. Govt. Print. Off.] 1955.

2 pts. tables. 24 cm.

Contents.—pt. 1. In the United States Government.—pt. 2. The Nation's paperwork for the Government—an experiment.

1. Public records—U.S. 2. Government questionnaires. I. Title.

JK468.P76A55 1955   55-60518 rev
MC#: 1955-5141
SuDocs no.: Y3.Or3/2:2P19/pt. 1
MC#: 1955-15973
SuDocs no.: Y3.Or3/2:2P19/pt. 2

U.S. *Commission on Organization of the Executive Branch of the Government (1953-1955)*

Paperwork management. Letter from the chairman, Commission on Organization of the Executive Branch of the Government transmitting a report on paperwork management pursuant to Public law 108, 83d Congress. Washington, U.S. Govt. Print. Off., 1955.

pts. 24 cm. (84th Cong., 1st sess. House document no. 92)

Issued also without congressional series numbering.

Contents.—pt. 1. In the United States Government.

1. Public records—U.S. 2. Government questionnaires. I. Title. (Series: U.S. 84th Cong., 1st sess., 1955. House. Document no. 92)

JK468.P76A55 1955a   025.171   55-60691 rev
MC#: 1955-4219 (Part 1)
SuDocs no.: 84th Cong., 1st sess. H. Doc. 92
MC#: 1955-14493 (Part 2)
SuDocs no.: 84th Cong., 1st sess. H. Doc. 207

U.S. *Commission on Organization of the Executive Branch of the Government (1953-1955) Task Force on Paperwork Management.*

Report on paperwork management, prepared for the Commission on Organization of the Executive Branch of the Government. [Washington, U.S. Govt. Print. Off.] 1955.

2 pts. illus., diagrs., tables. 24 cm.

Contents.—pt. 1. In the United States Government.—pt. 2. The Nation's paperwork for the Government, an experiment.

1. Public records—U.S. 2. Government questionnaires. I. Title: Paperwork management.

JK468.P76A55 1955b   55-60470 rev
MC#: 1955-5144
SuDocs no.: Y3.Or3/2:8P19/pt. 1
MC#: 1955-15977 (LC card 55-60518 listed in error)
SuDocs no.: Y3.Or3/2:8P19/pt. 2

771

U.S. *Commission on Organization of the Executive Branch of the Government (1953-1955)*

Personnel and civil service; a report to the Congress. [Washington, U.S. Govt. Print. Off.] 1955.

x, 101 p. diagrs., tables. 24 cm.

Issued also as House document no. 89, 84th Cong., 1st sess., under title: Commission report on personnel and civil service.

1. Civil service—U.S. 2. U.S.—Officials and employees. I. Title.

JK643.C53A55 1955b   *351.3 351.1   55-60490
MC#: 1955-5142
SuDocs no.: Y3.Or3/2:2P43

U.S. *Commission on Organization of the Executive Branch of the Government (1953-1955)*

Commission report on personnel and civil service. Letter from chairman, Commission on Organization of the Executive Branch of the Government transmitting a report on personnel and civil service, pursuant to Public law 108, 83d Congress. Washington, U.S. Govt. Print. Off., 1955.

viii, 52 p. diagrs., tables. 24 cm. (84th Cong., 1st sess, 1955. House document no. 89)
JK643.C53A55 1955d   351.1   55-60692
MC#: 1955-4218
SuDocs no.: 84th Cong., 1st sess. H. Doc. 89

U.S. *Commission on Organization of the Executive Branch of the Government (1953-1955) Task Force on Personnel and Civil Service.*
Report on personnel and civil service, prepared for the Commission on Organization of the Executive Branch of the Government. [Washington, U.S. Govt. Print. Off.] 1955.

xxiv, 252 p. diagrs., tables. 24 cm.
1. Civil service—U.S. 2. U.S.—Officials and employees. I. Title: Personnel and civil service.
JK643.C53A55 1955c   *351.3 351.1   55-60469
MC#: 1955-3609
SuDocs no.: Y3.Or3/2:8P43

772

U.S. *Commission on Organization of the Executive Branch of the Government (1953-1955)*
Progress report to the Congress, December 31, 1954. [Washington, U.S. Govt. Print. Off., 1955]

v, 57 p. 24 cm.
1. U.S.—Executive departments.
JK643.C53A55   353   55-60276
MC#: 1955-1765
SuDocs no.: Y3.Or3/2:1/954

773

U.S. *Commission on Organization of the Executive Branch of the Government (1953-1955)*
Real property management; a report to the Congress. [Washington, U.S. Govt. Print. Off.] 1955.

x, 53 p. 24 cm.
1. U.S.—Public buildings. 2. U.S.—Public lands. I. Title.
JK1613.A4 1955   55-61332
MC#: 1955-10631
SuDocs no.: Y3.Or3/2:2R22
MC#: 1955-11444
SuDocs no.: 84th Cong., 1st sess. H. Doc. 177

U.S. *Commission on Organization of the Executive Branch of the Government (1953-1955) Task Force on Real Property Management.*
Report on real property management, prepared for the Commission on Organization of the Executive Branch of the Government. [Washington, U.S. Govt. Print. Off.] 1955.

xi, 153 p. tables. 24 cm.
1. U.S.—Public buildings. I. Title: Real property management.
JK1613.A4 1955b   55-61589
MC#: 1955-15978
SuDocs no.: Y3.Or3/2:8R22

774

U.S. *Commission on Organization of the Executive Branch of the Government (1953-1955) Task Force on Procurement.*
Report on military procurement. Prepared for the Commission on Organization of the Executive Branch of the Government. [Washington, U.S. Govt. Print.Off.] 1955.

xiv, 132 p. diagrs. 24 cm.
1. U.S.—Armed Forces—Procurement.

UC263.A51644   55-61834
MC#: 1955-15976
SuDocs no.: Y3.Or3/2:8P94

775

U.S. *Commission on Organization of the Executive Branch of the Government (1953-1955)*
Research and development in the Government; a report to the Congress. [Washington, U.S. Govt. Print. Off.] 1955.

xii, 50p. 24 cm.
1. Research—U.S. I. Title.
Q180.U5A512   507.2   55-61333
MC#: 1955-10632
SuDocs no.: Y3.Or3/2:2R31
MC#: 1955-9461
SuDocs no.: 84th Cong., 1st sess. H. Doc. 174

776

U.S. *Commission on Organization of the Executive Branch of the Government (1953-1955)*
Transportation; a report to the Congress. [Washington, U.S. Govt.Print. Off.] 1955.

xii, 126 p. tables. 24 cm.
1. U.S.—Executive departments—Transportation. 2. U.S.—Officials and employees—Travel regulations. 3. U.S.—Armed Forces—Transportation.
JK468.T7A52   353   55-60869
MC#: 1955-6728
SuDocs no.: Y3.Or3/2:2T68
MC#: 1955-5980
SuDocs no.: 84th Cong., 1st sess. H. Doc. 125

U.S. *Commission on Organization of the Executive Branch of the Government (1953-1955) Committee on Business Organization of the Dept. of Defense.*
Report on transportation, prepared for the Commission on Organization of the Executive Branch of the Government by the Subcommittee on Transportation of the Committee on Business Organization for the Department of Defense. [Washington, U.S. Govt. Print. Off.] 1955.

vii, 362 p. maps (part fold.) diagrs., tables. 24 cm.
1. U.S.—Executive departments—Transportation. 2. U.S.—Officials and employees—Travel regulations. 3. U.S.—Armed Forces—Transportation.
JK468.T7A53   353   55-60870
MC#: 1955-6727
SuDocs no.: Y3.Or3/2:8T68

777

U.S. *Commission on Organization of the Executive Branch of the Government (1953-1955)*
Use and disposal of Federal surplus property; a report to the Congress. [Washington, U.S. Govt. Print. Off.] 1955.

xii, 96 p. tables. 24 cm.
1. U.S.—Government property. I. Title.
JK1661.A5 1955b   336.12   55-61104
MC#: 1955-8419
SuDocs no.: Y3.Or3/2:2Su7
MC#: 1955-7560
SuDocs no.: 84th Cong., 1st sess. H. Doc. 141

U.S. *Commission on Organization of the Executive Branch of the Government (1953-1955) Task Force on Use and Disposal of Federal Surplus Property.*
Report on use and disposal of Federal surplus property, prepared for the Commission on Organization of the Executive

Branch of the Government. [Washington, U.S. Govt. Print. Off.] 1955.

xxii, 259 p. diagrs., tables. 24 cm.
1. Surplus government property—U.S. I. Title: Use and disposal of Federal surplus property.

JK1661.A5 1955a   336.12   55-60949
MC#: 1955-8418
SuDocs no.: Y3.Or3/2:8Su7

778

U.S. *Commission on Organization of the Executive Branch of the Government* (1953-1955)
Water resources and power; a report to the Congress. [Washington, U.S. Govt. Print. Off.] 1955.

2 v. in 1. tables. 24 cm.
1. Water resources development—U.S. 2. Electric utilities—U.S. I. Title.

HD1694.A414   333.91   55-61488
MC#: 1955-12653
SuDocs no.: Y3.Or3/2:2W29/v. 1, 2
MC#: 1955-14494
SuDocs no.: 84th Cong., 1st sess. H. Doc. 208

U.S. *Commission on Organization of the Executive Branch of the Government* (1953-1955) *Task Force on Water Resources and Power.*
Report on water resources and power, prepared for the Commission on Organization of the Executive Branch of the Government. [Washington, U.S. Govt. Print. Off.] 1955.

3 v. (xxvi, 1783 p.) maps (part fold.) diagrs., tables. 24 cm.
1. Water resources development—U.S. 2. Electric utilities—U.S.

HD1694.A414 1955a   55-61591
MC#: 1955-15979
SuDocs no.: Y3.Or3/2:8W29/v. 1-3

779

U.S. *Library of Congress. Legislative Reference Service.*
Index to the Commission and Task Force reports; a report to the Congress by the Commission on Organization of the Executive Branch of the Government. [Prepared by American Law Division, Legislative Reference Service, Library of Congress. Washington, U.S. Govt. Print. Off.] 1955.

iii, 85 p. 24 cm.
1. U.S. Commission on Organization of the Executive Branch of the Government (1953-1955)

JK643.C53A55 1955h   55-63343
MC#: 1955-17575
SuDocs no.: Y3.Or3/2:2In2

HOOVER REPORT [Hoover, J. Edgar]
780

U.S. *Dept. of Justice.*
. . . Investigation activities of the Department of Justice. Letter from the attorney general transmitting in reponse to a Senate resolution of October 17, 1919, a report on the activities of the Bureau of investigation of the Department of Justice against persons advising anarchy, sedition, and the forcible overthrow of the government . . . Washington, Govt. print. off., 1919.

187 p. 23 cm. (66th Cong., 1st sess. Senate. Doc. 153)
Referred to the Committee on the Judiciary and ordered printed November 17, 1919.
1. Anarchism and anarchists—U.S. 2. Bolshevism. 3. Goldman, Emma, 1869- 4. Berkman, Alexander. I. Title.

HX843.A5 1919d   20-26021

- - - - - Copy 2.
MC#: Dec. 1919-page 324
SuDocs no.: 66th Cong., 1st sess. S. Doc. 153

HOOVER REPORTS
781

Hoover, Herbert, Clark, *Pres. U.S.,* 1874-1964.
The President's economic mission to Germany and Austria, report no. 1- [by] Herbert Hoover. [Washington, 1947-
v. 23 cm.
No. 1 issued also separately with title: Report on agricultural and food requirements.
Contents.—no. 1. German agriculture and food requirements.—no. 2. Austrian agriculture and food requirements. Economic reorganization.—no. 3. The necessary steps for promotion of German exports, so as to relieve American taxpayers of the burdens of relief and for economic recovery of Europe.
1. Germany—Econ. condit.—1945- 2. Food supply—Germany. 3. Austria—Econ. condit.—1918- 4. Food supply—Austria. I. Title.

HC286.5.H6   338.943   47-32399*
Not located in Monthly Catalog

782

[Hoover, Herbert Clark, *pres. U.S.*] 1874-1964.
Report on agricultural and food requirements. [Washington? 1947]

2 p. l., 11 numb. l. 26½ cm.
Caption title.
"A memorandum on the economic conditions affecting food supplies for the newly combined American and British zone [in Germany] together with estimates of supplies and costs."-Letter of transmittal, signed: Herbert Hoover.
1. Food supply—Germany. 2. Food supply—Austria. I. Title.

HD9013.5.H65   38.15   47-20721
Not located in Monthly Catalog

HOPLEY REPORT [Hopley, Russell J.]
783

U.S. *Office of Civil Defense Planning.*
Civil defense for national security. Washington, U.S. Govt. Print. Off. [1948]

vi, 301 p. charts. 24 cm.
1. U.S.—Civilian defense. I. Title.

UA927.A516 1948   355.23   48-47269*
MC#: 1949-527
SuDocs no.: M4.2:C49

HORNE REPORTS [Horne, John E.]
784

U.S. *White House Committee on Small Business.*
Progress report to the President; activities and recommendations. [Washington, U.S. Govt. Print. Off.] 1962.

10 p. 24 cm.
1. Small business.

HC106.5.A59247 1962a   62-64694
MC#: 1962-16111 (LC card 56-62059 referred to in error)
SuDocs no.: Pr35.8:Sm1/R29

785

U.S. *White House Committee on Small Business.*
Small business in the American economy: its contributions and its problems [and] the role of the Federal Government. Washington, 1962.

15 p. illus. 24 cm.
1. Small business. I. Title.
HC106.5.A59247
MC#: 1962-14562
SuDocs no.: Pr35.8:Sm1/Sm1

62-61486

HORNIG REPORT [Hornig, Donald F.]

Handling of toxicological information.

see
HANDLER REPORT [Handler, Phillip]

HORNIG REPORTS [Hornig, Donald F.]

786

United States. President's Science Advisory Committee. Panel on Oceanography.

Effective use of the sea; report. Washington, For sale by the Supt. of Docs., U.S. Govt. Print. Off., 1966.

xv, 144 p. illus. 24 cm.
Commonly known as the Hornig report.
Includes bibliographical references.
1. Oceanographic research—United States. 2. Marine resources—United States. I. Title. II. Title: Hornig report on the effective use of the sea.
GC58.A57   79-600399
                             MARC
MC#: 1966-13947
SuDocs no.: Pr35.8:Sci2/Se1

787

U.S. *Office of Science and Technology.*

Privacy and behavioral research. Washington, For sale by the Supt. of Docs., U.S. Govt. Print. Off., 1967.

v, 30 p. 24 cm.
1. Social science research. 2. Privacy, Right of—U.S. I. Title.
H62.U54   300'.72   67-60879
MC#: 1967-7107
SuDocs no.: PrEx8.2:B39

HORSKY REPORT [Horsky, Charles Antone]

see
SHEA REPORT [Shea, Francis Michael]

HORTON REPORT [Horton, Frank]

788

United States. Commission on Federal Paperwork.

Final summary report: a report of the Commission on Federal Paperwork.-Washington : The Commission, 1977.

ii, 74 p. : ill. ; 23 cm.
"Y3.P 19:1/977."
1. Government paperwork—United States.
JK468.P34U52 1977d   353.007'14   78-601718
                                   MARC
MC#: 1978-2210
SuDocs no.: Y3.P 19:1/977

HOUGH REPORT [Hough, Richard R.]

789

U.S. *Task Force on Air Traffic Control.*

A study of the safe and efficient utilization of airspace; report. Richard R. Hough, chairman. [Washington] Federal Aviation Agency, 1961.

xiii, 146 p. diagrs. 27 cm.
1. Air traffic control. I. Title. II. Title: Safe and efficient utilization of airspace.

TL725.3.T7U69   629.1366   62-60457
MC#: 1962-2451
SuDocs no.: FAA1.2:B35

HOUTHAKKER REPORT [Houthakker, Hendrick S.]

790

United States. Cabinet Committee on Economic Policy. Subcommittee on Copper.

Report of the Subcommittee on Copper to the Cabinet Committee on Economic Policy.-[Washington, D.C.?] : The Subcommittee, [1970]

29, [3] leaves : ill. ; 28 cm.
Caption title.
"18 May 1970."
Photocopy.
Supt. of Docs. no.: Pr 36.8:C 79
1. Copper industry and trade—United States. 2. Copper industry and trade.
HD9539.C7U5815 1970   381'.4243'0973-dc19   81-603478
                                AACR 2 MARC
Not located in Monthly Catalog
SuDocs no.: Pr36.8:C79

HOWE REPORT [Howe, Ernest Joseph]

see under
O'MAHONEY REPORTS [O'Mahoney, Joseph Christopher]

Gesell. Study of legal reserve life insurance companies.

HUBBELL REPORT [Hubbell, Lester E.]

791

U.S. *Department of Defense.*

Modernizing military pay; report of the first quadrennial review of military compensation. [Washington, D.C., For sale by the Supt. of Docs., U.S. Govt. Print. Off.] 1967.

v. illus.
Cover title.
Contents.—v. 1. Active duty compensation.—v. 2. Appendices 1-9 to report.—v. 4. Military estate program.—v. 5. Military estate program (appendices).
MC#: 1969-555 (vol. 1)
       1969-10958 (vol. 2) Volume 3 not located in Monthly Catalog
       1969-12374 (vol. 4)
       1969-12375 (vol. 5)
SuDocs no.: D1.2:P29/v.(nos.)

HUDSON REPORT

792

Hudson, Manley Ottmer, 1886-
. . . Munitions industry. International regulation of the trade in and manufacture of arms and ammunition, by Manley O. Hudson . . . A report presented on September 1, 1934, by the American committee in Geneva to the Special committee authorized by the Senate of the United States to investigate the munitions industry, together with a supplementary report presented on December 1, 1934 . . . Washington, U.S. Govt. print. off., 1935.

v, 104 p. 23½ cm.
At head of title: 73d Congress, 2d session. Senate committee print. No. 1.
"Printed for the use of the Special committee investigating the munitions industry."

"List of principal documents, and collections of documents submitted with this report": p. 70-71.

1. Firearms industry and trade—U.S. I. American committee in Geneva. II. U.S. Congress. Senate. Special committee to investigate the munitions industry. III. Title.
HD9743.A2H8   [338.4] 341.3   35-26217
MC#: 1935-page 276
SuDocs no.: Y4.M92:Ar5

HUGHES COMMISSION [Hughes, Harold E.]
793

Congressional support agencies : a compilation of papers prepared for the Commission on the Operation of the Senate. — Washington : U.S. Govt. Print. Off., 1976.

ix, 148 p. ; 24 cm.
At head of title: 94th Congres, 2d session. Committee print. Includes bibliographical references.
Contents: Carroll, J. D. Policy analysis for Congress, a review of the Congressional Research Service. — Pois, J. The General Accounting Office as a Congresional resource. — Skolnikoff, E. B. The Office of Technology Assessment. — Capron, W. M. The Congressional Budget Office. — Griffith, E. S. Four Agency comparative study.
1. United States. Congress. Senate—Information services. 2. United States. Library of Congress. Congressional Research Service. 3. United States. Congressional Budget Office. 4. United States. General Accounting Office. 5. United States. Congress. Office of Technology Assessment. I. United States. Commission on the Operation of the Senate.
JK1170.C66   328.73'07'6   78-602031
                                                                    MARC

Not located in Monthly Catalog

794

United States. Commission on the Operation of the Senate.
Toward a modern Senate : final report of the Commission on the Operation of the Senate. — Washington : U.S. Govt. Print. Off., 1976.

xv, 83 p. : diagrs. ; 24 cm. — (Document-94th Congress, 2d session, Senate ; no. 94-278)
"List of Commission papers": p. 80-81.
1. United States. Congress. Senate. I. Title. II. Series: United States. 94th Congress, 2d session, 1976. Senate. Document ; no. 94-278.
JK1170.U54 1976   328.73'07'1   77-600722
                                                                         MARC
MC#: 1977-4444
SuDocs no.: 94-2:S.doc.278

HUGHES REPORT [Hughes, Charles Evans]
795

U.S. *Dept. of justice.*
[Report of the aircraft inquiry] . . . [Washington? 1918?]
182, iii, 12 p. 23½ cm.
Report to the attorney general dated October 25, 1918 (182 p.) signed: Charles E. Hughes.
Report to the President dated October 31, 1918 (12 p. at end) signed: T. W. Gregory, attorney general.
1. Aeroplane industry and trade. 2. Aeronautics, Military. 3. U.S. Bureau of aircraft production. I. Hughes, Charles Evans, 1862- II. Title. III. Title: Aircraft inquiry, Report of the.
UG633.A4 1918h   20-11141
- - - - - Copy 2.
Not located in Monthly Catalog

HUGHES REPORT [Hughes, Richard J.]
796

U.S. *President's National Advisory Panel on Insurance in Riot-Affected Areas.*
Meeting the insurance crisis of our cities: a report. [Washington; For sale by the Supt. of Docs., U.S. Govt. Print. Off., 1968]
x, 165 p. 26 cm.
1. Insurance—U.S. I. Title.
HG8505 1968b   368   68-60558
MC#: 1968-4356
SuDocs no.: Pr36.8:C49/In7

HUMPHREY REPORT [Humphrey, Hubert H.]
797

United States. President's Council on Recreation and Natural Beauty.
From sea to shining sea; a report on the American environment, our natural heritage. Washington [For sale by the Supt. of Docs., U.S. Govt. Print. Off.] 1968.
304 p. illus. 27 cm.
Commonly known as the Humphrey report.
1. Environmental policy—United States. I. Title. II. Title: Humphrey report on the American environment.
HC110.E5A55   711'.2   68-67300
                                                                         MARC
MC#: 1968-18017
Sudocs no.: Pr36.8:R24/Se1

HUNDLEY REPORT [Hundley, James M.]
798

U.S. *Study Group on Mission and Organization of the Public Health Service.*
Final report. [Washington] U.S. Dept. of Health, Education, and Welfare, Public Health Service [1960]
v, 66 p. diagrs. 24 cm.
Cover title.
1. U.S. Public Health Service.
RA11.B15487   62-61923
Not located in Monthly Catalog

HUNT REPORT [Hunt, I. L.]
799

U.S. *Army. American Forces in Germany, 1918-1923.*
American military government of occupied Germany, 1918-1920. Report of [I. L. Hunt] the officer in charge of civil affairs, Third Army, and American Forces in Germany. [Coblenz? 1920]
4 v. 28 cm.
1. Germany—Hist.—Allied occupation, 1918-1930. I. Hunt, I. L. II. Title.
D650.M5U7 1920a   51-51121 rev
Not located in Monthly Catalog

HUNT REPORTS [Hunt, Reed Oliver]
800

United States. President's Commission on Financial Structure & Regulation.
The report. [Washington; For sale by the Supt. of Docs., U.S. Govt. Print. Off.] 1971 [i.e. 1972]
viii, 173 p. 22 cm.
Supt. of Docs. no.: Pr 37.8:F49/R29
1. Banking law—United States. 2. Banks and banking—United States.

KF974.A34   ⤸346'.73'082   79-188044
                                             MARC
MC#: 1972-6015
SuDocs no.: Pr 37.8:F49/R29

801

United States. President's Commission on Financial Structure &
Regulation.
     The report of the President's Commission on Financial Struc-
ture and Regulation (December 1972) including recommenda-
tions of Department of the Treasury. Committee on Banking,
Housing and Urban Affairs, United States Senate. Washington,
U.S. Govt. Print. Off., 1973.
     viii, 213 p. 24 cm.
     At head of title: 93d Congress, 1st session. Committee print.
Commonly known as the Hunt report.
     "Recommendations for change in the U.S. financial system":
p. 175-213.
     1. Financial institutions—United States. 2. Finance—United
States. I. United States. Treasury Dept. Recommendations for
change in the U.S. financial system. 1973. II. United States. Con-
gress. Senate. Committee on Banking, Housing and Urban Af-
fairs. III. Title: Hunt report.
HG181.U56 1973   332'.0973   73-602910
                                             MARC
MC#: 1972-6015
SuDocs no.: Pr37.8:F49/R29

HUNTINGTON REPORT [Huntington, Andrew T.]
     see under
  ALDRICH COMMISSION [Aldrich, Nelson
Wilmarth]
          Laws of the United States concerning money, banking,
     and loans.

HUSBAND REPORT [Husband, Walter W.]
     see under
  DILLINGHAM COMMISSION [Dillingham,
William Paul]
          Immigration situation in Canada.

          Immigration situation in other countries.

HUSTON PLAN [Huston, Thomas Charles]
802

United States. Congress. Senate. Select Committee to Study
Governmental Operations with Respect to Intelligence Activities.
     Intelligence activities : Senate Resolution 21 : hearings before
the Select Committee to Study Governmental Operations with
Respect to Intelligence Activities of the United States Senate,
Ninety-fourth Congress, first session.—Washington : U.S. Govt.
Print. Off., 197
     7 v. : 24 cm.
     Hearings held 1975-Sept. 23-Dec. 5
     v. 2: Huston Plan
     1. Internal security—United States. 2. Intelligence service—
United States. I. Title.
KF26.5.G68 1975   353.008'92   76-601277
                                                 MARC
MC#: 1976-1249
SuDocs no.: Y4.In8/17:In8/V.2-7

HYDE REPORT [Hyde, Howard Kemper]
     see under
  O'MAHONEY REPORTS [O'Mahoney, Joseph
Christopher]
          Dimock. Bureaucracy and trusteeship in large
     corporations.

HYNNING REPORT [Hynning, Clifford James]
     see under
  O'MAHONEY REPORTS [O'Mahoney, Joseph
Christopher]

IGNATIUS REPORT
803

Ignatius, Paul R
     Department of Defense reorganization study project : depart-
mental headquarters study: a report to the Secretary of Defense
/ [Paul R. Ignatius].—[Washington : U.S. Govt. Print. Off.],
1978.
     81, [13] p. ; 28 cm.
     Cover title.
     1. United States. Dept. of Defense. I. United States. Dept. of
Defense. II. Title.
UA23.3.I38   353.6-dc19   79-602045
                                             MARC
MC#: 1979-1856
SuDocs no.: D1.2:R29

ILSLEY REPORT [Ilsley, Ralph]
804

U.S. *Federal power commission.*
     Federal power commission electric rate survey. Rates for elec-
tric service to commercial and industrial cus-
tomers . . . Washington, U.S. Govt. print. off., 1936.
     v, 256 p. incl. tables, diagrs. 29 cm. (Rate series no. 4)
     1. Electric utilities—U.S.—Rates. I. Title. II. Title: Rates for
electric service to commercial and industrial customers.
TK23.A5 1936   621.3002   36-26552 Revised
MC#: 1936-page 757
SuDocs no.: FP1.10:4

INTERMAGGIO REPORTS [Intermaggio, Joseph
L.]
805

Washington Center for metropolitan Studies, *Washington, D.C.*
     A discussion guide to Washington area metropolitan problems;
staff report prepared for the Joint Committee on Washington
Metropolitan Problems, Congress of the United States.
Washington, U.S. Govt. Print. Off., 1960.
     v, 145 p. fold. col. map. 24 cm.
     At head of title: 86th Cong., 2d sess. Committee print.
     Includes bibliographies.
     1. Regional planning—Washington metropolitan area. I. U.S.
Congress. Joint Committee on Washington Metropolitan Pro-
blems. II. Title.
NA9127.W2W25   711.409753   60-62321
MC#: 1960-15384
SuDocs no.: Y4.W27/2:W29/5

806

Washington Center for Metropolitan Studies, *Washington D.C.*
     Support for planning in the Washington metropolitan area;
analysis of planning budgets, 1955 to 1959. Staff report prepared
for the Joint Committee on Washington Metropolitan Problems,
Congress of the United States. Washington, U.S. Govt. Print.
Off., 1959.
     iii, 4 p. tables. 24 cm.
     At head of title: 86th Cong., 1st sess. Committee print.
     1. Regional planning—Washington metropolitan area. I. U.S.
Congress. Joint Committee on Washington Metropolitan Problems. II. Title.

NA9127.W2W27 711.409753 59-62485
MC#: 1959-16231
SuDocs no.: Y4.W27/2:P69

IRWIN REPORT [Irwin, James W.]

807

U.S. *Civil Service Commission.*
 Hatch act decisions (political activity cases) prepared by James W. Irwin, chief hearing examiner. [Washington, U.S. Govt. Print. Off., 1949]
 viii, 304 p. 24 cm.
 Contents.—A text on principles and cases.—A casebook on Commission decisions.
 1. U.S.—Officials and employees—Political activity—Cases. I. Irwin, James W. II. Title.
              50-60578

MC#: 1950-8910
SuDocs no.: CS1.7/2:H28

JACKSON REPORT [Jackson, Donald Lester]

808

U.S. *Congress. House. Committee on Foreign Affairs.*
 Special study mission to Latin America on technical cooperation; report by Donald L. Jackson, chairman, Subcommittee on Inter-American Affairs of the Committee on Foreign Affairs, pursuant to H. Res. 113, a resolution authorizing the Committee on Foreign Affairs to conduct thorough studies and investigations of all matters coming within the jurisdiction of such committee. Washington, U.S. Govt. Print. Off., 1954.
 viii, 143 p. tables. 24 cm. (83d Cong., 2d sess. House report no. 2442)
 1. Technical assistance, American—Spanish America. I. Jackson, Donald Lester, 1910- II. Title. (Series: U.S. 83d Cong., 2d sess., 1954. House. Report no. 2442)
HC161.U55   54-60251
MC#: 1954-11882
SuDocs no.: Y4.F76/1:L34
MC#: 1954-14338
SuDocs no.: 83d Cong., 2d sess. H. Rept. 2442

JACKSON REPORT [Jackson, Henry M.]

809

U.S. *Congress. Joint Committee on Atomic Energy.*
 Report of the Underseas Warfare Advisory Panel to the Subcommittee on Military Applications. Washington, U.S. Govt. Print. Off., 1958.
 v, 16 p. 24 cm.
 At head of title: 85th Cong., 2d sess. Joint committee print.
 1. Submarine warfare. 2. Atomic submarines. 3. Intermediate-range ballistic missiles.
V210.U54   58-61936
MC#: 1958-14284
SuDocs no.: Y4.At7/2:Un2

JACOBS REPORT [Jacobs, Lawrence Merton]
 see under
ALDRICH COMMISSION [Aldrich, Nelson Wilmarth]

JACOBSON REPORT [Jacobson, Morris]
 see under
ALDRICH COMMISSION [Aldrich, Nelson Wilmarth]
  Riesser. German great banks.

JACOBY REPORT [Jacoby, Neil Herman]

810

United States. President's Task Force on Economic Growth.
 Policies for American economic progress in the seventies; the report of the President's Task Force on Economic Growth. [Washington; for sale by the Supt. of Docs., U.S. Govt. Print. Off.] 1970.
 v, 49 p. 24 cm.
 Neil Jacoby, chairman.
 1. United States—Economic policy—1961- I. Jacoby, Neil Herman, 1909- II. Title.
HC106.6.A53 338.973 75-608065
              MARC

MC#: 1970-11829
SuDocs no.: Pr37.8:Ec7/R29

JAMES REPORT [James, Clifford Lester]
 see under
O'MAHONEY REPORTS [O'Mahoney, Joseph Christopher]

JAVITS REPORTS

811

Javits, Jacob Koppel, 1904-
 Study mission to Europe, November-December, 1976 : a report on his trip to France, Britain, Federal Republic of Germany, Belgium, Italy and Yugoslavia, November 18-December 11, 1976, January 1977 / by Senator Jacob K. Javits to the Committee on Foreign Relations, United States Senate.—Washington : U.S. Govt. Print. Off., 1977.
 v, 14 p. ; 24 cm.
 At head of title: 95th Congress, 1st session. Committee print.
 1. Europe—Economic conditions—1945-. I. United States. Congress. Senate. Committee on Foreign Relations. II. Title.
HC240.J37 330.9'4'055 77-601310
              MARC

MC#: 1977-5302
SuDocs no.: Y4.F76/2:Eu7/24

812

U.S. *Congress. Joint Economic Committee.*
 The political stakes in East-West trade, a report on a factfinding trip to the U.S.S.R. and Eastern Europe, submitted to the Subcommittee on Foreign Economic Policy of the Joint Economic Committee, Congress of the United States, by Jacob K. Javits. Washington, U.S. Govt. Print. Off., 1962.
 vii, 19 p. tables. 24 cm.
 At head of title: 87th Cong., 2d sess. Joint committee print.
 1. East-West trade (1945-) 2. U.S.—Commercial policy. I. Javits, Jacob Koppell, 1904- II. Title. III. Title: Factfinding trip to the U.S.S.R. and Eastern Europe.
HF1456 1962.U53   62-2503
MC#: 1962-4892 (LC card 62-60596 cancelled in favor of 62-2503)
SuDocs no.: Y4.Ec7:T67/4

JEFFERY REPORT

813

Jeffery, L. W. *comp.*
 Comparison of potential voters and actual votes cast by counties in each State in 1948-1950 [compiled from official sources by L. W. Jeffery for Owen Brewster] Washington, U.S. Govt. Print. Off., 1952.
 v, 37 p. 24 cm. (82d Cong., 2d sess. Senate. Document no. 150)
 1. Voting—U.S. (Series: U.S. 82d Cong., 2d sess., 1952. Senate. Document no. 150)

JK1853.J45   324.73   52-61557
MC#: 1952-14950
SuDocs no.: 82d Cong., 2d sess. S. Doc. 150

JENKINS REPORT [Jenkins, Thomas Albert]
    see
DONAHEY REPORT [Donahey, Vic]

JENNER REPORT [Jenner, William E.]
814

U.S. *Congress. Senate. Committee on the Judiciary.*
   Interlocking subversion in government departments. Report of the Subcommittee to Investigate the Administration of the Internal Security Act and Other Internal Security Laws, to the Committee on the Judiciary, United States Senate, Eighty-third Congress, first session . . . Washington, U.S. Govt. Print. Off., 1953.
   iii, 50 p. 23 cm.
   At head of title: 83d Cong., 1st sess. Committee print.
   1. Subversive activities—U.S. 2. Communism—U.S.—1917- I. Title.
E743.5.A533   *364.13 351.74   53-63304
MC#: 1953-15843
SuDocs no.: Y4.J89/2:Su1/13

JOHNSON COMMITTEE
815

Johnson, Joseph
United States participation in the International Labor Organization.
   [*In* Monthly Labor Review, vol. 80, no. 3, March, 1957, pages 342-346]
MC#: 1957-8751 (refers to the reprint from the Monthly Labor Review)
SuDocs no.: L2.6/a:2225

816

Johnson, Joseph
Johnson Committee on U.S. participation in the ILO. Report. Washington, D.C. U.S. Dept. of Labor. 1957.
   A-6, B-46 (typescript)
Not located in Monthly Catalog

JOHNSON REPORT [Johnson, Donald Edward]
817

United States. President's Committee on the Vietnam Veteran.
   Report of the President's Committee on the Vietnam Veteran. [Washington, 1970]
   34 p. 27 cm.
   Donald E. Johnson, chairman.
   1. Veterans—United States. I. Johnson, Donald Edward, 1924- II. Title.
UB357.A64 1970   362.8   79-607306
                                   MARC
Not located in Monthly Catalog

JOHNSON REPORT [Johnson, Felix]
818

U.S. *Naval Reserve Evaluation Board.*
   Naval Reserve; a report to the Secretary of the Navy. [Washington] 1954.
   1 v. (various pagings) illus., fold. maps. 27 cm.

Cover title.
   1. U.S. Naval Reserve.
VA80.A458   *359.37 359.351   54-60938
Not located in Monthly Catalog

JOHNSON REPORT [Johnson, Joseph French]
   see under
   ALDRICH COMMISSION [Aldrich, Nelson Wilmarth]

JOHNSON REPORT [Johnson, Sherman E.]
819

U.S. *Agricultural Research Service.*
   Economic aspects of Soviet agriculture; report of a technical study group. [Washington, 1959]
   78 p. illus., group port., map. 27 cm.
   Cover title.
   Prepared by Sherman E. Johnson, U.S. Agricultural Research Service and chairman of the agricultural economists exchange group.
   Bibliographical footnotes.
   1. Agriculture—Economic aspects—Russia. [1. Agriculture—Economic aspects—U.S.S.R.]
HD1992.U54   338.10947   Agr59-190
MC#: 1959-8334
SuDocs no.: A 1.94:Ec7

JOHNSTON REPORT
820

Johnston, Olin Dewitt, 1896-
   Report on overseas pay and personnel practices, Public law 201, sec. 5 (b). Printed for the use of the Senate Committee on Post Office and Civil Service. Washington, U.S. Govt. Print. Off., 1953.
   v, 209 p. 23 cm.
   At head of title: 83d Cong., 1st sess. Senate committee print.
   "Overseas pay and personnel practices. A report prepared for the Post Office and Civil Service Committees of the Senate and the House of Representatives pursuant to Public law 201, 82d Congress [by the] Bureau of the Budget and the Civil Service Commission, April 1, 1952": p. 11-209.
   1. U.S.—Officials and employees—Salaries, allowances, etc. I. U.S. Congress. Senate. Committee on Post Office and Civil service. II. U.S. Bureau of the Budget. Overseas pay and personnel practices; a report. III. Title: Overseas pay and personnel practices.
JK775 1953.A55   *351.3 351.1   54-61286
MC#: 1954-5456
SuDocs no.: Y4.P84/11:Ov2

JOHNSTON REPORT [Johnston, Percy Hampton]
821

U.S. *Committee to Inquire into Economic Problems of Japan and Korea.*
   Report on the economic position and prospects of Japan and Korea and the measures required to improve them. [Washington] 1948.
   22 1. 32 cm.
   Percy H. Johnston, chairman.
   1. Japan—Econ. condit.—1945- 2. Korea-Econ. condit. I. Johnston, Percy Hampton, 1881-
HC462.U5 1948   330.952   48-47050*
Not located in Monthly Catalog

JOHNSTON REPORTS [Johnston, Eric]
822

U.S. *Economic Stabilization Agency.*
Strong dollars; report by Eric Johnston, Administrator. [Washington, U.S. Govt. Print. Off.] 1951.

39 p. illus. 26 cm.
1. U.S.—Economic policy. I. Title.
HC106.5.A58 1951   338.973   52-60192
MC#: 1952-538
SuDocs no.: ES 1.2:D69

823

U.S. *International Development Advisory Board.*
A new emphasis on economic development abroad. A report to the President of the United States on ways, means and reasons for U.S. assistance to international economic development. Washington [1957]

21 1. 27 cm.
1. Economic assistance, American. 2. Technical assistance, American. I. Title. II. Title: Ways, means and reasons for U.S. assistance to international economic development.
HC60.U6I5 1957a   338.91   58-61008
Not located in Monthly Catalog

JONES REPORT [Jones, Boisfeuillet]
824

U.S. *National Advisory Commission on Health Facilities.*
A report to the President. [Washington, For sale by the Supt. of Docs., U.S. Govt. Print. Off.] 1968.

85 p. 23 cm.
MC#: 1969-2401
SuDocs no.: Pr36.8:H34/2/R29/968

JOSEPHS REPORT [Josephs, Devereux C.]
825

U.S. *President's Committee on Education Beyond the High School.*
Report to the President. 1st-[3d]; Nov. 1956-Oct. 1957. Washington.

3 v. 23-27 cm.
Title varies: 1st, Interim report to the President.
Third report issued without t.p.; called Final report in letter of transmittal.
1. Education, Higher.
L111.P74   378   56-63885
MC#: 1957-1175 (1st interim report)
SuDocs no.: Pr34.8:Ed8
MC#: 1957-14525 (2d report)
SuDocs no.: Pr34.8:Ed8/957
MC#: 1958-868 (summary report)
SuDocs no.: Pr34.8:Ed8/957/sum.

JUDD REPORT [Judd, Walter Henry]
826

U.S. *Congress. House. Committee on Foreign Affairs.*
Special study mission to Southeast Asia and the Pacific; report by Walter H. Judd, chairman [and others] Washington, U.S. Govt. Print. Off., 1954.

viii, 107 p. maps. 24 cm.
At head of title: 83d Cong., 2d sess. Committee print.
1. East (Far East) I. Judd, Walter Henry, 1898- II. Title.
DS518.1.U53   915   54-61618
MC#: 1954-6884
SuDocs no.: Y4.F76/1:So8/5

MC#: 1954-11620
SuDocs no.: 83d Cong., 2d sess. H. Rept. 2025

KAHN REPORT
827

Kahn, Herman, 1922-
The nature and feasibility of war and deterrence, a study. Washington, U.S. Govt. Print. Off., 1960.

v, 37 p. 24 cm. (86th Cong., 2d sess. Senate Document no. 101)
"A slightly different version of this paper appeared as an article by the same title in the Stanford Research Institute journal in the fourth quarter of 1959."
1. Atomic warfare. 2. Military policy. 3. Deterrence (Strategy) 4. World politics—1955- I. Title. (Series: U.S. 86th Cong., 2d sess., 1960. Senate. Document no. 101)
UA11.K3 1960   341.672   60-61515
MC#: 1960-10982
SuDocs no.: 86th Cong., 2d sess. S. Doc. 101

KAIDANOVSKY REPORT [Kaidanovsky, Samuel P.]
see under
O'MAHONEY REPORTS [O'Mahoney, Joseph Christopher]

KAISER REPORT [Kaiser, Edgar F.]
828

United States. President's Committee on Urban Housing.
A decent home; report. Washington, [For sale by the Supt. of Docs., U.S. Govt. Print. Off., 1969]

ix, 252 p. illus. 25 cm.
Cover title.
Commonly known as the Kaiser report.
Bibliographical footnotes.
1. Housing—United States. 2. Building—United States. I. Title. II. Title: Kaiser report on urban housing.
HD7293.A5 1969   301.5'4'0973   74-600431
                                                  MARC
MC#: 1969-2397
SuDocs no.: Pr36.8:Ur1/D35

KAMERICK REPORT [Kamerick, Paul E.]
829

U.S. *Congress. Senate. Committee on Appropriations.*
Creation and management of United States Government records; report of the Investigations Division of Senate Appropriations Committee. Washington, U.S. Govt. Print. Off., 1954.

v, 31 p. 23 cm.
At head of title: Committee print. 83d Cong., 2d sess. Senate.
1. Public records—U.S. I. Title. II. Title: United States Government records.
JK468.P76A54   54-60498
MC#: 1954-17139
SuDocs no.: Y4.Ap6/2:R24/4

KAMMERMAN REPORT [Kammerman, David]
830

Senate Republican Policy Committee.
Senate rules and the Senate as a continuing body. [Prepared by David Kammerman, professional staff member, Senate Republican Policy Committee] Washington, U.S. Govt. Print. Off., 1953.

iii, 35 p. 24 cm. (83d Cong., 1st sess. Senate. Document no. 4)

1. U.S. Congress. Senate—Rules and practice. (Series: U.S. 83d Cong., 1st sess., 1953. Senate. Document no. 4)
KF4982.S4   328.735   53-60234
MC#: 1953-2253
SuDocs no.: 83d Cong., 1st sess. S. Doc. 4

KAPLAN REPORT [Kaplan, Herman Eliot]

831

U.S. *Committee on Retirement Policy for Federal Personnel.*
Retirement policy for Federal personnel. Letter from the chairman transmitting a report of the findings and recommendations pursuant to Public law 555, 82d Congress. Washington, U.S. Govt. Print. Off., 1954.

5 pts. illus. 24 cm. (83d Cong., 2d sess. Senate. Document no. 89)
Subtitle varies.
H. Eliot Kaplan, chairman.
Contents.—pt. 1. A descriptive and comparative analysis of retirement and related provisions in effect on January 1, 1954.—pt. 2-3. The relationships between the Federal staff retirement systems and the old-age and survivors insurance system. Proposal no. 1: the uniformed services retirement system. Proposal no. 2: The civil service retirement system.—pt. 4. A. The financial status of the Federal retirement plans. B. Recommended finding and financing policies.—pt. 5. Report on special benefit provisions; analytical studies and recommendations on special benefit provisions.
1. Civil service pensions—U.S. I. Kaplan, Herman Eliot, 1898-II. Title. (Series: U.S. 83d Cong., 2d sess., 1954. Senate. Document no. 89)
JK791.A515   351.5   54-61447 rev 2
MC#: 1954-5317, 9990, 11916, 14573, 14574
SuDocs no.: 83d Cong., 2d sess. S. Doc. 89

KAPLAN REPORT [Kaplan, Sheldon Z.]

832

U.S. *Congress. House. Committee on Foreign Affairs.*
Background information on the Inter-American Highway in connection with H. R. 7890, staff memorandum [prepared by Sheldon Z. Kaplan and George Lee Millikan, staff consultants] Washington, U.S. Govt. Print. Off., 1950.

iv, 40 p. fold. maps. 24 cm.
At head of title: Subcommittee print.
1. Inter-American Highway. I. Kaplan, Sheldon Z. II. Millikan, George Lee. III. Title.
TE21.U5 1950f   625.7   50-61184
Not located in Monthly Catalog

KAPPEL REPORTS [Kappel, Frederick R.]

833

U.S. *Commission on Executive, Legislative, and Judicial Salaries.*
Report. Washington, 1968.
vii, 78 p. tables.
MC#: 1969-4228 (LC card 75-600694 preassigned, not yet printed)
SuDocs no.: Y3.Ex3/3:1/968

834

United States. President's Commission on Postal Organization.
Towards postal excellence; the report of the President's Commission on Postal Organization. Washington, For sale by the Supt. of Docs., U.S. Govt. Print. Off., 1968.
5 v. illus. 24 cm. (Commission's report)
Commonly known as the Kappel report.

Includes the Commission's report (1 v.) and the Annex: Contractors' reports (4 v.)
1. Postal service—United States. I. Title. II. Title: Kappel report on postal organization.
HE6331 1968.A55   383'.49'73   68-62117
                                                   MARC
MC#: 1968-16463
SuDocs no.: Pr36.8:P84/R29
MC#: 1968-16464
SuDocs no.: Pr36.8:P84/R29/annex/v.(nos.)

KAPPLER REPORT [Kappler, Charles Joseph]

835

U.S. Laws, statutes, etc.
Indian affairs. Laws and treaties. Compiled and edited by Charles J. Kappler. Washington, Govt. Print. Off., 1903-41.
5 v. 30 cm.
Commonly known as the Kappler report.
Vols. I-II: 57th Congress, 1st session. Senate. Document 452; v. III: 62d Congress, 2d session. Senate. Document 719; v. IV: 70th Congress, 1st session. Senate. Document 53; v. V: 76th Congress, 3d session. Senate. Document no. 194.
Contents: I. Statutes, executive orders, proclamations, and statistics of tribes. Compiled to Dec. 1, 1902.—II. Treaties—III. Laws. Compiled to Dec. 1, 1913.-IV. Laws. Compiled to March 4, 1927.—V. Laws. Compiled from Dec. 22, 1927, to June 29, 1938.
1. Indians of North America—Legal status, laws, etc. 2. Indians of North America—Treaties. I. U.S. Treaties, etc. II. Kappler, Charles Joseph, 1868-1946. III. Title.
KF8203 1903   342'.73'087   3-13067
                                                   MARC
MC#: 1903-page 252
SuDocs no.: 57th Cong., 1st sess. S. Doc. 452
MC#: 1904-page 575 (vols. 1-2, 2d ed.)
SuDocs no.: 58th Cong., 2d sess. S. Doc. 319
MC#: Aug. 1914-page 102
SuDocs no.: 62d Cong., 2d sess. S. Doc. 719
MC#: Oct. 1929-page 221
SuDocs no.: 70th Cong., 1st sess. S. Doc. 53
MC#: 1941-page 664
SuDocs no.: 76th Cong., 3d sess. S. Doc. 194

United States. Laws, statutes, etc.
Indian affairs. Laws and treaties. Compiled and edited by Charles J. Kappler. Washington, Govt. Print. Off., 1904-41. [New York, AMS Press, 1971, i.e. 1972]
5 v. 27 cm.
Commonly known as the Kappler report.
Contents: v. 1. Laws. Compiled to Dec. 1, 1902.—v. 2. Treaties.—v. 3. Laws. Compiled to Dec. 1, 1913.—v. 4. Laws. Compiled to March 4, 1927.—v. 5. Laws. Compiled from Dec. 22, 1927, to June 29, 1938.
1. Indians of North America.—Legal status, laws, etc. 2. Indians of North America—Treaties. I. Kappler, Charles Joseph, 1868-1946. II. United States. Treaties, etc. III. Title. IV. Title: Kappler report on Indian affairs.
KF8203 1972   342'.73'087   78-128994
                                                   MARC
Not listed in Monthly Catalog

KATZENBACH REPORT

836

Katzenbach, Nicholas deB.
CIA support to private organizations. Statement by the President upon receiving the report of the committee appointed to

review relationships, with the text of the report. March 29, 1967.

(*In* Weekly Compilation of Presidential Documents, April 3, 1967. Vol. 3, no. 13, pages 556-558)
SuDocs no.: GS4.114:v.3, no.13

KATZENBACH REPORT [Katzenbach, Nicholas deB.]
see
CRIME COMMISSION REPORT

KAUN REPORT [Kaun, David E.]
see
BERGMANN REPORT [Bergmann, Barbara R.]

KAYE REPORT [Kaye, Gus]
see
GOLDWATER REPORT [Goldwater, Barry, Jr.]

KAYSEN REPORTS [Kaysen, Carl]

837

U.S. *Congress. Joint Economic Committee. Subcommittee on Economic Statistics.*
The coordination and integration of Government statistical programs; report. Washington, U.S. Govt. Print. Off., 1967.

v, 10 p. 24 cm.
At head of title: 90th Congress, 1st session. Joint committee print.
1. U.S. — Statistical services. I. Title.
HA37.U534   311′.39′73   67-62317
MC#: 1967-14918
SuDocs no.: Y4.Ec7:St2/5

838

U.S. *Task Force on the Storage of and Access to Government Statistics.*
Report of the Task Force on the Storage of and Access to Government Statistics. October 1966.

(*In* U.S. Congress. Joint Economic Committee. Subcommittee on Economic Statistics. The coordination and integration of Government statistical programs. Hearings . . . 90th Congress, 1st session. Washington, 1967. 24 cm. p. 195-205)
MC#: 1967-14917
SuDocs no.: Y4.Ec7:St2/4

KEEP COMMISSION [Keep, Charles Hallam]

Reports of the Keep Commission are filed according to the contents note of the first entry. Other related reports are interfiled.

839

U.S. *Committee on department methods.*
Reports to the President by the Committee on department methods. [Washington, Govt. print. off., 1905-09]

[254] p. 30 cm.
Various paging.
C. H. Keep, chairman.
Contents. — Purchase of typesetting machines for the Government printing office. — Public printing.-Government crop reports. — Interdepartmental telephone service. — Investigation of the Twelfth census report on agriculture. — Method of rendering and stating accounts. — Purchase of department supplies.-Use of committees in department work. — Annual leave, sick leave, and hours of labor. — Cost keeping in the government service. — Classification of positions and gradations of salaries. — Official bonds. — Treasury bookkeeping. — Government contracts. — Superannuation of civil-service employees of the government. —

Documentary historical publications of the United States government.
1. U.S. — Executive departments. 2. Civil service — U.S. I. Keep, Charles Hallam, 1861-
JK639.A6   11-32873
Not located in Monthly Catalog

840

U.S. *Committee on department methods.*
Report of the committee on department methods in the matter of purchase of typesetting machinery for Government printing office. August 4, 1905. Washington, Govt. print. off., 1905.

1 p. 1., 28 p. 23 cm.
Signed: C. H. Keep, F. H. Hitchcock, L. O. Murry, J. R. Garfield.
Z232.U6U74   10-5684
- - - - - Copy 2.
Not located in Monthly Catalog

841

Lanston monotype machine company.
Investigation held at the Government printing office, Washington, D.C., June 29th to July 15th, 1905, inclusive. In the matter of the investigation directed by the President as the result of a letter (called petition) addressed to him, signed by the Mergenthaler linotype company . . . June 24, 1905 . . . Before Mr. Commissioner Keep, chairman, Mr. Commissioner Garfield, Mr. Commissioner Murray, Mr. Commissioner Pinchot, Mr. Commissioner Hitchcock. Argument for Lanston monotype machine co. Joline, Larkin & Rathbone, attorneys . . . Adrian H. Larkin, L. T. Michener, Barry Mohun, of counsel. [Washington, Gibson bros., 1905]

cover-title, 101 p. 28½ cm.
1. Type-setting machines. 2. U.S. Government printing office. I. Joline, Larkin and Rathbone. II. U.S. Committee on department methods.
Z253.L25   8-14944
Document Catalogue, vol. 8, pages 433, 1710

842

U.S. *Committee on department methods.*
Report to the President by the Committee on department methods. Public printing. [Washington, 1906]

12 p. 30 x 23½ cm.
Signed: C. H. Keep, F. H. Hitchcock, Lawrence O. Murray, James Rudolph Garfield, Gifford Pinchot, Committee on department methods.
1. Printing, Public — U.S. I. Keep, Charles Hallam, 1861-
Z232.U6U742   655.1753   33-18430
- - - - - Copy 2.
MC#: 1906-page 14
SuDocs no.: Y3.D44:P96

843

U.S. *Committee on department methods.*
Report to the President by the Committee on department methods. Government crop reports. [Washington, Govt. print. off., 1906]

25 p. 29 cm.
C. H. Keep, chairman.
Report on the work of the Bureau of statistics of the Department of agriculture.
S21.S75 1906   11-25665
MC#: 1906-page 14
SuDocs no.: Y4.D44:C88

844

U.S. *Committee on department methods.*
Report on interdepartmental telephone service. [March 19, 1906]
6 p.
Document Catalogue, vol. 8, page 433

845

U.S. *Committee on department methods.*
Reports of the Keep commission. Message from the President . . . transmitting the reports of the Keep commission on department methods, relating to official crop statistics and the investigation of the Twelfth census report on agriculture, in compliance with Senate resolution no. 135 . . . [Washington, govt. print. off., 1906]
26 p. 23 cm. (59th Cong., 1st sess. Senate. Doc. 464)
Signed: C. H. Keep, Lawrence O. Murray, James Rudolph Garfield, Gifford Pinchot, Committee on department methods.
HD1425.A4   6-20712
MC#: 1906-page 253 (LC card 6-35252 cancelled in favor of 6-20712)
SuDocs no.: 59th Cong., 1st sess. S. Doc. 464

846

U.S. *Committee on department methods.*
Report on method of rendering and stating accounts.
Not located in Document Catalogue

847

U.S. *Committee on department methods.*
. . . Purchase of department supplies. Message from the President of the United States, transmitting the report to the President by the Committee on department methods . . . [Washington, Govt. print. off., 1906]
12 p. 23 cm. (59th Cong., 2d sess. Senate. Doc. 106)
Signed: C. H. Keep, Lawrence O. Murray, James Rudolph Garfield, Gifford Pinchot, Committee on department methods.
1. U.S. — Executive departments — Equipment and supplies. 2. Government purchasing — U.S. I. Keep, Charles Hallam, 1861- II. Title.
JK1671.A3 1906   6-35377
MC#: 1906-page 421
SuDocs no.: 59th Cong., 2d sess. S. Doc. 106

848

U.S. *Committee on department methods.*
Report on use of committees in Department work. [December 6, 1906]
7 p.
Document Catalogue, vol. 8, page 433

849

U.S. *Committee on department methods.*
Report on annual leave, sick leave, and hours of labor. [December 24, 1906]
10 p.
Document Catalogue, vol. 8, page 433

850

U.S. *Committee on department methods.*
Report on cost keeping in Government service. [December 29, 1906]
22 p.
Document Catalogue, vol. 8, page 433

851

U.S. *Committee on department methods.*
Report to the President by the Committee on department methods. Classification of positions and gradation of salaries for employees of the executive departments and independent establishments in Washington. [Washington, Govt. print. off., 1907]
16 p. 29½ x 23½ cm.
C. H. Keep, chairman.
JK776.U58   7-35300
- - - - - Copy 2.
Document Catalogue, vol. 8, page 433

852

U.S. *Congress. House. Committee on appropriations.*
Proposed reclassification of clerical force in the executive departments. Supplement to hearings before subcommittee of House Committee on appropriations in charge of deficiency appropriations for 1907 and prior years on General deficiency bill. [Jan. 15, 1907] Washington, Govt. print. off., 1907.
9 p. 23 cm.
Subcommittee: Messrs. Littauer, Tawney, Graff, Brundidge, and Livingston.
Statement of Hon. Charles H. Keep, chairman of the Committee on department methods.
I. Keep, Charles Hallam, 1861- II. U.S. Committee on department methods.
       7-35132
- - - - - Copy 2.
MC#: Feb. 1907-page 515

853

U.S. *Committee on department methods.*
Report on official bonds. [January 7, 1907]
11 p.
Document Catalogue, vol. 8, page 433

854

U.S. *Committee on department methods.*
Report on Treasury bookkeeping. [January 19, 1907]
10 p.
Document Catalogue, vol. 8, page 433

855

U.S. *Committee on department methods.*
Report on Government contracts. [April 30, 1907]
7 p.
Document Catalogue, vol. 8, page 433

856

U.S. *Committee on department methods.*
. . . Superannuation in classified civil service. Message from the President . . . transmitting a report by the Committee on departmental methods . . . also a draft of a proposed bill which provides for the payment of annuities to employees upon retirement . . . [Washington, Govt. print. off., 1908]
10 p. 23 cm. (60th Cong., 1st sess. Senate. Doc. 308)
Read, referred to the committee on appropriations and ordered printed, Feb. 21, 1908.
Prepared by the subcommittee on personnel, Arthur P. Davis, chairman.
1. Civil service — U.S. 2. Civil service pensions — U.S.
JK781.A5 1908   8-35185 Revised
Document Catalogue, vol. 9, page 438
60th Cong., 1st sess. S. Doc. 308. In Serial no. 5265, vol. 32

857

U.S. *Committee on department methods.*

. . . Draft of a proposed bill for the retirement of civil service employees, which was drafted by the sub-committee on personnel of the Committee on department methods, and report with which such draft was submitted to the whole committee . . . [Washington, D.C., 1907]

15, [1] p. 21½ cm.
JK791.A5 1907   17-19294
- - - - - Copy 2.
Not located in Monthly Catalog

858

U.S. *Committee on department methods.*

. . . Message from the President of the United States, transmitting a report by the Committee on department methods on the documentary historical publications of the United States government, together with a draft of a proposed bill providing for the creation of a permanent Commission on national historical publications . . . Washington, Govt. print. off., 1909.

45 p. 23 cm. (60th Cong., 2d sess. Senate. Doc. 714)
Feb. 11, 1909, read, ordered to lie on the table and be printed.
Report of the assistant committee on documentary historical publications of the United States, signed: Worthington C. Ford, chairman, Charles Francis Adams, Charles M. Andrews, William A. Dunning, Albert Bushnell Hart, Andrew C. McLaughlin, Alfred T. Mahan, Frederick J. Turner, J. Franklin Jameson.
Submitted by Lawrence O. Murray and Gifford Pinchot, Committee on department methods.
Pub. also with title beginning "Report to the President."
1. U.S. Hist. — Sources. 2. U.S. — Government publications. 3. Archives — U.S. 4. U.S. Commission on national historical publications. I. Ford, Worthington Chauncey, 1858-1941.
E172.U585   9-35289
MC#: Feb. 1909-page 431
SuDocs no.: Y3.D44:1:162

859

U.S. *Committee on department methods.*

Report to the President by the Committee on department methods. Documentary historical publications of the United States government. [Washington, Govt. print. off., 1909]

41 p. 29½ cm.
Commonly known as the Keep report.
1. U.S. — Hist. — Sources. 2. U.S. — Government publications. 3. Archives — U.S. 4. U.S. Commission on national historical publications. I. Ford, Worthington Chauncey, 1858-1941. II. Title. III. Title: Documentary historical publications. IV. Title: Keep report on the documentary historical publications of the United States government.
E172.U58   9-7023
MC#: Feb. 1909-page 431
SuDocs no.: 60th Cong., 2d sess. S. Doc. 714

KEFAUVER REPORT [Kefauver, Estes]
860

U.S. *Congress. Senate. Special Committee to Investigate Organized Crime in Interstate Commerce.*
Report. [1st-4th] Washington, U.S. Govt. Print. Off., 1950-51.
4 v. 24 cm.
Issued in the congressional series as Senate Reports.
The 1st-3d reports called Interim report; 4th report called Final report.
Final report has also a distinctive title: Organized crime in interstate commerce.

1. Crime and criminals — U.S.
HV6775.A32   364.973   50-61300
Interim Report
MC#: 1950-18983
SuDocs no.: 81st Cong., 2d sess. S. Rept. 2370
2d Interim Report
MC#: 1951-6681
SuDocs no.: 82d Cong., 1st sess. S. Rept. 141
3d Interim Report
MC#: 1951-9591
SuDocs no.: 82d Cong., 1st sess. S. Rept. 307
Final Report
MC#: 1951-16474
SuDocs no.: 82d Cong., 1st sess. S. Rept. 725

KEIM REPORT [Keim, Walter George]
see under
O'MAHONEY REPORTS [O'Mahoney, Joseph Christopher]
Keim. Geographical differentials in prices of building materials.

Nelson. Price behavior and business policy.

KEITH REPORT [Keith, Nathaniel Schnieder]
see
DOUGLAS REPORTS [Douglas, Paul H.]
National Commission on Urban Problems.

Research report no. 7

KELLEY REPORT [Kelley, Augustine Bernard]
861

U.S. *Congress. House. Committee on labor.*
. . . Aid to the physically handicapped. Report of the Committee on labor, Subcommittee on aid to the physically handicapped, pursuant to H. Res. 45 . . . Washington, U.S. Govt. print. off., 1946.
iii, 21 p. 23 cm. ([U.S.] 79th Cong., 2d sess. House. Rept. 2731)
Letter of transmittal signed: Augustine B. Kelly, chairman [of subcommittee]
1. Disabled — Rehabilitation, etc. — U.S. I. Kelley, Augustine Bernard, 1883- II. Title.
HD7256.U5A5 1946c   331.86   47-32963
MC#: 1947-page 38 (LC card 47-32971 cancelled in favor of 47-32963)
SuDocs no.: 79th Cong., 2d sess. H. Rept. 2731

KELLY REPORT [Kelly, Edna F.]
see
COFFIN REPORT [Coffin, Frank M.]
Special study mission to Europe.

KEMENY COMMISSION REPORTS [Kemeny, John G.]
862

United States. President's Commission on the Accident at Three Mile Island.
Report of the President's Commission on the Accident at Three Mile Island: the need for change: the legacy of TMI. — Washington: The Commission: for sale by the Supt. of Docs., U.S. Govt. Print. Off., 1979.
201 p.: ill.; 27 cm.
"October 1979".
Includes bibliographical references and glossary.
ISBN 0-9357-5800-3

1. Three Mile Island Nuclear Power Plant, Pa. 2. Atomic power-plants—Accidents. I. Title. II. Title: The need for change—the legacy of TMI.
MC#: 1980-6415
SuDocs no.: Pr39.8:T41/T41

United States. President's Commission on the Accident at Three Mile Island.
The need for change, the legacy TMI : report of the President's Commission on the Accident at Three Mile Island. — New York : Pergamon Press, 1979.

201 p. : ill. ; 28 cm.
ISBN 0-08-025946-4
1. Three Mile Island Nuclear Power Plant, Pa. 2. Atomic power plants—Accidents. I. Title.
TK1345.H37U54 1979   363.1'79   79-25694
                                                                    MARC
Not listed in Monthly Catalog

863

United States. President's Commission on the Accident at Three Mile Island.
Report of the Office of Chief Counsel on the Nuclear Regulatory Commission/by Stanley M. Gorinson . . . [et al.]. — Washington: President's Commission on the Accident at Three Mile Island: for sale by the Supt. of Docs., U.S. Govt. Print. Off., 1979.

139 p.; 27 cm.
Cover title: Staff report to the President's Commission on the Accident at Three Mile Island.
"October 1979".
Includes bibliographic references.
1. Three Mile Island Nuclear Power Plant, Pa. 2. United States. Nuclear Regulatory Commission. I. Gorinson, Stanley M. II. Title.
MC#: 1980-8726
SuDocs no.: Pr39.8:T41/N88

864

United States. President's Commission on the Accident at Three Mile Island.
Report of the Office of Chief Counsel on the role of the managing utility and its suppliers/ by Stanley M. Gorinson . . . [et. al.]. — Washington: President's Commission on the Accident at Three Mile Island: for sale by the Supt. of Docs., U.S. Govt. Print. Off., 1979.

321 p.; 27 cm.
Cover title: Staff report to the President's Commission on the Accident at Three Mile Island.
"October 1979."
Includes bibliographical references.
1. Three Mile Island Nuclear Power Plant, Pa. 2. Electric utilities—Pennsylvania. 3. Atomic power-plants—Pennsylvania. I. Gorinson, Stanley M. II. Title. III. Title: Role of the managing utility and its suppliers.
MC#: 1980-8727
SuDocs no.: Pr39.8:T41/Ut3

865

United States. President's Commission on the Accident at Three Mile Island. Technical Assessment Task Force.
Reports of the Technical Assessment Task Force. — Washington, D.C.: President's Commission on the Accident at Three Mile Island: For sale by the Supt. of Docs., U.S. Govt. Print. Off., 1979-1980.

4 v.: ill.; 27 cm.
Cover title: Staff reports to the President's Commission on the Accident at Three Mile Island.

"October 1979."
Includes bibliographical references.
Contents: v. 1. Technical staff analysis reports summary; Summary sequence of events—v. 2. Chemistry, thermal dynamics, core damage; WASH 1400 reactor safety study; Alternative event sequences—v. 3. Selection, training, qualification, and licensing of Three Mile Island reactor operating personnel; Technical assessment of operating, abnormal, and emergency procedures; Control room design and performance.—v. 4. Quality assurance; Condensate polishing system; Closed emergency feedwater valves; Pilot-operated relief valve design and performance; Containment: Transport of radioactivity from the TMI-2 core to the environs; Iodine filter performance; Recovery: TMI-2 cleanup and decontamination.
1. Three Mile Island Nuclear Power Plant, Pa. 2. Atomic power-plants—Accidents. I. Title. II. Title: Staff reports to the President's Commission on the Accident at Three Mile Island.
                                                                    81-603779
MC#: 82-6183
SuDocs no.: Pr39.8:T41/As7/v.1-4

866

United States. President's Commission on the Accident at Three Mile Island. Public Health and Safety Task Force.
Reports of the Public Health and Safety Task Force on public health and safety summary, health physics and dosimetry, radiation health effects, behavioral effects, public health and epidemiology. — Washington, D.c.: for sale by the Supt. of Docs., U.S. Govt. Print. Off., [1980]

423 p. : ill. ; 26 cm.
"October 1979."
Includes bibliographical references.
1. Atomic power-plants—Accidents—Hygenic aspects—Pennsylvania—Three Mile Island. 2. Atomic power-plants—Pennsylvania—Three Mile Island—Accidents. 3. Three Mile Island Nuclear Power Plant, Pa. 4. Radioactive pollution—Pennsylvania—Harrisburg region. 5. Radiation—Dosage. 6. Radiation—Toxicology. I. Title.
RA569.U4977 1980   363.1'79-dc19   80-601717
                                                                    MARC
MC#: 1980-12632
SuDocs no.: Pr39.8:T41/H34

867

United States. President's Commission on the Accident at Three Mile Island. Emergency Preparedness and Response Task Force.
Report of the Emergency Preparedness and Response Task Force/by Russell R. Dynes . . . [et al.]. — Washington: President's Commission on the Accident at Three Mile Island: for sale by the Supt. of Docs., U.S. Govt. Print. Off., 1979.

168 p. : ill. ; 27 cm.
Cover title: Staff Report to the President's Commission on the Accident at Three Mile Island.
"October 1979."
Includes bibliographical references.
1. Three Mile Island Nuclear Power Plant, Pa. 2. Disaster relief. I. Dynes, Russell Rowe, 1923- II. Title. III. Title: Staff report to the President's Commission on the Accident at Three Mile Island.
MC#: 1980-12631
SuDocs no.: Pr39.8:T431/Em2/3

868

United States. President's Commission on the Accident at Three Mile Island. Public's Right to Information Task Force.

Report of the Public's Right to Information Task Force / by David M. Rubin . . . [et al.]. — Washington, D.C. : For sale by the Supt. of Docs., U.S. Govt. Print. Off., [1980]

262 p. ; 27 cm.
"October 1979."
Includes bibliographical references.
1. Metropolitan Edison Company — Public relations. 2. Three Mile Island Nuclear Power Plant, Pa. 3. Atomic power plants — Pennsylvania — Accidents. I. Rubin, David M.
HD9698.U54M478 1980   363.1′79-dc19   80-601569
                                                    MARC
MC#: 1980-12633
SuDocs no.: Pr39.8:T41/In3

869

Staff reports to the President's Commission on the Accident at Three Mile Island: selected reports from the Technical Assessment Task Force, the Public Health and Safety Task Force, the Office of the Chief Counsel. 1st ed. Oxford; New York: Permagon Press, 1981.

viii, 438 p.; 26 cm.
"Reprinted from the U.S. government publications."
Includes bibliographical references and index.
1. Three Mile Island Nuclear Power Plant (Pa.) 2. Atomic power-plants — Pennsylvania — Accidents. I. United States. President's Commission on the Accident at Three Mile Island. II. United States. President's Commission on the Accident at Three Mile Island. Technical Assessment Task Force. III. United States. President's Commission on the Accident at Three Mile Island. Public Health and Safety Task Force. IV. United States. President's Commission on the Accident at Three Mile Island. Office of Chief Counsel. V. Title: Accident at Three Mile Island.
TK1345.H37S7 1981   363.1′79 19   01-189812
Not listed in Monthly Catalog

870

U.S. *Congress. Senate. Committee on Environment and Public Works. Subcommittee on Nuclear Regulation.*
Nuclear accident and recovery at Three Mile Island. A report. June 1980. U.S. Govt. Print. Off., 1980.

423 p.
96th Cong., 2d sess., Committee Print. Serial no. 96-14.
MC#: 1981-6337
SuDocs no.: Y4.P96/10:96-14

871

U.S. *Congress. Senate. Committee on Environment and Public Works. Subcommittee on Nuclear Regulation.*
Staff studies, Nuclear accident and recovery at Three Mile Island. July 1980. U.S. Govt. Print. Off., 1980.

564 p.
96th Cong., 2d sess. Committee Print. Serial no. 96-14.
MC#: 1981-6338
SuDocs no.: Y4.P96/10:96-14A

KEMMERER REPORT [Kemmerer, Edwin Walter]
    see under
    ALDRICH COMMISSION [Aldrich, Nelson Wilmarth]

KENNEDY REPORT [Kennedy, David M.]
872

U.S. *President's Commission on Budget Concepts.*
Report. Washington, U.S. Govt. Print. Off., 1967.
ix, 109 p. 24 cm.

1. Budget — U.S.
HJ2051.A6225   353.007′22   67-62908
MC#: 1967-18146
SuDocs no.: Pr36.8:B85/R29/967

KENNEDY REPORT [Kennedy, John Fitzgerald]
    see
    LANDIS REPORT [Landis, James McCauley]
    Report on regulatory agencies.

KENNEDY REPORTS [Kennedy, Joseph P.]
873

U.S. *Maritime commission.*
Economic survey of the American merchant marine. United States Maritime commission, November 10, 1937. Washington, U.S. Govt. print. off., 1937.

vi, 85 p. incl. tables. 23 cm.
Issued also as House doc. 392, 75th Cong., 2d sess.
1. Merchant marine — U.S. I. Title. II. Title: Kennedy report on the economic survey of the American merchant marine.
HE745.A38 1937   387.50973   37-28972
- - - - - Copy 2.
MC#: 1937-page 1390
SuDocs no.: MC1.2:M53/937

874

U.S. *Maritime commission.*
. . . Economic survey of the American merchant marine. United States Maritime commission, November 10, 1937. Letter from the chairman, United States Maritime commission transmitting Economic survey of the American merchant marine . . . Washington, U.S. Govt. print. off., 1937.

vi, 85 p. incl. tables. 23 cm. (75th Cong., 2d sess. House. Doc. 392)
Referred to the Committee on merchant marine and fisheries and ordered printed, November 15, 1937.
Issued also without document series note "(Bureau ed.)"
1. Merchant marine — U.S. I. Title.
HE745.A38 1937a   387.50973   37-28996
- - - - - Copy 2.
MC#: 1937-page 1390
SuDocs no.: 75th Cong., 2d sess. H. Doc. 392

KENNEDY REPORTS [Kennedy, Robert Francis]
875

U.S. *President's Committee on Juvenile Delinquency and Youth Crime.*
Report to the President. [Washington?] 1962.
22 p. 27 cm.
1. Juvenile delinquency — U.S.
HV9103.A64   63-60339
Not located in Monthly Catalog

876

U.S. *President's Study Group on National Voluntary Services.*
A report to the President. [Washington] 1963.
27 p. 21 x 10 cm.
1. Economic assistance, Domestic — U.S. 2. U.S. National Service Corps (Proposed)
HC106.5.A48   64-60356
Not located in Monthly Catalog

KEPPEL REPORT [Keppel, Frederick P.]
877

U.S. *Board of appeals on visa cases.*

Report to the President, Board of appeals on visa cases, November 9, 1942. [Washington, 1942]

cover-title, 32 p. 23 cm.

1. Passports.

JX4253.U6A5 1942g   323.67   44-11867

Not located in Monthly Catalog

KERNER COMMISSION [Kerner, Otto]

878

Supplemental studies for the National Advisory Commission on Civil Disorders. Washington, For sale by the Supt. of Docs., U.S. Govt. Print. Off. [1968]

viii, 248 p. forms. 26 cm.

"The studies were conducted independently of the Commission and of each other by research groups at the University of Michigan, the Johns Hopkins University, and Columbia University."

Contents. — Racial attitudes in fifteen American cities, by A. Campbell and H. Schuman. — Between black and white; the faces of American institutions in the ghetto, by P. H. Rossi and others. — Who riots? A study of participation in the 1967 riots, by R. M. Fogelson and R. B. Hill.

1. U.S. — Race question. 2. Riots — U.S. I. Campbell, Angus. Racial attitudes in fifteen American cities. II. Between white and black; the faces of American institutions in the ghetto. III. Fogelson, Robert M. Who riots? A study of participation in the 1967 riots. IV. Kerner Commission.

E185.61.S94 1968   364.14'3'0973   68-62329

MC#: 1968-16461

SuDocs no.: Pr36.8:C49/St9

879

United States. National Advisory Commission on Civil Disorders.

Report. [Washington, For sale by the Supt. of Docs., U.S. Govt. Print. Off., 1968]

xv, 425 p. illus., ports. 26 cm.

1. Riots — United States.

HV6477.A56   364.14'3'0973   68-61127
                                                 MARC

MC#: 1968-6716

SuDocs no.: Pr36.8:C49/R29

United States. Kerner Commission.

The riot report = a shortened version of the Report of the National Advisory Commission on Civil Disorders / by Barbara Ritchie ; introd. by Jeanne Noble. — New York : Viking Press, 1969.

254 p. : ill. ; 25 cm.

Bibliography: p. [247]-250.

Includes index.

ISBN 0-670-59903-4. ISBN 0-670-59904-2 lib. bdg.

1. Riots — United States. I. Ritchie, Barbara, ed. II. Title.

HV6477.U54 1969   364.1'43   74-193367
                                              MARC

Not listed in Monthly Catalog

KERR REPORT [Kerr, Robert S.]

880

U.S. *Congress. Senate. Select Committee on National Water Resources.*

Report, pursuant to S. res. 48, 86th Congress, together with supplemental and individual views. Washington, U.S. Govt. Print. Off., 1961.

x, 147 p. map, diagrs., tables. 24 cm. (87th Cong., 1st sess. Senate. Report no. 29)

1. Water-supply — U.S. (Series: U.S. 87th Cong., 1st sess., 1961. Senate. Report no. 29)

GB701.A513 1961   333.910973   61-60710

MC#: 1961-5802

SuDocs no.: 87th Cong., 1st sess. S. Rept. 29

KESTNBAUM COMMISSION [Kestnbaum, Meyer]

881

Governmental Affairs Institute, *Washington, D.C.*

A survey report on the impact of Federal grants-in-aid on the structure and functions of State and local governments, submitted to the Commission on Intergovernmental Relations. [Washington, U.S. Govt. Print. Off.] 1955.

vii, 489 p. tables. 24 cm.

Includes bibliography.

1. Federal government — U.S. 2. Grants-in-aid — U.S. I. U.S. Commission on Intergovernmental Relations. II. Title: The impact of Federal grants-in-aid on the structure and functions of State and local governments.

JK2408.G66   55-61479

MC#: 1955-12463

SuDocs no.: Y3.In8/7:G76

882

U.S. *Library of Congress. Legislative Reference Service.*

Index to the reports of the Commission on Intergovernmental Relations including the Commission's report, various study committees, staff and survey reports, and supporting documents. Prepared at request of the Senate Committee on Government Operations. [Washington, U.S. Govt. Print. Off., 1956]

iv, 143 p. 24 cm. (84th Cong. 2d sess. Senate. Document no. 111)

1. U.S. Commission on Intergovernmental Relations — Indexes. I. U.S. Congress. Senate. Committee on Government Operations. (Series: U.S. 84th Cong., 2d sess., 1956. Senate. Document no. 111)

Z7165.U5U617   56-61083

MC#: 1956-8667

SuDocs no.: 84th Cong., 2d sess. S. Doc. 111

883

U.S. *Commission on Intergovernmental Relations.*

A description of twenty-five Federal grant-in-aid programs, submitted to the Commission on Intergovernmental Relations. [Washington, U.S. Govt. Print. Off.] 1955.

vii, 179 p. tables. 24 cm.

1. Grants-in-aid — U.S. I. Title.

HJ275.A513 1955   55-61471

MC#: 1955-12450

SuDocs no.: Y3.In8/7:G76/3

884

U.S. *Commission on Intergovernmental Relations.*

A report to the President for transmittal to the Congress. [Washington, U.S. Govt. Print. Off.] 1955.

xi, 311 p. diagrs., tables. 24 cm.

1. Federal government — U.S. 2. Grants-in-aid — U.S.

JK325.A34   353   55-61469

MC#: 1955-11448

SuDocs no.: 84th Cong., 1st sess. H. Doc. 198

MC#: 1955-12449

SuDocs no.: Y3.In8/7:R29

United States. Commission on Intergovernmental Relations.

A report to the President for transmittal to the Congress / Commission on Intergovernmental Relations. — New York : Arno Press, 1977.

xi, 311 p. ; 24 cm. — (American federalism)
Reprint of the 1955 ed. published by the U.S. Govt. Print. Off., Washington.
Commonly known as the Kestnbaum report.
ISBN 0-405-10505-3
1. Federal government — United States. 2. Grants-in-aid — United States. I. Title: Kestnbaum report on intergovernmental relations. II. Series.
[JK325.U55 1977]   353   77-74962

                                      MARC
Not listed in Monthly Catalog

885

U.S. *Commission on Intergovernmental Relations.*
A staff report on civil defense and urban vulnerability, submitted to the Commission on Intergovernmental Relations. [Washington, U.S. Govt. Print. Off.] 1955.
viii, 35 p. 24 cm.
1. U.S. — Civilian defense. I. Title: Civil defense and urban vulnerability.
UA927.A487 1955   55-61477
MC#: 1955-12451
SuDocs no.: Y3.In8/7:D36

886

U.S. *Commission on Intergovernmental Relations.*
A staff report on Federal aid to airports, submitted to the Commission on Intergovernmental Relations. [Washington, U.S. Govt. Print. Off.] 1955.
viii, 137 p. maps, diagrs., tables. 24 cm.
1. Airports — U.S. — Finance. I. Title: Federal aid to airports.
TL725.3.G6U512   *387.73 629.136   55-61466
MC#: 1955-12452
SuDocs no.: Y3.In8/7:Ai7

887

U.S. *Commission on Intergovernmental Relations.*
Summaries of survey reports on the administrative and fiscal impact of Federal grants-in-aid, prepared [by W. Brooke Graves] from original survey reports submitted to the Commission on Intergovernmental Relations by management consulting and research organizations. [Washington, U.S. Govt. Print. Off.] 1955.
xi, 120 p. 24 cm.
1. Grants-in-aid — U.S. 2. Finance, Public — U.S. — States. I. Graves, William Brooke, 1889- II. Title: The administrative and fiscal impact of Federal grants-in-aid.
HJ275.A514   55-61472
MC#: 1955-12462
SuDocs no.: Y3.In8/7:G76/2

888

U.S. *Commission on Intergovernmental Relations. Advisory Committee on Local Government.*
An advisory committee report on local government, submitted to the Commission on Intergovernmental Relations. Washington, U.S. Govt. Print. Off., 1955.
vii, 62 p. tables. 24 cm.
1. Local finance — U.S. 2. Grants-in-aid — U.S. I. Title: Local government.
HJ9145.A52   *336.39 352.1   55-61474
MC#: 1955-12448
SuDocs no.: Y3.In8/7:L78

889

U.S. *Commission on Intergovernmental Relations. Study Committee on Federal Aid to Agriculture.*
A study committee report on Federal aid to agriculture, submitted to the Commission on Intergovernmental Relations. [Washington, U.S. Govt. Print. Off.] 1955.
vii, 38 p. 24 cm.
1. Agriculture and state — U.S. I. Title: Federal aid to agriculture.
S21.Z2 1955b   338.1   55-61465
MC#: 1955-12453
SuDocs no.: Y3.In8/7:Ag8

890

U.S. *Commission on Intergovernmental Relations. Study Committee on Federal Aid to Highways.*
A study committee report on Federal aid to highways, submitted to the Commission on Intergovernmental Relations. [Washington, U.S. Govt. Print. Off.] 1955.
viii, 40 p. tables. 24 cm.
1. Roads — U.S. — Finance. I. Title: Federal aid to highways.
HE355.A3A516 1955a   55-61508
MC#: 1955-12454
SuDocs no.: Y3.In8/7:H53

891

U.S. *Commission on Intergovernmental Relations. Study Committee on Federal Aid to Public Health.*
A study committee report on Federal aid to public health, submitted to the Commission on Intergovernmental Relations. [Washington, U.S. Govt. Print. Off.] 1955.
viii, 53 p. tables. 24 cm.
1. Hygiene, Public — Finance. I. Title: Federal aid to public health.
RA11.A3 1955c   55-61475
MC#: 1955-12455
SuDocs no.: Y3.In8/7:H34

892

U.S. *Commission on Intergovernmental Relations. Study Committee on Federal Aid to Welfare.*
A study committee report on Federal aid to welfare, submitted to the Commission on Intergovernmental Relations. [Washington, U.S. Govt. Print. Off.] 1955.
ix, 115 p. diagrs., tables. 24 cm.
1. Public welfare — U.S. I. Title: Federal aid to welfare.
HV85.A415   361.6   55-61467
MC#: 1955-12456
SuDocs no.: Y3.In8/7:W45

893

U.S. *Commission on Intergovernmental Relations. Study Committee on Federal Responsibility in the Field of Education.*
A study committee report on Federal responsibility in the field of education, submitted to the Commission on Intergovernmental Relations. [Washington, U.S. Govt. Print. Off.] 1955.
ix, 154 p. diagrs., tables. 24 cm.
1. Education and state — U.S. 2. Libraries and state — U.S. I. Title: Federal responsibility in the field of education.
LC89.A513   379.12   55-61473
MC#: 1955-12457
SuDocs no.: Y3.In8/7:Ed8

894

U.S. *Commission on Intergovernmental Relations. Study Committee on Natural Resources and Conservation.*

A study committee report on natural resources and conservation, submitted to the Commission on Intergovernmental Relations. Washington, U.S. Govt. Print. Off., 1955.

vii, 35 p. 24 cm.

1. Natural resources—U.S. 2. Grants-in-aid—U.S. I. Title: Natural resources and conservation.
HC103.7.A48   55-61478
MC#: 1955-12458
SuDocs no.: Y3.In8/7:R31

895

U.S. *Commission on Intergovernmental Relations. Study Committee on Payments in Lieu of Taxes and Shared Revenues.*

A study committee report on payments in lieu of taxes and shared revenues, submitted to the Commission on Intergovernmental Relations. [Washington, U.S. Govt. Print. Off.] 1955.

ix, 197 p. tables. 24 cm.

1. Taxation and government property—U.S. I. Title: Payments in lieu of taxes and shared revenues.
HJ2338.U512   55-61470
MC#: 1955-12459
SuDocs no.: Y3.In8/7:P29

896

U.S. *Commission on Intergovernmental Relations. Study Committee on Unemployment Compensation and Employment Service.*

A study committee report on unemployment compensation and employment service, submitted to the Commission on Intergovernmental Relations. Washington, U.S. Govt. Print. Off., 1955.

vii, 100 p. table. 24 cm.

1. Insurance, Unemployment—U.S. 2. Employment agencies—U.S. I. Title: Unemployment compensation and employment service.
HD7096.U5A525   *368.44 331.25444   55-61476
MC#: 1955-12460
SuDocs no.: Y3.In8/7:Un2

897

U.S. *Commission on Intergovernmental Relations. Subcommittee on Natural Disaster Relief.*

A subcommittee report on natural disaster relief, submitted to the Commission on Intergovernmental Relations. [Washington, U.S. Govt. Print. Off.] 1955.

vii, 34 p. tables. 24 cm.

1. Disaster relief—U.S. I. Title: Natural disaster relief.
HV555.U6A32   55-61468
MC#: 1955-12461
SuDocs no.: Y3.In8/7:D63

KEYSERLING REPORT [Keyserling, Leon H.]

898

U.S. *Council of Economic Advisers. Committee on the New England Economy.*

The New England economy; a report to the President transmitting a study initiated by the Council of Economic Advisers. [Washington] 1951.

xxxvi, 205 p. maps. 24 cm.

1. New England—Econ. condit. I. Title.
HC107.A11A5 1951F   338.974   51-61007
MC#: 1951-13573
SuDocs no.: Pr33.9:N42

KILBURN REPORT [Kilburn, Clarence Evans]
see
RAMSPECK REPORT [Ramspeck, Robert]

Investigation of civilian employment. 78th Cong., 2d sess. H. Rept. 1600.

KILLIAN REPORTS [Killian, James R., Jr.]

899

National Academy of Sciences, *Washington, D.C. Committee on Utilization of Scientific and Engineering Manpower.*

Toward better utilization of scientific and engineering talent, a program for action; report. [Washington, 1964]

153 p. col. illus. 25 cm. (National Academy of Sciences. Publication no. 1191)

Includes bibliographies.

1. Scientists—U.S. 2. Engineers—U.S. I. Title. (Series: National Research Council. Publication 1191)
Q149.U5N35   506.9   64-60040
Not located in Monthly Catalog

900

U.S. *President's Science Advisory Committee.*

Strengthening American science; a report. [Washington, U.S. Govt. Print. Off., 1958]

36 p. 23 cm.

1. Science—U.S. 2. U.S. Federal Council for Science and Technology (Proposed) I. Title.
Q127.U6A55   509.73   59-60261
MC#: 1959-2106
SuDocs no.: Pr34.8:Sci2/2

KING REPORT

901

King, Gilbert William, 1914-

Automation and the Library of Congress. [A report] submitted by Gilbert W. King [and others] Washington, Library of Congress; [for sale by the Superintendent of Documents, U.S. Govt. Print. Off.] 1963 [i.e. 1964]

vii, 88 p. diagrs., tables. 27 cm.

Commonly known as the King report.

A survey sponsored by the Council on Library Resources and undertaken by a team of which Gilbert W. King was chairman.

"Appendix: A cost analysis of an automated system for the Library of Congress, prepared under the direction of the survey team by Herbert T. Spiro and Allan D. Kotin of the Planning Research Corporation, Los Angeles": p. 27-88.

1. Libraries—Automation. 2. United States. Library of Congress. I. Council on Library Resources. II. United States. Library of Congress. III. Spiro, Herbert T. IV. Kotin, Allan D. V. Title. VI. Title: King report on automation and the Library of Congress.
Z699.K45   64-60015
                                MARC

- - - - - Copy 3.
Z663.A9
MC#: 1964-5454
SuDocs no.: LC1.2:Au8

KING REPORT

902

King, James Wilson, 1818-1905.

. . . Report of Chief Engineer J. W. King, United States navy, on European ships of war and their armament, naval administration and economy, marine constructions and appliances, dockyards, etc., etc. Washington, Govt. print. off., 1877.

273 p. fold. plans, diagrs. (part fold.) 23 cm. ([U.S.] 44th Cong., 2d sess. Senate. Ex. doc. 27)

Issued also Portsmouth, Eng., 1878, with title: The war-ships of Europe.

1. War-ships. 2. Navies. I. U.S. Navy dept. II. U.S. 44th Cong., 2d sess., 1876-1877. Senate. III. Title.

VA40.K539   9-15856

- - - - - Copy 2.

Checklist of United States Public Documents, 1789-1909, page 57

44th Cong., 2d sess. S. Ex. doc. 27. In Serial no. 1719, vol. 2

KINLEY REPORT [Kinley, David]

see under

ALDRICH COMMISSION [Aldrich, Nelson Wilmarth]

KIRKLAND REPORT [Kirkland, Burt P.]

903

U.S. *Forest service.*

. . . A national plan for American forestry. Letter from the secretary of agriculture transmitting in response to S. Res. 175 (Seventy-second Congress) the report of the Forest service of the Agricultural department on the forest problem of the United States . . . Washington, U.S. Govt. print. off., 1933.

2 v. maps, tables, diagrs. 23½ cm. (73d Cong., 1st sess. Senate. Doc. 12)

Paged continuously.

Referred to the Committee on printing March 13 (calendar day, March 30), 1933.

Another issue of this report is published without document series note as "Separate, no. 1-

References interspersed.

1. Forests and forestry—U.S. I. Title.

SD11.A47 1933   634.90973   33-26292

MC#: May 1933-page 863

SuDocs no.: 73d Cong., 1st sess. S. Doc. 12

KIRKPATRICK REPORT

904

Kirkpatrick, Patti.

Background and goals of the Federal nonnuclear research and development effort : printed at the request of Henry M. Jackson, chairman, Committee on Interior and Insular Affairs, United States Senate / [prepared by Patti Kirkpatrick and Walter Downing].—Washington : U.S. Govt. Print. Off., 1976.

v, 77 p. : graphs ; 24 cm.

At head of title: 94th Congress, 2d session. Committee print.

1. Power resources—Research—Law and Legislation—United States. 2. Energy policy—United States. 3. Energy development—Law and legislation—United States. I. Downing, Walter, joint author. II. United States. Congress. Senate. Committee on Interior and Insular Affairs. III. Title.

KF4280.E53K57   343'.73'092   77-601269
                                         MARC

MC#: 1977-4065

SuDocs no.: Y4.In8/13:N73/2

KIRSCHNER REPORTS

905

Kirschner Associates.

A national survey of the impacts of Head Start centers on community institutions. Prepared for Project Head Start. [Washington, U.S. Dept. of Health, Education, and Welfare] 1970.

xiii, 260 p. illus., forms. 27 cm.

Prepared under contract no. B89-4638.

1. Social service—U.S. 2. Project Head Start. I. Project Head Start. II. Title.

HV91.K5   362.7'0973   70-608995
                                         MARC

MC#: 1970-16648

SuDocs no.: HE21.202:Im7

906

Kirschner Associates.

A national survey of the impacts of Head Start centers on community institutions, summary report. Prepared for Project Head Start. [Washington, U.S. Dept. of Health, Education, and Welfare] 1970.

iv, 19 p. illus. 27 cm.

Prepared under contract no. B89-4638.

MC#: 1970-16649

SuDocs no.: HE21.202:Im7/summ.

KLEINMAN PLAN [Kleinman, David T.]

907

United States. Congress. House. Committee on Foreign Affairs. Subcommittee on Inter-American Affairs.

Capital markets and economic development: the Kleinman Plan. Hearing, Ninety-second Congress, second session. July 25, 1972. Washington, U.S. Govt. Print. Off., 1972 [i.e. 1973]

iii, 128 p. 24 cm.

Bibliography: p. 127-128.

1. Capital—Latin America. 2. Investment banking—Latin America. I. Title.

KF27.F646 1972 1   338.91'8'073   73-600760
                                         MARC

MC#: 1973-21222

SuDocs no.: Y4.F76/1:C17

KNECHT REPORT [Knecht, Robert W.]

908

U.S. *Interdepartmental Committee for Atmospheric Science.*

Final report of the Panel on Space Environmental Forecasting to the Interdepartmental Committee for Atmospheric Sciences of the Federal Council of Science and Technology. December 1964.

Cover title: ICAS report.

Not located in Monthly Catalog.

KNEELAND REPORT [Kneeland, Hildegarde]

909

U.S. *National resources committee.*

Family expenditures in the United States. Statistical tables and appendixes. A National resources committee publication released by the National resources planning board. Washington, U.S. Govt. print. off., 1941.

xxii, 209 p. incl. illus. (map) tables, forms. 28 cm.

"The report itself was prepared by Hildegarde Kneeland, Selma E. Fine, and Janet H. Murray."-p. v.

Supplements two earlier reports: Consumer incomes, 1935-36 and Consumer expenditures, 1935-36 *c.f.* p. iii.

1. Cost and standard of living—U.S. I. Kneeland, Hildegarde, 1889- II. Fine, Selma Evelyn. III. Murray, Janet Helen. IV. U.S. National resources planning board. V. Title.

HD6983.A5 1941   331.8310973   41-51427

MC#: 1941-page 1520

SuDocs no.: Pr32.302:F21

KNEESE REPORT
910

Kneese, Allen V.
Water resources: development and use. [Kansas City, Mo.] Federal Reserve Bank of Kansas City [1959]

xi, 68 p. maps, diagrs. 23 cm.
Bibliographical footnotes.
1. Water resources development. 2. Water resources development—U.S. I. Federal Reserve Bank of Kansas City.
HD1691.K6   333.910973   60-60319
Not located in Monthly Catalog

KNIGHT REPORT
911

Knight (Lester B.) & Associates, Inc.
Report of survey of personnel problems of the U.S. Government in the adoption and use of automatic data processing systems. Prepared on behalf of the U.S. Bureau of the Budget, April 15, 1959.

(*In* U.S. Congress. House. Committee on Post Office and Civil Service. Subcommittee on Census and Government Statistics. Use of electronic data-processing equipment. Hearings . . . 86th Congress, 1st session. Washington, 1959. 24 cm. p. 70-142)
1. U.S. Bureau of the Budget.
MC#: 1959-9920
SuDocs no.: Y4.P84/10:E12

KOCH REPORTS [Koch, Richard]
see under
ALDRICH COMMISSION [Aldrich, Nelson Wilmarth]
Renewal of Reichsbank charter.

Koch. German imperial banking laws.

KOFFSKY REPORT [Koffsky, Nathan M.]
912

U.S. *Dept. of Agriculture. Special Study Group on Sugar.*
Special study on sugar, a report. Printed for the use of the Committee on Agriculture. Washington, U.S. Govt. Print. Off., 1961.

iv, 89 p. diagrs., tables. 24 cm.
At head of title: 87th Cong., 1st sess. Committee print.
Bibliographical footnotes.
1. Sugar trade—U.S. 2. Sugar trade. 1. U.S. Congress. House. Committee on Agriculture.
HD9105.A5 1961   338.47664123   61-60897
MC#: 1961-5730
SuDocs no.: Y4.Ag8/1:Su3/18

KORB REPORT [Korb, L. David]
913

U.S. *Civil Service Commission. Program Planning Division.*
Reduction in force in the Federal service, a historical review. [Prepared by L. David Korb. Washington] 1957.

23 p. 27 cm.
1. U.S.—Officials and employees—Appointment, qualifications, tenure, etc. I. Title.
JK765.A515   *351.5 351.1   58-61731
Not located in Monthly Catalog

KOTIN REPORT [Kotin, Allan D.]
see
KING REPORT [King, Gilbert William]

KRASSA REPORTS
914

Krassa, Lucie G.
Governmental agencies concerned with land use, planning, or conservation in the Washington metropolitan area. Staff study for the Joint Committee on Washington Metropolitan Problems, United States Senate. Washington, U.S. Govt. Print. Off., 1958.

iii, 14 p. 23 cm.
At head of title: Committee print, 85th Cong., 2d sess. Senate.
1. Regional planning—Washington metropolitan area. I. U.S. Congress. Joint Committee on Washington Metropolitan Problems. II. Title.
NA9127.W1K7   58-61234
MC#: 1958-16889
SuDocs no.: Y4.W27/2:G74

915

Krassa, Lucie G.
Government agencies concerned with land use, planning, or conservation in the Washington metropolitan area; agencies of the State of Maryland. Staff study [for the] Joint Committee on Washington Metropolitan Problems, Congress of the United States. Washington, U.S. Govt. Print. Off., 1958.

iii, 30 p. diagrs., tables. 24 cm.
At head of title: 85th Cong., 2d sess. Joint committee print.
Bibliographical footnotes.
1. Regional planning—Washington metropolitan area. I. U.S. Congress. Joint Committee on Washington Metropolitan Problems. II. Title.
NA9127.W2K67   711.409753   58-62298
MC#: 1958-16888
SuDocs no.: Y4.W27/2:G74/2

916

Krassa, Lucie G.
Government agencies concerned with land use, planning, or conservation in the Washington metropolitan area: agencies of the State of Virginia. Staff study: Joint Committee on Washington Metropolitan Problems, Congress of the United States. Washington, U.S. Govt. Print. Off., 1959.

iii, 22 p. 24 cm.
At head of title: 85th Cong., 2d sess. Joint committee print.
1. Regional planning—Washington metropolitan area. I. U.S. Congress. Joint Committee on Washington Metropolitan Problems. II. Title.
NA9127.W2K68   711.409753   59-60305
MC#: 1959-3399
SuDocs no.: Y4.W27/2:G74/4

KREPS REPORT [Kreps, Juanita]
917

United States. Dept. of Commerce. Interagency Study Group.
Economic study of Puerto Rico : report to the President / prepared by the Interagency Task Force coordinated by the United States Department of Commerce. — Washington] : The Dept. : for sale by the Supt. of Docs., U.S. Govt. Print. Off., 1979.

2 v. : ill. ; 27 cm.
Includes bibliographical references.
1. Puerto Rico—Economic conditions—1952-. I. Title.
HC154.5.U54 1979   330.97295′053-dc19   80-601545
MARC
MC#: 1980-6982
SuDocs no.: C1.2:Ec7/11/v. 1-2

KREPS REPORT [Kreps, Theodore John]
   see under
   O'MAHONEY REPORTS [O'Mahoney, Joseph Christopher]

KRISTOF REPORT [Kristof, Frank S.]
   see
   DOUGLAS REPORTS [Douglas, Paul H.]
   National Commission on Urban Problems.

   Research report, no. 10.

KROEGER REPORT

918

Kroeger (Louis J.) and Associates.
   Personnel for the mutual security program. Washington, U.S. Govt. Print. Off., 1957.

   ix, 68 p. tables. 24 cm. (U.S. [Congress] Senate. Special Committee to Study the Foreign Aid Program. Study no. 2)
   At head of title: 85th Cong., 1st sess. Committee print.
   1. Mutual security program, 1951- I. Title. (Series)
   HC60.U48424 no. 2   57-61535
   MC#: 1957-7110
   SuDocs no.: Y4.F76/6:St9/no.2

KRUG REPORTS [Krug, Julius Albert]

919

U.S. *Dept. of the Interior.*
   National resources and foreign aid, report, October 9, 1947. [Washington, U.S. Govt. Print. Off., 1947]

   viii, 97 p. 30 cm.
   1. Natural resources—U.S. 2. U.S.—Economic policy. I. Title.
   HC106.5.A5 1947k   330.973   47-46561*
   MC#: 1948-1179
   SuDocs no.: I1.2:R31

920

U.S. *Dept. of the Interior.*
   The Navajo; report [on] a long-range program for Navajo rehabilitation. [Washington] Bureau of Indian Affairs, Navajo Agency, 1948.

   xi, 50 p. illus., map. 29 cm.
   1. Navajo Indians—Government relations. I. U.S. Office of Indian Affairs.
   E99.N3U52   970.5   48-46086*
   MC#: 1948-11118
   SuDocs no.: I20.2:N22/3

921

U.S. *War Production Board.*
   Production, wartime achievements and the reconversion outlook, a report to the War Production Board, by J. A. Krug. [Washington] 1945.

   113 p. 27 cm.
   Cover title.
   "WPB document no. 334."
   Issued also under title: Wartime production achievements and the reconversion outlook.
   1. U.S.—Indus. 2. World War, 1939-1945—Economic aspects—U.S. 3. Priorities, Industrial—U.S. I. Krug, Julius Albert, 1907-
   HC106.4.A287 1945c   355.26   45-37810*
   MC#: 1945-page 1330
   SuDocs no.: Pr32.4802:P94/13

922

U.S. *War production board.*
   Wartime production achievements and the reconversion outlook. Report of the chairman, War production board, October 9, 1945. [Washington, U.S. Govt. print. off., 1945]

   vi, 110 p. incl. tables, diagrs. 30 x 23 cm.
   Presented at its hundredth and final meeting. c.f. p. iii.
   1. U.S.—Indus. 2. Priorities. Industrial—U.S. 3. World war, 1939-1945—Economic aspects—U.S. I. Title.
   HC106.4.A287 1945b   355.26   46-25545
   Not located in Monthly Catalog

KUTCHIN REPORT [Kutchin, Howard M.]
   see
   BOWER REPORT [Bower, Ward T.]

KYLE REPORT [Kyle, James Henderson]

923

U.S. *Industrial commission.*
   Reports of the Industrial commission . . . Washington, Govt. print. off., 1900-02.

   19 v. maps, facsims., tab., diagrs. 23½ cm.
   Dates of publication: Vols. I-V, 1900; vols. VI-XVIII, 1901; vol. XIX, 1902.
   Chairman, James H. Kyle, succeeded by Albert Clarke.
   Contents—I. Preliminary report on trusts and industrial combinations, together with testimony, review of evidence, charts showing effect on prices, and topical digest. HLT 338
   II. Trusts and industrial combinations. Statutes and decisions of federal, state, and territorial law [prepared by J. W. Jenks] together with a digest of corporation laws. [Prepared by F. J. Stimson] HLT 338
   III. Report on prison labor. HFP 331
   IV. Report on transportation, including review of evidence, topical digest of evidence and testimony so far as taken May 1, 1900. HJR 380
   V. Report on labor legislation, including recommendations . . . and digests of the laws of the states and territories relating to labor generally, to convict labor, and to mine labor. HF 331
   VI. Report on the distribution of farm products. [Prepared by J. F. Crowell] HE 338
   VII. Report on the relations and conditions of capital and labor employed in manufactures and general business, including testimony so far as taken Nov. 1, 1900, and digest of testimony. HF 338
   VIII. Report on the Chicago labor disputes of 1900 with especial reference to the disputes in the building and machinery trades. HGS 331
   IX. Report on transportation (second volume on this subject) including testimony taken since May 1, 1900, review and topical digest of evidence, and special reports on railway legislation [by B. H. Meyer] and taxation [by R. C. McCrea] HJR 380
   X. Report on agriculture and agricultural labor, including testimony, with review and topical digest thereof. HE 338
   XI. Report on agriculture and on taxation in various states (second volume on agriculture) including special reports and summaries relating to fictitious sales of farm products, the tobacco trade, American farm labor, laws regarding agricultural boards, warehouse and elevator laws, adulteration of food products, and taxation systems. HE 336
   XII. Report on the relations and conditions of capital and labor employed in the mining industry, including testimony, review of evidence, and topical digest. HE 331
   XIII. Report on trusts and industrial combinations (second volume on this subject) including testimony taken since March 1, 1900, together with review and digest thereof, and special

reports on prices and on the stocks of industrial corporations. HLT 338

XIV. Report on the relations and conditions of capital and labor employed in manufactures and general business (second volume on this subject) including testimony taken after November 1, 1900, with review and digest thereof, and a special report on domestic service [by Gail Laughlin] HF 338

XV. Report on immigration, including testimony, with review and digest, and special reports. And on education, including testimony, with review and digest. JS 325

XVI. Report on the condition of foreign legislation upon matters affecting general labor. [Prepared by F. J. Stimson] HF 331

XVII. Reports on labor organizations, labor disputes, and arbitration [by C. E. Edgerton and E. D. Durand] and on railway labor [by S. M. Lindsay] HGS 331

XVIII. Final report on industrial combinations in Europe. HLT 338

XIX. Final report on the Industrial commission, prepared in accordance with an act of Congress approved June 18, 1898. HE 380

1. U.S.—Econ. condit. 2. Labor and laboring classes—U.S. 3. U.S.—Indus. I. Kyle, James Henderson, 1854-1901. II. Clarke, Albert, 1840-
HC101.A3   2-30276
Vol. 1 (Document edition)
MC#: 1900-page 188
56th Cong., 1st sess. H. Doc. 476, pt. 1. In Serial no. 3990, vol. 93
Vol. 1 (Department edition)
MC#: 1900-page 439
Vol. 2 (Document edition)
MC#: 1900-page 188
56th Cong., 1st sess. H. Doc. 476, pt. 2. In Serial no. 3991, vol. 94
Vol. 2 (Department edition)
MC#: 1900-page 439
Vol. 3 (Document edition)
MC#: 1900-page 259
56th Cong., 1st sess. H. Doc. 476, pt. 3. In Serial no. 3991, vol. 94
Vol. 3 (Department edition)
MC#: 1900-page 259
Vol.. 4 (Document edition)
MC#: 1900-page 410
56th Cong., 1st sess. H. Doc. 476, pt. 4. In Serial no. 3992, vol. 95
Vol. 5 (Document edition)
MC#: 1900-page 410
56th Cong., 1st sess. H. Doc. 476, pt. 5. In Serial no. 3992, vol. 95
Vol. 5 (Department edition)
MC#: 1901-page 261
Vol. 6 (Document edition)
MC#: 1901-page 179
56th Cong., 2d sess. H. Doc. 494. In Serial no. 4168, vol. 94
Vol. 7 (Document edition)
MC#: 1901-page 261
56th Cong., 2d sess. H. Doc. 495. In Serial no. 4169, vol. 95
Vol. 7 (Department edition)
MC#: 1901-page 227
Vol. 8 (Document edition)
MC#: 1902-page 62
57th Cong., 1st sess. H. Doc. 177. In Serial no. 4338, vol. 71
Vol. 8 (Department edition)
MC#: 1901-page 332
Vol. 9 (Document edition)
MC#: 1902-page 63
57th Cong., 1st sess. H. Doc. 178. In Serial no. 4339, vol. 72
Vol. 10 (Document edition)
MC#: 1902-page 62
57th Cong., 1st sess. H. Doc. 179. In Serial no. 4340, vol. 73
Vol. 10 (Department edition)
MC#: 1902-page 529
Vol. 11 (Document edition)

MC#: 1902-page 62
57th Cong., 1st sess. H. Doc. 180. In Serial no. 4341, vol. 74
Vol. 12 (Document edition)
MC#: 1902-page 63
57th Cong., 1st sess. H. Doc. 181. In Serial no. 4342, vol. 75
Vol. 12 (Department edition)
MC#: 1901-page 457
Vol. 13 (Document edition)
MC#: 1902-page 63
57th Cong., 1st sess. H. Doc. 182. In Serial no. 4343, vol. 76
Vol. 14 (Document edition)
MC#: 1902-page 134
57th Cong., 1st sess. H. Doc. 183. In Serial no. 4344, vol. 77
Vol. 15 (Document edition)
MC#: 1902-page 134
57th Cong., 1st sess. H. Doc. 184. In Serial no. 4345, vol. 78
Vol. 16 (Document edition)
MC#: 1902-page 63
57th Cong., 1st sess. H. Doc. 185. In Serial no. 4346, vol. 79
Vol. 16 (Department edition)
MC#: 1901-page 457
Vol. 17 (Document edition)
MC#: 1902-page 134
57th Cong., 1st sess. H. Doc. 186. In Serial no. 4347, vol. 80
Vol. 18 (Document edition)
MC#: 1902-page 63
57th Cong., 1st sess. H. Doc. 187. In Serial no. 4348, vol. 81
Vol. 19 (Document edition)
MC#: 1902-page 133
57th Cong., 1st sess. H. Doc. 380. In Serial no. 4349, vol. 82

LaFOLLETTE REPORTS [LaFollette, Robert Marion]

924

U.S. *Congress. Senate. Committee on education and labor.*
. . . Violations of free speech and rights of labor . . . Preliminary report, [Report[s] and Interim report] "Pursuant to S. Res. 266, 74th Cong." . . . [Washington, U.S. Govt. print. off., 1937-38]

4 v. plates, plan, tables, diagr. 23 cm. ([U.S.] 75th Cong., 1st[—3d] sess. Senate. Rept. 46)

"Preliminary report" and "Interim report" have caption title.

Submitted by Mr. LaFollette from the Committee on education and labor.

Reports have subtitles: The Chicago memorial day incident and Industrial espionage.

"Additional statement made by Senator Elbert D. Thomas": pt. 2, p. 41.

1. Liberty of speech. 2. Industrial relations—U.S. I. LaFollette, Robert Marion, 1895- I. Thomas, Elbert Duncan, 1883- III. Title.
HD6501.A57   331.880973   37-26218
MC#: 1937-page 163
SuDocs no.: 75th Cong., 1st sess. S. Rept. 46
MC#: 1937- page 894
SuDocs no.: 75th Cong., 1st sess. S. Rept. 46, pt. 2
MC#: 1937-page 1464
SuDocs no.: 75th Cong., 2d sess. S. Rept. 46, pt. 3
MC#: 1938-page 480
SuDocs no.: 75th Cong., 3d sess. S. Rept. 46, pt. 4

925

U.S. *Congress. Senate. Committee on education and labor.*
. . . Violations of free speech and rights of labor. Report of the Committee on education and labor pursuant to S. Res. 266 (74th Congress) a resolution to investigate violations of the right

of free speech and assembly and interference with the right of labor to organize and bargain collectively . . . Washington, U.S. Govt. print. off., 1939-41.

　7 v. illus. (maps) plates, tables, forms, diagrs. (1 fold.) 23 cm.
　Parts 1-6 issued as Senate rept. 6, 76th Cong., 1st sess.: pt. 7 as Senate rept. 151, 77th Cong., 1st sess.
　Submitted by Mr. LaFollette from the committee on education and labor.
　Contents. — [pt. 1] Strikebreaking services. pt. 2. Private policy systems. Harlan county, Ky. Republic steel corporation. — pt. 3. Industrial munitions. — pt. 4-[7] Labor policies of employers' associations. I. The National metal trades association. II. The Associated industries of Cleveland. III. The National association of manufacturers. IV. The "Little steel" strike and citizens' committees. 4 v.
　1. Industrial relations — U.S. 2. Strikes and lockouts — U.S. 3. Police, Private — U.S. 4. Employers' associations — U.S. 5. Civil rights — U.S. 6. Steel strike, 1937. I. LaFollette, Robert Marion, 1895- II. Title.
HD6501.A572　　　　　　331.892973　　　　　　40-26141
MC#: 1939-page 42 (LC card 37-26218 listed in error)
SuDocs no.: 76th Cong., 1st sess. S. Rept. 6
MC#: 1939-page 181 (LC card 37-26218 listed in error)
SuDocs no.: 76th Cong., 1st sess. S. Rept. 6, pt. 2
MC#: 1939-page 490 (LC card 37-26218 listed in error)
SuDocs no.: 76th Cong., 1st sess. S. Rept. 6, pts. 3, 4
MC#: 1939-page 1164 (LC card 37-26218 listed in error)
SuDocs no.: 76th Cong., 1st sess. S. Rept. 6, pts. 5, 6
MC#: 1941-page 482
SuDocs no.: 77th Cong., 1st sess. S. Rept. 151

926

U.S. *Congress. Senate. Committee on manufactures.*
　Conditions in coal fields in Harlan and Bell counties, Kentucky. Hearings before a subcommittee of the Committee on manufactures, United States Senate, Seventy-second Congress, first session, on S. Res. 178, a resolution for an investigation of conditions in the coal fields of Harlan and Bell counties, Kentucky. May 11, 12, 13, and 19, 1932. Printed for the use of the Committee on manufactures. Washington, U.S. Govt. print. off., 1932.

　iii, 286 p. incl. tables, form. 23½ cm.
　Running title: Conditions in Kentucky coal fields.
　Bronson Cutting, chairman of subcommittee.
　1. Coal mines and mining — Kentucky — Harlan co. 2. Coal mines and mining — Kentucky — Bell co. 3. Coal — miners — Kentucky. I. Title. II. Title: Conditions in Kentucky coal fields.
HD9547.K4A4 1932　　　　331.182233　　　　32-33178
- - - - - Copy 2.
MC#: July 1932-page 39
SuDocs no.: Y4.M31/2:K41

LAMBERT REPORT [Lambert, Robert W.]
927

U.S. *Arms Control and Disarmament Agency.*
　Documents on disarmament. 1945-59 — [Washington, For sale by the Superintendent of Documents, U.S. Govt. Print. Off.]
　v. in 24 cm. annual.
　Vols. for 1945-59-1960 issued as U.S. Dept. of State. Publication; for 1961- as U.S. Arms Control and Disarmament Agency. Publication . . . (JX1974.A1U52)
　Vols. for 1945-59-1960 issued by the Dept. of State, Historical Office.
　1. Disarmament. I. Title. (Series: U.S. Arms Control and Disarmament Agency. Publication)
JX1974.A1U542　　　　　　　　　　　　　60-64408 rev 2
MC#: 1960-18111 (1945-56 and 1957-59)
SuDocs no.: S1.2:D63/2/v.1, 2

MC#: 1961-15975 (1960)
SuDocs no.: S1.117:960
MC#: 1962-18677 (1961)
　　1963-20320 (1962)
　　1964-19200 (1963)
　　1966-109 (1964)
　　1967-1748, 15925, (1965, 1966)
　　1968-11820 (1967)
　　1969-16580 (1968)
　　1970-17459 (1969)
　　1972-4877 (1970)
　　1973-24165 (1971)
SuDocs no.: AC1.11/2:960-971

LAMPMAN REPORT
928

Lampman, Robert J.
　The low income population and economic growth, by Robert J. Lampman. The adequacy of resources for economic growth in the United States, by Joseph L. Fisher and Edward Boorstein. Materials prepared in connection with the study of employment, growth, and price levels for consideration by the Joint Economic Committee, Congress of the United States. Study papers nos. 12 and 13. Washington, U.S. Govt. Print. Off., 1959.

　viii, 71 p. diagr., tables. 24 cm.
　At head of title: 86th Cong., 1st sess. Joint Committee print.
　1. Income — U.S. 2. Natural resources — U.S. I. Fisher, Joseph L. The adequacy of resources for economic growth in the United States. II. U.S. Congress. Joint Economic Committee. III. Title. IV. Title: The adequacy of resources for economic growth in the United States.
HC110.I5L3　　　　　　　339.42　　　　　　60-60455
MC#: 1960-1594
SuDocs no.: Y4.Ec7:Em7/4/no. 12, 13

LANDIS REPORTS
929

Landis, James McCauley, 1899-
　Capital Transit. Report on the Capital Transit Co. Prepared at the request of John F. Kennedy, chairman of the Public Utilities, Insurance, and Banking Subcommittee of the Committee on the District of Columbia. Washington, U.S. Govt. Print. Off., 1952.

　xi, 26 p. 24 cm.
　At head of title: Committee print. 82d Cong., 2d sess. House report no. —
　1. Capital Transit Company, Washington, D.C. I. U.S. Congress. House. Committee on the District of Columbia.
HE4491.W4C42 1952 1　　　　338.4　　　　　53-60104
MC#: 1953-2229
SuDocs no.: Y4.D63/1:C17/2

930

Landis, James McCauley, 1899-
　Report on regulatory agencies to the President-elect, submitted by the chairman of the Subcommittee on Administrative Practice and Procedure to the Committee on the Judiciary of the United States Senate. Washington, U.S. Govt. Print. Off., 1960.
　v, 87 p. 24 cm.
　At head of title: 86th Cong., 2d sess. Committee print.
　1. Independent regulatory commissions — U.S. I. Kennedy, John Fitzgerald, 1917-1963. II. U.S. Congress. Senate. Committee on the Judiciary.
JK901.L3　　　　　　　353.09　　　　　　61-60258
MC#: 1961-7296
SuDocs no.: Y4.J89/2:R26

LANDMANN REPORT [Landmann, Julius]
see under
ALDRICH COMMISSION [Aldrich, Nelson Wilmarth]

LANSING PAPERS [Lansing, Robert]

931

U.S. *Dept. of State.*
    The Lansing papers, 1914-1920. Washington, U.S. Govt. Print. Off., 1939.
    2 v. 24 cm. (*Its* Papers relating to the foreign relations of the United States)
    [U.S.] Dept. of State. Publication 1420-1421.
    "The documents . . . constitute an extensive selection from the large body of correspondence of Robert Lansing, former Secretary of State, which was secured from the files of the Department of state following Mr. Lansing's death . . . A certain number of closely related documents from other official sources . . . have been included. The papers here published represent, therefore, an additional selection of documents from the period 1914 through 1920 bearing on subjects which have already been presented in the volumes of Foreign relations hitherto published dealing with that period."
    1. U.S.—For. rel.—1913-1921. 2. European War, 1914-1918—U.S. I. Lansing, Robert, 1864-1928. II. Title. (Series: U.S. Dept. of State. Foreign relations of the United States: diplomatic papers. Series: U.S. Dept. of State. Publication, no. 1420)
E766.U43   327.73   40-26340 rev*
- - - - - Copy 2.
D570.A2A692
MC#: 1940-page 427
SuDocs no.: S1.1/c:1, 2
Also issued as: 74th Cong., 2d sess. H. Doc. 502, pts 1, 2

LaQUE REPORT [LaQue, Francis L.]

932

U.S. *Panel on Engineering and Commodity Standards.*
    Report of the Panel on Engineering and Commodity Standards of the Commerce Technical Advisory Board to the Assistant Secretary for Science and Technology, February 2, 1965. Washington, D.C. 1965.
    2 parts
    Reproduced from typescript.
    Microfiche. Springfield, Va., Clearinghouse for Federal Scientific and Technical Information, 1965 (PB 166811-166812)
    Not located in Monthly Catalog

LATIMER REPORT [Latimer, Murray W.]

933

U.S. *Office of temporary controls.*
    Guaranteed wages. Report to the President by the Advisory board, Office of war mobilization and reconversion, Office of temporary controls. Murray W. Latimer, research director. January 31, 1947. Washington, U.S. Govt. print. off., 1947.
    xx, 473 p. incl. tables, diagrs. 26 cm.
    1. Wages—Annual wage. I. Title.
HD4928.A5U5 1947   331.23   47-32226
MC#: 1947-page 737
SuDocs no.: Pr33.302:W12

See also HANSEN-SAMUELSON REPORT [Hansen, Alvin H. and Samuelson, Paul A.]

LAUCK REPORT [Lauck, William Jett]
see under
DILLINGHAM COMMISSION [Dillingham, William Paul]
    Immigrants in industries.

LAY REPORT [Lay, James S.]

934

U.S. *National Security Council.*
    Organizational history of the National Security Council; study submitted to the Committee on Government Operations, United States Senate, by its Subcommittee on National Policy Machinery, pursuant to S. Res. 248, 86th Cong. Washington, U.S. Govt. Print. Off., 1960.
    v, 52 p. 24 cm.
    At head of title: 86th Cong., 2d sess. Committee print.
    I. U.S. Congress. Senate. Committee on Government Operations. II. Title.
UA23.A425   355.06173   60-62343
MC#: 1960-16944
SuDocs no.: Y4.G74/6:N21se/3

LAZARUS REPORT [Lazarus, Arthur]

935

U.S. *Congress. Joint Committee on Washington Metropolitan Problems.*
    Metropolitan transportation. Staff report prepared [by Arthur Lazarus, consultant] on investigation of status and prospects for the mass transportation survey. Washington, U.S. Govt. Print. Off., 1958.
    iii, 34 p. 24 cm.
    At head of title: 85th Congress, 2d sess. Committee print.
    1. Washington, D.C.—Transit systems. I. Title.
HE4491.W32 1958   388.4   58-61235
MC#: 1958-16890
SuDocs no.: Y4.W27/2:T68/2

LEA REPORT [Lea, Clarence Frederick]

936

U.S. *Congress. House. Select committee to investigate the Federal communications commission.*
    . . . Investigation of the Federal communications commission. Final report of the Select committee to investigate the Federal communications commission, House of representatives, pursuant to H. Res. 21 (78th Congress) . . . [Corrected print] Washington, U.S. Govt. print. off., 1945.
    1 p. l., 79 p. 23½ cm. ([U.S.] 78th Cong., 2d sess. House. Rept. 2095)
    Submitted by Mr. Lea.
    "Additional views by Hon. Louis E. Miller of Missouri": p. 54-57.
    "Additional minority views of Hon. Richard B. Wigglesworth, of Massachusetts": p. 58-79.
    1. U.S. Federal communications commission. 2. Radio—U.S. 3. Radio broadcasting. I. Lea, Clarence Frederick, 1874- II. Miller, Louis E., 1899- III. Wigglesworth, Richard Bowditch, 1891-
HE8677.A46 1945   384.06173   45-35369
MC#: 1945-page 162
SuDocs no.: 78th Cong., 2d sess. H. Rept. 2095

LEAVITT REPORT [Leavitt, Julian]
see
WICKERSHAM COMMISSION [Wickersham, George Woodward]
    Report on prosecution, no. 4

LEE REPORT [Lee, Philip R.]

937

United States. Task Force on Prescription Drugs.
Final report. Washington, Office of the Secretary, U.S. Dept. of Health, Education and Welfare; [for sale by the Supt. of Docs., U.S. Govt. Print. Off.] 1969.

xxii, 86 p. 26 cm.
Commonly known as the Lee report.
Updates material initially presented in interim reports.
Bibliographical footnotes.
1. Insurance, Pharmaceutical services – United States. 2. Drug trade – United States. I. Title: Lee report on prescription drugs.
HD7103.5.U5A52   368.4′26   72-600933
                                                                          MARC
MC#: 1969-5734
SuDocs no.: FS1.32:R29/969

LEHMAN REPORT [Lehman, John W.]

938

U.S. *Congress. Joint Economic Committee.*
The sustaining economic forces ahead; materials prepared for the Joint Committee on the Economic Report by the committee staff. Washington, U.S. Govt. Print. Off., 1952.

viii, 70 p. diagrs., tables. 24 cm.
At head of title: 82d Cong., 2d sess. Joint committee print.
1. U.S. – Econ. condit. – 1945- I. Title.
HC106.5.A53 1952   330.973   52-63221 rev
MC#: 1953-812
SuDocs no.: Y4.Ec7:Ec7/4

LELAND REPORT [Leland, Simeon Elbridge]

939

U.S. *National resources committee.*
Division of costs and responsibility for public works. A report to the National resources committee . . . Washington, U.S. Govt. print. off., 1938.

iv, 193 p. tables (1 fold.) 23 cm.
"Reprinted from Public works planning, published December 1, 1936, by the National resources committee."
Contents. – section 1. Principles and policies, by S. E. Leland. – section 2. Federal public works and grants in aid, by H. L. Case, H. W. Metz, and C. M. Wiltse. – section 3. Bases and methods of cost allocation, by H. W. Metz and C. M. Wiltse. – Appendix. British grants in aid, by C. M. Wiltse.
1. U.S. Public works. 2. U.S.-Econ. condit. – 1918- 3. U.S. Economic policy. I. Leland, Simeon Elbridge, 1897- II. Case, Harry Lawrence, 1907- III. Metz, Harold W. IV. Wiltse, Charles Maurice, 1907- V. Title.
HD3881.A5 1938   351.80973   38-26640
- - - - - Copy 2.
MC#: 1938-page 707
SuDocs no.: Y3.N21/12:2/a/P96

LEMBKEY REPORT [Lembkey, Walter I.]
see
EVERMANN REPORT [Evermann, Barton Warren]

LEONARD REPORT [Leonard, Donald E.]

940

United States. National Commission on the Financing of Postsecondary Education.
Financing postsecondary education in the United States. [Washington?]; For sale by the Supt. of Docs., U.S. Govt. Print. Off., Washington, 1973 [i.e., 1974]

xxxi, 442 p. illus. 27 cm.
Includes bibliographical references.
1. Universities and colleges – United States-Finance. I. Title.
LB2342.U42 1974   379′.124′0973   74-600908
                                                                          MARC
MC#: 1974-05656
SuDocs no.: Y3.Ed8/5:1/973

LERMAN REPORT [Lerman, Robert I.]
Incentive effects in public income transfer programs.
see under
GRIFFITHS REPORTS [Griffiths, Martha W.]
Studies in public welfare, paper no. 4.

LESTER REPORT [Lester, Richard A.]

941

U.S. *President's Commission on the Status of Women. Committee on Private Employment.*
Report of the Committee on Private Employment to the President's Commission on the Status of Women. Washington, For sale by the Superintendent of Documents, U.S. Govt. Print. Off., 1963 [i.e. 1964]

v. 55 p. tables. 26 cm.
Bibliography: p. 39-40.
1. Woman – Employment – U.S.
HD6093.A548   64-60464
MC#: 1964-5639
SuDocs no.: Pr35.8:W84/Em/7/2

LEVIN REPORT [Levin, Max]
see
McMINN REPORT [McMinn, John H.]

LEVIN REPORT [Levin, Melvin R.]
see
DOUGLAS REPORTS [Douglas, Paul H.]
National Commission on Urban Problems.

Research report, no. 17

LEVIN REPORTS

942

Levin, Gilbert V.
Sewage disposal and water pollution. Staff report prepared for the Joint Committee on Washington Metropolitan Problems on sewage disposal and water pollution in the Washington metropolitan area. Washington, U.S. Govt. Print. Off., 1958.

iii, 26 p. maps, diagrs., tables. 24 cm.
At head of title: 85th Cong., 2d sess. Committee print.
Bibliography: p. 25-26.
1. Sewage disposal – Washington, D.C. 2. Water – Pollution – Washington, D.C. I. U.S. Congress. Joint Committee on Washington Metropolitan Problems.
TD741.L66   628.3   58-61237
MC#: 1958-16892
SuDocs no.: Y4.W27/2:Se3

943

Levin, Gilbert V.
Water supply. Staff report prepared for the Joint Committee on Washington Metropolitan Problems on water supply in the Washington metropolitan area. Washington, U.S. Govt. Print. Off., 1958.

27 p. maps, tables. 24 cm.
At head of title: 85th Cong., 2d sess. Committee print.
Errata sheet inserted.

Bibliography: p. 26-27.
1. Water-supply—Washington, D.C. I. U.S. Congress. Joint Committee on Washington Metropolitan Problems.
TD225.W3L4　　　　　　　628.1　　　　　　58-61236
MC#: 1958-16893
SuDocs no.: Y4.W27/2:W29/2

944

Levin, Gilbert V.
Water supply and sewage disposal. Staff report prepared for the Joint Committee on Washington Metropolitan Problems on water supply and sewage disposal in the Washington metropolitan area. Washington, U.S. Govt. Print. Off., 1958.
viii, 56 p. illus., map. 24 cm.
At head of title: 85th Cong., 2d sess. Committee print.
1. Water-supply—Washington metropolitan area. 2. Sewerage—Washington metropolitan area. 3. Water-Pollution—Potomac River. I. U.S. Congress. Joint Committee on Washington Metropolitan Problems.
TD225.W3L42　　　　　　628.1　　　　　　58-62475
MC#: 1959-343
SuDocs no.: Y4.W27/2:W29/4

LEVITAN REPORT [Levitan, Sar A.]

945

U.S. *Library of Congress. Legislative Reference Service.*
Government regulation of internal union affairs affecting the rights of members; a report by Sar A. Levitan, Legislative Reference Service, Library of Congress. Printed for the use of the Committee on Education and Labor. Washington, U.S. Govt. Print. Off., 1958.
iii, 52 p. 24 cm.
At head of title: 85th Cong., 2d sess. Committee print.
Bibliographical footnotes.
1. Trade-unions—U.S. I. Levitan, Sar A. II. U.S. Congress. House. Committee on Education and Labor. III. Title.
HD6508.A277　　　　　　　　　　　　　58-61864
MC#: 1958-14569
SuDocs no.: Y4.Ed8/1:Un3/3

LEWIS REPORT

946

Lewis, Alvin Fayette, 1861-
History of higher education in Kentucky. Washington, Govt. Print. Off., 1899.
350 p. plates. 23 cm. (Contributions to American educational history, no. 25)
U.S. Bureau of education. Circular of information no. 3, 1899.
Thesis—Johns Hopkins Univ.
With bibliographies.
1. Education—Kentucky—Hist. 2. Universities and colleges—Kentucky. (Series: U.S. Office of Education. Contributions to American educational history, no. 25. Series: U.S. Office of Education. Circulars of information, 1899, no. 3)
L111.A5 1899, no. 3　　　　　　　　6-16482*
- - - - - Copy 2.
LA292.L67
MC#: 1900-page 249

LEWIS REPORT [Lewis, Burdette Gibson]

947

U.S. *Congress. Senate. Committee on appropriations.*
. . . Report of investigation of public relief in the District of Columbia . . . by Burdette G. Lewis, director. Submitted through the Advisory committee for the investigation, Ringgold Hart,

chairman, Willaim L. Beale, Robert E. Moran, M.D. Washington, D.C., 1938.
12 v. facsims., tables (part fold.) diagrs. (1 fold.) forms. 23½ cm.
At head of title: United States of America. 75th Congress. Subcommittees of the committees on appropriations of the Senate and the House of representatives. Honorable Elmer Thomas, chairman of the Senate subcommittee. Honorable Ross A. Collins, chairman of the House subcommittee.
Contents.—pt. 1-2. v. 1. The report in brief. The report in detail.—pt. 3. v. 1. The report at length. v. 2. The case for a consolidated intake for all agencies handling adults. v. 3. Special studies of acute relief problems. v. 4. Appraisal of personnel of public agencies. v. 5. Method of handling fraud cases in the Public assistance division, by J. T. McCoy. v. 6. Unemployment relief in the District of Columbia by construction operations.—pt. 4. v. 1-2. Supplementary data, statistical tables, charts, and other memoranda. v. 3. Relief activities in the District of Columbia. v. 4. A study of the administration of surplus commodities in the District of Columbia. v. 5. Analysis of complaints and information received.
1. Unemployed—Washington, D.C. 2. Washington, D.C.—Charities. 3. Washington, D.C.—Public works. 4. Washington, D.C.—Soc. condit. 5. Social service. I. Lewis, Burdette Gibson, 1882- II. McCoy, Jay T. III. U.S. Congress. House. Committee on appropriations. IV. Title: Investigation of public relief in the District of Columbia, Report of.
HV86.D8 1938　　　　　361.609753　　　　　39-26363
Not located in Monthly Catalog

LEWIS REPORTS

948

Lewis, F. J. and K. E. Willis.
Defense implications of the national power survey; an interim report. Prepared for the Federal Power Commission, September 17, 1963.
(*In* U.S. Federal Power Commission. National power survey; a report. Washington, 1964. Part II, p. 405-423)
SuDocs no.: FP1.2:P87/pt. 2

949

U.S. *Federal Power Commission.*
National power survey; a report. Washington, U.S. Govt. Print. Off., 1964.
2 v. illus., maps. 26 cm.
Includes bibliographies.
1. Electric utilities—U.S. 2. Power resources—U.S. I. Title.
HD9685.U5A545　　　　　　　　　　　65-60253
MC#: 1965-579-580
SuDocs no.: FP1.2:P87/pts. 1, 2

LEXIS REPORT [Lexis, Wilhelm Hector Richard Albrecht]
　　　see under
ALDRICH COMMISSION [Aldrich, Nelson Wilmarth]
　　　Renewal of Reichsbank charter.

LIBONATI REPORT [Libonati, Roland V.]

950

U.S. *Congress. House. Committee on the Judiciary.*
Report of a special subcommittee on the International Court of Justice and the International Criminal Police Organization. Washington, U.S. Govt. Print. Off., 1959.
iii, 19 p. 24 cm.

At head of title: 86th Cong., 1st sess. Committee print.
1. Hague. International Court of Justice. 2. International Criminal Police Organization.
JX1971.6.U52 1959a   341.63   59-61193
MC#: 1959-8743
SuDocs no.: Y4.J89/1:In8/8

LIEBERMAN REPORT [Lieberman, Barnet]
see
DOUGLAS REPORTS [Douglas, Paul H.]
National Commission on Urban Problems

Research report, no. 19

LIEDER REPORT [Lieder, Frederick William Charles]
see under
ALDRICH COMMISSION [Aldrich, Nelson Wilmarth]
Reichsbank.

LIESSE REPORT [Liesse, Andre]
see under
ALDRICH COMMISSION [Aldrich, Nelson Wilmarth]
Reichsbank.

LILIENTHAL REPORT [Lilienthal, David Eli]
951

U.S. *Dept. of state. Committee on atomic energy.*
. . . A report on the international control of atomic energy. Washington, U.S. Govt. print. off., 1946.

xiv, 55 p. 23 cm. [U.S. Dept. of state. Publication 2498]
U.S. 79th Cong., 2d sess. House. Doc. 709.
Prepared by a board of consultants for the secretary of state's Committee on atomic energy. cf. p. ii-[iii]
"Reprint."-p. iv.
David E. Lilienthal, chairman of the committee.
1. Atomic power—International control. I. Lilienthal, David Eli, 1899-
HD9698.A28U55 1946b   341   46-26610
MC#: 1946-page 984
SuDocs no.: 79th Cong., 2d sess. H. Doc. 709

LINNENBERG REPORT [Linnenberg, Clem Charles]
see under
O'MAHONEY REPORTS [O'Mahoney, Joseph Christopher]

LINOWITZ REPORT [Linowitz, Sol M.]
952

U.S. *Dept. of State. Advisory Committee on International Organizations.*
Financial management and the United Nations system: a report. [Washington] Dept. of State, 1963.

x, 30 p. tables. 24 cm.
Cover title.
1. United Nations—Finance. 2. United Nations—U.S. I. Title.
JX1977.8.F5U58   64-60724
MC#: 1964-11618
SuDocs no.: S1.2:F49

LINTON REPORT [Linton, Ron M.]
953

U.S. *Task Force on Environmental Health and Related Problems.*
A strategy for a liveable environment; a report to the Secretary of Health, Education, and Welfare. Washington [U.S. Dept. of

Health, Education, and Welfare]; for sale by the Supt. of Docs., U.S. Govt. Print. Off., 1967.

xxi, 90 p. illus., ports. 26 cm.
Bibliography: p. 67-70.
1. Pollution—U.S. I. U.S. Dept. of Health, Education, and Welfare. II. Title.
TD180.U57   620   HEW68-10
MC#: 1967-12622
SuDocs no.: FS1.2:En8

LIVERNASH REPORT
954

Livernash, Edward Robert.
Collective bargaining in the basic steel industry; a study of the public interest and the role of Government [by E. Robert Livernash and others. Washington] U.S. Dept. of Labor, 1961.

ix, 317 p. diagrs., tables. 24 cm.
1. Strikes and lockouts—[Iron and] steel industry—U.S. 2. Iron and steel workers—U.S. 3. Steel industry and trade—U.S. [3. Iron and steel industry—U.S.] 4. (Collective bargaining—U.S.). I. Title.
HD6515.I.5L5   331.18691   L61-17
MC#: 1961-4780
SuDocs no.: L1.2:St3/2

LIVINGOOD REPORT [Livingood, John M.]
see
HOOKER REPORT [Hooker, Evelyn]

LLOYD REPORT [Lloyd, Jessie C.]
see under
DILLINGHAM COMMISSION [Dillingham, William Paul]
Immigrants as charity seekers.

LOCKHART REPORTS [Lockhart, William B.]
955

United States. Commission on Obscenity and Pornography.
The report. [Washington, For sale by the Supt. of Docs., U.S. Govt. Print. Off.] 1970.

646 p. 25 cm.
Includes bibliographies.
1. Erotica. 2. Obscenity (Law)—United States.
HQ460.U53   364.17'4   70-609906
                          MARC
MC#: 1971-1372
SuDocs no.: Y3.Ob7:1/970

956

United States. Commission on Obscenity and Pornography.
Technical report. [Washington; For sale by the Supt. of Docs., U.S. Govt. Print. Off., 1971-

9 v. 25 cm.
Includes bibliographical references.
Contents:—v. 1. Preliminary studies.—v. 2. Legal analysis.—v. 3. The marketplace: the industry.—v. 4. The marketplace: empirical studies.—v. 5. Societal control mechanisms.—v. 6. National survey.—v. 7. Erotica and antisocial behavior.—v. 8. Erotica and social behavior.—v. 9. The consumer and the community.
Supt. of Docs. no.: Y3.Ob7:10
1. Erotica. 2. Obscenity (Law)—United States.
HQ471.U45   301.41'5   70-614103
                          MARC
MC#: 1971-14228
SuDocs no.: Y3.Ob7:1

MC#: 1971-15952
SuDocs no.: Y3.Ob7:10/v.2
MC#: 1971-14229
SuDocs no.: Y3.Ob7:3
MC#: 1971-15953
SuDocs no.: Y3.Ob7:10/v.4
MC#: 1971-15954
SuDocs no.: Y3.Ob7:10/v.5
MC#: 1971-15955
SuDocs no.: Y3.Ob7:10/v.6
MC#: 1972-1983
SuDocs no.: Y3.Ob7:10/v.7
MC#: 1972-1073
SuDocs no.: Y3.Ob7:10/v.8
MC#: 1972-8853
SuDocs no.: Y3.Ob7:10/v.9

LODGE REPORT [Lodge, Henry Cabot]

957

U.S. President's Commission for the Observance of the Twenty-Fifth Anniversary of the United Nations.
Report. [Washington; For sale by the Supt. of Docs., U.S. Govt. Print. Off., 1971]
xiii, 67 p. 23 cm.
Supt. of Docs. no.: Pr37.8:Un3/R29
1. United Nations—U.S.
JX1977.2.U5A57   341′.23   70-612279
                                                  MARC
MC#: 1971-11678
SuDocs no.: Pr37.8:Un3/R29

LODGE REPORT [Lodge, Henry Cabot, 1850-1924]
Debt of Santo Domingo.
see under
HOLLANDER REPORT [Hollander, Jacob Harry]

LODGE REPORT [Lodge, Henry Cabot, 1850-1924]
European immigration, 1899-1909.
see under
DILLINGHAM COMMISSION [Dillingham, William Paul]

LONG REPORT [Long, Franklin A.]

958

United States. President's Science Advisory Committee. Space Science Panel.
The space program in the post-Apollo period; a report of the President's Science Advisory Committee, prepared by the joint Space Panels. Washington, For sale by the Supt. of Docs., U.S. Govt. Print. Off., 1967.
viii, 99 p. 24 cm.
Commonly known as the Long report.
1. Astronautics and state—United States. 2. Astronautics—United States. I. United States. President's Science Advisory Committee. Space Technology Panel. II. Title. III. Title: Long report on the space program in the post-Apollo period.
TL789.8.U5A6 1967   629.4′0973   67-60900
                                                  MARC
MC#: 1967-7050
SuDocs no.: Pr35.8:Sci2/Sp1

LONG REPORT [Long, Oren E.]

959

U.S. *Congress. Senate. Committee on Interior and Insular Affairs.*

Study mission to Eastern (American) Samoa; report of Senators Oren E. Long, of Hawaii, and Ernest Gruening, of Alaska, to the Committee on Interior and Insular Affairs, United States Senate, pursuant to S. Res. 330, 86th Congress. Washington, U.S. Govt. Print. Off., 1961.
viii, 184 p. fold. maps, diagrs., tables. 24 cm. (87th Cong., 1st sess. Senate. Document no. 38)
1. American Samoa—Econ. condit. I. Long, Oren E. II. Gruening, Ernest Henry, 1887- (Series: U.S. 87th Cong., 1st sess., 1961. Senate. Document no. 38)
DU819.A1A5 1961   61-62077
MC#: 1961-14510
SuDocs no.: 87th Cong., 1st sess. S. Doc. 38

LONG REPORT [Long, Russell B.]

960

United States. Congress. Senate. Committee on Finance.
Staff data and materials on the Emergency unemployment compensation act of 1974 / Committee on Finance, United States Senate, Russell B. Long, chairman. - Washington : U.S. Govt. Print. Off., 1977.
iii, 46 p. : graphs ; 24 cm.
At head of title: 95th Congress, 1st session. Committee print. Chiefly tables.
1. Insurance, Unemployment—United States. 2. Insurance, Unemployment—United States—Statistics. I. United States. Laws, statutes, etc. Emergency unemployment compensation act of 1974. 1977. II. Title.
KF3671.A55F536   344′.73′024   77-601286
                                                  MARC
MC#: 1977-4017
SuDocs no.: Y4.F49:Un2/14

LORWIN REPORT [Lorwin, Lewis Levitzki]
see under
O'MAHONEY REPORTS [O'Mahoney, Joseph Christopher]

LOWENSTEIN REPORT [Lowenstein, James G.]
see
A-ARMS REPORT

LOZIER REPORT [Lozier, Ralph Fulton]
see
WHITE REPORT [White, Hays B.]

LUTES REPORT [Lutes, Le R.]

961

U.S. *War Dept. General Staff.*
Unified logistic support of the United States armed services . . . prepared under the direction of Le R. Lutes, GSC, Director of Service, Supply and Procurement [Division] War Dept., General Staff, by Robin Elliott, GSC. [Washington] 1947.
48 p. illus., fold. maps. 27 cm.
1. U.S. Army—Supplies and stores. 2. U.S. Navy—Supplies and stores. I. Elliott, Robin. II. Title.
UC263.A62 1947   355.8   52-64034
Not located in Monthly Catalog

LYTTON REPORT [Lytton, Victor Alexander George Robert Bulwer-Lytton, 2d earl of]

962

League of Nations. *Commission of Enquiry into the Sino-Japanese Dispute.*

Appeal by the Chinese Government. Report of Commission of Enquiry signed by the members of the commission on September 4th, 1932, at Peiping. [Geneva, 1932]

148 p. 33 cm. (Series of League of Nations publications: VII. Political. 1932. VII. 12)

[U.S.] Dept. of State. Publication no. 378.

Official no.: C.663.M.320.1932.vii.

Added t.p.: Manchuria. Report of the Commission on Enquiry appointed by the League of Nations. Washington, Govt. Print. Off., 1932.

"This publication is a verbatim reprint of the League of Nations document of October 1, 1932. Neither the maps which accompany the report nor the annexes are special studies cited therein are included in this reprint."

Lytton, chairman.

"List of corrigenda": leaf inserted.

1. Manchuria — Hist. — Sources. 2. China — Hist. — 1912-1937 — Sources. 3. Japanese in Manchuria. I. Lytton, Victor Alexander George Robert Bulwer-Lytton, 2d earl of, 1876-1947. (Series: League of Nations. Publications: vii. Political. 1932. VII. 12. Series: U.S. Dept. of State. Publication no. 378)

DS783.7.L4 1932a   32-28050 rev 2*

Not located in Monthly Catalog

MAAS REPORT [Maas, Melvin J.]

963

U.S. *President's Committee on Employment of the Physically Handicapped. Advisory Council.*

Special report to the President. [Washington, U.S. Govt. Print. Off.]

v. illus. 27 cm.

1. Physically handicapped — Employment — U.S.

HD7256.U5A347   59-62453 rev

MC#: 1964-20431

SuDocs no.: L16.44/2:Ad9 (date)

McCAIN REPORT [McCain, Charles Curtice]

see

ALDRICH REPORT [Aldrich, Nelson Wilmarth]

Wholesale prices, wages, and transportation.

McCARRAN REPORT [McCarran, Patrick]

964

U.S. *Congress. Senate. Committee on the Judiciary.*

The immigration and naturalization systems of the United States. Report pursuant to S. Res. 137, 80th Congress, 1st session, as amended, a resolution to make an investigation of the immigration system. Washington, U.S. Govt. Print. Off., 1950.

xvii, 925, xxvi p. 24 cm. (81st Cong., 2d sess. Senate. Report no. 1515)

Pat McCarran, chairman.

1. U.S. — Emig. & immig. 2. Naturalization — U.S. (Series: U.S. 81st Cong., 2d sess. [1950] Senate. Report no. 1515)

JV6416.A39 1950d   325.73   50-60699

MC#: 1950-11252

SuDocs no.: 81st Cong., 2d sess. S. Rept. 1515

McCLELLAN REPORT [McClellan, George Brinton]

965

U.S. *Military commission to Europe*, 1855-1856.

. . . Report of the secretary of war, communicating the report of Captain George B. McClellan, (First regiment United States

Cavalry,) one of the officers sent to the seat of war in Europe, in 1855 and 1856. Washington, A. O. P. Nicholson, printer, 1857.

2 p. l., 360 p. front., illus., maps (1 fold.) 29 cm. ([U.S. 34th Cong.] Special sess. Senate. Ex. doc. 1)

Issued in 1861 without document series note under title: The armies of Europe: comprising descriptions in detail of the military systems of England, France, Russia, Prussia, Austria and Sardinia.

1. Crimean war, 1853-1856. I. McClellan, George Brinton, 1826-1885. II. Title.

DK214.U6 1857   355.3   30-15976 Revised

Checklist of United States Public Documents, 1789-1909, page 33

SuDocs no.: 34th Cong., Spec. sess. S. Ex. Doc. 1. In Serial no. 916

McCLELLAN REPORTS [McClellan, John L.]

966

U.S. *Congress. Senate. Committee on Government Operations.*

Progress on Hoover Commission recommendations, report. Washington, U.S. Govt. Print. Off., 1949.

iii, 388 p. 24 cm. (81st Cong., 1st sess. Senate. Report no. 1158)

John L. McClellan, chairman.

Submitted by the committee under its earlier name: Committee on Expenditures in the Executive Departments.

1. U.S. — Executive departments. (Series: U.S. 81st Cong., 1st sess., 1949. Senate. Report no. 1158)

JK649 1949j   353   49-47125 rev*

MC#: 1949-25366

SuDocs no.: 81st Cong., 1st sess. S. Rept. 1158

967

United States. Congress. Senate. Committee on Government Operations. Permanent Subcommittee on Investigations.

Riots, civil and criminal disorders; college campus disorders. Second interim report, together with additional, individual, and minority views. Washington, U.S. Govt. Print. Off., 1971.

iii, 49 p. 24 cm. (92d Congress, 1st session. Senate. Report no. 92-42)

1. Riots — United States. 2. Universities and colleges — United States. I. Title. II. Series: United States. 92d Congress, 1st session, 1971. Senate. Report no. 92-42.

KF31.G658 1971   378.1'98'10973   70-611597

                                                                             MARC

MC#: 1971-7922

SuDocs no.: 92d Cong., 1st sess. S. Rept. 42

McCOY REPORT [McCoy, Jay T.]

see

LEWIS REPORT [Lewis, Burdette Gibson]

McCURDY REPORT [McCurdy, Robert M.]

968

United States. Congress. House. Committee on Veterans' Affairs.

Report of U.S. Veterans' Advisory Commission. Hearing, Ninetieth Congress, second session. March 19, 1968. Washington, U.S. Govt. Print. Off., 1968.

iii, 2713-2973 p. illus. 24 cm.

Commonly known as the McCurdy report.

"Report of the U.S. Veterans' Advisory Commission on the veterans benefits system": p. 2729-2832.

1. Veterans — United States. I. United States. Veterans' Advisory Commission. Report. 1968. II. Title. III. Title: McCurdy report on veterans' affairs.

UB357.A5137 1968   355.1'15'0973   68-61022
                                                   MARC
MC#: 1968-7364
SuDocs no.: Y4.V64/3:V64/13/968

McDERMOTT REPORT [McDermott, Walsh]
969

U.S. *President's Science Advisory Committee. Development Assistance Panel.*
  Research and development in the new development assistance
program; report. Prepared for the Department of State, 1961.
  (*In* U.S. Congress. House. Committee on Foreign Affairs. The
International development and security act. Hearings 87th
Congress, 1st session, part III. Washington, 1961. 24 cm. p.
971-82)
MC#: 1961-14462
SuDocs no.: Y4.F76/1:In8/32/pt. 3

McELROY REPORTS [McElroy, Neil Hosler]
970

United States. President's Commission on School Finance.
  Progress report. [Washington] 1971.
  iii, 61 p. 26 cm.
  1. Education—United States—Finance.
LB2825.A5 1971   379'.1'0973   72-600958
                                               MARC
MC#: 1973-16458
SuDocs no.: Pr37.8:Sch6/P94/971

971

United States. President's Commission on School Finance.
  Schools, people & money: the need for educational reform; final
report. [Washington, 1972]
  xxv, 147 p. 24 cm.
  Chairman: N. McElroy.
  Supt. of Docs. no.: Pr37.8:Sch6/Sch6/3
  1. Education—United States—1965- 2. Education—United
States—Finance. I. McElroy, Neil Hosler, 1904- II. Title.
LA209.2.A577   370'.973   72-601009
                                          MARC
MC#: 1972-6017
SuDocs no.: Pr37.8:Sch6/Sch6/3

972

U.S. *President's Committee for the White House Conference on Education.*
  A report to the President; full report. [Washington, U.S. Govt.
Print. Off.] 1956.
  vii, 126 p. maps, diagrs., tables. 24 cm.
  1. White House Conference on Education, Washington, D.C.,
1955.
L106 1955.W323   370.6373   56-60969
MC#: 1956-9543
SuDocs no.: Y3.W58/2:1/956

973

United States. President's Panel on Nonpublic Education.
  Nonpublic education and the public good; final report.
[Washington] President's Commission on School Finance; [for
sale by the Supt. of Docs., U.S. Govt. Print. Off., 1972]
  viii, 58 p. illus. 24 cm.
  Includes bibliographical references.
  1. Private schools—United States. I. Title.
LC49.A48   371'.02'0973   72-601503
                                          MARC

MC#: 1972-7277
SuDocs no.: Pr37.8:Sch6/N73/int. rep.
MC#: 1972-10245
SuDocs no.: Pr37.8:Sch6/N73

McGEE REPORTS [McGee, Gale William]
974

United States. Civil Service Commission.
  Statutory exceptions to the competitive service. A report to the
Committee on Post Office and Civil Service of the United States
Senate. Washington, U.S. Govt. Print. Off., 1973.
  v, 834 p. 24 cm.
  At head of title: 93d Congress, 1st session. Committee print.
  1. Civil service—United States. I. United States. Congress.
Senate. Committee on Post Office and Civil Service. II. Title.
KF5337.A625   342'.73'068   73-602970
                                            MARC

Not located in Monthly Catalog

975

U.S. *Congress. Senate. Committee on Appropriations.*
  Personnel administration and operations of Agency for Inter-
national Development. Report of Senator Gale W. McGee to the
Committee on Appropriations. Washington, U.S. Govt. Print.
Off., 1964.
  xi, 61 p. 24 cm. (88th Cong., 2d sess. Senate. Document no. 57)
  1. U.S. Agency for International Development—Officials and
employees. 2. Economic assistance, American. I. McGee, Gale
W. II. Title. (Series: U.S. 88th Cong., 2d sess., 1964. Senate.
Document no. 57)
HC60.U6A4 1964b   64-60677
MC#: 1964-4520
SuDocs no.: 88th Cong., 2d sess. S. Doc. 57

McGOVERN REPORT [McGovern, George]
976

United States. Congress. Senate. Select Committee on Nutrition
and Human Needs.
  The food gap: poverty and malnutrition in the United States;
interim report together with supplemental, additional, and individual views. Washington, U.S. Govt. Print. Off., 1969.
  v, 48 p. 24 cm.
  Commonly known as the McGovern report.
  At head of title: 91st Congress, 1st session. Committee print.
  1. Food supply—United States. 2. Food relief—United States.
3. Diet—United States. 4. Malnutrition—United States. I. Title. II. Title: McGovern report on poverty and malnutrition in
the United States.
TX360.U6A514 1969   338.1'9'73   74-603354
                                                 MARC
MC#: 1969-15477
SuDocs no.: Y4.N95:F73

McGUIRE REPORTS [McGuire, E. Perkins]
977

United States. Commission on Government Procurement.
  Final report[s of study groups, etc.] for the Commission on
Government Procurement. [Washington] 1971-72 [v. 1, 1972]
  35 v. illus. 27 cm.
  "Prepared as . . . advisory report[s] to the commission."
  Includes bibliographies.
  Contents: v. 1-3. Study Group #1, Utilization of Resources.
Final report.—v. [4-6] Study Group #2, Controls over the Pro-
curement Process. Final report.—[v. 7] Study Group #3, Regula-
tions. Final report.—v. [8-9] Study Group #4, Remedies. Final

report. — v. [10-14] Study Group #5, Organization & Personnel. Final report. — [v. 15] Study Group #6, Pre-contract Planning. Final report. — [v. 16] Study Group #7, Cost & Pricing Information. Final report. — v. [17-18] Study Group #8, Negotiations & Subcontracting. Final report. — [v. 19] Study Group #9, Reports and Management Controls. Final report. — [v. 20] Study Group #10. Contract Audit & Administration. Final report. — v. [21-23] Study Group #11, Research & Development. Final report: v. 1. Report of the study group. v. 2. Characteristics of performers and sponsors of research and development. v. 3. Background papers. — v. [24-26] Study Group #12. Major Systems Acquisition. Final report. — v. [27-29] Study Group #13-A, Commercial Products, Final report. — [v. 30] Study Group #13-B, Architect-Engineer Services. Final report. — [v. 31] Study Group #13-C, Construction. Final report. — v. [32-33] Statutory Studies Group. Final report. — [v. 34] Grants Task Force. Final report. — [v. 35] A special staff study of the roles and relationships of key agencies in procurement policy, control, and management; final report.

1. Government purchasing — United States.
JK1673.A486   353.007′12   73-601358
                                                         MARC

"This is part of a series of 100 numbered copies reproduced solely for working purposes . . . The manner in which this . . . report and the reports of all other study papers will be made available to the general public has not been finally determined."
— Final report of study group II.
Not located in Monthly Catalog

978

United States. Commision on Government Procurement.
Report. [Washington, For sale by the Supt. of Docs., U.S. Govt. Print. Off.] 1972.

4 v. illus. 26 cm.
Includes bibliographical references.
- - - - - Index, bibliography, acronyms. [Washington, For sale by the Supt. of Docs., U.S. Govt. Print. Off.] 1972.

xii, 142 p. 26 cm.
JK1673.A488 Suppl.
1. Government purchasing — United States.
JK1673.A488   353.007′12   73-601206
                                                         MARC

MC#: 1973-23396-399 (Vols. 1-4)
SuDocs no.: Y3.G74/4:1/972/v.(nos.)
MC#: 1973-26513 (Index)
SuDocs no.: Y3.G74/4:1/972/ind.

979

United States. Commission on Government Procurement.
Summary of the report of the Commission on Government Procurement. Washington; For sale by the Supt. of Docs., U.S. Govt. Print. Off., 1972.

viii, 143 p. 24 cm.
1. Government Purchasing — United States.
JK1673.A49   353.007′12   73-600813
                                                         MARC

MC#: 1973-26514 (LC card 73-601206 listed in error)
SuDocs no.: Y3.G74/4:1/972/summ.

McKAY REPORT [McKay, Henry Donald]
see
WICKERSHAM COMMISSION [Wickersham, George Woodward]
Report on the causes of crime, no. 13.

McKENNA REPORT [McKenna, William F.]
980

U.S. *Congress. Senate. Committee on Banking and Currency.*
Federal disaster insurance; report. Staff study. Washington, U.S. Govt. Print. Off., 1956.

ix, 419 p. illus., maps (part fold.) 24 cm. (84th Cong. 2d sess. Senate. Report no. 1313)
1. Insurance, Disaster — U.S. I. Title. (Series: U.S. 84th Cong., 2d sess., 1956. Senate. Report no. 1313)
HG9970.D52A48   56-60396
MC#: 1956-3585
SuDocs no.: 84th Cong., 2d sess. S. Rept. 1313
MC#: 1956-1521
SuDocs no.: Y4.B22/3:D63/4

McKEOWN REPORT [McKeown, Tom D.]
see
WHITE REPORT [White, Hays B.]

McKINNEY REPORT [McKinney, Frank E.]
981

U.S. *Comptroller of the Currency. Advisory Committee on Banking.*
National banks and the future; report to the Comptroller of the Currency. Washington, U.S. Treasury Dept., Comptroller of the Currency; for sale by the Superintendent of Documents, U.S. Govt. Print. Off. [1962]

xi, 189 p. 24 cm.
1. Banks and banking — U.S. I. Title.
HG2481.A414   332.10973   62-64630
MC#: 1962-20703
SuDocs no.: T12.2:N21/14

McKINNEY REPORTS
982

McKinney, Robert, 1910-
Review of the international atomic policies and programs of the United States; report to the Joint Committee on Atomic Energy, Congress of the United States. Washington, U.S. Govt. Print. Off., 1960.

5 v. (xi, 2080 p.) maps (2 fold.) diagrs., tables. 24 cm.
At head of title: 86th Cong., 2d sess. Joint committee print.
Vols. 2-5 have title: Background material for the review of the international atomic policies and programs of the United States.
Includes bibliographies.
1. Atomic energy — Economic aspects. 2. Atomic energy research — International cooperation. 3. Nuclear engineering. I. U.S. Congress. Joint Committee on Atomic Energy. II. Title.
HD9698.A2M27   338.4762148   60-64513
MC#: 1960-16827
SuDocs no.: Y4.At7/2:At7/21/v. 1-4
MC#: 1961-342
SuDocs no.: Y4.At7/2:At7/21/v.5

983

U.S. *Congress. Joint Committee on Atomic Energy.*
Peaceful uses of atomic energy; report of the Panel on the Impact of the Peaceful Uses of Atomic Energy to the Joint Committee on Atomic Energy. Washington, U.S. Govt. Print. Off., 1956.

2 v. illus. 24 cm.
At head of title: 84th Cong., 2d sess. Joint committee print.
Vol. 2 has subtitle: Background material for the report.
1. Atomic energy. I. Title.
HD9698.U52A52 1956   56-60555
MC#: 1956-5093, 5094
SuDocs no.: Y3.At7/2:At7/13/v. 1, 2

984

U.S. Industry-Government Special Task Force on Travel.

Report to the President of the United States from the Industry-Government Special Task Force on Travel. Washington; For sale by the Supt. of Docs., U.S. Govt. Print. Off., 1968.

x, 48 p. 24 cm.
1. Tourist trade—U.S.
G155.U6A617 1968b   338.4'7'917304   72-603813
                              MARC
MC#: 1968-5537 (LC card 68-60931 referred to in error)
SuDocs no.: Pr36.8:T69/R29/968

985

U.S. Industry-Government Special Task Force on Travel.

Report to the President of the United States from the Industry-Government Special Task Force on Travel.Rev. Washington; For sale by the Supt. of Docs., U.S. Govt. Print. Off., 1968.

x, 48 p. 24 cm.
1. Tourist trade—U.S.
G155.U6A617 1968   338.4'7'917304   68-61664
                              MARC
MC#: 1968-8235
SuDocs no.: Pr36.8:T69/R29/968-2

McLANE REPORT [McLane, Louis]

986

U.S. *Treasury Dept.*
Documents relative to the manufactures in the United States, collected and transmitted to the House of Representatives, in compliance with a resolution of Jan. 19, 1832, by the Secretary of the Treasury, in two volumes . . . Washington, Printed by D. Green, 1833.

2 v. 23 cm. [22d Cong., 1st sess. House. Doc. 308]
Louis McLane, Secretary of the Treasury.
Documents numbered 1-20 (1-9 in vol. I; 10-20 in vol. II) No. 1-17, Returns from Maine, Massachusetts, New Hampshire, Vermont, Rhode Island, Connecticut, New York, New Jersey, Pennsylvania, Delaware, and Ohio. No. 18-20, Additional papers: 18, Massachusetts. Manufacture of tacks, brads, and sprigs, in Abington, Mass.; 19, Rhode Island. Manufacture of cotton goods in Providence; 20, New Jersey. Review of the tariff policy, by Andrew Gray, of Newark.
1. U.S.—Manuf. 2. Tariff—U.S. 3. New England—Manuf. 4. Middle states—Manuf. 5. Ohio—Manuf. I. McLane, Louis, 1786-1857. II. Title.
HD9724.A4 1833   14-21464
Checklist of United State Public Documents, 1789-1909, page 12
22d Cong., 1st sess. H. doc. 308. In Serial nos. 222-223, vol. 7, pts. 1-2

MacLEOD REPORTS [MacLeod, Colin M.]

987

U.S. *President's Science Advisory Committee.*
Use of pesticides, a report. Washington, The White House; for sale by the Superintendent of Documents, U.S. Govt. Print. Off., 1963.

v, 25 p. 24 cm.
Cover title.
1. Pesticides. 2. Pesticides—Toxicology. I. Title.
SB959.U57   63-61540
MC#: 1963-11210
SuDocs no.: Pr35.8:Sci2/P43

988

U.S. *President's Science Advisory Committee. Panel on Herbicides.*

Report on 2,4,5-T. [Washington] Executive Office of the President, Office of Science and Technology; [for sale by the Supt. of Docs., U.S. Govt. Print. Off.] 1971.

vii, 68 p. 24 cm.
Includes bibliographies.
Supt. of Docs. no.: PrEx8.2:T93.
1. Trichlorophenoxyacetic acid. I. Title.
SB952.T72U5   632'.954   78-612214
                              MARC
MC#: 1971-15989
SuDocs no.: PrEx8.2:T93

MACMAHON REPORT [Macmahon, Arthur Whittier]
see
BROWNLOW REPORT [Brownlow, Louis]

McMAHON REPORT [McMahon, Robert S.]

989

U.S. *Congress. House. Committee on Interstate and Foreign Commerce. Special Subcommittee on Legislative Oversight.*

Regulation of broadcasting; half a century of government regulation of broadcasting and the need for further legislative action. Study for the Committee on Interstate and Foreign Commerce, House of Representatives, Eighty-fifth Congress, second session, on H. Res. 99 (85th Congress, 1st session) a resolution authorizing the Committee on Interstate and Foreign Commerce to conduct investigations and studies with respect to certain matters within its jurisdiction.Washington, U.S. Govt. Print. Off., 1958.

xiv, 171 p. 24 cm.
At head of title: Subcommittee print. 85th Cong., 2d sess. House of Representatives.
1. Radio—U.S.—Laws and regulations. 2. Television—Law and legislation—U.S. 3. U.S. Federal Communications Commission. I. Title.
            384.50973   59-61173
MC#: 1959-7471
SuDocs no.: Y4.In8/4:B78

McMINN REPORT [McMinn, John H.]

990

U.S. *Army Medical Service.*
Personnel in World War II [by John M. McMinn and Max Levin] Prepared and published under the direction of Leonard D. Heaton. Editor in chief; John Boyd Coates, Jr. Editor for personnel: Charles M. Wiltse. Washington, Office of the Surgeon General, Dept. of the Army; [for sale by the Superintendent of Documents, U.S. Govt. Print. Off.] 1963.

xxvi, 548 p. illus., ports. 27 cm. (*Its* Medical Department, United States Army)
"Bibliographical note": p. 511-513.
1. World War, 1939-1945—Medical and sanitary affairs. I. McMinn, John H. II. Levin, Max. III. Coates, John Boyd, ed. IV. Title. (Series: U.S. Army Medical Service. The Medical Department of the United States Army in World War II)
D807.U6A5197   63-60001
MC#: 1963-16832
SuDocs no.: D104.11:P43

McMORRAN REPORT [McMorran, Henry]
see
PUJO REPORT [Pujo, Arsène Paulin]

McNERNEY REPORT [McNerney, Walter J.]
991

U.S. *Task Force on Medicaid and Related Programs.*
Report. [Washington] U.S. Dept. of Health, Education, and Welfare; [for sale by the Supt. of Docs., U.S. Govt. Print. Off., 1970]
  xii, 130 p. 24 cm.
  Walter J. McNerney, chairman.
  1. Health care, Prepaid—U.S. I. McNerney, Walter J.
RA412.5.U6A585   368.3′82′00973   73-608524
                                             MARC
MC#: 1970-12596
SuDocs no.: HE1.2:M46/8

MACOMBER REPORT [Macomber, William B.]
992

United States. Dept. of State.
Diplomacy for the 70's; a program of management reform for the Department of State. [Washington, For sale by the Supt. of Docs., U.S. Govt. Print. Off., 1970]
  x, 610 p. illus. 26 cm. (Department of State publication 8551. Department and Foreign Service series, 143)
  Includes bibliographical references.
  I. Title. II. Series: United States. Dept. of State. Publication 8551. III. Series: United States. Dept. of State. Department and Foreign Service series, 143.
JK851.A425   353.1   74-610121
                                              MARC
MC#: 1971-2995
SuDocs no.: S1.69:143

MacQUIVEY REPORT [MacQuivey, Donald R.]
993

U.S. *Congress. Senate. Committee on Aeronautical and Space Sciences.*
Communication satellites: technical economic, and international developments. Staff report prepared for the use of the Committee on Aeronautical and Space Sciences, United States Senate. Washington, U.S. Govt. Print. Off., 1962.
  x, 287 p. illus., maps. 24 cm.
  At head of title: 87th Cong., 2d sess. Committee print.
  Bibliography: p. 241-242.
  1. Artificial satellites in telecommunications.
HE9721.U5A525   62-60693
MC#: 1962-7207
SuDocs no.: Y4.Ae8:C73

MACY REPORT [Macy, John W., Jr.]
994

U.S. *Presidential Task Force on Career Advancement.*
Investment for tomorrow; a report. Washington, Distributed by U.S. Civil Service Commission, 1967.
  v, 69 p. 26 cm.
  1. Civil service—U.S. 2. Employees, Training of. I. Title.
JK718.A57   353′.004   67-60752
MC#: 1967-7046
SuDocs no.: Pr36.8:C18/In8

MADOW REPORT [Madow, William G.]
995

U.S. *Congress. House. Committee on Interstate and Foreign Commerce.*
Evaluation of statistical methods used in obtaining broadcast ratings. Report pursuant to section 136 of the Legislative reorganization act of 1946, Public law 601, 79th Cong., and House

resolution 108, 87th Cong. Washington, U.S. Govt. Print. Off., 1961.
  x, 163 p. 24 cm. (87th Cong., 1st sess. House. Report no. 193)
  Includes bibliography.
  1. Radio programs—Rating. 2. Television programs—Rating. I. Title. (Series: U.S. 87th Cong., 1st sess., 1961. House. Report no. 193)
HE8697.A8U6   384.542   61-61089
MC#: 1961-7090
SuDocs no.: 87th Cong., 1st sess. H. Rept. 193

MAGNUSON REPORT [Magnuson, Paul B.]
996

U.S. *President's Commission on the Health Needs of the Nation.*
Building America's health; a report to the President. [Washington, U.S. Govt. Print. Off., 1952-53]
  5 v. illus., maps. 27 cm.
  Contents.—v. 1. Findings and recommendations.—v. 2. America's health status, needs and resources.—v. 3. America's health status, needs and resources; a statistical index.—v. 4. Financing a health program for America.—v. 5. The people speak; excerpts from regional public hearings on health.
  1. Hygiene, Public—U.S. 2. Medicine, State—U.S. I. Title.
RA11.A3 1953c   614.0973   53-60143
MC#: 1953-2770,6289,6290,4765,4766 (Vols. 1-5)
SuDocs no.: Pr33.19:B86/v.(nos.)
MC#: 1953-4119 (Vol. 1)
SuDocs no.: 83d Cong., 1st sess. H. Doc. 55

United States. President's Commission on the Health Needs of the Nation.
Building America's health : [report] / the President's Commission on the Health Needs of the Nation. - New York : Arno Press, 1976.
  5 v. in 2 : ill. ; 27 cm. — (Social problems and social policy-the American experience)
  Commonly known as the Magnuson report.
  Reprint of the 1952-1953 ed. published by the U.S. Govt. Print. Off., Washington.
  Includes bibliography and index.
  ISBN 0-405-07508-1
  1. Public health—United States. 2. Medicine, State—United States. I. Title. II. Title: Magnuson report on the health needs of the nation. III. Series.
[RA395.A3U52 1976]   362.1′0973   75-17239
                                          MARC
Not listed in Monthly Catalog

MAGNUSON REPORTS [Magnuson, Warren G.]
997

U.S. *Alaska International Rail and Highway Commission.*
Transport requirements for the growth of Northwest North America. Letter from the Chairman, Alaska International Rail and Highway Commission, transmitting the final report pursuant to Public Law 884, 84th Congress. Referred to the Committee on Interior and Insular Affairs. Washington, U.S. Govt. Print. Off., 1961-
  v. maps (part fold.) tables. 27 cm. (87th Cong., 1st sess. House document no. 176)
  1. Transportation—Northwest, Canadian. 2. Transportation—Alaska. I. U.S. Congress. House. Committee on Interior and Insular Affairs. II. Title. (Series: U.S. 87th Cong., 1st sess., 1961. House. Document no. 176)
HE215.Z7B87   61-62371
MC#: 1961-18777
SuDocs no.: 87th Cong., 1st sess. H. Doc. 176

998

U.S. Dept. of Health, Education, and Welfare. Public Health Service. National Institutes of Health.

Federal health manpower programs 1970. Prepared at the request of the Senate Committee on appropriations. Bethesda, Md.: National Institutes of Health. U.S. Department of Health, Education, and Welfare. [1970]

2 parts (typescript)
Second part: Inventory of federal programs that support health manpower training 1970.
1. Health manpower programs.
[RA410.8.F4]
BHME Library
Not listed in Monthly Catalog.

MAGRAW REPORT [Magraw, Richard M.]

999

U.S. Task Force on Health Manpower.

Report to the Assistant Secretary for Health and Scientific Affairs, Department of Health, Education, and Welfare. Manpower for health, National needs and Federal programs 1969.

ix, 131 p. (typescript)
Bound with Appendix A, 29p.
1. Supply and demand — Health personnel. 2. Federal aid to medical education. I. Magraw, Richard M. II. Title.
[RA410.8.U5U65]
BHME Library
Not listed in Monthly Catalog

MALONEY REPORT [Maloney, Francis Thomas]

1000

U.S. *Congress. Senate. Special committee to investigate gasoline and fuel-oil shortages.*

. . . Gasoline and fuel-oil shortages . . . Preliminary report, [Report and Additional report] "Pursuant to S. Res. 156" . . . [Washington, U.S. Govt. print. off., 1941-42]

5, 16, 10 p. tables, diagrs. 23 cm. ([U.S.] 77th Cong., 1st[-2d] sess. Senate. Rept. 676)
Caption title.
Submitted by Mr. Maloney from the Special committee to investigate gasoline and fuel-oil shortages.
1. Petroleum — U.S. 2. Gasoline. I. Maloney, Francis Thomas, 1894-
HD9565.A5 1941b   388.2   41-51244 Revised 2
MC#: 1941-page 1267
       1942-pages 54, 1137
SuDocs no.: 77th Cong., 1st sess. S. Rept. 676

MANLY REPORT [Manly, Basil M.]
    see
WALSH REPORT [Walsh, Francis Patrick]

MANSFIELD REPORT [Mansfield, Harvey Claflin]
    see
BROWNLOW REPORT [Brownlow, Louis]

MANSFIELD REPORTS [Mansfield, Michael Joseph]

1001

U.S. *Congress. Senate. Committee on Foreign Relations.*
Technical assistance. Final report pursuant to the provisions of S. Res. 214, 83d Congress, 2d session; S. Res. 36 and S. Res. 133, 84th Congress, 1st session; and S. Res. 162, 84th Congress, 2d session; extended by S. Res. 60 and 99 of the 85th Cong. Washington, U.S. Govt. Print. Off., 1957.

xiv, 668 p. illus., maps. 24 cm. (85th Cong., 1st sess. Senate. Report no. 139)
1. Technical assistance, American. (Series: U.S. 85th Cong., 1st sess., 1957. Senate. Report no. 139)
HC60.U51357   57-61458
MC#: 1957-7046A
SuDocs no.: 85th Cong., 1st sess. S. Rept. 139

1002

U.S. *Congress. Senate. Committee on Foreign Relations.*
The Vietnam conflict: the substance and the shadow. Report of Mike Mansfield [and others on a study mission to Europe and Asia] Washington, U.S. Govt. Print. Off., 1966.

v, 32 p. 24 cm.
At head of title: 89th Congress, 2d session. Committee print.
1. Vietnam — Hist. I. Mansfield, Michael Joseph, 1903- II. Title.
DS557.A6U45   66-60454
MC#: 1966-4218
SuDocs no.: Y4.F76/2:V67/7

MANSON REPORT [Manson, Joseph O.]
    see under
    ALDRICH COMMISSION [Aldrich, Nelson Wilmarth]
         Report to the National monetary commission on the
         fiscal systems of the United States.

MANSURE REPORT [Mansure, Edmund F.]

1003

U.S. *National Historical Publications Commission.*
A national program for the publication of historical documents; a report to the President. Washington, 1954.

viii, 106 p. 23 cm.
"A selective list of documentary historical publications of the United States Government": p. 98-106.
1. U.S. — Hist. — Historiography. 2. U.S. — Hist. — Sources — Bibl. I. Title.
E175.4.A417   973   54-60038
MC#: 1954-19749
SuDocs no.: GS4.14:H62

MANVEL REPORT [Manvel, Allen D.]
    see
    DOUGLAS REPORTS [Douglas, Paul H.]
         National Commission on Urban Problems.

         Research report, no. 6

         Research report, no. 9

         Research report, no. 12

MARK REPORT [Mark, Jerome Albert]
    see
    STEIN REPORT [Stein, Herbert]

MARK REPORT [Mark, Mary Louise]
    see under
    DILLINGHAM COMMISSION [Dillingham, William Paul]
         Immigrants in cities.

MAROUN STUDY

1004

United States. Office of the Comptroller of the Army.
Analysis of CONARC base operations (Maroun study) Dept. of the Army.

Washington: The Comptroller, 1971.

ca. 105 p. (in various pagings): diagrs., graphs. (ADSIRS: 3577)

Cover title.

1. United States. Army—Finance. 2. Military bases, American. I. Title. II. Title: CONARC base operations. III. Title: Maroun study. IV. Series.

[UC12.U5A5]

Dept. of the Army Library

Not located in Monthly Catalog

MARSH REPORT [Marsh, Millard C.]
see
BOWER REPORT [Bower, Ward T.]

MARSHALL REPORT [Marshall, Burke]
1005

U.S. *National Advisory Commission on Selective Service.*

In pursuit of equity: who serves when not all serve? Report. [Washington, For sale by the Supt. of Docs., U.S. Govt. Print. Off., 1967]

vii, 219 p. illus. 27 cm.

1. U.S. Selective Service System. I. Title.

UB343.A5238   355.2'23'0973   67-60904

MC#: 1967-7045

SuDocs no.: Pr36.8:Se4/Eq5

MARSHALL REPORT [Marshall, Burke]
see
PEERS COMMISSION [Peers, William R.]

MARSHALL REPORT
1006

Marshall, George Catlett, 1880-

Assistance to European economic recovery; statement before Senate Committee on Foreign Relations, January 8, 1948. [A program for United States aid to European recovery] the President's message to the Congress, December 19, 1947. [Washington, U.S. Govt. Print. Off., 1948]

20 p. 26 cm. ([U.S.] Dept. of State. Publication 3022. Economic cooperation series, 2)

"Related publications": p. 20.

1. Reconstruction (1939-)—Europe. 2. Europe—Econ. condit.—1945- I. U.S. President, 1945-1953 (Truman) (Series: U.S. Dept. of State. Publication 3022. Series: U.S. Dept. of State. Economic cooperation series, 2)

HC240.M257   338.94   48-45900*

MC#: 1948-9123

SuDocs no.: S1.65:no.2

MARTELL REPORT [Martell, Charles B.]
1007

U.S. *Federal Council for Science and Technology. Committee on Scientific and Technical Information.*

Status report on scientific and technical information in the Federal Government. [A Government research report. Washington, U.S. Dept. of Commerce, Office of Technical Services] 1963.

xi, 18 p. 27 cm.

"PB 181541."

Published by the committee under its earlier name: Committee on Scientific Information.

1. Communication in science. 2. Science and state—U.S. 3. Science—Information services—U.S. I. Title. II. Title: Scientific and technical information in the Federal Government.

Q223.U52   64-60293 rev

MC#: 1964-8541

SuDocs no.: Y3.F31/16:2In3

MARTIN REPORT [Martin, Betty Sullivan]
Look abroad.
see under
ORRRC REPORTS
ORRRC study report, 18.

MARTIN REPORT [Martin, Edwin M.]
see under
O'MAHONEY REPORTS [O'Mahoney, Joseph Christopher]
Brown. Industrial wage rates.

MARTIN REPORT [Martin, G. C.]
see
BROOKS REPORT [Brooks, Alfred H.]

MARTIN REPORT
1008

Martin, Roscoe Coleman, 1903-

Metropolis in transition; local government adaptation to changing urban needs. Prepared for the Housing and Home Finance Agency under the Urban studies and housing research program. [Washington, Housing and Home Finance Agency, 1963]

viii, 159 p. 24 cm.

1. Metropolitan areas—U.S. 2. Local government—U.S. I. U.S. Housing and Home Finance Agency. II. Title.

JS422.M28   64-60211

MC#: 1964-831

SuDocs no.: HH1.2:M56

MASON REPORT [Mason, James Murray]
1009

United States. Congress. Senate. Select Committee on the Harper's Ferry Invasion.

Invasion at Harper's Ferry. New York, Arno Press, 1969.

71, 255 p. 24 cm. (Mass violence in America)

"36th Cong., 1st sess. Senate. Rep. com. no. 278."

Submitted by J. M. Mason, chairman.

Reprint, with a new introd., of the 1860 ed., which was published under title: Report [of] the Select committee of the Senate appointed to inquire into the late invasion and seizure of the public property at Harper's Ferry.

Includes, also, Views of the minority, prepared by J. Collamer, journal of the Committee, appendix of documents, and testimony taken before the Committee.

1. Harpers Ferry, W. Va.—John Brown Raid, 1859. I. Mason, James Murray, 1798-1871. II. Collamer, Jacob, 1791-1865. III. Title. IV. Series.

E451.U57 1969   975.4'99   78-90198
                                                  MARC

Not listed in Monthly Catalog

MASOTTI REPORT
1010

Masotti, Louis H.

Shoot-out in Cleveland: black militants and the police; a report to the National Commission on the Causes and Prevention of Violence, by Louis H. Masotti and Jerome R. Corsi. Washington, For sale by the Supt. of Docs., U.S. Govt. Print. Off., 1969.

xv, 100 p. illus., map, ports. 24 cm. ([NCCPV staff study series] 5)

Number 5 on spine.
Includes bibliographical references.
1. Cleveland—Riot, 1968. I. Corsi, Jerome R., joint author.
II. United States. National Commission on the Causes and
Prevention of Violence. III. Title. IV. Series: United States. Na-
tional Commission on the causes and Prevention of Violence.
NCCPV staff study series, 5.
F499.C6M33 1969   977.1'32'04   72-602071
                                         MARC

MC#: 1969-13326
SuDocs no.: Pr36.8:V81/C59

MATTOX REPORT [Mattox, Gale A.]

1011

United States. Library of Congress. Congressional Research
Service.
Report by the Commission on the Organization of the Government for the Conduct of Foreign Policy: background and principal recommendations. 1975.
26 p. (Multilith 75-221 FA)
1. Foreign relations— U.S.
Not listed in Monthly Catalog

MAWHINNEY REPORT [Mawhinney, Robert J.]
see under
ALDRICH COMMISSION [Aldrich, Nelson
Wilmarth]
Laws of the United States concerning money, banking,
and loans.

MAY REPORT [Raymond and May Associates]
see
DOUGLAS REPORTS [Douglas, Paul H.]
National Commission on Urban Problems Research
report, no. 11

MAYER REPORT [Mayer, Jean]

1012

White House Conference on Food, Nutrition, and Health,
Washington, D.C., 1969.
Final report. [Washington; For sale by the Supt. of Docs., U.S.
Govt. Print. Off., 1970]
iv, 341 p. illus. 27 cm.
Jean Mayer, chairman.
Includes bibliographical references.
1. Nutrition—Congresses. 2. Food supply—United States—
Congresses. 3. Food relief—United States—Congresses. I. Mayer,
Jean.
TX345.W45 1969   338.1'9'73   72-606787
                                         MARC

MC#: 1970-7898
SuDocs no.: Y3.W58/16:1/970

MAYESKE REPORTS [Mayeske, George W.]

1013

A Study of our Nation's schools, by George W. Mayeske [and
others. Washington] U.S. Office of Education [1969]
xxiii, 884 p. illus. 29 cm.
Bibliography: p. 334-336.
1. Education—United States—Statistics. I. Mayeske, George
W., 1930- II. United States. Office of Education.
LA210.S78   370'.973   70-605907
                                         MARC

MC#: 1970-4064
SuDocs no.: HE5.2:Sch65/21

1014

A Study of our Nation's schools, by George W. Mayeske [and
others] With a foreword by Alexander M. Mood. [Washington]
Office of Education, Office of Program Planning and Evaluation;
[for sale by the Supt. of Docs., U.S. Govt. Print. Off., 1972, i.e.
1973]
xiv, 115 p. illus. 28 cm. (DHEW publication no. (OE) 72-142)
Previously issued in 1969 by the U.S. Office of Education as
a working paper.
Bibliography: p. 114-115.
Supt. of Docs. no.: HE5.210:10085
1. Education—United States—Statistics. I. Mayeske, George
W., 1930- II. United States. Office of Education. Office of Program Planning and Evaluation. III. Series: United States. Dept.
of Health, Education, and Welfare. DHEW publication no. (OE)
72-142.
LA210.S78 1973   370'.973   73-601831
                                         MARC

MC#: 1973-27435
SuDocs no.: HE5.210:10085

MAYO REPORT [Mayo, Leonard W.]

1015

U.S. *President's Panel on Mental Retardation.*
A proposed program for national action to combat mental retar-
dation; report to the President. Washington, For sale by the
Superintendent of Documents, U.S. Govt. Print. Off., 1962 [i.e.,
1963]
vii, 201 p. diagr., tables. 24 cm.
1. Mentally handicapped—U.S. 2. Mental deficiency—U.S.
I. Title: National action to combat mental retardation.
HV3006.A1A6   362.30973   63-60565
MC#: 1963-5676
SuDocs no.: Pr35.8:M52/P94

MAZIE REPORT [Mazie, Sara Mills]
see
ROCKEFELLER REPORT [Rockefeller, John D.
3d]
Population, distribution, and policy.

MEAD REPORT [Mead, George Houk]
see
ROPER REPORT [Roper, Daniel Calhoun]

MEADER REPORT

1016

Meader, George.
. . . Confidential report to the Special Senate committee in-
vestigating the national defense program on the preliminary in-
vestigation of military government in the occupied areas of
Europe, November 22, 1946 [by] George Meader, chief counsel.
[Washington, 1946]
1 v. 28 cm.
At head of title: Special Senate committee investigating the na-
tional defense program, Washington, D.C.
Leaves variously numbered.
"Release, December 4, 1946" (2 leaves) inserted.
1. Germany (Territory under U.S. occupation, 1945-) I. U.S.
Congress. Senate. Special committee investigating the national
defense program.
D802.G3M4   940.5343   47-71
Not located in Monthly Catalog

MEIER REPORT [Meier, John]
see
WEINBERGER REPORT [Weinberger, Casper W.]

MELLETT REPORT [Mellett, Lowell]
1017

U.S. *National emergency council.*
Report on economic conditions of the South. Prepared for the President by the National emergency council. [Washington, U.S. Govt. print. off., 1938]

cover-title, 64 p. 23½ cm.
1. Southern states—Econ. condit.—1918- I. Title.
HC107.A13A73 1938   330.975   38-26755
MC#: 1938-page 1120
SuDocs no.: Y3.N21/9:2So8

MELTZER REPORT
1018

Meltzer, Allan H.
A study of the dealer market of Federal Government securities; materials prepared for the Joint Economic Committee, Congress of the United States [by Allan H. Meltzer and Gert von der Linde] Washington, U.S. Govt. Print. Off., 1960.

ix, 144 p. tables. 23 cm.
Commonly known as the Meltzer report.
At head of title: 86th Cong., 2d sess., Joint Committee print.
1. Bonds—U.S. 2. Open market operations—U.S. I. Von der Linde, Gert, joint author. II. U.S. Congress. Joint Economic Committee. III. Title. IV. Title: Meltzer report on Federal Government securities.
HG4936.M4   61-60327
MC#: 1961-3994
SuDocs no.: Y4.Ec7:Se2

MENDES REPORT
1019

Mendes, Richard H. P.
Bibliography on community organization for citizen participation in voluntary democratic associations [by] Richard H. P. Mendes. [Washington] President's Committee on Juvenile Delinquency and Youth Crime; [for sale by the Superintendent of Documents, U.S. Govt. Print. Off.] 1965.

ii, 98 p. 26 cm.
1. U.S.—Soc. condit.—Bibl. 2. Community organization—Bibl. I. U.S. President's Committee on Juvenile Delinquency and Youth Crime. II. Title.
Z7165.U5M4   016.30926   66-60291
MC#: 1966-1396
SuDocs no.: Pr35.8:J98/C73

MENOCAL REPORT [Menocal, Aniceto García]
1020

U.S. *Dept. of state.*
Interoceanic canal congress, held at Paris, May, 1879. Instructions to Rear Admiral Daniel Ammen and civil engineer A. G. Menocal, U.S. Navy, delegates on the part of the United States to the Interoceanic canal congress, held at Paris, May, 1879, and reports of the proceedings of the congress. Washington, Govt. print. off., 1879.

21 p. 23 cm.
1. Canals, Interoceanic. 2. Interoceanic canal congress, Paris, 1879. I. Ammen, Daniel, 1820-1898. II. Menocal, Aniceto García, 1836-

TC773.U47 1879   6-7285
Checklist of United States Public Documents, 1789-1909, page 948
SuDocs no.: S5.15:879

MEREDITH REPORT [Meredith, Mrs. Christabel]
see under
ALDRICH COMMISSION [Aldrich, Nelson Wilmarth]
Philippovich von Philippsberg. History of the Bank of England.

MERIAM REPORTS [Meriam, Lewis]
1021

Brookings Institution, Washington, D.C. Institute for Government Research.
The problem of Indian administration. With a new introd. by Frank C. Miller. New York, Johnson Reprint Corp., 1971 [c1928]

xviii, xxii, 872 p. 23 cm.
Survey staff: Lewis Meriam and others.
Original ed. issues as no. 17 of Institute for Government Research, Brookings Institution, Studies in administration.
Bibliography: p. xvii-xviii (1st group)
1. Indians of North America—Government relations—1869-1934. 2. United States. Bureau of Indian Affairs. 3. Indians of North America. I. Meriam, Lewis, 1883II. Title. III. Series: Brookings Institution, Washington, D.C. Institute for Government Research. Studies in administration, no. 17.
E93.B873 1971   970.5   78-149059
                                                        MARC
Not located in Monthly Catalog

1022

Brookings institution, *Washington, D.C. Institute for government research.*
. . . The problem of Indian administration; report of a survey made at the request of Honorable Hubert Work, secretary of the interior, and submitted to him, February 21, 1928. Survey staff: Lewis Meriam, technical director; Ray A. Brown, Henry Roe Cloud, Edward Everett Dale . . . [and others] Baltimore, Md., The Johns Hopkins press, 1928.

xxii, 872 p. 22½ cm. (*Its* Studies in administration. [No. 17])
1. Indians of North America—Government relations. 2. U.S. Office of Indian affairs. 3. Indians of North America. I. Meriam, Lewis, 1883- II. Work, Hubert, 1860-1942. III. Title. IV. Title: Indian administration.
E93.B873   28-13503
Not located in Monthly Catalog

MERROW REPORTS [Merrow, Chester E.]
1023

U.S. *Congress. House. Committee on Foreign Affairs.*
Report of the Special Study Mission on International Organizations and Movements comprising Chester E. Merrow, chairman [and others] of the Committee on Foreign Affairs, pursuant to H. Res. 113, a resolution authorizing the Committee on Foreign Affairs to conduct thorough studies and investigations of all matters coming within the jurisdiction of such committee. Washington, U.S. Govt. Print. Off., 1954.

xv, 240 p. illus., map. 23 cm. (83d Cong., 2d sess. House report no. 1251)
Issued also as Committee print, 83d Cong., 2d sess., under title: Special Study Mission on International Organizations and Movements; report.
1. International agencies. 2. U.S.—For. rel.—1945- I. Merrow, Chester E. (Series: U.S. 83d Cong., 2d sess., 1954. House. Report no. 1251)

JX1995.U63 1954   *341.11   54-61389
MC#: 1954-5138
SuDocs no.: 83d Cong., 2d sess. H. Rept. 1251

1024

U.S. *Congress. House. Committee on Foreign Affairs.*
  Report of the Special Study Mission to Pakistan, India, Thailand, and Indochina, of the Committee on Foreign Affairs pursuant to H. Res. 113, a resolution authorizing the Committee on Foreign Affairs to conduct thorough studies and investigations of all matters coming within the jurisdiction of such committee. Washington, U.S. Govt. Print. Off., 1953.
  xi, 104 p. illus., maps (1 fold.) 24 cm. (83d Cong., 1st sess. House report no. 412)
  1. Asia, Southeastern. (Series: U.S. 83d Cong., 1st sess., 1953. House. Report no. 412)
DS518.1.U52   950   53-61002
MC#: 1953-8924
SuDocs no.: 83d Cong., 1st sess. H. Rept. 412
Also issued as Committee print:
MC#: 1953-8991
SuDocs no.: Y4.F76/1:P17/3

1025

U.S. *Congress. House. Committee on Foreign Affairs.*
  Special Study Mission on International Organizations and Movements; report by Chester E. Merrow, chairman [and others] Printed for the use of the Committee on Foreign Affairs. Washington, U.S. Govt. Print. Off., 1954.
  xiv, 240 p. illus., map.
  At head of title: 83d Cong., 2d sess. Committee print.
  Issued also as House report no. 1251, 83d Cong., 2d sess., under title: Report of the Special Study Mission on International Organizations and Movements.
  1. International agencies. 2. U.S.—For. rel.—1945- I. Merrow, Chester E. II. Title.
JX1995.U63 1954a   *341.11   54-61202
MC#: 1954-3728
SuDocs no.: Y4.F76/1:In8/23

MERWIN REPORT [Merwin, Charles Lewis]
  see under
O'MAHONEY REPORTS [O'Mahoney, Joseph Christopher]

METTLER REPORT [Mettler, Ruben F.]
1026

U.S. *President's Task Force on Science Policy.*
  Science and technology: tools for progress; the report of the President's Task Force on Science Policy. [Washington; For sale by the Supt. of Docs., U.S. Govt. Print. Off.] 1970.
  vii, 48 p. 24 cm.
  Ruben F. Mettler, chairman.
  Includes bibliographical references.
  1. Science and state—U.S. I. Mettler, Ruben F., 1924- II. Title.
Q127.U6A555   353.008'5   70-607262
                                        MARC
MC#: 1970-9070
SuDocs no.: Pr37.8:Sci2/R29

METZ REPORT [Metz, Harold W.]
  see
LELAND REPORT [Leland, Simeon Elbridge]

MEYERS REPORT [Meyers, Albert Leonard]
  see under
O'MAHONEY REPORTS [O'Mahoney, Joseph Christopher]

MIAMI REPORT
1027

Miami Study Team on Civil Disturbances.
  Miami report; the report of the Miami Study Team on Civil Disturbances in Miami, Florida, during the week of August 5, 1968. [Washington, For sale by the Supt. of Docs., U.S. Govt. Print. Off., 1969]
  viii, 30 p. illus.
  "Submitted to the National Commission on the Causes and Prevention of Violence."
  Cover title.
                                        70-600859
MC#: 1969-4859
SuDocs no.: Pr36.8:V81/M58

MIKESELL REPORT
1028

Mikesell, Raymond Frech.
  United States-Latin American relations: some observations on the operation of the Alliance for Progress, the first six months. A study prepared for the Subcommittee on American Republics Affairs of the Committee on Foreign Relations, United States Senate. Washington, U.S. Govt. Print. Off., 1962.
  vii, 22 p. 24 cm.
  At head of title: 87th Cong., 2d sess. Committee print.
  1. Alliance for Progress. I. U.S. Congress. Senate. Committee on Foreign Relations.
HC165.M5   62-62212
MC#: 1962-17330
SuDocs no.: Y4.F76/2:L34/5

MILES REPORT [Miles, Herman W.]
1029

U.S. *Defense Documentation Center.*
  Management of scientific research (unclassified title); an ASTIA report bibliography, compiled by Herman W. Miles. Arlington, Va., 1962.
  v, 77 p. 28 cm.
  "AD-269 700."
  Published by the center under its earlier name: Armed Services Technical Information Agency.
  1. Research—Bibl. I. Miles, Herman W. II. Title.
Z7405.R4U514   62-61601 rev
Not located in Monthly Catalog

MILGRAM REPORT [Milgram, Grace (Smelo)]
  see
DOUGLAS REPORTS [Douglas, Paul, H.]
  National Commission on Urban Problems.

  Research report, no. 13

MILLER REPORT [Miller, Louis E.]
  see
LEA REPORT [Lea, Clarence Frederick]

MILLER REPORT [Miller, Neal E.]
1030

U.S. *President's Science Advisory Committee. Life Sciences Panel.*

Strengthening the behavioral sciences; statement by the Behavioral Sciences Subpanel. Washington, 1962.

19 p. 24 cm.
1. Social sciences. I. Title.
H61.U57   62-61329
MC#: 1962-12650
SuDocs no.: Pr35.8:Sci2/B39

MILLER REPORTS [Miller, Herbert J., Jr.]
1031

U.S. *President's Commission on Crime in the District of Columbia.*
Report. Washington, U.S. Govt. Print. Off., 1966.

xxix, 1041 p. illus., maps. 23 cm.
"Final report."
Bibliographical footnotes: p. 937-1041.
1. Criminal law—District of Columbia. 2. Criminal Justice, Administration of—District of Columbia. 3. Crime and criminals—District of Columbia. 4. District of Columbia—Police.
KFD1762.A86   343'.09753   67-60320
MC#: 1967-2794
SuDocs no.: Pr36.8:C86/R29

1032

U.S. *President's Commission on Crime in the District of Columbia.*
Report on the Metropolitan Police Department. Washington, U.S. Govt. Print. Off., 1966.

vi, 95 p. illus. 24 cm.
Bibliographies included in "Footnotes" (p. 91-95)
1. District of Columbia. Police Dept. 2. Crime and criminals—District of Columbia. I. Title.
HV7619.D3 1966   66-62275
MC#: 1966-15262
SuDocs no.: Pr36.8:C86/P75

MILLER REPORTS [Miller, J. Irwin]
1033

United States. National Advisory Commission on Health Manpower.
Report. Washington, U.S. Govt. Print. Off., 1967-
v. illus. 23 cm.
Commonly known as the Miller report.
Bibliography: v. 1, p. 93.
1. Medical personnel—United States. 2. Medical care—United States. I. Title: Miller report on health manpower.
RA410.7.A53   338.4'7'3621   68-60181
                                                MARC
MC#: 1968-10066, 16459
SuDocs no.: Pr36.8:H34/R29/v.1, 2

1034

U.S. *Special Committee on U.S. Trade Relations With East European Countries and the Soviet Union.*
Report to the President. [Washington] Dept. of State [Office of Media Services, Bureau of Public Affairs; for sale by the Superintendent of Documents, U.S. Govt. Print. Off., 1966]

22 p. 24 cm. (Dept. of State publication 8061. Commercial policy series, 201)
1. U.S.—Comm.—Europe, Eastern. 2. Europe, Eastern—Comm.—U.S. (Series: U.S. Dept. of State. Commercial policy series, 201)
HF3092.A55 1966   382'.0973'047   66-61245
MC#: 1966-9718
SuDocs no.: S1.37:201

MILLIKAN REPORT [Millikan, Clark B.]
1035

U.S. *Congress. House. Committee on Government Operations.*
Organization and management of missile programs. Hearings before a subcommittee on the Committee on Government Operations, House of Representatives, Eighty-sixth Congress, second session . . . Washington, U.S. Govt. Print. Off., 1960.

iii, 228 p. illus. 24 cm.
Contents.—Department of Defense. May 3, 1960.—Air defense. May 4, 1960.—Air Force. May 6, 1960.
1. Aeronautics, Military—U.S. 2. Astronautics—U.S. I. Title.
UG633.A412 1960b   355.82   60-62054
The report entitled, "Report of the Secretary of the Air Force Management Study Committe", appears on pages 86-91 of the above cited committee hearing.
MC#: 1960-13433
SuDocs no.: Y4.G74/7:M69/960

MILLIKAN REPORT [Millikan, George Lee]
see
KAPLAN REPORT [Kaplan, Sheldon Z.]

MILLIMAN REPORT
1036

Milliman & Robertson, inc., *Seattle.*
Evaluation of premium rates for Government-wide uniform health benefit plan under the Retired Federal employees health benefits acts, Public law 86-724. Committee on Post Office and Civil Service, United States Senate. Submitted for the use of the committee by the United States Civil Service Commission. Washington, U.S. Govt. Print. Off., 1961.

viii, 10 p. tables. 24 cm.
At head of title: 87th Cong., 1st sess., Committee print.
1. Insurance, Government—U.S. 2. U.S.—Officials and employees, Retired. I. U.S. Congress. Senate. Committee on Post Office and Civil Service. II. U.S. Civil Service Commission.
HG8210.M5   62-60764
MC#: 1962-9501
SuDocs no.: Y4.P84/11:H34/3

MILLIS REPORT [Millis, H. A.]
see under
DILLINGHAM COMMISSION [Dillingham, William Paul]
Immigrants in industries.

MILLS REPORTS
1037

Mills, Frederick Cecil, 1892-
The statistical agencies of the Federal Government; a report to the Commission on Organization of the Executive Branch of the Government [by] Frederick C. Mills and Clarence D. Long. [New York] National Bureau of Economic Research [1949]

xiv, 201 p. diagrs. 24 cm. (Publications of the National Bureau of Economic Research, no. 50)
1. U.S.—Stat. 2. U.S.—Executive departments. I. Long, Clarence Dickinson, 1908- joint author. II. U.S. Commission on Organization of the Executive Branch of the Government. III. Title. (Series: National Bureau of Economic Research. Publications no. 50)
HA37.U55M48   311.3973   49-9945*
Not located in Monthly Catalog

1038

Mills, Frederick Cecil, 1892-

The statistical agencies of the Federal Government; a report with recommendations prepared for the Commission on Organization of the Executive Branch of the Government by Frederick C. Mills and Clarence D. Long. [Washington, U.S. Govt. Print. Off., 1948, i.e. 1949]

iii, 21 p. 23 cm.

On cover: Task force report on Statistical agencies, Appendix D.

An appendix to a report by the Commission on Organization of the Executive Branch of the Government with title, Statistical agencies published as p. 85-97 in Budgeting and accounting; a report to the Congress, February 1949.

1. U.S.—Stat. I. Long, Clarence Dickinson, 1908- joint author. II. U.S. Commission on Organization of the Executive Branch of the Government. Budgeting and accounting. III. Title: Task force report on Statistical agencies, Appendix D.

HA37.U55M5   310.6173   49-46010*

MC#: 1949-6883

SuDocs no.: Y3.Or3:7/D

MILLSTEIN REPORT [Millstein, Ira M.]

1039

United States. National Commission on Consumer Finance.

Consumer credit in the United States; report. [Washington; for sale by the Supt. of Docs., U.S. Govt. Print. Off.] 1972.

xxv, 294 p. illus. 27 cm.

Includes bibliographical references.

Supt. of Docs. no.: Y3.C76/2:1/972

1. Consumer credit—United States. 2. Consumer protection—United States. 3. Insurance, Credit. I. Title.

HG3755.U59 1972   332.7'43   72-600335

                                         MARC

MC#: 1973-25572

SuDocs no.: Y3.C76/2:1/972

MIRER REPORT [Mirer, Thad W.]

Alternative approaches to integrating income transfer programs.

see under

GRIFFITHS REPORTS [Griffiths, Martha W.]

Studies in public welfare, paper no. 4.

MITCHELL REPORT [Mitchell, James P.]

1040

U.S. *President's Committee on Migratory Labor.*

Report to the President on domestic migratory labor. 1st-Sept. 1956[Washington]

v. 26 cm.

1. Agricultural laborers—U.S. 2. Migrant labor—U.S.

HD1525.A34   331.763   L56-159

MC#: 1956-20530-First report

         1960-17719-Second report

SuDocs no.: L16.43:R29

MITCHELL REPORT

1041

Mitchell, Robert Buchanan, 1906-

Metropolitan planning for land use and transportation, a study, December, 1959. [Washington, 1960]

v, 47 p. 24 cm.

1. Cities and towns—Planning—U.S. I. Title.

NA9108.M5   711.40973   61-60359

MC#: 1961-5069

SuDocs no.: Pr34.2:M567

MIZEN REPORTS [Mizen, Mamie L.]

1042

U.S. *Congress. Senate. Committee on Appropriations.*

Federal facilities for Indians; report. 1955/61- Washington, U.S. Govt. Print. Off.

v. maps (part col. in pockets) 24 cm.

1. Indians of North America—Government relations—1934- 2. Indians of North America—Education. 3. Indians of North America—Health and hygiene. I. Title.

E93.U665815   970.5   66-60452 rev

MC#: 1962-11647 (LC card 62-61281 cancelled in favor of 66-60452 rev)

SuDocs no.: Y4.Ap6/2:In2/3

MC#: 1964-2228 (LC card 64-60477 cancelled in favor of 66-60452 rev)

SuDocs no.: Y4.Ap6/2:In2/3/962

MC#: 1966-11788

SuDocs no.: Y4.Ap6/2:In2/3/964

MC#: 1966-13192

SuDocs no.: Y4.Ap6/2:In2/3965-66

MC#: 1967-10804

SuDocs no.: Y4.Ap6/2:In2/3/967 add.

MC#: 1967-10805

SuDocs no.: Y4.Ap6/2:In2/3/967

MOFFIT REPORT [Moffit, Fred H.]

   see

BROOKS REPORT [Brooks, Alfred H.]

MONAGAN REPORT [Monagan, John S.]

1043

U.S. *Congress. House. Committee on Foreign Affairs.*

Conditions behind the Iron Curtain and in selected countries of Western Europe. Report of the special study mission to Europe . . . John S. Monagan, chairman, Harris B. McDowell, Jr. [and] William S. Broomfield of the Committee on Foreign Affairs, pursuant to H. Res. 60 (87th Congress) . . . Washington, U.S. Govt. Print. Off., 1963.

vii, 19 p. illus. 24 cm. (88th Cong., 1st sess. House report no. 234)

1. Europe—Descr. & trav.—1945- I. Monagan, John S. II. Title. (Series: U.S. 88th Cong., 1st sess., 1963. House. Report no. 234)

D922.U5   63-61415

MC#: 1963-9866

SuDocs no.: 88th Cong., 1st sess. H. Rept. 234

MONDALE REPORT [Mondale, Walter F.]

1044

United States. Congress. Senate. Select Committee on Equal Educational Opportunity.

Toward equal educational opportunity : the report of the Select Committee on Equal Educational Opportunity, United States Senate, prusuant to S. Res. 359, February 19, 1970 . . . December 31, 1972.—Washington : U.S. Govt. Print. Off., 1972.

xix, 440 p. : ill. ; 24 cm.—(Report - 92d Congress, 2d Session, Senate ; no. 92-000)

At head of title: Committee print.

Supt. of Docs. no.: Y4.Eq2:Eq2/2

1. Educational equalization—United States. I. Title. II. Series: United States. 92d Congress, 2d Session, 1972. Senate. Report : no. 92-000.

LA210.U56 1972   370.19   73-600943
                                                           MARC

MC#: 1973-21332

SuDocs no.: Y4.Eq2:Eq2/2

United States. Congress. Senate. Select Committee on Equal Educational Opportunity.

Toward equal educational opportunity: the report of the Select Committee on Equal Educational Opportunity, United States Senate. Edited, with a new introd. by Francesco Cordasco. New York, AMS Press [1974]

xxii, xix, 459 p. 24 cm.

Reprint of the 1972 ed. published by the U.S. Govt. Print. Off., Washington, which was issued as Report no. 92-000 of the United States Senate, 92d Congress, 2d Session.

Bibliography: p. [441]-449.

1. Educational equalization—United States. I. Cordasco, Francesco, 1920- ed. II. Title. III. Series: United States. 92d Congress, 2d Session, 1972. Senate. Report no. 92-000.

LA210.U56 1974   370-19   74-8765
                                                           MARC

Not listed in Monthly Catalog

MONROE REPORT [Monroe, David Goeting]
see
VOLLMER REPORT [Vollmer, August]

WICKERSHAM COMMISSION [Wickersham, George Woodward]

Report on police, no. 14.

MOOD REPORT [Mood, Eric W.]
see
DOUGLAS REPORTS [Douglas, Paul H.]

National Commission on Urban Problems.

Research report, no. 19.

MOONEY-BILLINGS REPORT [Mooney, Thomas J. and Billings, Warren K.]

1045

The Mooney-Billings report; suppressed by the Wickersham commission. New York city, Gotham house, inc. [1932]

7 p. 1., ii, iv, 243 p. 23½ cm.

"Draft of Mooney-Billings report, submitted to the National commission on law observance and enforcement by the Section on lawless enforcement of law. Consultants: Zechariah Chafee, jr., Walter H. Pollak [and] Carl S. Stern . . . June, 1931."-7th prelim. leaf.

Lettered on cover: The suppressed Mooney-Billings report.

1. Mooney, Thomas J., 1882-1942. 2. Billings, Warren K., 1894- I. Chafee, Zechariah, 1885-1957. II. Pollak, Walter Heilprin, 1887-1940. III. Stern, Carl Samuel. IV. U.S. Wickersham Commission. V. Title: The suppressed Mooney-Billings report.

Copyright A 58917   343.109794   33-2250

Not located in Monthly Catalog

See also WICKERSHAM COMMISSION [Wickersham, George Woodward]

MOOR REPORT [Moor, Roy E.]

1046

U.S. *Congress. Joint Economic Committee.*

The Federal budget as an economic document. Prepared for the Subcommittee on Economic Statistics of the Joint Economic Committee, Congress of the United States. Washington, U.S. Govt. Print. Off., 1962.

viii, 189 p. diagrs., tables. 24 cm.

At head of title: 87th Cong., 2nd sess. Joint committee print. Bibliography: p. 187-189.

1. Budget—U.S. 2. Budget. 3. U.S.—Economic policy.

HJ2051.A6115 1962   351.72   62-60414

MC#: 1962-2283

SuDocs no.: Y4.Ec7:B85

MOORE REPORT [Moore, John P.]

1047

U.S. *Congress. Senate. Committee on Rules and Administration.*

Interim report of 1956 presidential and senatorial campaign studies, from John P. Moore, special counsel [and others. Washington] 1956.

1 v. (various pagings) 28 cm.

At head of title: Senate Subcommittee on Priviliges and Elections.

1. Elections—U.S.—Campaign funds. 2. Presidents—U.S.—Election—1956. 3. U.S. Congress. Senate—Elections. I. Moore, John P., 1916-

JK1991.A4 1956a   324.273   56-63735

MC#: 1957-672

SuDocs no.: Y4.R86/2:P92/4

MOORE REPORT [Moore, William H.]
see
LEHMAN REPORT [Lehman, John W.]

MOORE REPORTS

1048

Moore, John Bassett, 1860-1947.

. . . A digest of international law . . . by John Basset Moore . . . Washington, Govt. print. off., 1906.

8 v. 24½ cm. ([U.S.] 56th Cong., 2d sess. House. Doc. 551)

Full title: A digest of international law as embodied in diplomatic discussions, treaties and other international agreements, international awards, the decisions of municipal courts, and the writings of jurists, and especially in documents, published and unpublished, issued by presidents and secretaries of state of the United States, the opinions of the attorneys-general, and the decisions of courts, federal and state.

By the act of Congress of February 20, 1897, a provision was made for "revising, reindexing, and otherwise completing and perfecting by the aid of such documents as may be useful, the second edition of the Digest of the international law of the United States." The work thus referred to . . . edited by Francis Wharton, LL. D., was published in three volumes in 1886. A second issued, embracing about 160 pages of new matter, added to the third volume, was made in 1887. *cf.* Pref.

Volume 8 contains General index; List of cases cited; List of documents; Addenda and errata.

1. International law—Sources. 2. U.S.—For. rel. I. Wharton, Francis, 1820-1889. II. U.S. President. III. U.S. Dept. of state. IV. U.S. Dept. of justice. V. Title.

JX237.M7   6-35196

MC#: 1906-pages 309, 351, 378, 401

SuDocs no.: 56th Cong., 2d sess. H. Doc. 551

1049

Moore, John Bassett, 1860-

History and digest of the international arbitrations to which the United States has been a party, together with appendices containing the treaties relating to such arbitrations, and historical legal notes . . . by John Bassett Moore . . . Washington, Govt. print. off., 1898.

6 v. fold. maps, facsim. 23 cm.

Paged continuously.

Published also as House misc. doc. 212, 53d Cong., 2d sess.

"List of authorities": v. 1, p. lxxxiii-xcviii.

1. Arbitration, International. 2. U.S.—For. rel. I. U.S. Treaties, etc. II. Title.

JX1987.A2   4-3795

- - - - - [Another issue] [U.S. 53d Cong., 2d sess. House. Misc. doc. 212]

JX1987.A2 1898a

MC#: 1899-pages 117, 185, 233

Also issued as: 53d Cong., 2d sess. H. Misc. Doc. 212 [6 pts.]

MOORE REPORTS [Moore, William H.]

1050

U.S. *Congress. Joint Economic Committee.*

Congressional action on major economic recommendations of the President, 1954. Materials prepared for the Joint Committee on the Economic Report by the Committee staff. Washington, U.S. Govt. Print. Off., 1954.

v, 15 p. 24 cm.

At head of title, 83d Cong., 2d sess. Joint committee print.

1. U.S.—Economic policy. I. Title.

HC106.5.A53 1954   338.973   54-60877 rev

MC#: 1954-18337

SuDocs no.: Y4.Ec7:Ec7/5/954

1051

U.S. *Congress. Joint Economic Committee.*

General credit control, debt management and economic mobilization; materials prepared for the Joint Committee on the Economic Report by the committee staff. Washington, U.S. Govt. Print. Off., 1951.

vi, 98 p. 24 cm.

At head of title: 82d Cong., 1st sess. Joint committee print.

1. Debts, Public—U.S. 2. Credit—U.S.

HJ8119.A48 1951   336.3   51-60335 rev

MC#: 1951-4790

SuDocs no.: Y4.Ec7:C86/2

1052

U.S. *Congress. Joint Economic Committee.*

Variability of private investment in plant and equipment; materials submitted to the Joint Economic Committee, Congress of the United States. Washington, U.S. Govt. Print. Off., 1962-

v. diagrs., tables. 24 cm.

At head of title, pt. 1: 87th Cong., 1st sess. Joint committee print.

Contents.—pt. 1. Investment and its financing.

1. Capital investments—U.S. 2. Saving and investment—U.S.

HG4028.C4U45   62-60580

MC#: 1962-4893, 6934

SuDocs no.: Y4.Ec7:In8/6/pt. 1, 2

MOOSE REPORT [Moose, Richard M.]
see
A-ARMS REPORT

MORAN REPORT [Moran, Robert D.]

1053

United States. President.

The President's report on occupational safety and health. 1971- Washington [s.n.] For sale by the Supt. of Docs., U.S. Govt. Print. Off.

v. ill. 27 cm.

Reports for 1971- issued in the Congressional series as House documents.

Reports for 1971- include reports on occupational safety and health by the United States Department of Labor and by the United States Department of Health, Education, and Welfare; reports for 1973- include Report on occupational safety and health by the Occupational Safety and Health Review Commission.

Supt. of Docs. no.: Pr38.2:Oc1; Pr38.2:Oc1/974

Key title: The President's report on occupational safety and health, ISSN 0360-5256.

1. Industrial hygiene—United States. 2. Industrial safety—United States. I. United States. Dept. of Labor. Report on occupational safety and health. II. United States. Dept. of Health, Education, and Welfare. Report on occupational safety and health. III. United States. Occupational Safety and Health Review Commission. Report on occupational safety and health. IV. Title.

HD7653.U55a   614.8′52   72-602347

                                                     MARC-S

MC#: 1972-14173

SuDocs no.: Pr37.2:Oc1

MC#: 1974-8186

SuDocs no.: Pr37.2:Oc1/973

MC#: 1977-3657

SuDocs no.: Pr38.2:Oc1/974

MC#: 1980-6413

SuDocs no.: Pr38.2:Oc1/975

MORGAN REPORT [Morgan, Russell H.]

1054

U.S. *National Advisory Committee on Radiation.*

Report to the Surgeon General, U.S. Public Health Service, on the control of radiation hazards in the United States. [n.p.] 1959.

20 p. 27 cm.

1. Radiation—Physiological effect.

RA1231.R2U518   614.715   60-60197

Not located in Monthly Catalog

MORGAN REPORT [Morgan, Thomas A.]

1055

U.S. *President's Advisory Committee on Management Improvement.*

Report to the President [of the] President's Advisory Committee on Management. Washington, U.S. Govt. Print. Off., 1952.

v, 20 p. 24 cm.

1. U.S.—Executive departments. 2. Public administration.

JK421.A44 1952   353   53-60131

MC#: 1953-1356 (LC card 51-60611 referred to in error)

SuDocs no.: Pr33.20:R29

MORISON REPORT [Morison, Robert]

1056

U.S. *President's Science Advisory Committee. Life Sciences Panel.*

Some new technologies and their promise for the life sciences. Washington, For sale by the Superintendent of Documents, U.S. Govt. Print. Off., 1963.

22 p. 24 cm.

1. Electronic data processing—Medicine. 2. Electronic data processing—Biology. I. Title.

R856.U55   63-60766

MC#: 1963-5678

SuDocs no.: Pr35.8:Sci2/T22

MORRISON REPORT [Morrison, James H.]

1057

U.S. *Civil Service Commission.*

A report on how people are recruited, examined, and appointed in the competitive civil service. Prepared for the Subcommittee on Civil Service, Committee on Post Office and Civil Service, House of Representatives. Washington, U.S. Govt. Print. Off., 1959.

iv, 130 p. map, diagrs., tables. 24 cm.
At head of title: Committee print.
1. U.S. – Officials and employees – Appointment, qualifications, tenure, etc. I. U.S. Congress. House. Committee on Post Office and Civil Service. II. Title: How people are recruited, examined, and appointed in the competitive civil service.
JK730.A5 1959   351.10973   59-61221
MC#: 1959-7480
SuDocs no.: Y4.P84/10:C49/9

MORROW REPORT [Morrow, Jay Johnson]

1058

U.S. *Alaska railroad commission.*

. . . Railway routes in Alaska. Message from the President of the United States transmitting report of Alaska railroad commission . . . Washington [Govt. print. off.] 1913.

172 p. incl. tables. fold. maps, fold. charts and portfolio of 19 fold. pl. (16 maps, 3 diagr.) 23 cm. (62d Cong., 3d sess. House. Doc. 1346)
Jay J. Morrow, chairman.
Message ordered printed Feb. 6, 1913. Message and report, with accompanying papers and illustrations, ordered printed Feb. 7, 1913.
"Message" is published also separately (with same document number) as "Transportation in Alaska."
Portfolio ordered printed, with illustrations, March 1, 1913.
"Publications relating to transportation and railway routes in Alaska": p. 167-172.
1. Railroads – Alaska. I. Morrow, Jay Johnson, 1870-1937. II. U.S. President, 1909-1913 (Taft) III. Title.
HE2771.A4A3 1913   13-35109
MC#: Feb. 1913-page 405
SuDocs no.: 62d Cong., 3d sess. H. Doc. 1346

MORSE REPORT [Morse, Richard S.]

1059

U.S. *Panel on Electrically Powered Vehicles.*

The automobile and air pollution; a program for progress. Report to the Commerce Technical Advisory Board. [Washington] U.S. Dept. of Commerce; [for sale by the Supt. of Docs., U.S. Govt. Print. Off.] 1967-

v. col. illus. 26 cm.
1. Air – Pollution. 2. Automobile exhaust gas. 3. Automobiles, Electric. I. U.S. Commerce Technical Advisory Board. II. Title.
TD886.5.U5   628'.53'2   67-62879
MC#: 1967-17470
SuDocs no.: C1.2:Au8/pt. 1
MC#: 1968-3467
SuDocs no.: C1.2:Au8/pt. 2

MORSE REPORT [Morse, Wayne Lyman]

1060

United Nations. *General Assembly. 15th sess., 1960-61. Delegation from the United States.*

The United States in the United Nations: 1960-a turning point. Supplementary report to the Committee on Foreign Relations, United States Senate, by Wayne Morse, member of the delegation. Washington, U.S. Govt. Print. Off., 1961.

ii, 55 p. 24 cm.
At head of title: 87th Cong., 1st sess. Committee print.
1. United Nations – U.S. I. Morse, Wayne Lyman, 1900- II. U.S. Congress. Senate. Committee on Foreign Relations.
JX1977.2.U5U55 1960-61b   61-60724
MC#: 1961-5868
SuDocs no.: Y4.F76/2:Un35/5

See also AIKEN REPORT [Aiken, George David] United States in the United Nations, 1960.

MORSS REPORT [Morss, Elliott R.]

see
ROCKEFELLER REPORT [Rockefeller, John D., 3d]

MOYNIHAN REPORTS [Moynihan, Daniel P.]

1061

U.S. *Dept. of Health, Education, and Welfare. Secretary's Advisory Committee on Traffic Safety.*

Report. [Washington] U.S. Dept. of Health, Education, and Welfare; [for sale by the Supt. of Docs., U.S. Govt. Print. Off.] 1968.

xiii, 147 p. illus. 24 cm.
Bibliography: p. 105-106.
1. Traffic safety – U.S.
HE5614.2.A55   614.8'62'0973   68-61279
MC#: 1968-9164
SuDocs no.: FS1.2:T67/968

1062

U.S. *Dept. of Labor. Office of Policy Planning and Research.*

The Negro family, the case for national action. [Washington, For sale by the Superintendent of Documents, U.S. Govt. Print. Off.] 1965.

78 p. illus. 27 cm.
Bibliography: p. 51-53.
1. Negroes – Moral and social conditions. 2. Family – U.S. I. Title.
E185.86.U52   L65-80
MC#: 1965-18392
SuDocs no.: L1.2:N31/3

United States. Dept. of Labor. Office of Policy Planning and Research.

The Negro family : the case for national action. – Westport, Conn. : Greenwood Press, 1981.

78 p. : ill. ; 29 cm.
Commonly known as the Moynihan report.
Reprint. Originally published: The Negro family / Office of Planning and Research, United States Department of Labor. Washington : U.S.G.P.O., 1965.
Includes bibliographical references.
ISBN 0-313-22853-1 (lib. bdg.)
1. Afro-American families. 2. Afro-Americans – Social conditions. I. Title. II. Title: Moynihan report on the Negro family.
E185.86.U52 1981   305.8'96073-dc19   81-607023
AACR2 MARC

Not listed in Monthly Catalog

MRAK REPORT [Mrak, Emil M.]

1063

United States. Secretary's Commission on Pesticides and Their Relationship to Environmental Health.

Report. [Washington] U.S. Dept. of Health, Education, and Welfare; for sale by the Supt. of Docs., U.S. Govt. Print. Off., 1969.

xvii, 677 p. 24 cm.

Includes bibliographies.

Contents. — Commission recommendations on pesticides. — Subcommittee and panel reports.

- - - - - Index, by Sharon L. Valley. Bethesda, Md., National Library of Medicine; [for sale by the Supt. of Docs., U.S. Govt. Print. Off., Washington, 1972]

310 p. 23 cm. (DHEW publication no. (NIH) 72-269)

At head of title: National Library of Medicine, Toxicology Information Program.

Bibliography: p. 207-310.

RA1270.P4U58 Suppl.

1. Pesticides and the environment. 2. Pesticides — Toxicology. I. Valley, Sharon L. II. United States. National Library of Medicine. Toxicology Information Program. III. Series: United States. Dept. of Health, Education, and Welfare. DHEW publication no. (NIH) 72-269.

RA1270.P4U58   632'.95   72-605266
                                                            MARC

MC#: 1970-1918
SuDocs no.: HE1.2:P43/pt. 1, 2
For the index:
MC#: 1972-12253
SuDocs no.: HE20.3602.P43

MUELLER REPORT [Mueller, Evan]
Participation in outdoor recreation.
see under
ORRRC REPORTS
ORRRC study report, 20.

MUELLER REPORTS [Mueller, Frederick H.]
1064

U.S. *Dept. of Commerce.*
Federal transportation policy and program. Washington, 1960.

viii, 32 p. 24 cm.

Commonly known as the Mueller report.

Bibliography: p. 32.

1. Transportation and state — U.S. I. Title. II. Title: Mueller report on Federal transportation policy and program.

HE18 1960.A53   385.0973   60-60795
MC#: 1960-4775
SuDocs no.: C1.2:T68/2/960

1065

U.S. *Dept. of Commerce.*
Report of the Highway cost allocation study. 1st-[5th]; Mar. 4, 1957-Jan. 23, 1961. Washington, U.S. Govt. Print. Off.

5 v. in 1. 24 cm.

Issued in the congressional series as House documents.

The 1st-4th vols. called Progress report; 5th called Final report.

Prepared by the Federal Highway Administrator.

Vol. 5 issued in 2 pts.

1. Roads — U.S. — Finance. I. U.S. Dept. of Commerce. Progress report of the Highway cost allocation study. II. U.S. Bureau of Public Roads. III. Title: Highway cost allocation study.

HE355.A3A255   57-61483 rev
MC#: 1957-6759 (1st progress report)
SuDocs no.: 85th Cong., 1st sess. H. Doc. 106
MC#: 1958-4239 (2d progress report)
SuDocs no.: 85th Cong., 2d sess. H. Doc. 344
MC#: 1959-5812 (3d progress report) (LC card 59-60890 cancelled in favor of 57-61483)

SuDocs no.: 86th Cong., 1st sess. H. Doc. 91
MC#: 1960-6503 (4th progress report)
SuDocs no.: 86th Cong., 2d sess. H. Doc. 355
MC#: 1961-5589 (Final report) (LC card 61-60738 cancelled in favor of 57-61483)
SuDocs no.: 87th Cong., 1st sess. H. Doc. 54

MUNDT REPORT [Mundt, Karl S.]
1066

U.S. *Congress. Senate. Committee on Government Operations.*

Transfer of occupation currency plates, espionage phase. Interim report of the Committee on Government Operations made by its Senate Permanent Subcommittee on Investigations, Subcommittee on Government Operations Abroad, pursuant to S. Res. 40. Washington, U.S. Govt. Print. Off., 1953.

iii, 16 p. 23 cm. (83d Cong., 1st sess. Senate. Report no. 837)

1. Occupation currency — Germany. 2. World War, 1939-1945 — Germany. 3. Espionage, Russian — U.S. I. Title. (Series: U.S. 83d Cong., 1st sess., 1953. Senate. Report no. 837)

HG1006.U53   332.4943   53-63831
MC#: 1954-573
SuDocs no.: 83d Cong., 1st sess. S. Rept. 837

MURDOCK REPORT [Murdock, John R.]
1067

U.S. *Congress. House. Committee on Interior and Insular Affairs.*
The physical and economic foundation of natural resources. Washington, 1952-53.

4 v. illus., maps. 29 cm.

A collection of papers by eminent authorities, prepared for the Committee on Interior and Insular Affairs.

Includes bibliographies.

Contents. — 1. Photosynthesis, basic features of the process. — 2. The physical basis of water supply and its principal uses. — 3. Groundwater regions of the United States, their storage facilities. — 4. Subsurface facilities of water management and patterns of supply; type area studies.

1. Water-supply — U.S. 2. Photosynthesis. I. Title.

GB701.A48 1952   *551.573   53-60448
MC#: 1953-5626, 5627, 5628, 17269 (Vols. 1-4)
SuDocs no.: Y4.In8/14:N21/(nos.)

MURPHY COMMISSION [Murphy, Robert D.]
1068

United States. Commission on the Organization of the Government for the Conduct of Foreign Policy.

Commission on the Organization of the Government for the Conduct of Foreign Policy ; [report]. - Washington : The Commission : for sale by the Supt. of Docs., U.S. Govt. Print. Off., 1975.

xii, 278 p. ; 24 cm.

- - - - - Appendices. — Washington : for sale by the Supt. of Docs., U.S. Govt. Print. Off., 1975 [i.e. 1976]

7 v. : ill. ; 27 cm.

Includes bibliographical references.
                                           JX1706.A37 1975 Suppl.

1. United States — Foreign relations administration. 2. United States — Diplomatic and consular service. 3. United States — Foreign relations-1945-

JX1706.A37 1975   353.008'92   75-602320
                                                      (MARC)

MC#: 1975-12681
SuDocs no.: Y3.F76/5:1/975

MURPHY REPORT [Murphy, Charles S.]
1069

U.S. *Congress. Office of legislative counsel.*

. . . General welfare clause. Memorandum on the general welfare clause prepared by the Office of the legislative counsel, United States Senate . . . Washington, U.S. Govt. print. off., 1945.

1 p. 1., 20 p. 23 cm. ([U.S.] 79th Cong., 1st sess. Senate. Doc. 46)

Signed: Charles S. Murphy.

1. U.S. Congress—Powers and duties. I. Murphy, Charles S. II. Title.

JK1064.A54 1945   328.34   45-36166
MC#: 1945-page 591
SuDocs no.: 79th Cong., 1st sess. S. Doc. 46

MURPHY REPORT [Murphy, Mrs. Kathryn (Robertson)]
see under
O'MAHONEY REPORTS [O'Mahoney, Joseph Christopher]

Kreps. Measurement of the social performance of business.

MURPHY REPORT
1070

Murphy, Tom O.

Economic appraisal of the sugar operations of the Virgin Islands Corporation. Public Works and Resources Subcommittee of the Committee on Government Operations. Washington, U.S. Govt. Print. Off., 1957.

vii, 25 p. tables. 24 cm.

At head of title: Committee print. 85th Cong., 1st sess. House of Representatives.

1. Virgin Islands Corporation. 2. Sugar trade—Virgin Islands of the United States. I. U.S. Congress. House. Committee on Government Operations.

HD9114.V52M8   338.476641   59-62484
MC#: 1959-15944
SuDocs no.: Y4.G74/7:Su3

MURRAY REPORT [Murray, Alan P.]
1071

U.S. *Congress. Joint Economic Committee.*

The Federal tax system: facts and problems, 1964; materials assembled by the committee staff. Washington, U.S. Govt. Print. Off., 1964.

x, 321 p. 24 cm.

At head of title: 88th Cong., 2d sess. Joint committee print.

1. Taxation—U.S.—Law. I. Title.

                                        64-62713
MC#: 1964-17442
SuDocs no.: Y4.Ec7:T19/5

MURRAY REPORT [Murray, James Edward]
1072

U.S. *Forest Service.*

Full use and development of Montana's timber resources. A survey prepared for the Montana delegation relating to developing the potential of forest resources in Montana. Washington, U.S. Govt. Print. Off., 1959.

xv, 35 p. illus., maps. 24 cm. (86th Cong., 1st sess. Senate. Document no. 9)

1. Timber—Montana. 2. Wood-using industries—Montana. I. Title. (Series: U.S. 86th Cong., 1st sess., 1959. Senate. Document. no. 9)
SD11.A4818   634.927   59-60495
MC#: 1959-3344
SuDocs no.: 86th Cong., 1st sess. S. Doc. 9

MURRAY REPORT [Murray, Janet Helen]
see
KNEELAND REPORT [Kneeland, Hildegarde]

MURRAY REPORT [Murray, John P.]
see
RUBINSTEIN-COMSTOCK REPORT [Rubinstein, Eli Abraham and Comstock, George A.]

MURRAY REPORT [Murray, Merrill Garver]
1073

U.S. *Committee on economic security.*

Social security in America; the factual background of the Social security act as summarized from staff reports to the Committee on economic security. Published for the Committee on economic security by the Social security board, Washington, D.C. Washington, U.S. Govt. print. off., 1937.

xix, 592 p. illus. (maps) tables (part fold.) diagrs. 23 ½ cm. (Social security board. [Publication no. 20])

"The publication of this summary of the staff reports of the Committee on economic security has been made possible by the Social security board. The board assumed the cost of publication and of completing the preparation of the summary, which was unfinished when the Committee on economic security went out of existence."—Pref.

"This summary was prepared principally by Miss Martha D. Ring . . . The unemployment compensation section was prepared by Merrill G. Murray."—Pref.

Appendixes: I. Procedures followed in estimating unemployment compensation coverage in the United States, 1922-1923.—II. Procedures followed in estimating duration of unemployment in the United States, 1922-23.—III. Procedures followed in estimating the maximum duration of benefits.—IV. The history and development of the United States Employment service.—V. Summary of state unemployment compensation laws, January 1, 1936.—VI. Unemployment insurance provisions of the Canadian employment and social insurance act.—VII. Old-age insurance in Great Britain. VIII. The Canadian pension systems.—IX. Survivors' insurance in foreign countries.—X. Financial history of the workers' invalidity, old-age, and survisors' insurance of Germany.—XI. Birth rate and infant and maternal mortality tables.—XII. Summary of provisions of the Social security act relating to federal grants to states for public-welfare purposes.—XIII. Creation and membership of the Committee on economic security and affiliated groups.—XIV. Staff of the Committee on economic security.—XV. List of staff reports.—XVI. The Social security act.

1. Insurance, Social—U.S. 2. Insurance, Unemployment—U.S. 3. Old-age pensions—U.S. I. Ring, Martha D. II. Murray, Merrill Garver, 1900-
HD7123.A3 no. 20   37-26586
- - - - - Copy 3.
HD7123.A55 1937
MC#: 1937-page 803
SuDocs no.: SS1.2:So1/3

MURRAY REPORT [Murray, Robert B., Jr.]
1074

U.S. *Air Coordinating Committee.*

Civil air policy; a report by direction of the President. Washington, U.S. Govt. Print. Off., 1954.

vi, 71 p. 26 cm.

1. Aeronautics, Commercial—U.S. I. Title.
TL521.A522   387.7   54-60083
MC#: 1954-9177
SuDocs no.: Y3.Ai7/3:2C49

MURRAY REPORT [Murray, Tom]

1075

U.S. *Congress. House. Committee on Post Office and Civil Service.*
United States Civil Service Commission; report. Washington, U.S. Govt. Print. Off., 1956.

iv, 79 p. diagrs., tables. 24 cm. (84th Cong., 2d sess. House report no. 1844)

1. U.S. Civil Service Commission. (Series: U.S. 84th Cong., 2d sess., 1956. House. Report no. 1844)
JK649 1956e   351.1   56-60706
MC#: 1956-5212
SuDocs no.: 84th Cong., 2d sess. H. Rept. 1844

MYERS REPORT [Myers, Charles Andrews]
see under
O'MAHONEY REPORTS [O'Mahoney, Joseph Christopher]
Brown. Industrial wage rates.

NASH REPORT [Nash, A. E. Keir]
see
ROCKEFELLER REPORT [Rockefeller, John D., 3d]

NATHAN REPORT

1076

Nathan, Richard P
Jobs & civil rights; the role of the Federal Government in promoting equal opportunity in employment and training, by Richard P. Nathan. Prepared for U.S. Commission on Civil Rights by the Brookings Institution, Washington, D.C. [Washington, For sale by the Supt. of Docs., U.S. Govt. Print. Off.] 1969.

vi, 318 p. 28 cm. (Clearinghouse publication no. 16)
Commonly known as the Nathan report.
Research performed under contract CCR-67-28.
Bibliography: p. 309-318.

1. Discrimination in employment—United States. I. Brookings Institution, Washington, D.C. II. Title. III. Title: Nathan report on jobs and civil rights. IV. Series: United States. Commission on Civil Rights. Clearinghouse publication no. 16.
KF4755.A83 no. 16   353.008′3   79-601739
                         MARC

MC#: 1969-7762
SuDocs no.: CR 1.10:no. 16

NATHAN REPORT

1077

Nathan (Robert R.) Associates, Washington, D.C.
The foreign market potential for United States coal. Report to the U.S. Dept. of the Interior, Office of Coal Research. Washington [1963]

4 v. 28 cm.
Cover title.
"Copy no. 94."

Bibliographical footnotes.

1. Coal trade. 2. Coal trade—U.S. I. U.S. Office of Coal Research. II. Title.
HD9540.N3   63-65069
Not located in Monthly Catalog

NATIONAL AGENDA FOR THE EIGHTIES

1078

United States. President's Commission for a National Agenda for the Eighties.
A national agenda for the eighties : report of the President's Commission for a National Agenda for the Eighties. — Washington : The Commission : For sale by The Supt. of Docs., U.S. G.P.O., 1980.

214 p. ; 23 cm.

1. United States—Economic Policy—1971- . 2. United States—Social policy. 3. United States—Politics and government—1945- . 4. United States—Foreign relations—1945- . I. Title.
HC106.7.U577 1980   973.926-dc19   81-356
                         AACR2 MARC

MC#: 1981-3830
SuDocs no.: Pr39.8:Ag3/Ag3

United States. President's Commission for a National Agenda for the Eighties.
A national agenda for the eighties : report of the President's Commission for a National Agenda for the Eighties. — Englewood Cliffs, N.J. : Prentice-Hall, [1981]

225 p. ; 23 cm.
"A Spectrum book."
Reprint. Originally published: Washington : President's Commission for a National Agenda for the Eighties, 1980.
Includes index.
ISBN 0-13-609537-2

1. United States-Economic policy—1971- . 2. United States—Social policy. 3. United States—Politics and government—1945- . 4. United States—Foreign relations—1945- . I. Title.
HC106.7.U577 1981   973.926-dc19   81-8549
                         AACR 2 MARC

Not listed in Monthly Catalog

1079

Panel on Energy, Natural Resources, and the Environment (U.S.)
Energy, natural resources, and the environment in the eighties : report of the Panel on energy, Natural Resources, and the Environment. — Washington : President's Commission for a National Agenda for the Eighties: For sale by The Supt. of Docs., U.S. G.P.O., 1980.

57 p. ; 23 cm.

1. Energy policy—United States. 2. Power resources—United States. 3. Environmental policy—United States. I. Title.
HD9502.U52P35 1981   333.79′0973-dc19   81-649
                         MARC

MC#: 1981-3833
SuDocs no.: Pr39.8:Ag3/En2

1080

Panel on the American Economy: Employment, Productivity, and Inflation (U.S.)
The American economy—employment, productivity, and inflation in the eighties : report of the Panel on the American Economy—Employment, Productivity, and Inflation, President's Commission for a National Agenda for the Eighties. — Washing-

ton : The Commission : For sale by The Supt. of Docs., U.S. G.P.O., 1980.

82 p. ; 23 cm.

1. United States—Economic policy—1971- . 2. Industrial productivity—United States. 3. Labor supply—United States. 4. Inflation (Finance)—United States. I. Title.

HC106.7.P345 1981　　　330.973′0926-dc19　　　81-357

　　　　　　　　　　　　　　　　　　　　　AACR2 MARC

MC#: 1981-3832

SuDocs no.: Pr39.8:Ag3/Ec7

1081

United States. Panel on Science and Technology: Promises and Dangers.

Science and technology : promises and dangers in the eighties : report of the Panel on Science and Technology: Promises and Dangers.—Washington : President's Commission for a National Agenda for the Eighties : Washington, D.C. : For sale by the Supt. of Docs., 1980.

96 p. ; 23 cm.

Includes bibliographies.

1. Technology and state—United States. 2. Science and state—United States. I. United States. President's Commisison for a National Agenda for the Eighties. II. Title.

T21.U56 1980　　　306.4-dc19　　　80-28290

MC#: 81-11112

SuDocs no.: Pr39.8:Ag3/Sci2

United States. Panel on Science and Technology: Promises and Dangers.

Science and technology : promises and dangers in the eighties : report of the Panel on Science and Technology: promises and dangers.—Englewood Cliffs, N.J. : Prentice-Hall, [1981]

96 p. ; 23 cm.

"A Spectrum book."

Reprint : Originally published : Washington : President's Commission for a National Agenda for the Eighties, 1981.

Includes index.

ISBN 0-13-795518-9

ISBN 0-13-795500-6 (pbk.)

1. Technology and state—United States. 2. Science and state—United States. I. United States. President's Commission for a National Agenda for the Eighties. II. Title.

T21.U558 1981　　　361.6′0973-dc19　　　81-8628

Not listed in Monthly Catalog

1082

United States. President's Commission for a National Agenda for the Eighties. Panel on Government and the Advancement of Social Justice: Health, Welfare, Education, and Civil Rights.

Government and the advancement of social justice : health, welfare, education, and civil rights in the eighties : report of the Panel on Government and the Advancement of Social Justice: Health, Welfare, Education, and Civil Rights. - Washington : President's Commission for a National Agenda for the Eighties : for sale by the Supt. of Docs., U.S. Gov't Print. Off., 1980.

130 p. : ill. ; 23 cm.

Includes bibliographical references.

1. United States—Social policy. I. Title.

HN59.U544 1980　　　361.6′1′0973-dc19　　　81-256

　　　　　　　　　　　　　　　　　　　　　MARC

MC#: 1981-3834

SuDocs no.: Pr39.8:Ag3/So1

United States. Panel on Government and the Advancement of Social Justice: Health, Welfare, Education, and Civil Rights.

Government and the advancement of social justice : health, welfare, education, and civil rights in the eighties : report of the Panel on Government and the Advancement of Social Justice: Health, Welfare, Education, and Civil Rights.—Englewood Cliffs, N.J. : Prentice-Hall, [1981]

130 p. ; 23 cm.

"A Spectrum book."

At head of title: President's Commission for a National Agenda for the Eighties.

Reprint : Originally published : Washington : President's Commission for a National Agenda for the Eighties, 1980.

Includes index.

1. Social justice. 2. United States—Social policy. I. United States. Presidents commission for a National Agenda for the Eighties. II. Title.

HN59.2.U54 1981　　　361.6′1′0973-dc19　　　81-10562

Not listed in Monthly Catalog

1083

United States. Panel on Policies and Priorities for Metropolitan and Nonmetropolitan America.

Urban America in the eighties : perspective and prospects : report of the Panel on Policies and Priorities for Metropolitan and Nonmetropolitan America.—Washington, President's Commission for a National Agenda for the Eighties, 1980.

112 p. ; 23 cm.

Includes bibliographies.

1. Urban policy—United States-Congresses.

I. United States. President's Commission for a National Agenda for the Eighties. II. Title.

HT123.U465 1980　　　307.7′6′0973-dc19　　　80-27894

MC#: 81-11113

SuDocs no.: Pr39.8:Ag3/Ur1

United States. Panel on Policies and Prospects for Metropolitan and Nonmetropolitan America.

Urban America in the eighties : perspectives and prospects : report of the Panel on Policies and Prospects for Metropolitan and Nonmetropolitan America. Englewood Cliffs, N.J. : Prentice Hall, [1981]

112 p. ; 23 cm.

"A Spectrum Book."

At head of title : President's Commission for a National Agenda for the Eighties.

Reprint : Originally published : Washington : President's Commission for a National Agenda for the Eighties. 1980.

Includes index.

1. Urban policy—United States—Congresses. I. United States. President's Commission for a National Agenda for the Eighties. II. Title.

HT123.U466 1981　　　307.7′6′0973-dc19　　　81-8831

Not listed in Monthly Catalog

1084

United States. Panel on Government and the Regulation of Corporate and Individual Decisions.

Government and the regulation of corporate and individual decisions in the eighties : report of the Panel on Government and the Regulation of Corporate and Individual Decisions.—Washington : President's Commission for a National Agenda for the Eighties : for sale by the Supt. of Docs., U.S. Govt. Print. Off., 1980.

113 p. ; 23 cm.

1. Industrial laws and legislation—United States. 2. Trade regulation—United States. 3. Social legislation—United States. I. Title. II. Title: Government regulation.

KF1600.A843   343.73′08-dc19   80-29251
                                             AACR2 MARC

MC#: 1982-26586
SuDocs no.: Pr39.8:Ag3/R36

United States. Panel on Government and the Regulation of Corporate and Individual Decisions.

Government and the regulation of corporate and individual decisions of the eighties : a report of the Panel on Government and the Regulation of Corporate and Individual Decisions. — Englewood Cliffs, N.J. : Prentice-Hall, [1981]

    113 p. ; 23 cm.
    "A Spectrum book."
    At head of title : President's Commission for a National Agenda for the Eighties.
    Reprint : Originally published : Washington : President's Commission for a National Agenda for the Eighties, 1980.
    Includes index.
    ISBN 0-13-360834-4
    ISBN 0-13-360826-3 (pbk.)
    1. Industrial laws and legislation — United States. 2. Trade regulation — United States. 3. Social legislation — United States. I. United States. President's Commission for a National Agenda for the Eighties. II. Title.
KF1600.A843 1981   343.73′07   81-8608
                          347.3037-dc19

Not listed in Monthly Catalog

1085

United States. President's Commission for a National Agenda for the Eighties. Panel on the Electoral and Democratic Process.

    The electoral and democratic process in the eighties : report of the Panel on the Electoral and Democratic Process. — Washington : President's Commission for a National Agenda for the Eighties : [for sale by the Supt. of Docs., U.S. Govt. Print. Off.], 1980.

    101 p. : ill. ; 23 cm.
    Includes bibliographies.
    1. United States — Politics and government. I. Title.
JK271.U56 1981   320.973-dc19   81-86
                                             MARC

MC#: 1981-3831
SuDocs no.: Pr39.8:Ag3/D39

United States. Panel on the Electoral and Democratic Process.

    The electoral and democratic process in the eighties : report of the Panel on the Electoral and Democratic Process. — Englewood Cliffs., N.J. : Prentice-Hall, [1981]

    101 p. ; 23 cm.
    "A Spectrum book."
    At head of title : President's Commission for a National Agenda for the Eighties.
    Includes Index.
    1. United States — Politics and government. I. United States. President's Commission for a National Agenda for the Eighties. II. Title.
JK271.U55 1981   320.973-dc19   81-8835
Not listed in Monthly Catalog

1086

United States. Panel on the Quality of American Life.
    The quality of American life in the eighties : report of the Panel on the Quality of American Life. — Washington : President's Commission for a National Agenda for the Eighties : For sale by the Supt. of Docs., U.S.G.P.O., 1980.

    140 p. : ill. ; 23 cm.
    Includes bibliographical references.

    1. Quality of life — United States. 2. United States — Social policy. I. Title.
HN60.U545 1980   361.6′1′0973-dc19   81-281
                                                  AACR2 MARC

MC#: 1981-10150
SuDocs no.: Pr39.8:Ag3/L62

United States. Panel on the Quality of American life.
    The quality of American life in the eighties : report of the Panel on the Quality of American life. — Englewood Cliffs, N.J. : Prentice-Hall, [1981]

    140 p. : 23 cm.
    "A Spectrum book."
    At head of title : President's Commission for a National Agenda for the Eighties.
    Reprint : Originally published : Washington : President's Commission for a National Agenda for the Eighties.
    Includes index.
    1. Quality of life — United States. 2. United States — Social policy.
HN60.U545 1981   361.6′1′0973-dc19   81-8579
Not listed in Monthly Catalog

1087

United States. President's Commission for a National Agenda for the Eighties. Panel on the United States and the World Community.

    The United States and the world community in the eighties : report of the Panel on the United States and the World Community. — Washington, D.C. : President's Commission for a National Agenda for the eighties : for sale by the Supt. of Docs., U.S. Govt. Print. Off., 1980.

    109 p. ; 23 cm.
    1. United States — Foreign relations — 1945- . I. Title.
E840.U67 1980   327.73-dc19   80-28709
                                           MARC

MC#: 1981-3835
SuDocs no.: Pr39.8:Ag3/W89

United States. Panel on the United States and the World Community.
    The United States and the world community in the eighties : report of the Panel on the United States and the World Community. - Englewood Cliffs, N.J. : Prentice-Hall [1981]

    109 p. ; 23 cm.
    "A Spectrum book."
    At head of title : President's Commission for a National Agenda for the Eighties.
    Reprint : Originally published : Washington : President's Commission for a National Agenda for the Eighties, 1980.
    Includes Index.
    1. United States — Foreign relations — 1945- . I. Title.
E840.U647 1981   327.73-dc19   81-8826
Not listed in Monthly Catalog.

NAVY COURT OF INQUIRY
see
ROBERTS COMMISSION [Roberts, Owen Josephus]

NEAL REPORT [Neal, Phil C.]
1088

U.S. *White House Task Force on Antitrust Policy.*
    Report of the White House Task Force on Antitrust Policy, July 5, 1968.

(*In* U.S. Congress. Congressional record. [Daily ed.] v. 115 (1969) no. 87, p. S5642-S5659)
SuDocs no.: X/a.91.1:87

NELSEN COMMISSION [Nelsen, Ancher]
1089

United States. Nelsen Commission.
Report of the Commision on the Organization of the Government of the District of Columbia. Washington, U.S. Govt. Print. Off., 1972-
v. illus. 24 cm. (92d Congress, 2d session. House document no. 92-317)
Contents: v. 1. summary.
Supt. of Docs. no.: 92-2:H. doc. 317
1. District of Columbia—Executive departments—Management. I. Title. II. Series: United States. 92d Congress, 2d session, 1972. House. Document no. 92-317.
JK2735.A5   353.9'753'04   72-603275
                                              MARC
MC#: 1973-19549
SuDocs no.: 92d Cong., 2d sess. H. Doc. 317

NELSON REPORT [Nelson, Saul]
see under
O'MAHONEY REPORTS [O'Mahoney, Joseph Christopher]

NETZER REPORT [Netzer, Dick]
see
DOUGLAS REPORTS [Douglas, Paul H.]
National Commission on Urban Problems.

Research report no. 1

NEUBERGER REPORT [Neuberger, Maurine B.]
1090

U.S. *President's Commission on the Status of Women. Committee on Social Insurance and Taxes.*
Report. Washington, For sale by the Superintendent of Documents, U.S. Govt. Print. Off., 1963.
vii, 81 p. tables. 26 cm.
Bibliographical footnotes.
1. Insurance, Social—U.S. 2. Income tax—U.S. 3. Woman—Employment—U.S.
HD7123.A517   63-65424
MC#: 1964-1545
SuDocs no.: Pr35.8:W84/Sol

NEUBERGER REPORT [Neuberger, Richard Lewis]
1091

U.S. *Congress. Senate. Committee on Interior and Insular Affairs.*
Study of development of upper Columbia River Basin, Canada and United States; report to the chairman of the Senate Committee on Interior and Insular Affairs, submitted by Richard L. Neuberger. Washington, U.S. Govt. Print. Off., 1955.
iv, 44 p. fold. map. 24 cm.
At head of title: Committee print.
1. Water resources development—Columbia River Valley. I. Neuberger, Richard Lewis, 1912-
HD1694.A2 1955c   56-60748
MC#: 1956-5484
SuDocs no.: Y4.In8/13:C72

NEWMAN REPORTS [Newman, Frank]
1092

United States. Office of Education.
Report on higher education. [Washington; For sale by the Supt. of Docs., U.S. Govt. Print. Off.] 1971.
xi, 130 p. 24 cm.
"OE-50065."
Prepared by an independent task force, Frank Newman, chairman, funded by the Ford Foundation.
Includes bibliographies.
1. Education, Higher—United States—1965- I. Title.
L112.R37   378.73   75-611992
                                      MARC
MC#: 1971-9502
SuDocs no.: HE5.250:50065

1093

The Second Newman report; national policy and higher education; report of a special task force to the Secretary of Health, Education, and Welfare. [Frank Newman, chairman] Cambridge, Mass., MIT Press [1973]
xxiii, 227 p. 21 cm.
The 1st Newman report was published in 1971 under title: Report on higher education, March 1971.
Bibliography: p. [181]-227.
1. Education, Higher—United States. I. Newman, Frank, 1927- II. United States. Dept. of Health, Education, and Welfare. Office of the Secretary. III. Report on higher education, March 1971. IV. Title: National policy and higher education.
L112.S42 1973   378.73   73-21475
                                          MARC
ISBN 0-262-08071-0; 0-262-58027-6 (pbk.)
Not located in Monthly Catalog

NEWTON REPORT
1094

Newton, George D 1931-
Firearms & violence in American life; a staff report submitted to the National Commission on the Causes & Prevention of Violence [prepared by] George D. Newton, Jr. [and] Franklin E. Zimring. [Washington] National Commission on the Causes and Prevention of Violence; for sale by the Supt. of Docs., U.S. Govt. Print. Off. [1969]
xxiii, 268 p. illus. 24 cm. ([NCCPV staff study series] 7)
Report of the Task Force on Firearms.
Bibliographical footnotes.
1. Firearms—Laws and regulations—United States. I. Zimring, Franklin E., joint author. II. United States. Task Force on Firearms. III. United States. National Commission on the Causes and Prevention of Violence. IV. Title. V. Series: United States. National Commission on the Causes and Prevention of Violence. NCCPV staff study series, 7.
KF3941.N4   353.007'53   70-601932
                                          MARC
MC#: 1969-13321
SuDocs no.: Pr36.8:V181/F51

NEYMARCK REPORT [Neymarck, Alfred]
see under
ALDRICH COMMISSION [Aldrich, Nelson Wilmarth]
Patron. Bank of France.

NICHOLS REPORT [Nichols, John Ralph]
1095

U.S. *Office of Territories.*
Management survey of the Government of American Samoa; a report of a Management Improvement Survey to the Department of the Interior, containing recommendations for the future civilian administration of American Samoa, prepared by John R. Nichols, director of the team [and others. Washington, 1951]

ii, 88 p. maps. 27 cm.
1. American Samoa—Pol. & govt. I. Nichols, John Ralph, 1898- II. Title.
JQ6230.A5 1951   354.961   51-60444
MC#: 1951-7443
SuDocs no.: I35.2:Sa4

NIX REPORT [Nix, Robert N. C.]
1096

U.S. *Congress. House. Committee on Post Office and Civil Service. Subcommittee on Census and Statistics.*
How to cut paperwork; [report] Eighty-ninth Congress, second session. Washington, U.S. Govt. Print. Off., 1966.

ix, 70 p. illus. 24 cm. (89th Cong., 2d sess. House report no. 2197)
1. Public records—U.S. I. Title. (Series: U.S. 89th Cong., 2d sess., 1966. House. Report no. 2197)
JK468.P76A555   66-62845
MC#: 1966-17257
SuDocs no.: 89th Cong., 2d sess. H. Rept. 2197

NIXON REPORTS [Nixon, Richard M.]
1097

U.S. *Government Contract Committee.*
Five years of progress, 1953-1958; a report to President Eisenhower. [Washington, U.S. Govt. Print. Off., 1958]

38 p. ports., tables. 28 cm.
1. Discrimination in employment—U.S.
HD4903.5.U58A549   331.113   58-62355
MC#: 1958-17340 (5th report-1958)
SuDocs no.: Pr34.8:C76/2/958

1098

U.S. *Government Contract Committee.*
Report. 1st- 1953/54- Washington.

v. 23 cm.
Reports for 1953/54- issued by the Committee under a variant name: President's Committee on Government Contracts.
1. Discrimination in employment—U.S. 2. Public contracts—U.S.
HD4903.5.U58A35   L54-166
MC#: 1954-17790 (LC card 54-60629 cancelled in favor of L54-166) (1st report—1954)
    1956-6031 (2d report—1955)
    1956-19347 (3d report—1956)
    1958-861 (4th report—1957)
    1960-4375 (6th report—1959)
    1961-2653 (Final report—1960)
SuDocs no.: Pr34.8:C76/2/(year)

NOBLEMAN REPORT [Nobleman, Eli E.]
1099

U.S. *Congress. Senate. Committee on Government Operations.*
The authority of the Senate to originate appropriation bills; a summary and analysis of the debates and actions of the Con-

stitutional Convention of 1787, and other pertinent source materials, with particular reference to the authority of the Senate to originate apporpriations measures. Washington, U.S. Govt. Print. Off., 1963.

iii, 49 p. 24 cm. (88th Cong., 1st sess. Senate. Document no. 17)
Bibliographical footnotes.
1. U.S. Congress. Senate. 2. U.S.—Appropriations and expenditures. I. Title. (Series: U.S. 88th Cong., 1st sess., 1963. Senate. Document no. 17)
                                                        63-61463
MC#: 1963-9959
SuDocs no.: 88th Cong., 1st sess. S. Doc. 17

NORRIS REPORT
1100

Norris, Frank Wade
Review of Army Officer Educational System. (Washington, U.S. Dept. of the Army) 1971.

3 v. in 1. charts, tables. (ASDIRS 3683)
1. Military education—U.S. 2. U.S. Army—Officers. I. Title. II. Title: Army officer educational system. III. Title: Norris report. IV. Series.
[U408.3.N85]
Dept. of the Army Library
Not located in Monthly Catalog

1101

U.S. *Dept. of the Army. Board to Review Army Officer Schools.*
Report; record of completed actions. Washington, 1970.

185 p. 28 cm.
[U408.3.U5811]
National War College
Not located in Monthly Catalog.

NOURSE REPORT [Nourse, Edwin Griswold]
1102

U.S. *Council of Economic Advisers.*
The impact of foreign aid upon the domestic economy, a report to the President. October 1947. Washington, U.S. Govt. Print. Off., 1948.

vii, 67 p. 24 cm.
At head of title: 80th Congress, 2d session. Committee print. Edwin G. Nourse, chairman.
1. U.S.—Econ. condit.—1945- 2. Reconstruction (1939-)—Europe. I. Nourse, Edwin Griswold, 1883- II. Title.
HC106.5.A59 1947h   330.94   48-45821*
Not located in Monthly Catalog

NOYES REPORT [Noyes, Alexander Dana]
see under
ALDRICH COMMISSION [Aldrich, Nelson Wilmarth]

NYE REPORT [Nye, Gerald P.]
1103

U.S. *War industries board.*
. . . Munitions industry. Final report of the chairman of the United States War industries board to the President of the United States. February, 1919 . . . Washington, U.S. Govt. print. off., 1935.

xxx, 1111 p. incl. tables, diagrs. 23½ cm.
At head of title: 74th Congress, 1st session. Senate committee print. No. 3.

"Printed for the use of the Special committee on investigating the munitions industry."

"This volume was printed from uncorrected galley proof supplied by the War department. The original manuscript is unavailable, consequently the typographical errors, duplication of charts, and breaks in the continuity of the text which occur are printed exactly as they were in the galley proof. The committee finds that it is beyond its province to incorporate such corrections in the text." — Explanatory note, p. 1.

1. U.S. War industries board. I. U.S. Congress. Senate. Special committee to investigate the munitions industry. II. Title.
HC106.2.A3 1919j   330.973   35-26219
MC#: 1935-page 276
SuDocs no.: Y4.M92:W19

ORRRC REPORTS

1104

U.S. *Outdoor Recreation Resources Review Commission.*
A progress report to the President and to the Congress. [Washington] 1961.

x, 85 p. map, diagrs., tables. 24 cm.
1. Recreation — U.S.
GV53.A545 1961   790.973   61-60358
MC#: 1961-5062
SuDocs no.: Y3.Ou8:1/961

1105

U.S. *Outdoor Recreation Resources Review Commission.*
Outdoor recreation for America, a report to the President and to the Congress. Washington, 1962.

xiii, 245 p. illus., maps (part col.) diagrs. 27 cm.
Bibliographical footnotes.
1. Outdoor recreation — U.S. I. Title.
GV53.A545 1962   796.0973   62-60017
MC#: 1962-6400
SuDocs no.: Y3.Ou8:2R24

1106

ORRRC study report. 1-27. Washington [For sale by the Superintendent of Documents, U.S. Govt. Print. Off.] 1962.

27 no. in 10 v. illus., maps (part fold.) 27 cm.
Issued by the Outdoor Recreation Resources Review Commission.
1. Outdoor recreation — U.S. I. U.S. Outdoor Recreation Resources Review Commission.
GV53.A25   63-65483
Not located in Monthly Catalog

Individual reports of the Outdoor Recreation Resources Review Commission are listed below, in numerical order.

1107

U.S. *Outdoor Recreation Resources Review Commission.*
Public outdoor recreation areas-acreage, use, potential. Report to the Outdoor Recreation Resources Review Commission by Commission staff. Washington, For sale by the Superintendent of Documents, U.S. Govt. Print. Off., 1962.

x, 200 p. forms, tables. 26 cm. (ORRRC study report 1)
1. Recreation areas. I. Title. (Series)
GV53.A25 no. 1   62-60023
MC#: 1962-24053
SuDocs no.: Y3.Ou8:10/1

1108

U.S. *Outdoor Recreation Resources Review Commission.*
List of public outdoor recreation areas, 1960; report to the Outdoor Recreation Resources Review Commission by Commission staff. Washington [U.S. Govt. Print. Off.] 1962.

vii, 173 p. 26 cm. (ORRRC study report 2)
1. Outdoor recreation — U.S. — Direct. I. Title: Public outdoor recreation areas. (Series)
GV53.A25 no. 2   62-60024
MC#: 1962-14556
SuDocs no.: Y3.Ou8:10/2

1109

California. University. *Wildland Research Center.*
Wilderness and recreation — a report on resources, values, and problems. Report to the Outdoor Recreation Resources Review Commission by the Wildland Research Center, University of California. Washington [U.S. Govt. Print. Off.] 1962.

x, 352 p. illus., maps, tables. 26 cm. (ORRRC study report 3)
Bibliographical footnotes.
1. Wilderness areas. 2. Recreation areas — U.S. I. U.S. Outdoor Recreation Resources Review Commission. II. Title. (Series)
GV53.A25 no. 3   333.78   62-60025
MC#: 1962-12641
SuDocs no.: Y3.Ou8:10/3

1110

George Washington University, *Washington, D.C.*
Shoreline recreation resources of the United States. Report to the Outdoor Recreation Resources Review Commission. Washington [U.S. Govt. Print. Off.] 1962.

viii, 156 p. maps, diagrs., tables. 26 cm. (ORRRC study report 4)
Bibliographical footnotes.
1. Coasts — U.S. 2. Recreation — U.S. I. Title. (Series)
GV53.A25 no. 4   62-60026
MC#: 1962-18371
SuDocs no.: Y3.Ou8:10/4

1111

Michigan. State University, *East Lansing. Dept. of Resource Development.*
The quality of outdoor recreation as evidenced by user satisfaction; report to the Outdoor Recreation Resources Review Commission. Washington [U.S. Govt. Print. Off.] 1962.

x, 95 p. illus., map. 26 cm. (ORRRC study report 5)
1. Outdoor recreation — U.S. I. Title. (Series)
GV53.A25 no. 5   62-60027 rev
MC#: 1962-16100
SuDocs no.: Y3.Ou8:10/5

1112

Michigan. University. *Dept. of Conservation.*
Hunting in the United States: its present and future role. Report to the Outdoor Recreation Resources Review Commission. Washington [U.S. Govt. Print. Off.] 1962.

x, 117 p. tables. 26 cm. (ORRRC study report, 6)
Bibliographical footnotes.
1. Hunting — U.S. 2. Game and game — birds — U.S. (Series)
GV53.A25 no. 6   62-60028
MC#: 1962-18372
SuDocs no.: Y3.Ou8:10/6

1113

U.S. *Bureau of Sport Fisheries and Wildlife.*
Sport fishing, today and tomorrow; report to the Outdoor Recreation Resources Review Commission. Washington [For sale by the Superintendent of Documents, U.S. Govt. Print. Off.] 1962.

x, 127 p. illus., maps. 26 cm. (ORRRC study report, 7)
Bibliography: p. 99-101.
1. Fishing—U.S. I. Title. (Series)
GV53.A25 no. 7   62-60029
MC#: 1962-20234
SuDocs no.: Y3.Ou8:10/7

1114

U.S. *Dept. of Agriculture. Economic Research Service.*
Potential new sites for outdoor recreation in the Northeast; report to the Outdoor Recreation Resources Review Commission. Washington [U.S. Govt. Print. Off.] 1962.

vi, 123 p. illus., maps. 27 cm. (ORRRC study report 8)
Bibliography: p. 121-123.
1. Recreation areas—Northeastern States. I. U.S. Outdoor Recreation Resources Review Commission. II. Title.
GV53.A25 no. 8   62-60030
MC#: 1962-18373
SuDocs no.: Y3.Ou8:10/8

1115

Conservation Foundation.
Alaska outdoor recreation potential; report to the Outdoor Recreation Resources Review Commission. Washington [U.S. Govt. Print. Off.] 1962.

63 p. illus. 26 cm. (ORRRC study report 9)
1. Recreation—Alaska. I. Title.
GV53.A25 no. 9   62-60031
MC#: 1962-12642
SuDocs no.: Y3.Ou8:10/9

1116

U.S. *Geological Survey.*
Water for recreation, values and opportunities; report to the Outdoor Recreation Resources Review Commission. Washington, 1962.

vi, 73 p. diagrs., maps. 26 cm. (ORRRC study report 10)
Bibliography; p. 57-65.
1. Water sports. I. Title. (Series)
GV53.A25 no. 10   62-60032
MC#: 1962-22701
SuDocs no.: Y3.Ou8:10/10

1117

U.S. *Dept. of Agriculture. Economic Research Service.*
Private outdoor recreation facilities; report to the Outdoor Recreation Resources Review Commission. Washington [U.S. Govt. Print. Off.] 1962.

xvii, 154 p. illus., tables. 26 cm. (ORRRC study report 11)
1. Outdoor recreation. I. U.S. Outdoor Recreation Resources Review Commission. II. Title. (Series)
GV53.A25 no. 11   62-60033
MC#: 1963-16473
SuDocs no.: Y3.Ou8:10/11

1118

National Planning Association.
Paying for recreation facilities. Report to the Outdoor Recreation Resources Review Commission. Washington, 1962.

xiv, 93 p. tables. 27 cm. (ORRRC study report, 12)
Bibliographical footnotes.
1. Recreation—Finance. I. Title. (Series)
GV53.A25 no. 12   62-60034
MC#: 1962-18374
SuDocs no.: Y3.Ou8:10/12

1119

California. State College, *San Francisco. Frederic Burk Foundation for Education.*
Federal agencies and outdoor recreation. Report to the Outdoor Recreation Resources Review Commission. Washington [U.S. Govt. Print. Off.] 1962.

x, 80 p. 26 cm. (ORRRC study report, 13)
Bibliographical footnotes.
1. Outdoor recreation—U.S. I. Title. (Series)
GV53.A25 no. 13   63-60035
MC#: 1962-18375
SuDocs no.: Y3.Ou8:10/13

1120

U.S. *Outdoor Recreation Resources Review Commission.*
Directory of State outdoor recreation administration; report to the Outdoor Recreation Resources Review Commission by commission staff, based on an American Political Science Association study. Washington, 1962.

xii, 146 p. 26 cm. (ORRRC study report 14)
1. Recreation—U.S.—Direct. I. Title: State outdoor recreation administration. (Series)
GV53.A25 no. 14   333.7805873   62-60036
MC#: 1962-22702
SuDocs no.: Y3.Ou8:10/14

1121

Whyte, William Hollingsworth.
Open space action. Report to the Outdoor Recreation Resources Review Commission. Washington [U.S. Govt. Print. Off.] 1962.

ix, 119 p. illus., maps, tables. 26 cm. (ORRRC study report, 15)
Bibliographical footnotes.
1. Recreation areas—U.S. 2. Recreation—Law and legislation—U.S.—States. I. Title. (Series)
GV53.A25 no. 15   790.68   62-60037
MC#: 1962-18376
SuDocs no.: Y3.Ou8:10/15

1122

Williams, Norman.
Land acquisition for outdoor recreation—analysis of selected legal problems; report to the Outdoor Recreation Resources Review Commission. Washington, 1962.

viii, 67 p. 26 cm. (ORRRC study report 16)
1. Recreation—Law and legislation—U.S. 2. Eminent domain—U.S. 3. Recreation areas—U.S. I. Title. (Series)
GV53.A25 no. 16   62-60038
MC#: 1962-18377
SuDocs no.: Y3.Ou8:10/16

1123

Shanklin, John F
Multiple use of land and water areas. Report to the Outdoor Recreation Resources Review Commission. Washington [U.S. Govt. Print. Off.] 1962.

vi, 41 p. 26 cm. (ORRRC study report, 17)

1. Land—U.S. 2. Recreation—U.S. I. Title. (Series)
GV53.A25 no. 17   62-600?)
MC#: 1962-18378
SuDocs no.: Y3.Ou8:10/17

1124

Martin, Betty Sullivan.
A look abroad: the effect of foreign travel on domestic outdoor recreation and a brief survey of outdoor recreation in six countries; report to the Outdoor Recreation Resources Review Commission. Washington [For sale by the Superintendent of Documents, U.S. Govt. Print. Off.] 1962.

xii, 82 p. 26 cm. (ORRRC study report 18)
Bibliography: p. 51-54.
1. Outdoor recreation. 2. Travel. I. Title. (Series)
GV53.A25 no. 18   62-60040
MC#: 1963-1380
SuDocs no.: Y3.Ou8:10/18

1125

U.S. *Outdoor Recreation Resources Review Commission.*
National recreation survey; report, prepared by Abbott L. Ferris assisted by Betty C. Churchill, Charles H. Proctor, and Lois E. H. Zazove, based on Bureau of Census data. Washington [For sale by the Superintendent of Documents, U.S. Govt. Print. Off.] 1962.

x, 394 p. diagrs., tables. 26 cm. (ORRRC study report, 19)
Bibliographical footnotes.
1. Outdoor recreation—Stat. I. Ferris, Abbott Lamoyne, 1915-II. Title. (Series)
GV53.A25 no. 19   62-60041
MC#: 1962-24054
SuDocs no.: Y3.Ou8:10/19

1126

Mueller, Eva, 1920-
Participation in outdoor recreation: factors affecting demand among American adults. Report to the Outdoor Recreation Resources Review Commission, by Eva Mueller and Gerald Gurin, assisted by Margaret Wood. Washington [U.S. Govt. Print. Off.] 1962.

viii, 94 p. diagrs., tables. 26 cm. (ORRRC study report 20)
1. Recreation—U.S. I. U.S. Outdoor Recreation Resources Review Commission. II. Title. (Series)
GV53.A25 no. 20   62-60042
MC#: 1962-18379
SuDocs no.: Y3.Ou8:10/20

1127

U.S. *Outdoor Recreation Resources Review Commission.*
The future of outdoor recreation in metropolitan regions of the United States, reports to the Outdoor Recreation Resources Review Commission, by commission staff, and selected universities and planning agencies. Washington [For sale by the Superintendent of Documents, U.S. Govt. Print. Off., 1962-

v. illus., maps. 26 cm. (ORRRC study report 21)
Bibliography: v. 1, p. 50-56.
Contents.—v. 1. The national view: present condition and future prospects of outdoor recreation for residents of the metropolitan centers of Atlanta, St. Louis, and Chicago.
1. Outdoor recreation—U.S. I. Title. (Series)
GV53.A25 no. 21   62-60043
MC#: 1963-3248 (Vol. 1)
       1963-7382 (Vol. 2)
       1963-3249 (Vol. 3)
SuDocs no.: Y3.Ou8:10/21

1128

U.S. *Outdoor Recretion Resources Review Commission.*
Trends in American living and outdoor recreation. Reports to the Outdoor Recreation Resources Review Commision by Lawrence K. Frank [and others] Washington [U.S. Govt. Print. Off.] 1962.

xiv, 257 p. diagrs., tables. 26 cm. (ORRRC study report 22)
"Report of the Outdoor Recreation Resources Review Commission to the President and the Congress."
Bibliographical footnotes.
1. Outdoor recreation. 2. U.S.—Civilization. I. Frank, Lawrence Kelso, 1890II. Title. (Series)
GV53.A25 no. 22   62-60044
MC#: 1962-24055
SuDocs no.: Y3.Ou8:10/22

1129

U.S. *Outdoor Recreation Resources Review Commission.*
Projections to the years 1976 and 2000: economic growth, population, labor force and leisure, and transportation. Reports to the Outdoor Recreation Resources Review Commission, by Commission staff; National Planning Association; [and] Bureau of Labor Statistics, U.S. Dept. of Labor, A. J. Goldenthal. Washington [For sale by the Superintendent of Documents, U.S. Govt. Print. Off.] 1962.

xviii, 434 p. illus. 26 cm. (ORRRC study report 23)
Bibliography: p. 288-289.
1. U.S.—Econ. condit.—1945- 2. U.S.-Economic policy—1961- I. Title. (Series)
GV53.A25 no. 23   62-60045
MC#: 1963-3250
SuDocs no.: Y3.Ou8:10/23

1130

U.S. *Outdoor Recreation Resources Review Commission.*
Economic studies of outdoor recreation; reports to the Outdoor Recreation Resources Review Commission by Commission staff and the following contributors: Marion Clawson, Arthur L. Moore [and] Ivan M. Lee. Washington [U.S. Govt. Print. Off.] 1962.

ix, 166 p. diagrs., tables. 27 cm. (ORRRC study report 24)
Bibliographical footnotes.
1. Outdoor recreation—Economic aspects—U.S. I. Title. (Series)
GV53.A25 no. 24   333.780973   62-60046
MC#: 1962-22703
SuDocs no.: Y3.Ou8:10/24

1131

U.S. *Outdoor Recreation Resources Review Commission.*
Public expenditures for outdoor recreation. Report to the Outdoor Recreation Resources Review Commission by Commission staff. Washington, For sale by the Superintendent of Documents, U.S. Govt. Print. Off., 1962.

v, 161 p. (chiefly tables) 26 cm. (ORRRC study report 25)
1. Outdoor recreation—Finance. I. Title. (Series)
GV53.A25 no. 25   62-60047
MC#: 1962-24056
SuDocs no.: Y3.Ou8:10/25

1132

U.S. *Outdoor Recreation Resources Review Commission.*
Prospective demand for outdoor recreation. Report to the Outdoor Recreation Resources Review Commission by Commission staff. Washington [U.S. Govt. Print. Off.] 1962.

ix, 61 p. diagrs., tables. 26 cm. (ORRRC study report 26)
Bibliographical footnotes.
1. Recreation—U.S. I. Title. (Series)
GV53.A25 no. 26   62-60048
MC#: 1962-18380
SuDocs no.: Y3.Ou8:10/26

1133

U.S. *Library of Congress.*
Outdoor recreation literature: a survey. Report to the Outdoor Recreation Resources Review Commission by the Librarian of Congress. Washington [U.S. Govt. Print. Off.] 1962.

ix, 137 p. 26 cm. (ORRRC study report 27)
"Historical development of outdoor recreation, by Arthur Hawthorne Carhart": p. 99-129.
Bibliography: p. 27-97.
1. Recreation—Bibl. 2. Recreation—U.S.—Hist. I. Carhart, Arthur Hawthorne, 1892- Historical development of outdoor recreation. II. Title. (Series)
GV53.A25 no. 27   62-60049
MC#: 1962-22704
SuDocs no.: Y3.Ou8:10/27

OAKES REPORT [Oakes, James]

1134

U.S. *Provost-Marshal-General's Bureau.*
Final report made to the Secretary of War by the Provost Marshal General, of the operations of the Bureau of the Provost Marshal General of the U.S., from the commencement of the business of the Bureau, March 17, 1863 to March 17, 1866; the Bureau terminating by law August 28, 1866. [Washington, 1866]

2 pts. in 1 v. 23 cm.
[E471.U583]
Dept. of the Army Library
Not located in Monthly Catalog

OBSCENITY REPORT
see
LOCKHART REPORT [Lockhart, William B.]

O'CONNELL REPORT [O'Connell, James T.]

1135

U.S. *Interdepartmental Committee on Civilian Compensation.*
Report on civilian compensation in the Executive Branch of the Federal Government. Prepared by the Steering Committee of the Interdepartmental Committee on Civilian Compensation [James T. O'Connell, chairman. Washington, 1957]

39 1. illus. 23 x 28 cm.
1. U.S.—Officials and employees—Salaries, allowances, etc. I. O'Connell, James T., 1906- II. Title.
JK775 1957.A57   64-5952 rev
MC#: 1958-15104 (LC card 58-61996 referred to in error)
SuDocs no.: Y3.In8/14:2C49

O'CONOR REPORT

1136

O'Conor, Herbert R.
"We've got to pay more for leadership."
(*In* Congressional record. v. 95 (1949) pt. 12, p. A149-A150)
SuDocs no.: X/a.81:1:12

ODEEN REPORT

1137

Odeen, Philip

National security policy integration: report of a study requested by the President's Reorganization Project [Philip Odeen]. [Washington] ; President's Reorganization Project, 1979.

iii, 53 p. ; 28 cm.
Cover title.
1. United States—Defenses. 2. United States—Military Policy. I. United States. President's Reorganization Project. II. Title. [UA23.023]
Dept. of the Army Library
Not located in Monthly Catalog

O'DWYER REPORT [O'Dwyer, William]

1138

U.S. *War refugee board.*
Final summary report of the executive director, War refugee board. Washington, 1945.

cover title, 2 p. 1., 74, 2 p. 26½ cm.
Reproduced from type-written copy.
"Summarizes the activities of the board from the time of its establishment on January 22, 1944, to its termination on September 15, 1945."—Release no. 19, leaf 1.
"Release no. 19" (3 numb. 1.) stapled to the report.
1. World war, 1939-1945—Refugees. 2. Refugees, Political.
D808.U66 1945   940.53159   45-36737
MC#: 1945-page 1107
SuDocs no.: Pr32.2:W195/7

OLDS REPORT [Olds, Leland]
see
BAKER REPORT [Baker, Jacob]

OLIVER REPORT [Oliver, Philip M.]

1139

United States. Civil Service Commission. Job Evaluation and Pay Review Task Force.
Report of the Job Evaluation and Pay Review Task Force to the United States Civil Service Commission. Washington, U.S. Govt. Print. Off., 1972.

2 v. in 1. illus. 26 cm.
Cover title.
At head of title: 92d Congress, 2d session. Committee print no. 16.
"Subcommittee on Employee Benefits of the Committee on Post Office and Civil Service, House of Representatives."
Contents: v. 1. Findings and recommendations.—v. 2. Models of evaluation systems and pay structures.
1. United States—Officials and employees—Salaries, allowances, etc. I. United States. Civil Service Commission. II. United States. Congress. House. Committee on Post Office and Civil Service. Subcommittee on Employee Benefits.
JK775 1972.A48   353.001'03   72-603480
                                               MARC

Not located in Monthly Catalog

O'MAHONEY REPORTS [O'Mahoney, Joseph Christopher]

1140

U.S. *Congress. Senate. Special committee on post-war economic policy and planning.*
. . . Post-war economic policy and planning. Report of Hon. Joseph C. O'Mahoney, United States senator from Wyoming, to the Special committee on post-war economic policy and planning, pursuant to S. Res. 102, a resolution creating a Special committee on post-war economic policy and planning . . . Washington, U.S. Govt. print. off., 1943.

ii, 144 p. incl. tables. 23 cm. ([U.S.] 78th Cong., 1st sess. Senate. Doc. 106)
1. U.S.—Economic policy. 2. Reconstruction (1939-)—U.S. I. O'Mahoney, Joseph Christopher, 1884- II. Title.
HC106.4.A2888 1943j   338.91   13-50872
MC#: 1943-page 1299
SuDocs no.: 78th Cong., 1st sess. S. Doc. 106

Individual reports of the Temporary National Economic Committee are listed below, in numerical order.

1141

U.S. *Temporary National Economic Committee.*
Investigation of concentration of economic power; monograph no. 1 [-43] Washington,U.S. Govt. Print. Off., 1940-[41]
43 v. in illus., diagrs., tables. 24 cm.
At head of title: 76th Cong., 3d sess. Senate committee print.
1. U.S.—Econ. condit.—1918- 2. U.S.—Economic policy. I. Title.
HC106.3.A5127   330.973   41-3
Not located in Monthly Catalog

1142

[Nelson, Saul] 1901-
. . . Price behavior and business policy . . . Washington, U.S. Govt. print. off., 1940.
xxv, 419 p. incl. tables, diagrs. 23 cm. ([U.S.] Temporary national economic committee. Investigation of concentration of economic power ▪ . . . Monograph no. 1)
At head of title: 76th Cong., 3d session. Senate committee print.
Running title: Concentration of economic power.
"A study made under the auspices of the Bureau of labor statistics for the Temporary national economic committee, Seventy-sixth Congress, third session, pursuant to Public resolution no. 113 (Seventy-fifth Congress), authorizing and directing a select committee to make a full and complete study and investigation with respect to the concentration of economic power in, and financial control over, production and distribution of goods and services."
"By Saul Nelson and Walter G. Keim assisted by Laura Mae Brown, John M. Blair, and William C. French, jr."—p. ii.
Issued also in mimeographed form without series note.
1. Prices—U.S. 2. U.S.—Commercial policy. 3. U.S.—Economic policy. I. Keim, Walter George, 1907- joint author. II. Brown, Laura Mae, 1910- III. Blair, John Malcolm, 1914- IV. French, William C. V. Title.
HC106.3.A5127 no. 1 (330.973) 338.50973 40-29251 Revised
MC#: 1940-page 1544
SuDocs no.: Y4.T24:M75, no. 1

1143

[Davenport, Donald Hills] 1896-
. . . Families and their life insurance. A study of 2132 Massachusetts families and their life insurance policies . . . Washington, U.S. Govt. print. off., 1940.
x, 168 p. incl. illus. (map) facsims., tables, diagrs., forms. 4 plates on 2 1. 23 cm. ([U.S.] Temporary national economic committee. Investigation of concentration of economic power . . . Monograph no. 2)
HC106.3.A5127 no. 2   40-29252
MC#: 1940-page 1544
SuDocs no.: Y4.T24:M75, no. 2

1144

[Tarasov, Helen] 1915-
. . . Who pays the taxes? (Allocation of federal, state, and local taxes to consumer income brackets) . . . Washington, U.S. Govt. print. off., 1940.
55 p. incl. tables, diagrs. 23 cm. ([U.S.] Temporary national economic committee. Investigation of concentration of economic power . . . Monograph no. 3)
At head of title: 76th Congress, 3d session. Senate committee print.
Running title: Concentration of economic power.
"A study made under the auspices of the Department of commerce for the Temporary national economic committee, Seventy-sixth Congress, third session, pursuant to Public resolution no. 113. (Seventy-fifth Congress), authorizing and directing a select committee to make a full and complete study and investigation with respect to the concentration of economic power in, and financial control over, production and distribution of goods and services."
By Helen Tarasov. *cf.* Acknowledgment.
Printed for the use of the Temporary national economic committee.
"Selective bibliography": p. 36-37.
1. Taxation—U.S. I. Title. II. Title: Allocation of federal, state, and local taxes to consumer income brackets.
HC106.3.A5127 no. 3   (330.973) 336.20973   40-29253
- - - - - Copy 2.
MC#: 1940-page 1412
SuDocs no.: Y4.T24:M75, no. 3

1145

[Goldenthal, Adolph James] 1916-
. . . Concentration and composition of individual incomes, 1918-1937 . . . Washington, U.S. Govt. print. off., 1940.
xv, 112 p. incl. tables, diagrs., 23 cm. ([U.S.] Temporary national economic committee. Investigation of concentration of economic power . . . Monograph no. 4)
At head of title: 76th Cong., 3d session. Senate committee print.
Running title: Concentration of economic power.
"A study made under the auspices of the Department of commerce for the Temporary national economic committee, Seventy-sixth Congress, third session, pursuant to Public resolution no. 113 (Seventy-fifth Congress), authorizing and directing a select committee to make a full and complete study and investigation with respect to the concentration of economic power in, and financial control over, production and distribution of goods and services."
By Adolph J. Goldenthal. *cf.* Acknowledgment.
Printed for the use of the Temporary national economic committee.
1. Income—U.S. 2. U.S.—Econ. condit.—1918-1945. I. Title.
HC106.3.A5127 no. 4   (330.973) 339.20973   40-29254
- - - - - Copy 2.
MC#: 1940-page 1544
SuDocs no.: Y4.T24:M75, no. 4

1146

[Brown, Douglass Vincent] 1904-
. . . Industrial wage rates, labor cost and price policies . . . Washington, U.S. Govt. print. off., 1940.
xxvi, 172 p. incl. illus. (map) tables, diagrs. plates. 23 cm. ([U.S.] Temporary national economic committee. Investigation of concentration of economic power . . . Monograph no. 5)
At head of title: 76th Cong., 3d session. Senate committee print.
Running title: Concentration of economic power.

"A study made under the auspices of the Bureau of labor statistics for the Temporary national economic committee. Seventy-sixth Congress, third session, pursuant to Public resolution no. 113 (Seventy-fifth Congress), authorizing and directing a select committee to make a full and complete study and investigation with respect to the concentration of economic power in, and financial control over, production and distribution of goods and services."

By Douglass V. Brown, John T. Dunlop, Edwin M. Martin, Charles A. Myers and John A. Brownell. cf. Acknowledgment.

Printed for the use of the Temporary national economic committee.

1. Wages—U.S. 2. Price policy. 3. Labor and laboring classes—U.S.—1914- I. Dunlop, John Thomas, 1914- joint author. II. Martin, Edwin M., joint author. III. Myers, Charles Andrew, 1913- joint author. IV. Brownell, John A., joint author. V. Title.
HC106.3.A5127 no. 5   (330.973) 331.2973   40-29289
- - - - - Copy 2.
MC#: 1940-page 1639
SuDocs no.: Y4.T24:M75, no. 5

1147

[Gilbert, Milton] 1909-
. . . Export prices and export cartels (Webb-Pomerene associations) . . . [Washington] U.S. Govt. print. off., 1940.

xiii, 310 p. incl. tables. 23 cm. ([U.S.] Temporary national economic committee. Investigation of concentration of economic power . . . Monograph no. 6)

At head of title: 76th Congress, 3d session. Senate committee print.

Running title: Concentration of economic power.

"A study made under the auspices of the Department of commerce and the Federal trade commission for the Temporary national economic committee, Seventy-sixth Congress, third session, pursuant to Public resolution no. 113 (Seventy-fifth Congress), authorizing and directing a select committee to make a full and complete study and investigation with respect to the concentration of economic power in, and financial control over, production and distribution of goods and services."

By Milton Gilbert and Paul D. Dickens, Department of commerce, and members of the staff of the Federal trade commission. cf. p. ii.

Printed for the use of the Temporary national economic committee.

"Selected list of references on the Export trade act": p. 297-300.

1. Prices—U.S. 2. Commercial associations—U.S. 3. U.S.— Commercial policy. 4. Competition, International. I. Dickens, Paul DeWitt, 1896- joint author. II. U.S.—Federal trade commission. III. Title.
HC106.3.A5127 no. 6   (330.973) 338.50973   40-29290
- - - - - Copy 2.
MC#: 1940-page 1638
SuDocs no.: Y4.T24:M75, no. 6

1148

[Kreps, Theodore John] 1897-
. . . Measurement of the social performance of business . . . Washington, U.S. Govt. print. off., 1940.

ix, 207 p. incl. tables. diagrs. (1 fold.) 23 cm. ([U.S.] Temporary national economic committee. Investigation of concentration of economic power . . . Monograph, no. 7)

At head of title: 76th Congress, 3d session. Senate committee print.

Running title: Concentration of economic power.

"A study made for the Temporary national economic committee, Seventy-sixth Congress, third session, pursuant to Public

resolution no. 113 (Seventy-fifth Congress), authorizing and directing a select committee to make a full and complete study and investigation with respect to the concentration of economic power in, and financial control over, production and distribution of goods and services."

"By Theodore J. Kreps assisted by Kathryn Robertson Wright."—p. ii.

Printed for the use of the Temporary national economic committee.

1. U.S.—Indus. 2. U.S.—Econ. condit. 3. U.S.—Economic policy. I. Murphy, Mrs. Kathryn (Robertson) II. Title. III. Title: Social performance of business.
HC106.3.A5127 no. 7   (330.973) 338.0973   41-50140
MC#: 1941-page 231
SuDocs no.: Y4.T24:M75, no. 7

1149

[Stone, Peter Anthony] 1892-
. . . Toward more housing . . . Washington, U.S. Govt. print. off., 1940.

xxi, 223 p. incl. tables. diagrs. (part fold.) 23 cm. ([U.S.] Temporary national economic committee. Investigation of concentration of economic power . . . Monograph no. 8)

At head of title: 76th Congress, 3d session. Senate committee print.

Running title: Concentration of economic power.

"A study made for the Temporary national economic committee, Seventy-sixth Congress, third session, pursuant to Public resolution no. 113 (Seventy-fifth Congress), authorizing and directing a select committee to make a full and complete study and investigation with respect to the concentration of economic power in, and financial control over, production and distribution of goods and services."

By Peter A. Stone and R. Harold Denton. cf. Acknowledgment.

Printed for the use of the Temporary national economic committee.

Includes bibliographies.

1. Housing—U.S. I. Denton, Robert Harold, 1910- joint author. II. Title.
HC106.3.A5127 no. 8   (330.973) 331.8330973   40-29291
- - - - - Copy 2.
MC#: 1940-page 1639
SuDocs no.: Y4.T24:M75, no. 8

1150

[Hynning, Clifford James] 1913-
. . . Taxation of corporate enterprise . . . Washington, U.S. Govt. print. off., 1941.

xi, 216 p. incl. tables. diagrs. (part fold.) 23 cm. ([U.S.] Temporary national economic committee. Investigation of concentration of economic power . . . Monograph no. 9)

At head of title: 76th Congress, 3d session. Senate committee print.

Running title: Concentration of economic power.

"A study made under the auspices of the Department of commerce for the Temporary national economic committee, Seventy-sixth Congress, third session, pursuant to Public resolution no. 113 (Seventy-fifth Congress), authorizing and directing a select committee to make a full and complete study and investigation with respect to the concentration of economic power in, and financial control over, production and distribution of goods and services."

By Clifford J. Hynning. cf. Acknowledgment.

Printed for the use of the Temporary national economic committee.

1. Corporations — Taxation. I. Title.
HC106.3.A5127 no. 9   (330.973) 658.1710973   41-50172
MC#: 1941-page 413
SuDocs no.: Y4.T24:M75, no. 9

1151

[James, Clifford Lester] 1903-
. . . Industrial concentration and tariffs . . . Washington, U.S. Govt. print. off., 1940.

x, 326 p. incl. tables. 23 cm. ([U.S.] Temporary national economic committee. Investigation of concentration of economic power . . . Monograph no. 10)
At head of title: 76th Congress, 3d session. Senate print.
Running title: Concentration of economic power.
"A study made for the Temporary national economic committee, Seventy-sixth Congress, third session, pursuant to Public resolution no. 113 (Seventy-fifth Congress), authorizing and directing a select committee to make a full and complete study and investigation with respect to the concentration of economic power in, and financial control over, production and distribution of goods and services."
By Clifford L. James assisted by Edward C. Welsh and Gordon Arneson. cf. Acknowledgment.
Printed for the use of the Temporary national economic committee.
1. Tariff — U.S. 2. U.S. — Indus. 3. U.S. — Commercial policy. 4. U.S. — Econ. condit. — 1918-1945. I. Welsh, Edward Cristy, 1909- joint author. II. Arneson, Gordon, joint author. III. Title.
HC106.3.A5127 no. 10   (330.973) 337.0973   40-29255
- - - - - Copy 2.
MC#: 1940-page 1544
SuDocs no.: Y4.T24:M75, no. 10

1152

[Dimock, Marshall Edward] 1903-
. . . Bureaucracy and trusteeship in large corporations . . . Washington, U.S. Govt. print. off., 1940.

ix, 144 p. incl. tables. diagrs. (part fold.) 23 cm. ([U.S.] Temporary national economic committee. Investigation of concentration of economic power . . . Monograph no. 11)
At head of title: 76th Congress, 3d session. Senate committee print.
Running title: Concentration of economic power.
"A study made for the Temporary national economic committee, Seventy-sixth Congress, third session, pursuant to Public resolution no. 113 (Seventy-fifth Congress), authorizing and directing a select committee to make a full and complete study and investigation with respect to the concentration of economic power in, and financial control over, production and distribution of goods and services."
By Marshall E. Dimock and Howard K. Hyde. cf. Acknowledgment.
Printed for the use of the Temporary national economic committee.
1. Corporations — U.S. I. Hyde, Howard Kemper, 1911- joint author. II. Title.
HC106.3.A5127 no. 11   40-29344
- - - - - Copy 2.
MC#: 1940-page 1639
SuDocs no.: Y4.T24:M75, no. 11

1153

[Taitel, Martin]
. . . Profits, productive activities and new investment . . . Washington, U.S. Govt. print. off., 1941.

xx, 188 p. incl. tables. diagrs. (part fold.) 23 cm. ([U.S.] Temporary national economic committee. Investigation of concentration of economic power . . . Monograph no. 12)
At head of title: 76th Congress, 3d session. Senate committee print.
Running title: Concentration of economic power.
"A study made for the Temporary national economic committee, Seventy-sixth Congress, third session, pursuant to Public resolution no. 113 (Seventy-fifth Congress), authorizing and directing a select committee to make a full and complete study and investigation with respect to the concentration of economic power in, and financial control over, production and distribution of goods and services."
By Martin Taitel. cf. Acknowledgment.
Printed for the use of the Temporary national economic committee.
1. Profit — U.S. 2. Investments — U.S. I. Title.
HC106.3.A5127 no. 12   (330.973) 339.2   41-50147
MC#: 1941-page 415
SuDocs no.: Y4.T24:M75, no. 12

1154

U.S. *Federal trade commission.*
. . . Relative efficiency of large, medium-sized, and small business . . . Washington, U.S. Govt. print. off., 1941.

xv, 449 p. illus. (map) tables (1 fold.) diagrs. (1 fold.) 23 cm. ([U.S.] Temporary national economic committee. Investigation of concentration of economic power . . . Monograph no. 13)
At head of title: 76th Congress, 3d session. Senate committee print.
Running title: Concentration of economic power.
"A study made under the auspices of the Federal trade commission for the Temporary national economic committee, Seventy-sixth Congress, third session, pursuant to Public resolution no. 113 (Seventy-fifth Congress), authorizing and directing a select committee to make a full and complete study and investigation with respect to the concentration of economic power in, and financial control over, production and distribution of goods and services."
By the Federal trade commission. cf. p. ii.
Printed for the use of the Temporary national economic committee.
1. U.S. — Indus. 2. U.S. — Econ. condit. — 1918-1945. I. Title.
HC106.3.A5127 no. 13   (330.973) 338.0973   41-50173
MC#: 1941-page 413
SuDocs no.: Y4.T24:M75, no. 13

1155

[Perlman, Jacob] 1898-
. . . Hourly earnings of employees in large and small enterprises . . . Washington, U.S. Govt. Print. off., 1940.

xv, 94 p. incl. tables. 23 cm. ([U.S.] Temporary national economic committee. Investigation of concentration of economic power . . . Monograph no. 14)
At head of title: 76th Congress, 3d session. Senate committee print.
Running title: Concentration of economic power.
"A study made under the auspices of the Bureau of labor statistics for the Temporary national economic committee, Seventy-sixth Congress, third session, pursuant to Public resolution no. 113 (Seventy-fifth Congress), authorizing and directing a select committee to make a full and complete study and investigation with respect to the concentration of economic power in, and financial control over, production and distribution of goods and services."
By Jacob Perlman. cf. Acknowledgment.

Printed for the use of the Temporary national economic committee.

1. Wages—U.S. 2. U.S.—Econ. condit.—1918-1945. I. Title.
HC106.3.A5127 no. 14   (330.973) 331.2973   40-29256
- - - - - Copy 2.
MC#: 1940-page 1544
SuDocs no.: Y4.T24:M75, no. 14

1156

[Merwin, Charles Lewis] 1912-
. . . Financial characteristics of American manufacturing corporations . . . Washington, U.S. Govt. print. off., 1940.

xiv, 442 p. incl. tables, diagrs. 23 cm. ([U.S.] Temporary national economic committee. Investigation of concentration of economic power . . . Monograph no. 15)

At head of title: 76th Congress, 3d session. Senate committee print.

Running title: Concentration of economic power.

"A study made under the auspices of the Department of commerce for the Temporary national economic committee, Seventy-sixth Congress, third session, pursuant to Public resolution no. 113 (Seventy-fifth Congress), authorizing and directing a select committee to make a full and complete study and investigation with respect to the concentration of economic power in, and financial control over, production and distribution of goods and services."

By Charles L. Merwin, jr. cf. Acknowledgment.

Printed for the use of the Temporary national economic committee.

1. Corporations—U.S.—Finance. I. Title.
HC106.3.A5127 no. 15   (330.973) 658.150973   40-28954
- - - - - Copy 2.
MC#: 1941-page 97
SuDocs no.: Y4.T24:M75, no. 15

1157

[Hamilton, Walton Hale] 1881-1958.
. . . Antitrust in action . . . Washington, U.S. Govt. Print. Off., 1940.

vii, 146 p. incl. tables. 23 cm. ([U.S.] Temporary national economic committee. Investigation of concentration of economic power . . . Monograph no. 16)

At head of title: 76th Congress, 3d session. Senate committee print.

Running title: Concentration of economic power.

"A study made for the Temporary national economic committee, Seventy-sixth Congress, third session, pursuant to Public resolution no. 113 (Seventy-fifth Congress), authorizing and directing a select committee to make a full and complete study and investigation with respect to the concentration of economic power in, and financial control over, production and distribution of goods and services."

By Walton Hamilton and Irene Till. cf. Acknowledgment.

Printed for the use of the Temporary national economic committee.

1. Trusts, Industrial—U.S. 2. Trusts, Industrial—U.S.—Law. I. Till, Irene, 1906- II. Title.
HC106.3.A5127 no. 16   40-29346
- - - - - Copy 2.
MC#: 1940-page 1639
SuDocs no.: Y4.T24:M75, no. 16

1158

[Cover, John Higson] 1891-
. . . Problems of small business . . . Washington, U.S. Govt. print. off., 1941.

xix, 412 p. incl. tables, diagrs. 23 cm. ([U.S.] Temporary na-

tional economic committee. Investigation of concentration of economic power . . . Monograph no. 17)

At head of title: 76th Congress, 3d session. Senate committee print.

Running title: Concentration of economic power.

"A study made under the auspices of the Department of commerce and the Securities and exchange commission for the Temporary national economic committee, Seventy-sixth Congress, third session, pursuant to Public resolution no. 113 (Seventy-fifth Congress), authorizing and directing a select committee to make a full and complete study and investigation with respect to the concentration of economic power in, and financial control over, production and distribution of goods and services."

By John H. Cover, Nathanael H. Engle, Earl D. Strong, and others. cf. Acknowledgment.

Printed for the use of the Temporary national economic committee.

1. Small business. 2. U.S.—Econ. condit.—1918-1945. 3. Credit—U.S. I. Engle, Nathanael Howard, 1893- joint author. II. Strong, Earl D., 1885- joint author. III. Title.
HC106.3.A5127 no. 17   (330.973) 658   41-50145
MC#: 1941-page 413
SuDocs no.: Y4.T24:M75, no. 17

1159

[Pearce, Charles Albert]
. . . Trade association survey . . . Washington, U.S. Govt. print. off., 1941.

xiv, 501 p. incl. tables, forms. 23 cm. ([U.S.] Temporary national economic committee. Investigation of concentration of economic power . . . Monograph no. 18)

At head of title: 76th Congress, 3d session. Senate committee print.

Running title: Concentration of economic power.

"A study made under the auspices of the Department of commerce for the Temporary national economic committee, Seventy-sixth Congress, third session, pursuant to Public resolution no. 113 (Seventy-fifth Congress), authorizing and directing a select committee to make a full and complete study and investigation with respect to the concentration of economic power in, and financial control over, production and distribution of goods and services."

"By Dr. C. A. Pearce and associates in the Department of commerce."—p. xiii.

Printed for the use of the Temporary national economic committee.

1. Trade and professional associations—U.S. I. Title.
HC106.3.A5127 no. 18   (330.973) 338.06273   41-50064
MC#: 1941-page 231
SuDocs no.: Y4.T24:M75, no. 18

1160

[Linnenberg, Clem Charles] 1912-
. . . Government purchasing—an economic commentary . . . Washington, U.S. Govt. print. off., 1940.

xix, 330 p. incl. tables. diagrs. (part fold.) 23 cm. ([U.S.] Temporary national economic committee. Investigation of concentration of economic power . . . Monograph no. 19)

At head of title: 76th Congress, 3d session. Senate committee print.

Running title: Concentration of economic power.

"A study made for the Temporary national economic committee, Seventy-sixth Congress, third session, pursuant to Public resolution no. 113 (Seventy-fifth Congress), authorizing and directing a select committee to make a full and complete study and investigation with respect to the concentration of economic power in, and financial control over, production and distribution of goods and services."

By Clem C. Linnenberg, jr. and Dana M. Barbour. *cf.* Acknowledgment.

Printed for the use of the Temporary national economic committee.

"Selected bibliography on governmental procurement": p. 132-137.

1. Buying. 2. U.S. — Econ. condit. I. Barbour, Dana Mills, 1907- joint author. II. Title.

HC106.3.A5127 no. 19   (330.973) 351.71   41-50174

MC#: 1941-page 414

SuDocs no.: Y4.T24:M75, no. 19

1161

[Anderson, Hobson Dewey] 1897-

. . . Taxation, recovery, and defense . . . Washington, U.S. Govt. print. off., 1940.

xviii, 374 p. incl. illus. (maps) tables. diagrs. (1 fold.) 23 cm. ([U.S.] Temporary national economic committee. Investigation of concentration of economic power . . . Monograph no. 20)

At head of title: 76th Congress, 3d session. Senate committee print.

Running title: Concentration of economic power.

"A study made for the Temporary national economic committee, Seventy-sixth Congress, third session, pursuant to Public resolution no. 113 (Seventy-fifth Congress), authorizing and directing a select committee to make a full and complete study and investigation with respect to the concentration of economic power in, and financial control over, production and distribution of goods and services."

By H. Dewey Anderson. *cf.* Acknowledgment.

Printed for the use of the Temporary national economic committee.

1. Taxation — U.S. 2. U.S. — Econ. condit. — 1918-1945. 3. U.S. — Defenses. I. Title.

HC106.3.A5127 no. 20   40-29345

- - - - - Copy 2.

MC#: 1940-page 1639

SuDocs no.: Y4.T24:M75, no. 20

1162

[Wilcox, Clair] 1898-

. . . Competition and monopoly in American industry . . . Washington, U.S. Govt. print. off., 1940.

xi, 344 p. incl. tables. 23 cm. ([U.S.] Temporary national economic committee. Investigation of concentration of economic power . . . Monograph no. 21)

At head of title: 76th Congress, 3d session. Senate committee print.

Running title: Concentration of economic power.

"A study made for the Temporary national economic committee, Seventy-sixth Congress, third session, pursuant to Public resolution no. 113 (Seventy-fifth Congress), authorizing and directing a select committee to make a full and complete study and investigation with respect to the concentration of economic power in, and financial control over, production and distribution of goods and services."

By Clair Wilcox. *cf.* Acknowledgment.

Printed for the use of the Temporary national economic committee.

1. Competition. 2. Monopolies — U.S. 3. U.S. — Indus. I. Title. *Full name:* Clair Lown Wilcox.

HC106.3.A5127 no. 21   (330.973) 380.18   41-50310

MC#: 1941-page 414

SuDocs no.: Y4.T24:M75, no. 21

1163

[Lorwin, Lewis Levitzki] 1883-1970.

. . . Technology in our economy . . . Washington, U.S. Govt. print. off., 1941.

xvi, 313 p. incl. tables, diagrs. 23 cm. ([U.S.] Temporary national economic committee. Investigation of concentration of economic power . . . Monograph no. 22)

At head of title: 76th Congress, 3d session. Senate committee print.

Running title: Concentration of economic power.

"A study made for the Temporary national economic committee, Seventy-sixth Congress, third session, pursuant to Public resolution no. 113 (Seventy-fifth Congress), authorizing and directing a select committee to make a full and complete study and investigation with respect to the concentration of economic power in, and financial control over, production and distribution of goods and services."

By Lewis L. Lorwin and John M. Blair, assisted by Ruth Aull. *cf.* Acknowledgment.

Printed for the use of the Temporary national economic committee.

1. Technology. 2. U.S. — Economic policy. 3. U.S. — Econ. condit. — 1918-1945. I. Blair, John Malcolm, 1914- joint author. II. Aull, Ruth. III. Title.

HC106.3.A5127 no. 22   (330.973) 338.4   41-50317

MC#: 1941-page 415

SuDocs no.: Y4.M224:M75, no. 22

1164

[Meyers, Albert Leonard]

. . . Agriculture and the national economy . . . Washington, U.S. Govt. print. off., 1940.

vii, 48 p. incl. tables. 23 cm. ([U.S.] Temporary national economic committee. Investigation of concentration of economic power . . . Monograph no. 23)

At head of title: 76th Congress, 3d session. Senate committee print.

Running title: Concentration of economic power.

"A study submitted by a committee appointed by the secretary of agriculture, to the Temporary national economic committee, Seventy-sixth Congress, third session, pursuant to Public resolution no. 113 (Seventy-fifth Congress), authorizing and directing a select committee to make a full and complete study and investigation with respect to the concentration of economic power in, and financial control over, production and distribution of goods and services."

By Albert L. Meyers. *cf.* Acknowledgment.

Printed for the use of the Temporary national economic committee.

Bibliography: p. 43.

1. Agriculture — U.S. 2. Farm produce — Marketing. 3. U.S. — Economic policy. I. Title.

HC106.3.A5127 no. 23   40-29343

- - - - - Copy 2.

MC#: 1940-page 1638.

SuDocs no.: Y4.T24:M75, no. 23

1165

[Kaidanovsky, Samuel P]

. . . Consumer standards . . . Washington, U.S. Govt. print. off., 1941.

xii, 433 p. tables (part fold.) fold. diagrs. 23 cm. ([U.S.] Temporary national economic committee. Investigation of concentration of economic power . . . Monograph no. 24)

At head of title: Concentration of economic power.

Running title: Concentration of economic power.

"A study made under the auspices of the Department of agriculture for the Temporary national economic committee, Seventy-sixth Congress, third session, pursuant to Public resolution no. 113 (Seventy-fifth Congress), authorizing and directing a select committee to make a full and complete study and investigation with respect to the concentration of economic power in, and financial control over, production and distribution of goods and services."

By Samuel P. Kaidanovsky assisted by Alice L. Edwards. *cf.* Acknowledgment.

Printed for the use of the Temporary national economic committee.

1. Standardization. I. Edwards, Alice Leora, 1882- II. Title.
HC106.3.A5127 no. 24   (330.973) 339.4   41-50316
MC#: 1941-page 415
SuDocs no.: Y4.T24:M75, no. 24

1166

U.S. *Temporary national economic committee.*

. . . Recovery plans . . . Washington, U.S. Govt. print. off., 1940.

x, 260 p. incl. tables, diagrs. 23 cm. (Investigation of concentration of economic power . . . Monograph no. 25)

At head of title: 76th Congress, 3d session. Senate committee print.

Running title: Concentration of economic power.

"A study made for the Temporary national economic committee, Seventy-sixth Congress, third session, pursuant to Public resolution no. 113 (Seventy-fifth Congress), authorizing and directing a select committee to make a full and complete study and investigation with respect to the concentration of economic power in, and financial control over, production and distribution of goods and services."

"This monograph has been prepared from materials submitted to the Temporary national economic committee."—Acknowledgment.

Printed for the use of the Temporary national economic committee.

1. U.S.—Econ. condit.—1918-1945. 2. U.S.—Economic policy. I. Title.
HC106.3.A5127 no. 25   (330.973) 330.973   41-50148
MC#: 1941-page 413
SuDocs no.: Y4.T24:M75, no. 25

1167

[Blaisdell, Donald Christy] 1899-
. . . Economic power and political pressures . . . Washington, U.S. Govt. print. off., 1941.

ix, 222 p. 23 cm. ([U.S.] Temporary national economic committee. Investigation of concentration of economic power . . . Monograph no. 26)

At head of title: 76th Congress, 3d session. Senate committee print.

Running title: Concentration of economic power.

"A study made for the Temporary national economic committee, Seventy-sixth Congress, third session, pursuant to Public resolution no. 113 (Seventy-fifth Congress), authorizing and directing a select committee to make a full and complete study and investigation with respect to the concentration of economic power in, and financial control over, production and distribution of goods and services."

By Donald C. Blaisdell assisted by Jane Greverus. *cf.* Acknowledgment.

Printed for the use of the Temporary national economic committee.

1. Lobbying. 2. Corruption (in politics)—U.S. I. Greverus, Jane. II. Title.

HV106.3.A5127 no. 26   (330.973) 328.3680973   41-50175
MC#: 1941-page 414
SuDocs no.: Y4.T24:M75, no. 26

1168

[Thorp, Willard Long] 1899-
. . . The structure of industry . . . Washington, U.S. Govt. print. off., 1941.

xv, 759 p. incl. tables, diagrs. 23 cm. ([U.S.] Temporary national economic committee. Investigation of concentration of economic power . . . Monograph no. 27)

At head of title: 76th Congress, 3d session. Senate committee print.

Running title: Concentration of economic power.

"A study made under the auspices of the Department of commerce for the Temporary national economic committee, Seventy-sixth Congress, third session, pursuant to Public resolution no. 113 (Seventy-fifth Congress), authorizing and directing a select committee to make a full and complete study and investigation with respect to the concentration of economic power in, and financial control over, production and distribution of goods and services."

"By Willard L. Thorp, Walter F. Crowder, and associates."—p. ii.

Printed for the use of the Temporary national economic committee.

1. U.S.—Indus. 2. U.S.—Manuf. I. Crowder, Walter Frederick, joint author. II. Title.
HC106.3.A5127 no. 27   (330.973) 338.40973   41-50311
MC#: 1941-page 414
SuDocs no.: Y4.T24:M75, no. 27

1169

[Gesell, Gerhard Alden] 1910-
. . . Study of legal reserve life insurance companies . . . Washington, U.S. Govt. print. off., 1940.

vii, 466 p. incl. tables, forms. 23 cm. ([U.S.] Temporary national economic committee. Investigation of concentration of economic power . . . Monographic no. 28)

At head of title: 76th Congress, 3d session. Senate committee print.

Running title: Concentration of economic power.

"A study made under the auspices of the Securities and exchange commission for the Temporary national economic committee, Seventy-sixth Congress, third session, pursuant to Public resolution no. 113 (Seventy-fifth Congress), authorizing and directing a select committee to make a full and complete study and investigation with respect to the concentration of economic power in, and financial control over, production and distribution of goods and services."

By Gerhard A. Gesell and Ernest J. Howe. *cf.* Acknowledgment.

Printed for the use of the Temporary national economic committee.

1. Insurance, Life—U.S. I. Howe, Ernest Joseph, 1900- joint author. II. Title.
HC106.3.A5127 no. 28   (330.973) 368.30973   41-50146
MC#: 1941-page 414
SuDocs no.: Y4.T24:M75, no. 28

1170

U.S. *Temporary national economic committee.*

. . . Statement on life insurance . . . Washington, U.S. Govt. print. off., 1941.

v, 84 p. incl. tables, diagrs. 23 cm. (*Its* Investigation of concentration of economic power . . . Monograph 28-A)

At head of title: 76th Congress, 3d session. Senate committee print.

Running title: Concentration of economic power.

"A study made for the Temporary national economic committee, Seventy-sixth Congress, third session, pursuant to Public resolution no. 113 (Seventy-fifth Congress), authorizing and directing a select committee to make a full and complete study and investigation with respect to the concentration of economic power in, and financial control over, production and distribution of goods and services."

Contents. — I. Comments on Monograph no. 28 on legal reserve life insurance companies, submitted by five life insurance company officials. — II. Rejoinder to comments on Monograph no. 28, by Sumner T. Pike and Gerhard A. Gesell. — III. State supervision of insurance and the National Association of insurance commissioners.

1. Insurance, Life — U.S. I. Pike, Sumner Tucker, 1891- II. Gesell, Gerhhard Alden, 1910-
HC106.3.A5127 no. 28-A   (330.973) 368.3   41-50664
MC#: 1941-page 924
SuDocs no.: Y4.T24:M75/no. 28-A

1171

[Goldsmith, Raymond William] 1904-
. . . The distribution of ownership in the 200 largest nonfinancial corporations . . . Washington, U.S. Govt. print. off., 1940.

xviii, 1557 p. tables (part fold.) diagrs. 23 cm. ([U.S.] Temporary national economic committee. Investigation of concentration of economic power . . . Monograph no. 29)

At head of title: 76th Congress, 3d session. Senate committee print.

Running title: Concentration of economic power.

"A study made under the auspices of the Securities and exchange commission for the Temporary national economic committee, Seventy-sixth Congress, third session, pursuant to Public resolution no. 113 (Seventy-fifth Congress), authorizing and directing a select committee to make a full and complete study and investigation with respect to the concentration of economic power in, and financial control over, production and distribution of goods and services."

"[By] Raymond W. Goldsmith, Rexford C. Parmelee, Irwin Friend [and others]" — p. ii.

Printed for the use of the Temporary national economic committee.

1. Stock ownership — U.S. I. Parmelee, Rexford Clark, 1908- joint author. II. Friend, Irwin, joint author. III. Title.
HC106.3.A5127 no. 29   (330.973) 338.70973   41-50459
MC#: 1941-page 585
SuDocs no.: Y4.T24:M75/ no. 29

1172

[Granby, Helene]
. . . Survey of shareholding in 1,710 corporations with securities listed on a national securities exchange . . . Washington, U.S. Govt. print. off., 1941.

xviii, 258 p. incl. tables, diagrs. 23 cm. ([U.S.] Temporary national economic committee. Investigation of concentration of economic power . . . Monograph no. 30)

At head of title: 76th Congress, 3d session. Senate committee print.

Running title: Concentration of economic power.

"A study made under the auspices of the Securities and exchange commission for the Temporary national economic committee, Seventy-sixth Congress, third session, pursuant to Public resolution no. 113 (Seventy-fifth Congress), authorizing and directing a select committee to make a full and complete study and investigation with respect to the concentration of economic power in, and

financial control over, production and distribution of goods and services."

By Helene Granby. cf. Acknowledgment.

Printed for the use of the Temporary national economic committee.

1. Stock ownership — U.S. I. Title.
HC106.3.A5127 no. 30   (330.973) 332.630973   41-50149
MC#: 1941-page 415
SuDocs no.: Y4.T24:M75, no. 30

1173

[Hamilton, Walton Hale] 1881-1958.
. . . Patents and free enterprise . . . Washington, U.S. Govt. print. off., 1941.

vii, 179 p. incl. tables. 23 cm. ([U.S.] Temporary national economic committee. Investigation of concentration of economic power . . . Monograph no. 31)

At head of title: 76th Congress, 3d session. Senate committee print.

Running title: Concentration of economic power.

"A study made for the Temporary national economic committee, Seventy-sixth Congress, third session, pursuant to Public resolution no. 113 (Seventy-fifth Congress), authorizing and directing a select committee to make a full and complete study and investigation with respect to the concentration of economic power in, and financial control over, production and distribution of goods and services."

"By Walton Hamilton with the assistance of Elmer E. Batzell [and others]" — p. ii.

Printed for the use of the Temporary national economic committee.

1. Patents — U.S. 2. Laissez-faire. I. Batzell, Elmer E., joint author. II. Title.
HC106.3.A5127 no. 31   (330.973) 608   41-50391
MC#: 1941-page 585
SuDocs no.: Y4.T24:M75/no. 31

1174

[Wallace, Donald Holmes] 1903- ed.
. . . Economic standards of government price control . . . Washington, U.S. Govt. print. off., 1941.

xxvii, 514 p. incl. tables. fold. diagrs. 23 cm. ([U.S.] Temporary national economic committee. Investigation of concentration of economic power . . . Monograph no. 32)

At head of title: 76th Congress, 3d session. Senate committee print.

Running title: Concentration of economic power.

"A study made under the auspices of the Bureau of labor statistics for the Temporary national economic committee, Seventy-sixth Congress, third session, pursuant to Public resolution no. 113 (Seventy-fifth Congress), authorizing and directing a select committee to make a full and complete study and investigation with respect to the concentration of economic power in, and financial control over, production and distribution of goods and services."

Edited by Donald H. Wallace. cf. Acknowledgment.

Printed for the use of the Temporary national economic committee.

1. Price regulation — U.S. 2. U.S. — Economic policy — 1933-1940. 3. U.S. — Econ. condit. — 1918-1945. I. Title.
HC106.3.A5127 no. 32   (330.973) 338.50973   41-50312
MC#: 1941-page 415
SuDocs no.: Y4.T24:M75, no. 32

1175

[Keim, Walter George] 1907-
. . . Geographical differentials in prices of building materials . . . Washington, U.S. Govt. print. off., 1940.

xxii, 459 p. incl. illus. (maps) tables, diagrs. 23 cm. ([U.S.] Temporary national economic committee. Investigation of concentration of economic power . . . Monograph no. 33)

At head of title: 76th Congress, 3d session. Senate committee print.

Running title: Concentration of economic power.

"A study made under the auspices of the Bureau of labor statistics for the Temporary national economic committee, Seventy-sixth Congress, third session, pursuant to Public resolution no. 113 (Seventy-fifth Congress), authorizing and directing a select committee to make a full and complete study and investigation with respect to the concentration of economic power in, and financial control over, production and distribution of goods and services."

"By Walter G. Keim." – p. ii.

Printed for the use of the Temporary national economic committee.

1. Building materials industry – U.S. I. Title.
HC106.3.A5127 no. 33   (330.973) 338.5   41-50309
MC#: 1941-page 413
SuDocs no.: Y4.T24:M75, no. 33

1176

U.S. *Federal trade commission.*

. . . Control of unfair competitive practices through trade practice conference procedure of the Federal trade commission . . . Washington, U.S. Govt. print. off., 1941.

vii, 65 p. 23 cm. (Temporary national economic committee. Investigation of concentration of economic power . . . Monograph no. 34)

At head of title: 76th Congress, 3d session. Senate committee print.

Running title: Concentration of economic power.

"A study made under the auspices of the Federal trade commission for the Temporary national economic committee, Seventy-sixth Congress, third session, pursuant to Public resolution no. 113 (Seventy-fifth Congress), authorizing and directing a select committee to make a full and complete study and investigation with respect to the concentration of economic power in, and financial control over, production and distribution of goods and services."

By the Federal trade commission. *cf.* Acknowledgment.

Printed for the use of the Temporary national economic committee.

1. Competition, Unfair – U.S. 2. Monopolies – U.S. I. Title.
HC106.3.A5127 no. 34   (330.973) 380.18   41-50176
MC#: 1941-page 413
SuDocs no.: Y4.T24:M75, no. 34

1177

[Hoffman, Austin Clair] 1905-

. . . Large-scale organization in the food industries . . . Washington, U.S. Govt. print. off., 1940.

xi, 174 p. incl. tables, diagrs. 23 cm. ([U.S.]Temporary national economic committee. Investigation of concentration of economic power . . . Monograph no. 35)

At head of title: 76th Congress, 3d session. Senate committee print.

Running title: Concentration of economic power.

"A study made for the Temporary national economic committee, Seventy-sixth Congress, third session, pursuant to Public resolution no. 113 (Seventy-fifth Congress), authorizing and directing a select committee to make a full and complete study and investigation with respect to the concentration of economic power in, and financial control over, production and distribution of goods and services."

By A. C. Hoffman. *cf.* Acknowledgment.

Printed for the use of the Temporary national economic committee.

Bibliography: p. 166-168.

1. Food industry and trade – U.S. I. Title.
HC106.3.A5127 no. 35   (330.973) 338.4   41-50150
MC#: 1941-page 413
SuDocs no.: Y4.T24:M75, no. 35

1178

U.S. *Federal trade commission.*

. . . Reports of the Federal trade commission on natural gas and natural gas pipe lines in U.S.A., agricultural implement and machinery inquiry, motor vehicle industry inquiry . . . Washington, U.S. Govt. print. off., 1940.

xi, 275 p. incl. tables. fold. map, fold. diagrs. 23 cm. (Temporary national economic committee. Investigation of concentration of economic power . . . Monograph no. 36)

At head of title: 76th Congress, 3d session. Senate committee print.

Running title: Concentration of economic power.

"Reports made under the auspices of the Federal trade commission for the Temporary national economic committee, Seventy-sixth Congress, third session, pursuant to Public resolution no. 113 (Seventy-fifth Congress), authorizing and directing a select committee to make a full and complete study and investigation with respect to the concentration of economic power in, and financial control over, production and distribution of goods and services."

Printed for the use of the Temporary national economic committee.

1. Gas, Natural – U.S. 2. Agricultural machinery – Trade and manufacture – U.S. 3. Automobile industry and trade – U.S.
HC106.3.A5127 no. 36   (330.973) 338.2   41-50177
MC#: 1941-page 413
SuDocs no.: Y4.T24:M75, no. 36

1179

[Altman, Oscar Louis] 1909-

. . . Saving, investment, and national income . . . Washington, U.S. Govt. print. off., 1941.

x, 135 p. incl. tables. 23 cm. ([U.S.] Temporary national economic committee. Investigation of concentration of economic power . . . Monograph no. 37)

At head of title: 76th Congress, 3d session. Senate committee print.

Running title: Concentration of economic power.

Commonly known as the Altman report.

By Oscar L. Altman. *cf.* Acknowledgment.

Printed for the use of the Temporary national economic committee.

"A study made for the Temporary national economic committee, Seventy-sixth Congress, third session, pursuant to Public resolution no. 113 (Seventy-fifth Congress), authorizing and directing a select committee to make a full and complete study and investigation with respect to the concentration of economic power in, and financial control over, production and distribution of goods and services."

1. Saving and investment. 2. Investments – U.S. 3. National income – U.S. 4. U.S. – Econ. condit. – 1918-1945. I. Title: Saving, investment, and national income. II. Title: Altman report on saving, investment, and national income.
HC106.3.A5127 no. 37   (330.973) 339.4973   41-50315
MC#: 1941-page 415
SuDocs no.: Y4.T24:M75, no. 37

1180

[Handler, Milton] 1903-

. . . A study of the construction and enforcement of the federal anti-trust laws . . . Washington, U.S. Govt. print. off., 1941.

vii, 106 p. incl. tables. 23 cm. ([U.S.] Temporary national economic committee. Investigation of concentration of economic power . . . Monograph no. 38)

At head of title: 76th Congress, 3d session. Senate committee print.

Running title: Concentration of economic power.

"A study made under the auspices of the Treasury department for the Temporary national economic committee, Seventy-sixth Congress, third session, pursuant to Public resolution no. 113 (Seventy-fifth Congress), authorizing and directing a select committee to make a full and complete study and investigation with respect to the concentration of economic power in, and financial control over, production and distribution of goods and services."

"By Milton Handler."—Acknowledgment.

Printed for the use of the Temporary national economic committee.

1. Trusts, Industrial—U.S.—Law. 2. Monopolies—U.S. I. Title.

HC106.3.A5127 no. 38   (330.973) 338.80973   41-50308
MC#: 1941-page 412
SuDocs no.: Y4.T24:M75, no. 38

1181

[Cook, Roy Clyde] 1909-

. . . Control of the petroleum industry of major oil companies . . . Washington, U.S. Govt. print. off., 1941.

xi, 101 p. incl. tables. fold. map, diagrs. (part fold.) 23 cm. ([U.S.] Temporary national economic committee. Investigation of concentration of economic power . . . Monograph no. 39)

At head of title: 76th Congress, 3d session. Senate committee print.

Running title: Concentration of economic power.

"A study made for the Temporary national economic committee, Seventy-sixth Congress, third session, pursuant to Public resolution no. 113 (Seventy-fifth Congress), authorizing and directing a select committee to make a full and complete study and investigation with respect to the concentration of economic power in, and financial control over, production and distribution of goods and services."

By Roy C. Cook. *cf.* Acknowledgment.

Printed for the use of the Temporary national economic committee.

Bibliography: p. 53-55.

1. Petroleum industry and trade—U.S. 2. Oil industries—U.S. I. Title.

HC106.3.A5127 no. 39   (330.973) 338.2   41-50178
MC#: 1941-page 414
SuDocs no.: Y4.T24:M75, no. 39

1182

U.S. *Temporary national economic committee.*

. . . Review and criticism on behalf of Standard oil co. (New Jersey) and Sun oil co. of Monograph no. 39 with rejoinder by monograph author . . . Washington, U.S. Govt. print. off., 1941.

vi, 96 p. incl. tables. 23 cm. (*Its* Investigation of concentration of economic power . . . Monograph no. 39-A)

At head of title: 76th Congress, 3d session. Senate committee print.

Running title: Concentration of economic power.

"A study made for the Temporary national economic committee, Seventy-sixth Congress, third session, pursuant to Public resolution no. 113 (Seventy-fifth Congress), authorizing and directing a select committee to make a full and complete study

and investigation with respect to the concentration of economic power in, and financial control over, production and distribution of goods and services."

Contents.—I. The alledged control of the petroleum industry. A reply to Mr. Roy C. Cook's monograph, "Control of the petroleum industry by major oil companies." [By W. S. Farish and J. Howard Pew]—II. Rejoiner by Roy C. Cook, author of Monograph no. 39.

1. Petroleum industry and trade—U.S. 2. Oil industries—U.S. I. Farish, William Stamps, 1881- II. Pew, John Howard, 1882- III. Cook, Roy Clyde, 1909-

HC106.3.A5127 no. 39-A   (330.973) 338.2   41-50954
MC#: 1941-page 1084
SuDocs no.: Y4.T24:M75, no. 39-A

1183

[Domeratzky, Louis] 1881-

. . . Regulation of economic activities in foreign countries . . . Washington, U.S. Govt. print. off., 1941.

x, 177 p. incl. tables. fold. diagr. 23 cm. ([U.S.] Temporary national economic committee. Investigation of concentration of economic power . . . Monograph no. 40)

At head of title: 76th Congress, 3d session. Senate committee print.

Running title: Concentration of economic power.

"A study made for the Temporary national economic committee, Seventy-sixth Congress, third session, pursuant to Public resolution no. 113 (Seventy-fifth Congress), authorizing and directing a select committee to make a full and complete study and investigation with respect to the concentration of economic power in, and financial control over, production and distribution of goods and services."

By Louis Domeratzky, Rudolf Callmann, Agnes Roman [and others] *cf.* Acknowledgment.

Printed for the use of the Temporary national economic committee.

1. Industry and state. I. Callmann, Rudolf, joint author. II. Roman, Agnes, joint author. III. Title.

HC106.3.A5127 no. 40   (330.973) 338   41-50179 Revised
MC#: 1941-page 414
SuDocs no.: Y4.T24:M75, no. 40

1184

[Blair, John Malcolm] 1914-

. . . Price discrimination in steel . . . Washington, U.S. Govt. print. off.; 1941.

ix p., 1 l., 54 p. incl. tables, diagrs. 23 cm. ([U.S.]Temporary national economic committee. Investigation of concentration of economic power . . . Monograph, no. 41)

At head of title: 76th Congress, 3d session. Senate committee print.

Running title: Concentration of economic power.

By John M. Blair and Arthur Reeside. *cf.* Acknowledgment.

1. Steel—Prices—U.S. 2. Price discrimination—U.S. 3. Steel industry and trade—U.S. I. Reeside, Arthur, 1903- joint author. II. Title.

HC106.3.A5127 no. 41   338.5   41-50141
MC#: 1941-page 231
SuDocs no.: Y4.T24:M75, no. 41

1185

U.S. *Federal trade commission.*

. . . The basing point problem . . . Washington, U.S. Govt. print. off., 1941.

xiv, 151 p. incl. tables, diagrs. maps (part fold.) 23 cm. (Temporary national economic committee. Investigation of concentration of economic power . . . Monograph no. 42)

At head of title: 76th Congress, 3d session. Senate committee print.

Running title: Concentration of economic power.

"A study made by the Federal trade commission for the Temporary national economic committee, Seventy-sixth Congress, third session, pursuant to Public resolution no. 113 (Seventy-fifth Congress), authorizing and directing a select committee to make a full and complete study and investigation with respect to the concentration of economic power in, and financial control over, production and distribution of goods and services."

"By the Federal trade commission." — p. ii.

Printed for the use of the Temporary national economic committee.

1. Basing-point system. 2. Steel industry and trade — U.S.
HC106.3.A5127 no. 42   (330.973) 338.5   41-50313
MC#: 1941-page 415
SuDocs no.: Y4.T24:M75, no. 42

1186

[Bertrand, Daniel] 1901-
. . . The motion picture industry — a pattern of control . . . Washington, U.S. Govt. print. off., 1941.

xii, 92 p. incl. tables. 23 cm. ([U.S.] Temporary national economic committee. Investigation of concentration of economic power . . . Monograph no. 43)

At head of title: 76th Congress, 3d session. Senate committee print.

Running title: Concentration of economic power.

"A study made for the Temporary national economic committee, Seventy-sixth Congress, third session, pursuant to Public resolution no. 113 (Seventy-fifth Congress), authorizing and directing a select committee to make a full and complete study and investigation with respect to the concentration of economic power in, and financial control over, production and distribution of goods and services."

By Daniel Bertrand, W. Duane Evans and E. L. Blanchard. cf. Acknowledgment.

Printed for the use of the Temporary national economic committee.

1. Moving-picture industry — U.S. 2. Moving-pictures, Talking. I. Evans, Wilmoth Duane, 1909- joint author. II. Blanchard, Edna L., joint author. III. Title.
HC106.3.A5127 no. 43   (330.973) 791.4   41-50180
MC#: 1941-page 414
SuDocs no.: Y4.T24:M75, no. 43

1187

U.S. *Temporary national economic committee.*
. . . Investigation of concentration of economic power. Final report and recommendations of the Temporary national economic committee transmitted to the Congress of the United States pursuant to Public resolution no. 113 (Seventy-fifth Congress) authorizing and directing a select committee to make a full and complete study and investigation with respect to the concentration of economic power in, and financial control over, production and distribution of goods and services . . . Washington, U.S. Govt. print. off., 1941.

ix, 783 p. incl. tables. diagrs. (1 fold.) 23 cm. ([U.S.]77th Cong., 1st sess. Senate. Doc. 35)

Presented by Mr. O'Mahoney. Ordered printed, with illustrations, March 31, 1941.

1. U.S. — Economic policy. 2. U.S. — Econ. condit. I. Title.
HC106.3.A5128 1941   330.973   41-50460
MC#: 1941-page 585
SuDocs no.: 77th Cong., 1st sess. S. Doc. 35

ONDERDONK REPORT [Onderdonk, Andrew]
see
WALKER COMMISSION [Walker, John Grimes]

OPPENHEIM REPORT [Oppenheim, Saul Chesterfield]

1188

U.S. *Attorney General's National Committee to Study the Antitrust Laws.* Report. [Washington, U.S. Govt. Print. Off.] 1955.

xiii, 393 p. 24 cm.
Cover title.
1. Trusts, Industrial — U.S. — Law.
                              338.85   55-60722
MC#: 1955-6616 (LC card 55-69722 referred to in error)
SuDocs no.: J1.2:An8/7

OPPENHEIMER REPORT [Oppenheimer, Reuben]
see
WICKERSHAM COMMISSION [Wickersham, George Woodward]
Report on deportation, no. 5

ORLEANS REPORT

1189

Orleans, Leo A
Professional manpower and education in Communist China. [Washington, U.S. Govt. Print. Off., 1961]

xii, 260 p. diagrs., tables. 24 cm.
"NSF-61-3."
1. Education — China. 2. Scientists — China. I. Title.
LA1131.07   370.951   61-61233
MC#: 1961-9633
SuDocs no.: NS1.2:C44

ORRICK REPORT

1190

Orrick, William Horsley, 1915-
Shut it down! A college in crisis: San Francisco State College, October 1968-April 1969; a report to the National Commission on the Causes and Prevention of Violence, by William H. Orrick, Jr. [Washington, For sale by the Supt. of Docs., U.S. Govt. Print. Off.] 1969.

xiii, 172 p. illus. 24 cm. ([NCCPV staff study series] 6)
Published in 1970 under title: College in crisis.
1. California. State College, San Francisco — Students. 2. Student movements — United States. I. United States. National Commission on the Causes and Prevention of Violence. II. Title. III. Series: United States. National Commission on the Causes and Prevention of Violence. NCCPV staff study series, 6.
LD729.C97507   378.1'98'10979461   76-602072
                                                            MARC
MC#: 1969-13327
SuDocs no.: Pr36.8:V81/Sa5f

OSBORNE REPORT [Osborne, Stanley de J.]
see
BLACK REPORT [Black, Eugene R.]

OTIS REPORT [Otis, Elwell Stephen]
see
SCHURMAN REPORT [Schurman, Jacob Gould]

OTIS REPORT [Otis, Jack]

1191

U.S. *President's Committee on Juvenile Delinquency and Youth Crime.*

President's Committee on Juvenile Delinquency and Youth Crime and its implications for education, by Jack Otis, program analyst, Welfare Administration, Office of Juvenile Delinquency and Youth Development, Department of HEW, speech delivered Nov. 5, 1963.

13 1.

MC#: 1964-5762

SuDocs no.: FS14.11:Ot4

OUTDOOR RECREATION REPORT
see
ORRRC REPORTS

OWINGS REPORTS [Owings, Nathanial Alexander]

1192

U.S. *President's Council on Pennsylvania Avenue.*

Pennsylvania Avenue; report. [Washington, U.S. Govt. Print. Off., 1964]

56 p. illus., plans (part fold.) 32 cm.

1. Cities and towns—Planning—Washington, D.C. 2. Washington, D.C.—Streets—Pennsylvania Avenue. I. Title.

NA9127.W2A54   71.551   64-61649

MC#: 1964-13378

SuDocs no.: Pr35.8:P38/P38

1193

U.S. *President's Temporary Commission on Pennsylvania Avenue.*

Pennsylvania Avenue; report. [Washington; For sale by the Supt. of Docs., U.S. Govt. Print. Off., 1969]

69 p. illus. 26 x 36 cm.

1. Cities and towns—Planning—Washington, D.C. 2. Washington, D.C.—Streets—Pennsylvania Avenue. I. Title.

NA9127.W2A542   711'.551   77-602958
                                            MARC

MC#: 1969-13323

SuDocs no.: Pr36.8:P38/P38

PACE REPORT [Pace, Frank, Jr.]
see
WRISTON REPORT [Wriston, Henry Merritt]
Goals for Americans.

PAISH REPORT [Paish, George]
see under
ALDRICH COMMISSION [Aldrich, Nelson Wilmarth]
Hirst. Credit of nations.

PALEY REPORTS [Paley, William S.]

1194

U.S. *President's Materials Policy Commission.*

Resources for freedom; a report to the President. [Washington, U.S. Govt. Print. Off.] 1952.

5 v. maps, diagrs. 30 cm.

Includes bibliographies.

Contents.—v. 1. Foundations for growth and security.—v. 2. The outlook for key commidities.—v. 3. The outlook for energy sources.—v. 4. The promise of technology.—v. 5. Selected reports to the commission.

1. Natural resources—U.S. 2. Natural resources. I. Title.

HC103.7.A53 1952   333.72   52-61183

MC#: 1952-11419, 11420, 14337, 11421, 14338 (Vols. 1-5)

SuDocs no.: Pr33.15:(nos.)

MC#: 1952-16367 (Vols. 1-3, 5)

SuDocs no.: 82d Cong., 2d sess. H. Doc. 527

MC#: 1952-17497

SuDocs no.: 82d Cong., 2d sess. H. Doc. 527, v. 4

1195

U.S. *President's Materials Policy Commission.*

Resources for freedom; summary of volume I of a report to the President. [Washington, U.S. Govt. Print. Off.] 1952.

82 p. 23 cm.

1. Natural resources—U.S. 2. Natural resources. I. Title.

HC103.7.A53 1952a   338.973   52-61344

MC#: 1952-14336

SuDocs no.: Pr33.15:1/summ.

PALGRAVE REPORT [Palgrave, Sir Robert Harry Inglis]
see under
ALDRICH COMMISSION [Aldrich, Nelson Wilmarth]
Withers. English banking system.

PALMER REPORT [Palmer, Dwight R. G.]

1196

U.S. *Committee on Government Contract Compliance.*

Equal economic opportunity; a report. Washington, 1953.

viii, 111 p. tables. 24 cm.

1. Discrimination in employment—U.S. 2. Public contracts—U.S. I. Title.

HC4903.5.U58A5   331.11   53-60210 rev

MC#: 1953-2772

SuDocs no.: Pr33.17/2:953

PARKE REPORT [Parke, Robert, Jr.]
see
ROCKEFELLER REPORT [Rockefeller, John D., 3d]
Demographic and social aspects of population growth.

PARKER PANEL [Parker, David S.]

1197·

United States. *Dept. of the Army. Special Review Panel of Department of the Army Organization.*

Report of the Special Review Panel on Department of the Army Organization. [Washington] 1971.

2 v. in 1. (ASDIRS 3338).

Cover title.

1. United States. Army—Organization. I. Title. II. Title: Parker Panel. III. Series.

[UA24.A794]

Dept. of the Army Library

Not located in Monthly Catalog

PARKER REPORT

1198

Parker, Charles, 1916-

The court reporting system in United States District Courts, 1960 [by Charles Parker, Jr. and Norman R. Tharp. Washington] Administrative Office of the U.S. Courts [1960]

139 p. illus. 27 cm.

1. Law reporting—U.S. 2. U.S. District Courts. I. Tharp, Norman R., joint author. II. Title. *Full name:* Charles Frederick Parker.

         347.9973   60-64517
Not located in Monthly Catalog

PARKER REPORT [Parker, James Southworth]

1199

U.S. *Congress. House. Committee on interstate and foreign commerce.*
   . . . Regulation of stock ownership in railroads . . . Washington, U.S. Govt. print. off., 1931.
   3 v. maps (part fold.) tables, diagrs. (part fold.) forms. 23½ cm. (71st Cong., 3d sess. House. Rept. 2789)
   House calendar no. 553.
   On cover: House reports on public bills, etc. III[-V] Stock ownership in railroads . . . House report 2789, 71st Congress, 3d session.
   Paged continuously.
   Walter M. W. Splawn, special counsel.
   Submitted by Mr. Parker, pursuant to House resolution no. 114. Referred to the House calendar and ordered printed, with illustrations, February 20, 1931.
   "Legal study on constitutional power of Congress to regulate stock ownership in railroads engaged in interstate commerce, by M. S. Breckenridge, assisted by Willard W. Gatchell and William H. Watts": pt. 1, p. 1-62.
   "Should the railway holding company be outlawed? By James C. Bonbright": pt. 1, p. 63-81.
   Bibliography on investment trusts: pt. 3, p. 1736.
   1. Railroads—U.S.—Finance. I. Parker, James Southworth, 1867-1933. II. Breckenridge, M. S. III. Gatchell, Willard Waddington, 1898- IV. Watts, William H. V. Bonbright, James Cummings, 1891- VI. Splawn, Walter Marshall William, 1883- VII. Title. VIII. Title: Legal study on constitutional power of Congress to regulate stock ownership in railroads engaged in interstate commerce. IX. Title: Should the railway holding company be outlawed?
HE2236.U7 1931   385.0973   31-26664
MC#: Mar. 1931-page 794
SuDocs no.: 71st Cong., 3d sess. H. Rept. 2789 (Monthly Catalog listing of H. Rept. 2780 in error)

PARKER REPORT [Parker, Julia O'Connor]
   see
RUSSELL REPORT [Russell, John Dale]

PARMELEE REPORT [Parmelee, Julius H.]
   see under
DILLINGHAM COMMISSION [Dillingham, William Paul]
      Occupations of the first and second generations of immigrants.

PARMELEE REPORT [Parmelee, Maurice Farr]

1200

U.S. *Railroad Retirement Board.*
   Economic factors influencing railroad employment, by Maurice Parmelee. An analysis of some of the factors which affect production and determine the volume of employment, and, therefore, railroad employment and the work load and obligations of the railroad retirement and unemployment insurance systems. Chicago, United States Railroad Retirement Board, Office of Director of Research, 1946.
   vi, 152 1. 26 cm.

1. Railroads—U.S.—Hist. 2. Railroads—U.S.—Employees. 3. U.S.—Econ. condit.—1918-1945. 4. Labor supply—U.S. I. Parmelee, Maurice Farr, 1882- II. Title.
HE2751.A54 1946   385.13   49-49524*
Not located in Monthly Catalog

PARMELEE REPORT [Parmelee, Rexford Clark]
   see under
O'MAHONEY REPORTS [O'Mahoney, Joseph Christopher]
      Goldsmith. Distribution of ownership in the 200 largest non-financial corporations.

PARNES REPORT

1201

Parnes, Herbert S 1919-
   Effective utilization of engineering manpower; a survey of the literature. Prepared for the President's Committee on Scientists and Engineers. Washington [1957?]
   29 1. 28 cm.
   Includes bibliography.
   1. Engineering as a profession. 2. Engineers—U.S. I. Title. II. Title: Engineering manpower.
TA157.P3   620.69   58-60302
Not located in Monthly Catalog

PASMA REPORT [Pasma, Theodore K.]

1202

U.S. *Dept. of Commerce. Area Development Division.*
   Organized industrial districts; a tool for community development, by Theodore K. Pasma, Area Development Division. [Washington] 1954.
   vii, 111 p. illus., fold. map. 26 cm.
   Bibliography: p. 108-109.
   1. Industrial districts. I. Pasma, Theodore K. II. Title.
HD1393.5.U52   333.77   55-60102 rev
MC#: 1955-307
SuDocs no.: C41.22:In2

PATMAN REPORTS [Patman, Wright]

1203

U.S. *Congress. House. Committee on Banking and Currency. Subcommittee on Domestic Finance.*
   Commercial banks and their trust activities: emerging influence on the American economy; staff report. Washington, U.S. Govt. Print. Off., 1968.
   2 v. 26 cm.
   At head of title: Subcommittee print.
   1. Trust companies—U.S. 2. Banks and banking—U.S. I. Title.
HG4342.A4   332.1′2′0973   75-600154
                                         MARC
MC#: 1969-392
SuDocs no.: Y4.B22/1:B22/17/v. 1,2

1204

U.S. *Congress. House. Select Committee on Small Business.*
   Tax-exempt foundations and charitable trusts: their impact on our economy. [1st]- installment; Dec. 31, 1962- Washington, U.S. Govt. Print. Off.
   v. 29 cm.
   At head of title: Committee print.
   1. Charitable uses, trusts, and foundations—U.S.—Taxation. I. Title.
                                       63-60464 rev

MC#: 1963-2063
SuDocs no.: Y4.Sm1:T19/2
MC#: 1963-18960 — 2d installment
    1964-8402 — 3d installment
    1967-4562 — 4th installment
    1967-10679 — 5th installment
    1968-7363 — 6th installment
    1969-13942 — 7th installment
MC#: 1973-31015 (LC card 72-603277 listed in error)
SuDocs no.: Y4.B22/1:T19/10/8th inst.

1205

U.S. *Congress. Joint Economic Committee.*
    Monetary policy and the management of the public debt; report of the Subcommittee on General Credit Control and Debt Management of the Joint Committee on the Economic Report, Congress of the United States. Washington, U.S. Govt. Print. Off., 1952.
    vi, 80 p. 24 cm. (82d Cong., 2d sess. Senate. Document no. 163)
    1. Finance — U.S. 2. Credit — U.S. 3. Currency question — U.S. I. Title. (Series: U.S. 82d Cong., 2d sess., 1952. Senate. Document no. 163)
HG181.A412 1952k   332.4973   52-61315 rev
MC#: 1952-13532
SuDocs no.: 82d Cong., 2d sess. S. Doc. 163

1206

U.S. *Congress. Joint Economic Committee.*
    Monetary policy and the management of the public debt; their role in achieving price stability and high-level employment. Replies to questions and other material for the use of the Subcommittee on General Credit Control and Debt Management, Joint Committee on the Economic Report. Washington, U.S. Govt. Print. Off., 1952.
    2 v. (xvii, 1302 p.) maps (part fold.) diagrs. 24 cm.
    At head of title: 82d Cong., 2d sess. Joint committee print.
    Issued also as Senate Document no. 123, 82d Cong., 2d sess.
    1. Monetary policy — U.S. 2. Debts, Public — U.S. I. Title. II. Title: Patman report on monetary policy and the management of the public debt.
HG181.A412 1952c   332.4973   52-60615 rev
MC#: 1952-5073
SuDocs no.: Y3.Ec7:M74/3/pt. 1-2

1207

U.S. *Congress. Joint Economic Committee.*
    Monetary policy and the management of the public debt; their role in achieving price stability and high-level employment. Replies to questions and other material for the use of the Subcommittee on General Credit Control and Debt Management, Joint Committee on the Economic Report. Washington, U.S. Govt. Print. Off., 1952.
    2 v. (xvii, 1320 p.) maps (part fold.) diagrs. 24 cm. (82d Cong., 2d sess. Senate. Document no. 123)
    Issued also as Committee print, 82d Cong., 2d sess.
    1. Finance — U.S. 2. Credit — U.S. 3. Currency question — U.S. I. Title. (Series: U.S. 82d Cong., 2d sess., 1952. Senate. Document no. 123)
HG181.A412 1952h   332   52-60995 rev
MC#: 1952-8952
SuDocs no.: 82d Cong., 2d sess. S. Doc. 123

1208

U.S. *Congress. Joint Economic Committee. Subcommittee on Foreign Economic Policy.*

New directions in the Soviet economy; studies. Washington, U.S. Govt. Print. Off., 1966.
    4 v. in 5 (xiii, 1093 p.) illus., maps. 24 cm.
    At head of title: 89th Congress, 2d session. Joint committee print.
    Includes bibliographies.
    Contents. — pt. 1. Economic policy. — pt. 1. A-B. Economic performance. 2v. — pt. 3. The human resources. — pt. 4. The world outside, and a selected bibliography of recent Soviet monographs, and appendixes.
    1. Russia — Econ. condit. — 1955-1965. I. Title.
HC336.2.U53   330.947   66-62352
MC#: 1966-12843 — part 1
    1966-12844 — part 2-A
    1966-12845 — part 2-B
    1966-14372 — part 3
    1966-12846 — part 4
SuDocs no.: Y4.Ec7:So8/7/(pt.)

PATRON REPORT [Patron, Maurice]
    see under
ALDRICH COMMISSION [Aldrich, Nelson Wilmarth]

PAULEY REPORTS

1209

Pauley, Edwin Wendell, 1903-
    Report on Japanese assets in Manchuria to the President of the United States, July 1946, by Edwin W. Pauley, Ambassador of the United States and personal representative of the President on reparations. [Washington, U.S. Govt. Print. Off., 1946]
    1 v. (various pagings) illus., maps (part fold.) 27 cm.
    1. Japanese property in Manchuria. 2. Investments, Japanese — Manchuria. 3. Manchuria — Indus. I. U.S. Reparations Mission to Japan. II. Title: Japanese assets in Manchuria.
HC428.M3P3   338   50-60214
MC#: 1950-6185
SuDocs no.: S1.2:J27/5

1210

Pauley, Edwin Wendell, 1903-
    Report on Japanese assets in Soviet-occupied Korea to the President of the United States, June 1946, by Edwin W. Pauley, Ambassador of the United States and personal representative of the President on reparations. [Washington, U.S. Govt. Print. Off., 1946]
    iv, 141 p. illus. 27 cm.
    1. Japanese property in Korea. 2. Alien property — Korea. I. U.S. Reparations Mission to Japan. II. Title: Japanese assets in Soviet-occupied Korea.
HC467.P3   330.9519   50-26130
MC#: 1950-6186
SuDocs no.: S1.2:J27/4

PEARCE REPORT [Pearce, Charles Albert]
    see under
O'MAHONEY REPORTS [O'Mahoney, Joseph Christopher]

PEERS COMMISSION [Peers, William R.]
1211

United States. Dept. of the Army.
    Report of the Department of the Army review of the preliminary investigations into the My Lai incident : volume I, The report of the investigation. — [Washington] : The Dept. : [for sale by the Supt. of Docs., U.S. Govt. Print. Off.], 1970 i.e. 1974.

413 p. in various pagings : ill., maps (some fold.) ; 27 cm.
Cover title.
"Peers inquiry."
"Volumes II and IV . . . will not be released. Volume III
. . . due to its volume (seven books) . . . will not be repro-
duced."
1. My lai (4), Vietnam—Massacre, 1968. I. Peers, William
R. II. Title: Report of the Department of the Army review . . .
III. Title: My Lai incident.
DS557.8.M9U54 1974   355.1'334   74-603407
                                                    MARC
MC#: 1976-1730
SuDocs no.: D101.2:M99/v. 1

United States. Dept. of the Army.
The My Lai Massacre and its cover-up : beyond the reach of
law? : The Peers Commission report / Joseph Goldstein, Burke
Marshall, Jack Schwartz.—New York : Free Press, c1976.

xi, 586 p. : maps ; 24 cm.
W. R. Peers, chairman of the inquiry.
Consists of the report first issued in 1974 under title: Report
of the Department of the Army review of the preliminary investiga-
tions into the My Lai incident : volume I, The report of the
investigation. Vols. 2 and 4 of the original report were not released
and v. 3 was not reproduced.
Includes texts of documents from World War II and Nuremberg
and from the Vietnam War.
Includes bibliographical references.
ISBN 0-02-912230-9. ISBN 0-02-912240-6 pbk.
1. My lai (4), Vietnam—Massacre, 1968. I. Peers, William
R. II. Goldstein, Joseph. III. Marshall, Burke, 1922- IV.
Schwartz, Jack, 1946- V. Title.
DS557.8.M9U54 1976   355.1'334   75-38298
                                                    MARC
Not listed in Monthly Catalog

PENNSYLVANIA AVENUE REPORT
        see
OWINGS REPORT [Owings, Nathaniel Alexander]

PENROSE REPORT [Penrose, Boies]
1212

U.S. *Congress. Joint commission on business methods of Post-office department and postal service.*
. . . Preliminary report of Joint commission on business method
of Post-office department and postal service . . . Washington,
Govt. print. off., 1908.
vi, 387 p. fold. tables, fold. diagrs. 23 cm. (60th Cong., 1st
sess. Senate. Rept. 201)
Submitted by Mr. Penrose, Feb. 10, 1908, referred to the Com-
mittee on the post-offices and post-roads and ordered printed with
accompanying illustrations.
Printed also as House rept. 698, submitted by Mr. Overstreet.
Appendix: Laws of Congress governing the Post-office depart-
ment and the postal service: p. 177-294.
1. U.S. Post-office dept. 2. Postal service—U.S. I. Penrose,
Boies, 1860-1921. II. U.S. 60th Cong., 1st sess., 1907-1908.
HE6331 1908   8-35175
Document Catalogue, vol. 9-page 1341
SuDocs no.: 60th Cong., 1st sess. S. Rept. 201

PENTAGON PAPERS
1213

United States-Vietnam relations, 1945-1967; study prepared by
Department of Defense. Washington, U.S. Govt. Print. Off.,
1971.

12 v. maps. 28 cm.
At head of title: Committee print.
"Printed for the use of the House Committee on Armed Ser-
vices."
"The 12-volume text here contains the first 43 volumes of the
original 47-volume study."
Commonly known as the Pentagon papers.
Supt. of Docs. no.: Y4.Ar5/2:B67/3/945
1. United States—Foreign relations—Vietnam. 2. Vietnam—
Foreign relations—United States. 3. Vietnam—Politics and
government. 4. Vietnamese Conflict, 1961- I. United States. Dept.
of Defense. II. United States. Congress. House. Committee on
Armed Services.
E183.8.V5P4 1971d   327.73'0597   70-614379
                                                    MARC
MC#: 1971-16432
SuDocs no.: Y4.Ar5/2:V67/3/945-67bk. 1-12

PERKINS REPORT [Perkins, Frances]
1214

U.S. *Committee on economic security.*
Report to the President of the Committee on economic secu-
rity. Washington, U.S. Govt. print. off., 1935.
vii, 53 p. 23 cm.
Frances Perkins, chairman.
HD7123.A55 1935c
- - - - - Copy 2.
- - - - - Supplement . . . Washington, U.S. Govt. print. off.,
1935.
1 p. 1., 18 p. tables (2 fold.) 23 cm.
1. Insurance, State and compulsory—U.S. I. *Perkins, Frances,
1882- II. Title.
HD7123.A55 1935 c Suppl.   331.250973   35-26030
- - - - - Copy 2.
MC#: 1935-page 37
SuDocs no.: Y3.Ec74:2R29, Y3.Ec74:2R29/supp.

PERKINS REPORT [Perkins, James A.]
1215

U.S. *President's Advisory Panel on a National Academy of Foreign Affairs.*
Report [Washington] 1962.
8 p. 26 cm.
Commonly known as the Perkins report.
1. U.S. National Academy of Foreign Affairs (Proposed) I. Ti-
tle: Perkins report on a National Academy of Foreign Affairs.
JX1634.U56   63-60488
MC#: 1963-3261
SuDocs no.: Pr35.8:F76/2/R29

PERLMAN REPORT [Perlman, Jacob]
        see under
O'MAHONEY REPORT [O'Mahoney, Joseph
Christopher]

PERLMAN REPORT [Perlman, Philip B.]
1216

U.S. *President's Commission on Immigration and Naturalization.*
Whom we shall welcome; report. [Washington, U.S. Govt.
Print. Off., 1953]
xv, 319 p. illus., map. 23 cm.
1. U.S.—Emig. & immig. 2. Emigration and immigration
law—U.S. I. Title.
JV6415.A4 1953   325.73   53-60119
MC#: 1953-2773
SuDocs no.: Pr33.18:R29

PERSHING REPORT [Pershing, John J.]

1217

U.S. *American battle monuments commission.*
    36th division, summary of operations in the world war. Prepared by the American battle monuments commission. [Washington] U.S. Govt. print. off., 1944.
    x, 28 p. incl. tables. maps (1 fold. in pocket) 23½ cm.
    "Sources": p. 23-24.
    1. U.S. Army. 36th division. 2. European war, 1914-1918 — Regimental histories — U.S. — 36th division.
D570.3.36th.A53   940.41273   44-40924
MC#: 1944-page 618
SuDocs no.: Y3.Am3:W89/36th Div.

PESTICIDE COMMISSION REPORT
        see
MRAK REPORT [Mrak, Emil M.]

PETERSON REPORT [Peterson, Esther]
        Consumer issues '66.
    see
HELLER REPORT [Heller, Walter W.]
        Consumer Advisory Council. Report. 1963.

PETERSON REPORT [Peterson, Leonard T.]

1218

U.S. *Commission on amputations and prostheses.*
    Report on European observations . . . [Washington? 1946?]
    135 p. illus. 26½ cm.
    1. Artificial limbs. [1. Extremities, Prosthetic] 2. Amputation.
[WE168.8qU58r 1946]   Med 47-298
Not located in Monthly Catalog

PETERSON REPORT

1219

Peterson, Peter G
    The United States in the changing world economy [by] Peter G. Peterson. [Washington; For sale by the Supt. of Docs., U.S. Govt. Print. Off., 1971]
    2 v. illus. 27 cm.
    Cover title.
    Contents: v. 1. A foreign economic perspective. — v. 2. Background material.
    1. United States — Foreign economic relations. 2. United States — Commerce. 3. Economic history — 1945- I. Title.
HF1455.P47   382.1'0973   72-600901
                                                      MARC
MC#: 1972-6021
SuDocs no.: Pr37.8:In8/3/R29/v. 1,2

PETERSON REPORT [Peterson, Rudolph A.]

1220

U.S. *Task Force on International Development.*
    U.S. foreign assistance in the 1970s: a new approach; report to the President. Washington; [For sale by the Supt. of Docs., U.S. Govt. Print. Off.] 1970.
    v, 39 p. 24 cm.
    1. Economic assistance, American. 2. Military assistance, American. I. Title.
HC60.U6T36   338.91'73   73-606538
                                                      MARC
MC#: 1970-7712
SuDocs no.: Pr37.8:In8/F76

PETERSON REPORTS [Peterson, Esther]

1221

U.S. *President's Commission on the Status of Women.*
    American women; report. [Washington, For sale by the Superintendent of Documents, U.S. Govt. Print. Off.] 1963.
    v, 86 p. illus., ports., map. 26 cm.
    1. Women in the U.S. I. Title.
HQ1420.A52   63-65278
MC#: 1963-20075
SuDocs no.: Pr35.8:W84/Am3

1222

U.S. *President's Commission on the Status of Women. Committee on Protective Labor Legislation.*
    Report to the President's Commission on the Status of Women. [Washington, President's Commission on the Status of Women; for sale by the Superintendent of Documents, U.S. Govt. Print. Off.] 1963.
    v, 38 p. 26 cm.
    Bibliographical footnotes.
    1. Woman Employment — U.S.
                                                      63-65277
MC#: 1963-20081
SuDocs no.: Pr35.8:W84/P94

1223

United States. President's Committee on Consumer Interests.
    A summary of activities, 1964-1967. [Washington] 1967.
    61 p. 27 cm.
    Cover title.
    1. Consumer protection — United States. I. Title.
HC110.C6A584   339.4'0973   67-61332
                                                      MARC
MC#: 1967-10029
SuDocs no.: Pr36.8:C76/Ac8/964-67

PETERSON REPORTS [Peterson, Russell W.]

1224

National Advisory Commission on Criminal Justice Standards and Goals.
    Community crime prevention [report. Washington; For sale by the Supt. of Docs., U.S. Govt. Print. Off., 1973]
    xviii, 364 p. illus. 27 cm.
    Bibliography: p. 333-342.
    1. Crime prevention — United States. 2. Crime prevention — United States — Citizen participation. 3. Social service — United States. I. Title.
HV7431.N27 1973   364   73-603421
MC#: 1974-04593
SuDocs no.: Y3.C86:2C73

1225

National Advisory Commission on Criminal Justice Standards and Goals.
    Corrections. [Washington; For sale by the Supt. of Docs., U.S. Govt. Print. Off., 1973]
    xix, 636 p. illus. 26 cm.
    Includes bibliographical references.
    1. Corrections — United States.
HV9304.N28 1973   365'.973   73-602803
                                                      MARC
MC#: 1974-1386
SuDocs no.: Y3.C86:2C81

1226

National Advisory Commission on Criminal Justice Standards and Goals.

Courts. [Washington; For sale by the Supt. of Docs., U.S. Govt. Print. Off., 1973]

xxi, 358 p. illus. 26 cm.
Bibliography: p. 323-337.
1. Criminal justice, Administration of—United States. I. Title.
KF9223.A846   345′.73′05   73-602601
                                                       MARC
MC#: 1974-538
SuDocs no.: Y3.C86:2C83

1227

National Advisory Commission on Criminal Justice Standards and Goals.

Criminal justice system. [Washington, U.S. Govt. Print. Off., 1973]

xv, 286 p. illus. 27 cm.
Includes bibliographical references.
1. Criminal justice, Administration of—United States. I. Title.
KF9223.A847   345′.73′05   73-603019
                                                       MARC
MC#: 1974-04594
SuDocs no.: Y3.C86:2C86/2

1228

National Advisory Commission on Criminal Justice Standards and Goals.

A national strategy to reduce crime. [Washington; For sale by the Supt. of Docs., U.S. Govt. Print. Off., 1973]

xv, [5], 194 p. illus.
MC#: 1973-31599
SuDocs no.: Y3.C86:2C86

1229

National Advisory Commission on Criminal Justice Standards and Goals.

Police; [a report. Washington; for sale by the Supt. of Docs., U.S. Govt. Print. Off., 1973]

xix, 668 p. illus. 27 cm.
Bibliography: p. 617-638.
1. Police—United States. 2. Law enforcement—United States. I. Title.
HV8138.N27 1973   363.2′0973   73-602929
                                                          MARC
MC#: 1974-1387
SuDocs no.: Y3.C86:2P75

1230

United States. Congress. Office of Technology Assessment.

OTA priorities 1979 : with brief descriptions of priorities and of assessments in progress. — Washington : Congress of the U.S., Office of Technology Assessment, [1979]

v, 49 p. ; 24 cm.
Cover title.
"OTA-P-81."
1. Technology assessment. I. Title.
T174.5.U56 1979   301.24′3   79-601047
                                                      MARC
MC#: 1979-8726
SuDocs no.: Y3.T22/2:2P93/979

PEW REPORT [Pew, John Howard]
      see under
      O'MAHONEY REPORTS [O'Mahoney, Joseph Christopher]
            Review and criticism on behalf of Standard Oil Co.

PHILIPPOVICH VON PHILIPPSBERG REPORT [Philippovich von Philippsberg, Eugen]
      see under
      ALDRICH COMMISSION [Aldrich, Nelson Wilmarth]

PHILLIPS REPORT [Phillips, Thomas Wharton]
      see
      WHITE REPORT [White, Hays B.]

PICK-SLOAN REPORTS [Pick, Lewis A. and Sloan, W. G.]

1231

U.S. *Army. Corps of engineers.*

. . . Missouri river basin. Report of a committee of two representatives each from the Corps of engineers, U.S. Army, and Bureau of reclamation, appointed to review the features of the plans presented by the Corps of engineers (House document no. 475) and the Bureau of reclamation (Senate document no. 191) for the comprehensive development of the Missouri river basin . . . Washington, U.S. Govt. print. off., 1944.

1 p. 1., 6 p. 23 cm. ([U.S.] 78th Cong., 2d sess. Senate. Doc. 247)
"Supplemental to Senate doc. no. 191 and House doc. no. 475, 78th Congress."
1. Missouri river. I. U.S. Bureau of reclamation.
TC425.M7A5 1944k   627.1   45-35351 rev
MC#: 1945-page 137
SuDocs no.: 78th Cong., 2d sess. S. Doc. 247

1232

U.S. *Army. Corps of engineers.*

. . . Reconciliation report on problems of Missouri valley project. Message from the President of the United States, transmitting reconciliation report on the problems of the Missouri valley project. [Washington, U.S. Govt. print. off., 1944]

10 p. 23 cm. ([U.S.] 78th Cong., 2d sess. House. Doc. 784)
Caption title.
Running title: Report on problems of Missouri valley project.
Prepared by the Engineer dept. and the Bureau of reclamation.
1. Hydraulic engineering—Missouri valley. I. U.S. Bureau of reclamation. II. Title:Missouri valley project.
TC425.M7A5 1944 1   627.1   45-35340
MC#: 1945-page 137
SuDocs no.: 78th Cong., 2d sess. H. Doc. 784

PIERCE REPORT [Pierce, John R.]

1233

U.S. *President's Science Advisory Committee.*

Computers in higher education; report. Washington [For sale by the Supt. of Docs., U.S. Govt. Print. Off.] 1967.

vi, 79 p. 24 cm.
1. Electronic data processing—Education.
LB1028.5.U53   378′.001′8   67-60928
                                                     MARC
MC#: 1967-8615
SuDocs no.: Pr35.8:Sci2/C73

PIKE REPORT [Pike, Otis]

1234

United States. Congress. House. Select Committee on Intelligence.
    CIA : the Pike report / with an introduction by Philip Agee. — Nottingham : Spokesman Books for the Bertrand Russell Peace Foundation, 1977.
    284 p. ; 20 cm.

GB77-26148

    Includes bibliographical references.
    ISBN 0-85124-172-7 ISBN 0-85124-173-5 pbk.
    1. United States. Central Intelligence Agency. I. Pike, Otis. II. Title.

JK468.I6U55 1977	327'.12'06173	78-301398
		MARC

Not listed in Monthly Catalog.

PIKE REPORT [Pike, Sumner Tucker]
see under
O'MAHONEY REPORTS [O'Mahoney, Joseph Christopher]
    Statement on life insurance.

PILCHER REPORT [Pilcher, John L.]

1235

U.S. *Congress. House. Committee on Foreign Affairs.*
    Report of the special study mission to Asia, western Pacific. Middle East, southern Europe and North Africa pursuant to H. Res. 113 . . . Washington, U.S. Govt. Print. Off., 1960.
    vii, 84 p. diagrs., tables. 24 cm. (86th Cong., 2d sess. House report no. 1386)
    1. Economic history—1945- 2. Technical assistance, American. 3. Economic assistance, American. (Series: U.S. 86th Cong., 2d sess., 1960. House. Report no. 1386)

HC60.U6A5 1960	309.220973	60-60886 rev

MC#: 1960-6558
SuDocs no.: 86th Cong., 2d sess. H. Rept. 1386

PISAR REPORT

1236

Pisar, Samuel.
    A new look at trade policy toward the Communist bloc; the elements of a common strategy for the West. Materials prepared for the Subcommittee on Foreign Economic Policy of the Joint Economic Committee. Washington, U.S. Govt. Print. Off., 1961.
    viii, 103 p. tables. 24 cm.
    At head of title: Joint committee print.
    1. East-West trade (1945-) 2. Communist countries—Commercial policy. I. U.S. Congress. Joint Economic Committee. II. Title.

HF499.P52	382	62-60132

MC#: 1962-2285
SuDocs no.: Y4.Ec7:T67

PLOSCOWE REPORT [Ploscowe, Morris]
see
WICKERSHAM COMMISSION [Wickersham, George Woodward]
    Report on criminal statistics, no. 3.

    Report on the causes of crime, no. 13.

PLUM BOOK

1237

U.S. *Congress. Senate. Committee on Post Office and Civil Service.*

United States Government policy and supporting positions. Committee on Post Office and Civil Service, United States Senate, 86th Congress, 2d session. Washington, U.S. Govt. Print. Off., 1960.
    viii, 141 p. 32 p.
    At head of title: Committee print.
    1. U.S.—Officials and employees. I. Title.

JK661 1960.A53		64-61116

Not located in Monthly Catalog

1238

United States. Civil Service Commission.
    United States Government policy and supporting positions. 90th Congress, 2d session. Washington, U.S. Govt. Print. Off., 1968.
    vii, 162 p. 31 cm.
    At head of title: Committee print.
    "Printed for the use of the Committee on Post Office and Civil Service, House of Representatives."
    1. United States—Officials and employees. I. United States. Congress. House. Committee on Post Office and Civil Service. II. Title.

JK661 1968.A5	353.002	70-600107
		MARC

MC#: 1969-414
SuDocs no.: Y4.P84/10:P75

1239

United States. Civil Service Commission.
    United States Government policy and supporting positions. 93d Congress, 1st session. Washington, U.S. Govt. Print. Off., 1973.
    vii, 191 p. 31 cm.
    At head of title: Committee print.
    "Printed for the use of the [Senate] Committee on Post Office and Civil Service."
    1. United States—Officials and employees. I. United States. Congress. Senate. Committee on Post Office and Civil Service. II. Title.

JK661 1973.A5	353.002	73-600827
		MARC

MC#: 1973-23071 (LC card 73-601184 cancelled in favor of 73-600827)
SuDocs no.: Y4.P84/11:P75/973

1240

United States. Civil Service Commission.
    United States Government policy and supporting positions : Committee on Post Office and Civil Service, House of Representatives, 94th Congress, 2d session. — Washington : U.S. Govt. Print. Off., 1976.
    ix, 139 p. ; 31 cm.
    At head of title: Committee print.
    "Printed for the use of the Committee on Post Office and Civil Service."
    Tables.
    1. United States—Officials and employees. I. United States. Congress. House. Committee on Post Office and Civil Service. II. Title.

JK661.C59 1976	353.001'03	76-603437
		MARC

MC#: 1977-2551
SuDocs no.: Y4.P84/10:P75/976

1241

United States government policy and suporting positions / Committee on Post Office and Civil Service, House of Representatives,

96th Congress, 2d session. — Washington : U.S. G.P.O. : For sale by the Supt. of Docs. U.S. G.P.O., 1980.

  vii, 161 p. ; 31 cm.
  Spine title: U.S. government policy and supporting positions.
  At head of title: Committee print.
  Includes index.
  Tables.
  "November 18, 1980.
  S/N 052-070-05436-1
  Item 1022
Supt. of Docs. no.: Y4.P84/10:P75/980
  1. United States — Officials and employees. 2. Government executives — United States — Registers. I. United States. Congress. House. Committee on Post Office and Civil Service. II. Title: U.S. government policy and supporting positions.
JK661.U54   353.001′03-dc19   80-604162
                                                AACR2 MARC
MC#: 1981-3098
SuDocs no.: Y4.P84/10:P75/980

POLLACK REPORT [Pollak, Walter Heilprin]
        see
  MOONEY-BILLINGS REPORT [Mooney, Thomas J. and Billings, Warren K.]
  WICKERSHAM COMMISSION [Wickersham, George Woodward]
        Report on lawlessness, no. 11.

POUND REPORT [Pound, Glenn S.]
1242

National Research Council. Committee on Research Advisory to the U.S. Department of Agriculture.
  Report. Washington, National Academy of Sciences, 1972.
  v, 91 p.
  Includes Appendix A.
  Photocopy of typescript. Springfield, Va., National Technical Information Service, 1972. (PB-213-338)
- - - - - Appendices B-R. Washington, National Academy of Sciences, 1972. 92-464 p.
  Photocopy of typescript, Springfield, Va., National Technical Information Service. 1972. (PB-213-339)
  Not located in Monthly Catalog

PRETTYMAN REPORTS [Prettyman, Elijah Barrett]
1243

U.S. *Administrative Conference.*
  Selected reports. Submitted by the chairman of the Subcommittee on Administrative Practice and Procedure of the Committee on the Judiciary of the United States Senate. Washington, U.S. Govt. Print. Off., 1963.
  xi, 417 p. maps. 24 cm. (88th Cong., 1st sess. Senate. Document no. 24)
  Bibliographical footnotes.
  1. Administrative procedure — U.S. 2. Independent regulatory commissions — U.S. I. U.S. Congress. Senate. Committee on the Judiciary. (Series: U.S. 88th Cong., 1st sess., 1963. Senate. Document no. 24)
                                                      63-62295
MC#: 1963-15342
SuDocs no.: 88th Cong., 1st sess. S. Doc. 24

1244

U.S. *President's Advisory Commission on Narcotic and Drug Abuse.*
  Final report. Washington, U.S. Govt. Print. Off., 1963.
  iv, 123 p. diagrs. 24 cm.

Bibliography: p. 95.
  1. Narcotic habit — U.S. 2. Drug trade — U.S. I. Title.
HV5825.A6   64-60320
MC#: 1964-5636
SuDocs no.: Pr35.8:N16/R29/963-2

PRICE REPORT [Price, Charles Melvin]
1245

U.S. *Library of Congress. Legislative Reference Service.*
  United States defense policies. 1945-56- Washington, U.S. Govt. Print. Off.
  v. 24 cm. annual.
  Issued in the congressional series as House documents.
  Compiler: 1945-56- C.H. Donnelly.
  1. U.S. — Military policy. 2. U.S. — Defenses. I. Donnelly, Charles H., comp.
UA23.A274   355.0973   58-61885
MC#: 1957-6757
SuDocs no.: 85th Cong., 1st sess. H. Doc. 100
MC#: 1958-14302
SuDocs no.: 85th Cong., 2d sess. H. Doc. 436
MC#: 1959-15775
SuDocs no.: 86th Cong., 1st sess. H. Doc. 227
MC#: 1960-16855
SuDocs no.: 86th Cong., 2d sess. H. Doc. 432
MC#: 1961-14162
SuDocs no.: 87th Cong., 1st sess. H. Doc. 207
MC#: 1962-20962
SuDocs no.: 87th Cong., 2d sess. H. Doc. 502

PRICE REPORT
1246

Price, Daniel O
  Changing characteristics of the Negro population, by Daniel O. Price. Prepared in cooperation with the Social Science Research Council. [Washington] U.S. Bureau of the Census; [for sale by the Supt. of Docs., U.S. Govt. Print. Off., 1969]
  viii, 259 p. illus. 24 cm. (A 1960 census monograph)
  Includes bibliographical references.
  1. Negroes — Social conditions — 1964- 2. Negroes — Employment. I. Social Science Research Council. II. Title. III. Series.
E185.86.P7   301.451′96′073   75-606158
                                                      MARC
MC#: 1970-6437
SuDocs no.: C3.30:N31

PRICE REPORT [Price, Don Krasher]
1247

United States. *President's Task Force on Government Reorganization.*
  Report of the President's Task Force on Government Reorganization. 1964.
  ii, 116 leaves, 28 cm.
  1. United States — Executive Departments. I. Price, Don K.
[JK691.U55]
George Mason University Library
Not located in Monthly Catalog

PROJECT BLUEBOOK
        see
  CONDON REPORT [Condon, Edward Uhler]
  FULLER REPORT [Fuller, John Grant]

PROJECT HEAD START
see
KIRSCHNER REPORT

PROJECT INDEPENDENCE REPORTS
1248

Project Independence blueprint : final task force report[s] / Federal Energy Administration. — Washington : The Administration : for sale by the Supt. of Docs., U.S. Govt. Print. Off., 1974-

16 v. in 19 : ill. ; 28 cm.

Includes bibliographical references.

Contents: [1] Interagency Task Force on Coal. Coal. — [2] Interagency Task Force on Energy Conservation. Energy conservation. 3. v. — [3] Interagency Task Force on Facilities. Facilities. — [4] Federal Energy Administration and Federal Reserve Board. Finance. — [5] Interagency Task Force on Geothermal Energy. Geothermal energy. — [6] An Historical perspective. — [7] U.S. Dept. of Labor. Labor. — [8] Interagency Task Force on Materials, Equipment and Construction. Materials, equipment, and construction. — [9] Interagency Task Force on Natural Gas. Natural gas. — [10] Interagency Task Force on Nuclear Energy. Nuclear energy. — [11] Interagency Task Force on Oil. Oil. — [12] Interagency Task Force on Oil Shale. Oil shale. — [13] Interagency Task Force on Solar Energy. Solar energy — [14] Interagency Task Force Transportation Crosscut Group. Transportation. 2v. — [15] Water Resources Council. Water resources. — [16] Interagency Task Force on Synthetic Fuels from Coal. Synthetic fuels from coal.

1. Energy policy — United States. 2. Power resources — United States. I. United States. Federal Energy Administration.
HD9502.U52P76   333.7   75-603592
                                                             MARC

Vol. 1. Coal.
MC#: 1975-13983
SuDocs no.: FE1.18:C63

Vol. 2. Energy conservation.
MC#: 1975-10477
SuDocs no.: FE1.18:En2/v.1
MC#: 1975-10476
SuDocs no.: FE1.18:En2/v.2
MC#: 1975-10475
SuDocs no.: FE1.18:En2/v.3

Vol. 3. Facilities.
MC#: 1976-00980
SuDocs no.: FE1.18:F11

Vol. 4. Finance.
MC#: 1976-05782
SuDocs no.: FE1.18:F49

Vol. 5. Geothermal energy.
MC#: 1975-13984
SuDocs no.: FE1.18:G29

Vol. 6. Historical perspective.
MC#: 1976-00981
SuDocs no.: FE1.18:H62

Vol. 7. Labor.
MC#: 1975-12064
SuDocs no.: FE1.18:L11

Vol. 8. Materials, equipment, and construction.
MC#: 1975-13982
SuDocs no.: FE1.18:M41

Vol. 9. Natural gas.
MC#: 1975-13986
SuDocs no.: FE1.18:G21

Vol. 10. Nuclear energy.
MC#: 1975-13987
SuDocs no.: FE1.18:N88

Vol. 11. Oil.
MC#: 1975-13988
SuDocs no.: FE1.18:Oi5

Vol. 12. Oil shale.
MC#: 1975-13989
SuDocs no.: FE1.18:Oi5/2

Vol. 13. Solar energy.
MC#: 1975-10478
SuDocs no.: FE1.18:So4

Vol. 14. Transportation.
MC#: 1975-12063
SuDocs no.: FE1.18:T68/v.1
MC#: 1975-13985
SuDocs no.: FE1.18:T68/v.2

Vol. 15. Water resources.
MC#: 1975-17697
SuDocs no.: FE1.18:W29/2

Vol. 16. Synthetic fuels from coal.
MC#: 1975-12066
SuDocs no.: FE1.18:Sy7

1249

United States. Federal Energy Administration.
Project Independence report. — [Washington] : Federal Energy Administration : for sale by the Supt. of Docs., U.S. Govt. Print. Off., 1974.

xxii, 443, 337 p. : ill. ; 26 cm.
1. Energy policy — United States. 2. Power resources — United States. I. Title.
HD9502.U52U52 1974a   333.7   75-600589
                                                             MARC

MC#: 1975-04035
SuDocs no.: FE1.18:In2

1250

United States. Federal Energy Administration.
Project independence : a summary / Federal Energy Administration. — Washington : The Administration : for sale by the Supt. of Docs., U.S. Govt. Print. Off., 1974.

50 p. : graphs. ; 26 cm.
Includes bibliographical references.
1. Energy policy — United States. 2. Energy consumption — United States — Statistics. 3. Petroleum industry and trade — United States. I. Title.
HD9502.U52U52 1974c   333.7   75-603205
                                                             MARC

MC#: 1975-13992
SuDocs no.: FE1.18:Su6

PROUTY REPORT
1251

Prouty, Winston L 1906-
Washington inner city poverty survey. [By Winston L. Prouty] Prepared for the Subcommittee on Employment, Manpower, and

Poverty of the Committee on Labor and Public Welfare, United States Senate. Washington, U.S. Govt. Print. Off., 1968.

xvi, 274 p. 23 cm.

At head of title: 90th Congress, 2d session. Committee print.

1. Washington, D.C. — Social conditions. 2. Washington, D.C. — Economic conditions. I. U.S. Congress. Senate. Committee on Labor and Public Welfare. Subcommittee on Employment, Manpower, and Poverty. II. Title.

HN80.W3P7   309.1'753   79-600427
                                                  MARC

MC#: 1969-1743
SuDocs no.: Y4.L11/2:W27

PROXMIRE REPORTS [Proxmire, William]

1252

An Economic profile of mainland China; studies prepared for the Joint Economic Committee, Congress of the United States. Washington, U.S. Govt. Print. Off., 1967.

2 v. (xviii, 684 p.) illus., maps. 24 cm.

At head of title: 90th Congress, 1st session. Joint committee print.

Includes bibliographies.

1. China (People's Republic of China, 1949-) — Econ. condit. I. U.S. Congress. Joint Economic Committee.

HC427.9.E32   338.951   67-60884
MC#: 1967-5974
SuDocs no.: Y4.Ec7:C44/v. 1
MC#: 1967-7588
SuDocs no.: Y4.Ec7:C44/v. 2

1253

U.S. *Congress. Joint Economic Committee.*

Old age income assurance: an outline of issues and alternatives; material prepared by the committee staff for the Subcommittee on Fiscal Policy. Washington, U.S. Govt. Print. Off., 1966.

v, 39 p. 24 cm.

At head of title: 89th Congress, 2d sess. Joint committee print.

1. Old age pensions — U.S. 2. Retirement income — U.S. I. U.S. Congress. Joint Economic Committee. Subcommittee on Fiscal Policy. II. Title.

HD7106.U5A5324   331.2'52'0973   66-65700
MC#: 1966-17153
SuDocs no.: Y4.Ec7:O1 1

PUEBLO REPORT [U.S.S. *Pueblo*]

1254

United States. Congress. House. Special Subcommittee on the U.S.S. Pueblo.

Inquiry into the U.S.S. Pueblo and EC-121 plane incidents; report. Washington, U.S. Govt. Print. Off., 1969.

v, 1619-1696 p. 24 cm.

"H.A.S.C. no. 91-12."

1. Pueblo (Ship) 2. Aeronautics, Military — Observations. I. Title.

KF32.A775 1969   358.4'5   79-602866
                                                  MARC

MC#: 1969-12207
SuDocs no.: Y4.Ar5/2a:969-70/12

PUJO REPORT [Pujo, Arsène Paulin]

1255

U.S. *Congress. House. Committee on banking and currency.*

. . . Report of the committee appointed pursuant to House resolutions 429 and 504 to investigate the concentration of control of money and credit . . . Washington, Govt. print. off., 1913.

258 p. incl. tables. fold. diagrs. 23 cm. (62d Cong., 3d sess. House. Rept. 1593)

House calendar no. 424.

Submitted by Mr. Pujo, chairman of the subcommittee of the Committee on banking and currency. Ordered printed, with illustrations, February 28, 1913.

"Views of the minority," signed Everis A. Hayes, Frank E. Guernsey, William H. Heald": p. 247-248.

"Views of Mr. McMorran": p. 249-258.

Published also in v. 3 of "Money trust investigation . . . (In three volumes) . . . 1913." The "Report," wanting the minority reports, was pub. also without document series note (245 p.) and the "Minority report of Henry McMorran" was pub. also in the same manner (8 p.)

1. Banks and banking — U.S. 2. Credit — U.S. 3. Clearinghouse — U.S. 4. New York stock exchange. I. Pujo, Arsène Paulin, 1861- II. Hayes, Everis Anson, 1855 III. McMorran, Henry. IV. Title.

HG181.A4 1913b   13-35140 Revised
- - - - - Copy 2.
MC#: Mar. 1913-page 493
SuDocs no.: 62d Cong., 3d sess. H. Rept. 1593

PURVIS REPORT [Purvis, Melvin]

1256

U.S. *Congress. Senate. Committee on Post Office and Civil Service.*

Utilization of manpower in the Federal Government. An interim report on the progress of the investigation into the personnel needs and practices of the various governmental agencies being conducted by the Subcommittee on Federal Manpower Policies pursuant to Senate resolution 53, as amended by Senate resolution 206, with the purpose of formulating policies for the most effective utilization of civilian personnel during the period of the national emergency. Washington, U.S. Govt. Print. Off., 1952.

iii, 17 p. 24 cm. ([U.S.] 82d Cong., 2d sess. Senate. Report no. 1342)

1. Civil service — U.S. I. Title. (Series: U.S. 82d Cong., 2d sess. 1952. Senate. Report no. 1342)

JK765.A5 1952b   351.1   52-60673
MC#: 1952-5494
SuDocs no.: 82d Cong., 2d sess. S. Rept. 1342

QUATTLEBAUM REPORTS [Quattlebaum, Charles Albert]

1257

U.S. *Library of Congress. Legislative Reference Service.*

Federal educational activities and educational issues before Congress; a report prepared by Charles A. Quattlebaum, educational research analyst. Printed for the use of the Committee on Education and Labor. Washington, U.S. Govt. Print. Off., 1951-52.

4 pts. in 3 v. 24 cm.

At head of title: 82d Cong., 1st[-2d] sess. Committee print.

Issued also as House Document no. 423, 82d Cong., 2d sess.

1. Education and state — U.S. I. Quattlebaum, Charles Albert, 1902- II. U.S. Congress. House. Committee on Education and Labor.

LC71.U53   379.73   51-60383 rev
MC#: 1951-6647
SuDocs no.: Y4.Ed8/1:Ed8/5/v. 1
MC#: 1951-19585
SuDocs no.: Y4.Ed8/1:Ed8/5/v. 2
MC#: 1952-7205
SuDocs no.: Y4.Ed8/1:Ed8/5/v. 3

1258

U.S. *Library of Congress. Legislative Reference Service.*
Federal educational activities and educational issues before Congress; a report prepared by Charles A. Quattlebaum, educational research analyst. Printed for the use of the Committee on Education and Labor. Washington, U.S. Govt. Print. Off., 1952.

xxviii, 567 p. 23 cm. (82d Cong., 2d sess. House document no. 423)
Issued also as Committee print, 82d Cong., 1st-2d sess.
1. Education and state—U.S. I. Quattlebaum, Charles Albert, 1902- II. U.S. Congress. House. Committee on Education and Labor. (Series: U.S. 82d Cong., 2d sess., 1952. House. Document no. 423)
LC71.U532   379.73   52-60992
MC#: 1952-8716
SuDocs no.: 82d Cong., 2d sess. H. Doc. 423

1259

U.S. *Library of Congress. Legislative Reference Service.*
Federal educational policies, programs and proposals; a survey and handbook. Prepared by Charles A. Quattlebaum, specialist in education. Printed for the use of the Committee on Education and Labor. Washington, U.S. Govt. Print. Off., 1960.

3 pts. 24 cm.
At head of title: 86th Cong., 2d sess. Committee print.
1. Education and state—U.S. I. Quattlebaum, Charles Albert, 1902- II. U.S. Congress. House. Committee on Education and Labor.
LC71.U533   379.0973   60-62001
MC#: 1960-15251
SuDocs no.: Y4.Ed8/1:Ed8/9/pt. 1
MC#: 1960-16887
SuDocs no.: Y4.Ed8/1:Ed8/9/pt. 2,3

1260

U.S. *Library of Congress. Legislative Reference Service.*
Federal educational policies, programs and proposals; a survey and handbook. Prepared by Charles A. Quattlebaum. Washington, U.S. Govt. Print. Off., 1968.

3 v. 24 cm. (90th Congress, 2d session. House document no. 398)
"Printed for the use of the Committee on Education and Labor."
Includes bibliographical references.
Contents.—pt. 1. Background; issues; relevant considerations.—pt. 2. Survey of Federal educational activities.—pt. 3. Analysis and classification of the programs.
1. Education and state—U.S. I. Quattlebaum, Charles Albert, 1902- II. U.S. Congress. House. Committee on Education and Labor. III. Title. (Series: U.S. 90th Congress, 2d session, 1968. House. Document no. 398)
LC71.U5332   379′.0973   76-600437
                                                            MARC
MC#: 1969-1692
SuDocs no.: 90th Cong., 2d sess. H. Doc. 398

QUESADA REPORT [Quesada, Elwood R.]
1261

Greiner-Mattern, Associates.
Additional airport for Washington, D.C.; site selection study. Prepared for the White House. [Baltimore?] 1957.

xv, 74 p. maps (part fold., part col.) diagrs., tables. 29 cm.
Includes bibliographies.
1. Airports—Washington, D.C. I. U.S. Executive Office of the President. II. Title.
TL726.4.W3G7   629.1362   58-44343
Not listed in Monthly Catalog

RECAT REPORT
1262

United States. Ad Hoc Committee on the Cumulative Regulatory Effects on the Cost of Automotive Transportation.
Cumulative regulatory effects on the cost of automotive transportation (RECAT); final report of the ad hoc committee. Prepared for Office of Science and Technology. [Washington] 1972.

1 v. (various pagings) illus. 27 cm.
Cover title.
Includes bibliographical references.
Supt. of Docs. no.: PrEx8.2:Au8
1. Transportation, Automotive—United States—Cost of Operation. I. United States. Office of Science and Technology. II. Title.
HE5623.A4 1972b   338.1′1   72-601509
                                                            MARC
MC#: 1972-8897
SuDocs no.: PrEx8.2:Au8

RABAUT REPORT [Rabaut, Louis Charles]
1263

U.S. *Congress. House. Committee on appropriations.*
Official trip of examination of federal activities in South and Central America. Report of a subcommittee of the Committee on appropriations, House of representatives, Seventy-seventh Congress, first session, relative to a trip taken by the subcommittee to South and Central America. December 4, 1941 . . . Washington, U.S. Govt. print. off., 1941.

ii, 42 p. 23 cm.
Running title: Report on trip to South and Central America.
Louis C. Rabaut, chairman of committee.
1. U.S.—Diplomatic and consular service. 2. U.S.—For. rel.—Spanish America. 3. Spanish America—For. rel.—U.S. I. Rabaut, Louis Charles, 1886-
JX1706.A34 1941c   341.80973   41-46357
MC#: 1942-page 486
SuDocs no.: Y4.Ap6/1:So8a

RACKOW REPORT [Rackow, Leon L.]
        see
CASEY REPORT [Casey, Jesse F.]

RAGAN REPORT
1264

Ragan, Robert C
Financial recordkeeping for small stores, by Robert C. Ragan. Washington, Small Business Administration; [for sale by the Superintendent of Documents, U.S. Govt. Print. Off.] 1966.

viii, 131 p. illus. 24 cm. (Small business managament series, no. 32)
Bibliography: p. 131.
1. Accounting. I. Title. (Series: U.S. Small Business Administration. Small business management series, no. 32)
HD30.U5 no. 32   657.2   66-60748
MC#: 1966-6602
SuDocs no.: SBA1/12:32

RAMSAY REPORT [Ramsay, Gordon A.]
1265

U.S. *Interdepartmental board of contracts and adjustments.*
Preliminary report of the chairman of the Interdepartmental board of contracts and adjustments to the director of the Bureau of the budget. June 27, 1922. Washington, Govt. print. off., 1922.

vi, 9 p. 23½ cm.

Gordon A. Ramsay, chairman.
1. Contracts, Letting of. 2. U.S.—Executive departments—Equipment and supplies. I. Ramsay, Gordon A. II. Title.
JK643.C21 b,   22-26674
- - - - - Copy 2.
MC#: July 1922-page 48
SuDocs no.: T51.9/1:922

RAMSEY REPORT [Ramsey, W. K., Jr.]
see under
DILLINGHAM COMMISSION [Dillingham, William Paul]
Immigrant banks.

RAMSPECK REPORTS [Ramspeck, Robert]
1266

U.S. *Congress. House. Committee on the civil service.*
. . . Investigation of civilian employment . . . Report. "Pursuant to H. Res. 16, 78th Cong., 1st sess." . . . [Washington, U.S. Govt. print. off., 1943]
13 p. 23 cm. ([U.S.] 78th Cong., 1st sess. House. Rept. 766)
Caption title.
Subtitle: Interim report on investigation of civilian employment.
Submitted by Mr. Ramspeck from the Committee on the civil service.
1. Civil service—U.S. I. Ramspeck, Robert, 1890- II. Title.
JK649 1943k   351.1   43-50849
MC#: 1943-page 1286
SuDocs no.: 78th Cong., 1st sess. H. Rept. 766

1267

U.S. *Congress. House. Committee on the civil service.*
. . . Investigation of civilian employment. Committee on the civil service, House of representatives, Seventy-eighth Congress, second session. Concerning inquiries made of certain proposals for the expansion and change in civil service status of the WASPS, pursuant to H. Res. 16, a resolution to authorize the Committee on the civil service to investigate various activities in the departments and agencies of the government . . . Washington, U.S. Govt. print. off., 1944.
ii, 14 p. 23½ cm. ([U.S.] 78th Cong., 2d sess. House. Rept. 1600)
Running title: Change in civil service status of the WASPS.
"Interim report" (p. 1-13)submitted by Mr. Ramspeck, "Minority report" (p. 14) signed: Clarence E. Kilburn . . . [and others]
1. U.S. Women's air service pilots. I. Ramspeck, Robert, 1890- II. Kilburn, Clarence Evans, 1893- III. Title: Change in civil service status of the WASPS.
UG633.A4 1944f   358.4   44-41027
MC#: 1944-page 764
SuDocs no.: 78th Cong., 2d sess. H. Rept. 1600

1268

U.S. *Congress. House. Committee on the civil service.*
. . . Investigation of civilian employment. Report of the Committee on the civil service, House of representatives, Seventy-eighth Congress, first and second sessions, pursuant to H. Res. 66, a resolution to authorize the Committee on the civil service to investigate various activities in the departments and agencies of the government . . . Washington, U.S. Govt. print. off., 1944.
v, 17 p. 23½ cm. ([U.S.] 78th Cong., 2d sess. House. Rept. 2084)
Submitted by Mr. Ramspeck from the Committee on the civil service.
1. Civil service—U.S. I. Ramspeck, Robert, 1890-
JK649 1944m   351.1   45-35303

MC#: 1945-page 32
SuDocs no.: 78th Cong., 2d sess. H. Rept. 2084

1269

U.S. *Congress. House. Committee on the civil service.*
. . . Investigation of civilian employment. Report of the Committee on the civil service, House of representatives, Seventy-ninth Congress, first session, pursuant to H. Res. 66, a resolution to authorize the Committee on the civil service to investigate various activities in the departments and agencies of the government . . . Washington, U.S. Govt. print. off., 1945.
ix, 110 p. incl. tables. 23½ cm. ([U.S.] 79th Cong., 1st sess. House. Rept. 514)
Submitted by Mr. Ramspeck.
1. U.S.—Officials and employees—Salaries, allowances, etc. I. Ramspeck, Robert, 1890-
JK775 1945d   351.1   45-36535
MC#: 1945-page 576
SuDocs no.: 79th Cong., 1st sess. H. Rept. 514

RANDALL REPORTS [Randall, Clarence Belden]
1270

U.S. *Executive Office of the President.*
International travel; report to the President of the United States [by] Clarence B. Randall, special assistant to the President. Washington [U.S. Govt. Print. Off.] 1958.
v, 52 p. 24 cm.
1. Travel. I. Randall, Clarence Belden, 1891- II. Title.
G155.A1U58   910.2   58-61017
MC#: 1958-7613
SuDocs no.: Pr34.8:T69
MC#: 1958-6741
SuDocs no.: 85th Cong., 2d sess. H. Doc. 381

1271

U.S. *Advisory Panel on Federal Salary Systems.*
Report [to the] Committee on Post Office and Civil Service, House of Representatives. Washington, U.S. Govt. Print. Off., 1963.
ii, 24 p. 24 cm.
At head of title: Committee print.
1. U.S.—Officials and employees—Salaries, allowances, etc. I. U.S. Congress. House. Committee on Post Office and Civil Service.
JK775 1963.A38   64-60439
MC#: 1964-2119
SuDocs no.: Y4.P84/10:Sa3/9

1272

U.S. *Commission on Foreign Economic Policy.*
Report to the President and the Congress. Washington, 1954.
v, 94 p. 23 cm.
Clarence B. Randall, chairman.
1. U.S.—Foreign economic relations. I. Randall, Clarence Belden, 1891-
HC106.5.A5753   338.973   54-61116
MC#: 1954-1921
SuDocs no.: Y3.F76/2:R29
MC#: 1954-1618
SuDocs no.: 83d Cong., 2d sess. H. Doc. 290

See also REED REPORT [Reed, Daniel Alden]

RASMUSSEN REPORT [Rasmussen, Norman C.]
1273

United States. Atomic Energy Commission. Technical Information Center.

Reactor safety study. An assessment of accident risks in U.S. Commercial Nuclear Power Plants. Washington, D.C., U.S. Atomic Energy Commission. 1974.

244 p. (WASH-1400) (Draft)
- - - - - Appendix I: Accident definition and use of event trees. 229 p. Appendix II, v. 1: Fault tree methodology. 173 p. v. 2: PWR fault trees. 635 p. v. 3. BWR fault trees. 506 p. Appendix III: Failure data. 219 p. Appendix IV: Common mode failures. 99 p. Appendix V: Quantitative results of accident sequences. 170 p. Appendix VI: Calculation of reactor accident consequences. 110 p. Appendix VII: Release of radioactivity in reactor accidents. 367 p. Appendix VIII: Physical processes in reactor meltdown accidents. 210 p. Appendix IX: Safety design rationale for nuclear power plants. 86 p. Appendix X: Design adequacy. 262 p.
Not located in Monthly Catalog.

RAY REPORT [Ray, Daniel A.]
1274

U.S. *Hawaiian Commission.*
Report of Daniel A. Ray on conditions of affairs in Hawaii. [Washington, U.S. Govt. Print. Off.] 1899.

56 p.
Checklist of United States Public Documents, 1789-1909-page 1514
SuDocs no.: Y3.H31:Af2

RAYMOND REPORT [Raymond and May Associates]
see
DOUGLAS REPORTS [Douglas, Paul H.]
National Commission on Urban Problems.

Research report, no. 11

REACTOR SAFETY STUDY
see
RASMUSSEN REPORT [Rasmussen, Norman C.]

REDFORD REPORT
1275

Redford, Emmett Shelburn, 1904-
The President and the regulatory commissions. [A report prepared for the President's Advisoty Committee on Government Organization. n.p., 1960]

33 1. 27 cm.
1. Independent regulatory commissions—U.S. 2. Executive power—U.S. I. Title.
JK901.R42   62-60821
Not located in Monthly Catalog

REED COMMITTEE REPORT [Reed, Gordon W.]
1276

United States. *Dept. of the Air Force. Committee to Study MATS.*
Reed Committee report on MATS. New York: Gordon W. Reed, 1960.

43 p.: charts.
Cover title.
1. United States. Dept. of the Air Force. Military Air Transport Service. 2. United States—Armed Forces—Transportation. 3. Transportation, Military. I. Reed, Gordon W. II. Title.
[U333.A22]

Dept. of the Army Library
Not listed in Monthly Catalog

REED REPORT [Reed, Daniel Alden]
1277

U.S. *Commission on Foreign Economic Policy.*
Minority report, by Daniel A. Reed and Richard M. Simpson. Washington, 1954.

v, 20 p. 23 cm.
Clarence B. Randall, chairman.
1. U.S.—Foreign economic relations. I. Reed, Daniel Alden, 1875- II. Simpson, Richard M. III. Randall, Clarence Belden, 1891-
HC106.5.A5752   338.973   54-61167
MC#: 1954-4201
SuDocs no.: Y3.F76/2:R29/2
MC#: 1954-3585
SuDocs no.: 83d Cong., 2d sess. H. Doc. 290, pt. 2

REED REPORT [Reed, Richie H.]
see
ROCKEFELLER REPORT [Rockefeller, John D., 3d]
Economic aspects of population change.

REED REPORT [Reed, Stanley]
1278

U.S. *President's committee on civil service improvement.*
. . . Report of President's Committee on civil service improvement. Mr. Justice Stanley Reed, chairman . . . Washington, U.S. Govt. print. off., 1941.

xvi, 128 p. incl. illus. (map) tables. 23 cm. ([U.S.] 77th Cong., 1st sess. House. Doc. 118)
Issued also, in mimeographed form, without congressional series numbering.
JK649 1941a
- - - - - . . . Documents and reports to accompany Report on civil service improvement . . . Washington, U.S. Govt. print. off., 1942.

3 v. in 4. illus. (maps) tables, diagrs., forms. 29 cm.
Appendices 1 and 2 of v. 1 issued as Technical paper no. 6 of the Bureau of the budget.
"List of special studies prepared for the committee and other material used": v. 3, pt. 2, p. 200-205.
1. Civil service—U.S.
JK649 1941 a Docs.   351.1   41-50186
MC#: 1941-page 400
SuDocs no.: 77th Cong., 1st sess. H. Doc. 118
MC#: 1943-page 357 (LC card 43-51811 cancelled in favor of 41-50186)
SuDocs no.: Y3.P92/4:C49/v. 1,2
MC#: 1943-page 491 (LC card 43-51811 cancelled in favor of 41-50186)
SuDocs no.: Y3.P92/4:C49/v. 3, pt. 1,2

1279

U.S. *President's committee on civil service improvement.*
Report of President's committee on civil service improvement. Mr. Justice Stanley Reed, chairman . . . [Washington] 1941.

cover-title, xviii, 251, 251a-251b, 252-278 numb. 1. incl. map, tables. 27 1/2 cm.
Reproduced from type-written copy.
Issued also as House doc. 118, 77th Cong., 1st sess.
1. Civil service—U.S. 2. U.S.—Officials and employees.
JK649 1941   42-21223
Not located in Monthly Catalog

REESIDE REPORT [Reeside, Arthur]
see under
O'MAHONEY REPORTS [O'Mahoney, Joseph Christopher]
Blair. Price discrimination in steel.

REEVES REPORT [Reeves, Floyd Wesley]

1280

U.S. *Advisory committee on education.*
. . . Report of the advisory committee on education. Message from the President of the United States, transmitting the Report of the Advisory committee on education appointed in September 1936 to study the experience under the existing program of federal aid for vocational education . . . Washington, U.S. Govt. print. off., 1938.
xii, 148 p. incl. illus. (maps) tables, diagrs. 23½ cm. (75th Cong., 3d sess. House. Doc. 529)
Referred to the Committee on education and ordered printed, with illustrations, February 23, 1938.
Issued also without document series note with title: Report of the committee.
Floyd W. Reeves, chairman.
"Minority report submitted by Mr. T. J. Thomas": p. 142-143.
1. Education—U.S. 2. Vocational education—U.S. I. Reeves, Floyd Wesley, 1890II. Thomas, T. J. III. Title.
L111.C5 1938   379.120973   38-26172
- - - - - Copy 2.
MC#: 1938-page 263
SuDocs no.: 75th Cong., 3d sess. H. Doc. 529

1281

U.S. *Advisory committee on education.*
. . . Report of the committee. February 1938. Washington, U.S. Govt. print. off., 1938.
xi, 243 p. incl. illus. (maps) tables, diagrs. 23½ cm.
At head of title: The Advisory committee on education.
Issued also as House doc. 529, 75th Cong., 3d sess., with title: Report of the Advisory committee on education. Messge from the President of the United States transmitting the report of the Advisory committee on education appointed in September 1936 to study the experience under the existing program of federal aid for vocational education.
Floyd W. Reeves, chairman.
"Minority report submitted by Mr. T. J. Thomas": p. 222-224.
1. Education—U.S. 2. Vocational education—U.S. I. Reeves, Floyd Wesley, 1890II. Thomas, T. J. III. Title.
L111.C5 1938a   379.120973   38-26217
MC#: Mar. 1938-page 263
SuDocs no.: Y3.Ad9/2:2R29

REEVES REPORT [Reeves, Floyd Wesley]
Report of the committee on administrative management.
see under
BROWNLOW REPORTS [Brownlow, Louis]

REEVES REPORT [Reeves, Floyd Wesley]
Studies on administrative management in the government.
see under
BROWNLOW REPORTS [Brownlow, Louis]

REID REPORT [Reid, Charles Frederick]
see
BLAUCH REPORT [Blauch, Lloyd E.]

REID REPORT

1282

Reid, George Willard, 1917-
Water requirements for pollution abatement. Washington, U.S. Govt. Print. Off., 1960.
viii, 28 p. diagrs., tables. 27 cm. (Water resources activities in the United States)
At head of title: 86th Cong., 2d sess. Committee print no. 29.
1. Water—Pollution. 2. Water—Pollution—U.S. 3. Water—supply—U.S. I. U.S. Congress. Senate. Select Committee on National Water Resources. II. Title. (Series)
TD223.R4   628.168   60-64699
MC#: 1961-424
SuDocs no.: Y4.N21/8:86/29

REID REPORT [Reid, Ira De Augustine]
see
WICKERSHAM COMMISSION [Wickersham, George Woodward]
Report on the causes of crime, no. 13.

REILLY REPORT [Reilly, James Francis]

1283

U.S. *Post Office Department Advisory Board.*
Research, development, and mechanization in the United States Post Office Department; an interim report to the Postmaster General. [Washington, For sale by the Superintendent of Documents, U.S. Govt. Print. Off.] 1963.
ix, 65 p. illus., group port. 24 cm.
1. U.S. Post Office Dept. I. Title.
HE6326 1963.A5   63-60568
MC#: 1963-5673
SuDocs no.: P1.2:R31/8

RENO REPORT

1284

Reno, Marcus Albert, 1835-1889, defendant.
Abstract of the official record of proceedings of the Reno Court of Inquiry, convened at Chicago, Illinois, 13 January 1879, by the President of the United States, upon the request of Major Marcus A. Reno, 7th Cavalry, to investigate his conduct at the Battle of the Little Big Horn, 25-26 June, 1876. With a pref. by W. A. Graham. Harrisburg, Pa., Stackpole Co. [1954]
xxx, 303 p. illus., port., maps (part fold.) 24 cm.
1. Little Big Horn, Battle of the, 1876- I. U.S. Army. Courts of Inquiry. Reno. 1879. II. Graham, William Alexander, 1875-
E83.876.R42   973.82   54-8682
Not listed in Monthly Catalog

REUSS REPORTS [Reuss, Henry S.]

1285

U.S. Library of Congress. Science Policy Research Division.
A case study of the utilization of Federal laboratory resources. Washington, U.S. Govt. Print. Off., 1966.
ix, 141 p. illus. 24 cm.
At head of title: Committee print. 89th Congress, 2d session. House of Representatives.
Commonly known as the Reuss report.
"A study submitted to the Research and Technical Programs Subcommittee of the Committee on Government Operations."
1. Research—U.S. 2. Science and state—U.S. 3. Laboratories—U.S. I. U.S. Congress. House. Committee on Government Operations. Research and Technical Programs

Subcommittee. II. Title. III. Title: Reuss report on the utilization of Federal laboratory resources.

Q180.U5A547 1966   507.2'073   67-60182
MC#: 1967-4537
SuDocs no.: Y4.G74/7:L11

1286

United States. Congress. House. Conservation and Natural Resources Subcommittee.

Effects of population growth on natural resources and the environment. Hearings before a subcommittee of the Committee on Government Operations, House of Representatives, Ninety-first Congress, first session. September 15 and 16, 1969. Washington, U.S. Govt. Print. Off., 1969.

iv, 256 p. 24 cm.
Includes bibliographies.
1. Pollution — United States. 2. United States — Population. I. Title.

KF27.G636 1969b   301.3   73-604517
                                         MARC
MC#: 1970-417
SuDocs no.: Y4.G74/7:P81

RHODES REPORT [Rhodes, Charles Dudley]
see
UPTON REPORTS [Upton, Emory]

RICE REPORT [Rice, Stuart A.]
1287

Surveys and Research Corporation, *Washington, D.C.*

A metropolitan statistical program for the National Capital region. Staff study for the Joint Committee on Washington Metropolitan Problems, Congress of the United States. [Principal authors: Stuart A. Rice, Jeremy C. Ulin, and Libert Ehrman] Washington, U.S. Govt. Print. Off., 1958.

v, 36 p. 24 cm.
At head of title: 85th Cong., 2d sess. Joint committee print.
1. Washington metropolitan area — Stat. I. U.S. Congress. Joint Committee on Washington Metropolitan Problems. II. Title.

HA37.U8W37   311.39753   59-60203
MC#: 1959-1572
SuDocs no.: Y4.W27/2:St2

RICE REPORTS [Rice, Donald B.]
1288

Defense resource management study : case studies of logistics support alternatives / Donald B. Rice, study director. — Washington : Supt. of Docs., U.S. Govt. Print. Off., 1979.

vii, 278 p. ; 26 cm.
"A companion report to the final report."
Includes bibliographical references.
1. Logistics — Case studies. 2. United States — Armed Forces — Equipment — Maintenance and repair — Case studies. 3. United States — Armed Forces — Supplies and stores — Management — Case studies. 4. United States — Weapons systems — Case studies. I. Rice, Donald B.

U168.D43   355.4'11   79-601989
                                         MARC
MC#: 1979-14771
SuDocs no.: D1.2:R31/7/case

Rice, Donald B
Defense resource management study : final report / by Donald B. Rice. — Washington : U.S. Govt. Print. Off., 1979.

xxiii, 112 p. : ill. ; 26 cm.

Prepared for the Secretary of Defense.
Includes bibliographical references.
1. United States. Dept. of Defense — Management. 2. United States — Armed Forces — Procurement. 3. Logistics. 4. United States — Armed Forces — Personnel management. 5. United States — Armed Forces — Medical care. I. United States. Dept. of Defense. II. Title.

UB23.R53   355.6'0973   79-601966
                                         MARC
MC#: 1980-20729
SuDocs no.: D1.2:R31/7

1289

United States. National Advisory Committee on Oceans and Atmosphere.

Engineering in the ocean : a report for the Secretary of Commerce : by the National Advisory Committee on Oceans and Atmosphere. — Washington : for sale by the Supt. of Docs., U.S. Govt. Print. Off., 1974.

iii, 54 p. ; 23 cm.
"Memorandum report by the Ocean Engineering Panel of the National Advisory Committee on Ocean and Atmosphere": p. 7-18.
1. Ocean engineering. I. United States. National Advisory Committee on Oceans and Atmosphere. Ocean Engineering Panel. II. United States. Dept. of Commerce. III. Title.

TC1645.U54 1974   620'.416'2   75-601513
                                         MARC
Not located in Monthly Catalog
SuDocs no.: Y3.OC2.2:En3

RICHARD REPORT [Richard, Dorothy Elizabeth]
1290

U.S. *Office of Naval Operations.*

United States naval administration of the Trust Territory of the Pacific Islands, by Dorothy E. Richard, lieutenant commander, U.S.N. With a foreword by Arthur W. Radford and an introd. by Leon S. Fiske. [Washington] 1957-[63]

3 v. illus., ports., maps, diagrs. 23 cm.
Contents. — v. 1. The wartime military government period, 1942-1945. — v. 2. The postwar military government era, 1945-1947. — v. 3. The trusteeship period, 1947-1951.
1. Pacific Islands (Ter.) — Pol. & govt. I. Richard, Dorothy Elizabeth, 1909- II. Title.

JQ6451.A5A5   354.965   57-62103 rev
MC#: 1957-18012
SuDocs no.: D207.2:P11/2/v. 1
MC#: 1958-820
SuDocs no.: D207.2:P11/2/v. 2
MC#: 1963-14623
SuDocs no.: D207.2:P11/2/v. 3

RICHBERG REPORT [Richberg, Donald Randall]
1291

U.S. *Executive council.*

Report of the executive secretary of the Executive council to the President. August 25, 1934. Washington, U.S. Govt. print. off., 1934.

v, 48, iii p. incl. tables. 23½ cm.
Donald R. Richberg, executive secretary.
1. U.S. — Econ. condit. — 1918- 2. U.S. — Executive departments. 3. U.S. — Pol. & govt. — 1933- I. Richberg, Donald Randall, 1881- II. Title.

HC106.3.A5 1934f   330.973   34-28038
- - - - - Copy 2.
MC#: Sept. 1934-page 195
SuDocs no.: Y3.Ex3/2:R29

RICKOVER REPORT [Rickover, Hyman George]

1292

U.S. *Congress. House. Committee on Appropriations.*

Report on Russia by Vice Admiral Hyman G. Rickover, USN. Hearings before the Committee on Appropriations, House of Representatives, Eighty-sixth Congress, first session. Washington, U.S. Govt. Print. Off., 1959.

ii, 82, ii p. table. 23 cm.
1. Education—Russia—1945- 2. Education—U.S.—1945- I. Rickover, Hyman George.
LA132.U65   378.47   59-62213
MC#: 1959-15938
SuDocs no.: Y4.Ap6/1:R92/2

RIDKER REPORT [Ridker, Ronald Gene]

see
ROCKEFELLER REPORT [Rockefeller, John D., 3d]

RIEHLMAN REPORT [Riehlman, R. Walter]

1293

U.S. *Congress. House. Committee on Government Operations.*

Organization and administration of the military research and development programs; twenty-fourth intermediate report. Washington, U.S. Govt. Print. Off., 1954.

v, 72 p. 23 cm. (83d Cong., 2d sess. House. Report no. 2618)
1. Military research—U.S. I. Title. (Series: U.S. 83d Cong., 2d sess., 1954. House. Report no. 2618)
U393.A52   54-60461
MC#: 1954-14512
SuDocs no.: 83d Cong., 2d sess. H. Rept. 2618

RIESSER REPORT [Riesser, Jacob]

see under
ALDRICH COMMISSION [Aldrich, Nelson Wilmarth]

RIFKIND REPORTS [Rifkind, Simon H.]

1294

U.S. *Commission to Inquire into a Controversy between Certain Air Carriers and Certain of their Employees.*
Report to the President. Washington, 1961.

vii, 31 p. 24 cm.
1. Aeronautics, Commercial—U.S.—Employees.
HD5325.A35A5 1961a   61-61582
MC#: 1961-13623
SuDocs no.: Pr35.8:Ai7/R29/961

1295

U.S. *Commission to Inquire into a Controversy between Certain Carriers and Certain of their Employees.*
Report of the Presidential Railroad Commission. Washington, U.S. Govt. Print. Off., 1962.

viii, 327 p. 24 cm.
- - - - - Appendix volume[s] Washington, 1962.
4 v. diagrs., tables. 28 cm.
Bibliographical footnotes.
Contents.—1. Index-digest to the record of the commission's hearings.—2. Pay structure study, railroad operating employees.—3. Studies relating to railroad operating

employees.—4. Studies relating to collective bargaining agreements and practices outside the railroad industry.
HD5325.R1A44 Appx.
1. Railroads—U.S.—Employes.
HD5325.R11A44   331.181385   62-61259 rev
MC#: 1962-12649
SuDocs no.: Pr34.8:R13
MC#: 1962-16110, 20242, 16115, 16114 (LC card 61-61582 referred to in error). Appendix vols. 1-4
SuDocs no.: Pr34.8:R13/app./v. (nos.)

RILES REPORT [Riles, Wilson C.]

1296

U.S. *Task Force on Urban Education.*

Final report of the Task Force on Urban Education of the Department of Health, Education, and Welfare Office of Education.

(*In* U.S. Congress. Congressional record. [Daily ed.] v. 116 (1970) no. 1, p. H9-H15; v. 116 (1970) no. 2, p. E21-E77)
SuDocs no.: X/a.91/2:1,2

RILEY REPORT [Riley, Donald C.]

1297

U.S. *Foreign Economic Administration.*

Report of the Subcommittee on Foreign Trade Statistics of the Clearing Office for Foreign Transactions and Reports, Foreign Economic Administration. [Washington] 1944.

39 p. 27 cm.
1. Commercial statistics. 2. U.S.—Comm.
HF3003.A45   382   53-52768
Not located in Monthly Catalog

RING REPORT [Ring, Martha D.]

see
MURRAY REPORT [Murray, Merrill Garver]

RIOT REPORT

see
KERNER REPORT [Kerner, Otto]

RITCHIE REPORT [Ritchie, Barbara]

see
KERNER COMMISSION [Kerner, Otto]

RIVLIN REPORT [Rivlin, Alice M.]

1298

United States. Dept. of Health, Education, and Welfare. Office of the Assistant Secretary for Planning and Evaluation.

Toward a long-range plan for Federal financial support for higher education; a report to the President. [Washington] 1969.

xii, 73 p. 24 cm.
1. Federal aid to higher education—United States. I. Title.
LB2338.A5243   379'.1214'0973   77-600586
                                      MARC
MC#: 1969-4381A
SuDocs no.: FS1.2:Ed8/4

RIZLEY REPORTS [Rizley, Ross]
see under
HOFFMAN REPORTS [Hoffman, Clare E.]

Second intermediate report.

Seventh intermediate report.

Thirteenth intermediate report.

ROBERT REPORT [Robert, William Pierre]

1299

U.S. *Committee to report on changes in labor and trade practice standards.*
[The Robert committee report with a letter of transmittal. Washington, 1936]

2, 210 numb. 1. incl. tables, forms. 27 cm.
Mimeographed.
"For the press. March 17, 1936."
Letter of transmittal signed: Daniel C. Roper.
W. P. Robert, chairman.
1. Labor and laboring classes—U.S.—1914- 2. U.S.—Indus. I. U.S. Dept. of commerce. II. Robert, William Pierre, 1873-
HD3616.U45A5 1936   38-24267
- - - - - Copy 2.
Not located in Monthly Catalog.

ROBERTS COMMISSION [Roberts, Owen Josephus]

1300

U.S. *Congress. Joint committee on the investigation of the Pearl harbor attack.*
Pearl harbor attack. Hearings before joint committee on the investigation of the Pearl harbor attack, Congress of the United States, Seventy-ninth Congress of the United States, Seventy-ninth Congress, first session, pursuant to S. Con. Res. 27, 79th Congress, a concurrent resolution authorizing an investigation of the attack on Pearl harbor on December 7, 1941, and events and circumstances relating thereto . . . Washington, U.S. Govt. print. off., 1946.

v. illus., plates, maps, plans, facsims., tables, forms, diagrs. 23 cm.
Part of the illustrative matter is folded.
Alben W. Barkley, chairman.
Contents. — pt. 1-8. Hearings, Nov. 15, 1945-Feb. 6, 1946. 1. v. — pt. 10-11. Hearings, Feb. 15-May 31, 1946. 2 v. — pt. 12-Joint committee exhibits nos. 1v. — pt. 22- Proceedings of Roberts commission. v. — pt. 26. Proceedings of Hart inquiry. — pt. 27-31. Proceedings of Army Pearl harbor board. 5 v. — pt. 32-33. Proceedings of Navy court of inquiry. 2 v. — pt. 34. Proceedings of Clarke investigation. — pt. 35. Proceedings of Clausen investigation. — pt. 36. Proceedings of Hewitt inquiry. v. — pt. 39. Reports, findings, and conclusions of Roberts commission. Army Pearl harbor board, Navy court of inquiry, and Hewitt inquiry, with endorsements.
1. Pearl harbor, Attack on, 1941. 2. World War, 1939-1945-Japan.
D767.92.A5 1946   940.542   46-27775
MC#: 1946-page 1160
          1947-pages 257-8 (parts 12-39 of hearings)
SuDocs no.: Y4.P31:P31

ROBERTS REPORT

1301

Roberts, Merrill Joseph, 1915-
Evaluation of rate regulation. [Washington? 1959?]
133 p. diagr., tables. 27 cm.
Caption title.
Bibliographical footnotes.
1. Transportation—U.S.—Rates. I. Title.
HE195.5.U6R6   385.132   60-60955
Not located in Monthly Catalog

ROBERTS REPORT [Roberts, Owen Josephus]

1302

U.S. *American commission for the protection and salvage of artistic and historic monuments in war areas.*
Report of the American commission for the protection and salvage of artistic and historic monuments in war areas. Washington [U.S. Govt. print. off.] 1946.

v, 238 p. incl. plates, maps. 26 cm. [United States. United States government historical reports on war administration]
Owen J. Roberts, chairman.
Bibliography: p. 165-168.
1. World war, 1939-1945—Destruction and pillage. 2. Art treasures in war. 3. Monuments—Preservation. I. Roberts, Owen Josephus, 1875-
D810.A7U6 1946   940.53187   46-27664
MC#: 1946-page 1148
SuDocs no.: Y3.Am3/4:R29

ROCHE REPORT [Roche, Josephine]

1303

U.S. *Interdepartmental committee to coordinate health and welfare activities.*
National health conference, July 18-19-20, 1938, called by the Interdepartmental committee to coordinate health and welfare activities. Mayflower hotel, Washington, D.C. [Washington, 1938]

2 p. 1., vii, 75 p. 26 cm.
Recommendations regarding the nation's health services submitted to the National health conference by the Technical committee on medical care of the Interdepartmental committee to coordinate health and welfare activities.
1. Hygiene, Public—U.S. 2. U.S.—Sanit. affairs. I. National health conference, Washington, D.C., 1938.
RA422.N27 1938d   614.06373   38-26791
Not located in Monthly Catalog

ROCKEFELLER COMMISSION REPORT [Rockefeller, Nelson A.]

1304

United States. Commission on CIA Activities within the United States.
Report to the President / by the Commission on CIA Activities within the United States. — Washington : U.S. Govt. Print. Off., 1975.

xi, 299 p. ; 24 cm.
1. United States. Central Intelligence Agency.
JK468.I6U54 1975   327'.12'06173   75-601924
                                                   MARC
MC#: 1975-09736
SuDocs no.: Pr38.8:C33/C33

ROCKEFELLER REPORT [Rockefeller, Jeannette]

1305

United States. President's Task Force on the Mentally Handicapped.
Action against mental disability; the report. Washington; For sale by the Supt. of Docs., U.S. Govt. Print. Off., 1970.

v, 62 p. 24 cm.
1. Mentally handicapped—United States. 2. Mentally ill—United States. I. Title.
HV3006.A1A655   362.3'0973   70-609294
                                            MARC
MC#: 1970-17214
SuDocs no.: Pr37.8:M52/R29

ROCKEFELLER REPORT [Rockefeller, Laurance S.]

1306

United States. Citizens Advisory Committee on Environmental Quality.
    Community action for environmental quality. Washington: [For sale by the Supt. of Docs., U.S. Govt. Print. Off., 1970]
    42 p. 26 cm.
    Laurance S. Rockefeller, Chairman.
    Bibliography: p. 40-42.
    1. Environmental policy—United States. I. Rockefeller, Laurance S., 1910- II. Title.
HC110.E5A5   301.3   78-606791
                                            MARC

MC#: 1970-7706
SuDocs no.: Pr37.8:En8/C73

ROCKEFELLER REPORT [Rockefeller, Laurance S.]
    Outdoor recreation for America.

    Progress report [on outdoor recreation].

    see under
ORRRC REPORTS

ROCKEFELLER REPORTS [Rockefeller, John D., 3d]

1307

Westoff, Charles F
    Demographic and social aspects of population growth. Edited by Charles F. Westoff and Robert Parke, Jr. [Washington, Commission on Population Growth and the American Future; for sale by the Supt. of Docs., U.S. Govt. Print. Off., 1972]
    674 p. illus. 26 cm. (The Commission on Population Growth and the American Future. Research reports, 1)
    Includes bibliographical references.
    Supt. of Docs. no.: Y3.P81:9/1
    1. United States—Population—Addresses, essays, lectures. 2. Birth control—United States—Addresses, essays, lectures. I. Parke, Robert, joint author. II. Title. III. Series: United States. Commission on Population Growth and the American Future. Research reports, 1.
HB3505.A5254 vol. 1   301.32′9′73s   72-600123
                     [301.32′9′73]   MARC
MC#: 1973-25669
SuDocs no.: Y3.P81:9/1

1308

Morss, Elliott R
    Economic aspects of population change. Edited by Elliott R. Morss and Ritchie H. Reed. [Washington] Commission on Population Growth and the American Future; [for sale by the Supt. of Docs., U.S. Govt. Print. Off.,1973]
    xii, 379 p. 27 cm. (Commission on Population Growth and the American Future. Research reports, 2)
    Includes bibliographical references.
    Supt. of Docs. no.: Y3.P81:9/2
    1. United States—Population—Addresses, essays, lectures. 2. Population forecasting—United States—Addresses, essays, lectures. 3. United States—Economic conditions—Addresses, essays, lectures. I. Reed, Ritchie H., joint author. II. Title. III. Series: United States. Commission on Population Growth and the American Future Research reports, 2.
HB3505.A5254 vol. 2   301.32′973s   72-600124
                     [301.32′9′73]   MARC
MC#: 1973-29446
SuDocs no.: Y3.P81:9/2

1309

Ridker, Ronald Gene, 1931-
    Population, resources, and the environment, edited by Ronald G. Ridker. [Washington, Commission on Population Growth and the American Future; for sale by the Supt. of Docs., U.S. Govt. Print. Off., 1972]
    377 p. illus. 27 cm. (Commission on Population Growth and the American Future. Research reports, 3)
    Includes bibliographical references.
    1. United States—Population—Addresses, essays, lectures. 2. Environmental policy—States—Addresses, essays, lectures. 3. Natural resources—United States—Addresses, essays, lectures. I. Title. II. Series: United States. Commission on Population Growth and the American Future. Research reports, 3.
HB3505.A5254 vol. 3   301.32′9′73s   72-600125
                    [301.3′0973]   MARC
MC#: 1973-22192
SuDocs no.: Y3.P81:9/3

1310

Nash, A E Keir.
    Governance and population: the governmental implications of population change, edited by A. E. Keir Nash. [Washington, Commission on Population Growth and the American Future; for sale by the Supt. of Docs., U.S. Govt. Print. Off., 1972]
    342 p. illus. 26 cm. (Commission on Population Growth and the American Future. Research reports, 4)
    Includes bibliographical references.
    Supt. of Docs. no.: Y3.P81:9/4
    1. United States—Population—Addresses, essays, lectures. 2. United States—Politics and government—Addresses, essays, lectures. I. Title. II. Series: United States. Commission on Population Growth and the American Future. Research reports, 4.
HB3505.A5254 vol. 4   301.32′9′73s   72-600126
MARC   [301.32′9′73]
MC#: 1973-23907
SuDocs no.: Y3.P81:9/4

1311

    Population, distribution, and policy. Edited by Sara Mills Mazie. [Washington, Commission on Poulation Growth and the American Future; for sale by the Supt. of Docs., U.S. Govt. Print. Off., 1973]
    xvi, 719 p. illus. 26 cm. (Commission on Population Growth and the American Future. Research reports, 5)
    Prepared for Commission on Population Growth and the American Future.
    Includes bibliographical references.
    1. United States—Population—Addresses, essays, lectures. 2. Migration, Internal—United States—Addresses, essays, lectures. I. Mazie, Sara Mills, ed. II. United States. Commission on Population Growth and the American Future. III. Series: United States. Commission on Population Growth and the American Future. Research reports, 5.
HB3505.A5254 vol. 5   301.32′9′73   72-600127
                                              MARC
MC#: 1973-30601
SuDocs no.: Y3.P81:9/5

1312

    Aspects of population growth policy. Edited by Robert Parke, Jr. and Charles F. Westoff. [Washington, Commission on Population Growth and the American Future; for sale by the Supt. of Docs., U.S. Govt. Print. Off., 1972]
    xvii, 607 p. illus. 26 cm. (Commission on Population Growth and the American Future. Research reports, 6)

Includes bibliographical references.

Supt. of Docs. no.: Y3.P81:9/6

1. United States—Population—Addresses, essays, lectures. I. Parke, Robert, ed. II. Westoff, Charles F., ed. III. United States. Commission on Population Growth and the American Future. IV. Series: United States. Commission on Population Growth and the American Future. Research reports, 6.

HB3505.A5254 vol. 6   301.32′9′73s   72-600128

                      [301.32′9′73]   MARC

MC#: 1973-32532

SuDocs no.: Y3.P81:9/6

1313

United States. Commission on Population Growth and the American Future.

Population and the American future; the report. Washington; For sale by the Supt. of Docs., U.S. Govt. Print. Off. [1972]

186 p. illus. 30 cm.

Includes bibliographical references.

1. United States—Population. I. Title.

HB3505.A525   301.32′9′73   72-77389

                                       MARC

MC#: 1972-13072

SuDocs no.: Y3.P81:1/972

ROCKEFELLER REPORTS [Rockefeller, Nelson Aldrich]

1314

U.S. *Committee on Dept. of Defense Organization.*

Report of the Rockefeller Committee on Department of Defense Organization. Washington, U.S. Govt. Print. Off., 1953.

vi, 25 p. 24 cm.

At head of title: Committee print.

83d Cong., 1st sess. Senate.

1. U.S. Dept. of Defense.

UA23.3.A462   353.6

MC#: 1953-9170   53-60991

SuDocs no.: Y4.Ar5/3:R59

1315

U.S. *Congress. House. Committee on Foreign Affairs. Subcommittee on Inter-American Affairs.*

Governor Rockefeller's report on Latin America. Hearing, Ninety-first Congress, first session. November 12, 1969. Washington, U.S. Govt. Print. Off., 1970.

iii, 54 p. 24 cm.

1. U.S.—Foreign relations—Latin America. 2. Latin America—Foreign relations—U.S. 3. Latin America—Economic conditions. I. Title.

KF27.F646 1969b   327.73′08   70-605804

                                       MARC

MC#: 1970-3861

SuDocs no.: Y4.F76/1:R59

1316

U.S. Congress. Senate. Committee on Foreign Relations. Subcommittee on Western Hemisphere Affairs.

Rockefeller report on Latin America. Hearing, Ninety-first Congress, first session. Nov. 20, 1969. Washington, U.S. Govt. Print. Off., 1970.

iii, 204 p. illus., maps. 24 cm.

Appendix (p. 55-204):—Quality of life in the Americas, by N. A. Rockefeller.

1. U.S.—Foreign relations—Latin America. 2. Latin America—Foreign Relations—U.S. I. Rockefeller, Nelson Aldrich, 1908-1979. Quality of life in the Americas. II. Title.

KF26.F697 1969   327.73′08   71-605318

                                       MARC

MC#: 1970-3974

SuDocs no.: Y4.F76/2:R59

Rockefeller, Nelson Aldrich, 1908-1979.

The Rockefeller report on the Americas; the official report of a United States Presidential mission for the Western Hemisphere, by Nelson A. Rockefeller. With an introd. by Tad Szulc. New York Times ed. Chicago, Quadrangle Books, 1969.

x, 144 p. illus., maps. 22 cm.

1. Latin America—Relations (general) with the United States. 2. United States—Relations (general) with Latin America. I. Title.

F1418.R74   301.29′73′08   78-108447

                                       MARC

Not listed in Monthly Catalog

1317

United States. Domestic Council. Committee on the Right of Privacy.

National information policy : report to the President of the United States / submitted by the Staff of the Domestic Council Committee on the Right of Privacy, Nelson A. Rockefeller, chairman. — Washington : National Commission on Libraries and Information Science : for sale by the Supt. of Docs., U.S. Govt. Print. Off., 1976.

xix, 233 p. ; 27 cm.

Bibliography: p. 215-233.

1. Privacy, Right of—United States. 2. Computers—Access control. 3. Public records—United States. 4. Business records—United States. I. United States. National Commission on Libraries and Information Science. II. Title.

JC599.U5U55 1976   323.44′0973   77-601651

                                       MARC

MC#: 1977-12392

SuDocs no.: Y3.L61:2In3/2

1318

U.S. *International Development Advisory Board.*

Partners in progress; a report to the President. [Washington, U.S. Govt. Print. Off.] 1951.

v, 120 p. maps, diagrs. 23 cm.

1. Industrialization. 2. Technical assistance, American. I. Title.

HC60.U5 1951c   338.91   51-60507

MC#: 1951-7150

SuDocs no.: Y4.In85:P94

1319

U.S. *President's Advisory Committee on Government Organization.*

Report of Nelson A. Rockefeller, Chairman, President's Advisory Committee on Government Organization summarizing the Committee's principal activities from January 1953 to date. [Washington] 1958.

5 1. (U.S. President. Press release, December 29, 1958)

SuDocs no.: Pr34.7:Dec. 29, 1958

ROGERS REPORT [Rogers, Edith Nourse]

1320

U.S. Congress. House. Committee on Veterans' Affairs.

Operations of Veterans' Administration hospital and medical program. 1953 Washington, U.S. Govt. Print. Off.

v. in illus., diagrs. 24 cm. biennial.

1. Hospitals, Military—U.S. 2. Veterans—Medical care—U.S.
3. U.S. Veterans Administration. I. Title.
UH473.A25   362.110973   58-61238 rev
MC#: 1953-15599 (LC card 53-61908 cancelled in favor of
58-61238)
SuDocs no.: Y4.V64/3:H79/5

For later reports, see TEAGUE REPORT

ROGOVIN REPORTS [Rogovin, Mitchell]

1321

United States. Congress. House. Committee on Government
Operations. Environment, Energy, and Natural Resources
Subcommittee.
    Nuclear Regulatory Commission—the Rogovin report : hear-
ing before a Subcommittee of the Committee on Government
Operations, House of Representatives, Ninety-sixth Congress,
second session, February 13, 1980.—Washington : U.S. Govt.
Print. Off., 1980.
    iii, 90 p. ; 23 cm.
    1. United States. Nuclear Regulatory Commission. 2. Atomic
power-plants—United States—Safety measures. 3. Nuclear
facilities—United States—Safety measures. 4. Atomic power-
plants—United States—Accidents. I. Title. II. Title: The Rogovin
report.
KF27.G655 1980b   363.1′79-dc19   80-602901
                                                                                   MARC

MC#: 1980-22784
SuDocs no.: Y4.G74/7:R63

1322

U.S. Nuclear Regulatory Commission. Special Inquiry Group.
    Three Mile Island. A report to the Commissioners and to the
Public.
    4 v.
Not located in Monthly Catalog

ROMAN REPORT [Roman, Agnes]
    see under
O'MAHONEY REPORTS [O'Mahoney, Joseph Christopher]
        Domeratzky. Regulation of economic activities in
        foreign countries.

ROOSEVELT REPORT [Roosevelt, Franklin D., Jr.]

1323

U.S. *President's Appalachian Regional Commission.*
    Appalachia; a report, 1964. Washington, For sale by the
Superintendent of Documents, U.S. Govt. Print. Off., [1964]
    xviii, 93 p. illus., maps. 24 cm.
    1. Appalachian Mountains, Southern—Econ. condit. 2. Appa-
lachian Mountains—Econ. condit. I. Title.
HC107.A13A73 1964   64-60876
MC#: 1964-9699
SuDocs no.: Pr35.8:Ap4/R29

ROPER REPORTS [Roper, Daniel Calhoun]

1324

U.S. *Committee on industrial analysis.*
    The National recovery administration. Report of the President's
committee in industrial anaylsis. [Washington, 1937]
    cover-title, 1 p. 1., x, 240 p. 26 cm.
    Photoprinted.

Prepared by John M. Clark, William H. Davis, George M.
Harrison and George H. Mead. cf. Foreword, p. [i]-ii.
    Issued also as House doc. 158, 75th Congress, 1st session, with
title: The National recovery administration. Message from the
President of the United States transmitting a report on the opera-
tion of the National recovery administration . . .
    Daniel C. Roper, chairman.
    1. U.S. National recovery administration. I. Clark, John
Maurice, 1884- II. Davis, William Hammatt, 1879- III. Har-
rison, George McGregor, 1891- IV. Mead, George Houk, 1877-
V. Roper, Daniel Calhoun, 1867-1943. VI. Title.
HD3616.U45A5 1937   338.973   37-26274
MC#: Mar. 1937-page 311
SuDocs no.: Y3.In2/5:2N21

1325

U.S. *Interdepartmental committee on communication.*
    . . . Study of communications by an interdepartmental com-
mittee. Letter from the President of the United States to the chairman of the Committee on interstate commerce transmitting a
memorandum from the secretary of commerce relative to a study
of communications by an interdepartmental committee. Printed
for the use of the Committee on interstate commerce. Washington,
U.S. Govt. print. off., 1934.
    iii, 14 p. 23½ cm.
    At head of title: 73d Congress, 2d session. Separate commit-
tee print.
    1. Communication and traffic—U.S. 2. Telegraph—U.S. 3.
Telephone—U.S. 4. Cables, Submarine. 5. Radio—U.S. I. U.S.
Congress. Senate. Committee on interstate commerce. II. Title.
HE18 1934d   334.0973   34-24675
Not located in Monthly Catalog

ROSENBLATT REPORT [Rosenblatt, Frank F.]
    see under
ALDRICH COMMISSION [Aldrich, Nelson Wilmarth]
        Koch. German imperial banking laws.

ROSS REPORT [Ross, Malcolm]

1326

U.S. *Committee on Fair Employment Practice (1943-1946)*
    Final report, June 28, 1946. Washington, U.S. Govt. Print.
Off., 1947.
    xvi, 128 p. 23 cm.
    Bound with the Committee's First report. Washington, 1945.
    1. Discrimination in employment—U.S.
HD4903.U47   331.11   47-32547*
MC#: 1947-page 450
SuDocs no.: Pr32.412:R29/946

ROSSI REPORT [Rossi, P. H.]
        Between black and white; the faces of American
        institutions in the ghetto.
    see
KERNER COMMISSION [Kerner, Otto]
        Supplemental studies.

ROSTOW REPORT [Rostow, Eugene V.]

1327

United States. President's Task Force on Communications Policy.
    Final report, August 14, 1967. [Washington] For sale by the
Supt. of Docs., U.S. Govt. Print. Off., 1968.
    1 v. (various pagings) 27 cm.
    Commonly known as the Rostow report.

1. Telecommunication—United States. I. Title: Rostow report on communications policy.

HE7763.A55   384'.0973   76-602178
                                                 MARC

MC#: 1969-10288
SuDocs no.: Pr36.8:C73/C73

ROTH REPORTS

1328

Roth, William V 1921-
   Listing of operating Federal assistance programs compiled during the Roth study. Prepared by the staff of Representative William V. Roth, Jr. Washington, U.S. Govt. Print. Off., 1968.
   iii, 399 p. 24 cm. (90th Congress, 2d session. House of Representatives. Document no. 399)
   Commonly known as the Roth report.
   "Reprinted from the Congressional record of June 25, 1968."
   1969 ed. published under title: 1969 listing of operating Federal assistance programs compiled during the Roth study.
   1. Grants-in-aid—United States. 2. Subsidies—United States. 3. Economic assistance, Domestic—United States. I. Title. II. Title: Roth report on Federal assistance programs. III. Series: United States. 90th Congress, 2d session, 1968. House. Document no. 399.

HJ275.R6   338.973   76-602474
                                                   MARC

MC#: 1969-370
SuDocs no.: 90th Cong., 2d sess. H. Doc. 399

1329

Roth, William V 1921-
   1969 listing of operating Federal assistance programs compiled during the Roth study. Prepared by the staff of Representative William V. Roth, Jr. Washington, U.S. Govt. Print. Off., 1969.
   x, 1132 p. 24 cm. (91st Congress, 1st session. House of Representatives. Document no. 91-177)
   1968 ed. published under title: Listing of operating Federal assistance programs compiled during the Roth study.
   1. Grants-in-aid—United States. 2. Subsidies—United States. 3. Economic assistance, Domestic—United States. I. Title. II. Title: Listing of operating Federal assistance programs compiled during the Roth study. III. Series: United States. 91st Congress, 1st session, 1969. House. Document no. 91-177.

HJ275.R6 1969   338.973   73-605845
                                                   MARC

MC#: 1970-3770
SuDocs no.: 91st Cong., 1st sess., H. Doc. 177

1330

U.S. *Office of the Special Representative for Trade Negotiations.*
   Future United States foreign trade policy; report to the President. Washington, For sale by the Supt. of Docs., U.S. Govt. Print. Off., 1969.
   ix, 101 p. 27 cm.
   Commonly known as the Roth report.
   1. U.S.—Commercial policy. I. Title. II. Title: Roth report on future United States foreign trade policy.

HF1456 1969.A57   382'.0973   79-600810
                                                   MARC

MC#: 1969-4945
SuDocs no.: PrEx9.2:T67

ROWE REPORTS [Rowe, James H.]

1331

U.S. *Dept. of State.*
   An analysis of the personnel improvement plan of the Department of State, prepared for the use of the Committee on Foreign Affairs. Washington, U.S. Govt. Print. Off., 1951.
   iv, 68 p. 24 cm.
   At head of title: 82d Cong., 1st sess. Committee print.
   1. U.S. Dept. of State—Officials and employees. I. U.S. Congress. House. Committee on Foreign Affairs. II. Title.

JK851.A4 1951d   353.1   51-60730
MC#: 1951-13392
SuDocs no.: Y4.F76/1:St2/4

1332

United States-Puerto Rico Commission on the Status of Puerto Rico.
   Status of Puerto Rico. Letter from the chairman transmitting the report of the Commission. Washington, U.S. Govt. Print. Off., 1966.
   vii, 273 p. 24 cm. (89th Cong., 2d sess. House document no. 464)
   Cover title.
   1. Puerto Rico. I. Title. (Series: U.S. 89th Cong., 2d sess., 1966. House. Document no. 464)

F1958.U56   320.9'7295   66-62987
Not located in Monthly Catalog
SuDocs no.: 89th Cong., 2d sess. H. Doc. 464

1333

United States-Puerto Rico Commission on the Status of Puerto Rico.
   Status of Puerto Rico; report. [Washington] 1966.
   v, 273 p. 24 cm.
   Bibliography: p. 235-273.
   1. Puerto Rico—Pol. & govt.—1898- 2. Puerto Rico—Constitutional law. I. Title.

JL1043 1966.U5   309.17295   66-65472
MC#: 1967-2959
SuDocs no.: Y3.Un3/5:1/966

1334

United States-Puerto Rico Commission on the Status of Puerto Rico.
   Status of Puerto Rico; report. Washington, Office of the Commonwealth of Puerto Rico, 1967.
   24 p. (p. 24 blank) 23 cm. (Puerto Rico booklets, no. 5)
   1. Puerto Rico—Pol. & govt.—1898- I. Title. (Series: Puerto Rico. Office of the Commonwealth of Puerto Rico, Washington, D.C. Puerto Rico booklets series, no. 5)

F1951.A35 no. 5   327'.7295'073   67-65732
Not located in Monthly Catalog

1335

United States-Puerto Rico Commission on the Status of Puerto Rico.
   Status of Puerto Rico; selected background studies prepared for the United States-Puerto Rico Commission on the Status of Puerto Rico. [Washington] 1966.
   v, 973 p. 24 cm.
   Includes bibliographies.
   Contents.—The Puerto Rican political movement in the 19th century, by L. Cruz Monclova.—Historical survey of the Puerto Rico status question, 1898-1965, by R. J. Hunter.—Significant factors in the development of education in Puerto Rico, by

I. Rodriguez Bou. — Unionism and politics in Puerto Rico, by W. Knowles. — Puerto Rico: an essay in the definition of a national culture, by S. W. Mintz. — The United States and the dilemmas of political control, by W. T. Perkins. — Selected trends and issues in contemporary Federal and regional relations, by C. J. Friedrich. — The Netherlands, French, and British areas of the Caribbean, by Institute of Caribbean Studies, University of Puerto Rico. — Toward a balance sheet of Puerto Rican migration, by C. Senior and D. O. Watkins. — Inventory of government departments, by Dept. of Public Administration, University of Puerto Rico.

1. Puerto Rico. I. Title.
F1958.U562   917.2′95′03   66-65729
MC#: 1967-2960
SuDocs no.: Y3.Un3/5:2St9

RUBINSTEIN-COMSTOCK REPORT [Rubinstein, Eli Abraham and Comstock, George A.]

1336

Television and social behavior; reports and papers. A technical report to the Surgeon General's Scientific Advisory Committee on Television and Social Behavior. Edited by John P. Murray, Eli A. Rubinstein, and George A. Comstock. Editorial coordination: Susan Lloyd-Jones. Rockville, Md., National Institute of Mental Health; [for sale by the Supt. of Docs., U.S. Govt. Print. Off., Washington, 1972.]

v. illus. 23 cm. (DHEW Publication no. HSM 72-9057, 72-9060)

Contents: v. 2. Television and social learning. v. 5. Television's effects: further explorations.

Includes bibliographies.

1. Television and children. 2. Aggressiveness (Psychology) 3. Violence. I. Murray, John P., ed. II. Rubinstein, Eli Abraham, ed. III. Comstock, George A., ed. IV. United States. Surgeon General's Office Scientific Advisory Committee on Television and Social Behavior. V. United States. National Institute of Mental Health. VI. Series: U.S. Dept. of Health, Education, and Welfare: DHEW publication no. (HSM) 72-9057. VII. United States. Dept. of Health, Education, and Welfare. DHEW publication no. (HSM) 72-9060.
HQ784.T4T44   301.1   72-600874
                                        MARC
MC#: 1972-8769-8773 (Vols. 1-5)
SuDocs no.: HE20.2402:T23/2/v.(nos.)

RUGGLES REPORT [Ruggles, Richard]

1337

Social Science Research Council. *Committee on the Preservation and Use of Economic Data.*

Report of the Committee on the Preservation and Use of Economic Data to the Social Science Research Council, April 1965.

(*In* U.S. Congress. House. Committee on Government Operations. Special Subcommittee on Invasion of Privacy. The computer and invasion of privacy. Hearings . . . 89th Congress, 2d session. Washington, 1966. 24 cm. p. 195-253)
MC#: 1966-14422
SuDocs no.: Y4.G74/7:P93/2

RUINA REPORT [Ruina, J. P.]

1338

U.S. Dept. of Health, Education, and Welfare. Secretary's Advisory Committee on the Management of National Institutes of Health Research Contracts and Grants.

Report. [Washington] U.S. Dept. of Health, Education, and Welfare, Office of the Secretary, Office of the Assistant Secretary for Health and Scientific Affairs; [for sale by the Superintendent of Documents, U.S. Govt. Print. Off.] 1966.

v, 81 p. illus. 24 cm.

Commonly known as the Ruina report.

1. U.S. National Institutes of Health. 2. Medical research — Research grants — United States. 3. Public health research — Research grants — United States. I. Title: Ruina report on the management of National Institutes of Health research contracts and grants.
RA11.D5 1966   610.6173   66-61752
                                           MARC
MC#: 1966-10656
SuDocs no.: FS1.2:N2li

RUSK REPORTS [Rusk, Howard A.]

1339

U.S. *Committee on Veterans' Medical Services.*

Report to the President. Washington, U.S. Govt. Print. Off. [1950]

65 p. map. 24 cm.

Howard A. Rusk, chairman.

1. Hospitals, Military — U.S. 2. Disabled — Rehabilitation, etc. — U.S.
UH473.A5 1950d   355.115   50-61472
MC#: 1950-25571
SuDocs no.: Pr33.2:V641/2

1340

United States. National Citizens Advisory Committee on Vocational Rehabilitation.

A report to the Secretary of Health, Education, and Welfare. Washington, For sale by the Supt. of Docs., U.S. Govt. Print. Off., 1968.

xi, 115 p. illus. 26 cm.

Commonly known as the Rusk report.

"Final report."

1. Vocational rehabilitation — United States. I. Title. II. Title: Rusk report on vocational rehabilitation.
HD7256.U5A562   331.86′8′0973   68-62833
                                                 MARC
MC#: 1968-15820
SuDocs no.: FS1.2:V85

1341

U.S. *Office of Defense Mobilization. Health Resources Advisory Committee.*

Mobilization and health manpower; report. [1]- [Washington, 1955]-

v. illus. 26 cm.

1. Medical personnel — U.S. 2. Medical colleges — U.S. I. Title.
R151.A25   55-61138 rev
MC#: 1956-3814
SuDocs no.: Pr34.202:H34

RUSSELL REPORT [Russell, Donald Steuart]

1342

U.S. *Dept. of state.*

The Russell plan for the organization of positive intelligence research in the Department of state. [Washington, U.S. Govt. print. off., 1946]

1 p. 1., 5 p. 26 cm. [*Its* Publication 2554]

"Program planned by Donald S. Russell, assistant secretary for administration." — p. 1.

1. U.S. Dept. of state. 2. Research. I. Russell, Donald Steuart, 1906- II. Title.

JK851.A4 1946d   353.1   46-27745

MC#: 1946-page 1207

SuDocs no.: S1.2:R91

RUSSELL REPORT [Russell, Harold]
1343

United States. President's Committee on Employment of the Handicapped.

Building and maintaining community support; a guide. [Washington, 1966]

v, 32 p. 24cm.

Includes bibliographies.

1. Handicapped—Employment—United States. I. Title.

HD7256.U5A568 1966   362   77-19892

                                                 MARC

MC#: 1966-9197

SuDocs no.: L16.44/2:C73

RUSSELL REPORT
1344

Russell, John Dale, 1895-

Vocational education, by John Dale Russell and associates . . . Prepared for the Advisory committee on education. Washington, U.S. Govt. print. off., 1938.

x, 325 p. incl. tables. 23½ cm. ([U.S.] Advisory committee on education. Staff study no. 8)

Appendix: A. The experience of labor with trade and industrial education, by Howell H. Broach and Julia O'Connor Parker.— B. Major legislation for vocational education grants to states as of January 1, 1938.

"Publications of the committee": p. 325.

1. Vocational education—U.S. I. Broach, Howell Hamilton, 1893- II. Parker, Julia O'Connor.

L111.A93 no. 8   (370.973) 371.426973   38-26003

- - - - - Copy 2.

LC1045.R87

MC#: Dec. 1938-page 1509

SuDocs no.: Y3.Ad9/2:7/8

RYBECK REPORT [Rybeck, Walter]
see
DOUGLAS REPORTS [Douglas, Paul H.]
National Commission on Urban Problems.

Research report no. 4

SABINE REPORT
1345

Sabine, Lorenzo, 1803-1877.

Report on the principal fisheries of the American seas.

(*In* U.S. Treasury dept. Annual report of the secretary . . . on the state of the finances. [Washington, 1853] 8° 1851/52, p. 181-493.)

Contents.—pt. 1. France. Spain. Portugal.—pt. 2. Newfoundland. Nova Soctia. Cape Breton. Prince Edward island. Magdalene islands. Bay of Chaleurs. Labrador. New Brunswick.—pt. 3. United States. Plymouth colony.—pt. 4. Historical view of the controversy as to the intent and meaning of the first article of the convention of 1818.

1-4288

Checklist of United States Public Documents, 1789-1909, page 1000

SuDocs no.: T1.1:851/1852

SADY REPORT [Sady, Emil John]
1346

U.S. *Dept. of the Interior.*

Report of a transportation survey on the means of establishing sea and air transportation in the Trust Territory [of the Pacific Islands] under civilian administration for the Department of the Interior and the Department of the Navy, prepared by members of the survey team: Emil J. Sady, chief, Pacific Branch, Division of Territories [and others. Washington] 1950.

110 1. fold. charts. 27 cm.

1. Transportation—Micronesia. I. Sady, Emil John, 1916- II. U.S. Navy Dept.

HE298.M6U5 1950   387   50-61108

MC#: 1950-20036

SuDocs no.: I35.2:P11/2

SAMUELSON REPORT [Samuelson, Paul A.]
see
HANSEN-SAMUELSON REPORT [Hansen, Alvin H. and Samuelson, Paul A.]

SANGER REPORT [Sanger, Joseph Prentiss]
see
UPTON REPORTS [Upton, Emory]

SARNOFF REPORT [Sarnoff, David]
1347

U.S. *Citizens Advisory Commission on Manpower Utilization in the Armed Forces.*

Sarnoff Commission report; final report. Washington, U.S. Govt. Print. Off., 1953.

v, 85 p. 24 cm.

At head of title: Committee print. 83d Cong., 1st sess. Senate.

1. U.S. Dept. of Defense.

UA23.A472 1953   355   53-60533

MC#: 1953-5740

SuDocs no.: Y4.Ar5/3:Sa7

SARNOFF REPORT [Sarnoff, David]
National Security Training.

see
WADSWORTH REPORT [Wadsworth, James W.]

SAULINER REPORT [Sauliner, Raymond J.]
1348

United States. President's Task Force on Low Income Housing.

Toward better housing for low income families; the report of the President's Task Force on Low Income Housing. [Washington; For sale by the Supt. of Docs., U.S. Govt. Print. Off.,] 1970.

30 p. 24 cm.

1. Housing—United States. I. Title.

HD7293.A5 1970c   301.5'4'0973   77-608158

                                                 MARC

MC#: 1970-11833

SuDocs no.: Pr37.8:H81/R29

SAWYER REPORT [Sawyer, Charles]

1349

U.S. *Dept. of Commerce.*

Issues involved in a unified and coordinated Federal program for transportation; a report to the President from the Secretary of Commerce. [Washington, U.S. Govt. Print. Off.] 1949.

viii, 49 p. 24 cm.

1. Transportation—U.S.
HE18 1949.A54   385   50-60034
MC#: 1950-723
SuDocs no.: C1.2:T68

SCAMMON REPORTS [Scammon, Richard M.]

1350

U.S. *President's Commission on Registration and Voting Participation.*
Report. [Washington] 1963.

iii, 69 p. 24 cm.

Cover title: Report on registration and voting participation.

1. Voting—U.S. I. Title: Report on registration and voting participation.
JK1853.A44   64-60374
MC#: 1964-3091
SuDocs no.: Pr35.8:R26/R29

1351

United States. Select Commission on Western Hemisphere Immigration.
Report. Washington, For sale by the Supt. of Docs., U.S. Govt. Print. Off., 1968.

iv, 197 p. illus., maps. 27 cm.

Commonly known as the Scammon report.

Bibliographical footnotes.

1. United States—Emigration and immigration. I. Title: Scammon report on Western Hemisphere immigration.
JV6415.A4 1968   325.73   68-62267
                                         MARC
MC#: 1968-13510
SuDocs no.: Y3.W52:1/968

SCHEELE REPORT [Scheele, Leonard A.]

1352

U.S. *Special Commission to Study Nutrition in Bizonal Germany.*
Report. Wiesbaden, 1948.

ii, 9 l. 27 cm.

1. Food supply—Germany (Federal Republic, 1949-) 2. Nutrition.
TX360.G3U58   58-29501
Not located in Monthly Catalog

SCHERMER REPORT [George Schermer Associates]
see
DOUGLAS REPORTS [Douglas, Paul H.]
National Commission on Urban Problems.

Research report, no. 3

SCHOOLCRAFT REPORT

1353

Schoolcraft, Henry Rowe, 1793-1864.

Historical and statistical information respecting the history, condition and prospects of the Indian tribes of the United States; collected and prepared under the direction of the Bureau of Indian Affairs per act of Congress of March 3d, 1847. Illustrated by S. Eastmen. Philadelphia, Lippincott, Grambo, 1851-57.

6 v. illus., plates (part col.) ports., maps (part fold., part col.) 33 cm.

Vols. 2-5 have title: Information respecting the history, condition and prospects of the Indian tribes of the United States. Vol. 6 has title: History of the Indian tribes of the United States: their present condition and prospects and a sketch of their ancient status.

Vols. 5-6 published by Lippincott.

- - - - - Index to Schoolcraft's Indian tribes of the United States, compiled by Frances S. Nichols. Washington, U.S. Govt. Print. Off., 1954.

vi, 257 p. 24 cm. ([U.S.] Bureau of American Ethnology. Bulletin 152)
E51.U6 no. 152
- - - - - Copy 2.
E77.S381 Index

1. Indians of North America. I. Nichols, Frances Sellman (Gaither) 1869 (Series: U.S. Bureau of American Ethnology. Bulletin 152)
E77.S381   2-14425 rev*
Checklist of United States Public Documents, 1789-1909-page 495
SuDocs no.: I20.2:In2 1-6
MC#: 1954-4718
SuDocs no.: SI2.3:152
Also issued as:
82d Cong., 1st sess. H. Doc. 140
Not located in Monthly Catalog

SCHULTZ REPORT [Schultz, George P.]

1354

United States. Cabinet Task Force on Oil Import Control.

The oil import question; a report on the relationship of oil imports to the national security. Washington; For sale by the Supt. of Docs., U.S. Govt. Print. Off., 1970.

xiv, 399 p. illus., maps. 24 cm.

Includes bibliographical references.

1. Petroleum industry and trade—United States. I. Title.
HD9566.A48 1970   382′.42′2820973   75-606229
                                         MARC
MC#: 1970-6125
SuDocs no.: Pr37.8:Oi5/Im7

SCHUMAN REPORT [Schuman, H.]
Racial attitudes in fifteen American cities.

see
KERNER COMMISSION [Kerner, Otto]
Supplemental studies.

SCHURMAN REPORT [Schurman, Jacob Gould]

1355

U.S. *Philippine commission, 1899-1900.*

. . . Report of the Philippine commission to the President January 31, 1900[-December 20, 1900] Washington, Govt. print. off., 1900-01.

4 v. in 3. plates (part col.) maps, diagr. 23 ½ cm. (56th Cong., 1st sess. Senate. Doc. no. 138)

Composition of the report is as follows: v. 1, Papers by the various members of the commission on existing and desired conditions, e.g. "Efforts toward conciliation and the establishment of peace." "Peoples of the islands." "Education." "Government." "Condition and needs of the United States in the Philippines from a naval and maritime standpoint," etc. v. 2, Testimony and exhibits. v. 3-4. Translation and condensation, under the direction of Dean C. Worcester, of treatises submitted by the condensation, under the direction of Dean C. Worcester, of treatises submitted by the Jesuits on the subject: orography, hydrography, geognosy, phytography, zoography, climatology, cyclical variation of terrestrial magnetism, seismic foci, ethnography, chorography, state of culture, chronology. The originals were published in Washington, 1900, under title: "El archipélago filipino."

The atlas to accompany this report, prepared at the Observatoria de Manila, was published by the U.S. Coast and geodetic survey. "Special pub. no. 3, 1900."

- - - - - Another issue.

Without document series note.

DS653.A5

1. Philippine islands. I. Schurman, Jacob Gould, 1854-1942. II. Dewey, George, 1837-1917. III. Otis, Elwell Stephen, 1838-1909. IV. Denby, Charles, 1830-1904. V. Worcester, Dean Conant, 1866-1924.

J662.N19   1-22358

Listed under U.S. Congress. Senate. Documents.

MC#: 1901-pages 410, 502, 467 (Vols. 1 and 2, 3, 4)

SuDocs no.: 56th Cong., 1st sess. S. Doc. 138

Listed under Philippine Commission, 1899-1900.

MC#: 1900-pages 97, 393 (Vols. 1, 2)

MC#: 1901-page 391 (Vols. 3, 4)

SuDocs no.: 56th Cong., 1st sess. S. Doc. 138

SCHWARTZ REPORT [Schwartz, Jack]
see
PEERS COMMISSION [Peers, William R.]

SCRANTON REPORT [Scranton, William W.]
1356

U.S. *President's Commission on Campus Unrest.*

The report of the President's Commission on Campus Unrest. [Washington; For sale by the Supt. of Docs., U.S. Govt. Print. Off., 1970]

x, 537 p. illus., 23 cm.

Cover title: Campus unrest.

Bibliography: p. 468-518.

1. Student movements—U.S. I. Title: Campus unrest.

LA229.A54   322'.4   74-608779
                                           MARC

MC#: 1970-18302

SuDocs no.: Pr37.8:C15/R29

SCRIBNER REPORT [Scribner, Fred C., Jr.]
1357

United States. Ad Hoc Advisory Group on the Presidential Vote for Puerto Rico.

The presidential vote for Puerto Rico; report. [Washington, U.S. Govt. Print. Off.] 1971.

iii, 58 p. 24 cm.

English and Spanish.

Supt. of Docs. no.: Pr37.8:P96/R29

1. Suffrage—Puerto Rico. I. Title.

                 342'.73'07   73-614329
                                             MARC

MC#: 1971-17050

SuDocs no.: Pr37.8:P96/R29

SEABORG REPORT [Seaborg, Glenn T.]
1358

U.S. *President's Science Advisory Committee.*

Scientific progress, the universities, and the Federal Government; statement. Washington [U.S. Govt. Print. Off.] 1960.

v, 33 p. 24 cm.

1. Research—U.S. 2. Science and state—U.S. I. Title.

Q180.U5A57 1960   507.2   61-60209

MC#: 1961-2655

SuDocs no.: Pr34.8:Sci2/4

SEGAL REPORT [Segal, Bernard G.]
1359

U.S. *Commission on Judicial and Congressional Salaries.*

Report of the Commission on Judicial and Congressional Salaries. Letter from Chairman transmitting a report of the findings and recommendations pursuant to Public law 220, 83d Congress. Washington, U.S. Govt. Print. Off., 1954.

vii, 36 p. 23 cm. (83d Cong., 2d sess. House document no. 300)

1. Judges—U.S.—Salaries, pensions, etc. 2. U.S. Congress—Salaries, pensions, etc. (Series: U.S. 83d Cong., 2d sess., 1954. House. Document no. 300)

                         328.333
                                       54-61157

MC#: 1954-1627

SuDocs no.: 83d Cong., 2d sess., H. Doc. 300

SHAFER REPORTS [Shafer, Raymond Philip]
1360

United States. Commission on Marihuana and Drug Abuse.

Drug use in America: problem in perspective; second report. [Washington; For sale by the Supt. of Docs., U.S. Govt. Print. Off., 1973]

xvii, 481 p. 24 cm.

Bibliography: p. 413-439.

Supt. of Docs. no.: Y3.M33/2:1/973

- - - - - Appendix; the technical papers of the second report. [Washington; For sale by the Supt. of Docs., U.S. Govt. Print. Off., 1973-

v. illus. 27 cm.

Includes bibliographical references.

Contents: v. 1. Patterns and consequences of drug use.—v. 2. Social responses to drug use.—v. 3. Legal system and drug control.—v. 4. Treatment and rehabilitation.

HV5825.U56 1973 Suppl.

1. Drug abuse—United States. 2. Narcotics, Control of—United States. 3. Drug abuse—Treatment—United States. I. Title.

HV5825.U56 1973   362.2'9'0973   73-601309
                                             MARC

MC#: 1973-25391

SuDocs no.: Y3.M33/2:1/973

MC#: 1973-27226

SuDocs no.: Y4.In8/4:D84/3

MC#: 1974-534—Appendix, vol. 1

        1973-32440—Appendix, vol. 2

        1974-1367—Appendix, vol. 3

        1973-32441—Appendix, vol. 4

SuDocs no.: Y3.M33/2:1/973/app./v.(nos.)

1361

United States. Commission on Marihuana and Drug Abuse.

Marihuana: a signal of misunderstanding; first report. [Washington; For sale by the Supt. of Docs., U.S. Govt. Print. Off.] 1972.

x, 184 p. 24 cm.

- - - - - Appendix; the technical papers of the first report of the National Commission on Marihuana and Drug Abuse. [Washington; For sale by the Supt. of Docs., U.S. Govt. Print. Off.] 1972-

v. illus. 26 cm.

HV5822.M3U49 Suppl.

Supt. of Docs. no.: Y3.M33/2:2M33
1. Marihuana. 2. Drug abuse — United States. 3. Drugs and youth — United States. I. Title.
HV5822.M3U49   362.2′9   72-601280
                                                                                    MARC

MC#: 1972-7065A
SuDocs no.: Y3.M33/2:2M33
MC#: 1972-10022
SuDocs no.: Y3.M33/2:2M/33/app./v. 1,2

SHANKLIN REPORT [Shanklin, John F.]

Multiple use of land and water areas.
see under
ORRRC REPORTS

ORRRC study report, 17.

SHANNON REPORT [Shannon, James A.]

1362

United States. National Institutes of Health. Office of Program Planning.

The advancement of knowledge for the Nation's health; a report to the President on the research programs of the National Institutes of Health. Washington, U.S. Dept. of Health, Education, and Welfare, Public Health Service; for sale by the Supt. of Docs., U.S. Govt. Print. Off., 1967.

ix, 202 p. illus. 26 cm. (Public Health Service publication no. 1659)

"Prepared under the direction of the Office of Program Planning, National Institute of Health."
1. Public health — Research — United States. I. Title. II. Series: United States. Public Health Service. Publication no. 1659.
RA11.D5 1967b   614′.0973   67-62121
                                                                                    MARC

MC#: 1967-14616
SuDocs no.: FS2.22:H34/2

SHARON REPORT [Sharon, Milton I.]

1363

United States. Merit Staffing Review Team.

A self-inquiry into merit staffing : report of the Merit Staffing Review Team. United States Civil Service Commission : Committee on Post Office and Civil Service, House of Representatives, Ninety-fourth Congress, second session. — Washington : U.S. Govt. Print. Off., 1976.

iii, 96 p. ; 23 cm.
At head of title: 94th Congress, 2d session. Committee print no. 94-14.
1. Civil service recruiting — United States. 2. Civil service — United States — Examinations. I. Title.
JK765.U59 1976   353.006   76-602468
                                                                                    MARC

MC#: 1977-4156
SuDocs no.: Y4.P84/10:M54/2

SHARP REPORT [Sharp, Ulysses S. Grant]

1364

U.S. *Pacific Command.*

Report on the war in Vietnam, as of 30 June 1968. Section I: Report on air and naval campaigns against North Vietnam and Pacific Command-wide support of the war, June 1964-July 1968, by U. S. G. Sharp, USN, Commander in Chief Pacific. Section II: Report on operations in South Vietnam, January 1964-June 1968, by W. C. Westmoreland USA, Commander, U.S. Military Assistance Command, Vietnam. [Washington, For sale by the Supt. of Docs., U.S. Govt. Print. Off., 1969]

v, 347 p. illus., maps (part fold.) 27 cm.
- - - - - Index. [Washington, For sale by the Supt. of Docs., U.S. Govt. Print. Off., 1969]

34 p. 27 cm.
DS557.A6U55 Index
1. Vietnamese Conflict, 1961- —Campaigns. I. Sharp, Ulysses S. Grant, 1906- II. Westmoreland, William Childs, 1914- III. U.S. Military Assistance Command, Vietnam. IV. Title.
DS557.A6U55   959.7′04   70-601356
                                                                                    MARC

MC#: 1969-6440
SuDocs no.: D101.2:V67
MC#: 1969-15044
SuDocs no.: D101.2:V67/ind.

SHAW REPORT [Shaw, Clifford Robe]

see
WICKERSHAM COMMISSION [Wickersham, George Woodward]

Report on the causes of crime, no. 13.

SHAW REPORT [Shaw, Frank L.]

see under
DILLINGHAM COMMISSION [Dillingham, William Paul]

Immigration legislation.

SHEA REPORT [Shea, Francis Michael]

1365

U.S. *Attorney general's committee on bankruptcy administration.*

Administration of the Bankruptcy act; report of the Attorney general's committee on bankruptcy administration, 1940. Committee: Francis M. Shea, chairman, Jesse H. Jones, Jerome N. Frank [and others] . . . Charles A. Horsky, director. George S. Elpern, Leon Frechtel, assistant directors. Washington, U.S. Govt. print. off., 1941.

[i], iia-iic, iii-xvii, 330 p. fold. tab. 23 cm.
1. Bankruptcy — U.S. I. Shea, Francis Michael, 1905- II. Horsky, Charles Antone. III. Title.
                [347.7] 332.750973   41-2456
MC#: 1941-page 67 (LC card 41-50011 cancelled in favor of 41-2456)
SuDocs no.: J1.2:B22/3

SHELDON REPORT [Sheldon, Charles S.]

1366

U.S. *Congress. House. Committee on Science and Astronautics.*

Science, astronautics, and defense: the 1961 review of scientific and astronautic research and development in the Department of Defense. Staff report of the Committee on Science and Astronautics, U.S. House of Representatives, Eighty-seventh Congress, first session. Washington, U.S. Govt. Print. Off., 1961.

v, 68 p. 24 cm.
At head of title: Committee print.
1. Military research — U.S. 2. Astronautics, Military — U.S. 3. U.S. — Defenses. I. Title.
U393.A53   61-62301
MC#: 1961-18977
SuDocs no.: Y4.Sci2:Sci2

SHEPLEY REPORT [Shepley, Marjorie]

see
FRY REPORT [Fry, Bernard Mitchell]

SHEPPARD REPORT [Sheppard, Morris]
1367

U.S. *Congress. Senate. Special committee to investigate campaign expenditures.*
. . . . Investigation of senatorial campaign expenditures and use of governmental funds. Report of the Special committee to investigate senatorial campaign expenditures and use of governmental funds in 1938, pursuant to Senate resolution no. 283, Seventy-fifth Congress, and Senate resolution no. 290, Seventy-fifth Congress . . . Washington, U.S. Govt. print. off., 1939.
2 v. in 1. tables, forms. 23 cm. ([U.S.] 76th Cong., 1st sess. Senate. Rept. 1)
Part II has subtitle: Summary of cases by states and miscellaneous cases.
Morris Sheppard, chairman.
1. Elections—U.S.—Campaign funds. 2. U.S. Congress. Senate—Elections. I. Sheppard, Morris, 1875-1941.
JK1991.A4 1938   324.273   39-26090 rev 2
MC#: Jan. 1939-page 43
SuDocs no.: 76th Cong., 1st sess., S. Rept.1

SHKUDA REPORT [Shkuda, Anne N.]
see under
GRIFFITHS REORTS [Griffiths, Martha W.]
Studies in public welfare, paper no. 8.

SHOUP MISSION REPORT [Shoup, Carl D.]
1368

U.S. *Tax Mission to Japan.*
Report on Japanese taxation, by the Shoup Mission. [Tokyo] General Headquarters, Supreme Commander for the Allied Powers, 1949.
4 v. 23 cm.
English and Japanese.
1. Taxation—Japan.
HJ2986.U5   336.2   50-60272 rev 2
Not located in Monthly Catalog

SHRIVER REPORT
1369

Shriver, Robert Sargent
Summary of Report to the President on the Peace Corps. [Washington] 1961.
10 1. (U.S. President. Press release, March 4, 1961)
SuDocs no.: Pr34.7:Mar. 4, 1961

SHUBIK REPORT [Shubik, Philippe]
1370

United States. National Cancer Institute.
Survey of compounds which have been tested for carcinogenic activity. 1939-
[Washington, For sale by the Supt. of Docs., U.S. Govt. Print. Off.]
5 v. 24 x 30 cm. (1968/69-) : DHEW publication no. (NIH) (1939/47-1965/69 : Public Health Service publication no. 149)
Vols. for 1948/53, 1954/60 called also supplement no. 1 and 2.
1. Carcinogens—Collected works. I. Title. II. Series : United States. Dept. of Health, Education, and Welfare. DHEW publication. III. Series : United States. Public Health Service. Publication no. 149.
RC268.57.U55   616.9'94'071   52-60248
Original vols. not located in Monthly Catalog

2d ed.-suppl. 1
MC#: 1958-1758
SuDocs no.: FS2.22:C17/suppl. 1
2d ed.-suppl. 2
MC#: 1970-4556
SuDocs no.: HE20.3152:C17/suppl. 2
1970-71 vol.
MC#: 1975-16128
SuDocs no.: HE20.3152:C17/970-71
1978 entry
MC#: 1980-24536
SuDocs no.: HE20.3152:C17/978

SHUMAN REPORT [Shuman, Howard E.]
see
DOUGLAS REPORTS [Douglas, Paul H.]
National Commission on Urban Problems.
Research report, no. 4

SICILIANO REPORT [Siciliano, Rocco C.]
1371

U.S. *Office of Defense Mobilization. Manpower Policy Committee.*
A manpower program for full mobilization. Staff assistance provided by Office of Defense Mobilization and U.S. Dept. of Labor. [Washington] 1954.
19 p. 27 cm.
1. Industrial mobilization—U.S. 2. Labor supply—U.S. 3. Manpower—U.S. I. Title.
UA18.U5A574   355.26   54-63342
MC#: 1955-4662
SuDocs no.: Pr34.202:M31/2

SILVERMAN REPORT
1372

Silverman, Abner D
Selected aspects of administration of publicly-owned housing: Great Britain, Netherlands, and Sweden. [Washington, Housing and Home Finance Agency, Public Housing Administration] 1961.
xi, 238 p. 24 cm.
Bibliography: p. 226-228.
1. Housing. I. U.S. Public Housing Administration. II. Title.
HD7287.S498   331.833   61-60922
MC#: 1961-6512
SuDocs no.: HH3.2:Ad6

SIMONDS REPORT [Simonds, Frances W.]
see under
DILLINGHAM COMMISSION [Dillingham, William Paul]
Children of immigrants in schools.

SIMPSON REPORT [Simpson, Richard M.]
see
REED REPORT [Reed, Daniel Alden]

SIMPSON REPORT [Simpson, Sidney Post]
see
WICKERSHAM COMMISSION [Wickersham, George Woodward]
Report on the cost of crime, no. 12.

SINNOTT REPORT [Sinnott, William V.]
1373

U.S. *Congress. Senate. Committee on Appropriations.*

United States aid to India; report [compiled and prepared by William V. Sinnott] of the Investigations Division of Senate Appropriations Committee. Washington, U.S. Govt. Print. Off., 1954.

iii, 21 p. 24 cm.
At head of title: Committee print. 83d Cong., 2d sess. Senate.
1. Technical assistance, American—India. I. Title.
HC435.U485   338.954   54-61788
MC#:1954-8552
SuDocs no.: Y4.Ap6/2:In2/2

SKOLNICK REPORT

1374

Skolnick, Jerome H
    The politics of protest; a report submitted by Jerome H. Skolnick. [Washington, For sale by the Supt. of Docs., U.S. Govt. Print. Off., 1969]
    xxvi, 276 p. 24 cm. ([NCCPV staff study series] 3)
    Commonly known as the Skolnick report.
    Report of the Task Force on Demonstrations, Protests, and Group Violence to the National Commission on the Causes and Prevention of Violence.
    Includes bibliographies.
    1. United States—Social conditions—1960- 2. Violence—United States. I. United States. Task Force on Demonstrations, Protests, and Group Violence. II. United States. National Commission on the Causes and Prevention of Violence. III. Title. IV. Title: Skolnick report on violent aspects of protests and confrontation. V. Series: United States. National Commission on the Causes and Prevention of Violence. NCCPV staff study series, 3.
HN90.V5S5 1969   301.6′0973   72-601930
                                                                      MARC
MC#: 1969-13324
SuDocs no.: Pr36.8:V81/P94

SLAVET REPORT [Slavet, Joseph S.]
see
DOUGLAS REPORTS [Douglas, Paul H.]
    National Commission on Urban Problems.

    Research report, no. 17

SMALL REPORT [Small, John D.]

1375

U.S. *Civilian production administration.*
    From war to peace, civilian production achievements in transition, report to the president by John D. Small. [Washington] Civilian production administration, 1946.
    2 p. 1., 73 p. map, diagrs. 27½ cm.
    1. U.S.—Economic policy. 2. Reconstruction (1939-)—U.S. I. Title.
HC106.5.A59 1946p   338.973   47-32985
MC#: 1947-page 204 (LC card 47-32986 referred to in error)
SuDocs no.: Pr32.4802:C49

SMART REPORT [Smart, Walter]
see
DOUGLAS REPORTS [Douglas, Paul H.]
    National Commission on Urban Problems.

    Research report no. 4

SMATHERS REPORTS [Smathers, George A.]
1376

Military Procurement Advisory Committee.

How to improve Federal procedures for buying national defense materials; report to Senator George A. Smathers. [Washington] 1961.
    58 p. 26 cm.
    1. Government purchasing—U.S. 2. Defense Contracts—U.S. I. Title.
[UC263.M64]
Dept. of the Army Library
Not located in Monthly Catalog

1377

U.S. *Congress. Senate. Committee on Interstate and Foreign Commerce.*
    Foreign Commerce Study; Latin America: Panama, Colombia, Ecuador, Peru, Chile, Argentina, Brazil, Venezuela, Dominican Republic, and Haiti. Report of George A. Smathers, on a study mission, to the Committee on Interstate and Foreign Commerce, United States Senate. Washington, U.S. Govt. Print. Off., 1960.
    vi, 55 p. 24 cm.
    At head of title: 86th Cong., 2d sess. Committee print.
    1. United States—Comm.—Latin America. 2. Latin America—Comm.—U.S. I. Smathers, George A. II. Title-Latin America.
HF3080.A45   60-64415
MC#: 1960-15369
SuDocs no.: Y4.In8/3:F76/3/960-3

SMITH REPORT [Smith, Philip S.]
see
BROOKS REPORT [Brooks, Alfred H.]

SMITH REPORT [Smith, Robert L.]
see
ACKERMAN REPORT [Ackerman, William G.]
    Federal water resources research program, fiscal year 1966.

SMYTH REPORT

1378

Smyth, Henry De Wolf, 1898-
    Atomic bombs, a general account of the development of methods of using atomic energy for military purposes under the auspices of the United States government, 1940-1945, by H. D. Smyth . . . Written at the request of Major General L. R. Groves, United States Army . . . [Washington?] c 1945.
    1 v. diagrs. 26 x 20 cm.
    Various pagings; reproduced from type-written copy.
    1. Atomic bomb. 2. Atomic energy. I. U.S. Army.
UF767.S5   623.45   45-7713
Not located in Monthly Catalog

SNYDER REPORT [Snyder, Melvin C.]
see under
HOFFMAN REPORTS [Hoffman, Clare E.]
    Sixteenth intermediate report.

    Twenty-fourth intermediate report.

SPAULDING REPORT

1379

Spaulding, Morril B.
    A comparative analysis of non-economic Federal transportation regulations. Prepared for the Dept. of Commerce transportation study. [Washington, 1959]
    iii, 129 p. tables. 29 cm.

1. Transportation—U.S.—Laws and regulations. I. U.S. Dept. of Commerce.

60-61592

Not located in Monthly Catalog

SPIRO REPORT [Spiro, Herbert T.]
see
KING REPORT [King, Gilbert William]

SPLAWN REPORT [Splawn, Walter Marshall William]
1380

U.S. *Congress. House. Committee on interstate and foreign commerce.*
. . . Report on communication companies . . . Washington, U.S. Govt. print. off., 1934-35.

6 v. maps (part fold.) tables (part fold.) fold. diagrs., forms. 23cm. (73d Cong., 2d sess. House. Rept. 1273)
House calendar no. 212.
Submitted by Mr. Rayburn pursuant to House resolution 59, 72d Congress and House joint resolution 572, 72d Congress. [Pt. I] referred to the House calendar and ordered printed with illustrations, April 18, 1934. Pt. II-III referred to the House calendar and ordered printed with illustrations June 4 (calendar day of June 8), 1934.
Parts I and II issued in 1 v. each. Pt. III, issued in 4 v., covers sections A-D, divisions 1 to 5, of which divisions 4 and 5 are combined in 1 v.
Part I has title: Preliminary report on communication companies.
1. Communication and traffic—U.S. I. Rayburn, Sam Taliaferro, 1882- II. Title.
HE18 1934 fb ·   384.0973   34-26747
- - - - - Copy 2.
MC#: 1935-page 644
SuDocs no.: 73d Cong., 2d sess. H. Rept. 1273, pt. 3, no. 1-4

Only Part III is referred to as the SPLAWN REPORT

SPLAWN REPORT [Splawn, Walter Marshall William]
Regulation of stock ownership in railroads.
see
PARKER REPORT [Parker, James Southworth]

SPRAGUE REPORT [Sprague, Oliver Mitchell Wentworth]
see under
ALDRICH COMMISSION [Aldrich, Nelson Wilmarth]

STAATS REPORT [Staats, Elmer B.]
1381

United States. General Accounting Office.
Need for a comparability policy for both pay and benefits of Federal civilian employees-Civil Service Commission, Office of Management and Budget : report to the Congress / by the Comptroller General of the United States.—[Washington : General Accounting Office, 1975]

iv, 35 p. : graphs ; 27 cm.
Cover title.
Publication date stamped on cover.
"FPCD-75-62."
"B-167266."
1. United States—Officials and employees—Salaries, allowances, etc. I. Title: Need for a comparability policy . . .

JK775 1975.G45 1975b   353.001′2   75-602316
MARC
MC#: 1975-10604
SuDocs no.: GA1.13:FPCD75-62

STANDARDS AND GOALS REPORT
see
PETERSON REPORTS [Peterson, Russell W.]

STARNES REPORTS [Starnes, Joe]
1382

U.S. *Congress. House. Special committee on un-American activities (1938-1944)*
. . . Investigation of un-American propaganda activities in the United States . . . Report. "Pursuant to H. Res. 282 (75th Cong.)" and H. Res. 26 (76th Cong.) . . . [Washington, U.S. Govt. Print. Off., 1940]

25 p. 23½ cm. (76th Cong., 3d sess. House. Rept. 1476)
Union calendar no. 5.
Committed to the Committee of the whole House on the state of the Union and ordered printed January 3, 1940.
Running title: Un-American activities and propaganda.
1. National socialism. 2. Propaganda, German. 3. Germans in the U.S. 4. Communism. 5. Propaganda, Russian. 6. Fascism. 7. Propaganda, Italian. I. Title. II. Title: Un-American activities and propaganda.
E743.5A5 1940   335.0973   40-26155
- - - - - Copy 2.
MC#: 1940-page 39
SuDocs no.: 76th Cong., 3d sess. H. Rept. 1476

1383

U.S. *Congress. House. Special committee on un-American activities (1938-1944)*
. . . Special report on subversive activities aimed at destroying our representative form of government . . . Report [and Minority views] "Pursuant to H. Res. 282 (75th Cong.) and H. Res. 26 (76th Cong.)" . . . [Washington, U.S. Govt. print. off., 1942]

22, 7 p. tab. 23 cm. ([U.S.] 77th Cong., 2d sess. House. Rept. 2277)
Caption title.
"Report" (22 p.) submitted by Mr. Starnes, "Minority views" (7 p.) by Mr. Voorhis, from the Special committee on un-American activities.
1. Communism—U.S.—1917- I. Starnes, Joe, 1895- II. Voorhis, Horace Jeremiah, 1901- III. Title: Subversive activities aimed at destroying our representative form of government.
JK1051.A5 1942f   328.73   42-38372
MC#: 1942-pages 778, 911
SuDocs no.: 77th Cong., 2d sess. H. Rept. 2277

STARR REPORT [Starr, Chauncey]
1384

National Academy of Engineering. *Committee on Public Engineering Policy.*
A study of technology assessment; report of the Committee on Public Engineering Policy, National Academy of Engineering. [Washington] Committee on Science and Astronautics. U.S. House of Representatives; [for sale by the Supt. of Docs., U.S. Govt. Print. Off.] 1969.

xiii, 208 p. 24 cm.
Bibliography: p. 159-173.

1. Technology assessment. I. U.S. Congress. House. Committee on Science and Astronautics. II. Title.

T174.5.N3   301.2′4   74-604430
MARC

MC#: 1969-16824
SuDocs no.: Y4.Sci2:T22/2

STEADMAN REPORT

1385

Steadman, Richard C
The national military command structure : report of a study requested by the President and conducted in the Department of Defense. — Washington : The Dept. : for sale by the Supt. of Docs., U.S. Govt. Print. Off., 1978.

iii, 79 p. ; 27 cm.
Cover title: Report to the Secretary of Defense on the national military command structure.
1. United States. Dept. of Defense. 2. United States — Armed Forces — Organization. 3. United States — Armed Forces — Management. I. United States. Dept. of Defense. II. Title. III. Title: Report to the Secretary of Defense on the national military command structure.

UA23.3.S73   355.3′3041′0973   79-602790
MARC

MC#: 1980-5676
SuDocs no.: D1.2:M59/12

STEARNS-EISENHOWER REPORT [Stearns, Robert L. and Eisenhower, Dwight David]

1386

U.S. *Dept. of Defense. Service Academy Board.*
A report and recommendations to the Secretary of Defense. [Washington] 1950.

82 p. diagr. 27 cm.
1. Military education — U.S.

U408.3.A5 1950   355.07   50-60819
Not located in Monthly Catalog

STEELMAN REPORTS [Steelman, John Roy]

1387

U.S. *President, 1945-1953 (Truman)*
Synthetic rubber, recommendations transmitted to Congress together with a report on maintenance of the synthetic rubber industry in the United States and disposal of Government-owned synthetic rubber facilities from the Assistant to the President [John R. Steelman. Washington, U.S. Govt. Print. Off.] 1950.

iii, 121 p. illus., fold. col. map. 24 cm.
"Glossary": p. 119-121.
1. Rubber industry and trade — U.S. I. Steelman, John Roy, 1900-

HD9161.U52A52 1950   338.47678   50-60130
MC#: 1950-3958
SuDocs no.: Pr33.2:R821/950
MC#: 1950-4801
SuDocs no.: 81st Cong., 2d sess., H. Doc. 448

1388

U.S. *President's Scientific Research Board.*
Science and public policy. A report to the President by John R. Steelman. Washington, U.S. Govt. Print. Off., 1947.

5 v. illus. 24 cm.
Contents — v. 1. A program for the nation. — v. 2. The Federal research program. — v. 3. Administration for research. — v. 4. Manpower for research. — v. 5. The nation's medical research.

1. Research — U.S. 2. Science and States — U.S. 3. Medical research — U.S. I. Steelman, John Roy, 1900- II. Title.

Q180.U5A47   507.2   47-46212*
MC#: 1947-5339, 6798, 6796, 8306, 8307 (Vols. 1-5)
SuDocs no.: Pr33.2:Sci2/v.(nos.)

United States. President's Scientific Research Board.
Science and public policy / John R. Steelman. — New York : Arno Press, 1980.

5 v. in one : ill. ; 24 cm. — (Three centuries of science in America)
Commonly known as the Steelman report.
Reprint of the 1947 ed. published by the U.S. Govt. Print. Off., Washington, D.C.
Contents: v. 1. A program for the Nation. — v. 2. The Federal research program. — v. 3. Administration for research. — v. 4. Manpower for research. — v. 5. The Nation's medical research.
ISBN 0-405-12586-0
1. Research — United States. 2. Science and state — United States. 3. Federal aid to research — United States. I. Steelman, John Roy, 1900- II. Title. III. Title: Steelman report on science and public policy. IV. Series.

Q180.U5U57 1980   507′.2073   79-7998
MARC

Not listed in Monthly Catalog

STEER REPORT

1389

Steer, Henry Bake, 1893- *comp.*
Lumber production in the United States, 1799-1946. [Washington, U.S. Govt. Print. Off., 1948]

iii, 233 p. illus., map. 30 cm. (U.S. Dept. of Agriculture. Miscellaneous publication no. 669)
Cover title.
Contribution from Forest Service.
"Reference list": p. 229-233.
1. (Lumber trade — U.S.) [1. Lumbering — U.S. — Hist.] 2. [Lumber — U.S.] 3. [Lumber — Stat.] (Series)

HD9754.S75   338.174984   Agr48-485*
- - - - - Copy 2.
S21.A46 no. 669
MC#: 1949-2302
SuDocs no.: A1.38:669

STEIN REPORT

1390

Stein, Herbert.
The meaning and measurement of productivity [by Herbert Stein and Jerome A. Mark] Prepared for the National commission on Productivity by the Bureau of Labor Statistics, U.S. Dept. of Labor. [Washington] 1971.

iv, 15 p. illus. 26 cm.
Includes bibliographical references.
Supt. of Docs. no.: Pr37.8:P94/M46
1. Labor productivity — United States. I. Mark, Jerome Albert. II. National Commission on Productivity. III. United States. Bureau of Labor Statistics. IV. Title.

HC110.L3S74   338′.00973   71-614157
MARC

MC#: 1971-15964
SuDocs no.: Pr37.8:P94/M46

STEINHART REPORT

1391

Steinhart, John S

The universities and environmental quality: commitment to problem focused education; a report to the President's Environmental Quality Council, by John S. Steinhart and Stacie Cherniack. Washington, Office of Science and Technology; for sale by the Supt. of Docs., U.S. Govt. Print. Off., 1969.

49, 22 p. 27 cm.

1. Environmental policy — United States. 2. Human ecology — Study and teaching — United States. I. Cherniack, Stacie, joint author. II. United States Council on Environmental Quality. III. Title.

HC110.E5S7	301.3	73-604087
		MARC

MC#: 1969-16399
SuDocs no.: PrEx8.2:En8

STENNIS REPORT [Stennis, John C.]

1392

U.S. *Congress. Senate. Committee on Armed Services.*

Investigation of the preparedness program. Interim report by Preparedness Investigating Subcommittee, under the authority of S. Res. 75, 88th Cong., 1st sess., on the Cuban military buildup. Washington, U.S. Govt. Print. Off., 1963.

v, 18 p. 24 cm.

At head of title: 88th Cong., 1st sess. Committee print.

1. Military bases, Russian — Cuba. 2. Intelligence service — U.S. I. Title. II. Title: Cuban military buildup.

F1788.U45	63-61609

MC#: 1963-13792
SuDocs no.: Y4.Ar5/3:P91/8

STEPHAN REPORT [Stephan, Frederick F.]

1393

U.S. *Dept. of Commerce. Special Advisory Committee on Employment Statistics.*

The measurement of employment and unemployment by the Bureau of the Census in its Current population survey; report of the Special Advisory Committee on Employment Statistics. [Washington] 1954.

35, A4 p. 27 cm.

Cover title.

- - - - - Appendixes and bibliography. [Washington] 1954.

A87 p. illus. 27 cm.

HD5711.U54 Appx.

1. Labor supply — Stat. 2. Unemployed — Stat. 3. Labor supply — U.S.

HD5711.U54	331.112	54-60044

MC#: 1955-380
SuDocs no.: C1.2:Em7/4
MC#: 1955-381
SuDocs no.: C1.2:EM7/4/app.

STERLING REPORT [Sterling, Thomas]

1394

U.S. *Congress. Joint commission on postal service.*

. . . Postal service. Report of the Joint commission on postal service submitting pursuant to law, a report relative to methods and systems of handling, dispatching, transporting, and delivering the mails . . . Washington, Govt. print. off., 1924.

ii, 41 p. 23½ cm. (68th Cong., 1st sess. Senate. Doc. 36)

Presented by Mr. Sterling. Ordered printed February 7 (calendar day, February 8, 1924)

1. Postal service — U.S. I. Sterling, Thomas, 1851-

HE6331 1924	24-26123

- - - - - Copy 2.

MC#: Feb. 1924-page 442
SuDocs no.: 68th Cong., 1st sess. S. Doc. 36

STERN REPORT [Stern, Carl Samuel]

see

MOONEY-BILLINGS REPORT [Mooney, Thomas J. and Billings, Warren K.]

WICKERSHAM COMMISSION [Wickersham, George Woodward]

Report on lawlessness, no. 11.

STETTINIUS REPORT [Stettinius, Edward Reilly]

1395

U.S. *Delegation to the United Nations conference on international organization, San Francisco, 1945.*

Charter of the United nations. Report to the President on the results of the San Francisco conference by the chairman of the United States delegation, the secretary of state. [Washington, U.S. Govt. print. off.] 1945.

266 p. 23 cm. [U.S. Dept. of state. Publication 2349. Conference series 71]

Edward R. Stettinius, jr., chairman.

1. United nations conference on international organization, San Francisco, 1945. I. Stettinius, Edward Reilly, 1900-

JX1976.4.U55	341.1	45-36388

MC#: 1945-page 906
SuDocs no.: S5.30:71

STEVER REPORT [Stever, H. Guyford]

see

ACKERMAN REPORT [Ackerman, William G.]

Federal water resources research program, fiscal year 1970.

STEWART REPORT [Stewart, Irwin]

1396

U.S. *President's Communications Policy Board.*

Telecommunications, a program for progress; a report. Washington, U.S. Govt. Print. Off., 1951.

vii, 238 p. 25 cm.

1. Telecommunication — U.S. I. Title.

HE7763.A44 1951	384	51-60572

MC#: 1951-8727
SuDocs no.: Pr33.13:T23

STEWART REPORT [Stewart, William Blair]

see

WIGHT REPORT [Wight, Royce Atwood]

STIGLER REPORT [Stigler, George J.]

1397

U.S. *Task Force on Productivity and Competition.*

Report of the Task Force on Productivity and Competition.

(*In* U.S. Congress. Congressional record. [Daily ed.] Washington. 28 cm. v. 115 (1969) no. 98, p. S6473-S6482)

SuDocs no.: X/a.91/1:98

STILL REPORT [Still, Samuel Hutchins]

see

HALSEY REPORT [Halsey, Edwin Alexander]

Electoral college.

STOCKPILE REPORT

1398

U.S. *Office of Emergency Planning.*

Stockpile report to the Congress. Washington.

v. illus. 26 cm. semiannual.

Began publication with report for July/Dec. 1946.

Reports for 19 -52 issued by the Munitions Board; Jan./June 1953 by the Office of the Secretary of Defense; July/Dec. 1953-July/Dec. 1957 by the Office of Defense Mobilization; 1958-60 by the Office of Civil Defense Mobilization.

Report for Jan./June 1948 has supplement with title: The National stockpile.

1. Strategic materials—U.S. 2. U.S.—Defenses. I. U.S. Munitions Board. Stockpile report to the Congress. II. U.S. Dept. of Defense. Stockpile report to the Congress. III. U.S. Office of Defense Mobilization. Stockpile report to the Congress. IV. U.S. Office of Civil and Defense Mobilization. Stockpile report to the Congress. V. Title. VI. Title: The National stockpile.

UA23.2.A35   51-60126 rev 3
MC#: 1949-15172
SuDocs no.: M5.2:St6/949
MC#: 1956-616
SuDocs no.: Pr34.202:St6/954
MC#: 1956-617
SuDocs no.: Pr34.202:St6/955
MC#: 1956-20248
SuDocs no.: Pr34.210:956
MC#: 1957-8464
SuDocs no.: Pr34.210:956-2
MC#: 1958-1404
SuDocs no.: Pr34.210:957
MC#: 1958-7172
SuDocs no.: Pr34.210:957-2
MC#: 1959-3200
SuDocs no.: Pr34.709:958
MC#: 1959-8469
SuDocs no.: Pr34.709:958-2
MC#: 1959-15510
SuDocs no.: Pr34.709:959
MC#: 1960-9265
SuDocs no.: Pr34.709:959-2
MC#: 1960-18362
SuDocs no.: Pr34.709:960
MC#: 1961-8553
SuDocs no.: PrEx4.9:960
MC#: 1962-476
SuDocs no.: PrEx4.9:961
MC#: 1962-15509
SuDocs no.: PrEx4.9:961-2
MC#: 1963-6352
SuDocs no.: PrEx4.9:962
MC#: 1963-12083
SuDocs no.: PrEx4.9:962-2
MC#: 1964-2291
SuDocs no.: PrEx4.9:963
MC#: 1965-2106
SuDocs no.: PrEx4.9:964
MC#: 1966-1983
SuDocs no.: PrEx4.9:964-2
MC#: 1966-1984
SuDocs no.: PrEx4.9:965
MC#: 1966-10433
SuDocs no.: PrEx4.9:965-2
MC#: 1967-4725
SuDocs no.: PrEx4.9:966
MC#: 1967-9416
SuDocs no.: PrEx4.9:966-2
MC#: 1968-14048
SuDocs no.: PrEx4.9:967
MC#: 1969-592
SuDocs no.: PrEx4.9:968

1399

U.S. *Office of Emergency Preparedness.*
  Stockpile report to the Congress.
  Published semiannually in Washington.
  Supersedes the publication with the same title issued by the Office of Emergency Planning.
  Continued by a publication with the same title issued by the General Services Administration, Office of Preparedness.
I. Title.
HC110.S8U53a
MC#: 1969-10993 (LC card 51-60126 referred to in error)
SuDocs no.: PrEx4.9:968-2
MC#: 1970-14299
SuDocs no.: PrEx4.9:969
MC#: 1971-2354
SuDocs no.: PrEx4.9:969-2
MC#: 1971-2355
SuDocs no.: PrEx4.9:970
MC#: 1972-9619
SuDocs no.: PrEx4.9:970-2
MC#: 1972-12836
SuDocs no.: PrEx4.9:971
MC#: 1975-03914
SuDocs no.: PrEx4.9:971-2
MC#: 1975-03915
SuDocs no.: PrEx4.9:972
MC#: 1975-03916
SuDocs no.: PrEx4.9:972-2

1400

United States. General Services Administration. Office of Preparedness.
  Stockpile report to the Congress. Jan./June 1973-July/Dec. 1974.
  Washington, Office of Preparedness, General Services Administration.
  v. ill. 27 cm.
  Semiannual.
  Continues: Stockpile report to the Congress, ISSN 0500-1110, issued by: United States. Office of Emergency Preparedness.
  Continued by: Stockpile report to the Congress, ISSN 0500-1110, issued by: United States. Federal Preparedness Agency.
  Key title: Stockpile report to the Congress, ISSN 0500-1110.
  1. Strategic materials—United States—Periodicals. I. Title.
HC110.S8U53a   338.4   74-645008
                                                MARC-S
MC#: 1976-8096
SuDocs no.: GS1.22:973
MC#: 1976-8097
SuDocs no.: GS1.22:974, GS1.22:974-2

1401

United States. Federal Preparedness Agency.
  Stockpile report to the Congress. Jan./June 1975- Washington, General Services Administration, Federal Preparedness Agency.
  v. ill. 27 cm.
  Semiannual.
  Continues: Stockpile report to the Congress, ISSN 0500-1110, issued by: United States. General Services Administration. Office of Preparedness.
  Continued by: Stockpile report to the Congress, ISSN 0500-1110, issued by: United States. Federal Emergency Management Agency.
  Key title: Stockpile report to the Congress, ISSN 0500-1110.
  1. Strategic materials—United States—Periodicals. I. Title.
HC110.S8U53a   338.4   76-642098

MC#: 1976-8098
SuDocs no.: GS1.22:975-1
MC#: 1976-6625
SuDocs no.: GS1.22:975-2
MC#: 1978-21105
SuDocs no.: GS13.2:St6/976
MC#: 1979-6007
SuDocs no.: GS13.2:St6/976-2
MC#: 1982-10463
SuDocs no.: GS13.2:St6/979

1402

United States. Federal Emergency Management Agency.
　Stockpile report to the Congress. Washington, Federal
Emergency Management Agency.
　　v. ill. 27 cm.
　　Semiannual.
　　Continues: Stockpile report to the Congress, ISSN 0500-1110,
issued by: United States. Federal Preparedness Agency.
　　Key title: Stockpile report to the Congress, ISSN 0500-1110.
　　1. Strategic materials—United States—Periodicals. I. Title.
HC110.S8U53a　　　　355.2′4′0973　　　　80-641793
　　　　　　　　　　　　　　　　　　　　　　　　MARC-S

MC#: 1982-10296
SuDocs no.: FEM1.12:979-2, FEM1.12:980

STONE REPORT [Stone, Peter Anthony]
　　see under
　O'MAHONEY REPORTS [O'Mahoney, Joseph
Christopher]

STOREY REPORT [Storey, James R.]
　　　How public welfare benefits are distributed in low in-
　　　come areas.
　　see under
　GRIFFITHS REPORTS [Griffiths, Martha W.]
　　　Studies in public welfare, paper no. 6.

STOREY REPORT [Storey, James R.]
　　　Implications of income maintenance experiments.
　　see under
　GRIFFITHS REPORTS [Griffiths, Martha W.]
　　　Studies in public welfare, paper 5, part 3.

STOREY REPORT [Storey, James R.]
　　　Intergovernmental relationships.
　　see under
　GRIFFITHS REPORTS [Griffiths, Martha W.]
　　　Studies in public welfare, paper 5, part 2.

STOREY REPORT [Storey, James R.]
　　　Model income supplement bill.
　　see under
　GRIFFITHS REPORTS [Griffiths, Martha W.]
　　　Studies in public welfare, paper no. 15.

　　　Studies in public welfare, paper no. 16.

STOREY REPORT [Storey, James R.]
　　　New supplemental security income program.
　　see under
　GRIFFITHS REPORTS [Griffiths, Martha W.]
　　　Studies in public welfare, paper no. 10.

STOREY REPORT [Storey, James R.]
　　　Public income transfer programs.
　　see under
　GRIFFITHS REPORTS [Griffiths, Martha W.]
　　　Studies in public welfare, paper no. 1.

STOREY REPORT [Storey, James R.]
　　　Welfare in the 70's: a national study of benefits available
　　　in 100 local areas.
　　see under
　GRIFFITHS REPORTS [Griffiths, Martha W.]
　　　Studies in public welfare, paper no. 15.

STRATTON REPORTS [Stratton, Julius A.]
1403

United States. Commission on Marine Science, Engineering, and
Resources.
　Panel reports. [Washington, For sale by the Supt. of Docs.,
U.S. Govt. Print. Off., 1969]
　　3 v. illus., maps. 27 cm.
　　Commonly known as the Stratton report.
　　Bibliographical footnotes.
　　Contents: v. 1. Science and environment.—v. 2. Industry and
technology.—v. 3. Marine resources and legal-political ar-
rangements for their development.
　　1. Oceanography and state—United States. 2. Marine
resources—United States. I. Title. II. Title: Stratton report on
marine science, engineering, and resources.
GC58.A45　　　　333.9′1　　　　75-602045
　　　　　　　　　　　　　　　　　　　　　　　　MARC

MC#: 1969-10285
SuDocs no.: Pr36.8:M33/P19/v.1-3

1404

U.S. Commission on Marine Science, Engineering and
Resources.
　Our Nation and the sea: a plan for national action; report.
Washington, For sale by the Supt. of Docs., U.S. Govt. Print.
Off., 1969.
　　xi, 305 p. illus. 26 cm.
　　1. Oceanography and state—U.S. 2. Oceanographic
research—U.S. 3. Marine resources—U.S. I. Title.
GC58.A44　　　　551.4′6′00973　　　　77-600752
　　　　　　　　　　　　　　　　　　　　　　　　MARC

MC#: 1969-6164
SuDocs no.: Pr36.8:M33/Se1
MC#: 1969-5333
SuDocs no.: 91st Cong., 1st sess. H. Doc. 42

STRAUS REPORT [Straus, Michael W.]
1405

U.S. *Bureau of Reclamation.*
　A study of future power transmission for the West.
[Washington, 1952]
　　30 p. illus., col. maps. 23 x 29 cm.
　　Cover title.
　　Bibliography: p. 29-30.
　　1. Electric utilities—West, The. 2. Electric power distribution.
I. Title: Future power transmission for the West.
HD9685.U4A643 1952　　　　621.31　　　　53-60144
MC#: 1953-2831
SuDocs no.: I27.2:P87/2

STRAUS REPORT

1406

Straus, Ralph I

Expanding private investment for free world economic growth; a report and recommendations prepared pursuant to section 413 (c) of the Mutual security act of 1954, as amended. Washington, 1959.

    viii, 71, [1] p. diagrs., tables. 28 cm.

    On cover: A special report prepared at the request of the Dept. of State.

    Bibliography: p. 66-[72]

    1. Investments, American. I. U.S. Dept. of State.

HG4538.S78   332.67373   59-61439

MC#: 1960-1330

SuDocs no.: S1.2:In8/23

STRAUSS COMMISSION [Strauss, Lewis L.]

1407

U.S. *Commission on Incentive-Hazardous Duty and Special Pays.*

    Differential pays for the armed services of the United States; report. Washington, U.S. Govt. Print. Off., 1953.

    xiii, 182 p. illus. 24 cm.

    At head of title: Committee print. 83d Cong., 1st sess.

    "In three parts . . . part III, the classified supplement (not printed)"

    1. U.S. — Armed Forces — Pay, allowances, etc. I. Title.

UC74.A53   355.135   53-61011

MC#: 1953-9166

SuDocs no.: Y4.Ar5/3:P29/5

STRAUSS REPORT [Strauss, Lewis L.]

    see

DRAPER REPORT [Draper, William Henry]

        Coordination of procurement between the War and Navy Departments.

STRAYER REPORT

1408

Strayer, George Drayton, 1876-

    The report of a survey of the public schools of the District of Columbia, conducted under the auspices of the chairmen of the subcommittees on District of Columbia appropriations of the respective appropriations committees of the Senate and House of Representatives. Washington, U.S. Govt. Print. Off., 1949.

    xxi, 980 p. maps. 24 cm.

    1. Washington, D.C. — Public schools. 2. Education — Washington, D.C.

LA255.S75   379.753   49-46237*

MC#: 1949-9469

SuDocs no.: DC18.2:P96

STRÖLL REPORT [Ströll, Moritz]

    see under

ALDRICH COMMISSION [Aldrich, Nelson Wilmarth]

        Renewal of Reichsbank charter.

STRONG REPORT [Strong, Earl D.]

    see under

O'MAHONEY REPORTS [O'Mahoney, Joseph Christopher]

        Cover. Problems of small business.

STUART REPORT [Stuart, Charles Edward]

    see

BAKER REPORT [Baker, Jacob]

STUART REPORT [Stuart, Francis Lee]

    see

WALKER COMMISSION [Walker, John Grimes]

STURGIS REPORT [Sturgis, S. D.]

1409

International Passamaquoddy Engineering Board.

    Investigation of the international Passamaquoddy tidal power project; report to the International Joint Commission. [Washington] 1959.

    7 v. in 20 no. illus., maps (part fold., part col.) diagrs., tables. 28 cm.

    1. Passamaquoddy Bay. 2. Water-power electric plants — Maine. 3. Water-power electric plants — New Brunswick. I. Title.

TK1425.P3I5   621.312134   60-21416

Not located in Monthly Catalog

SUBIN REPORT

1410

Subin, Harry I

    Criminal justice in a metropolitan court; the processing of serious criminal cases in the District of Columbia Court of General Sessions, by Harry I. Subin. Washington, Office of Criminal Justice, U.S. Dept. of Justice, 1966.

    xv, 209 p. illus. 24 cm.

    1. Criminal procedure — District of Columbia. 2. District of Columbia. Court of General Sessions. I. Title.

                  343.0975303   67-60160

MC#: 1967-1348

SuDocs no.: J1.2:C86/7

SUITS REPORT [Suits, C. G.]

1411

Little (Arthur D.) inc.

    Basic research in the Navy; report to the Secretary of the Navy by the Naval Research Advisory Committee. [Cambridge, Mass., 1959]

    2 v. illus., diagrs. (part col.) 31 cm.

    Cover title.

    Bibliography: v. 2, p. 99-102.

    1. Research — U.S. I. U.S. Naval Research Advisory Committee. II. Title.

Q180.U5L55   507.2   59-64186 rev

Not located in Monthly Catalog

SURGEON GENERAL'S REPORT

1412

U.S. *Surgeon General's Advisory Committee on Smoking and Health.*

    Smoking and health; report of the advisory committee to the Surgeon General of the Public Health Service. [Washington] U.S. Dept. of Health, Education, and Welfare, Public Health Service; [for sale by the Superintendent of Documents, U.S. Govt. Print. Off., 1964]

    xvii, 387 p. illus. 24 cm. (Public Health Service publication no. 1103)

    Includes bibliographies.

    1. Tobacco — Psychological effect. 2. Smoking. I. Title. (Series: U.S. Public Health Service. Publication no. 1103)

RA1242.T6U5   64-60499

MC#: 1964-5664

SuDocs no.: FS2.2:Sm7/2

SURREY REPORT [Surrey, Stanley S.]

1413

U.S. *Treasury Dept.*

Tax reform studies and proposals. Joint publication [for the] Committee on Ways and Means of the U.S. House of Representatives and Committee on Finance of the U.S. Senate. Washington, U.S. Govt. Print. Off., 1969.

4 v. illus. 24 cm.

At head of title: 91st Congress, 1st session. Committee print.

Vol. 4, entitled The economic factors affecting the level of domestic petroleum reserves, was prepared by CONSAD Research Corporation for the Office of Tax Analysis of the Treasury Dept.

Includes bibliographies.

1. Taxation — U.S. — Law. I. U.S. Congress. House. Committee on Ways and Means. II. U.S. Congress. Senate. Committee on Finance. III. CONSAD Research Corporation. The economic factors affecting the level of domestic petroleum reserves. IV. Title. V. Title: The economic factors affecting the level of domestic petroleum reseves.

KF6335.A87   340   76-600717
                                  MARC

MC#: 1969-4006
SuDocs no.: Y4.W36:T19/42/pt. 1-3
MC#: 1969-12244
SuDocs no.: Y4.W36:T19/42/pt. 4

SUTERMEISTER REPORT [Sutermeister, Oscar]

see
DOUGLAS REPORTS [Douglas, Paul H.]
National Commission on Urban Problems.

Research report, no. 19.

SWAFFORD REPORT [Swafford, Rosa Lee]

see
BALL REPORT [Ball, Joseph Hurst]
Wartime record of strikes and lock-outs.

SWARTWOUT REPORT [Swartwout, Samuel]

1414

U.S. *Congress. House. Select Committee to Investigate the Defalcations of Samuel Swartwout and Others.*

Journal. Washington, Printed by W. O. Nils, 1839.

v, 476 p. 27 cm.

1. Swartwout, Samuel, 1783-1856. 2. U.S. Custom House, New York.

HJ6623.N5A5   58-51352

Checklist of United States Public Documents, 1789-1909, page 16
25th Cong., 3d sess. H. Rept. 313. In Serial no. 352, vol. 2

SYKES REPORT [Sykes, Ernest]

see under
ALDRICH COMMISSION [Aldrich, Nelson Wilmarth]
Withers. English banking system.

SYMONS REPORT

1415

Symons, James M

Water quality behavior in reservoirs [sic]; a compilation of published research papers. Compiled by James M. Symons. Cincinnati, U.S. Consumer Protection and Environmental Health Service, Bureau of Water Hygiene; for sale by the Supt. of Docs., U.S. Govt. Print. Off., Washington, 1969 [i.e. 1970]

xii, 616 p. illus. (part col.) 24 cm. (Public Health Service publication no. 1930)

"Contains all the technical papers prepared from data collected for the project "Influence of impoundments and controlled releases on water quality," from September 1962 through December 1966."

Includes bibliographies.

1. Reservoirs. 2. Water quality. I. Title. (Series: U.S. Public Health Service. Publication no. 1930)

TD395.S97   628'.13   76-607131
                                  MARC

MC#: 1970-8565
SuDocs no.: HE20.1102:W9

TABER REPORT [Taber, John]

see
COCHRAN REPORT [Cochran, John Joseph]

TAFT COMMISSION [Taft, William Howard]

see
CLEVELAND COMMISSION [Cleveland, Frederick Albert]

TAFT REPORT [Taft, Robert, Jr.]

1416

Welfare alternatives : a report with recommendations based upon the public welfare study of the Subcommittee on Fiscal Policy of the Joint Economic Committee, Congress of the United States, and related materials / by Robert Taft, Jr. — Washington : U.S. Govt. Print. Off., 1976.

vii, 39 p. ; 24 cm.

At head of title: 94 Congress, 2d session. Joint committee print.

Includes bibliographical references.

1. Public welfare — United States. 2. Income maintenance programs — United States. I. United States. Congress. Joint Economic Committee. Subcommittee on Fiscal Policy.

HV95.T34   362.5   76-602618
                                  MARC

MC#: 1976-8656
SuDocs no.: Y4.Ec7:W45/3

TAGGART REPORT [Taggart, Robert]

Labor market impacts of the private retirement system.

see under
GRIFFITHS REPORTS [Griffiths, Martha W.]
Studies in public welfare, paper no. 11.

TAITEL REPORT [Taitel, Martin]

see under
O'MAHONEY REPORTS [O'Mahoney, Joseph Christopher]

TARASOV REPORT [Tarasov, Helen]

see under
O'MAHONEY REPORTS [O'Mahoney, Joseph Christopher]

TAYLOR REPORT [Taylor, George W.]

1417

U.S. *Board of Inquiry to Report on a Labor Dispute Affecting the Steel Industry.*

Report to the President; the 1959 labor dispute in the steel industry, submitted by the Board of Inquiry under Executive orders 10843 and 10848. Washington, U.S. Govt. Print. Off., 1959.

iii, 40 p. 23 cm.

1. Steel Strike, 1959. 2. Iron and steel workers—U.S.
HD5325.I5 1959.U5   L59-58
MC#: 1959-17819
SuDocs no.: Pr34.2:St3

TAYLOR REPORT [Taylor, Hobart, Jr.]

1418

U.S. *President's Committee on Equal Employment Opportunity.*
Report. 1961/62-[Washington]

v. 26 cm.
First report covers period Apr. 7, 1961-Jan. 15, 1962.
Each vol. has also a distinctive title: 1961/62, The first nine
months.
1. Discrimination in employment—U.S.
HD4903.5.U58A38   62-61046
MC#: 1964-13382
SuDocs no.: Pr35.8:Em7/R29/963

For the first report: The first nine months, see TROUTMAN
REPORT [Troutman, Robert B., Jr.]

TAYLOR REPORT [Taylor, Telford]

1419

Germany *(Territory under Allied occupation, 1945-U.S. Zone) Office
of Military Government. Office, Chief of Counsel for War Crimes.*
Final report to the Secretary of the Army on Nuernberg war
crimes trials under Control Council Law no. 10, by Telford
Taylor, chief of counsel for war crimes. Washington [U.S. Govt.
Print. Off.] 1949 [i.e. 1950]

viii, 345 p. 23 cm.
Until the establishment of the Office, Chief of Counsel for War
Crimes, in Oct. 1946, the preparation for the trials was the task
of the Subsequent Proceedings Division of U.S. Chief of Counsel
for the Prosecution of Axis Criminality. This report covers the
entire period from Oct. 1945 to June 1949.
1. War crime trials—Nuremberg, 1946-1949. I. U.S. Chief of
Counsel for the Prosecution of Axis Criminality.
           341.4   50-60580
MC#: 1950-8484
SuDocs no.: D102.2:N93

TAYLOR REPORT [Taylor, Theodore W.]

1420

U.S. *Office of Territories.*
Management survey of the Government of the Trust Territory
of the Pacific Islands; a report of a Management Improvement
Survey to the Department of the Interior, containing recommendations for the future civilian administration of the Trust Territory, prepared by Theodore W. Taylor, director of the team
[and others. Washington, 1951]

2·v. maps (part fold.) 27 cm.
1. Pacific Islands (Ter.)—Pol. & govt. I. Taylor, Theodore W.
II. Title.
JQ6451.A58A5 1951   354.965   51-60445 rev
MC#: 1951-7444
SuDocs no.: I35.2:P11/3/v. 1,2

TAYLOR REPORT [Taylor, William L.]
     see
   HANNAH REPORT [Hannah, John A.]
      Racial isolation in the public schools.

TEAGUE REPORT [Teague, Olin E.]

1421

U.S. *Congress. House. Committee on Veterans' Affairs.*

Operations of Veterans' Administration hospital and medical
program. 1953Washington, U.S. Govt. Print. Off.

v. in illus., diagrs. 24 cm. biennial.
1. Hospitals, Military—U.S. 2. Veterans—Medical care—U.S.
3. U.S. Veterans Administration. I. Title.
UH473.A25   362.110973   58-61238 rev
MC#: 1955-7786 (LC card 55-60863 cancelled in favor of
58-61238)
SuDocs no.: Y4.V64/3:H79/5/955
1957-85th Cong., 1st sess. comm. Print No. 30
Not located in Monthly Catalog
1961-87th Cong., 1st sess. Comm. Print No. 1, Pt. 1,2
Not located in Monthly Catalog

For earlier report see ROGERS REPORT

THARP REPORT [Tharp, Norman R.]
     see
   PARKER REPORT [Parker, Charles]

THOMAS REPORT [Thomas, Elbert Duncan]
     see
   LaFOLLETTE REPORT [LaFollette, Robert
Marion]
           Violations of free speech and rights of labor. 75th Cong.,
           1st sess. S. Rept. 46.

THOMAS REPORT [Thomas, T. J.]
     see
   REEVES REPORT [Reeves, Floyd Wesley]

THORP REPORT [Thorp, Willard Long]
     see under
   O'MAHONEY REPORTS [O'Mahoney, Joseph
Christopher]

THREE MILE ISLAND
     see
   KEMENY COMMISSION REPORT [Kemeny,
John G.]
   ROGOVIN REPORT [Rogovin, Mitchell]

TILL REPORT [Till, Irene]
     see under
   O'MAHONEY REPORTS [O'Mahoney, Joseph
Christopher]
           Hamilton. Antitrust in action.

TINGLE REPORT [Tingle, George R.]
     see
   BOWER REPORT [Bower, Ward T.]

"TO FULFILL THESE RIGHTS"
     see
   HEINEMAN REPORT [Heineman, Ben W.]

TOBEY REPORT [Tobey, Charles William]

1422

U.S. *Congress. Joint Committee on Housing.*
Effects of taxation upon housing. Report of a subcommittee
of the Joint Committee on Housing, Congress of the United States,
pursuant to H. Con. Res. 104, 80th Congress. Washington, U.S.
Govt. Print. Off., 1948.

v, 29 p. 23 cm.
At head of title: 80th Cong., 2d sess. Joint committee print.

1. Housing—U.S. 2. Land—Taxation—U.S. 3. Income tax—U.S. 4. Taxation, Exemption from—U.S.
HD7293.A5 1948t   331.833   49-46827*
MC#: 1949-19482
SuDocs no.: Y4.H81/4:T19

TOLAN COMMITTEE [Tolan, John Harvey]

Reports on national defense migration are listed in chronological order.

1423

U.S. *Congress. House. Select committee investigating national defense migration.*

National defense migration. Committee print. Select committee investigating national defense migration, House of representatives, Seventy-seventh Congress, first session, pursuant to H. Res. 113, a resolution to inquire further into the interstate migration of citizens. Analysis of material bearing on the economic and social aspects of the case of Fred F. Edwards vs. the people of the state of California (no. 17, October term, 1941, Supreme court of the United States) From the record and reports of the Select committee to investigate the interstate migration of destitute citizens and the Select committee investigating national defense migration . . . Washington, U.S. Govt. print. off., 1941.

vii, 84 (*i.e.* 85) p. incl. tables, diagr. 23 cm.
Includes extra numbered page 26A.
John H. Tolan, chairman.
1. Migrant labor—U.S. 2. Migration, Internal—U.S. 3. Edwards, Fred F. I. Title.
HD5856.U5A5 1941b   331.796   46-40893
Not located in Monthly Catalog

1424

U.S. *Congress. House. Select committee investigating national defense migration.*

. . . National defense migration. Report of the Select committee investigating national defense migration, House of representatives, Seventy-seventh Congress, second session, pursuant to H. Res. 113, a resolution to inquire further into the interstate migration of citizens, emphasizing the present and potential consequences of the migration caused by the national defense program. Preliminary report and recommendations on problems of evacuation of citizens and aliens from military areas. March 19, 1942. Washington, U.S. Govt. print. off., 1942.

iv, 33 p. 23½ cm. ([U.S.] 77th Cong., 2d sess. House. Rept. 1911)
John H. Tolan, chairman.
1. World war, 1939-1945—U.S. 2. Japanese in the U.S. 3. Aliens—U.S. I. Tolan, John Harvey, 1877-1947. II. Title.
D769.8.A6A5 1942d   940.547273   42-37919
MC#: 1942-page 349
SuDocs no.: 77th Cong., 2d sess. H. Rept. 1911

1425

U.S. *Congress. House. Select committee investigating national defense migration.*

. . . National defense migration. First interim report of the Select committee investigating national defense migration, House of representatives, Seventy-seventh Congress, first session, pursuant to H. Res. 113, a resolution to inquire further into the interstate migration of citizens, emphasizing the present and potential consequences of the migration caused by the national defense program. October 21, 1941. Washington, U.S. Govt. print. off., 1941.

iii, 118 p. incl. tables. 23 cm. ([U.S.] 77th Cong., 1st sess. House. Rept. 1286)
Union calendar no. 453.

John H. Tolan, chairman.
1. Migration, Internal—U.S. 2. Labor and laboring classes—U.S. I. Tolan, John Harvey, 1877-1947. II. Title.
HD8072.A17 1941b   331.796   41-46315
MC#: 1941-page 1594
SuDocs no.: 77th Cong., 1st sess. H. Rept. 1286

1426

U.S. *Congress. House. Select committee investigating national defense migration.*

. . . National defense migration. First interim report of the Select committee investigating national defense migration, House of representatives, Seventy-seventh Congress, first session, pursuant to H. Res. 113, a resolution to inquire further into the interstate migration of citizens, emphasizing the present and potential consequences of the migration caused by the national defense program. October 1941 . . . Washington, U.S. Govt. print. off., 1941.

iii, 118 p. incl. tables. 23½ cm.
At head of title: "Committee print"
Submitted by Mr. Tolan.
1. Migration, Internal—U.S. 2. World war, 1939-1945—Economic aspects—U.S. I. Tolan, John Harvey, 1877-1947. II. Title.
HD5723.A5 1941f   331.796   45-45103
Not located in Monthly Catalog

1427

U.S. *Congress. House. Select committee investigating national defense migration.*

. . . National defense migration. Second interim report of the Select committee investigating national defense migration, House of representatives, Seventy-seventh Congress, first session, pursuant to H. Res. 113, a resolution to inquire further into the interstate migration of citizens, emphasizing the present and potential consequences of the migration caused by the national defense program. Recommendations of full utilization of America's industrial capacity and labor supply in the war effort. December 19, 1941. Washington, U.S. Govt. print. off., 1941.

iii, 149 p. incl. tables. 23 cm. ([U.S.] 77th Cong., 1st sess. House. Rept. 1553)
John H. Tolan, chairman.
1. Migration, Internal—U.S. 2. Labor and laboring classes—U.S.—1914- 3. World war, 1939-1945—Economic aspects—U.S. 4. Unemployed—U.S. I. Tolan, John Harvey, 1877-1947. II. Title.
HD5723.A5 1941   331.796   41-46415
MC#: Dec. 1941-page 1740
SuDocs no.: 77th Cong., 1st sess. H. Rept. 1553

1428

U.S. *Congress. House. Select committee investigating national defense migration.*

. . . National defense migration. Third interim report of the Select committee investigating national defense migration, House of representatives, Seventy-seventh Congress, second session, pursuant to H. Res. 113, a resolution to inquire further into the interstate migration of citizens, emphasizing the present and potential consequences of the migration caused by the national defense program. On the need for a single procurement agency to effect all-out war production and achieve full use of labor supply. March 9, 1942. Washington, U.S. Govt. print. off., 1942.

iii, 109, vi p. incl. tables. 23 cm. ([U.S.] 77th Cong., 2d sess. House. Rept. 1879)
John H. Tolan, chairman.

1. Labor and laboring classes—U.S.—1914- 2. U.S.—Indus. 3. World war, 1939-1945—Economic aspects—U.S. 4. Defense contracts—U.S. I. Tolan, John Harvey, 1877-1947. II. Title.
HD5723.A5 1942b   331.796   42-37920
MC#: 1942-page 349
SuDocs no.: 77th Cong., 2d sess. H. Rept. 1879

1429

U.S. *Congress. House. Select committee investigating national defense migration.*
. . . National defense migration. Fourth interim report of the Select committee investigating national defense migration, House of representatives, Seventy-seventh Congress, second session pursuant to H. Res. 113, a resolution to inquire further into the interstate migration of citizens, emphasizing the present and potential consequences of the migration caused by the national defense program. Findings and recommendations on evacuation of enemy aliens and others from prohibited military zones. May 1942. Washington, U.S. Govt. print. off., 1942.
vi, 362 p. incl. illus. (maps) tables, forms. 23 cm. ([U.S.] 77th Cong., 2d sess. House. Rept. 2124)
John H. Tolan, chairman.
1. Aliens—U.S. 2. Japanese in the U.S. 3. World War, 1939-1945—U.S. I. Title.
D769.8.A6A5 1942h   940.547273   42-38159
MC#: 1942-page 636
SuDocs no.: 77th Cong., 2d sess. H. Rept. 2124

1430

U.S. *Congress. House. Select committee investigating national defense migration.*
. . . National defense migration. Fifth interim report of the Select committee investigating national defense migration, House of representatives, Seventy-seventh Congress, second session, pursuant to H. Res. 113, a resolution to inquire further into the interstate migration of citizens, emphasizing the present and potential consequences of the migration caused by the national defense program. Recommendations on the mobilization of manpower for the all-out war effort. August 10, 1942. Washington, U.S. Govt. print. off., 1942.
iii, 38 p. 23½ cm. ([U.S.] 77th Cong., 2d sess. House. Rept. 2396)
John H. Tolan, chairman.
1. Labor supply—U.S. 2. World war, 1939-1945—Manpower—U.S. 3. Migration, Internal—U.S. I. Title.
HD5723.A5 1942bd   331.796   42-38533
MC#: 1942-page 1024
SuDocs no.: 77th Cong., 2d sess. H. Rept. 2396

1431

U.S. *Congress. House. Select committee investigating national defense migration.*
. . . National defense migration. Sixth interim report of the Select committee investigating national defense migration, House of representatives, Seventy-seventh Congress, second session, pursuant to H. Res. 113, a resolution to inquire further into the interstate migration of citizens, emphasizing the present and potential consequences of the migration caused by the national defense program. Changes needed for effective mobilization of manpower. October 20, 1942. Washington, U.S. Govt. print. off., 1942.
iii, 43 p. 23 cm. ([U.S.] 77th Cong., 2d sess. House. Rept. 2589)
John H. Tolan, chairman.
1. Labor and laboring classes—U.S.—1914- 2. U.S.—Economic policy. 3. World war, 1939-1945—Economic aspects—U.S. I. Tolan, John Harvey, 1877-1947. II. Title.

HD5723.A5 1942c   331.796   42-38786
MC#: 1942-page 1251
SuDocs no.: 77th Cong., 2d sess. H. Rept. 2589

1432

U.S. *Congress. House. Select committee investigating national defense migration.*
. . . National defense migration. Final report of the Select committee investigating national defense migration, House of representatives, Seventy-seventh Congress, second session, pursuant to H. Res. 113, a resolution to inquire further into the interstate migration of citizens, emphasizing the present and potential consequences of the migration caused by the national defense program. January 1943. Washington, U.S. Govt. print. off., 1943.
ii, 24 p. 23 cm. ([U.S.] 78th Cong., 1st sess. House. Rept. 3)
Submitted by Mr. Tolan from the Select committee investigating national defense migration.
"Additional views of Carl T. Curtis": p. 21.
"Additional comments of George H. Bender": p. 22-24.
1. Labor supply—U.S. 2. World war, 1939-1945—Manpower—U.S. I. Tolan, John Harvey, 1877-1947. II. Curtis, Carl Thomas, 1905- III. Bender, George H., 1896- IV. Title.
HD5723.A55 1943   331.796   43-51664
MC#: 1943-page 160
SuDocs no.: 78th Cong., 1st sess. H. Rept. 3

TOWNSEND REPORT [Townsend, Alair A.]
see under
GRIFFITHS REPORTS [Griffiths, Martha W.]
Studies in public welfare, paper no. 6.

Studies in public welfare, paper no. 14.

Studies in public welfare, paper no. 16.

TRAIN REPORT [Train, Russell E.]
1433

United States. Council on Environmental Quality.
Environmental quality. 1st-1970-
[Washington, For sale by the Supt. of Docs, U.S. Govt. Print. Off.]
v. ill. 24 cm.
Annual.
"The . . . annual report of the Council on Environmental Quality."
Supt. of Docs. no.: PrEx14.1:
Key title: Environmental quality (Washington), ISSN 0095-2044.
1. Environmental protection—United States—Periodicals. I. Title. II. Key title.
TD169.U53a   301.31   75-608885
                                      MARC-S
MC#: 1970-13772
    1972-586 (1971 Annual Report)
    1972-12788 (1972 Annual Report)
    1973-32159 (1973 Annual Report)
    1975-13650 (1974 Annual Report)
    1976-1026 (1975 Annual Report)
    1977-11822 (1976 Annual Report)
    1978-11806 (1977 Annual Report)
    1979-8392 (1978 Annual Report)
    1980-19686 (1979 Annual Report)
    1981-14311 (1980 Annual Report)
    1982-24121, 26591 (1981 Annual Report)
SuDocs no.: PrEx14.1:(year)

1434

United States. Council on Environmental Quality.

    Integrated pest management. [Washington, For sale by the Supt. of Docs., U.S. Govt. Print. Off.] 1972.

    x, 41 p. illus. 27 cm.

    Bibliography: p. 37-39.

    1. Pest control—United States. 2. Pesticides—Environmental aspects—United States. I. Title.

SB950.2.A1A53   632′.9′0973   73-600796
                                                 MARC

MC#: 1973-21390
SuDocs no.: PrEx14.2:P43

TRAPNELL REPORT [Trapnell, W. C.]

    see

  ILSLEY REPORT [Ilsley, Ralph]

TROUTMAN REPORT [Troutman, Robert B., Jr.]

1435

U.S. *President's Committee on Equal Employment Opportunity.*

    Report. 1961/62- [Washington]

    v. 26 cm.

    First report covers period Apr. 7, 1961-Jan. 15, 1962.

    Each vol. has also a distinctive title: 1961/62, The first nine months.

    1. Discrimination in employment—U.S.

HD4903.5.U58A38   62-61046

MC#: 1962-10591
SuDocs no.: Pr35.8:Em7/R29/961-62

For the second report: Report to the President by the President's Committee on Equal Employment Opportunity, see TAYLOR REPORT [Taylor, Hobart, Jr.]

TRUE REPORT

1436

True, Alfred Charles, 1853-1929.

    . . . A history of agricultural experimentation and research in the United States 1607-1925 including a history of the United States Department of agriculture. By Alfred Charles True, late specialist in States relations work, United States Department of agriculture . . . Washington, U.S. Govt. print. off., 1937.

    vi, 321 p. front., illus., ports. 23 cm. (U.S. Dept. of agriculture. Miscellaneous publication no. 251)

    "This is the third and final monograph in a series intended to give a comprehensive summary of the history of agricultural education, extension, and research in the United States. Agricultural instruction in schools and colleges . . . was dealt with in the monograph published in 1929 as Miscellaneous publication no. 36 of the United States Department of agriculture. The history of agricultural extension work was issued by this Department in 1928 as Miscellaneous publication no. 15."—Preface, p. iii.

    Bibliography: p. 278-295.

    1. Agriculture—Experimentation[—Hist.] 2. Agriculture[—Research]—Hist. 3. (Agriculture—U.S.) 4. U.S. Dept. of agriculture. I. Title.

S533.T8377   Agr37-469

- - - - - Copy 2.

S21.A46 no. 251

MC#: 1937-page 837
SuDocs no.: A1.38:251

TRUNDLE REPORT [Trundle, H. H.]

    see

  WALKER COMMISSION [Walker, John Grimes]

TUDOR REPORT [Tudor, W. Wallace]

1437

U.S. *President's Panel on Mental Retardation.*

    Report of the mission to the Netherlands. W. Wallace Tudor, chairman [and others. Washington] U.S. Dept. of Health, Education, and Welfare, Public Health Service, 1962 [i.e. 1963]

    vi, 97 p. illus., map. 26 cm.

    1. Mentally handicapped—Netherlands. I. Tudor, W. Wallace. II. Title.

HV3008.N4U58   63-65290

MC#: 1963-20082
SuDocs no.: Pr35.8:M52/N38

TUKEY REPORT [Tukey, John W.]

1438

U.S. *President's Science Advisory Committee. Environmental Pollution Panel.*

    Restoring the quality of our environment. Report. [Washington] The White House, 1965.

    xii, 317 p. maps. 24 cm.

    Bibliography: p. 131-133.

    1. Pollution—U.S. I. Title.

TD180.U55   66-60170

MC#: 1966-1399
SuDocs no.: Pr35.8:Sci2/En8

UPTON REPORTS

1439

Upton, Emory, 1839-1881.

    The military policy of the United States, by Bvt. Maj. Gen. Emory Upton . . . 4th impression. Washington, Govt. print. off., 1917.

    1 p. l., xxiii, 495 p. fold. map. 23 cm.

    War dept. doc. no. 290.

    Edited by Joseph P. Sanger, assisted by William D. Beach and Charles D. Rhodes, of the Military information division of the General staff, from an unpublished manuscript to which General Upton had devoted the last years of his life.

    1. U.S.—History, Military. 2. U.S. Army. I. Sanger, Joseph Prentiss, 1840-1926. II. Beach, William Dorrance, 1856- III. Rhodes, Charles Dudley, 1865- 1948. IV. Title.

UA23.U75 1917   War 18-9

MC#: Jan. 1918-page 392
SuDocs no.: W1.2:M59/3-917

1440

Upton, Emory, 1839-1881.

    . . . The military policy of the United States, by Bvt. Maj. Gen. Emory Upton . . . 4th impression. Washington, Govt. print. off., 1916.

    1 p. l., xxiii, 495 p. 2 fold. maps. 23 cm. (64th Cong., 1st sess. Senate. Doc. no. 379)

    Edited by Joseph P. Sanger, assisted by William D. Beach and Charles D. Rhodes, of the Military information division of the General staff, from an unpublished manuscript to which General Upton had devoted the last years of his life.

    1. U.S.—History, Military. 2. U.S.—Army. I. Sanger, Joseph Prentiss, 1840-1926. II. Beach, William Dorrance, 1856- III. Rhodes, Charles Dudley, 1865-1948. IV. Title.

E181.U7   War 16-142

UA23.U75

MC#: May 1916-page 710
SuDocs no.: 64th Cong., 1st sess. S. Doc. 379

USED CAR STUDY
1441

U.S. *Dept. of Transportation.*
Safety for motor vehicles in use. Report to the Congress of the United States pursuant to Public law 89-563. Washington, U.S. Govt. Print. Off., 1968.

vii, 107 p. illus. 24 cm. (90th Congress. 2d session. Senate. Document no. 103)
Bibliography: p. 99-103.
1. Motor vehicles—Standard—Law and legislation—U.S. I. U.S. Congress. II. Title. (Series: U.S. 90th Congress, 2d session, 1968. Senate. Document no. 103)
KF2212.A85   629.282′0973   68-67038
                                       MARC
MC#: 1968-15308
SuDocs no.: 90th Cong., 2d sess. S. Doc. 103

VALACHI REPORT [Valachi, Joseph]
1442

U.S. *Congress. Senate. Committee on Government Operations. Permanent Subcommittee on Investigations.*
Organized crime and illicit traffic in narcotics; report, together with additional combined views and individual views. Washington, U.S. Govt. Print. Off., 1965.

iv, 127 p. maps (part fold.) 24 cm. (89th Cong., 1st sess. Senate Report no. 72)
1. Narcotic habit—U.S. I. Title. (Series: U.S. 89th Cong., 1st sess., 1965. Senate. Report no. 72)
HV5825.A5254   65-60827
MC#: 1965-7511
SuDocs no.: 89th Cong., 1st sess. S. Rept. 72

VALLEY REPORT [Valley, Sharon L.]
     see
MRAK REPORT [Mrak, Emil M.]

VAN HECKE REPORT [Van Hecke, Maurice T.]
1443

U.S. *President's Commission on Migratory Labor.*
Migratory labor in American agriculture; report. [Washington, U.S. Govt. Print. Off.] 1951.

xii, 188 p. illus. 23 cm.
1. Agricultural laborers—U.S. 2. Migrant labor—U.S. 3. Mexicans in the U.S. I. Title.
HD1525.A54 1951   331.763   51-60571
MC#: 1951-8726
SuDocs no.: Pr33.14:Ag8

VAN KLEECK REPORT [Van Kleeck, May]
     see
WICKERSHAM COMMISSION [Wickersham, George Woodward]
     Report on the causes of crime, no. 13.

VAN WATERS REPORT [Van Waters, Miriam]
     see
WICKERSHAM COMMISSION [Wickersham, George Woodward]
     Report on child offender, no. 6.

VANCE REPORT [Vance, Harold S.]
1444

U.S. *Office of Defense Mobilization. Advisory Committee on Production Equipment.*
Production capacity: a military reserve; a report to the Director of Defense Mobilization. [Washington, U.S. Govt. Print. Off.] 1953.

iv, 31 p. illus. 23 cm.
1. Industrial mobilization—U.S. I. Title.
UA18.U5A573 1953   355.26   53-60228
MC#: 1953-2432
SuDocs no.: Pr33.1003:P94/3

VANDERBILT REPORT [Vanderbilt, Arthur T.]
1445

U.S. *War Dept. Advisory Committee on Military Justice.*
Report. Washington, D.C., 1946.

15 p. 26 cm.
1. Military law—U.S. 2. Courts-martial and courts of inquiry—U.S. I. Title: Vanderbilt report.
[KM8500.U588R4 1946]
Dept. of the Army Library
Not located in Monthly Catalog

VANECH REPORT [Vanech, A. Devitt]
1446

U.S. *President's temporary commission on employee loyalty.*
The report of the President's temporary commission on employee loyalty. [Washington, 1947]

1 p. 1., 39 numb. 1. incl. tables. 27 cm.
1. Civil service—U.S. 2. Loyalty.
JK730.A4 1947   351.1   47-32494
MC#: 1948-4414
SuDocs no.: Pr33.2:Em7

VIDAL REPORT [Vidal, Emmanuel]
     see under
ALDRICH COMMISSION [Aldrich, Nelson Wilmarth]

VIVIAN REPORT [Vivian, Weston E.]
1447

United States. Committee on Administration of Training Programs.
Report. Washington, 1968.

78 p. 26 cm.
Commonly known as the Vivian report.
1. Occupational training—United States. I. Title: Vivian report on administration of training programs.
HD5723.A5137 1968   353.008′3   68-61651
                                       MARC
MC#: 1968-10958
SuDocs no.: FS1.2:Ad6

VOLLMER REPORT [Vollmer, August]
1448

U.S. *Wickersham Commission.*
Report on police. Washington, U.S. Govt. Print. Off., 1931.
iii, 140 p. illus. 24 cm. [Its Publications, no. 14]
At head of title: National Commission on Law Observance and Enforcement.
Issued also as no. 14 in the series of Reports, v. 4.

"Police conditions in the United States; a report to the National Commission on Law Observance and Enforcement by David G. Monroe and Earle W. Garrett . . . under the direction of August Vollmer": p. [11]-140.

1. Police — U.S. I. Monroe, David Geeting. II. Garrett, Earle W. III. Vollmer, August, 1876-1955. IV. Title.

351.740973   31-27255

- - - - - Copy 2.

HV7568.A5 1930

MC#: Aug. 1931-page 111

SuDocs no.: Y3.N21/7:5/14

See also WICKERSHAM COMMISSION [Wickersham, George Woodward]

VON DER LINDE REPORT [Von der Linde, Gert]
see
MELTZER REPORT [Meltzer, Allan H.]

VOORHEES REPORTS [Voorhees, Tracy S.]
1449

U.S. *Dept. of the Army.*

Decartelization in Germany. Study by Tracy J. Voorhees of the report by the Committee of Decartelization in Germany. Washington, 1949.

14 p. 28 cm.

Cover memorandum for the press by Secretary of Army Gray attached.

1. Germany — Industries. 2. Germany — Hist. — Allied occupation — 1945- I. Voorhees, Tracy J. II. Title.

[DD257.2.U58]

Dept. of the Army Library

Not located in Monthly Catalog

1450

Voorhees, Tracy S

Informe para el Presidente de los Estados Unidos sobre el problema de los refugiados cubanos. [Washington, U.S. Govt. Print. Off., 1961]

21 p. 24 cm.

Issued also in English.

1. Refugees, Cuban.

HV640.5.C9V618   61-60510

MC#: 1961-6489

SuDocs no.: Pr34.2:C891

1451

Voorhees, Tracy S

Report to the President of the United States on the Cuban refugee problem. Washington, U.S. Govt. Print. Off., 1961.

iii, 15 p. 24 cm.

1. Refugees, Cuban. I. Title: Cuban refugee problem.

HV640.5.C9V6   61-60509

MC#: 1961-6489

SuDocs no.: Pr34.2:C891

VOORHIS REPORT [Voorhis, Horace Jeremiah]
1452

U.S. *Congress. House. Special committee on un-American activities (1938-1944)*

. . . Special report on subversive activities aimed at destroying our representative form of government . . . Report. "Pursuant to H. Res. 420, 77th Cong" . . . [Washington, U.S. Govt. print. off., 1943]

16 p. 23½ cm. ([U.S.] 77th Cong., 2d sess. House. Rept. 2748)

Caption title.

Submitted by Mr. Dies, chairman, from the Special committee on un-American activities.

"Minority views" (p. 14-16) signed: Jerry Voorhis.

1. Subversive activities — U.S. 2. Communism — U.S. — 1917- 3. Fascism — U.S. I. Dies, Martin, 1901- II. Voorhis, Horace Jeremiah, 1901- III. Title: Subversive activities aimed at destroying our representative form of government.

E743.5.U547   335   43-51591

MC#: 1943-page 161

SuDocs no.: 77th Cong., 2d sess. H. Rept. 2748

See also STARNES REPORT [Starnes, Joe]

Special report on subversive activities.

VREELAND REPORTS [Vreeland, Edward Butterfield]
see under
ALDRICH COMMISSION [Aldrich, Nelson Wilmarth]

Interview on the banking and currency systems of Canada.

Vreeland. Plan of the National monetary commission.

WADE REPORTS [Wade, Benjamin Franklin]
1453

U.S. *Congress. Joint committee on the conduct of the war.*

Report of the Joint committee on the conduct of the war, at the second session Thirty-eighth Congress . . . Washington, Govt. print. off., 1865.

3 v. 23 cm. [38th Cong., 2d sess. Senate doc. no. 142]

B. F. Wade, chairman.

A supplemental report was published in 1866, in 2 vols.

Each volume includes reports of the committee, testimony and documentary appendices.

Contents. — [v. 1] Journal of the committee, Jan. 20, 1864-May 22, 1865. Army of the Potomac: General Hooker. General Meade, Battle of Petersburg. — [v. 2] Red River expedition [with Minority report, by D. W. Gooch] Fort Fisher expedition. Heavy ordnance. — [v. 3] Sherman-Johnston. Light-draught monitors. Massacre of Cheyenne Indians. Ice contracts. Rosecrans's campaigns. Miscellaneous.

1. U.S. — Hist. — Civil war — Campaigns and battles. 2. U.S. — Hist. — Civil war — Regimental histories — Army of the Potomac. 3. Chancellorville, Battle of 1863. 4. Gettysburg, Battle of, 1863. 5. Petersburg Crater, Battle of 1864. 6. Fisher, Fort — Expeditions, 1864-1865. 7. U.S. — Army — Ordnance and ordnance stores. 8. U.S. — Hist. — Civil war — Naval operations. 9. Cheyenne Indians — Wars, 1864. 10. Rosecrans, William Starke, 1819-1898. I. Wade, Benjamin Franklin, 1800-1878. II. Gooch, Daniel Wheelwright, 1820-1891.

E470.U585   2-17197

Checklist of United States Public Documents, 1789-1909-page 1549-50

SuDocs no.: Y4.C75:R29 4-6

Checklist of United States Public Documents, 1789-1909, page 42

38th Cong., 2d sess. S. Rept. 142. In Serial nos. 1212-1214, vols. 2-4

1454

U.S. *Congress. Joint committee on the conduct of the war.*

Supplemental report of the Joint committee on the conduct of the war, in two volumes. Supplemental to Senate report no. 142, 38th Congress, 2d session . . . Washington, Govt. print. off., 1866.

2 v. illus., fold. maps. 23 cm.

These volumes, issued without document numbers, form v. 2-3 of Senate reports, 39th Cong., 1st sess. (nos. 1241-1242 of the Congressional series).

Reports of W. T. Sherman, George H. Thomas, John Pope, J. G. Foster, A. Pleasanton, E. A. Hitchcock, P. H. Sheridan, James B. Richetts; and Communication and memorial of Norman Wiard [upon the subject of great guns]

E470.U587   3-28502

Checklist of United States Public Documents, 1789-1909 — page 1550

SuDocs no.: Y4.C75:Su7 1-2

Checklist of United States Public Documents, 1789-1909, page 43 39th Cong., 1st sess. S. Rept. (unnumbered). In Serial nos. 1241-1242, vol. [2]-[3]

WADSWORTH REPORT [Wadsworth, James W.]

1455

U.S. *National Security Training Commission.*

Report. 1st- Oct. 1951- [Washington, U.S. Govt. Print. Off.] v. illus. 24 cm.

1. Military service, Compulsory — U.S. 2. U.S. National Security Training Corps.

UB353.A33   355.22   51-61682

MC#: 1951-20204 (1st report)
SuDocs no.: Y3.N21/19:1/1
MC#: 1952-2259 (1st report)
SuDocs no.: 82d Cong., 2d sess. H. Doc. 315
MC#: 1956-19306 (Annual report)
SuDocs no.: Y3.N21/19:1/956
MC#: 1957-11780 (Final report)
SuDocs no.: Y3.N21/19:1/957

WALFORD REPORTS [Walford, Lionel Albert]

1456

U.S. *Fish and wildlife service.*

. . . Fishery resources of the United States. Letter of the secretary of the interior, transmitting, pursuant to law, a report on a survey of the fishery resources of the United States and its possessions . . . Washington, U.S. Govt. print. off., 1945.

2 p. 1., ii-iv, 135 p., 1 1. illus. (incl. maps) diagrs. 30 cm. ([U.S.] 79th Cong., 1st sess. Senate. Doc. 51)

Text on p. [2] of cover.

Prepared by the Fish and wildlife service of the Dept. of the interior. cf. Pref.

Issued also without congressional series numbering.

1. Fisheries — U.S. I. Title.

SH11.A5 1945a   338.372   45-36536

MC#: 1945-page 964
SuDocs no.: 79th Cong., 1st sess. S. Doc. 51

1457

U.S. *Fish and wildlife service.*

Fishery resources of the United States of America, by the Fish and wildlife service, United States Department of the interior. Edited by Lionel A. Walford. Designed under the supervision of the Bureau of graphics, Office of war information. [Washington, 1945]

2 p. 1., ii-iv, 135 p. illus. (incl. maps) diagrs. 31 x 24½ cm. Issued also as Senate doc. 51, 79th Cong., 1st sess.

1. Fisheries — U.S. I. Walford, Lionel Albert, 1905- ed. II. Title. III. Title: Walford report on fishery resources of the United States.

SH11.A5 1945   338.372   45-35739

MC#: 1945-page 388
SuDocs no.: I49.2:F53/5/945

WALKER COMMISSION [Walker, John Grimes]

1458

U.S. *Nicaragua canal commission, 1897-1899.*

Report of the Nicaragua canal commission, 1897-1899. Rear Admiral John G. Walker, U.S.N., president; Colonel Peter C. Hains, U.S.A., Corps of engineers; Professor Lewis M. Haupt, civil engineer. With an atlas. Baltimore, The Friedenwald company, 1899.

xii, 502 p. illus., plates, maps, plans, tables. *and* atlas. 29 x 23 cm.

Atlas in portfolio: pl., 7 maps on 32 fold. sheets, 6 profiles on 8 fold. sheets, tab.

The commission was constituted by act of Congress, June 4, 1897. This, its complete report, dated May 9, 1899, is published, in a limited edition by the Isthmian canal commission, constituted by act of Congress, March 3, 1899. *cf.* Catalogue, U.S. pub. doc. 1900.

Contents. — Report of the Nicaragua canal commission. — App. I. Report of E. S. Wheeler, chief engineer. — App. II. Report on the geology and physiography of the Nicaragua canal route by Charles Willard Hayes. — App. III. Report of hydrographic investigations in Nicaragua made for the Nicaragua canal commission by Arthur P. Davis. — App. IV. Report on the western division by J. W. G. Walker. — App. V. Report on San Juan River and Lake Nicaragua by Francis Lee Stuart. — App. VI. Report of H. H. Trundle. — App. VII. Report of Boyde Ehle. — App. VIII. Report of S. S. Evans. — App. IX. Report on the precise level line from the Caribbean Sea to the Pacific Ocean by Stephen Harris. — App. X. Report of Andrew Onderdonk. — App. XI. Report of L. Hankins.

1. Nicaragua canal. I. Walker, John Grimes, 1835-1907. II. Hains, Peter Conover, 1840- III. Haupt, Lewis Muhlenberg, 1844- IV. Davis, Arthur Powell, 1861- V. Ehle, Boyd. VI. Evans, S. S. VII. Hankins, L. VIII. Harris, Stephen. IX. Hayes, Charles Willard, 1859- X. Onderdonk, Andrew. XI. Stuart, Francis Lee. XII. Trundle, H. H. XIII. Wheeler, Ebenezer Smith, 1839- XIV. U.S. Isthmian canal commission, 1899- 1902, pub.

                                                    1-27239* Cancel

TC784.U58 1899

MC#: 1900-page 335
SuDocs no.: Y3.N51/R29/1

1459

U.S. *Isthmian canal commission, 1899-1902.*

. . . Message from the President of the United States, transmitting a preliminary report of the Isthmian canal commission. December 4, 1900. — Read, referred to the Committee on interoceanic canals, and ordered to be printed. Washington, Govt. print. off., 1900.

44 p. 23 cm. (56th Cong., 2d sess. Senate. Doc. no. 5)

John G. Walker, president of commission.

1. Panama canal. 2. Nicaragua canal. I. Walker, John Grimes, 1835-1907.

TC773.U5 1900   2-24223

MC#: 1900-page 604
SuDocs no.: Y3.Is7:P91

1460

U.S. *Isthmian canal commission, 1899-1902.*

. . . Report of the Isthmian canal commission, 1899-1901. Rear-Admiral John G. Walker, United States Navy, president . . . Washington, Govt. print. off., 1904.

688 p. plates, diagrs. (part fold.) and portfolio of 86 fold. pl., maps, and profiles. 30 cm. (58th Cong., 2d sess. Senate. Doc. 222)

An incomplete edition of this report was published (in 2 parts) 1901-02, as Senate doc. 54, 57th Cong., 1st sess.

" . . . Supplementary report of Isthmian canal commission [upon the proposition of the New Panama canal company to sell and dispose of all its rights, property, and unfinished work to the United States] "Senate doc. no. 123, 57th Cong., 1st sess.": p. 673-681. This report was published also separately in 1902.

Appendixes: A. Study of locks for Nicaragua and Panama routes, by S. H. Woodward. — B. Historical notes relative to the Universal interoceanic canal company, 1880-1894, prior to the organization of the new company. — C. List of documents furnished to the commission by the New Panama canal company. — D. Report on the hydrography of the Panama canal route, by A. P. Davis. — E. Waste weir dimensions and discharges for Lake Bohio. — F. Description of alternative location for canal between Gatun and Bohio. — G. Discussion of the time required for transit through an isthmian canal by the two routes. — H. Discharge of the canalized San Juan river. — I. Report of hydrographic investigations in Nicaragua, by A. P. Davis. — J. Surveys of the upper San Juan to the Indio river, by A. B. Nichols. — K. Treaty between Nicaragua and the United States, 1867, Dickinson-Ayon. — L. Treaty negotiated between the United States and Nicaragua December, 1884, Frelinghuysen-Savala. — M. Treaty between Great Britain and Nicaragua, relative to the Mosquito Indians and the rights and claims of British subjects, Feb. 11, 1860. — N. Treaty between Nicaragua and Great Britain, Jan. 28, 1860. — O. Treaty between Nicaragua and France, April 11, 1859. — P. List of treaties made, or negotiated by Nicaragua with other countries. — Q. Treaty between the United States and Great Britain, April 19, 1850, Clayton-Bulwer. — R. Contract between Nicaragua and the Nicaragua canal association. — S. Act of Congress incorporating the Maritime canal company of Nicaragua. — T. Contract between Nicaragua and Eyre and Cragin, representing the Interoceanic canal company. — U. Contract between Nicaragua and the Atlas steamship company. — V. Treaty between the United States and Costa Rica, July 1851. — W. Treaty between Spain and Costa Rica, May, 1850. — X. Treaty between Costa Rica and Nicaragua, June, 1869. — Y. List of treaties made by Costa Rica with other countries. — Z. Contract between Costa Rica and the Nicaragua canal association. — AA. Protocol of agreement between the United States and Costa Rica, December, 1900. — BB. Treaty between the United States and New Granada, concluded December, 1846. — CC. Treaties between France and New Granada, 1856, and France and Colombia, 1892. — DD. Treaty between Spain and Colombia, 1881. — EE. List of treaties made by New Granada, or Colombia, with other countries. — FF. Amended contract between Colombia and the Panama railroad company. — GG. Contract between Colombia and the Interoceanic canal association, March 20, 1878. (Wyse concession) — HH. Additional contract modifying that of March 20, 1878, Dec. 10, 1890. — II. Contract granting extension to the Panama canal company in liquidation, April 4, 1893. — JJ. Contract granting further extension of time to the New Panama canal company, April 25, 1900. — KK. Memorandum showing legal status of the New Panama canal company, with laws, decrees of court, and charter. — LL. Treaty negotiated by Hise between the United States and Nicaragua, June 1849. — MM. Contract between Nicaragua and the American Atlantic and Pacific ship canal company, Aug. 27, 1849. — NN. Report on industrial and commercial value of canal by Prof. Emory R. Johnson. — Supplementary report.

1. Panama canal. 2. Nicaragua canal. 3. Darien canal. 4. Panama — Descr. & trav. — Maps. 5. Central America — Descr. & trav. — Maps. 6. Compagnie nouvelle du canal de Panama. I. Walker, John Grimes, 1835-1907.

TC773.U5 1904   5-32741
MC#: 1906-pages 299-300
SuDocs no.: Y3.Is7:R29/1
MC#: 1905-page 398
SuDocs no.: Y3.Is7:R29/2

1461

U.S. *Isthmian canal commission,* 1899-1902.

. . . Report of the Isthmian canal commission, 1899-1901, Rear Admiral John G. Walker, United States navy, president . . . Washington, Govt. print. off., 1901-02.

2 v. plates, maps, diagrs. 23½ cm. (57th Cong., 1st sess. Senate. Doc. 54)

"Index to supplementary report of Isthmian canal commission. "Senate document no. 123, Fifty-seventh Congress, first session": pt. 2, p. 535. That report is published with title, "Report of the Isthmian canal commission . . . upon the proposition of the New Panama canal company to sell and dispose of all its rights, property, and unfinished work to the United States." It consists of 10 pages and does not contain an index. It is published also, with index, in the "Report of the . . . commission 1899-1901" which was printed with additional material in 1904, and issued as Senate doc. 222, 58th Cong., 2d sess. (p. 673-681)

Appendixes (pt. 2): B. Historical notes relative to the Universal canal company (1880-1894) until the organization of the new company. — C. List of documents received by the Isthmian canal commission from the New Panama canal company. — D. Report on hydrography of Panama canal route, by A. P. Davis. — E. Waste weir and discharge for Lake Bohio. — F. Description of alternate location for canal between Gatun and Bohio. — G. Time required for transit through an Isthmian canal. — H. Discharge of the canalized San Juan River. — I. Report of hydrographic investigations in Nicaragua, by A. P. Davis. — J. Surveys of upper San Juan to headquarters of the Indio, by A. B. Nichols. — U. Translation of contract between Nicaragua and the Atlas steamship company (September 30, 1897) — cc1. Treaty between France and New Granada. — cc2. Convention between Republic of Columbia and French Republic. — DD. Treaty between Spain and Colombia. — FF. Contract between Colombia and Panama railroad company. — GG. Wyse concession of March 20, 1878. — HH. Additional contract modifying that of March 23, 1878. — II. Contract granting extension to Panama canal company. — JJ. Contract relative to extension of time to the New Panama canal company. — KK. Memorandum of legal status of New Panama canal company. — MM. Contract between nicaragua and the American Atlantic and Pacific ship canal company. — NN. Report on industrial and commercial value of canal, by Emory R. Johnson.

1. Panama canal. 2. Nicaragua canal. 3. Compagnie nouvelle du canal de Panama. I. Walker, John Grimes, 1835-1907.
TC773.U5 1901   4-1205
- - - - - Copy 2. 2 v. in 1.
MC#: 1901-page 517
SuDocs no.: 57th Cong., 1st sess. S. Doc. 54
MC#: 1902-page 209
SuDocs no.: 57th Cong., 1st sess. S. Doc. 54, pt. 2

1462

U.S. *Isthmian canal commission,* 1899-1902

Abstract from the report of the Isthmian canal commission for 1899-1901, containing chapter 12 of said report . . . Washington, Govt. print. off., 1904.

9 p. 23 cm. (58th Cong., 2d sess., Senate. Doc. 82)
Ordered to be printed, January 12, 1904.
TC784.U58 1904   9-197
Not located in Monthly Catalog

1463

U.S. *Isthmian canal commission,* 1899-1902.

. . . Report of the Isthmian canal commission. Message from the President of the United States, transmitting the report . . . upon the proposition of the New Panama canal company to sell and dispose of all its rights, property, and unfinished work to the United States. January 20, 1902. — Read; referred to the Committee on interoceanic canals and ordered to be printed. [Washington, Govt. print. off., 1902]

    10 p. 23 cm. (57th Cong., 1st sess. Senate. Doc. 123)

    John G. Walker, president of the commission.

    Supplementary to the Report of the Isthmian canal commission, 1899-1901, issued as Senate doc. 54, 57th Cong., 1st sess., in which the index to the present work was printed (p. 535)

    This supplementary report, with index, is found also in the "Report of the . . . commission 1899-1901", published with additional material in 1904 and issued as Senate doc. 222, 58th Cong., 2d sess. (p. 673-681)

    1. Panama canal. 2. Nicaragua canal. 3. Compagnie nouvelle du canal de Panama. I. Walker, John Grimes, 1835-1907.

TC773.U5 1902   2-24874

MC#: 1902-page 47

SuDocs no.: 57th Cong., 1st sess. S. Doc. 123

1464

U.S. *Isthmian canal commission,* 1904-1905.

    Proceedings Isthmian canal commission March 22, 1904 to March 29, 1905. Meetings nos. 1 to 90. With Circulars [nos. 1-13, June 25, 1904, to April 3, 1905] [Washington, 1905]

    cover-title, 206, 3-202, 407-554 p. 23 cm.

    Paged incorrectly: 3-202 should be 207-406.

    Rear Admiral John G. Walker, chairman of the Commission. Continued by "Minutes of meetings of the Isthmian canal commission and of its Executive and Engineering committees".

    1. Panama canal. I. Walker, John Grimes, 1835-1907.

TC774.U53   6-14143

- - - - - Copy 2.

Proceedings:

MC#: 1905-page 90

SuDocs no.: W73.9/1:904/1-49

MC#: 1905-page 90

SuDocs no.: W73.9/1:904/50-63

MC#: 1905-page 90

SuDocs no.: W73.9/1:904/64-66

MC#: 1905-page 219

SuDocs no.: W73.9/1:905/67-70

MC#: 1905-page 219

SuDocs no.: W73.9/1:905/71-73

MC#: 1905-page 267

SuDocs no.: W73.9/1:905

MC#: 1905-page 303

SuDocs no.: W73.9/1:905/4

MC#: 1905-page 303

SuDocs no.: W73.9/1:905/5

Circulars:

MC#: 1905-page 90

SuDocs no.: W73.4:1-10

MC#: 1905-page 219

SuDocs no.: W73.4:11

MC#: 1905-page 267

SuDocs no.: W73.4:12

MC#: 1905-page 303

SuDocs no.: W73/4:13

1465

U.S. *Isthmian canal commission,* 1904-1905.

    . . . Report of the chief engineer Isthmian canal commission. June 1, 1904-February 1, 1905. Washington, D.C., 1905.

    cover-title, 30 p. 23 cm.

    John F. Wallace, chief engineer.

    1. Panama canal — Construction. I. Wallace, John Findley, 1852-

TC774.U54   6-14145

- - - - - Copy 2.

MC#: 1905-page 303

SuDocs no.: W73.12:905/2

WALKER REPORT

1466

Walker, Daniel.

    Rights in conflict; the violent confrontation of demonstrators and police in the parks and streets of Chicago during the week of the Democratic National Convention of 1968. A report submitted by Daniel Walker, director of the Chicago Study Team, to the National Commission on the Causes and Prevention of Violence. [Chicago, 1968]

    xiii, 88, 233 p. illus. 28 cm.

    Commonly known as the Walker report.

    Cover title.

    1. Chicago — Riot, Aug. 1968. 2. Chicago — Police. 3. Democratic Party. National Convention, Chicago, 1968. I. United States. National Commission on the Causes and Prevention of Violence. II. Title. III. Title: Walker report on the violent confrontation of demonstrators and police in the parks and streets of Chicago.

F548.52.W3   977.3'11'04   68-67375

                                                  MARC

Not located in Monthly Catalog

Walker, Daniel.

    Rights in conflict; Chicago's 7 brutal days. New York, Grosset & Dunlap [1968]

    xiii, A88, 233, S7 p. illus., maps. 28 cm.

    Commonly known as the Walker report.

    A report submitted to the National Commission on the Causes and Prevention of Violence.

    1. Chicago — Riot, August 1968. 2. Chicago — Police. 3. Democratic National Convention (1968 : Chicago, Ill.) I. United States. National Commission on the Causes and Prevention of Violence. II. Title. III. Title: Chicago's 7 brutal days. IV. Title: Walker report on the violent confrontation of demonstrators and police in the parks and streets of Chicago.

F548.52.W3 1968e   977.3'11'04   72-2274

                                                  MARC

Not listed in Monthly Catalog

Walker, Daniel.

    Rights in conflict; convention week in Chicago, August, 25-29, 1968; a report. Special introd. by Max Frankel. New York, Dutton [c1968]

    xx, 362, A96 p. illus., maps, ports. 22 cm.

    Commonly known as the Walker report.

    A report submitted to the National Commission on the Causes and Prevention of Violence.

    1. Chicago — Riot, August 1968. 2. Chicago — Police. 3. Democratic Party. National Convention, Chicago, 1968. I. United States. National Commission on the Causes and Prevention of Violence. II. Title. III. Title: Walker report on the violent confrontation of demonstrators and police in the parks and streets of Chicago.

F548.52.W3 1968c   977.3'11'04   70-75001

                                                  MARC

Not listed in Monthly Catalog.

Walker, Daniel.

    Rights in conflict; the violent confrontation of demonstrators and police in the parks and streets of Chicago during the week of the Democratic National Convention of 1968. A report submitted by Daniel Walker, director of the Chicago Study Team, to the National Commission on the Causes and Prevention of

Violence. Introd. by Robert J. Donovan. [New York] New American Library [1968]

xxviii, 324 p. illus., maps. 18 cm. (A Signet special broadside, #7) (Signet books)

Commonly known as the Walker report.

1. Chicago—Riot, August 1968. 2. Chicago—Police. 3. Democratic Party. National Convention, Chicago, 1968. I. United States. National Commission on the Causes and Prevention of Violence. II. Title. III. Title: Walker report on the violent confrontation of demonstrators and police in the parks and streets of Chicago.

F548.52.W3 1968b   977.3'11'04   75-2327
                                                MARC

Not listed in Monthly Catalog

Walker, Daniel.

Rights in conflict; the violent confrontation of demonstrators and police in the parks and streets of Chicago during the week of the Democratic National Convention of 1968. A report submitted by Daniel Walker, director of the Chicago Study Team, to the National Commission on the Causes and Prevention of Violence. Special introd. by Max Frankel. New York, Bantam Books [1968]

xx, 362, A96 p. illus., maps. 18 cm. (A Bantam extra)

Commonly known as the Walker report.

1. Chicago—Riot, August 1968. 2. Chicago—Police. 3. Democratic National Convention (1968 : Chicago, Ill.) I. United States. National Commission on the Causes and Prevention of Violence. II. Title. III. Title: Walker report on the violent confrontation of demonstrators and police in the parks and streets of Chicago.

F548.52.W3 1968d   977.3'11'04   68-59647
                                                MARC

Not listed in Monthly Catalog

WALKER REPORT [Walker, Paul A.]

1467

U.S. *Federal communications commission.*

[Telephone investigation reports] Washington, 1937-38

9 v. (in 4.) tables (part fold.), diagrs. (part fold.) 28½ cm.

Binder's title: U.S. Fed. commun. comm. Telephone invest. reports . . .

Reproduced from type-written copy.

Contents.—[v. 1] Message toll telephone rates of Long lines department and associated companies of American telephone and telegraph company at January 15, 1937 (interstate and intrastate telephone toll rates schedules).—[v. 2] The classified toll rate structure and basic rate practices for message toll telephone service (as developed by the American telephone and telegraph company and "the associated Bell companies in the United States).—[v. 3] General review of operating results of the Bell system and its principal functional divisions for the years 1936 and 1937 and certain prior years and detailed comparison of operating results of Long lines department for the years 1936 and 1937.—[v. 4] Analysis of "license contract" servicing relations between the American telephone and telegraph company's general department and its Long lines department.—[v. 5] The "Price trend review" of the American telephone and telegraph company, and prices and pricing policies of Western electric company, incorporated.—[v. 6] Fundamental legal problems underlying the regulation of interstate telephone rates.—[v. 7] The problem of the "rate of return in public utility regulation with special reference to the Long lines department of the American telephone and telegraph company.—[v. 8] Factors underlying the "rate of return" in public utility regulations, as disclosed in court and commission decisions.—[v. 9] Final report of the Telephone rate and research department.

- - - - - Copy 2.

                                                42-1205

MC#: 1938-page 54 (Vol. 2)
SuDocs no.: CC1.2:T236/7
Other volumes not located in Monthly Catalog

WALKER REPORT

1468

Walker, Richard Louis, 1922-

The human cost of communism in China. Prepared at the request of the late Senator Thomas J. Dodd, Subcommittee to Investigate the Administration of the Internal Security Act and Other Internal Security Laws of the Committee on the Judiciary, United States Senate. Washington, U.S. Govt. Print. Off., 1971.

xiii, 28, v p. 24 cm.

At head of title: 92d Congress, 1st session. Committee print.

Includes bibliographical references.

Supt. of Docs. no.: Y4.J89/2:C73/57

1. China—Politics and government—1949-1976. I. United States. Congress. Senate. Committee on the Judiciary. Subcommittee to Investigate the Administration of the Internal Security Act and Other Internal Security Laws. II. Title.

DS777.55.W353   320.9'51'05   79-614289
                                                MARC

MC#: 1971-15149
SuDocs no.: Y4.J89/2:C73/57

WALLACE REPORT [Wallace, Donald Holmes]
see under
O'MAHONEY REPORTS [O'Mahoney, Joseph Christopher]

WALLACE REPORT [Wallace, Henry Agard]
see
GRAY REPORT [Gray, Lewis Cecil]

WALLACE REPORT [Wallace, John Findley]
see
WALKER COMMISSION [Walker, John Grimes]

WALLIS REPORT [Wallis, W. Allen]
1469

United States. President's Commission on Federal Statistics.

Federal statistics; report. [Washington; For sale by the Supt. of Docs., U.S. Govt. Print. Off., 1971.]

2 v. illus. 24 cm.

Includes bibliographies.

Supt. of Docs. no.: Pr37.8:St2/R29

1. United States—Statistical services. I. Title.

HA37.U18   310   78-181860
                                                MARC

MC#: 1972-1990
SuDocs no.: Pr37.8:St2/R29/v. 1,2

WALLISON REPORT [Wallison, Peter J.]
1470

United States. *Dept. of the Treasury. Office of the General Counsel.*

Management review on the performance of the U.S. Department of the Treasury: in connection with the March 30, 1981 assissination attempt on President Ronald Reagan. Washington, D.C.: Dept. of the Treasury, Office of the General Counsel, 1981. [For sale by the Supt. of Docs., U.S. Govt. Print. Off., 1981]

iv, 101 p., 28 cm.

Cover title.

Item 925

1. Reagan, Ronald—Assassination attempt, 1981. 2. United States. Dept. of the Treasury. 3. Secret Service—United States.
E877.2.U54 1981   353.0074'2'19   81-603180
MC#: 1981-14422
SuDocs no.: T1.2:M31/2

WALSH REPORTS [Walsh, Francis Patrick]
1471

U.S. *Commission on industrial relations.*
Final report of the Commission on industrial relations, including the report of Basil M. Manly, director of research and investigation, and the individual reports and statements of the several commissioners. (Reprinted from Senate doc. no. 415, 64th Congress) Washington, Govt. print. off., 1916.

269 p. 23 cm.
Frank P. Walsh, chairman.
Senate doc. 415, 64th Cong., 1st sess., has title: Industrial relations. Final report and testimony.
1. Industrial relations—U.S. 2. U.S.—Indus. I. Walsh, Francis Patrick, 1864-1939. II. Manly, Basil Maxwell, 1886- III. Title.
HD8051.C4 1916a   16-26009
MC#: May 1916-page 637 ("Notes of general interest")
MC#: May 1916-page 670 (LC card 16-26500 referred to in error)
SuDocs no.: 64th Cong., 1st sess. S. Doc. 415

1472

U.S. *Commission on industrial relations.*
. . . Industrial relations. Final report and testimony, submitted to Congress by the Commission on industrial relations created by the act of August 23, 1912 . . . Washington, Govt. print. off., 1916.

11 v. 24 cm. (64th Cong., 1st sess. Senate. Doc. 415)
Frank P. Walsh, chairman.
The "Final report," issued also with different arrangement in 1915, includes the report of Basil M. Manly, director of research and investigation, and individual reports and statements of the several commissioners.
1. Industrial relations—U.S. 2. U.S.—Indus. I. Walsh, Francis Patrick, 1864-1939. II. Manly, Basil M. III. Title.
HD8051.C4 1916   16-26500 Revised
- - - - - Copy 2.
- - - - - Copy 3.
MC#: Sept. 1916-page 175 (Vols. 1-4)
      Oct. 1916-page 226 (Vols. 5-7)
      Nov. 1916-page 274 (Vols. 8-9)
      Dec. 1916-page 332 (Vol. 10)
      Jan. 1917-page 420 (Vol. 11)
SuDocs no.: 64th Cong., 1st sess. S. Doc. 415

WARBURG REPORT [Warburg, Paul Moritz]
see under
ALDRICH COMMISSION [Aldrich, Nelson Wilmarth]

WARD REPORT [Ward, Jesse Lee]
1473

U.S. *National recovery review board.*
. . . First[-Third] report to the President of the United States . . . [Washington, 1934]

3 v. 28 cm.
At head of title: National recovery review board.
Mimeographed.
Jesse L. Ward of Ward & Paul, official reporter.

1. U.S. National recovery administration—Codes. 2. U.S.—Econ. condit.—1918- I. Ward, Jesse Lee.
HD3616.U455A3   338.973   35-10710 rev
Document Catalog, vol. 22-page 1737

WARE REPORT [Ware, Willis H.]
1474

United States. Dept. of Health, Education, and Welfare. Secretary's Advisory Committee on Automated Personal Data Systems.
Records, computers, and the rights of citizens; report. [Washington] U.S. Dept. of Health, Education & Welfare; for sale by the Supt. of Docs., U.S. Govt. Print. Off., 1973.

xxxv, 346 p. 24 cm. (DHEW Publication, no. (OS) 73-94)
Bibliography: p. 298-330.
1. Privacy, Right of—United States. 2. Business records—United States. 3. Public records—United States. 4. Computers and civilization. I. Title. II. Series: United States. Dept. of Health, Education, and Welfare. DHEW publication no. (OS) 73-94.
JC599.U5U54 1973   323.44'0973   73-602254
                                                      MARC
MC#: 1973-30292
SuDocs no.: HE12.R24/3

WARNER REPORT [Warner, Sam Bass]
1475

U.S. *Wickersham Commission.*
Report on criminal statistics. Washington, U.S. Govt. Print. Off., 1931.

v, 205 p. 25 cm. [*Its* Publications, no. 3]
At head of title: National Commission on Law Observance and Enforcement.
Issued also as no. 3 in the series of Reports, v. 3.
Contents.—Report on criminal statistics.—Survey of criminal statistics in the United States, by S. B. Warner. Appendix I. Checklist of printed reports containing criminal statistics. Appendix II. State laws providing for collection of criminal statistics from police courts, prosecuting attorneys and jails. Comp. by Charles Hamilton.—A critique of Federal criminal statistics, by Morris Ploscowe. Appendix A. A criticism of the Federal Penal code. Appendix B. Comparability of Department of Justice statistics.
1. Criminal statistics—U.S. 2. Criminal law—U.S. I. Warner, Sam Bass, 1889- II. Hamilton, Charles. III. Ploscowe, Morris. IV. Title.
                              364.973   31-26689
- - - - - Copy 2.
HV6787.A5 1931
MC#: Mar. 1931-page 828
SuDocs no.: Y3.N21/7:C86/2

See also WICKERSHAM COMMISSION [Wickersham, George Woodward]

WARREN COMMISSION [Warren, Earl]
1476

U.S. *Warren Commission.*
Report of the President's Commission on the Assassination of President John F. Kennedy. Washington, U.S. Govt. Print. Off. [1964]

xxiv, 888 p. illus., facsims., maps, ports. 24 cm.
Bibliographical references includes in "Footnotes" (p. 817-879)
1. Kennedy, John Fitzgerald, Pres. U.S., 1917-1963-Assassination. 2. Oswald, Lee Harvey.
E842.9.A55   64-62670
MC#: 1964-18882
SuDocs no.: Pr36.8:K38/R29

WARREN REPORT [Warren, Gouverneur Kemble]

1477

U.S. *Army. Corps of Topographical Engineers.*
Explorations in Nebraska. Preliminary report of Lieut. G. K. Warren, Topographical Engineers, to Captain A. A. Humphreys, Topographical Engineers, Office of Explorations and Surveys, War Dept. Washington, D.C., November 24, 1858.

[*In* U.S. War Dept. Report of the Secretary of War. Washington, D.C., 1858.]
35th Cong., 2d sess. House. Ex. Doc. 2, pages 620-747.
Checklist of United States Public Documents, 1789-1909-page 35
35th Cong., 2d sess. H. Ex. doc. 2. In Serial no. 998-999, vol. 2, part 2,3

WASHOE PROJECT REPORT

1478

U.S. *Bureau of Reclamation.*
Washoe project, Nevada-California. Letter from the Assistant Secretary of the Interior transmitting a report and findings on the Washoe project, Nevada and California, pursuant to section 9 (a) of the Reclamation project act of 1939 (53 stat. 1187) Washington, U.S. Govt. Print. Off., 1955.

xxvii, 227 p. illus., maps (part fold., part col.) 24 cm. (84th Cong., 1st sess. House document no. 181)
1. Washoe reclamation project (Nevada-California) (Series: U.S. 84th Cong., 1st sess., 1955. House. Document no. 181)
TC425.W34A515   56-60740
MC#: 1956-1389
SuDocs no.: 84th Cong., 1st sess. H. Doc. 181

WATERGATE REPORTS

1479

United States. Wagergate Special Prosecution Force.
Final report / Watergate Special Prosecution Force. — Washington : for sale by the Supt. of Docs., U.S. Govt. Print. Off., 1977.

76 p. ; 27 cm.
1. Watergate Affair, 1972-
E860.U54 1977   364.1′32′0973   77-603004
                                                          MARC

MC#: 1978-17902
SuDocs no.: J1.2:W29/977

1480

United States. Watergate Special Prosecution Force.
Report / Watergate Special Prosecution Force. — Washington : U.S. Govt. Print. Off., 1975.

iii, 277 p. ; 24 cm.
Bibliography: p. 265-273.
1. Watergate Affair, 1972- 2. United States. Watergate Special Prosecution Force.
E860.U54 1975   364.1′32′0973   75-603269
                                                          MARC

MC#: 1975-1225
SuDocs no.: J1.2:W29

WATKINS REPORT [Watkins, Ralph J.]

1481

U.S. *Dept. of Commerce. Intensive Review Committee on the Bureau of the Census.*
Appraisal of census programs; report of the Intensive Review Committee to the Secretary of Commerce. [Washington, U.S. Govt. Print. Off.] 1954.

x, 119 p. illus. 24 cm.

- - - - - Exhibits to the report of the Intensive Review Committee to the Secretary of Commerce on the programs, policies, and procedures of the Bureau of the Census. [Washington] 1954.

2 v. (945 p.) 27 cm.
Cover title.
HA37.U54 1954 Suppl.
1. U.S.—Census. I. Title.
HA37.U54 1954   311′.39′73   54-61307 rev
MC#: 1954-4941
SuDocs no.: C3.2:P94/3

WATSON REPORT [Watson, Arthur K.]

1482

U.S. *Advisory Committee on Private Enterprise in Foreign Aid.*
Foreign aid through private initiative; report. Washington, Agency for International Development, 1965.

57 p. 28 cm.
1. Investments, American. I. Title.
HG4538.U717   65-62675
MC#: 1965-16359
SuDocs no.: S18.2:F76/4

WATSON REPORT [Watson, James]

1483

U.S. *President's Science Advisory Committee. Cotton Insect Panel.*
Cotton insects; a report. Washington, White House; for sale by the Superintendent of Documents, U.S. Govt. Print. Off., 1965.

vii, 19 p. 24 cm.
1. Cotton—Diseases and pests. 2. Insects, Injurious and beneficial—Control. I. Title.
SB608.C8U64   65-61512
MC#: 1965-9845
SuDocs no.: Pr35.8:Sci2/C82

WATSON REPORT [Watson, James R.]

1484

U.S. *Congress. Senate. Committee on Post Office and Civil Service.*
Administration of the civil service system; report to the Committee on Post Office and Civil Service pursuant to S. Res. 33 and S. Res. 153 of the 84th Cong., and extended by S. Res. 25 of the 85th Cong. Washington, U.S. Govt. Print. Off., 1957.

ii, 144 p. illus. 24 cm.
At head of title: Committee print no. 2. 85th Cong., 1st session. Senate.
1. Civil service—U.S. I. Title.
JK649 1957d   57-60946
MC#: 1957-15597
SuDocs no.: Y4.P84/11:C49/2

WATTS REPORT [Watts, William H.]
see
PARKER REPORT [Parker, James Southworth]

WEBB REPORT

1485

Webb, John Nye, 1899-
. . . Migrant families, by John N. Webb and Malcolm Brown . . . Washington, U.S. Govt. print. off., 1938.

xxx, 192 p. incl. illus. (maps) tables, diagrs., forms. 25½ cm. ([U.S.] Works progress administration. Research monograph XVIII)

At head of title: Works progress administration. F. C. Harrington, administrator. Corrington Gill, assistant administrator. Division of social research. Howard B. Myers, director.

1. Migrant labor—U.S. 2. Unemployed—U.S. I. Brown, Malcolm Johnston, 1910- joint author.
HV85.A36 no. 18   331.137973   39-26659
- - - - - Copy 2.
HB1965.W4
MC#: 1939-page 926
SuDocs no.: Y3.W89/2:17/18

WEDEMEYER REPORT

1486

Wedemeyer, Albert Coady, 1896-
Report to the President submitted September 1947: Korea. Washington, U.S. Govt. Print. Off., 1951.

vii, 27 p. 23 cm.
At head of title: Committee print.
"The portions . . . dealing with China have previously been released, and are not included herein."
1. Korea—Pol. & govt.—1910-1948. 2. Korea—Econ. condit. I. U.S. President, 1945-1953 (Truman)
DS917.W4   951.9   51-60685 rev
MC#: 1951-13545
SuDocs no.: Y4.Ar5/3:K84/2

WEEKS REPORTS [Weeks, Sinclair]

1487

U.S. *Dept. of Commerce.*
Modern transport policy; documents relating to the report of the Presidential Advisory Committee on Transport Policy and Organization and implementing legislation. Washington, 1956.

v, 118 p. diagrs. 27 cm.
Cover title.
1. Transportation—U.S. I. U.S. Presidential Advisory Committee on Transport Policy and Organization. Revision of Federal transportation policy. II. Title.
HE18 1956.A56   385   56-62449
MC#: 1957-1759
SuDocs no.: C1.2:T68/3

1488

U.S. *Presidential Advisory Committee on Transport Policy and Organization.*
Revision of Federal transportation policy; a report to the President. [Washington, U.S. Govt. Print. Off.] 1955.

iv, 20 p. 24 cm.
1. Transportation—U.S.
HE18 1955.A57   385.132   55-60832
MC#: 1955-5939
SuDocs no.: C1.2:T68/2

WEIL REPORT [Weil, Frank L.]

1489

U.S. *President's Committee on Religion and Welfare in the Armed Forces.*
Free time in the armed forces; a study of the armed forces' special services and recreation programs. Washington, U.S. Govt. Print. Off., 1951.

x, 79 p. 24 cm.
1. Soldiers—Recreation. I. Title.
UA23.3.A56 1951   355.12   51-60694
MC#: 1951-10187
SuDocs no.: Y3.P92/5:2F87

WEINBERG REPORT [Weinberg, Alvin]

1490

U.S. *President's Science Advisory Committee.*
Science, government, and information: the responsibilities of the technical community and the Government in the transfer of information; a report. Washington, For sale by the Superintendent of Documents, U.S. Govt. Print. Off., 1963.

v, 52 p. 24 cm.
1. Communication in science. 2. Science and state—U.S. 3. Science—U.S.—Information services. I. Title: Responsibilities of the technical community and the Government in the transfer of information.
Q223.U53   63-60595
MC#: 1963-5677
SuDocs no.: Pr35.8:Sci2/Sci2

WEINBERGER REPORTS [Weinberger, Casper W.]

1491

Meier, John, 1935-
Screening and assessment of young children at developmental risk. Washington, President's Committee on Mental Retardation; for sale by the Supt. of Docs., U.S. Govt. Print. Off., 1973.

vii, 188 p. illus. 26 cm. (DHEW publication no. (OS) 73-90)
Prepared for a conference which was planned and arranged by the Association of University Affiliated Facilities, and held in Boston, Oct., 1972.
Bibliography: p. 175-187.
Supt. of Docs. no.: Pr36.8:M52/Scr2/2
1. Mentally handicapped children—Testing—Congresses. I. Title. II. Series: United States. Dept. of Health, Education, and Welfare. DHEW publication no. (OS) 73-90.
RJ506.M4M38   362.7'8'2   73-601681
                                      MARC
MC#: 1973-26794
SuDocs no.: Pr36.8:M52/Scr2/2

1492

Screening and assessment of young children at developmental risk; background papers of the Boston conference, October 19-21, 1972. Washington, President's Committee on Mental Retardation; for sale by the Supt. of Docs., U.S. Govt. Print. Off., [1973]

v, 70 p. illus. 27 cm. (DHEW publication no. (OS) 73-91)
Organized by the Asosciation of University Affiliated Facilities. Includes bibliographies.
1. Mentally handicapped children—Testing—Congresses. I. Association of University Affiliated Facilities. II. Series: United States. Dept. of Health, Education and Welfare. DHEW publication no. (OS) 73-91.
RJ506.M4S34   362.1   73-601705
                                      MARC
MC#: 1973-29447
SuDocs no.: Pr36.8:M52/Scr2

WEINFELD REPORT [Weinfeld, Edward]

1493

U.S. *Council of National Defense Advisory Commission. Consumer Division.*
Suggested emergency fair rent legislation, a report. Washington, U.S. Govt. Print. Off., 1941.

v, 21 p. ill., 24 cm. (*Its* bulletin no. 10)
1. Rent, U.S. I. Title.
MC#: March 1941-page 314
SuDocs no.: Y3.C831:109/10

WEISS REPORT [Weiss, Stephen J.]
 see
WHEAT REPORT [Wheat, Francis M.]

WELCH REPORT [Welch, Ronald B.]
 see
DOUGLAS REPORTS [Douglas, Paul H.]
 National Commission on Urban Problems.

 Research report, no. 12.

WELLDON REPORT [Welldon, Samuel Alfred]
 see under
ALDRICH COMMISSION [Aldrich, Nelson Wilmarth]

WELSH REPORT [Welsh, Edward Cristy]
 see under
O'MAHONEY REPORTS [O'Mahoney, Joseph Christopher]
 James. Industrial concentration and tariffs.

WENK REPORT [Wenk, Edward, Jr.]
1494

U.S. *Library of Congress. Legislative Reference Service.*
 Ocean sciences and national security. Report of the Committee on Science and Astronautics, U.S. House of Representatives, Eighty-sixth Congress, second session. Washington, U.S. Govt. Print. Off., 1960.

 xi, 180 p. tables. 24 cm. (86th Cong., 2d sess. House report no. 2078)
 "Serial h."
 Bibliographical footnotes.
 1. Oceanographic research. 2. Sea-power. 3. Marine resources. I. U.S. Congress. House. Committee on Science and Astronautics. (Series: U.S. 86th Cong., 2d sess., 1960. House. Report no. 2078)
 GC57.U528   60-61848
 MC#: 1960-13401
 SuDocs no.: 86th Cong., 2d sess. H. Rept. 2078

WESCOE REPORT [Wescoe, W. Clarke]
1495

United States. *Advisory Committee on Higher Education.*
 Report of the Advisory Committee on Higher Education. Report to the Secretary of Health, Education, and Welfare. [n.p.] 1968.

 iv, 29 leaves
 Cover title.
 1. Higher education.
 [LC173.U55]
 National Institute of Education.
 Not located in Monthly Catalog

WEST REPORT [West, Mary Mills]
 see under
DILLINGHAM COMMISSION [Dillingham, William Paul]
 Immigration situation in other countries.

WEST-CLAUSEN REPORT [West, Bland and Clausen, Hugh T.]
1496

Report of investigation of allegations that Army personnel have harassed and intimidated defense counsel in the EE 304 cases at West Point. [Washington: Dept. of the Army], 1976.

92, [10] leaves.
 Report to Secretary of the Army by Bland West, Deputy General Counsel (Military and Civil Affairs) and Hugh J. Clausen, Chief Judge, U.S. Army Court of Military Review.
 Includes letters from Secretary of the Army to chairmen, Subcommittee on Military Personnel, House of Representatives, and Subcommittee on Manpower and Personnel, U.S. Senate. Popular title: West-Clausen report.
 1. United States. Military Academy, West Point. Honor Code. 2. Duress. 3. Due process of law—United States. I. West, Bland. II. Clausen, Hugh J. III. United States. Dept. of the Army. Deputy General Counsel (Military and Civil Affairs) IV. United States. Army Court of Military Review. V. Title: West-Clausen report.
 [U410.F7R19]
 Dept. of the Army Library
 MC#: 1977-12477
 SuDocs no.: Y4.Ar5/2a:977-78/3

United States. *Congress. House. Committee on Armed Services. Subcommittee on Military Personnel.*
 Hearings on United States Military Academy honor code before the Subcommittee on Military Personnel of the Committee on Armed Services, House of Representatives, Ninety-fourth Congress, second session, hearings held August 25 and September 1, 1976, including the final report to the Secretary of the Army by the Special Commission on the United States Military Academy and the report by the general counsel of the Army on allegations that defense counsel at West Point were harassed and intimidated.—Washington : U.S. Govt. Print. Off., 1977.

 iii, 420 p. : ill. ; 24 cm.
 "H.A.S.C. no. 95-3."
 1. Self-government (in higher education) 2. United States. Militarty Academy, West Point. I. United States. Special Commission on the United States Military Academy. II. Title: Hearings on United States Military Academy honor code . . .
 KF27.A76398 1976a   355.1'3322   77-602488
                                                              MARC
 MC#: 1977-12477
 SuDocs no.: Y4.Ar5/2a:977-78/3

WESTMORELAND REPORT [Westmoreland, William Childs]
 see
SHARP REPORT [Sharp, Ulysses S. Grant]

WESTOFF REPORT [Westoff, Charles F.]
 see
ROCKEFELLER REPORT [Rockefeller, John D., 3d]

WHARTON REPORT
1497

Pennsylvania. University. *Wharton School of Finance and Commerce.*
 A study of mutual funds, prepared for the Securities and Exchange Commission. Report of the Committee on Interstate and Foreign Commerce, pursuant to section 136 of the Legislative reorganization act of 1946, Public law 601, 79th Congress, and House Resolution 108, 87th Congress. Washington, U.S. Govt. Print. Off., 1962.

 xxxiii, 595 p. illus. 24 cm. (87th Cong., 2d sess. House report no. 2274)
 1. Investment trusts—U.S. I. U.S. Securities and Exchange Commission. II. U.S. Congress. House. Committee on Interstate

and Foreign Commerce. (Series: U.S. 87th Cong., 2d sess., 1962. House. Report no. 2274)

HG4530.P4   62-62400

MC#: 1962-19124

SuDocs no.: 87th Cong., 2d sess. H. Rept. 2274

WHEARTY REPORT [Whearty, Raymond P.]
1498

U.S. *Interdepartmental Committee on Internal Security.*

    A report on the Government employee security program as submitted to the President by the National Security Council. [Washington, 1952]

    3, 2, 35, x 1. 27 cm.

    In collaboration with the staff of the Civil Service Commission. Raymond P. Whearty, chairman.

    1. Loyalty—security program, 1947- I. Whearty, Raymond P. II. Title: Government employee security program.

JK734.A55   *351.1 351.4   54-2241

Not located in Monthly Catalog

WHEAT REPORT [Wheat, Francis M.]
1499

U.S. *Securities and Exchange Commission.*

    Disclosure to investors: a reappraisal of Federal administrative policies under the '33 and '34 acts. The Wheat report. [New York, Commerce Clearinghouse, 1969]

    xvii, 397, [181] p. 23 cm.

- - - - - Another issue.

    On cover: Federal securities law reports.

                 KF1439.A395 1969a

    1. Securities—U.S. I. Title. II. Title: The Wheat report. III. Title: Federal securities law reports.

KF1439.A395 1969   336.3'1   77-8472
                                                MARC

Not listed in Monthly Catalog

Federal Bar Association Conference on New Era in SEC Disclosure: the Wheat Report, Miami Beach, Fla., 1969.

    Transcript. Edited by Stephen J. Weiss. Washington, Federal Bar Association [1970]

    v, 164 p. 28 cm.

    On cover: New era in SEC disclosure: the Wheat report.

    The conference was held by the Securities Law Committee of the Federal Bar Association on Sept. 5, 1969.

    1. Securities—United States. I. Weiss, Stephen J., 1938- ed. II. Federal Bar Association. Securities Law Committee. III. Title: New era in SEC disclosure: the Wheat report.

KF1070.A2F4 1969   336.3'1   72-118871
                                                  MARC

Not listed in Monthly Catalog

WHEELER REPORT [Wheeler, Ebenezer Smith]
see
WALKER COMMISSION [Walker, John Grimes]

WHERE'S WHAT REPORTS
1500

Murphy, Harry J.

    Where's what : sources of information for Federal investigators / prepared by Harry J. Murphy. —[s.l. : s.n., 1965?]

    iv, 452 p., [3] fold. leaves of plates : ill. ; 28 cm.

    Includes bibliographical references and index.

1. Public records—United States. 2. Records. 3. Investigations. I. Title.

JK734.M87   353.008'1   75-603537
                                                  MARC

Not located in Monthly Catalog

Murphy, Harry J.

    Where's what : sources of information for Federal investigators / prepared by Harry J. Murphy. —New York : Quadrangle/New York Times Book Co., [1975?]

    452 p. : ill. ; 28 cm.

    Includes bibliographical references and index.

    ISBN 0-8129-0636-5

    1. Public records—United States. 2. Records—United States. 3. Investigations. I. Title.

JK734.M87 1975   353.008'1   76-366302
                                                  MARC

Not listed in Monthly Catalog

WHITE REPORT [White, Hays B.]
1501

U.S. *Congress. House. Committee on election of President, vice-president, and representatives in Congress.*

    Four-year term for members of the House of representatives. Hearings before the Committee on election of President, vice-president, and representatives in Congress of the House of representatives, Sixty-eighth Congress, second session on H. J. Res. 309. January 28, 1925 . . . Washington, Govt. print. off., 1925.

    ii, 17 p. 23 cm.

    Hays B. White, chairman.

    Testimony of Hon. T. D. McKeown, Hon. T. W. Phillips, jr., Hon. R. F. Lozier.

    1. U.S. Congress. House. I. McKeown, Tom D., 1878- II. Phillips, Thomas Wharton, 1874- III. Lozier, Ralph Fulton, 1866- IV. Title.

JK1323.1925.A5   25-5713

- - - - - Copy 2.

MC#: Feb. 1925-page 538

SuDocs no.: Y4.E12/1:H81

WHITE REPORT [White, Herbert S.]
see
FRY REPORT [Fry, Bernard Mitchell]

WHITENEY REPORT [Whiteney, Robert A.]
1502

President's Conference on Technical and Distribution Research for the Benefit of Small Business, *Washington, D.C., 1957.*

    Proceedings, September 23, 24, 25, 1957. [Washington] U.S. Dept. of Commerce; distributed by the Office of Technical Services [1957]

    x, 287, p. 26 cm.

    1. Small business—Congresses. 2. Research, Industrial—Congresses.

HD20.P7 1957   338.973   58-60279

MC#: 1958-2894

SuDocs no.: C41.22:R31/2

WHYTE REPORT [Whyte, William Hollingsworth]
    Open space action.
see under
ORRRC REPORTS
    ORRRC study report, 15.

WICKERSHAM COMMISSION [Wickersham, George Woodward]

Publications of the Wickersham Commission are listed numerically, with related reports interfiled.

1503

U.S. *Wickersham Commission.*
[Publications, no. 1-14] [Washington, U.S. Govt. Print. Off., 1930]-31.

14 v. tables. 23-25 cm.

Issued also with same numbering as "Reports," v. 1-6, respectively.

Contents. —[no. 1] ([U.S.] 71st Congress, 2d session. House. Doc. 252) Proposals to improve enforcement of criminal laws of the United States. Message from the President of the United States transmitting comments upon proposals to improve enforcement of the criminal laws of the United States. —[no. 2] ([U.S.] 71st Congress, 3d session. House. Doc. 722) Enforcement of the prohibition laws of the United States. Message from the President of the United States transmitting a report of the National Commission on Law Observance and Enforcement relative to the facts as to the enforcement, the benefits, and the abuses under the prohibition laws, both before and since the adoption of the eighteenth amendment to the Constitution. —[no. 3] Report on criminal statistics. —[no. 4] Report on prosecution. —[no. 5] Report on the enforcement of the deportation laws of the United States. —[no. 6] Report on the child offender in the federal system of justice. —[no. 7] Progress report on the study of the Federal courts. —[no. 8] Report on criminal procedure. —[no. 9] Report on penal institutions, probation and parole. —[no. 10] Report on crime and the foreign born. —[no. 11] Report on lawlessness in law enforcement. —[no. 12] Report on the cost of crime. —[no. 13] Report on the causes of crime. —[no. 14] Report on police.

1. Law enforcement —U.S.
KF9223.A73W5   31-16124
Not located in Monthly Catalog

1504

U.S. *Wickersham Commission.*
Reports. Washington, U.S. Govt. Print. Off., 1931.

6 v. illus., forms, plans. 24 cm.

At head of title: National Commission on Law Observance and Enforcement.

Issued also separately in the series of Publications as Publication no. 1-14, respectively.

Includes bibliographies.

Contents. —I. no. 1. Preliminary report on prohibition. no. 2. Report on the enforcement of the prohibition laws of the United States. no. 3. Report on criminal statistics. no. 4. Report on prosecution. —II. no. 5. Report on the enforcement of the deportation laws of the United States. no. 6. Report on the child offender in the Federal system of justice. no. 7. Progress report on the study of the Federal courts. no. 8. Reports on criminal procedure. —III. no. 9. Report on penal institutions, probation and parole. no. 10. Report on crime and the foreign born. —IV. no. 11. Report on lawlessness in law enforcement. no. 14. Report on police. —V. no. 12. Report on the cost of crime. —VI. no. 13. Report on the causes of crime.

1. Law enforcement.
HV6775.A5 1931   364.973   31-28081
Not located in Monthly Catalog

1505

. . . Proposals to improve enforcement of criminal laws of the United States. Message from the President of the United States

transmitting comments upon proposals to improve enforcement of the criminal laws of the United States . . . [Washington, U.S. Govt. print. off., 1930]

27 p. 23 cm. ([U.S.] 71st Cong., 2d sess. House. Doc. 252)

Referred to the committees on ways and means, judiciary, interstate and foreign commerce, expenditures in the executive departments, District of Columbia, and immigration and naturalization, and ordered printed January 13, 1930.

Comments of the National commission on law observance and enforcement and the officials of the Department of justice and of the Treasury department.

1. Criminal law —U.S. I. U.S. National commission on law observance and enforcement. II. U.S. Dept. of justice. III. U.S. Treasury dept.
KF9223.A73W5 no. 1   30-26166
MC#: Jan. 1930-page 540
SuDocs no.: 71st Cong., 2d sess. H. Doc. 252

1506

U.S. *Wickersham Commission.*
Enforcement of the prohibition laws of the United States. Message from the President of the United States transmitting a report of the National Commission on Law Observance and Enforcement relative to the facts as to the enforcement, the benefits, and the abuses under the prohibition laws, both before and since the adoption of the eighteenth amendment to the Constitution. Washington, U.S. Govt. Print. Off., 1931.

viii, 162 p. 24 cm. [*Its* Publications, no. 2]

71st Congress, 3d session. House. Doc. 722.

Issued also as no. 2 in the series of Reports, v. 1.

Issued also separately without document series note ("Bureau ed.") with title: Report on the enforcement of the prohibition laws.

Referred to the Committee on Judiciary and ordered printed Jan. 20, 1931.

"Separate statements of the commissioners": p. 85-162.

1. Prohibition —U.S. I. Title. (Series: U.S. 71st Cong., 3d sess., 1930-1931. House. Document 722)
KF9223.A75W5 no. 2   178.50973   31-26316
MC#: Jan. 1931-page 563
SuDocs no.: 71st Cong., 3d sess. H. Doc. 722

1507

U.S. *Wickersham Commission.*
Report on the enforcement of the prohibition laws of the United States. Dated, January 7, 1931. [Washington, 1931]

286 p. 23 cm.

At head of title: National Commission on Law Observance and Enforcement.

Issued also with same title in the series of Reports, v. I, Report, no. 2 and in the series of Publications as Publication no. 2, House doc. 722, 71st Congress, 3d session with title: Enforcement of the prohibition laws of the United States. Message from the President of the United States transmitting a report.

"Separate statements of the commissioners": p. 151-286.

1. Prohibition —U.S. I. Title.
                              178.50973   33-17244
Not located in Monthly Catalog

1508

U.S. *Wickersham Commission.*
Enforcement of the prohibition laws. Official records of the National Commission on Law Observance and Enforcement pertaining to its investigation of the facts as to the enforcement, the benefits, and the abuses under the prohibition laws, both before and since the adoption of the eighteenth amendment to the Constitution. Washington, U.S. Govt. Print. Off., 1931.

5 v. illus., maps (1 fold.), ports. 24 cm. (71st Congress, 3d session. Senate. Doc. 307)

On cover: Prohibition enforcement.

1. Prohibition—U.S. I. Title. (Series: U.S. 71st Congress, 3d session, 1930-1931. Senate. Document 307)

KF3905.5.W53   178.50973   31-28542

MC#: Nov. 1931-page 333

SuDocs no.: 71st Cong., 3d sess. S. Doc. 307

1509

U.S. *Wickersham Commission.*

Report on criminal statistics. Washington, U.S. Govt. Print. Off., 1931.

v, 205 p. 25 cm. [*Its* Publications, no. 3]

At head of title: National Commission on Law Observance and Enforcement.

Issued also as no. 3 in the series of Reports, v. 3.

Contents. — Report on criminal statistics. — Survey of criminal statistics in the United States, by S. B. Warner. Appendix I. Checklist of printed reports containing criminal statistics. Appendix II. State laws providing for collection of criminal statistics from police courts, prosecuting attorneys and jails. Comp. by Charles Hamilton. — A critique of Federal criminal statistics, by Morris Ploscowe. Appendix A. A criticism of the Federal Penal Code. Appendix B. Comparability of Department of Justice statistics.

1. Criminal statistics—U.S. 2. Criminal law—U.S. I. Warner, Sam Bass, 1889- II. Hamilton, Charles. III. Ploscowe, Morris. IV. Title.

KF9223.A73W5 no. 3   364.973   31-26689

- - - - - Copy 2.

HV6787.A5 1931

MC#: Mar. 1931-page 828

SuDocs no.: Y3.N21/7:C86/2

1510

United States. *Wickersham Commission.*

Report on prosecution. Washington, United States Govt. Print. Off., 1931.

v, 337 p. 23 cm. [*Its* Publications, no. 4]

At head of title: National Commission on Law Observance and Enforcement.

Issued also as no. 4 in the series of Reports, vol. 1.

George W. Wickersham, chairman.

"Criminal justice surveys analysis being an analysis of the surveys of the administration of criminal justice relating to the subjects of prosecution and courts for National Commission on Law Observance and Enforcement, by Alfred Bettman of the Cincinnati, Ohio, bar": p. 39-221.

"Bibliography of prosecution including references to grand jury, legal aid, public defender and related subjects, by Julian Leavitt, research consultant": p. [223]-318.

1. Criminal procedure—United States. 2. Public defenders—United States. 3. Grand jury—United States. 4. Criminal procedure—Bibliography. I. Wickersham, George Woodward, 1858-1936. II. Bettman, Alfred, 1873-1945. III. Leavitt, Julian, 1878-1939. IV. Title: Prosecution.

KF9223.A73W5 no. 4   31-27056

MC#: June 1931-page 1065

SuDocs no.: Y3.N21/7:5/4

1511

U.S. *Wickersham Commission.*

Report on the Enforcement of the deportation laws of the United States. Washington, U.S. Govt. Print. Off., 1931.

iii, 179 p. 25 cm. [*Its* Publications, no. 5]

At head of title: National Commission on Law Observance and Enforcement.

Issued also as no. 5 in the series of Reports, v. 2.

"The administration of the deportation laws of the United States. Report to the National Commission on Law Observance and Enforcement, by Reuben Oppenheimer": p. [15]-179.

1. Deportation—U.S. 2. Aliens—U.S. I. Oppenheimer, Reuben, 1897- II. Title.

KF9223.A73W5 no. 5   341.4   31-26961

MC#: Aug. 1931-page 110

SuDocs no.: Y3.N21/7:5/5

1512

U.S. *Wickersham Commission.*

Report on the child offender in the Federal system of justice. Washington, U.S. Govt. Print. Off., 1931.

iii, 175 p. illus., forms, maps. 25 cm. [*Its* Publications, no. 6]

At head of title: National Commission on Law Observance and Enforcement.

Issued also as no. 6 in the series of Reports, v. 2.

"Problems presented to the Federal system of justice by the child offender; report to the National Commission on Law Observance and Enforcement by Miriam Van Waters, consultant": p. 7-175.

1. Juvenile delinquency—U.S. I. Van Waters, Miriam. II. Title.

KF9223.A73W5 no. 6   364   31-27148

MC#: July 1931-page 46

SuDocs no.: Y3.N21/7:5/6

1513

U.S. *Wickersham Commission.*

Progress report on the study of the Federal courts. Washington, U.S. Govt. Print. Off., 1931.

vii, 123 p. illus. 24 cm. [*Its* Publications, no. 7]

At head of title: National Commission on Law Observance and Enforcement.

Issued also as no. 7 in the series of Reports, v. 2.

Running title: Business of Federal courts.

"Manual for field workers": p. 65-123

1. Courts—U.S. I. Title. II. Title: Business of Federal courts.

KF9223.A73W5 no. 7   347.99'73   31-27260

MC#: Aug. 1931-page 110

SuDocs no.: Y3.N21/7:5/7

1514

U.S. *Wickersham Commission.*

Progress report on the study of the business of the Federal courts for National Commission on Law Observance and Enforcement. [Washington, U.S. Govt. Print. Off., 1931]

III p., 87 1. illus. 31 cm.

Found also in the Progress report on the study of the Federal courts which is issued in the series of Publications as Publication no. 7 and in the series of Reports, V. II, no. 7, respectively.

Charles E. Clark, chairman, Advisory Committee, Federal court study.

1. Courts—U.S. I. Title.

                 347.990973   31-29217

Not located in Monthly Catalog

1515

U.S. *Wickersham Commission.*

Report on criminal procedure. Washington, U.S. Govt. Print. Off., 1931.

v, 51 p. 23 cm. [*Its* Publications, no. 8]

At head of title: National Commission on Law Observance and Enforcement.

Issued also as no. 8 in the series of Reports, v. 2.
1. Criminal procedure—U.S. I. Title.
KF9223.A73W5 no. 8   343.10973   31-27177
MC#: July 1931-page 46
SuDocs no.: Y3.N21/7:5/8

1516

U.S. *Wickersham Commission.*
Report on penal institutions, probation and parole.
Washington, U.S. Govt. Print. Off., 1931.

vi, 344 p. illus. 25 cm. [*Its* Publications, no. 9]
At head of title: National Commission on Law Observance and
Enforcement.
Issued also as no. 9 in the series of Reports, v. 3.
"Police jails and village lockups; special report . . . by Hastings
H. Hart": p. 327-344.
1. Prisons—U.S. 2. Reformatories—U.S. 3. Probation—U.S.
4. Parole—U.S. I. Hart, Hastings Hornell, 1851-1932. II. Title.
KF9223.A73W5 no. 9   365.973   31-27206
MC#: July 1931-page 46
SuDocs no.: Y3.N21/7:5/9

1517

U.S. *Wickersham Commission.*
Report on crime and the foreign born. Washington, U.S. Govt.
Print. Off., 1931.

iii, 416 p. 25 cm. [*Its* Publications, no. 10]
At head of title: National Commission on Law Observance and
Enforcement.
Issued also as no. 10 in the series of Reports, v. 3.
"Report on crime and criminal justice in relation to the foreign
born for National Commission on Law Observance and Enforce-
ment, by Edith Abbott, with supplementary reports by Alida C.
Bowler [and others]": p. 7-416.
1. Crime and criminals—U.S. 2. U.S.—Foreign population.
3. Mexicans in the United States. I. Abbott, Edith, 1876-1957.
II. Bowler, Alida Cynthia. III. Title.
KF9223.A73W5 no. 10   364.973   31-27290
MC#: Aug. 1931-page 110
SuDocs no.: Y3.N21/7:5/10

1518

U.S. *Wickersham Commission.*
Report on lawlessness in law enforcement. Washington, U.S.
Govt. Print. Off., 1931.

v, 347 p. 25 cm. [*Its* Publications, no. 11]
At head of title: National Commission on Law Observance and
Enforcement.
Issued also as no. 11 in the series of Reports, v. 4.
"The third degree; report to the National Commission on Law
Observance and Enforcement, by Zechariah Chafee, Jr., Walter
H. Pollak, Carl S. Stern, consultants": p. 13-261.
"Unfairness in prosecutions; report to the National Commis-
sion on Law Observance and Enforcement, by Zechariah Chafee,
Jr., Walter H. Pollak, Carl S. Stern, consultants": p. 263-347.
1. Evidence, Criminal. 2. Police—U.S. I. Chafee, Zechariah,
1885-1957. II. Pollak, Walter Heilprin, 1887-1940. III. Stern,
Carl Samuel. IV. Title.
KF9223.A73W5 no. 11   343.1   31-27265
MC#: Aug. 1931-page 110
SuDocs no.: Y3.N21/7:5/11

1519

U.S. *National commission on law observance and enforcement.*
. . . Report on the cost of crime. Washington, U.S. Govt. print.
off., 1931.

iii, 509, 510a-510c, 553-657 p. incl. tables. 25 cm. [Publica-
tions, no. 12]
At head of title: National commission on law observance and
enforcement.
Issued also as no. 12 in the series of Reports, vol. v.
George W. Wickersham, chairman.
"Report on the cost of crime and criminal justice in the United
States. Prepared for the National commission on law observance
and enforcement under the direction of Goldthwaite H. Dorr and
Sidney P. Simpson": p. 9-657.
Bibliography, by Mary Daugherty, research assistant: p.
457-483.
1. Crime and criminals—U.S. 2. Justice, Administration of—
U.S. I. Wickersham, George Woodward, 1858-1936. II. Dorr,
Goldthwaite Higginson, 1876- III. Simpson, Sidney Post, 1896-
IV. Daugherty, Mary. V. Title.
KF9223.A73W5 no. 12   364.973   31-27076
- - - - - Copy 2.
MC#: Aug. 1931-page 110
SuDocs no.: Y3.N21/7:5/12

1520

U.S. *Wickersham Commission.*
Report on the causes of crime. Washington, U.S. Govt. Print.
Off., 1931.

2 v. illus., forms, plans (part fold.) 25 cm. [*Its* Publications,
no. 13]
At head of title: National Commission on Law Observance and
Enforcement.
Issued also as no. 13 in the series of Reports, v. 6.
"Reference list of books and articles cited": v. 1, p. 143-161.
Contents. — I. The causes of crime; separate report of H. W.
Anderson. Some causative factors in criminality, by Morris
Ploscowe. Work and law observance, by Mary Van Kleeck,
Emma A. Winslow, and I. De A. Reid.—II. Social factors in
juvenile delinquency, by C. R. Shaw and H. D. McKay.
1. Crime and criminals—U.S. 2. Juvenile delinquency—U.S.
I. Anderson, Henry Watkins, 1870-1954. II. Ploscowe, Morris.
III. Van Kleeck, Mary, 1883- IV. Winslow, Emma Annie,
1887- V. Reid, Ira De Augustine, 1901-1968. VI. Shaw, Clif-
ford Robe, 1896- VII. McKay, Henry Donald, 1899- VIII. Ti-
tle. (Series)
KF9223.A73W5 no. 13   364.973   31-27279
MC#: Aug. 1931-page 110
SuDocs no.: Y3.N21/7:5/13/v. 1,2

1521

U.S. *Wickersham Commission.*
Report on police. Washington, U.S. Govt. Print. Off., 1931.
iii, 140 p. illus. 24 cm. [*Its* Publications, no. 14]
At head of title: National Commission on Law Observance and
Enforcement.
Issued also as no. 14 in the series of Reports, v. 4.
"Police conditions in the United States; a report to the National
Commission on Law Observance and Enforcement by David G.
Monroe and Earle W. Garrett . . . under the direction of August
Vollmer": p. [11]-140.
1. Police—U.S. I. Monroe, David Geeting. II. Garrett, Earle
W. III. Vollmer, August, 1876-1955. IV. Title.
KF9223.A73W5 no. 14   351.740973   31-27255
MC#: Aug. 1931-page 111
SuDocs no.: Y3.N21/7:5/14

1522

The Mooney-Billings report; suppressed by the Wickersham commission. New York city, Gotham house, inc. [1932]

7 p. 1., ii, iv, 243 p. 23½ cm.

"Draft of Mooney-Billings report, submitted to the National commission on law observance and enforcement by the Section on lawless enforcement of law. Consultants: Zechariah Chafee, Jr., Walter H. Pollak [and] Carl S. Stern . . . June, 1931."—7th prelim. leaf.

Lettered on cover: The suppressed Mooney-Billings report.

1. Mooney, Thomas J., 1882-1942. 2. Billings, Warren K., 1894- I. Chafee, Zechariah, 1885-1957. II. Pollak, Walter Heilprin, 1887-1940. III. Stern, Carl Samuel. IV. U.S. Wickersham Commission. V. Title: The suppressed Mooney-Billings report.

KF224.M6 M65   343.109794   33-2250
Not listed in Monthly Catalog

WIDNALL REPORT [Widnall, William B.]

1523

National Commission on Electronic Fund Transfers.

EFT and the public interest : a report of the National Commission on Electronic Fund Transfers. — Washington : NCEFT, 1977.

xix, 149 p. : ill. ; 22 x 28 cm.
Includes bibliographical references.
1. Electronic funds transfers. 2. Consumer protection — United States. 3. Privacy, Right of — United States. I. Title.
HG1710.N37 1977   332.1'7   77-601494
                                         MARC
MC#: 1977-8866
SuDocs no.: Y3.E12/4:2P96

WIESEL REPORT [Wiesel, Elie]

1524

United States. President's Commission on the Holocaust.

Report to the President, September 27, 1979 / President's Commission on the Holocaust, Elie Wiesel, chairman. — [Washington, D.C.] : U.S. Govt. Print. Off. : [for sale by the Supt. of Docs., U.S. Govt. Print. Off.], 1979.

vii, 40 p. ; 23 cm.
Includes bibliographical references.
1. Washington, D.C. Holocaust Memorial — Addresses, essays, lectures. 2. United States. President's Commission on the Holocaust — Addresses, essays, lectures. 3. Holocaust, Jewish (1939-1945) — Addresses, essays, lectures. I. Title.
D810.J4U63 1979   353.0085'9   80-600962
                                         MARC
MC#: 1980-8724
SuDocs no.: Pr39.8:H74/H74

WIESNER REPORT [Wiesner, Jerome B.]

1525

U.S. *Federal Council for Science and Technology. Committee on Natural Resources.*

Research and development on natural resources; report. [Washington] Office of Science and Technology, Executive Office of the President; [for sale by the Superintendent of Documents, U.S. Govt. Print. Off.] 1963.

x, 134 p. illus. 24 cm. ([U.S.] Federal Council for Science and Technology. Publication no. 1)
1. Natural resources — U.S. I. Title. (Series)
HC103.7.A514 1963   63-65329
MC#: 1963-20122
SuDocs no.: PrEx8.2:N21

WIGGLESWORTH REPORT [Wigglesworth, Richard Bowditch]
    see
LEA REPORT [Lea, Clarence Frederick]

WIGHT REPORT [Wight, Royce Atwood]

1526

U.S. *Commodity exchange administration.*

. . . Trading for others in commodity futures. Commodity exchange administration. [Washington, U.S. Govt. print. off., 1939]

29 p. diagrs. 23 cm. (U.S. Dept. of agriculture. Circular no. 539)

Caption title.

"The information on which this report is based was obtained by numerous members of the staff of the Commodity exchange administration, both in Washington and in the field. The preparation of the report was largely the work of Royce A. Wight . . . The project was conducted under general supervision of Blair Stewart."—Foot-note, p. 1.

1. Speculation. [1. Future trading] 2. (Commission merchant — U.S.) 3. (Produce trade — U.S.) I. Stewart, William Blair, 1900- II. Wight, Royce Atwood, 1912- III. Title.
HG6046.U6 1939a   332.64   Agr39-616 Revised
MC#: 1939-page 1393
SuDocs no.: A1.4/2:539

WILCOX REPORT [Wilcox, Clair]
    see under
O'MAHONEY REPORTS [O'Mahoney, Joseph Christopher]

WILEY REPORTS [Wiley, Alexander]

1527

U.S. *Congress. Senate. Committee on Foreign Relations.*

Strength of the international Communist movement [by Alexander Wiley, chairman] Special Subcommittee on Security Affairs. Washington, U.S. Govt. Print. Off., 1953.

ii, 60 p. fold. map. 24 cm.
At head of title: 83d Cong., 1st sess. Committee print.
1. Communist parties. 2. Communism — Hist. I. Title.
HX40.U62   335.4   53-63712
MC#: 1953-20008
SuDocs no.: Y4.F76/2:C73

1528

Wiley, Alexander, 1884-

An economic survey of Wisconsin; a series of reports from Federal Government agencies on the growth and development of the State of Wisconsin, 1848-1948, on the occasion of the 100th anniversary of Wisconsin's statehood. Washington, U.S. Govt. Print. Off., 1948.

iii, 32 p. 24 cm. ([U.S.] 80th Cong., 2d sess., 1948. Senate. Document no. 130)
1. Wisconsin — Econ. condit. (Series)
HC107.W6W65   330.9775   48-46118*
MC#: 1948-10570
SuDocs no.: 80th Cong., 2d sess. S. Doc. 130

WILL REPORT [Will, Robert Frederick]

1529

U.S. *Office of Education.*

The State department of education report, prepared by Robert F. Will, research assistant, State school administration, in cooperation with the Study Commission of the National Council of Chief State School Officers. [Washington, 1953]

vii, 58 p. tables. 23 cm.
Bibliography: p. 57-58.

1. School reports. 2. State departments of education. I. Will, Robert Frederick, 1917-
LB2809.A2U62   379.73   E53-50
MC#: 1953-17405
SuDocs no.: FS5.2:St2/2

WILLENBERG REPORTS [Willenberg, Ernest Paul]
1530

U.S. *President's Panel on Mental Retardation.*
  Report of Task Force on Education and Rehabilitation, August, 1962. Washington, U.S. Dept. of Health, Education, and Welfare, Public Health Service; for sale by the Superintendent of Documents, Govt. Print. Off. [1963]

  iii, 78 p. 26 cm.
  1. Mentally handicapped—Rehabilitation. I. Title.
HV3006.A1A63   63-65388
MC#: 1963-21074
SuDocs no.: Pr35.8:M52/Ed8

1531

U.S. *President's Panel on Mental Retardation.*
  Report of the mission to Denmark and Sweden. Ernest P. Willenberg, chairman [and others. Washington] U.S. Dept. of Health, Education, and Welfare, Public Health Service; for sale by the Superintendent of Documents, U.S. Govt. Print. Off., 1962 [i.e. 1963]

  48 p. 27 cm.
  Includes bibliography.
  1. Mentally handicapped—Denmark. 2. Mentally handicapped—Sweden. 3. Mental deficiency—Denmark. 4. Mental deficiency—Sweden. I. Willenberg, Ernest Paul, 1918- II. Title.
HV3008.D4U53   63-62052
MC#: 1963-14651
SuDocs no.: Pr35.8:M52/D41

WILLIAMS BOARD REPORT [Williams, Edward T.]
1532

U.S. *Dept. of the Army. Officer Education and Training Review Board.*
  Report. Edward T. Williams, President of the Board. Washington, 1958.

  260 p. charts. 27 cm.
  1. Military education—U.S. 2. U.S. Army—Officers. I. Williams, Edward T. II. Title: Williams Board Report.
[U408.3.A53 1958]
Dept. of the Army Library
Not located in Monthly Catalog

WILLIAMS REPORT [Williams, Albert L.]
1533

U.S. Commission on International Trade and Investment Policy.
  United States international economic policy in an interdependent world; report to the President. Washington, 1971.

  xii, 394 p. illus. 24 cm.
  Supt. of Docs. no.: Pr37.8:In8/2/Ec7
- - - - - Papers submitted to the Commission on International Trade and Investment Policy and published in conjunction with the Commission's report to the President; compendium of papers. Washington; [For sale by the Supt. of Docs., U.S. Govt. Print. Off.] 1971.

  2 v. illus. 24 cm.
HF1455.A5153 Suppl.

1. U.S.—Foreign economic relations. 2. U.S.—Commerce. 3. Investments, American. I. Title.
HF1455.A5153   382'.0973   78-614330
                                                            MARC
MC#: 1971-15965
SuDocs no.: Pr37.8:In8/2/Ec7

WILLIAMS REPORT [Williams, Ernest William]
1534

U.S. *Office of the Under Secretary of Commerce for Transportation.*
  Rationale of Federal transportation policy, by Ernest W. Williams, Jr., and David W. Bluestone. Appendix to Federal transportation policy and program. Washington, U.S. Dept. of Commerce, 1960.

  v, 71 p. 24 cm.
  Bibliography: p. 71.
  1. Transportation—U.S. I. Bluestone, David W. II. Williams, Ernest William, 1916- III. U.S. Dept. of Commerce. Federal transportation policy. IV. Title.
HE18 1960.A56   385.0973   60-62042
MC#: 1960-10664 (LC card 60-60795 referred to in error)
SuDocs no.: C1.2:T68/2/960/app.

WILLIAMS REPORT [Williams, Norman]
  Land acquisition for outdoor recreation.
  see under
ORRRC REPORTS
  ORRRC study report, 16.

WILLIAMSBURG PAPERS
1535

Workshop on Comprehensive Community Services for Problem Drinkers and Their Families, Williamsburg, Va., 1969.
  Comprehensive community services for alcoholics; the Williamsburg papers, [by Richard Brotman, and others] Chevy Chase, Md., National Institute of Mental Health; for sale by the Supt. of Docs., U.S. Govt. Print. Off., Washington, 1970.

  iv, 68 p. 26 cm. (Public Health Service publication no. 2060)
  Sponsored by the National Center for Prevention and Control of Alcoholism.
  1. Alcoholics—United States—Rehabilitation—Congresses. I. Brotman, Richard Emanuel. II. United States. National Center for Prevention and Control of Alcoholism. III. Title. IV. Title: The Williamsburg papers. V. Series: United States. Public Health Service. Publication no. 2060.
HV5279.W66 1969   362.2'92'0973   75-608081
                                                                MARC
MC#: 1970-11775
SuDocs no.: HE20.240:A1 1/2

WILLIS REPORT [Willis, Benjamin C.]
1536

U.S. *Panel of Consultants on Vocational Education.*
  Education for a changing world of work; report prepared at the request of the President of the United States. [Washington] U.S. Dept. of Health, Education, and Welfare, Office of Education; [for sale by the Superintendent of Documents, U.S. Govt. Print. Off., 1963]

  xx, 296 p. map, diagrs., tables. 24 cm.
  "OE-80021."
  Bibliography: p. 269-279.
- - - - - Appendices I-III. [Washington, 1963]

  3 v. 27 cm.
  "OE-80022, OE-80025-26."
  Bibliographical footnotes.

Contents. — 1. Technical training in the United States, by L. A. Emerson. — 2. Manpower in farming and related occupations, by C. E. Bishop and G. S. Tolley. — 3. The economic and social background of vocational education in the United States, by H. F. Clark. A sociological analysis of vocational education in the United States, by W. Brookover and S. Nosow. The case for education for home and family living, by B. M. Moore. The contribution to the national economy of the use of resources within and by the family, by E. E. Hoyt.
LC1045.A554 Appx.
- - - - - Summary report. [Washington, 1962]

    24 p. 20 x 27 cm.
    "OE-80020."
    1. Vocational education — U.S. I. U.S. Office of Education. II. Emerson, Lynn Arthur, 1890- III. Title.
LC1045.A554   HEW63-55
MC#: 1963-10066
SuDocs no.: FS5.280:80021
MC#: 1963-13844 (Appendix I)
SuDocs no.: FS5.280:80022
MC#: 1963-13845 (Appendix II)
SuDocs no.: FS5.280:80025
MC#: 1963-13846 (Appendix III)
SuDocs no.: FS5.280:80026
MC#: 1963-2156 (Summary report)
SuDocs no.: FS5.280:80020

WILLIS REPORT [Willis, K. E.]
    see
LEWIS REPORT [Lewis, F. J.]
Defense implications of the national power survey.

WILSON REPORT [Wilson, Charles Erwin]

1537

U.S. *President's Committee on Civil Rights.*
    To secure these rights, the report of the President's Committee on Civil Rights. Washington, U.S. Govt. Print. Off., 1947.
    xii, 178 p. illus., maps. 25 cm.
    Charles E. Wilson, chairman.
    1. Civil rights — U.S. I. Wilson, Charles Erwin, 1880- II. Title.
JC599.U5A32 1947   323.4   47-46486*
MC#: 1947-8309
SuDocs no.: Pr33.2:R449

WILSON REPORT [Wilson, Edwin B.]

1538

U.S. *National resources committee. Science committee.*
    The problems of a changing population. Report of the Committee on population problems to the National resources committee. May, 1938. Washington, U.S. Govt. print. off., 1938.
    iv, 306 p. incl. tables, diagrs., forms. maps (3 fold.) 29 cm.
    Prepared by the subcommittee on population problems of the Science committee. cf. p. iii.
    Edwin B. Wilson, chairman of subcommittee.
    "Government serial reports and current population research": p. 260-275.
- - - - - Statistical supplement to The problems of a changing population. Report of the Committee on population problems to the National resources committee. January, 1937. Washington, U.S. Govt. print. off., 1937.
    2 p. 1., 107 p. incl. tables. 29 cm.
    Errata slip inserted.
HB3505.A5 1938 Suppl.
    1. U.S. — Population. 2. Population. I. Title.
HB3505.A5 1938   312.8   38-26657
MC#: 1938-page 892
SuDocs no.: Y3.N21/12:2P81/3

WILSON REPORT [Wilson, O. Meredith]

1539

U.S. *Advisory Panel on Educational Statistics.*
    Report. [Washington] U.S. Dept. of Health, Education, and Welfare, Office of Education, 1963.
    vii, 22 p. 27 cm.
    Issued, by error, as U.S. Office of Education. Circular 737, OE-20061.
    1. U.S. Office of Education — Statistical program. 2. Education — U.S. — Stat. I. U.S. Office of Education.
L112.A4   HEW64-72 rev
MC#: 1964-8494
SuDocs no.: FS5.220:20061

WILTSE REPORT [Wiltse, Charles Maurice]
    see
LELAND REPORT [Leland, Simeon Elbridge]

WINSLOW REPORT [Winslow, Emma Annie]
    see
WICKERSHAM COMMISSION [Wickersham, George Woodward]
    Report on the causes of crime, no. 13.

WINSTON REPORT [Winston, D. Ellen]

1540

U.S. *President's Council on Aging.*
    Federal payments to older persons in need of protection; a report of a survey and conference. Washington [For sale by the Superintendent of Documents, U.S. Govt. Print. Off., 1965]
    iv, 66 p. 26 cm.
    Bibliographical footnotes.
    1. Old age pensions — U.S. 2. Old age assistance — U.S. I. Title.
HD7106.U5A546   65-61513
MC#: 1965-9846
SuDocs no.: Pr35.8:Ag4/P29

WIRTZ REPORTS [Wirtz, W. Willard]

1541

U.S. *President's Committee on Corporate Pension Funds and Other Private Retirement and Welfare Programs.*
    Public policy and private pension programs; a report to the President on private employee retirement plans. Washington, For sale by the Superintendent of Documents, U.S. Govt. Print. Off., 1965.
    1 v. (various pagings) illus. 26 cm.
    1. Old age pensions — U.S. I. Title.
HD7106.U5A545   65-60708
MC#: 1965-5322
SuDocs no.: Pr35.8:P38/2/P38

1542

U.S. *President's Committee on Youth Employment.*
    The challenge of jobless youth; [report and recommendations. Washington, U.S. Govt. Print. Off.] 1963.
    20 p. illus. 28 cm.
    1. Youth — Employment — U.S. I. Title.
HD6273.A55   63-61200
MC#: 1963-9327
SuDocs no.: Pr35.8:Y8/2/J57

1543

U.S. *President's Task Force on Manpower Conservation.*
    One-third of a nation; a report on young men found unqualified for military service. [Washington] 1964.

36, A-51 p. diagrs., forms tables. 26 cm.
1. U.S.—Armed Forces—Recruiting, enlistment, etc. 2. Youth—Employment—U.S. 3. Manpower—U.S. I. Title.
UB323.A5 1964   L64-12
MC#: 1964-7678
SuDocs no.: Pr35.8:M31/On2

WITHERS REPORT [Withers, Hartley]
see under
ALDRICH COMMISSION [Aldrich, Nelson Wilmarth]

WITTE REPORT [Witte, Edwin E.]
see
BROWNLOW REPORT [Brownlow, Louis]

WOLVERTON REPORT [Wolverton, Charles Anderson]
see
DONAHEY REPORT [Donahey, Vic]

WOMBLE REPORT [Womble, J. P., Jr.]
1544

U.S. *Dept. of Defense. Ad Hoc Committee on the Future of Military Service as a Career That Will Attract and Retain Capable Career Personnel.*
The Womble report on service careers.
(*In* Army information digest. v. 9 (1954) no. 2, p. 24-36)
Signed J. P. Womble, Jr., chairman.
I. Womble, J. P. II. Title.
SuDocs no.: D101.12:V. 9, no. 2

WOOD REPORT [Wood, John Stephens]
1545

U.S. *Congress. House. Special committee on un-American activities (1938-)*
. . . Sources of financial aid for subversive and un-American propaganda . . . Report . . . [Washington, U.S. Govt. print. off., 1946]
5 p. 23 cm. ([U.S.] 79th Cong., 2d sess. House. Rept. 1996)
Caption title.
Running title: Financial aid for subversive and un-American propaganda.
Submitted by Mr. Wood from the Committee on un-American activities.
1. Propaganda. 2. Fascism—U.S. 3. Communism—U.S.—1917- I. Wood, John Stephens, 1885- II. Title. III. Title: Financial aid for subversive and un-American propaganda.
E743.5.U55 1946b   351.74   46-26233
MC#: 1946-page 608 (LC card 46-26292 cancelled in favor of 46-26233)
SuDocs no.: 79th Cong., 2d sess. H. Rept. 1996

WOODCOCK REPORT [Woodcock, Leonard]
1546

United States. Congress. Senate. Committee on Foreign Relations.
U.S. MIA's in Southeast Asia : hearing before the Committee on Foreign Relations, United States Senate, Ninety-fifth Congress, first session, on report of the Presidential Commission on U.S. Missing and Unaccounted for in Southeast Asia.—Washington : U.S. Govt. Print. Off., 1977.
iii, 25 p. ; 24 cm.
1. Vietnamese Conflict, 1961-1975—Missing in action—United States. 2. United States. Presidential Commission on Americans Missing and Unaccounted for in Southeast Asia. I. Title.

KF26.F6 1977g   959.704'3373   77-602630
                                                  MARC
MC#: 1977-15693
SuDocs no.: Y4.F76/2:As4/19

WOOLDRIDGE REPORT [Wooldridge, Dean E.]
1547

U.S. *NIH Study Committee.*
Biomedical science and its administration; a study of the National Institutes of Health. Washington, The White House; [for sale by the Superintendent of Documents, U.S. Govt. Print. Off.] 1965.
xviii, 213 p. 24 cm.
1. U.S. National Institutes of Health. I. Title.
RA11.D5 1965b   610.6173   65-60922
MC#: 1965-6858
SuDocs no.: P36.2:B52

WORCESTER REPORT [Worcester, Dean Conant]
see
SCHURMAN REPORT [Schurman, Jacob Gould]

WORK IN AMERICA REPORT
1548

Work in America; report of a special task force to the Secretary of Health, Education, and Welfare. Washington, U.S. Govt. Print. Off., 1973.
v, xiv, 211 p. 24 cm.
At head of title: 93d Congress, 1st session. Committee print.
"Subcommittee on Employment, Manpower, and Poverty of the Committee on Labor and Public Welfare, United States Senate."
"Prepared by the W. E. Upjohn Institute for Employment Research."
Bibliography: p. 178-211.
1. Labor and laboring classes—United States. I. United States. Dept. of Health, Education, and Welfare. II. United States. Congress. Senate. Committee on Labor and Public Welfare. Subcommittee on Employment, Manpower, and Poverty. III. Upjohn Institute for Employment Research.
HD8072.W816   331.1'1'0973   73-601017
                                                  MARC
MC#: 1973-26283
SuDocs no.: Y4.L11/2:W89/3

WORK REPORT [Work, Hubert]
see
MERIAM REPORT [Meriam, Lewis]
Problem of Indian administration. Studies in administration, no. 17.

WRIGHT REPORT [Wright, Carroll Davidson]
1549

U.S. *Bureau of labor.*
A report on marriage and divorce in the United States, 1867 to 1886; including an appendix relating to marriage and divorce in certain countries in Europe. By Carroll D. Wright, commissioner of labor. February, 1889. Rev. ed. Washington, Govt. print. off., 1891.
1074 p. 23 cm. [First special report of the commissioner of labor. Rev. ed.]
An earlier edition was printed in 1889; a later edition, in 1897.

1. Marriage—U.S. 2. Divorce—U.S. I. Wright, Carroll Davidson, 1840-1909.
HQ833.A4 1889a   312.5   4-18106
Checklist of United States Public Documents, 1789-1909-page 618
SuDocs no.: La1.5:1

WRIGHT REPORT [Wright, Carroll Davidson]
Retail prices and wages.

see
ALDRICH REPORT [Aldrich, Nelson Wilmarth]

WRIGHT REPORT [Wright, Lloyd]
1550

U.S. *Commission on Government Security.*
Report pursuant to Public law 304, 84th Congress, as amended. [Washington, U.S. Govt. Print. Off., 1957]
xxxiii, 807 p. 24 cm.
1. Loyalty—security program, 1947- 2. Subversive activities—U.S.
JK734.A514   *351.1 351.4   57-60551
MC#: 1957-11633
SuDocs no.: Y3.G74/2:R29

WRISTON REPORTS [Wriston, Henry Merritt]
1551

U.S. *Dept. of State. Secretary of State's Public Committee on Personnel.*
Toward a stronger Foreign Service; report. [Washington, U.S. Govt. Print. Off.] 1954.
70 p. illus. 23 cm. ([U.S.] Dept. of State. Publication 5458. Department and Foreign Service series, 36)
1. U.S.—Diplomatic and consular service. I. Title. (Series: U.S. Dept. of State. Publication 5458. Series: U.S. Dept. of State. Department and Foreign Service series, 36)
JK851.A435   327.73   SD54-7
MC#: 1954-10854
SuDocs no.: S1.69-36

1552

U.S. *President's Commission on National Goals.*
Goals for Americans; programs for action in the sixties, comprising the report of the President's Commission on National Goals and chapters submitted for the consideration of the Commission. [Englewood Cliffs, N.J.?] Prentice-Hall, 1960.
xii, 372 p. 21 cm.
1. U.S.—Economic policy. 2. U.S.—Social policy. 3. U.S.—Pol. & govt.—1953- I. Title.
E841.U54   338.973   60-53566
Not listed in Monthly Catalog

YOUNG REPORT [Young, Philip]
1553

U.S. *Committee on Engineers and Scientists for Federal Government Programs.*

Summary report of survey of attitudes of scientists and engineers in Government and industry. [Washington, U.S. Govt. Print. Off.] 1957.
vi, 78 p. diagrs., tables. 26 cm.
1. Science as a profession. 2. Engineering as a profession. 3. Science and state. I. Title: Survey of attitudes for scientists and engineers in Government industry.
Q147.U523   506.9   57-62054
MC#: 1957-17162
SuDocs no.: Pr34.8:En3

ZIMRING REPORT [Zimring, Franklin E.]
see
NEWTON REPORT [Newton, George D.]

ZOOK REPORT [Zook, George F.]
1554

U.S. *President's Commission on Higher Education.*
Higher education for American democracy, a report. Washington, U.S. Govt. Print. Off., 1947.
6 v. illus. 23 cm.
George F. Zook, chairman.
Contents.—V. 1. Establishing the goals.—V. 2. Equalizing and expanding individual opportunity.—V. 3. Organizing higher education.—V. 4. Staffing higher education.—V. 5. Financing higher education.—V. 6. Resource data.
1. Education, Higher. 2. Education—U.S.—1945- I. Zook, George Frederick, 1885II. Title.
LA226.A48   378.73   48-50042*
MC#: 1948-4410, 4411, 4412, 6409, 6410, 11487
SuDocs no.: Pr33.2:Ed83/v. (nos.)

ZORNOW REPORT [Zornow, Gerald B.]
1555

United States. President's Commission on Olympic Sports.
The final report of the President's commission on Olympic Sports, January 1977, Washington, D.C.—Washington : U.S. Govt. Print. Off., 1977.
2 v. : ill. ; 28 cm.
Includes bibliographical references.
Contents: v. 1. Executive summary and major conclusions and recommendations.—v. 2. Findings of fact and supporting material.
1. United States. President's Commission on Olympic Sports. 2. Olympic games.
GV721.4.U6U54 1977   796'.0973   77-600747
                                                              MARC
MC#: 1977-3658
SuDocs no.: Pr38.8:OL 9/OL 9/v. 1
MC#: 1977-8586
SuDocs no.: Pr38.8:OL 9/OL 9/v. 2

Unidentified Reports

The following reports have been brought to the attention of the editors from various sources, but, at the time of publication of this edition of *Popular Names . . .* , all efforts to identify them fully have proved unsuccessful. If any user of this catalog can provide additional information concerning any of these reports, the editors would appreciate receiving such information as input toward the inclusion of these reports in the next edition.

BARTLETT REPORT [Bartlett, Claude Jackson]

A statistical report concerning disparate treatment in grade of black employees compared to non-black employees. 1977.

BLEUM REPORT [Bleum, A. William]

Study on the preservation of broadcast history. 1970.

BOAKLEY REPORT

Concerns communism. 1965 or 1966.

BROOKS REPORT [Brooks, Jack]

U.S. Congress. House. Commission on Information and Facilities. Organizational effectiveness of the Congressional Research Service: Communication from the Chairman. 1977.

BUCY REPORT [Bucy, J. Fred]

Task Force on Defense Science Review Board submitted in 1976 on export policy to communist countries.

CASEY REPORT [Casey, William]

Subject unknown.

COHEN REPORT

On accounting.

COLLEGE REPORT

Exact subject unknown.

COLLINS REPORT [Collins, Ralph T.]

Issued by the President's Committee on Employment of the Handicapped and entitled "Fifteen years, 1947-1962".

COOLIDGE REPORT [Coolidge, Charles A.]

U.S. Dept. of Defense. DOD implementation of recommendations of Coolidge Committee on classified information. 1957.

CRITICAL CHOICES FOR AMERICA

National Commission on Critical Choices for America.

CRITTENDON BOARD [Crittendon, Capt. S. H.]

Report of the Board appointed to prepare and submit recommendations to the Secretary of the Navy for the revision of policies, procedures and directives dealing with homosexuals. 1957.

DCPA STUDY

Relating to civil defense, based upon the Skelton (Missouri) amendment. Technical report.

DALEY REPORT [Daley, Bo]

U.S. Continental Army Command. Army School System: Report of a Board of Officers. 1962.

DARROW BOARD INVESTIGATION [Darrow, Clarence]

U.S. National Recovery Review Board. Appointed by the President to investigate the extent to which NRA codes were "designed to promote monopolies or to eliminate or oppress small enterprises or operate to discriminate against them or permit monopolies or monopolistic practices" 1934.

EDELMAN BOARD REPORT

U.S. Army Command & General Staff College. Report of the Educational Survey Commission of the U.S. Army.

FAUNTROY REPORT [Fauntroy, Walter E.]

Report. Ad Hoc Hearings on Fitness-For-Duty Examinations. 1976.

FILERS COMMISSION [Filers, John]

National Commission on Philanthropy and Public Need. 1975.

FINE COMMISSION REPORT

On banking.

FOSTER REPORT

Issued by the Federal Power Commission and deals with natural gas. 1963.

FOWLER-McCRACKEN REPORT

Subject unknown.

FRY REPORT [Fry, Robert]

Energy situation in Ford's last year in office.

GOLDBERG-MACY TASK FORCE

Federal labor-management relations. 1962.

H-BOMB REPORT

Atomic Energy Commission. Secret devices that trigger hydrogen bombs. 1975.

HABER REPORT [Haber, William]

Final report of Jewish affairs in Germany and Austria. 1949.

HAMPTON COMMITTEE

Federal labor-management relations. 1969.

HANSEN REPORT

Report on government reform.

HARBORD REPORT [Harbord, James Guthrie]

The American General Staff. 1921.

HARRISON REPORT [Harrison, B. L.]

U.S. Dept. of the Army. Study Group for the Review and Education of Officers. Report.

HAUBEN COMMITTEE REPORT

Subject unknown.

HAWLEY BOARD REPORT

On Army tactical mobility.

HAWTHORNE REPORT

Welfare policy with Micmac Indians - Maine. Late 1950's or 1960's.

HAZLITT REPORT

Subject unknown.

HEFFRON REPORT

A report prepared for the National Commission on Product Safety.

HEIMANN REPORT [Heimann, John G.]

Report on Bert Lance.

HELLER REPORT

Subject unknown.

HERMANN REPORT [Hermann, John G.]

Comptroller's report.

HERTER COMMITTEE

Subject unknown.

HOEBER REPORT [Hoeber, Francis]

Potentials for expansion of national security programs.

HOPKINS REPORT [Hopkins, Ernest M.]

U.S. Navy Dept. Special Civilian Committee to Study the Naval Administration of Guam and American Samoa. Report. 1947.

HUGHES REPORT [Hughes, Harold E.]

Government waste. 1969-1975.

JOHNSON COMMITTEE REPORT

Subject unknown.

JOHNSON REPORT [Johnson, Leon]

A study completed in August 1953 by the Reserve Review Board [U.S. Air Force?] Board headed by Gen. Johnson. Made recommendations concerning Air Force Reserves.

KAISER REPORT

Concerns shipbuilding.

KARMAN REPORT

Subject unknown.

KEENAN REPORT

On German coal mining machinery. 1948.

KELLY REPORT

Subject unknown.

KERNER REPORT

On taxes.

KIDD COMMITTEE REPORT [Kidd, Charles]

U.S. Dept. of H.E.W. Ad Hoc Interconstituent Committee on Financial Support of Teaching and Training. Report. 1955.

KING SURVEY [King, Gilbert William]

U.S. National Commission on Libraries and Information Science. Library photocopying.

KINNEY REPORT [Kinney, John]

U.S. National Advisory Council on Health Research Facilities. Research space needs of new and expanding medical schools; a report. 1969.

KORRY REPORT [Korry, Edward M.]

Prepared in 1966 for President Johnson, by a team of specialists headed by Edward M. Korry, U.S. Ambassador to Ethiopia. Reviews AID's Africa program to determine how the Agency could contribute more effectively to African development.

LEONARD REPORT [Leonard, J. L.]

Agriculture-labor. 1934.

LEOPOLD REPORT [Leopold, Luna]

Issued by the U.S. Geological Survey and entitled "Jet port on the edge of the Everglades." 1969.

LITTLE HOOVER COMMISSION

On reorganization. 1976.

LIVINGSTON REPORT

Single department procurement of paint; a pilot study of coordinated military procurement. 1951.

LOCKHART REPORT [Lockhart, Jack H.]

War departments, Bureau of public relations. 1946. Carlisle Barracks, Pa. The Armed Forces Information School, 1948.

LOWENTHAL REPORT [Lowenthal, Mark M.]

Defense Department reorganization: The Fitzhugh Report, 1969-1970.

LYLE REPORT

CSC President's Reorganization Committee.

McCOY REPORT

Subject unknown.

McINTYRE COMMISSION REPORT

A report issued by the Congressional Committee on Reporting Requirements.

MEANY REPORT [Meany, Thomas]

Cost of living.

METCALF REPORT

On accounting.

NADER REPORT [Nader, Ralph]

Task Force report on environmental pollution.

NORRIS REPORT [Norris, Frank Wade]

U.S. Dept. of the Army. Boards to Review Army Officer Schools. Report; record of completed actions., 1970.

NYE REPORT [Nye, Gerald P.]

Senate Commission on Foreign Investments. 1931.

OIL IMPORT PROGRAM

U.S. Dept. of the Interior. Cost of the Oil Import Program to the American Economy. 1969.

ORRICK REPORT [Orrick, William H.]

Study of Defense Department communication system. 1963.

PATCHBOARD STUDY

War Department reorganization. 1946.

POUND REPORT [Pound, Glenn S.]

National Research Council. Committee on Research Advisory to the U.S. Department of Agriculture. Report. 1972.

PRATT REPORT

Subject unknown.

PUMPKIN PAPERS

Subject unknown.

RAGAN REPORT [Ragan, Lawrence]

Subject unknown.

RAILEY REPORT

The Railey Report and Army Morale, 1941: Anatomy of a Crisis.

RANDALL REPORT [Randall, Clarence B.]

U.S. Congress. House. Committee on Post Office and Civil Service. Report of the Advisory Panel on Federal Salary Systems. 1963.

REARDON REPORT

Mass communications law; cases and comment.

REECE REPORT [Reece, Brazilla Carroll]

U.S. Congress. House. Special Committee to Investigate Tax Free Foundations. Tax exempt foundations.

REY REPORT [Rey, Jean]

Subject unknown.

RICHARDS BOARD

Subject unknown.

RIDENOUR REPORT

Report of Special Committee of the Scientific Advisory Board to the Chief of Staff, USAF, 1949.

ROBBINS REPORT [Robbins, D. Walter]

Postwar German foreign trade - its progress, problems, and recommended objectives to the immediate future. 1948.

ROBERTSON COMMITTEE REPORT

Ad Hoc, Army, Navy, Air Force Interim. 1956.

ROGERS REPORT

Army Aviation Requirements Review Board. 1962.

ROSEN REPORT

Concerns food. 1945.

ROSENTHAL REPORT

Subject unknown.

ROSSITER REPORT [Rossiter, William S.]

Report to the President upon conditions prevailing in the Government Printing Office. 1908.

RUSH REPORT

Concerns a study of means of establishing public-private mechanism for providing funds for overseas activities. 1968.

SIEMER REPORT [Siemer, Deanne]

U.S. Bureau of the Budget. Medical school study-patterns of federal funding. 1967.

SIMPSON COMMISSION REPORT [Simpson, Gordon]

Survey of Dachau war crimes program undertaken on August 1, 1948, by Justice Gordon Simpson of the Supreme Court of Texas and Judge Edward Van Roden of Delaware County, Pa. Reference made to report but text not given in DA Press Release of October 6, 1948.

SMITHSONIAN REPORT

Concerns energy. 1972.

SPRAGUE REPORT [Sprague, Mansfield]

Issued by the President's Commission on United States Information Operations Abroad. 1960.

STEARN REPORT

Subject unknown.

STEVER REPORT [Stever, Horton Guyford]

Air Materiel Command sponsored by ARDC, 1958.

STEWART REPORT

Report of the Advisory Committee on contractual and administrative procedures for research and development for the Department of the Army. 1948.

STILLWELL REPORT

Subject unknown.

SYMINGTON REPORT

Reorganization of the Department of Defense.

TASCA REPORT

Strengthening the Korean economy. Report to the President, Pusan, 1935.

TAYLOR REPORT [Taylor, Maxwell D.]

Cuban Study Group.

TREACY REPORT [Treacy, Vincent]

Authority of GSA to vest final administrative authority for public access to Presidential tapes and materials in the Presidential Materials Review Board. 1975.

UDALL REPORT [Udall, Stewart L.]

Concerns the investment in natural resources science and technology and the mission of the Department of the Interior. 1967.

VISSCHER REPORT [Visscher, Maurice Bolkes]

Communications problems in biomedical research; report of a study. 1963.

VISSERING AND VICKERY REPORT

Report on food conditions in Japan and Korea. 1948.

VOORHEES REPORT [Voorhees, Tracy J.]

Fiscal management of the national military establishment. 1948.

WEICKER REPORT [Weicker, Lowell P., Jr.]

Watergate hearings 1974.

WETZEL REPORT

A study dealing with women in the Army. 1981.

WHEELER REPORT

Concerns the reliability of Navy products.

WIRTZ COMMITTEE [Wirtz, W. Willard]

Federal labor-management relations 1967.

WOODHOUSE REPORT [Woodhouse, Chase Going]

U.S. Dept. of the Army. Public Information Division. Army releases report on German women's activities. 1948.

Index

This section provides access by subject and corporate entry to the publications or groups of publications listed by popular name in the body of this work. Subject descriptors, which are shown in roman type, do not in all cases correspond to subject headings on Library of Congress printed cards or to other official LC subject headings but rather to key words of the reports. The italicized corporate entries are in some cases inverted to give additional subject access, e.g., "Budget Concepts, President's Commission on" in addition to "U.S. President's Commission on Budget Concepts."